GROWING BEAUTIFUL HOUSEPLANTS

GROWING BEAUTIFUL HOUSEPLANTS

An Illustrated Guide to the Selection and Care of over 1,000 Varieties

ROB HERWIG

Facts On File

New York • Oxford

Growing Beautiful Houseplants

Copyright © 1987 by Zomer & Keuning
Boeken B.V., Ede
Translation copyright © 1992 by Facts On File

Facts On File, Inc.   Facts On File Limited
460 Park Avenue South   c/o Roundhouse Publishing Ltd.
New York, NY 10016   P.O. Box 140
USA   Oxford OX2 7SF
                         United Kingdom

Library of Congress Cataloging-in-Publica-
tion Data

Herwig, Rob, 1935–
    [Volkomen kamerplantenboek. English]
    Growing beautiful houseplants : an illus-
trated guide to the selection and care of over
1000 varieties / Rob Herwig.
       p. cm.
    Translation of: Het volkomen
kamerplantenboek.
    ISBN 0-8160-2454-5
    1. House Plants—Dictionaries. I. Title.
SB419.H5813 1991
635.9'65—dc20   89-77998

A British CIP catalogue record for this book
is available from the British Library.

Facts On File books are available at special
discounts when purchased in bulk quantities
for businesses, associations, institutions or
sales promotions. Please call our Special Sales
Department in New York at 212/683-2244
(dial 800/322-8755 except in NY, AK or HI)
or in Oxford at 865/728399.

Jacket design by Thomas Goddard
Composition by Catherine Hyman
Manufactured by Mandarin Offset
Printed in Hong Kong

10 9 8 7 6 5 4 3 2 1

This book is printed on acid-free paper.

Heartfelt thanks to everyone who contributed to the book.

Many people helped in its completion, and I
relied on the experience and knowledge of
countless gardeners. Listed here are a number
of nurseries, gardens and companies who allowed us access to their collections and to their
invaluable expertise:

Buthuis Cactus Nursery, Cothen, Netherlands

Cornelis Bak bv, Assendelft (special bromeliads)

Cresco bv, De Kwakel

Wed. P. Eveleens & Zonen, Aalsmeer

Toon Containers bv, De Kwakel

Kloezemans Orchid Nursery, Bemmel

Koninklijke Lemkes & Zn. bv, Alphen aan de Rijn

Lodder bv, Vleuten (bonsai)

Van Maanen en Mantel bv, De Kwakel

Fa. Maarse Kzn, Rijssenhout

A.A. Mathijssen, Reeth/Elst (*Fuschia* and *Pel-argonium*)

Sahim, Alphen aan de Rijn

Scholte-Ubink Cactus Nursery, Aalsmeer

Van der Velden, St. Oedenrode

Wubben Orchid Nursery, Hollandse Rading

Thanks also to Chris Woods and Karen Van
Westering for their help.

Photo credits

t = top, b = bottom, m = middle, r = right, l =
left, tl = top left, bl = bottom left, ml = middle
left, tr = top right, mr = middle right, br =
bottom right

Johannes Apel, Baden-Baden, Germany
9 bl and br, 39 tl, 61 tr, 92 tl, 99 tl, 102 bl, 103
bl, 104 tr, 105 l, 106 br, 109 bl and br, 110 br,
115 bl, 121 tr, 123 tr and bl, 130 tr, 136 t, 142
mr, 145 t, 147 t, 150 br, 185 bl, 186 bl, 187 br,
188 t, 194 tr, 205 ml and bl, 206 br, 207 t and
bl, 212 t, 223 tl, 231 br, 242 b, 245 bl, 248 tr,
252 tl, 254 ml, 265 m, 269 ml, 272 l, 290 bl and
br, 293 mr, 297 l, 304 tl, 317 ml, 318 tl and bl,
321 bl, 325 ml, 336 b, 351 t, 357 br, 359 br.

L. den Arend, Netherlands
333 tm.

Ing. G. Beckman KG, Wangen, Germany
45 br.

Arend Bouhuys, Weesp, Netherlands
34 b, 35 bl, 48.

Burda GmbH (Mein Schoener Garten),
Offenburg, Germany
2, 8 m, 9 b, 21 l, 27 bl and br, 32 bl and bm, 37 br,
40 tr, ml and mr, 42 bl and br, 43 br, 76 258 br.

Herman Eisenbeiss, Munich, Germany
132 tr, 135 t, 192 tr, 213 ml.

Foto Lans, Hillegom, Netherlands
24 tr, 330 bl, 358 bl.

Prof. G. Groener, Stuttgart, Germany
114 b, 173 br, 204 tr and mr, 269 mr and br,
273 br, 324 mr.

F.M. van der Kruijf, Lisse, Netherlands
28, 29 bl and br.

Proefstation voor de Bloemisterij, Aalsmeer,
Netherlands
84 t and b, 85, 87.

Roehm GmbH Chemische Fabrik,
Darmstadt, Germany
46.

H. Schlachter, Guenzburg, Germany
44, 45 bl.

Harry Smith Horticultural Photographic
Collection, Chelmsford, England
132 mt, 152 br, 231 bl, 275 t, 304 tr, 328 tl.

Wolfram Stehling, Hamburg, Germany
9 t, 14 r, 161, 32 tr, 35 br, 36 br, 38, 43 bl, 54,
55, 191 br, 334 tl, 345 tl.

W.A. Tomey, The Hague, Netherlands
58.

Vakblad voor de Bloemisterij, Leiden, Netherlands
81 and r.

Christopher Woods
60–61.

World Wide Plant Pictures, Haarlem, Netherlands
90 ml, 92 br, 99 tl, 102 br, 107 tl, 111 tr, 115 t and
br, 130 tl, 132 tl and bl, 133 t, 136 bl, 137 mr, 138
tr and mr, 139 br, 142 tr, 144 tl, 145 br, 148 l, 152
l, 154 br, 156 bm, 158 tl and bl, 161 br, 165 br,
169 tr and l, 174 m, 179 br, 182 t, 185 t, 186 br,
187 tl and bl, 188 bl, 192 br, 193 tr, 194 tl, 195 br,
198 b, 202 l, 204 bm, 205 t and br, 209 br, 217 tr,
221 bl, 223 m and b, 236 tr, 237 tl and b, 239 t and
mr, 241 br, 246 t and b, 249 br, 251 tr, 257 t, 264
t, 267 t, 271 t, 273 t and ml, 276 ml and br, 277 t,
278 tr and bl, 282 tl, m and br, 283 bl, 285 tm, 291
tr and bl, 294 b, 295 tl, 297 tr, 300 t, 301 bl, 203
tr, 303 t and ml, 304 bl, 308 bl and m, 309 t, 310
tl, 312 bl, 314 br, 315 b, 316 tl and tm, 319 mr,
320 br, 321 br, 323 br, 324 tr and br, 326 tl, 329
bl, 330 ml and br, 331 bl, 332 bm, 333 bl, 334 br,
340 tr, 342 mr, 344 bl, 345 bm, 346 br, 347 tl and
bl, 348 tl, tr and bl, 349 tl, 352 tl, 353 t, bl and br,
354 t and ml, 357 m.

All other photos by Rob Herwig.

Design and layout
Chiel Veffer, ADM

Drawings
Piet Eggen

Translation
Gerda Van Leuwen

CONTENTS

PREFACE

In recent years the available assortment of houseplants has undergone great changes. The trade has grown enormously; many new species have been imported from the tropics and subtropics, or even grown from seed. Research facilities and individual growers are trying hard to add new strains to the old assortment, strains that are even more beautiful and hardier that the old cultivars.

This is why an older houseplant book may be of little use to you, since it quite possibly fails to deal with at least 30 percent of the plants now available. Hence the necessity to publish a new book about houseplants, a book that deals extensively with the most current new species. One thousand plants are illustrated and even more are described. Absolute comprehensiveness is of course impossible; with the inclusion of all cacti and orchids, at least 5,000 species are available.

I cannot resist adding one personal remark: Let us be sure to regard plants as living creatures, not just as "decorative greenery." To my mind, too many plants are placed in locations where they will never do well; for example, in offices where it is often too dark for them to survive. Tired, wilting plants do not encourage us to grow our own varieties, and by ignoring the basic requirements of houseplants we stimulate the rise of phony substitutions, such as plastic plants and silk flowers. There are plenty of plants that are able to thrive in offices or in homes—you need only to consult the appendices at the end of this book.

Finally I want to express my thanks to Juliette Roorda, who assisted me in compiling this book. She spent a year visiting growers and assembled the plants for the photographs.

Rob Herwig

REAL HOUSEPLANTS DO NOT EXIST

No plant grows indoors naturally. All plants we call "houseplants" are put there by us—certainly without their asking. If they were able to walk off, plants would go back to their natural habitat, and flourish—far better than they ever do in our living rooms. When I work with houseplants, I try to "crawl under the skin" of the plant as much as possible. To successfully grow your houseplants, I suggest you do the same. Only then can you begin to give these plants a semblance of their environment and a chance to thrive.

bigger than the original ones, but this is not an achievement; they only neglected to use a retardant. The artificial influence has been felt in other areas as well. Potting soil is no longer earth, but a mixture of different kinds of materials suitable for feeding and supporting the roots of plants. Often they consist of artificial materials like perlite, vermiculite and even fertilizer.

Artificial houseplants

Today, many of the plants we use in our homes do not exist in nature. Developed by cross-pollination, they have been specially bred for use as houseplants. Others, such as potted chrysanthemums, are not suited for long-term survival indoors; I call these disposable plants. Still other plants are kept small artificially with growth retardants. When propagating cuttings from such plants without spraying them, the new plants reach their natural height. Caretakers often take pride in the fact that their plants from cuttings are

Large numbers of houseplants are initially cultivated in factory-like conditions. They do not fulfill their function as decorative ornaments or even companions until they reach people's homes.

Below: *In nature, everything grows on its own. In order to be successful with houseplants, natural conditions must be imitated as closely as possible.*

Why put plants in your home?

We bring plants into our homes for beauty and comfort, and to remind us of nature. Although 3,000 years ago Egyptians did put plants in pots—which were left outside—it was not until the 15th century, when Italian sailors started to bring home exotic greenery from Asia, that plants were brought inside. The first greenhouse dates from 1585. As travel around the globe increased, more unusual plants turned up in Europe. At first, only the very rich had them. They built beautiful houses, called orangeries, to protect the plants from the severe winter weather.

In the summer the plants were displayed outside, but in the winter they were kept cool and frost-free in these large indoor spaces, especially in England. This was more or less the beginning of the houseplant rage; it was not long before less affluent people took cuttings from these expensive plants and tried to grow them in their homes. Hardy plants such as *Aspidistra*, *Dracaena* and palms have been decorating living spaces for a long time. Still, not so long ago in England, it was absolutely forbidden to bring plants inside. Plants belong in the garden, it was said, which every English resident possessed. Only after apartment living became commonplace did the houseplant boom take off in earnest, lasting to this day.

We cannot live without nature

Almost all of us feel a need for nature. If you have a garden where you can grow plants to your heart's desire, you may not have a need to fill your house with plants as well. But when you live on the 12th floor with a view of a concrete sea, then you try to bring as many plants inside as possible. This is especially true in Northern countries where one is forced by the weather to spend a large part of the year indoors.

Houseplants are a multimillion dollar market. Statistics show that in some countries families own 40 to 50 houseplants on average, and a large number of these get replaced regularly.

Even in tropical countries where the jungle is "just around the corner," there can be a great interest in houseplants. I have noticed this from the sale of my books in Brazil, a country with large urban areas where many people live in apartment buildings with conditions very similar to ours. In the summer their air conditioning, like our winter heating, keeps the temperature around 68°F.

ORIGIN AND SIGNIFICANCE OF HOUSEPLANTS

To understand plants better it is useful to find out where they come from—it will surely make houseplant care easier. And when your plants grow and thrive you get something back: satisfaction. I will try to explain how to develop a successful relationship with your plants in the following pages.

Where do our houseplants come from?

Most houseplants come from the warmer areas of the world. They are not frost-resistant, and therefore cannot survive outdoors year-round in most parts of North America. The majority of houseplants originate from one of three climatic areas. First of all there's the tropical climate zone, where there is a high uniform temperature. The number of daylight hours varies much throughout the year. Periods of drought can occur, but in the tropical forest it remains humid. Many plants from tropical areas work well in homes, since we also try to keep the indoor temperature uniform. The major problem for this type of plant is the dry air in our homes. Periods of dormancy are not usually necessary for tropical plants.

In the subtropics we find other conditions. Although it is seldom so cold that it freezes, there are seasons. In summer the subtropics are extremely hot and can also be very dry. In most cases subtropical plants have adapted to survive heat and drought, which makes them good candidates for our homes. In the subtropical winter there is less light, and it is much colder than in summer. Accordingly the plants go into a dormancy period in the winter. Subtropical plants survive well in modern houses, but it is difficult to give them a cool rest period in winter. For that reason, many subtropical plants are grown as container plants, kept outside in the summer and moved to a cool, frost-free space in the winter. Many people have success with oleander and laurel, two well-known container plants.

Even more extreme conditions are found in savannas and deserts. The plants that grow in these areas have a special power of adaptation without which they would not survive. The best-known group of this type are the succulents, especially cacti. These plants are capable of storing moisture in their tissues, and can minimize evaporation. In this way it is possible for cacti to get through months of drought. These plants also need a cool, but most of all dry, dormancy period when kept inside. Lovers of cacti and other succulents often achieve splendid results in their greenhouses. Fortunately there are succulents that can go on growing without a dormant period. They usually do not flower, but since their foliage and shape is interesting enough, it doesn't matter.

Love can make plants grow

Good technical care is the most important factor in successfully growing houseplants. But we can take it one step further. We can also achieve spiritual contact with plants, although on a very different level than with people. It happens.

Numerous experiments have been performed to show that we can influence how plants grow with our thoughts. A group held prayer sessions under the guidance of a priest for two identical groups of plants, one group in each of two different rooms. First, the group prayed positively with group A, wishing these

On page 10: Houseplants, especially exotic ones, only grow and bloom in such unnatural spots as a window if given the proper attention and care.

Most houseplants originate from tropical and subtropical areas. Many houseplants are native to the mountains of the tropics, where cooler conditions prevail. These plants require a cooler cultivation with much light.

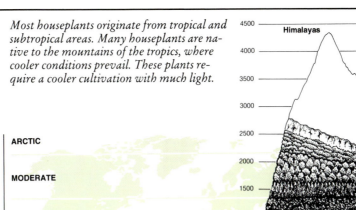

plants the best of what is possible. Next the group prayed negatively with group B; all these plants were fed bad thoughts and cursed. After a few weeks, they found that the plants from group A flourished while the plants from group B almost died. A similar experiment was conducted with two kinds of music: baroque and rock and roll. The ones listening to Bach grew towards the loudspeakers while the plants in the rock room moved away from the music. Try it yourself.

These experiments are meant to provide proof, but even without scientific proof, many of us know that it is possible to influence plants through our thoughts. That is what we mean when we talk of people with "green thumbs," people who have exceptional relationships with plants. When I write that this or that plant in the living room is hard to get to bloom, a letter always follows from someone who succeeded with it. Most of the time a photograph is included as proof. Growing difficult greenhouse orchids in a normal living room, or delicious bananas under a plastic tent, are both possible when you have a green thumb.

Favorable effects of houseplants

In addition to the beauty and decorative value plants bring to our homes, they

The oleander (Nerium oleander) is a well known subtropical plant that can be grown as a container plant in more moderate climate zones.

release humidity and oxygen into the air, although not in large quantities. Equally important is the educational value of having plants around, especially for children. With the help of plants they can be taught very quickly about love and caring. Tending houseplants teaches them to put another's needs before their own. Many simple but interesting phenomena can be illustrated with the help of plants: How does a seed germinate? How do cuttings develop roots? What is the influence of light and temperature? We should not underestimate the educational value of plants.

Unfavorable effects of houseplants

Many plants are poisonous, including several used as houseplants. The poison is not usually deadly, but the effects can be very disagreeable. (In this book I always note in the description if a plant is poisonous. If nothing is mentioned, the plant is not poisonous; this does not mean, however, that it is edible!) Sometimes the ber-

ries are poisonous but more often it is the leaves or stems. Generally, you only have to be concerned with poisonous plants when you have small children or pets. You'd have to be crazy to eat a *dieffenbachia*, even as a joke. You'd end up in the hospital. The degree of toxicity is different for people and animals. It is important that you know which plant causes what symptoms. With the help of this book you should be able to discover it easily, but if the toxicity of a plant eaten by a human or animal is unknown, your doctor can help. Your doctor can then contact the poison control center and calculate the antidote accordingly.

Aside from eating, touching some plants can result in poisoning as well, mostly in the form of rashes. *Primula obconcia* is quite notorious for causing rashes, since it contains the substance primine. Some people are very sensitive to this substance, which, when touched, results in skin irritation, although it does not bother others at all. In addition, the latex of the *Euphorbias* can cause irritation of the mucous membranes. There are other examples of irritating plants, but most are not really dangerous.

WHY ALL THE DIFFICULT NAMES?

A question frequently asked of writers of plant books is, "Why do you always use those difficult names? Wouldn't it be easier to go by the common names?" While we certainly refer to common names, in general the complicated Latin names are used to avoid confusion.

The problem with folk names

Too often there are many different common or folk names for one plant. Depending on where you come from the lovely blue-flowered plant *Myosotis* can be called a "mouse ear," but can also be called a "forget-me-not," starchflower, or blue starchflower, because its flowers were put into the laundry to give the wash a beautiful blue-white shade. Another name, "canal flower," does not have anything to do with where it grows. In Zeeland, the Netherlands, it has the mysterious name "greasy sock." In Germany, one says *Vergissmeinnicht*, in France, *ne m'oublie pas*, and so it goes with other countries and other languages. Altogether we can easily assume that around the world there are at least 50 different names for this one little plant.

When you consider that this book is published in different languages, the use of such folk names becomes problematic. The listing for the forget-me-not would appear in the back of the Dutch version, but in the French edition somewhere in the middle, and in English near the front. Another problem involves choosing the "right" common name. Forget-me-not is overall the most common English name for this plant, but there are also plants for which there are more than one commonly accepted name.

Yet throughout all countries there is one official Latin name for every plant. In the case of the forget-me-not it is *Myosotis*. In order to make the book as useful as possible, I've listed the plants alphabetically by their Latin names and included the common names, as well. Both entries are indexed so that you can always find a plant when you know only the folk name.

How the official naming works

The plant world is divided systematically into classes, subclasses, orders, families, genera, species, subspecies and varieties. In this book, we have not used the first three categories because the larger groups have less significance in the actual care of the plants. Plants that belong to the same family, however, often need the same care. Below the family is the genus—for example, *Ficus*—which is the most useful name for you to know the plant by. It is comparable to the surname of people.

The specific name can be compared with our first names. With *Ficus elastica*

Below, left: Schefflera, Fatsia *and* Dizygotheca *are often confused, since at one point they were each known as a 'fingerplant.'*
Below: Pothos, Scindapsus, Rhaphidophora, Epipremnum: *four different plants that all look the same.*

Far left: X Fatshedera *is a hybridization between the genera* Fatsia *and* Hedera. Left: *Dozens of* Codiaeum variegatum *species exist with different leaf shapes.*

we indicate that we are dealing with a specific kind of *Ficus*. In the same way we might indicate a person with the name Smith, John. The name comparison stops here. With *Ficus elastica* we then move to varieties such as 'Decorata' and 'Variegata.' In this book you will come across many of these varieties, which are written with a capital letter and set within single quotation marks.

Instead of the generic name, a plant may be given a designation indicating a hybrid. Many species are assembled under this one name when one does not know the genus. Sometimes these hybrids are subdivided again, into groups comparable to a species indication. If you read a plant's description where the species is given below the genus, this means that some of the species of that genus will be discussed together in the following text.

Variety versus cultivar?

Varieties are variant subdivisions of a species that arise from natural causes. With plants the indication "cultivar" means an abnormality of the species that is not naturally reproducible from seed, and is created by human interference: irradiation, selection, hybridization. Further propagation occurs through dividing, striking cuttings or in any other vegetative manner.

What does X mean?

An X indicates nothing more than that the particular plant is a product of hybridization. The first successful cross-hybridization of two genera happened in France in 1910, when a *Hedera helix* (regular ivy) was cross-fertilized with *Fatsia japonica*, a well-known houseplant originally from Japan. The cross-hybridization was named X *Fatshedera lizei*. The two generic names were combined and the X explains that two different genera were involved. Nowadays this happens frequently with orchids; more than two genera can be involved. X *Brassolaeliocattleya* is assembled from the genera *Brassavola*, *Laelia*, and *Cattleya*. Only real plant fanatics know how to pronounce names like these, I would imagine.

It is also possible to cross-fertilize two species within a genus. In this case the X is placed between the generic name and the name of the species. *Begonia* X *credneri* is a cross-fertilization of *Begonia metallica* and *Begonia scharffiana*, for example, This kind of cross-fertilization is used less frequently with houseplants than garden plants.

With intensive hybridization, an impatiens can be created with a two-color flower in a star-shaped pattern.

Names sometimes change

An additional difficulty with plant names is that they change from time to time. *Hortensia* became *Hydrangea*, and *Azalea* is now classified in the genus *Rhododendron*. A famous, variegated houseplant was called *Scindapsus aureus*, to everybody's satisfaction. A while ago, it became *Rhaphidophora aurea*, and just after we got used to that, the name was changed to *Epipremnum pinnatum*. Now you will find this plant under that last name in this book.

Each year a few plants are given new, lesser-known names. Why? In the 18th century, a noted Swedish botanist, Carolus Linnaeus, developed a botanical naming system for plants. His system, which was accepted internationally, brought order to what had been a chaotic system for naming plants. Since many plants already had several names, in the 19th century it was internationally decided that the oldest given name was the "right" name. Linnaeus named many plants, but some of these had already been named, and many plants discovered after the death of Linnaeus have since been given names by someone else. It is understandable that the same plants in disparate parts of the world are discovered by different people and given different names. In this way it may happen that a name given in the 19th century may have already been given another Latin name. Thus scholarly research often provides evidence to change the accepted name to an older name. Sometimes the name is changed several times for the same plant. If scientific research proves that a certain plant has been classified with the wrong genus, the name changes as well. Fortunately for us, these changes do not happen as frequently as they used to.

Eventually, all plants will be researched in such a thorough manner that names and generations will no longer be disputed. But I estimate that this will take another 100 years, and until that date, we have to cope with a confusing profusion of names.

FLOWERING PLANTS

It is useful to subdivide the large assortment of houseplants into groups, because within groups the plants often demand similar care. I have discussed the following nine groups: flowering plants, foliage plants (including ferns and palms), bromeliads, succulents, orchids, bulbs and tubers, container plants, bonsai and "disposable plants."

Flowering is almost always temporary

Although more and more foliage plants are sold, it is still very nice to have something flowering in a room. Unfortunately, with few exceptions, these plants cannot flower year-round. Blooming has a definite function in nature, connected to the reproductive system of plants. The color and scent systems of flowers serve to attract insects and other animals that take care of pollination. It is because of this cycle that the flowering of any plant can only be temporary. To have continuous blooming indoors you need several plants at various stages of the blooming cycle.

Flowering after the first year

It is often possible to make a flowering plant bloom again after allowing it to have a period of dormancy. The *Clivia* is a good example. Such a plant can bloom year after year when it feels comfortable with its surroundings. It also grows bigger and produces even more flowering stems. These plants give more than satisfaction. After flowering, a few plants, especially the *Clivia*, can still form seeds. The seeds can be sowed after maturing and with some luck new plants can be grown; an especially easy one to propagate is *Eurphorbia lophogona*.

Play the bee

Pollination is difficult inside houses since there are no bees or soft breezes. You can play the bee using a soft brush and attempt to bring pollen to the pistol at the right moment, so that afterwards seed forming can begin. There is more to caring for flowering plants than simply admiring their visual beauty.

In general, flowering plants should be purchased the moment the blossoming starts. In this way you can enjoy the blossoms as long as possible. It is not wise to put the plants in full sunlight, because only a few flowering plants can endure that. It is better to place them in screened sunlight, or in an east- or west-facing window. With some species blossoms may drop when the plants are moved and the light strikes a new spot. Not much can be done about this, but when you bring such a plant into bloom take care that it is turned towards the light consistently on the same side. Flowering plants can stop blooming when they find themselves in totally new conditions. Never keep flowering azaleas too warm; flowering begonias also stay more beautiful when kept on the cool side. And beware the cycla-

Left: *Cyclamen persicum*
Below: *Adenium obeseum*

men. This lovely plant does not withstand heated room temperatures well at all. I bought some blossoming cyclamens with big flowers in November and kept them on a protected balcony; only with the night frost did I bring them inside. The plants flowered until Christmas. Had I put them in a warm room, they would have lasted a week, at most. The same is true of flowering heather, *Erica gracilis*, which also does better outside than in a room. These are just examples of the problems that may occur. Look for more details with the individual plant descriptions.

Flowering plants can get confused

In nature plants bloom in certain seasons. They try to keep to these seasons indoors as well, but due to variable temperatures and light, and skipped dormant periods, plants can get confused. Sometimes they bloom at the strangest times depending on the conditions. Therefore don't take as absolute the indications about flowering times in this book.

With a simple light bulb you can make a wax begonia believe that it is not winter at all and it will just continue to bloom.

Below: Erica gracilis, *a heath plant, is hard to bring through dormancy—a disposable plant.*
Right: The Fuchsia *will flower after its dormant period.*

Poinsettias are forced commercially to bloom at Christmas time, but it is absolutely no problem to have them bloom in May, if you provide the appropriate light conditions.

Blooming is not always a sign of health

Often I receive questions about foliage plants that start to bloom unexpectedly. *Dieffenbachia* and *Dracaena* are two examples of plants grown for their leaves but that can bloom. Of all houseplants only the fern cannot bloom at all. The question is therefore: Does the flowering exhaust the plant and should you remove the flowers? I do not advise doing this. It is much nicer to enjoy the flowers, especially when flowering does not usually occur. In truth, however, plants with

spectacular foliage often have rather undistinguished flowers. But if exhaustion is the concern, be reassured it has already happened before flowering. A plant that does not often bloom can start to flower because of very good care, but also because of exceptionally bad care as well. It blooms in a last desperate effort to reproduce.

A note of caution. Many flowers have a wonderful scent, but some also smell terrible. You will probably not try to grow an *Amorphophallus* in your living room, but if you did you would leave immediately. The smell of a *Gynura* reminds one of decay. There are any number of plants that you had better not put in the living room while they are in bloom. Check the alphabetical plant listing for more details.

FOLIAGE PLANTS

Foliage plants are generally grown for their attractive leaves. They are often easy plants to take care of because many species do not require dormant periods, as most flowering plants do. Several foliage plants can bloom beautifully, although when grown indoors they rarely have the opportunity, due to improper conditions. (None of the ferns can flower; they are pure foliage plants.)

Diversity of foliage plants

Among foliage plants I include all plants with green and colored leaves as well as those that belong to the groups of palms and ferns. It is a very heterogeneous group so that there are no overall rules for their care. A rule of thumb to what kind of conditions a certain foliage plant will need can be determined by examining the leaf. The darker green the leaf is, the more chlorophyll there is, which means it is easier for the plant to assimilate (transform light into food). For you, that means the plant can live with minimal light. But remember all plants need some. If a plant has white, yellow or red colored leaf parts, more light is necessary. If such a variegated plant gets too little light, the colors become less prominent until the foliage finally becomes completely green.

Ferns and Dracaenas *are attractive foliage plants for the home.*

At this point the plant is just keeping itself alive. (See later chapter on light.)

Among the foliage plants we find strong houseplants that can hold out for years in a dark corner, as in the case of the *Cissus rhombifolia*. But there are also foliage plants with large thin leaves that need high humidity. These thrive in a greenhouse and only in the summer can they tolerate our room conditions.

When you buy a plant, observe the form and color of the leaf. If the leaf is quite small and shiny, leathery and dark green, chances are that such a plant is suitable for a heated room and rather dark situations. If the leaf is transparent and thin, strongly feathered and light green, it is not well suited to normal home conditions. As durable as many foliage plants can be, we have to remember we are nonetheless dealing with living creatures. They need sufficient light, water and temperature, otherwise they will soon look very sad.

Ferns

Ferns are foliage plants, but they form a unique, homogenous group. Ferns are spore plants while all other houseplants are considered seed plants, which means the two groups reproduce in essentially different ways. The development of a plant from seed is described on page 78. With ferns, however, there are spores on the underside of the fronds, or leaves, that look like fine seeds when they fall off. But unlike seeds, which are already fertilized when they are ripe, spores are not fertilized. From the dust-like spores there first develops a prothallium. It looks like a small green leaf or piece of seaweed. Masculine as well as feminine parts develop within the prothallium and only when the prothallium matures does fertilization take place; at that point, if they are on moist soil, a fern starts to grow.

Ferns in general have thin, feathered leaves. We call a leaf feathered when it is curved in to the midrib (the vein running down the center of the leaf). These parts can be feathered again. In this case the leaf is called double feathered, which frequently occurs with ferns. Even triple feathered is not uncommon. The evaporation through such a finely divided leaf

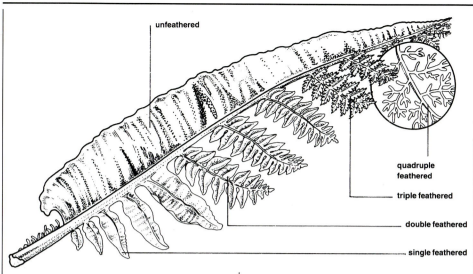

unfeathered

quadruple
feathered

triple feathered

double feathered

single feathered

When a leaf is indented to the main stem, smaller leaves are created. Leaves are generally arranged to maximize the use of incoming light, and come in a variety of shapes, including the feathered shapes of the fern frond to the left.

is enormous; therefore, most ferns in nature grow in shaded, humid places. When we put them in a heated room they only stay healthy for a short time, especially in winter when the air is so dry.

The primary concern is to provide sufficient humidity. Nonetheless, I would urge you to try ferns. They are dramatic plants and, with proper care, they can survive for months. Naturally there are people who keep them well for years, but I've found these people are the exceptions.

Contrary to what I have just said, there are also ferns that tolerate dry air well. The best-known is the Staghorn fern. Its fronds resemble antlers—hence its common name; the fronds are covered with a thin wax layer that helps keep evaporation limited. As a result it flourishes very well indoors. Other good ferns for home conditions are *Cyntomium*, with its strong leathery shiny leaves, and the less-known *Phlebodium* with its large feathered roots.

Ferns do not like sun. Place them in a northern window, or further from a window, away from direct sunlight.

The most important aspect of care is an even water supply. The soil in small pots dries out quickly; therefore, after buying a fern replace the pot with a bigger one. Even better is to use a pot with a water reservoir on the bottom. Then the soil stays equally moist, which for ferns is ideal. In times of temporary drought they react by dropping their leaves in no time.

Palms

Palms are tall wood-like plants with a trunk that seldom branches. In nature they grow in subtropical and tropical areas. The leaves are composed mostly in feathered, fan forms. When growing in nature, palms readily bloom and produce fruit (dates, coconuts etc.) but when grown inside they rarely bloom.

Although older palms can easily withstand the full sun, young palms, as most house plants are, should be kept out of the bright sun. Strong light is fine but not direct sun. The roots of palms like to dig deeply, so it is a good idea to grow them in narrow, deep containers. In the summer palms can be put outside on a sheltered, not too sunny, terrace. Most can be treated as container or greenhouse plants (see page 26). Palms are strong plants, even though it is not easy to cultivate them indoors for years. Although they can tolerate dry room air quite easily, many species need a dormant period, which is hard to achieve in a living room with consistent light and temperature. They do best in a soil mixture that includes clay, an ingredient that is not naturally easy to come by for most plant lovers. The little room palm, *Microcoelum*, likes to stand with a little

water in the bottom of the pot, unlike most houseplants.

Palm ferns

Palm ferns are remarkable plants that have existed for 200 million years. They look like palms but in reproduction they more closely resemble ferns. The primary species used as houseplants is *Cycas revoluta*. It is the easiest plant to grow, but it is also particularly decorative. In botanical gardens where growing conditions are more ideal, we are able to see large specimens in containers.

Left, above: This Cissus rhombifolia *has complex, hand-shaped leaves.*
Left, below: Cycas revoluta, a potentially painful palm fern.
Below: A detail of a Platycerium, *also known as a stag-horn fern.*

BROMELIADS

Bromeliads are noteworthy plants, originating almost exclusively in Central and South America; only one species has its origin in Africa. Many are tree-growing epiphytes, but other bromeliads grow directly in the earth. Bromeliads grow in both the tropical rain forest and the desert. The leaves form from a central base into a rosette, and the bromeliads have one unusual quality in common; every rosette flowers only one time and then dies.

The way bromeliads grow

As you can see in the photo of the traverse section, most bromeliads form a short compact trunk with large leaves resembling a drainpipe. The distance between the buds is very small, which makes the leaves stand close together to form a rosette. Sometimes they form a bulb (see bulbs) but the leaves of a bulb-like bromeliad lack the typical thickening of the scales found in a true bulb. The rosette forms a cup-like container into which water and insects find their way. In some bromeliads the ends of the leaves are farther away from each other. No rosette appears, but rather a stem with leaves regularly placed. Spanish moss is a good example of such a bromeliad.

At a certain height, where the trunk stops forming leaves, the flower stem begins. With the gigantic bromeliad *Puya raimondii*, development of the flower can take several years, but with the normal houseplant species, flowers usually bloom quite quickly. Often blooming is characterized by special-colored outer leaves that surpass the beauty of the real flowers. The flower stem can be extended so that the flower develops far above the rosette. This is not the case with the *Neoregelia*, however, whose little violet flowers are situated deep in the funnel. You might blame yourself if the flower stem does not grow tall, but this is characteristic of certain species of bromeliad.

Propagation

Bromeliads are grown from seed. Some species can reproduce only from seed, but generally there is another system working as well. About the same time that the plant flowers, small shoots develop on the sides of the main stalk. If they appear under the axils of the lowest leaves, they will grow more or less horizontally. Miniature plants develop on the tip of the side shoots and end up growing adjacent to the mother plant. Sometimes the mother becomes surrounded by a circle of children.

If the side shoots grow from the axils of the upper leaves, they will grow vertically. The children end up growing above the mother plant. This is especially the case with terrestrial (earth-growing) bromeliads. When the "children" grow in this manner, "cushions" are eventually formed. In the middle of such a cushion sits a little mountain of humus (decayed vegetable matter) originating from previous generations.

At first the miniature plants will draw their food from the mother plant, which is drained empty and afterwards dies. You can multiply the bromeliads with cuttings of the small plants. But you should not cut them before the mother rosette clearly starts to die off, which can take a considerable time.

Location

In nature bromeliads can grow under totally different conditions depending on the species. Many species grow suspended in trees, a way of growing called epiphytic. Other species grow in the earth; these I call terrestrial. Bromeliads are content in various climatic conditions; tropical rainforest, high elevations over 10,000 feet or the desert. All are suitable for particular species, which have accommodated themselves through clever adaptations. Often roots play an inferior role, serving only as an anchoring device. In some cases leaves take on this role, functioning as tendrils. There are also species

As the plant cross section to the left shows, the leaves of a bromeliad usually grow from a short trunk, which creates a tubular rosette that can hold water reserves. The flowers, often surrounded by striking bracts, may sit atop a long stalk, or sit down in the bottom of the rosette tube.

that form no roots at all. Spanish moss grows very cheerfully hanging from trees or telephone wires. And small gray-scaled *Tillandsias* can be tied to a piece of wood and grown in a greenhouse.

Water storage
Many bromeliads have the ability to hold water, not in their tissues but in their funnel-like rosettes or in the hollow spaces that are often present in the gray, bulb-shaped bromeliads. Large species can hold several quarts of water and in such a mini-pond various animal species can survive (frogs, for example). The bulb-shaped bromeliads serve as a good hiding place for ant colonies. It is possible that dead ants after decomposing serve as food for the plant. A question often asked is whether the rosette can withstand water. Soft water is not harmful, except when the plant is dormant and needs no water at all. In nature rain falls into the rosette as a matter of course.

Dormant periods
Bromeliads from the tropical rain forest, where uniform temperature and high humidity prevail, do not need dormant periods. Species native to areas where there are temporary droughts definitely need it. In these areas the temperature can also very significantly. Misting these plants with water now and then is usually sufficient to keep them alive during their dormant period.

Tips for cultivation
Most of the bromeliads that you buy in the store are tropical in origin, grown with a lot of attention, much light and humidity. Almost always they are in bloom when sold. It is important to re-

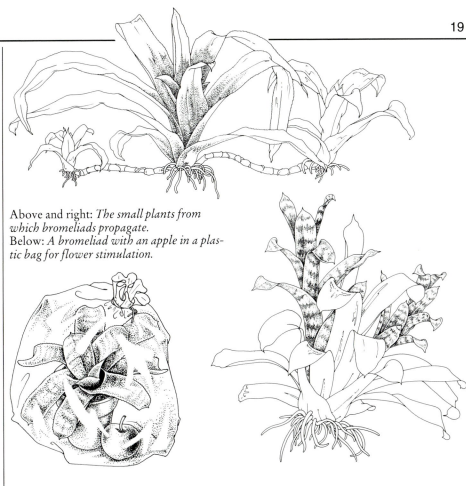

Above and right: *The small plants from which bromeliads propagate.*
Below: *A bromeliad with an apple in a plastic bag for flower stimulation.*

member that the plant, once in bloom, has already begun its dying off period. Care at this point does not matter. You can delay its death for several months by continuing to water the bromeliad. Do not place it in the sun, but use it to brighten a dark corner. When the bromeliad becomes less beautiful dispose of it.

It is a totally different story if you want to propagate small plants from the original. First of all I caution you that this is hard to do under living-room conditions. These small plants need a high level of humidity and temperature, and develop best in a greenhouse. Even then it will take several years before young rosettes are ready to bloom. If the plants have matured, but are not flowering, I suggest you add some bromeliad fertilizer in the

funnel of the plant. Another method to encourage blossoming is to secure the bromeliad together with some apples inside a plastic bag. The ethylene gas from the apples stimulates the flowering.

Putting together a collection
If you want to grow the big green bromeliads you need a lot of space, preferably in a greenhouse. It must be well heated in winter, and thus is an expensive hobby. Therefore, collectors often concentrate on the small, gray-scaled bromeliads (often *Tillandsia*) that require less space. These plants need a lot of light and can be hung in a wire—no need for soil. A week without water is no problem for this species. Normally these plants get dipped in water every day during the summer; in the winter every other day. During a dry summer, I hang many plants of this species outside in a not-too-dark tree. In the winter, these plants need as much light as possible. The temperature may drop to 60°F, temporarily even a bit lower. If you do not have a greenhouse it is possible to grow these small plants; either in a window greenhouse or terrarium.

Far left: *Each rosette flowers only once, after which the plant dies off.*
Left: Tillandsias *make excellent additions to any collection, and can grow with practically no humus.*

SUCCULENTS

All succulent plants are able to retain water in their tissues, in the trunk, the stem or the leaves. This characteristic is very noticeable with the bulb-shaped succulents such as cacti. It is less noticeable with the Wandering Jew, *Tradescantia*, which has thick fleshy stems. We call this type of plant a half-succulent. Succulents are divided into two groups: cacti, a family unto itself; and the remaining succulents of various families.

Cacti

These plants are distinguished from other succulents by "areoles," or little knobs or pillows, from which the thorns, flowers and leaves grow. Other succulents can have thorns too, especially various kinds of *Euphorbia*, but these grow straight from the plant and never from areoles.

There are cacti that develop ordinary, thin leaves, but they also have small groups of thorns on the stems; *Pereskia* is a good example. Another group is the pad cacti, such as the *Opuntia*. In the meaty throned pads we can still recognize the leaves. There are the column cacti with their thick throned stems; the *Cererus* is a good example. Finally there are the ball cacti whose growth pattern is the most efficient in limiting as much evaporation as possible. There are ball cacti that evaporate ten thousand times less water than a normal leaf plant.

An ability to conserve moisture is the most important characteristic of cacti and other succulents and enables them to survive long periods of drought. Everything about the plant is directed toward retaining moisture during short wet periods and to conserving moisture during the dry periods. The plant's optimal shape, pores that can close and a covering of shadow-producing thorns, all contribute to a cactus's water retention.

Column and ball cacti often have ribs and knobs, which hold the areoles. The areoles create the thorns, which we view as unformed leaves, and then flower bulbs open. Eventually new shoots appear, especially after an injury.

There are two kinds of thorns: central thorns and fringe thorns. The central ones are often larger and attractively colored, and have a defensive function. The fringe

Right: An Opuntia, *which has extremely fine hooked thorns called glochids that can break off and stick painfully into the skin.*
Far right: A truly rare cactus with real leaves and few thorns, Pereskia aculeata.

thorns are usually smaller, often colored white, and serve to shade the body of the cactus. The big hook-like bent thorns of some frightening-looking species are not the meanest; rather the small barbed thorns, called *Glochiden*, deserve that reputation. All of the species *Opuntia* have these barbs, which pierce your skin when you touch them and subsequently break off. Because of the barbs you will have difficulty in removing the thorn.

Many cacti have beautiful flowers. The blossoming period generally falls in spring and early summer. With some species the flowers are enormous in comparison to the body of the cactus. Other species will not flower in northern climates.

Strange forms also exist: cristate forms (those with a crest) are bizarre, freaks of nature that can be propagated. Little yellow or red cacti are often grafted on a green base; people sometimes think that the red or yellow part is the flower, but it is part of the cactus body itself.

Right: A succulent that's not a cactus, the Euphorbia officinarum, *variety* Beaumieriana.

Succulents

Strictly speaking, cacti belong to the group of succulents, but when we refer to succulent plants we usually mean the succulents that do not belong to the family *Cactaceae*. But sometimes you have to look twice to see the difference between a succulent and a cactus. Succulents, in general, show normal branching, such as we see in shrubs; the distance between the nodes, however, is often very small so that the leaves form a rosette. Moisture is stored in the leaf, but also in the trunk or stems. Typical trunk succulents, such as members of the species *Euphorbia*, form normal thin leaves, which soon fall. These are more or less rudimentary leaves, which the plant does not really need. In nature, the *Pachypodium* produces sturdy leaves, which it drops when there is a lack of moisture. The thorny body is then able to wait for a long period until it rains again before it forms new leaves.

The care of succulent plants

If you want to have success with succulent plants you should take into account the conditions of their natural growth. Succulents are able to store water and survive a long time without added moisture. The worst thing you can do is to give them too much water; the plant will

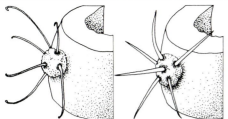

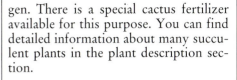

Cacti have areoles, from which thorns arise. Central thorns and edge thorns can be distinguished by their different colors. Glochids are hooked, thin thorns.

Below, left: *A small collection in bloom.* Below, right: Above: *The cristate form.* Middle: *A Kalanchoë species with new buds along the edges of the leaf.* Below: Euphorbia trigona *produces small leaves that drop off during times of drought.*

quickly rot away. In nature, periods of drought are dormant periods for a succulent plant. It is often, but not always, cooler in a drought period, depending on the climate zone in which the plant is growing. If we grow cacti in a moderate climate zone such as is found in large parts of Europe and North America, then we have to deal with a dark winter. Most succulent plants need plenty of light to grow healthy. If they have sufficient light, they will retain their density. But if we allow succulent plants to grow during the short winter days, they will soon lose their shape, grow thin and become sensitive to infections. For that reason it is best to let most succulent plants rest in winter.

You force them into dormancy by dropping the temperature and watering them less, since evaporation diminishes. It is even possible for some succulent plants to go totally dormant and do without any extra moisture. In some natural habitats this is a necessity where there can be years between rainfalls. Nonetheless cacti can survive there.

The optimum temperature for most cacti and succulents during dormancy varies between 40 and 50°F. But there are exceptions; some cacti only can withstand temperatures below freezing if they are kept very dry. With other cacti the tem-

perature has to remain a bit above 50°F. Finally, some true houseplant succulents do not care what the winter temperature is. They flourish beautifully when you keep them cool and dry during dormancy, but they also can thrive in a heated room year round. *Kalanchoe daigremontiana* is a good example as are many half-succulents like the *Peperomia* species. But almost all the cacti and the rich flowering succulents only stay healthy when their temperature and water supply are drastically reduced in winter.

During dormancy plants are preparing themselves for the next bloom. Buds are formed, but only begin to develop when the water supply and temperature slowly rise. Without a dormancy period most cacti will absolutely not flower. It is hard to say how much water you should give them during the rest period. When in doubt it is best not to give water at all. The soil should feel rather dry and the cactus body may shrink somewhat. In spring when the temperature rises and the light is stronger, mist lightly once a week. At the end of September after a summer of growth and bloom, most plants start their dormancy period again. In the summer succulent plants should be fed occasionally with a fertilizer that contains nitro-

gen. There is a special cactus fertilizer available for this purpose. You can find detailed information about many succulent plants in the plant description section.

ORCHIDS

All orchids belong to the family *Orchidaceae*, the largest of all the plant families. Ten percent of all flowering plants are orchids. The plant's special appeal is its flowers, for without them there is little else of interest. The dramatic flowers by themselves are often sold by florists while the plants have traditionally been found in the greenhouses of collectors. However, some species can be cultivated quite successfully in home environments.

Orchids have flowers that are characteristically different from those produced by other plants. There are three sepals and three petals. The top (middle) sepal is sometimes known as the flag. As a rule the sepals differ in form and color from the three petals, which are also called crown leaves. The two petals on either side of the flower are usually alike. But the middle or lowest petal nearly always has a different shape and is called a lip, labellum or shoe. In the middle of the orchid flower is the reproductive organ called the "column," containing both male and female genitalia.

A distinct method of growing
Orchids are divided into two groups depending on how they grow; monopodial and sympodial plants. Monopodial means that the orchid grows vertically from the seedling without making side shoots. Roots and leaves all come from this one stalk. A sympodial orchid is also a vertical growing plant. Leaves and flowers develop at the rootstock mostly above ground, but after blooming the growth continues horizontally. Therefore such sympodial plants soon grow out of their container. In many cases a kind of tuber, called a pseudobulb (pseudo because they are not really tubers in a botanical sense) or back bulb, grows at the rootstock. It is from these tubers that leaves grow again. The pseudobulbs are food storage organs, indicating that the plant needs to undergo a dry rest period.

Orchids can also be distinguished by where they grow—either terrestrial, earth-growing orchids, or epiphytic, tree-living orchids. The terrestrial orchids are able to recede into the earth when there is drought or other distress and then sprout up again later when conditions improve. The tree orchids use their roots to attach themselves to bark and branches. In cultivation, many long roots grow from tree orchids, which for the most part hang on the outside of the

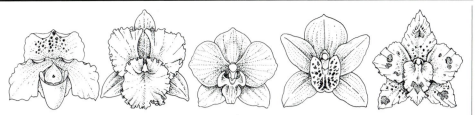

Though the flowers of orchids are sometimes very different in shape, sepals, petals and the labellum are often easy to recognize. From left to right: Paphiopedilum, X Vuylstekeara, Phalaenopsis, Cymbidium *and* Odontoglossum.

pot rather than on the inside. These aerial roots are protected against dehydration by a layer of dead cells that give the root a shiny silver exterior.

The cultivation of orchids

The species usually grown indoors all come from tropical and subtropical climate zones. This does not mean that they all like high temperatures, however, as there are also cool mountain areas in the tropics. What most orchids like is high humidity, preferably 80 percent or more. Therefore, many types are unsuitable for indoor cultivation because there the humidity often drops below 50 percent, especially in winter. Appropriate light is an important growing factor, but direct sunlight is not what most orchids want. This is the reason why orchid greenhouses are often chalked white or are provided with screens.

Many orchids also develop better if they are given a rest period in which the temperature drops and less water is provided. To know how to care for a specific orchid, read the plant description. Often even that is not sufficient, however—if you want to grow orchids, I advise you to buy a book specifically about orchids.

Appropriate soil mixture

Because of their growth habits, you cannot cultivate orchids in standard potting soil. For at least a hundred years man has been trying to produce orchid "soils" that match the characteristics of their natural environment. With fern roots (often os-monda fern), sphagnum moss, fir bark, redwood bark or coconut fiber man tried to please the plants, often with success. There are also commercial potting soils available formulated specifically for various types of orchids. At present, synthetic materials are used as well, such as rock wool (manufactured rock powder and resembling cotton), gravel or clay granules. None of these products retains water, which means that you have to water the plants rather often. Because no nutrients come from these synthetic materials, a weak solution of fertilizer should be added to the water during the growth period of an orchid. But the products do offer the advantage that the excess water will drain off immediately. Sufficient drainage is absolutely necessary for the successful cultivation of orchids. If the instructions for your orchid say: "Give orchid food every fortnight," it only applies to plants that are cultivated in organic soil. If you grow your orchids in synthetic material, which does not contain nourishment, then you must always add food to the water.

Wooden teak lattice baskets are often used for cultivating orchids, but regular plastic and clay pots can work, too, as long as they have good drainage. Actually, many species can be cultivated on just a piece of fir bark or a piece of material from a tree fern. Tie the plant to its support with copper wire or old pantyhose, then hang it in a humid location, preferably a greenhouse. Watering is easily accomplished by dipping the plant and the support piece in a tub with water. In the growth period remember to add some fertilizer to the water first.

Repotting becomes necessary when the plant starts to grow outside the container. With sympodial orchids the dying part is set against the side of the new pot, so that the pseudobulb with the new shoots has room to grow. Monopodial orchids can be centered in the middle of the pot. Orchid roots are often fragile, so repotting should be done with great care. Overgrown roots should be shortened.

Watering your orchid

In nature orchids receive a lot of rainwater, which ends up mostly at the end of the roots. They also receive moisture from condensation, which occurs regularly because of fog, high humidity, etc. This is all pure water with a low calcium content. Unfortunately, our tapwater frequently has a high level of carbonate hardness and for that reason is unsuitable for watering orchids. You should use rainwater or water that is stripped of calcium.

Propagation of orchids

All orchids can be grown from seed, but because the seed is extremely fine and germinates slowly, absolute sterility is necessary for success. Commercial growers germinate the seeds in sealed bottles. The plants can also be propagated via tissue cultivation, a difficult task for an amateur. In a home environment, however, it is quite simple to divide plants that show more than one growth point.

Numerous cross-breedings

Because orchids cross-breed quite easily, there are hundreds or even thousands of cross-pollinations, not just between the different species, but also between various families. As a result no other plant family has as many different variations as orchids. The offspring often carry names that are created from syllables of the original species. The prefix of the name of the new orchid is always a multiplication sign to indicate that it is an intergeneric crossing. Thus X *Brassolaelio cattleya* was created by cross-breeding the original species *Brassavola cattleya* and *Laelia*. It is impossible to record all of these cross-breedings in this particular book, although many of the original species existing in nature are discussed.

Left: *Next to photographs of a few orchid flowers, the drawings illustrate sympodial and monopodial methods of growth. The drawing to the left shows a horizontal rootstock (sympodial). The drawing to the right shows a pseudotuber, which grows vertically like a pyramid (monopodial).*

Above: *Many orchids grow better when cultivated in lattice baskets (left) than flower pots (middle). Many species can be grafted onto a piece of fern tree with copper wire or nylon thread (right). By dipping and spraying these plants during their growing period, enough food and water can be provided.*

BULBS AND TUBERS

These are self-contained plants with the ability to store their food in order to survive barren, dry times. Everybody knows hyacinths, daffodils and tulips, but there are many more of these plants that are suitable for a (temporary) place in the living room.

Bulbs

A true bulb is an underground stem with a point around which thick leaves grow. The leaves are called scales; together they form a bulb, containing the food supply. A flower-bud develops in the center which opens from the top of a stalk in the growing season. Leaves also develop at the same time, which during the growing season transport food to the underground bulb. After blooming, the section above ground gradually dies off, during which period a new bulb or a new bulb-scales develop in the soil, ready to bloom the following season. However, a new bulb will only develop if the leaves are allowed to fully mature and yellow. Usually this is best left to bulbs planted in the garden.

Tubers

Actually there are two types of tubers—those formed of stem tissue and those of root tissue. Along stem tubers, eyes or buds form, which sprout and grow new shoots that develop into the leaves and flowers. These tubers can be divided to form new plants, but in order to sprout each piece must have an eye or bud. Potatoes are an example of stem tubers while dahlias are examples of root tubers. A corn tuber differs from a bulb in that it is made up of solid, fleshy tissue. If we cut

A bulb (drawing) consists of a short stalk with swollen scale leaves or leaf bases.

Lilies can produce roots above the soil, where new bulbs are formed. New bulbs can also grow from bulb cuttings, which can then flower after a few years of cultivation.

right through it, it appears to be solid, not skirted, as is the case with bulbs. Buds that produce flowers and leaves are situated at the top of the tuber. After blooming this growth completely dies down, while a brand new tuber (or tubers) starts to form on top of the old one. Examples of tubers are the crocus, gladiolus and cyclamen.

Rhizomes

These are thick roots that usually grow horizontally in the soil and are elongated and often branched. In various spots on the upper surface of the rhizome vertical buds or shoots will appear that eventually grow leaves and flowers. Examples are rex begonias and bearded iris.

Keep spring flowers cool

It is useful to divide both the bulb and tuber plants into spring and summer plants, because their treatment is quite different. Many of the bulb plants that flower in the spring garden, such as crocuses, hyacinths, daffodils and tulips, can be forced into early blooming and enjoyed in our homes. In general these plants need a cool, dark start, so that roots can form. To have flowers in bloom during the dark winter months, plant the bulbs (usually in soil, sometimes in water or on pebbles) at staggered intervals during the fall. The bulbs are buried just below the surface; very large bulbs, such as the amaryllis, may stick up a bit. Moisten the soil and put in a dark place; the hardy bulbs like crocus or daffodils need a low temperature. At temperatures between 40° and 50°F, they form excellent roots.

If you have a garden, put the potted bulbs in a trench or cold frame. The pots should be buried about 16 inches deep to prevent them from freezing. Cover the surface with straw or a thick layer of leaves, so you will be able to dig up the pots before a heavy freeze.

If you have no garden, this rooting process can be done in a cool basement or in a frost-free box on the balcony. If there is danger of a freeze, wrap the pots in black plastic for protection. Check from time to time to be sure the soil is still moist.

Bulbs have been in cold temperatures long enough if you can feel a thickening, which is the flower-bud, under the leaves. Bring the bulbs into moderate light, but continue to keep them rather cool for a while. The temperature should not be higher than 60°F. Mist them often and to limit evaporation, put a plastic bag over the plant. Crocuses stop flowering very quickly, when they are placed in a warm room. Tulips can tolerate more heat.

After these spring bulbs have flowered, the bulbs are generally thrown out. It is almost impossible to get them to flower another time.

The one exception is the amaryllis, which can bloom for many years if after blooming the plant is allowed to follow its natural growth and leaves develop and mature. Amaryllis bulbs can grow to gigantic sizes.

Summer blossomers can handle heat

Bulbs, tubers and rhizomes that bloom in the summer are usually planted in March and April. They need no cool, dark rooting period and can be put in a warm environment as soon as potted. Often high humidity is necessary, especially for members of the *Gesneria* family. For small plants a window greenhouse is big enough.

One of the easiest-to-cultivate plants in this group is the tuberous begonia, which flourishes beautifully on balconies and patios. The tubers are put in warm, moist sphagnum moss so that they will sprout quickly. Only after sprouting are they planted in pots. It is even easier to start them in small pots filled with peat. Leaves and flowers develop over the summer. After the vegetation has ended, the plants die off once again. Dormancy can be encouraged by watering them less toward the end of August and into September. The tuber can remain in the soil, stored there till the next spring. The optimum storage temperature is generally between 50° and 60°F.

Propagating

Bulbs and tubers often develop new shoots that can be removed and grown as separate plants. But in general it takes years before such an offspring will flower. The tubers and even the rhizomes are easier to propagate. These are best divided in the spring, after they have developed some shoots and you are able to detect the eyes. Each section has to have at least one growth-point, otherwise it will not be able to sustain itself and develop a new plant.

Ensiling pots with flower bulbs is a good way to get flowering plants to bloom prematurely. Do make sure, however, that the ground above the hole does not freeze up completely, trapping the bulbs underground until spring.

If you do not have access to a garden, then an ensiling box can be built for use elsewhere, for example, on a balcony. Again, try to keep the soil from freezing.
Below, right: A hyacinth glass.

CONSERVATORY AND CONTAINER PLANTS

These plants need similar care, as was the case with plants of the succulent and bromeliad types. But they come from different families and otherwise have very little in common. Technically, they are not houseplants, since they cannot tolerate growing inside in a warm room year-round. The following pages provide information on how to give them the care they really need.

A long history

The history of the conservatory started when travelers brought exotic plants back to Europe from foreign lands, beginning with the Crusaders in the 12th century who brought back plants from the Middle East. Italian sailors imported fascinating plants from the vast areas of Asia. In Italy the plants could be kept outside for a long period, but in the winter they probably succumbed to the cold. It was not until 1585 that the first greenhouse was built and only then was it discovered that it was possible to cultivate these exotic plants in northern Europe, despite the cold winters. By the 17th century conservatories or orangeries, as they are also known, were being built all over Germany, England and France.

A conservatory is a cool storeroom

To this day on old country estates and some botanical gardens, one can still admire the cool storerooms of centuries ago. They are in general tall, dark build-ings usually made of stone with large doors through which to haul the plants. Initially they were not glass houses at all and were not very light inside. In winter, with burning stoves the temperature was kept to around 45°F. Even if it was warmer outside, it did not get warmer than the 45°F inside these dark rooms, because of the thick walls. In the fall the plants were brought inside, and in the spring, as soon as the danger of frost was gone, they were hauled outside. To make them easy to move, they were planted in large, wooden tubs, which is why they are often called tub plants. Some botanical gardens, especially in Europe, still operate in this manner, but modern conservatories now have large glass windows.

You can have your own conservatory

This elaborate history will give you an idea of the rigorous demands of these plants. Most species grown in a conservatory originated from subtropical climates, where it is usually not warm in the winter. (There can be snow even on the Riviera.) Conservatory plants need a change of season to end one growth period and to form new buds for the next season. When I speak of conservatory plants, you probably immediately think of the gigantic plants that one sees in botanical gardens. The name is somewhat confusing, but it does not refer to size, but rather to the kind of cultivation the plants need. A simple Chinese rose with a length of 8 inches or an oleander can both be conservatory plants, as can a fuchsia or a yucca. Without your realizing it you probably have some conservatory plants

On page 26: *A collection of container plants from the author's garden. In the summer they are kept in a sunny location; in the winter, these plants are stored in a greenhouse with a temperature of 40–50°F (5–10°C).*

Below, left: *Even banana trees can be cultivated as container plants.*
Below, right: Above: *An Italian terracotta flower pot.* Below: *Dantura is a beloved (but poisonous) container plant. There are species with yellow or light red flowers as well.*

at home. If you want to treat these plants well, you should try to create a cool space in your home.

It can be a cool hallway or foyer. If you have a garage with extra room alongside the car, you can install a large window and skylight and create your own conservatory that can store a lot of container plants. A porch is an excellent place for container plants. A real conservatory or greenhouse would be even better of course, because it can be kept cool, yet frost-free in the winter.

Containers

Plants look very pretty in teakwood containers, varnished neutral or, even more chic, painted green. It is a pity that these containers are so expensive. Fortunately, the plants don't care and grow as well in a big plastic container, provided there is sufficient drainage. Make holes in the bottom and place old pot shards or gravel in the bottom of the container before adding the soil. Less expensive than teak and more decorative than plastic is Italian red terracotta, which is marketed in many forms and sizes. It is not freeze-proof, but then neither are the plants, so that is no problem. To prevent moisture from quickly evaporating via the clay sides in the summer, I always line the insides of such pots with black plastic, before I add

the soil and plants. With this protection the roots will not dry out so quickly. Additionally you inhibit those ugly white calcium spots that you see on many flower pots.

Soil mixtures

Most container plants flourish in standard potting soil, which is commercially available in bags. But palm and citrus plants, especially, need more calcium in the soil and grow better in a mixture where clay (fine) or loam is added. Sometimes it is possible to buy separately potting soil containing clay. But you can also just dig up some clay and loam and make your own mixture. (See page 66.)

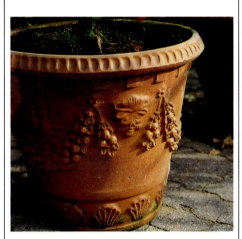

Young container plants properly cared for grow fast, so that you will soon have a decent sized plant. For that reason, for the first few years you will need to repot the plants every year. The best time to do this is in spring before new growth starts. Once a plant has reached a substantial size, it will only need to be repotted every few years. In the summer, fertilize these plants every two weeks. Discontinue fertilizing after August, so that the plant will become dormant before the winter arrives.

Cultivation

Some container plants can withstand frost, but more than one light frost is not advisable. These plants have to be brought inside when fall weather approaches. I always try to delay this moment as long as possible by protecting the plants with plastic when there is a danger of night frost; I take the plastic off again when all danger of frost is over. Often a light freeze occurs early in the fall followed by mild weather sometimes lasting through early December, depending on your location. In that case, the plants can stay outside, but keep a very close eye on the weather forecast.

During winter storage do not allow the temperature to rise very much, because warmer temperatures will induce the plants to grow again. This is unwise since in the winter the light is weaker and any new growth will become long, weak and more susceptible to diseases later. If the winter storage area gets warmer than 55°F, you should ventilate it. Do not be fooled: the temperature will rise inside on a sunny, bright day even if the outside temperature is quite low. Naturally you have to stop ventilation at night. Especially in the months of March and April, it is important to continue to keep the container plants cool, for frost can still occur through May. The plants can be brought outside in good weather, but at the threat of frost bring them inside or cover them. The minimum temperature tolerated varies from plant to plant and is indicated in the plant descriptions. A laurel can tolerate a temperature below zero, while plants originating in more tropical climates can hardly endure a temperature below 55°F.

Summer location

In the summer most container plants like a sheltered, sunny spot. A patio or a sheltered terrace is fine. A number of plants do not like full sunlight, for instance, the fuchsias, so be sure to check this information in the plant descriptions.

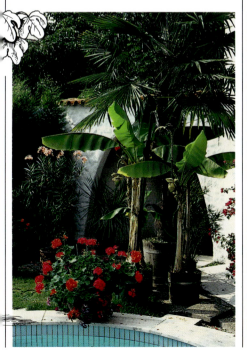

BONSAI

Bonsai literally means "a plant that grows in a flat bowl," and it is often, but not always, a hardy, deciduous plant. The Japanese have been cultivating these dwarf trees for almost 1,000 years, trying to better understand nature by working with it and miniaturizing it. Over the centuries bonsai has become an integral part of the Japanese culture and religion. In the West, where bonsai has gained popularity in recent years, we treasure these small trees for other reasons: as beautiful objects, for prestige or as a fascinating hobby.

How do you keep them alive?
Almost all bonsai are cultivations of hardy plants that grow outside in a seasonal climate. If they are kept in a warm room year-round, they do not get the necessary rest period.

Only a few plants are considered indoor bonsai, and these originate from tropical regions where the seasons are constant and warm (just as in your living room). For instance, various types of *Ficus* in bonsai form will stay healthy inside year-round. In regard to appropriate growing conditions, there is no real difference between "normal" plants and bonsai. An apple tree belongs outside and a *Ficus* inside.

Where to keep a bonsai
The outdoor bonsai grows best in a sheltered, half-shady spot outside. They can endure a frost, but during the extreme of winter they should be brought in to a conservatory or greenhouse, where temperatures are between 40 and 50°F. The plants should not grow, but be allowed to go dormant during this period. Deciduous shrubs or trees will lose their leaves. The best place to keep indoor bonsai in the winter is on a window sill that faces east or west, so that the bright midday sun cannot reach the plants.

Styles of growing
In the course of time various styles of bonsai have been created by the Japanese. It is not the purpose of this book to describe every style, but in general the styles are taken from themes in nature: weathered tree, crooked tree, wind-blown tree, groups of trees creating a miniature forest, etc. The bonsai bought or cultivated by Westerners do not always match the specific traditional styles. They are not "authentic" in that regard, but are still interesting, decorative plants.

Pruning is essential
A bonsai only stays a bonsai if it is pruned from time to time to maintain its size and shape. This is usually done in the spring just before new growth starts. Pruning has two purposes: keeping the plants small and giving them the appropriate shape. To do this, it is necessary to know the way a tree branches, since once pruned it will sprout again from eyes, active or not. If you carefully observe trees in nature, then it will not be difficult to determine the growth direction of a future branch on a bonsai. With this knowledge it is possible to make woody plants grow according to a predetermined idea. Often in spring there will be many buds on a tree. If they all develop, the tree will become a criss-cross of small branches. To create an interesting bonsai one has to make a careful choice between buds that are allowed to develop and those that are removed. Buds are removed with a small pair of scissors. By taking a bud off the end of a branch, one stimulates the development of more branches.

Besides pruning the branches, it is necessary to cut back the roots as well, otherwise there will soon be no room in the small bonsai container. Pruning of the roots slows the top growth considerably. Always keep in mind the balance between root volume and the volume above the soil. When pruning the roots you should

Only a few bonsai can be kept in a warm room all year round. Most species require a cool dormancy. Only tropical plants are suitable for indoor bonsai cultivation, such as this Ficus retusa, *which is rather easy to grow.*

always be careful not to remove all the root hairs, since water and nutrients are taken up through these fine roots. New root hairs are formed most quickly in the spring, but even then it is wise to save some root hairs to make regeneration of the plant easier. After pruning, keep the bonsai in the shade to minimize evaporation; mist often and, if necessary, enclose it in a plastic bag until growth is re-established.

Shaping the bonsai

In addition to direct pruning, it is possible to shape bonsai by training the young branches. This training is frequently done by wrapping the branches in thick copper or aluminum wire that is specially manufactured for this purpose. It should be done carefully and gradually, because if you bend the branches too forcefully, they will break. In six months or less, the branches will hold their position without the support of the wire. The metal should be removed then to prevent denting and damaging the trunk. Older established bonsai rarely need such wire support and can be maintained with pruning.

Repotting

Bonsai are often cultivated in shallow, glazed bowls that are made with many drainholes. Copper wire is inserted in the drainholes to fasten the root ball to the

pot. In that way the tree (or trees) can be held in the desired position. Pieces of wire mesh are used to cover the drainholes and prevent the soil from washing away.

The potting soil should be adjusted to the needs of the particular plant being grown. When this book recommends acid soil for a plant, restrain from adding any calcium. It is important that the growth medium be able to adequately hold moisture and still drain well. A mixture of standard potting soil, sharp sand and fine clay or loam will be sufficient for most plants. Instead of sand, one can also use perlite, but that is less attractive in the pot. The soil should be evenly spread around the roots and watered in, so that it lies smoothly against the delicate roots. The surface is then covered with moss or very small pebbles.

Fertilizing the bonsai

Because of the small pot in which the bonsai grows, its roots have little access to soil. As a result, the nutrients in the soil will soon be exhausted. A lot of fertilizing

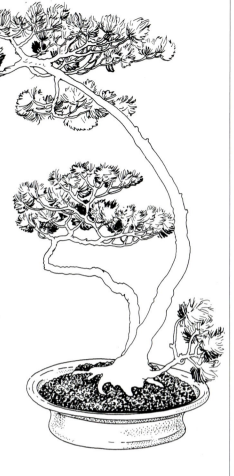

A bonsai in the sloping Shankan style.

is unnecessary, because it causes too much growth. Fertilizing is only necessary when the plants are actually growing, usually in summer. Towards the end of the summer one should stop fertilizing to coax the plant into its winter rest. Bonsai plants in a consistently warm environment can be fertilized longer into the fall, but should be given a break for a while during the winter.

In bonsai cultivation, chunks of organic compost is often used to fertilize; it is spread among the roots and slowly dissolves. Another method is to add a liquid fertilizer regularly during the growth period (preferably a complete fertilizer with trace elements). Use a light concentration; for instance, .5 to .75 fluid ounces per quart of water. Another tip: always use rainwater or soft water to water the bonsai to prevent the accumulation of calcium in the soil.

When growing bonsai, the aim is strictly defined forms. These can be achieved by pruning with special tools and by forcing the twigs into certain positions with thread. After some time, the tied branches will remain in their position without support.

DISPOSABLE PLANTS

People do not like to discard what they admire. So why are so many plants sold that will prove to be a disappointment? These plants are very pretty at the moment of purchase, but doomed to wither away within a short period, no matter what care they receive.

What are disposable plants?

By "disposable plants" I mean a whole range of plants that will only last for a short time indoors. A good example is the potted chrysanthemum sold by many florists. With assistance from artificial light and darkness, the plants are forced into bloom. They are sprayed with substances to stunt growth. You then buy a plant in a beautiful flowering state. Enjoy it while the flowers last for after they are gone, there is little to do but throw it away. With watering you can prolong the existence of the plant, but nothing will get the plant to bloom again. In the summer, you can plant the chrysanthemum out in the garden. The growth inhibitors will be worn off by that time, and it may grow into a rather large plant, that will probably freeze the next winter because it is not hardy. Occasionally somebody succeeds in bringing a poinsettia into bloom for a second time, for this is not completely impossible in home conditions. But 95 percent of them end up in the garbage after Christmas. The same happens to the pretty begonias, which look so beautiful in the winter. It will be a very disappointing experience to try to get them to flower again. I will always mention in the plant descriptions whether a particular plant is difficult or even impossible to keep, so you will know what to expect from it. Annual plants, *Browallia*, *Exacum*, *Thunbergia* and such, die off in nature after blooming, and they will have the same fate indoors.

Bromeliads are slightly different in this aspect. Every rosette blooms only one time and then dies off. But people with "green thumbs" cultivate the new suckers that form around the original plant; these new plants will eventually flower. This is not at all difficult to do with the hardy *Billbergias*, but most other species are more of a problem. There is always a chance you will succeed, however, and it is fun just to try.

This advice applies to a lot of other houseplants, which although difficult to maintain well, will prosper with good care. Take, for instance, the beautiful fern *Nephrolepis*. With little care it will only be fit for the garbage within a month. But if you give it proper attention, it can last indoors three months to six months and sometimes even longer. After a while, this plant will demonstrate visibly the love and attention it has received.

Why buy them?

There are numerous reasons why we buy disposable plants. I do not object at all to using colorful, happy annuals indoors. Many people buy a potted chrysanthemum because it lasts longer than a bouquet of flowers and is the same price. Indeed, it is for much the same reason that we eat fast food because cooking is too time-consuming. For everything there is a reason.

While these plants are meant to be enjoyed and then discarded, I find it absolutely appalling when plants that normally have a long life expectancy are placed in a spot where they have no chance of survival—something that happens often in office situations. I cannot comprehend how someone can love a four-foot-high *Yucca* and yet keep it in a dark corner at a constant temperature of 68°F, only to find it clearly deteriorating in a few months' time. Sadly enough such treatment happens frequently. I hope that this book may contribute to a more respectful treatment of our plants.

PLANTS THAT LAST

Below: *Good examples of perennial houseplants are the* Clivia *(left) and the* Crassula. *With good care, which mainly involves providing properly timed dormant periods, these plants can live for decades.*

The opposite of the disposable plant is what I call the "laster." This is the houseplant that can live for years, sometimes decades, and that often becomes an heirloom after the death of the owner. People do get attached to these plants and do everything to preserve them. The *Clivia* will become a friend that also rewards you every year with more and more flowers. Often you can propagate these particular plants either through cuttings or seeds, a true hobby that can give much pleasure.

Do not buy them too large

If you want your plants to last a long time, do not choose species that grow too fast and become too big. A six-foot *Ficus* is of course a beautiful indoor tree. But did you ever see the same *Ficus* in nature? In Indonesia, for instance, they easily reach 60 feet or higher. The same could happen with good care in your living room. But because the ceilings in our homes are seldom higher than 10 feet, there will always come the sad day when you have to say farewell to the plant or give it an ugly amputation. No, it is far better to select a smaller plant. *Crassula ovata*, also known as "German oak," is a beautifully branched little shrub with thick branches and plump leaves, which with the right care can grow really old. Other long-lived plants are the already-mentioned *Clivia*,

On page 30: *Disposable plants:* Left, *potted chrysanthemums;* right, *annual houseplants.*

the sturdy *Philodendron* and *Monstera* and a whole group of other plants. It is important to leave these "eternal" plants in the same environment and not to change their treatment very much. They should be repotted regularly though, because our tapwater contains calcium and magnesium sulfates. They accumulate in the pot and over many years can poison the plants. You can eliminate this danger by using pure rainwater.

Other plants can last and give you continuing pleasure if you give them time in a garden. Towards the fall these "lasters" are brought in from the garden and forced to bloom another time. There are many plants that respond well to this treatment, such as the *Hortensia*, the *Cacti*, the *Cyclamen* and the *Azalea*. Every year the plants grow taller, and after 10 years they will have become true family treasures.

PLANTS IN THE WINDOW

Most houseplants are grown in a window because they need the light. But not all windows are good for plants, and we should consider what the particular conditions are and what measures we can take to make a window site as agreeable to the plants as possible.

Windows on all sides

A house can have windows on all sides. It is important that you know what direction your house faces when you buy your plants. This is explained in detail on page 52. It is absolutely wrong to grow plants that need a lot of light in a north-facing window, and shade plants will die in no time in a southern window. Few plants can endure either full sunlight or its total absence. The ideal windows are those that face east or west. Since light requirements are dealt with elsewhere I will limit this discussion to the other growth conditions needed in the area around the window.

Modern building techniques are not helpful to many plants

In earlier times windows were rather small, consisting of a single sheet of glass pane fitted into a wooden frame, which often had imperfections that allowed heat to escape. The house was heated with a stove that was located as far from the windows as possible. In older houses one can still come across these conditions today. Because warm air rises and after partly cooling descends again, the stove location creates a current that rises near the stove, passes along the ceiling towards the window, descends quickly and then moves back along the floor to the stove. People sit next to the stove in cold weather, but near the windows in hot weather as it is much cooler. For plants that like a rest period in the winter these are ideal conditions. Tropical plants,

however, which like a consistently warm temperature throughout the year, will suffer in an old-fashioned home like that.

In houses built recently with central heating, the situation is reversed, as the gas heaters are under the windows. The heat rises at the window, passes along the ceiling towards the windowless wall opposite, drops there and comes back along the floor. As a result, plants are continuously in a warm air current. Tropical plants such as *Ficus* or *Dracaena* are quite happy with that situation, but plants that like to rest in the wintertime start to bloom too early because of the heat and get totally confused. (See page 62.)

Construction of the window sill

How well a plant will do at a window near a heater depends on how the window sill is constructed. If it is a narrow plank, which does not fit the window frame, then the hot air from the radiator below

Various plant windows. The top photo shows an east-facing window, bottom left a north-facing window, bottom right a south-facing window.

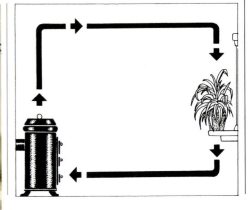

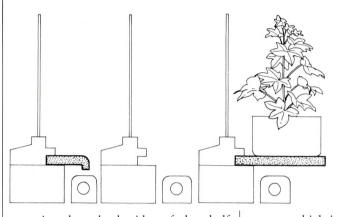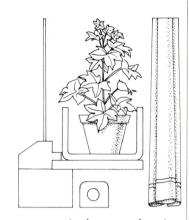

Plant locations in homes are not generally accounted for when houses are built. Usually, window ledges are much too narrow, and often above radiators, which creates overly dry conditions for many plants.

A wider window ledge can be created by adding some sort of flat shelf, and a waterproof container would improve it even more, resulting in more room for plants and a healthier, more humid location.

can rise along both sides of the shelf, brushing against the leaves of the plants. This is the worst condition for a plant. It is somewhat better if the sill actually fits the window, for instance with ceramic window tiles. The hot air in that case can only pass by one side. Furthermore, the width of the window ledge is important. It is often much too narrow for plants. The wider the better for the plants.

Many houses of modern design do not have window sills, because the windows reach the floor. In that case, the heat vents are on the floor in front of the window, covered with a grate, to let hot air pass. It is not advisable to place your plants on this grate as they will dry out from the warm air current.

Single or double glass
For plants, it makes a big difference if the window has a single or double pane of glass. A single pane of glass is not a good insulator, resulting in the temperature near the window being considerably lower than elsewhere in the room. You will be surprised at the difference, if you check the temperature with a thermometer on a cold winter day. Energy costs

money, which is why more new houses are equipped with insulated-glass windows. Storm windows are often added to older houses for the same reason. The temperatures at the window ledge will rise considerably with either kind of window. Some plants will be happy, while other plants, such as the *Cyclamen*, which like a cool place, will hardly survive behind a well-insulated window.

Curtains closed or open?
If window curtains are kept open at night, the temperature near the window stays nearly constant; when curtains are drawn, blocking the window ledge from the warm room, the temperature will drop considerably. The humidity increases when the curtains are drawn, however (see page 64), and this can be advantageous for many plants, provided they can endure the low temperature. Obviously, if curtains are drawn, it makes a big difference to the plants if the window has a storm window or not. If it is a single glass pane, then frost may appear on the window on a cold night, which is extremely harmful to plants. If you are afraid that this will happen during your winters,

then hang your curtains between the window and the plants.

Too much light in the summer
In the summer there is usually too much light and warmth at a south-facing window. The solution is to create shade. A window can be shaded from the outside with an awning. This method has the advantage of keeping the heat from the room as well. To provide effective shade from the inside use Venetian or Levelor blinds. But the room will be hotter with this method.

Choosing plants for a window sill
By determining the amount of light entering through the window, the direction of the window is facing and the possible temperature variations, you can determine which plants will flourish in a particular window. Compare these conditions to the light, temperature, humidity and rest periods described in this book. By consulting the charts in the back, you can easily select suitable plants for a particular window.

If there is not enough room on the window sill for all your plants, you can build more shelves, one above the other, placing the plants on different levels. Plant lovers frequently cover their whole window with plants. This is an attractive way to discourage peepers.

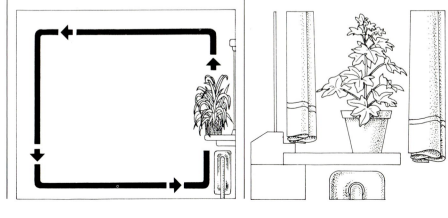

Far left: Air circulation by stove. To the right: A radiator beneath a window reverses the direction of the stove-circulated air. Left: With a curtain between window and plant, the plant can stay warm at night. With a curtain placed between the plant and the rest of the room, the plant cools off at night. The proper use of curtains depends entirely on the care requirements of a given plant.

OTHER PLACES TO GROW HOUSEPLANTS

Although 80 percent of all houseplants are placed at a window, there are other places to grow them. Many times these are areas where there is not much light, so consequently you have to select plants that like a shady spot.

Container plants

Plants in large pots or containers can be moved in principle anywhere in the room provided there is sufficient light. (See page 53.) An easy rule of thumb to remember is twice the distance to the window equals four times less light. Thus, if you go too far from the window, there will be not enough light for your plants to thrive. Artificial light (see page 54) can make a difference, but you should not expect miracles. The size of your windows, small or large, also makes a big difference. Large windows carry light much farther into a room. Also the back of a room on the tenth floor of an unobstructed apartment building is much lighter than the back of a room in a house surrounded by woods. Every room is different and only after you measure the light can you decide where to put the container plant.

Mixed container gardens are a problem

We continue to see container gardens with a mixture of plants in one large pot. And we can hardly object as long as all the plants in the arrangement need the same conditions and do not obstruct one another. But unfortunately people tend to mix together plants that do not suit each other well. The best solution if you have such a garden is to leave the prettiest and largest plant in the container and replant the rest in other pots. In this way, you can give each plant the growing conditions it deserves. You will be more successful if you select an appropriate plant for an empty space rather than combining several. A pretty possibility can be to add a low ground cover, such as *Soleirolia*, to cover the soil.

If the light comes from one side only, then the plant will grow toward the light. Foliage plants (these are most suitable for mixed containers anyway), can be turned once in a while without a problem, to prevent lopsided growth.

Far left: *A badly planted container:* Dracaena, Euphorbia *and* Ficus *all require different care.*
Left: *An umbrella plant in a bedroom.*
Below: *Even olive trees can be grown inside, if given enough light and cool temperatures in the winter.*

A good container is important

When used as a design element a houseplant is often placed inside a decorative container. Although the decorative aspect is entirely your judgment, it is still advisable to keep a few practical things in mind. For every plant there is a certain balance between the part above ground and the dimensions of the root-system. A *Ficus* six feet tall in a pot with a diameter of 12 inches is wrong. The plant will soon topple over, and furthermore there is not enough room for roots to grow in such a small pot. In fact there is not enough soil and the plant will dry out too quickly. It is better to buy a container large enough to allow the plant to grow and expand than one that is too small. When purchased, most plants are already too big for their pots. The commercial grower likes to keep costs down regarding potting soil and the weight to be transported.

A decorative container should be watertight at the bottom, but pots with no drainage are not suitable for the plants because they often get water logged. Therefore, I advise you to make a viewing tube (see page 69). Even more effective is to use a watering system, or hydrocultivation.

Hanging and climbing plants

There are many interesting plants with a climbing or hanging growth pattern that can grow against walls or drop dramatically from ceilings, always provided of course that there is enough light. Climbing plants usually do not cling without some support, so you have to help them here and there, especially when the wall has a smooth surface. Besides walls and partitions, ropes tied to a window sill can serve as a growing space for a climbing plant. Climbing plants often stand in pots or boxes on the floor and the growth guided upwards along a wall or other structure.

The containers of hanging plants can be mounted high on a wall or on the ceiling, so they can drop their long stalks. Be warned, however, if you are concerned about your wallpaper or other wallcovering, that the care of such plants can pose a problem. Misting can discolor the wallpaper, although there is no problem when your wall is made of brickwork. Do not spray with water containing calcium, however, as you might end up with chalky spots on the brick wall. With hanging plants the pots are often difficult to reach, which does not simplify the watering process. Too often these high-placed pots are forgotten, and then, of course, the plants die. Useful in such situations are special hanging pots complete with a saucer where surplus water can collect. The easiest way to water a staghorn fern is to take the whole plant down, dip it in water and after draining hang it again. This is a good way to water other hanging plants as well. Hang them in such a way as to make it easy to take them down.

Plants in bathrooms and kitchens

In bathrooms and kitchens the relative humidity in the air is often higher than in other rooms. Many plants appreciate this atmosphere and if there is sufficient light, these rooms can be decorated with a variety of plants. Bathrooms are often too dark for plants, but in newer houses the bathrooms often have fairly large windows. Tropical plants, which like warmth and high humidity, will really flourish there. In kitchens too there is often a lot of steam, which keeps the air moist for plants. Of course one should select plants that like to stay warm year-round, because kitchens as well as bathrooms are used daily and are always heated in the winter.

The cool hall or vestibule

Some houses have a cool hall or vestibule that is scarcely heated. In common hallways of apartment buildings the temperature also tends to be lower, often near the ideal winter temperature for many plants, between 50° and 60° F. Almost all plants that need a rest period in the winter are suitable for growing in such spaces. Water less frequently and take care that the plants don't freeze—that is all you have to do.

Houseplants can grow almost anywhere in a home if the proper species are selected. They can be cultivated in a bathroom (right, top and bottom), *and even coming out of a marble floor. These plants' large containers are invisible, sunk beneath the floor's surface.*

PERMANENT PLANTERS AND OTHER ARRANGEMENTS

In newly built houses or when remodeling a home, it is exciting to arrange for permanent places for indoor plants. A built-in planter often looks very pretty, and if it is well made—by that I mean its location as well as the construction—then the plants will flourish better than they would in separate pots on the window sill. On these pages you will find tips for building these permanent containers.

Always in the light

The most important question is where the planter will be built. It should never be far from a window, or you will have to use artificial light, which many times leads to disappointment. (See also pages 54–55.) Therefore first measure the light in your proposed location. Before you start to build, consider the needs of the plants you would like to grow. Try to think "plant," and not just what you think is pretty. Naturally it would be ideal if you could combine satisfactorily both your choice of plant and the conditions available. In any case it is better if you know beforehand, what plants you want to grow in the permanent unit. If you are a lover of orchids, you should consider the particular demands of these plants when building the planter. (Anyway, you will discover that it is probably better with orchids to build a plant window or a greenhouse!)

Type of construction important

If you want to build permanent planters in an existing home, you must take into account the construction of the house before deciding on the material for the planter. For instance, it is better not to choose brick, which is heavy, if the planter will sit on a wooden floor—unless, however, you can reinforce the floor and make a foundation for the brick planter. If there is a concrete floor that can bear a heavy weight, then you can use brick easily.

Make these planters watertight by draping the insides with plastic; they should not create spots on the floor. Leaking planters are a big problem and not easily repaired. You will need a way to keep an eye on the water level in the bottom of the planter. Before you notice, it can be half full of water, and not many plants like that! By putting a thick layer of pebbles on the bottom, you can drain the surplus water away from the plant roots.

Newly built houses are an easier proposition. Inform your contractor or architect as early as possible in the building process about your wishes. He will take care of the structural part, and you can take care of the interests of the plants. I advise you to use only water-resistant materials, which can endure wet soil, such as natural stone, concrete or stainless steel.

Floor level planters in front of the window

Often we see a plant window that is level with the floor. The outlet of the heating system is often situated right in front of the window. This is a way to keep the window clear of condensation. It is convenient to make this space at least 12–20 inches wide, because then window washing is still possible by standing in the space. From here, you can tend to the plants from the far side of the planted area as well.

In front of the radiator, separated by a watertight wall, is the pit for the plants. The depth should be at least 24 inches, although it can be deeper; the width should be no wider than 24 inches, so that you are still able to reach into the back of the planter to care for the plants. The

Two examples of built-in plant cases. The larger picture shows a case in front of a shaded window, with an easily cleaned formica surface. The picture above shows a plant case in a south-facing window, filled with sun-loving plants such as cacti.

The drawing illustrates a plant case built above a radiator, with temperature regulation from a heat cable. The heat of the plant case can be controlled by means of a timer and/or thermostat.

floor-level plant window should be completely waterproof but at the same time be provided with one or more drainpipes for surplus water. If possible connect the drain system to the house's sewage system. In the bottom of the pit there should be a drainage layer at least 4 inches thick, covered with a filter. The potting-soil lies on top of the filter.

Another solution for drainage is to use individual containers, which are small enough to be pulled out. Each container has its own drain and drainage layer, and stands free from the bottom and sides of the built-in pit. These smaller planters make repotting a lot easier, and you can rearrange and interchange them periodically with other planters, perhaps containing bulbs, cacti or azaleas from outside, etc.

Plants in soil

Your first instinct is probably to remove the plants from their pots and plant them in the loose soil of the planter. The positive result is they will grow better, but the disadvantage is that all the roots will get entangled and after a year or two it will be almost impossible to remove a plant without damaging it and all the others. The solution for that problem is to keep plants in individual pots (as large as buckets) and bury them in the pit. You can fill in and spread pebbles around them if you think that is pretty. Replacing, renewing and removing plants becomes much easier this way.

Soil level

Soil settles down in planters. If you do not occasionally fill them up, you will get an ugly bare rim of up to 4 inches. You will be able to see, by looking at the planters, which ones you forgot to fill up in time.

Lighting from above

As I've said before, you should not expect too much growth from the plants in a large planter lit only by artificial light. But it looks very pretty to direct a few spotlights from the ceiling or from a rail above the planter, so that at night the

Right: A large movable container with a single Philodendron *is supplemented by a small creeping plant. In this way, the soil is unseen. Far right: Various houseplants can thrive in small terrariums. Here, an umbrella plant grows with a water hyacinth.*

plants look like a green living curtain. The plants will not grow faster, but it sure looks lovely.

Cold feet are not healthy

That includes plants as well! The soil can cool off tremendously in these large floor-level cases. Therefore it would be sensible to provide some heat. You do not have to spend too much energy on that; usually, it is enough to insulate the concrete or brick planter thoroughly on the inside, with styrofoam for instance. An electric heating cord is probably sufficient, too, and with a thermostat you can regulate the temperature. The soil should not be warmer than 68°F. Even some floor heaters will keep the soil warm, but of course that is more expensive.

Replanting

After two, or at the longest three, years the planter should be emptied and replanted. Maybe you can use some of the same plants again. In any case new soil must be put in, because damaging chemicals in the tap water slowly poison the soil, roots can block the drainholes, or

little creatures can collect in hollow areas. In short: Spring cleaning is necessary from time to time. It is also an opportunity to review the whole plant arrangement. Over time you will have noticed which plants flourished best in a certain spot and which plants did not. The second planting will always be more beautiful than the first.

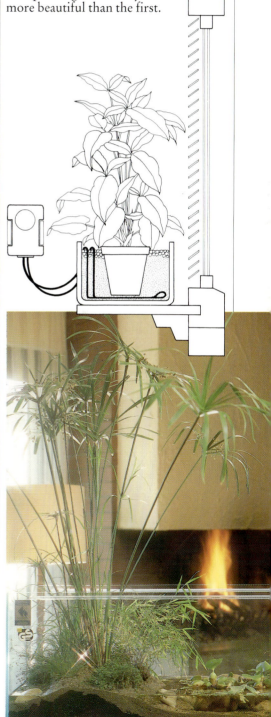

WINDOW GREENHOUSES

By window greenhouses, I mean a space, often separated from the room, designed specially for the purpose of cultivating houseplants that otherwise would not survive under home conditions. The climate—temperature and humidity—in such a window is completely regulated, but the light comes in from an existing window.

A German invention

The *Blumenfenster* (flower window) is very popular in Germany, although I am not sure it was actually invented there. One can trace it back to the plant case or "Edwardian Case," which was very popular in the last century. The reason for the success of window greenhouses is that you are able to create a higher humidity in the isolated area where the plants are than in the rest of the room. But I should mention the fact that the term "window greenhouse" is also sometimes used to describe large spaces occupying the whole width of the room and not separated from the room.

I see these more or less as permanent planters as described on page 36. Here on these pages, I am speaking of the true window greenhouse, separate from the room so that its own climate can be maintained.

Directions of the wind

Almost any window can be used for a greenhouse, and any floor. Often they stick out from the side of the house so they catch more light and take up less space in the room. They are easy to install in a house under construction, if the architect knows what is required for a window greenhouse. But it is also possible to convert an existing window into a window greenhouse. Prefabricated window greenhouses exist, which match standard window sizes.

One often thinks that the best window for a greenhouse should face south, but this is only true if there are trees in the yard that will provide some shade in the middle of a hot day. If this is not the case, then the greenhouse will become too warm in the summer, and you will be obliged to provide screens and ventilation. A window facing southeast is ideal: It warms up in the morning, but just at the moment when the sun gets too strong, it disappears behind the side of the house. East and west also work well; even a window facing north is not as bad as it seems, at least if there are no trees or high buildings close by. A north window is ideal for orchids and other plants that do not need sunlight. Before you choose a particular window, measure the light first (see page 53) because various factors can influence the quantity of light.

Tips for construction

An enclosed window greenhouse provides a growing space between two windows: the outside window and an inside window that separates the area from the rest of the room. The outside window can be closed off permanently, but not the inside one, or else you cannot reach the plants. The outside window should consist of insulated glass to conserve heat and to achieve a constant temperature. Aluminum frames are ideal for this humid space since they will not rust or need painting; the inside should have sliding windows. It is advisable to put the plants in cases that stand a bit off the floor and leave a small space between the outside and the inside wall (see drawing). The air can circulate freely that way and ventilation is important. There should be two openings for ventilation, so the air can come in and go out. It can happen via grids in the outside wall. Or it is very easy to install a ventilation system in the outside wall that works in a reversed mode. If necessary, it is possible to ventilate via the room; the ventilating system is regulated for temperature by a thermostat. If you use a humidistat, you can control the humidity as well.

A closed plant window facing east is very suitable for growing many different kinds of orchids, though it is fine for other plants needing half shade as well.

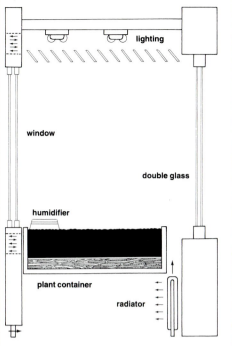

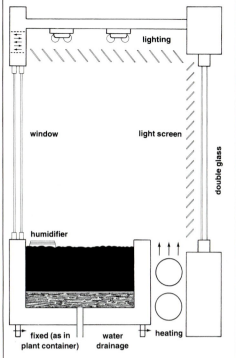

Two ways to build a plant window. At left, a window is built around an existing radiator. Even better is the window to the right, which is provided with a deeper plant container and drainage.

Humidity

Evaporation from the plants automatically creates a higher humidity in the greenhouse than in the rest of the room. However, with so much heat the humidity can still be too low. It is therefore advisable to install an electric humidifier that is controlled by a humidistat and supplies moisture when necessary.

Water

It is unquestionably possible to automate the supply of water too, but I do not support that. When everything is done automatically, you will have hardly any contact with the plants and much will escape your attention. It is necessary in my opinion to slide the greenhouse windows open at least once a day for half an hour or so and spend some time with your plants. Usually there are many plants in a greenhouse, so watering can be time-consuming. It will be easier for you if you can install a faucet near the window, so that the plants can be showered. Ideally it should have both hot and cold water, so that you can use warm water in the winter. If you have bad tap water or water some plants, such as bromeliads or orchids, with pure soft water, then I advise you to install a large tank for catching rainwater. With a simple pond pump you are able to bring this water into the greenhouse from a nearby tank or pond: Switch it on and the water runs.

Lighting

For best care of your plants, most light should come from outside. But it is a very attractive sight to light your window greenhouse at night with spotlights set in a lowered ceiling. Special low wattage lamps give a beautiful effect.

Heating

Usually a radiator is located in front of the window and can be used to heat the window greenhouse as well. Preferably it should be a hot-air radiator that can be installed next to the plant case, as is indicated in the drawing. You need to be able to regulate the heater by using an automatic radiator valve, which is standard on radiators these days. For convenience there should be easy access to the valve from the room. Also, an extra heating unit can be installed underneath the planting area to warm the soil. When the case is insulated adequately, a heating cord with a low wattage (100–200 watts) will be sufficient. You will also want a thermostat here to regulate the temperature and to save on energy.

Screens

A lot of construction work will be avoided if the greenhouse is located in such a position that it is shaded in the afternoon. With too much sun you have to screen the glass to prevent high temperatures and scorching of the plants. The screening is best done with an awning fixed to the outside of the window. It is easier to install screens inside, but they are less effective. In some way the warm air has to be forced through the outside vent. A small electric fan designed for such a greenhouse works the best, as it sucks the hot air from the greenhouse and replaces it with cool air from outside (or from inside).

PLANTS IN BOTTLES, SHOWCASES OR TERRARIUMS

What is important for an enclosed window greenhouse applies to bottles, vitrines (glass showcases) and terrariums as well. The air is generally more humid than in open spaces, making them ideal places to grow tropical plants. Today the Victorian plant vitrine is back again because it forms an elegant and interesting showcase in an interior. With such a showcase, it is also possible to keep plants in areas with little light.

Bottle garden

A bottle garden is simple and inexpensive to create. You need only a bottle with a screwtop. A wicker bottle is good, although they are rather large. It is also easier to work with if the neck of the bottle is not too narrow. Put some drainage material, then soil, in the bottom of the bottle. You can insert these using a paper funnel so that the sides of the bottle do not get dirty. The plants should be rather small at the time you plant them; you can do this with a small fork or spoon tied to long sticks. This requires some patience, but when the plants are set, all your work is done. The bottle stays sealed creating its own environment so that no evaporation escapes the bottle. Only after the plants are firmly established do they need some water. But don't wait until they start to wilt! The bottle should get good light, but do not put it in the sun for long, because the temperature will rise too much and the plants will "cook."

After a short period, the plants will have grown so much that the bottle will be completely filled and then it becomes ugly. It is time to start over—clean it out and replant.

Vitrines

Plant vitrines are commercially available. Supplied with heating units, sometimes a humidifier, and with special lightbulbs on the top to replace daylight, they are usually made of glass or plastic and can be free-standing. When the vitrine is not too high and the lights are strong enough, many plants are able to grow independent of daylight. A time clock regulates the lights (see details on page 54–55). These vitrines should be filled with plants that do not need much light, because even at its best artificial light is not very strong. You can also use the showcases as temporary places for plants, orchids for instance, during their bloom. After flowering they go back to the greenhouse and are replaced with other plants. The

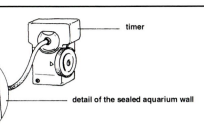

timer

lid with light

detail of the sealed aquarium wall

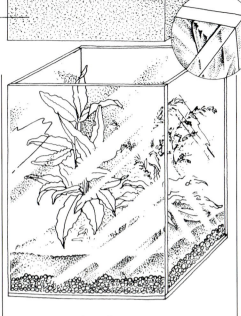

same goes for bromeliads. Try placing a knotty branch in the vitrine, covered with Spanish moss. On the branch you can hang various epiphytic plants that do not grow much.

Plant vitrines can be very large, but I prefer the small ones. They are more affordable and can be replanted easily. This will be necessary every month, or at least every six months, if you want to keep the display attractive. The plants can outgrow the space in that time. Plant vitrines are expensive because they are often made in small quantities and include electrical fixtures.

Terrariums

Much cheaper is the terrarium since it can be created from almost any container—fish tank, brandy snifter, bubble bowl, etc.—and is without heat or electrical fixtures. Still, you can grow a nice collection of plants in it, and if there is enough light, the plants will stay very healthy for a long period. You can also convert an old aquarium with an overhead light in to a mini-vitrine.

Take care that the light is strong enough and that the right wavelength is used. (See pages 52–54.)

Do it yourself

A handy do-it-yourselfer can easily construct his or her own vitrine. A square model is not difficult to make from glass and aluminum segments. There are segments for sale that you can connect with plastic binders. After that the glass is inserted. You also can glue together sheets of glass with silicone, the same way as for an aquarium. In the bottom you must

make space for electric equipment, including a heating system, a ventilator, a thermostat, perhaps a humidifier and an evaporator. Wires can be led through the hollow aluminum segments. On top is the light box, which is in fact the most important aspect of the whole construction. In the hood special plant lamps are used, which are available at good nurseries. The strength of the light has to be such that halfway down the vitrine it still measures 500 lux (see page 55). Heat should not be allowed to accumulate under the hood, but at the same time there should not be any air leakage because in that case the vitrine will quickly dry out. Put glass or plastic between the light and the plants to prevent too much heat. The light should be on for 16 out of every 24 hours. A simple timer can regulate the lighting.

A vitrine does not have to be heated too much, because it is generally placed in an environment with a temperature of 68°F. The lights, as I've said, also give off

An aquarium case can be adapted to form a small plant vitrine by sealing the corners and installing a fluorescent light inside the aquarium lid. The light usually provides enough warmth to keep the vitrine at the right temperature.

some heat. It is best to find out how hot it gets inside the showcase before you add additional heating. A temperature of 77°F is fine. At night 64°F is sufficient. Additional heat if needed can be supplied with a small space heater built in below. The heat will rise along the glass, preventing condensation. Instead of such a heating system, which can warm small vitrines too much, try a heating cable. Position the cable so that the heat can rise along the windows. Use the same cable to warm the soil as well. Make sure to build in a thermostat to control the temperature. You can get extra humidity by evaporating some water from the bottom of the vitrine. This works very simply if you use water and a small tray, heated with a hot plate. If the vitrine is closed off tightly, then the water cannot escape and extra evaporation will probably not be necessary. Many commercial vitrines are round but because the lightbox and the bottom have to be round too, this construction can give an inexperienced do-it-yourselfer a lot of problems. Hence I don't recommend it.

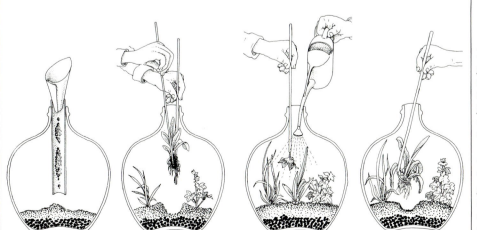

Left: *Bottles can be used to cultivate various plants, although vitrines are easier to maintain. With the aid of a spoon or fork, attached to a longer stick if necessary, the plants can be put in place. If the bottle is sealed, the plants form a world of their own; even water is hardly necessary.*

On page 40: Above: *A large plant vitrine with orchids, bromeliads and other tropical plants.* Below left: *An aquarium as plant vitrine; next to it are various planting possibilities under glass, such as a bottle, large glasses and a mini-greenhouse.*

SUNROOMS AND WINTERGARDENS

Older houses often have sun rooms, constructed of glass and wood, but they are often in a deteriorating state. We are seeing the revival of the sunroom, however, built with new materials such as aluminum and synthetics. This is a welcome occurrence because these rooms provide terrific growing conditions for plants.

New materials set the trend

Wood, particularly pine (which was often used in the past), is an unsuitable material for the construction of sunrooms. It rots and splits easily. Therefore today almost all construction is in aluminum. In addition to the traditional use of single or double panes of glass for the sides, synthetic acrylic sheets with multiple layers are increasingly popular. You cannot see through this material, but a good deal of light comes through. As a result one does not have to screen and insulate as one does with glass. The framing material is made of stainless steel. To maintain it, just hose it down and let it dry. Since the insulation is good, the heating costs are consequently low. Only the purchase is costly.

The building permit

You will usually need a permit to build an addition such as a sunroom to the house. With a new house, the sunroom can be part of the original construction plan. That usually makes it cheaper to con-struct, since common elements such as foundations are taken into account at the same time.

The location of the sunroom must be carefully planned. If you want to catch as much sun as possible, then an unob-structed spot facing south is advised. Your sunroom will get less sun if it is connected to the house on the east or west side. Even the north side can be used, but in that case, your selection of plants will be more limited, the heating will be more expensive and it will be less suitable as a sitting room.

The least expensive way to add on a sunroom is to buy a prefabricated one. You could call it an extension green-house. They come in all sizes and designs, often with very beautiful sliding panels, some of which can be opened completely in the summer. These sunrooms are con-nected to an existing door of the house, so that one can walk from the living room into the greenhouse creating a so-called indoor-outdoor living space. On these pages you will also find an example of a sunroom that is custom made, which of course is much more expensive.

Energy saving

Sunrooms absorb a lot of light and there-fore can get quite warm inside. This hap-pens on a sunny day even in early spring, late fall and winter, when you are also heating the house. This solar heat can be fed into the living area by placing a fan in the wall of the sunroom, possibly at the highest point where the warm air will accumulate. (With modern technology, there are many ways to utilize this excess heat, such as for water pumps and water reservoirs. It is even possible to construct a house in which the solar heat from out-side and the water use inside is practically

Wintergardens and sunrooms are built more and more frequently, offering terrific possibil-ities for the cultivation of plants, especially when the growing area can be kept cooler in the winter. With the addition of insulation, little extra energy is needed to heat sunrooms in the winter.

in balance. But it is too complicated to explain all of this here. Ask your energy specialist.)

Insulation is the best way to save energy in the winter. Instead of glass you can use the already-mentioned strong insulating synthetic sheets. The floor should be made of a heat-retaining material such as tile, brick or slate. In the winter keep the sunroom at a temperature of 40–50°F and there will not be much need for additional heat. Supplemental heat can be brought in by floor heating or portable electric heaters.

Screening and ventilation
Good insulation can cause the sunroom to get too hot in the summer, so ventilation is also necessary. In some styles, whole parts of the sunroom can be opened up; in others there are ventilation windows. Forced ventilation by using a ventilating system is very effective too. (Some air-conditioning units can perform this function.) Extra screening is not nec-essary when double synthetic insulating sheets are used. But you will probably want to have some normal glass in the outside wall as well, to be able to see outside. The sun easily penetrates the glass, however, so that you will need blinds or shades to keep the sun out.

Plant containers in the sunroom
In your sunroom, you can grow plants in free-standing pots and planters, but also in floor-level planters. It is important to provide enough soil depth, at least 24 inches for bigger plants, and sufficient insulation from the floor, so that not much cold enters through the bottom. Also consider effective drainage. The sunroom has enhanced charm as a wintergarden. On days when it is too cold to sit outside, you can sit and eat in your sunroom amidst the plants.

Plants in the sunroom
A sunroom is usually not a living area, so it is not necessary to maintain a consistent temperature. Often I see sunrooms that are kept at a temperature of 60°F in the winter or even warmer. In such a room some people keep plants that need a cool, winter dormant period (see orangerie plants page 26). This is not smart, for the plants will not flourish.

It is also possible to construct a sunroom for tropical plants, but you will have to keep the temperature at least 64° (greenhouse temperature). That is costly, even when you insulate the room well. More sensible and easier to maintain is a sunroom in which you grow mostly plants that need a dormant period, including succulents and other plants, which are very happy with a temperature of 40–50°F. On a sunny day, the temperature will rise somewhat, but do not turn on the heat, because you do not want the plants to start growing too early. The greatest danger of this is in the spring.

If you do not want to heat the sunroom at all during the winter and live where winters are cold, then there will not be many plants that remain healthy. If they were hardy enough for these conditions, they would not be in the sunroom in the first place, but out in the garden.

Spending time in a greenhouse can be an absolute joy. If it is kept around room temperature, only those plants not requiring a dormant period will flourish. Durable houseplants can only benefit from the extra light and higher humidity.

GREENHOUSES

The dream of many a houseplant enthusiast is a real greenhouse. In such buildings one can indeed create the ideal conditions for exotic plants. Temperature, light and humidity are all easier to regulate here than in a house. On these pages I will explain briefly the most important aspects of the greenhouse.

Greenhouses vary in temperature

Traditionally greenhouses are classified in three ways, depending on the minimum temperatures maintained in each during the winter. In each of these three types one can grow different groups of plants. Research has determined that 95 percent of all tropical and subtropical plants can be grown under one of these three conditions. The remaining plants are more or less hardy garden plants and do not need to grow in sheltered conditions.

1. The cold greenhouse, which has a minimal winter temperature of 40–45°F, is used for subtropical plants, succulents and some orchids.

2. The moderate greenhouse has a minimum temperature of 55–60°F and is used for sensitive succulents and various tropical plants that cannot survive temperatures lower than 55°F.

3. Traditionally a greenhouse that has a minimum winter temperature of 64°F is often referred to as a "hot house." It is used for many plants from the tropical forest, including orchids.

Maximum temperatures are not discussed here, as the temperature in any greenhouse can rise to 85° or over 100°F temporarily, depending on the sunlight. As a result, one has to ventilate the greenhouse regularly, because no plant needs a temperature above 85°F. In the plant descriptions the minimum temperature is indicated so that you can determine in which type of greenhouse you should grow a particular plant. Once in a while a greenhouse is built consisting of two or three compartments with different temperature levels, but this does not happen often as it is very expensive.

For the sake of completeness, I should mention the totally unheated greenhouse, which maintains a temperature matching that outside. Obviously you cannot keep any houseplants in these greenhouses. They are only useful from early spring on and for alpine plants.

Greenhouse location

In most cases greenhouses are built in the garden, although it is possible to put a small greenhouse on a balcony or a rather big one on the roof of a garage. There are free-standing greenhouses, as well as connecting greenhouses, that are built with one or two sides against existing walls. If a greenhouse is open to both the garden and the house and is designed for living, then it is being used like a sunroom (see page 42). Here we are only concerned with the kind of greenhouse used specifically for growing plants.

We begin with greenhouses connected to the house. On which side of the house you locate the greenhouse is important, as it will determine what you are able to grow. In a greenhouse facing north, you can only cultivate plants that have little or no need for sun, and there are many plants like that. If it faces south, the greenhouse gets really hot in the summer, so that you need to have a good air-circulation system and screening devices (see below). East- and west-facing sides receive sun only part of the day, which makes them good choices. Obviously, you also need to consider any trees or buildings nearby, because the shade they cast can change the light situation. These considerations also apply to the free-standing greenhouses, although you have to position these buildings even more carefully.

The ideal location is one where the morning sun warms the greenhouse and then disappears behind a large tree that is exactly south of the greenhouse. Late in the afternoon the greenhouse will once again get sun. To achieve this situation, site the greenhouse in a north-south direction lengthwise. It is also important to protect your greenhouse against north and east winds by planting a hedge or putting up a partition 10–12 feet high. Either of these will block the cold wind and save energy.

On page 44: *A free-standing greenhouse made of aluminum and paneled with semi-opaque glass, which makes screening unnecessary. The use of insulated double- or triple-paned glass also eliminates the need for screening, and some extra work.*

Below, left and right: *The aluminum frames for these greenhouses are finished in color, and can stay attractive for a long period. Specialized companies can deliver almost every type of greenhouse.*

Greenhouse construction

Greenhouses can be made out of wood, aluminum or steel. Aluminum, because of durability and low maintenance, is used mostly for private greenhouses. However, untreated aluminum, especially near salt water, soon becomes ugly and pitted. To avoid this, lacquer or enamel the aluminum. The protective coating becomes dark brown or neutral and does not deteriorate.

Greenhouses are almost never custom-made today, because there is a large selection of prefabricated ones in various forms and designs. The most popular is a simple rectangular shape, with a slanting roof that can later be expanded if desired by inserting more building units.

Traditionally greenhouses were covered in glass, and it remains popular because the view inside and out is unobstructed. Nowadays, synthetic materials, like rigid acrylic, provide better insulation and are easier to install. These synthetic panes let through as much light as glass, but they are sometimes opaque. If you think that is a disadvantage, you can always combine them: a roof of synthetic panes and sides of glass. It is possible of course to use insulated glass, but that will be very expensive if the greenhouse is of any size.

Building a greenhouse

In many places a building permit is mandatory, so I advise you to apply for the permit first. A greenhouse of any type needs an appropriate foundation that is both level and square. A concrete or brick foundation is relatively easy to make yourself. I built a greenhouse on four beams that rested in a layer of rubble to prevent sinking and lifting by frost. Such movement in the foundation can cause the greenhouse to shift and be damaged.

Greenhouse kits generally can be assembled following the detailed instructions that are included. Some technical knowledge and experience is advisable; moreover, the actual construction will take some time. But it is manageable and can save you a lot in labor costs. In case of an emergency, you can always call a contractor. One word of caution—be sure the greenhouse is built at right angles and everything is level. Otherwise you will have problems later with doors and windows that do not fit or hang properly.

Layout of a greenhouse

Greenhouse plants are usually grown on tables for easy access. These have to be purchased or made separately. Aluminum is a good material for plant benches but once filled with damp soil, they can weigh quite a lot. They should be solid, therefore, and connected to the sides of the greenhouse. There is usually a path in the middle of a greenhouse with benches arranged on either side of it. For small plants you can create additional space by building benches in the shape of a gradually sloping amphitheater on which the plants are placed. This is an excellent arrangement for growing orchids.

CLIMATE CONTROL IN A GREENHOUSE

In a greenhouse, you have complete control over the climate. With the help of certain equipment it is possible to create the ideal conditions for a specific group of plants. What atmosphere you create will depend on what you want to grow, orchids, fuchsias or cacti, for example.

Sunlight and screens

Most succulent plants love to bathe under glass in full sun. But you have to protect almost all other plants against that same sun. If there is no tree or building for protection in the middle of the day, then it is necessary to provide some shade. There are screens or mats available that are put up on the outside of the greenhouse as well as blinds that are connected on the inside. In both cases you have to lower the blinds when the sunlight is strong and raise them again when the sunlight is weaker. This, of course, means that somebody must always be around to do this job. Otherwise you can leave home in the morning with an overcast sky and not lower the blinds. If the sun should break through around noon, by the time you return your precious orchids or fuchsias will be in a desperate state. It is possible to automate the operation of the screens, but it is very expensive. Also the windows of the greenhouse can be sprayed with a screening substance. There is a product available that becomes transparent with rainy weather and turns white again when the weather clears. A white greenhouse does not look as pretty, but it does mean less work. You can wash the finish off in October and apply a new coat again in March.

Heating

A greenhouse can be heated in various ways. No matter what type of heater is used, thermostats are advisable and easy to use; some kind of ventilation is also necessary. The simplest heat source is a kerosene heater. It does not provide much heat and, therefore, is only suitable for a small hothouse and minor temperature increases. One must also remember to refill the oil reservoir or the heater will go out. Growers used oil heaters for a long time in many greenhouses. They gave sufficient heat, but were often in disrepair. Gas heaters are the most effi-

cient today, if available. They have a large capacity, thermostatic control, reliability, but require ventilation as well.

Another option is to extend the central heating from the house. This is not as complicated as you might think with all the do-it-yourself equipment available. Your boiler should have sufficient capacity though. An alternative is a separate central heating system for the greenhouse with a boiler as source of heat. Water is supplied through hoses and heat emission via radiators. No ventilation is necessary when the boiler is not situated in the greenhouse. Thermostatic control is easy.

Finally, there is electric heating. This is the most expensive way of heating, but is easy to maintain and reliable. Usually a fan heater is installed. There are special

designs for greenhouses, but I think that standard modern fan heaters are reliable enough to use in a greenhouse. A capacity of 3,000 watts for most small greenhouses is enough. No ventilation is necessary, and temperature is easy to control with the thermostat. It is advisable to install a day thermostat and a night thermostat as well, as many houses have. That way the night temperature can be lowered to the appropriate minimum level for the plants, while in the daytime a higher temperature is maintained. By not heating more than is absolutely necessary at night, you save energy. Additionally, most plants flourish when there is a difference between day and night temperature, as is always the case in nature. When you grow precious plants, it is important to install a battery-operated alarm that will alert you in case the heating system fails. Of course that will always happen on a freezing cold night, and if you do not act immediately, your plants are done for.

Screening mats are attached to the outside of this greenhouse, a less effective way of screening light.

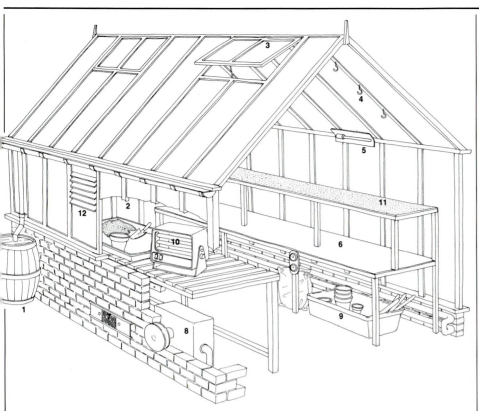

A typical amateur hothouse with the usual components:
1. rainwater barrel
2. working area for repotting, etc.
3. window, preferably automatically opening
4. hooks for hanging plants
5. thermostat for heat regulation
6. bench
7. controllable air supply
8. gas heater with convectors
9. storage for potting soil, pots, etc.
10. heater
11. extra shelf for plants
12. ventilation window with blinds

is a large-sized reservoir inside; then you can use this water for the plants. Use a watering can to scoop the rainwater from the reservoir. It is also helpful to install water fixtures in the greenhouse if at all possible. That way you can use tap water for the plants as well. A gardenhose with nozzle is the most practical way to water in a greenhouse.

Lighting

If you bring electric power into the greenhouse, install light fixtures at the same time, so that you will be able to work in the evening as well. Be careful that the installation is waterproof, because water and electricity are incompatible, as you know. It is also possible to give the plants extra light, which will help their growth. For that purpose, use fluorescent lighting or high-pressure mercury lamps; this supplemental light can be especially useful at the early stage of growing cuttings and seedlings. You can even create an extra growing area under a dark table with this artificial lighting.

Ventilation

Ventilation is necessary at two times: when the temperature rises too high (always in the daytime) and when there is too much humidity. Usually, ventilation is achieved by opening up the windows or a door in the greenhouse, so that the warm or damp air can be replaced with cooler or drier air. In the past this was all done manually, and involved the risk of airing too late or leaving the windows open on a cold night. Today, automatic window regulators are available that open and close the windows depending on the temperature. Another way to provide ventilation is with an electric fan that draws the hot air out. For this to work there has to be a vent somewhere to supply fresh air. Even the smallest model window fan is suitable for this purpose. A thermostat is set to regulate the fan, depending on the temperature.

Humidity

Evaporation from the plants or soil brings humidity to the greenhouse. It is dark and damp under the tables in a greenhouse with a brick foundation—an ideal atmosphere for increasing humidity. In this situation you hardly have to ventilate to achieve a higher humidity level in cold weather. Other simple ways to increase humidity—pour water on the floor or fill the tables with ample peatmoss. They both help to raise the humidity level. If this is not enough, boil some extra water to create steam. A tray with water on the stove is the cheapest method, but an electric humidifier is certainly satisfactory too.

Watering

You can catch and transport the rainwater that falls on the roof of the greenhouse. The water never freezes that way, if there

Left: Bubble plastic can be installed on the outside or inside of a greenhouse for additional insulation.
Right: An oil heater.

Left and right: Kerosene heaters do not give off much heat. To spread the heat more effectively, fans can be installed.

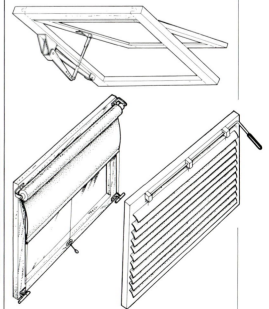

Above: Automatic ventilation window. Left: Blinds for screening sun inside the greenhouse. Right: Window with blinds.

PLANTS IN THE OFFICE

Houseplants are not only found in living spaces; increasingly they appear in offices, factories and public buildings. There are even office gardens, where people work amidst the foliage. It is generally assumed that these plants contribute to creating a more pleasant work environment. But they have to be looked after too, and that does not always happen.

Growing conditions

Companies often spend a lot of money on the purchase of plants. They not only have to be decorative, but varied as well. They only stay in good condition if they are placed in an appropriate place and taken care of. Unfortunately, they are often neglected, with the result that within a year, half of the plants are dead. Generally the same conditions exist in offices as in our homes: a year-round temperature of ± 68°F and a slightly lower humidity level in the wintertime. These conditions indicate that only a small number of houseplants are suitable for office gardens. All plants that are not suited to these conditions—*Yuccas*, palms, succulents, bay trees and other plants that need a dormant period—are doomed to die sooner or later. Generally, there are enough windows that provide light, but people want plants in dark hallways, entrances or obscure corners of the office because they look so pretty. These plants will suffer and die. At least half the plants I see in offices are a poor choice or in the wrong location.

Plant services

Companies that provide plants for offices or other spaces are in business to make money. Cost factors may mean they do not always take into consideration the growing conditions of the plants they choose for a customer. That is not smart business because when the plants die, the client will be dissatisfied and may buy somewhere else next time. If the plant service measures the light intensity and looks for suitable locations before choosing the plants, it will select the right varieties to flourish in your office. The choice is not too difficult, because most species

are unsuitable for offices. Next the service should lay out a plan, so the client knows where each plant belongs. In that case, the supplier can comfortably guarantee the well-being of the plants. If the client moves the containers around, then the supplier's warranty will not be valid.

Generally, if the building or office is totally unsuitable, I would strongly advise against the purchase of houseplants.

Mixed containers do not work out well

Often the customer wants to see a container planted with various species. This arrangement usually does not work very well—what would be right for one plant is absolutely wrong for another. You can save money and have more chance of success if you select only one species for each container.

Gigantic Yuccas *can be grown in offices, though they often die after a few years due to lack of light and warmer winter temperatures. Fortunately, this spot offers enough light and the ability to move the plants for the winter.*

Maintenance is important

Personal contact between people and plants is important. I do not favor situations where it is forbidden for people to tend the plants, such as when their care is left to a company that has a maintenance contract. Maybe the plants are better taken care of this way, but the gap between the plants and the people who see them is much too big. As a result, many people are inclined to use the containers as an ashtray or garbage pail. Furthermore, the so-called "maintenance" is often unsatisfactory. The person assigned to this task sometimes does not know much about plants and does not perform much more than some pruning, replacing hydrosolutions and spraying against diseases. Anyone who has had a houseplant is able to do at least that.

Temperature in the office

Offices often have day and night temperature regulation. That is not bad for the plants. But sometimes there is weekend regulation as well. During the weekend, the temperature is set not to go below 50°F. That saves a lot of energy (and money) in a large building, but most plants will suffer under these conditions. For tropical plants, which are often used in offices, 60°F is the absolute minimum. Also, the sunlight can raise the temperature too high. When there are people around, accommodations can be made, but over a weekend the plants will get too hot. Moving some plants for the weekend or using screening can prevent this damage.

Watering

In offices and public buildings, the biggest problem is often the amount of water the plants get. Therefore, I suggest a system that largely prevents lapses in the watering of plants. Hydroculture is such a system, as it has a water reservoir in the bottom of the container. In this system the roots get access to the water via a grill, and only absorb what they need. An indicator shows the water level in the bottom reservoir. Do not give more water than is indicated, otherwise it will overflow and spill on the carpeting. Give water an average of once or twice a week. Then you will have no problems over the weekend. Nutrients are added to the water in the growing season (see page 75). Using this system, the plant is easy to maintain; repotting every year is all it really needs.

Artificial light in offices

One often sees large plants growing in dark spots with only artificial lights. It is definitely possible to grow plants under these conditions, but not with a small light. Only big, special plant lamps that have considerable power can provide strong enough light. This light is often too strong for people who have to work next to it. In general, the use of artificial light is not a big success for growing plants in offices.

Various plants have proved to be strong enough to survive the less-than-ideal conditions in office spaces. (See the chart on page 367 for an easy reference list.)

Left, below: Ficus benghalensis *is a good office plant.*
Below: *Containers for hydroponics (water culture).*

EVERY PLANT IS A CLEVER FACTORY

Plants are unique in nature in being able to convert certain elements into carbohydrates by harnessing the energy of the sun through the process of photosynthesis. A plant is, in essence, a factory that supplies our atmosphere with oxygen in exchange for the carbon dioxide that we discharge when we breathe. In a world without plants people would suffocate. To care for plants well, it is useful to understand the process that takes place inside the plants.

The absorption of food

Most plants absorb nutrients via their roots. A few are capable of absorbing nutrients in other ways. A bromeliad can absorb food that decays in its shaft or reservoir. Carnivorous plants absorb food via the organs that catch the inserts. All nutrients have to be dissolved in water before they can enter the plant. At the tip of most roots are many fine hairs which actually absorb the nutrients into the plant. They are apparent in houseplants as matted white "felt" around the soil ball. They are often especially noticeable in plants grown in terracotta pots as the roots will try to extract food from the pot itself if the soil becomes exhausted.

Nutrients only pass through the cell wall of the root hairs when the concentration of the solution outside the roots is weaker or lower than inside. This process is called osmosis. The supply of nourishment flows in the reverse direction when the concentration in the plant is weaker than outside. This happens if you fertilize too heavily. The plant will lose its last nourishment and "scorch."

Absorption of nutrients via the roots slows with low temperatures and completely stops below freezing.

Food production happens in the green parts

The nutrients are absorbed into the roots and transported through vessels in the stems to the leaves, the chief food production organ of the plant. In the process known as photosynthesis, stomatas, or pores, on the underside of the leaves withdraw carbon dioxide from the air. The water, which entered via the roots, is split with the assistance of chlorophyll into hydrogen and oxygen. The oxygen is released into the atmosphere via the pores, while the hydrogen is used by the plant to change the carbon dioxide into a carbohydrate. The carbohydrates (starches and sugars) are transported at night to various parts of the plants where they are used for growth. Sometimes they are reserved in storage organs, for instance with bulb and tuber plants.

Another process that takes place inside the plant is the fixation of nitrogen. Nitrates that enter via the roots are reduced inside the plants and finally, via a series of chemical reactions, protein is produced. This is an extremely important ability, as neither animals nor people are capable of producing protein. Humans can only transform proteins into different types, so without plant proteins, we could not continue to live.

The breathing of plants

The reverse of photosynthesis, or respiration, is the transpiration of the plant, the loss of water due to evaporation. In transpiration, a part of the sugars, formed via photosynthesis, are used again; this process requires oxygen. When everything goes according to plan, photosynthesis creates more energy than is used in transpiration, resulting in a surplus of carbohydrates and oxygen. Only then is cultivation possible. If there is no surplus,

Left: *A* Hoya multiflora, *also called 'shooting star' plant. This not very well-known houseplant can produce flowers continuously throughout the summer, though it does need a dormant period in the winter to stay healthy.*

Above: *Bromeliads and orchids thrive when grown on trees. An imitation tree can be made of a drainpipe covered with moss. A water system can also be integrated (notice the tube running along the drainpipe).*

The complicated factory that is a plant: At the top is the lead growing point and the flowers, which constitute the reproductive organs of a plant. After pollination, seeds are formed.

The most important chemical processes take place in the leaves, respiration and transpiration. With the aid of light and chlorophyll as a catalyst, water is split into hydrogen and oxygen. See the accompanying text on page 50.

Roots support the plants and absorb food from the soil. Plants can have different kinds of roots, each thriving only in a specific environment comparable to their native habitats.

then the growth stagnates and the plant will die in the long term.

The flower

The flower contains the reproductive organs of the plant: the stamens and the pistils. The stamen consists of a filament and an anther, containing male pollen; the anther is divided into two compartments. A pistil consists of the ovary, holding one or more female gametes (seed buds or eggs), the style and the stigma. The stigma is destined to receive the pollen. These important organs are surrounded by the perianth, the so-called green petals, as well as often extraordinarily colored sepals.

There is an enormous variation in the forms of flowers, so that the original layout is sometimes hard to recognize. Stamens can be transformed into petals, so that double flowers are created. Petals and sepals are not always easy to distinguish from each other, especially when the sepals are colored. Flowers of one gender, either male or female, are called diclinous. The partner is located in another flower or even in another plant.

The leaf

Leaves are lateral growths of the stem. Their growth is limited, but there are almost no limits to the number of shapes. The many illustrations in this book clearly show that. If the leaf consists of more than one part, then it is called a compound leaf. It can be palmate, in the form of a hand, or be feather-shaped, as with ferns. If the leaf is divided again, then it is called double feathered; even triple feathered leaves are possible.

Another type of leaf, shallow carved leaves, include serrated, crenated, lobed, etc.

At the stem is the petiole or stalk, leading to the leaf base. Instead of a leaf base, it is also possible to find two small supporting leaves underneath the leafstalk. The leaves on the stem can be variously arranged: opposite, spiraled, rosette, etc. Sometimes leaves take the form of thorns or tendrils. Nature is very inventive.

The stem

This is the part of the plant that supports the leaves. The leaves bud from notches along the length of the stem. Side stems form at these notches too, forming the beginning of a new branch. In the stem are the vascular bundles, which transport the supply of water and food. If the stem is

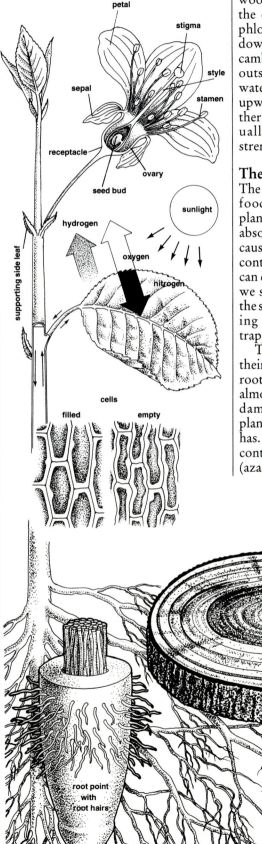

woody, then it is protected with bark on the outside. Underneath is the bast, or phloem, through which the sap flows down. Next follows a very thin layer of cambium, a tissue that makes bast on the outside and wood on the inside. The water and nutrients from the roots flow upward via this young wood. Even further inside is the heartwood, which gradually dies but whose rigidity gives strength to the tree or shrub.

The root

The roots are responsible for the intake of food. Furthermore, they anchor the plant. Only the tips of the roots actually absorb food. Plants grow in nature because the roots draw nourishment from continually fresh soil. Houseplants only can do this for a short time, which is why we see a large amount of matted root at the sides of a pot. These are roots attempting to grow further that have been trapped by the pot.

The form of the roots is determined by their natural habitat. Plants with long taproots have to be able to grow deep, and almost no plant roots live in a constantly damp environment. When potting a plant, know what kind of roots the plant has. You can then select an appropriate container: a deep pot (palms), a wide pot (azaleas), a basket (orchids), etc.

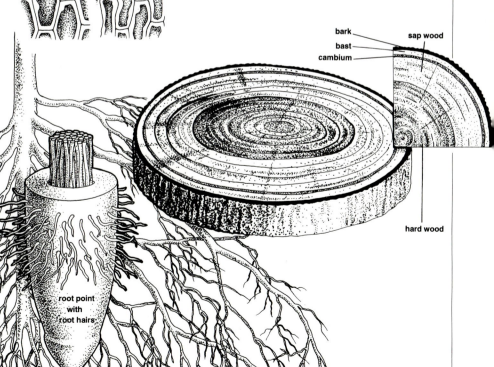

PLANTS NEED LIGHT

Almost all plants need light, and certainly all the plants we grow as houseplants need it. The amount of light needed, however, varies greatly. Some plants like a lot of sunlight, others grow well in the shade. If you do not consider these natural requirements when deciding where to put your plant, the plant will not thrive.

What is light?

Light is, physically speaking, a wave motion with a very short wavelength that we express in a millionth of a millimeter, called a nanometer. The light that the human eye can observe is between 380 and 780 nanometers. What we experience as white light is in reality a composite of all colors. Blue is 590 nanometers and orange 610 nanometers. So the cooler the light, the lower the wavelength.

If white light reaches an object that we see as red, it means nothing more than that this object absorbs all colors except red. If all colors of the spectrum are reflected by an object in the same amount, then we call the object gray. If less than 10 percent of the light hitting an object is reflected, we call the object black. It is that simple.

Our eye is most sensitive to light with a wavelength of about 550 nanometers, in the green-yellow range. But plants are most sensitive to wavelengths of 700 nanometers (red), with areas slightly less-sensitive at 450 nanometers. At yellow-green, there is a dip in sensitivity.

Thus light that is the brightest for humans is not necessarily so for plants. With daylight, this phenomenon is not very important, but it is important with artificial light.

Light throughout the seasons

During the year, the sun shifts. In midwinter it stands low above the horizon and the strength of the light is rather weak. But because of this lower position, the sun is able to penetrate far into a room, especially on the higher floors of apartment buildings, where trees or other buildings do not block the light. For plants that do not stand close to a window, this is particularly important. In midsummer the sun stands much higher above the horizon and the light intensity

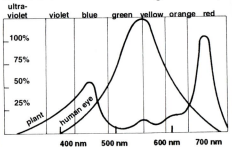

The human eye has a different sensitivity to light than a plant. Plants mainly assimilate the blue and red frequencies of the spectrum.

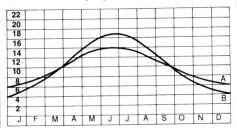

Geographic location affects the amount of light plants get. The slight difference in latitude between southern Germany (A) and Denmark (B), for example, results in both different seasonal lengths and different light intensities.

Left: *Variegated plants need more light than green plants of the same species, which have more chlorophyll. Direct sunlight would be too much for this croton and Dracaena*

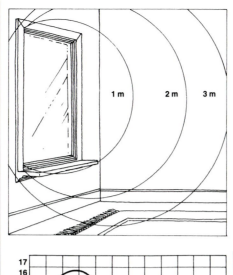

The strength of light decreases exponentially as the distance from the light source increases; the light strength decreases by a power of two. That is, if a plant is two feet from a window (the light source), there is four times less light than if it was placed right next to the source. This proportion is important to keep in mind when placing houseplants.

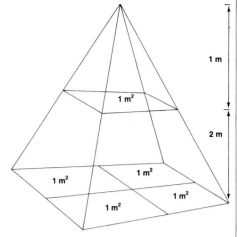

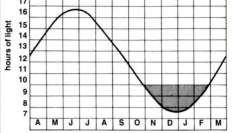

is high, but the light does not reach far into a room. Also because of the slant of the light rays in the summer, the light is reflected more on the window ledge. An east-facing window will receive the sun earlier in summer, not only because the sun rises earlier, but also because it rises further north than it does in the winter.

This is also why the sun shines a few hours longer through the west-facing window. These natural factors influence the amount of light available at any given time. Therefore, it is not sufficient to know the light intensity at one time of the year. If you want to be absolutely certain about available light of a particular time and location, you should measure.

Plants grow toward light
In nature light reaches a plant from above, as well as from all sides. Inside this is not the case, and the plants show a definite inclination to grow toward the source of light.

Most plants can be turned to face away from the light source. After some days, the leaves will again turn around toward the light. But flowering plants, and particularly plants in bud, do not tolerate this treatment. Notorious are the camellia, gardenia, hibiscus and hoya, which quickly drop their buds as soon as the location of the light changes. If you move these plants temporarily, for instance, to clean the window sill or to dip them in water, be careful to always put them back in the same position. A match stuck in the soil helps to remind you which side was facing the light. Transferring these plants to another window is almost always disastrous. If the plant flourishes in a particular spot, leave it there. Plants that need a rest period are, of course, an exception. These need to be transferred twice a year: in the autumn to cooler storage and in the spring back again to the room.

The intensity of the light
The amount of light that touches a particular surface is measured in lux. This unit is based on the sensitivity of the human eye, not on the sensitivity of the plant, to light. On a sunny day in the summer, behind a south-facing window, we would measure a light intensity of 160,000 to 320,000 lux. The minimum at which the strongest plant stays alive (but hardly grows) is 700 lux. For purposes of growing plants, we are dealing with light values between these two extremes.

It is difficult for us to determine the intensity of the light with the naked eye, because the iris of our eye automatically adjusts the amount of light admitted. A plant has no iris and only experiences too much light or too little. With a simple light meter, the kind used by photographers, we can easily determine what the light intensity is at a particular place (see page 55). Of course that intensity constantly changes, depending on the hour of the day and the month of the year. Moreover, it is affected by weather conditions. So you are not finished after you have determined an intensity of 100,000 lux behind an east window in the morning. If you measure again at 5 o'clock in the afternoon, you will record not more than 25,000 lux, which is four times less. And if you measure again at a spot further into the room, you will discover sadly enough that the intensity of light subsides by the square of the distance. Simply speaking, twice as far into the room there is four times less light. Light intensity dimin-

Left: Day length varies with the seasons. In the northern hemisphere, the longest day falls around June 21, the shortest around December 21. The dark patch on the chart represents the darkest part of the year, when many plants suffer from a lack of light.

Below: By sticking a match or other small object in the pot you can remind yourself which side of the plant should be turned to the light.

ishes rapidly as you move away from a window and that is precisely why many plants droop; they simply are placed too far inside a room. A light meter can make all the difference.

Indication of light intensity
I have used three categories to explain the intensity of light needed by plants: full sun, half shade and shade. I do not mean constant full sun or constant shade, but rather an average for the whole day.

These categories can be defined as:

1. Full sun: south window, unscreened daylight, maximum light intensity of 320,000 lux on a clear day.
2. Half shade: full sun for only a few hours in the morning or late afternoon with the rest shade, or the whole day in filtered sunlight, screened by a tree, blinds or lace curtain.
3. Shade: no sun at all, either a north window or a window that stays in the shadow, minimum light intensity of 5,000 lux on a clear day.

LIGHT AND ARTIFICIAL LIGHT

On these pages, I have provided some tips about how to screen out too much light, followed by some thoughts about artificial plant lighting and why this form of lighting often results in disappointment. I have also concluded with information about the influence that the length of the day has on growth and especially on the flowering of a plant.

Screening against too much light

There are only a few plants that can endure full sunlight. Cacti and other succulents are the most familiar, although there are other plants that can limit the evaporation from their leaves and in this way endure the sunlight. You can tell which plants can take sunlight by observing the shape of the leaves: Thick, pruinose (whitish) or very narrow leaves can stand a lot of light, but large, transparent, finely cut leaves have to be kept in the shade. For a plant, light means the possibility of keeping photosynthesis going. But light also means warmth, especially behind glass. Because of that warmth, evaporation increases. Plants in small pots are more inclined to dry out quickly in the light. The solution to these concerns is to screen. You can very successfully grow plants that need half shade in a south window, if you see to it that the sun does not shine directly on the plants from about 10 o'clock in the morning until 5 o'clock in the afternoon. You accomplish this with screening. You can screen from the outside of the window with awnings or weatherproof blinds or from the inside with glass curtains, blinds or removable synthetic screens. If you screen from the inside, you can also block out a lot of heat, which makes the room more comfortable in the summer.

Tinted glass or glass that is covered with a sunscreen foil are also available. I personally think that the part of the light that is filtered out with this coated glass is the part that is important for the plant. I advise you to be particularly careful with this coating. In the winter, plants could have a hard time when they are placed behind such glass and in fact with the overcast winter weather, one does not need to screen as often. But when the sun does come out, you will need to provide some protection for the plants. It is possible to regulate the screening automatically, but it is rather costly. The other solution is to only put those plants in an unscreened window that are suitable for this condition. Then you do not have to worry.

Plants under artificial light

Unfortunately, normal light bulbs give very little of the type of light that makes plants grow. There are other lamps, however, that do provide light that stimulates growth. The cheapest are the fluorescent lights, which come in various colors indicated by numbers. The best ones for plants are numbers 22, 25, 32, 33 and 36. Special plant lights with color number 77, also known as "gro-lux," are often used to give a dramatic effect, but they provide a less favorable spectra for plants than the other mentioned numbers.

Another type are special plant lamps, which can be screwed right into the fixture. That is the case with the super-high-pressure mercury lamps. They also cost a lot more for that reason. These lamps are frequently used for street lighting because they do not use much current in relation to the amount of light they cast, which makes them cheaper in the long run. For professional use there is also the super-high-pressure mercury-iodide lamp or high-pressure sodium lamp, but they are rarely seen in houses.

Light intensity

We can determine the intensity of artificial light with a lux meter. Cheap lux meters are not very reliable. Therefore, I recommend a good photographic light meter, which is often supplied with a conversion chart for lux. If not, then one can convert the result of every light meter, or camera with a built-in light meter, to lux according to the chart on page 55.

If the plant gets only artificial light, the light should be on for about 18 hours a day, with six hours' rest. The minimal light intensity at the level of the leaves has

On page 54: Cheap light meters give an appropriate indication of light intensity, but are not very accurate. The light meter of a camera actually works better. A conversion to lux units from camera meter readings can be made using the chart below.

To determine the light intensity with a photographic lightmeter

Adjust the camera or the meter to 50 ASA and 1/125 seconds. Measure the light that reflects from a piece of pure white paper that you hold at the same spot where the plant is. The best time to measure is in July at 12 o'clock noon. The readings can be translated as follows:

f 16–22	full sun (ca. 160,000–320,000 lux)
f 5.6–16	screened daylight or half shade (20,000–160,000 lux)
f 2.8–5.6	shade (5,000–20,000 lux)

At other less bright hours of the day and in different seasons (except June) there is naturally less light.

---

to be at least 700 lux for the hardiest plant. But there will be hardly any growth at that level. Therefore, a minimum of 1,000 lux should be provided for strong plants. You can achieve that intensity with a 36-watt fluorescent light suspended about 24 inches above the plants. Plant lights with 160 watts give more light and can be hung 32 inches above the plant. A mercury lamp gives even more light (depending on the size) and can be hung higher (5 feet) above the plants. These are relatively small distances so the lamps usually cannot be inserted into the ceiling. Moreover, you have to consider that the indicated distance applies to the distance between the light and the leaves. With tall plants we run into problems. What is a good light intensity for leaves that grow at a

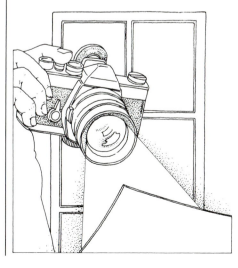

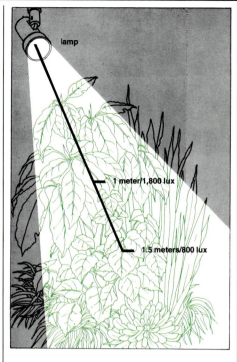

lamp

1 meter/1,800 lux

1.5 meters/800 lux

level of 5 feet high, is too low for the leaves on the same plant at 2.5 feet. Also, the upper leaves screen out the light for the lower leaves. A plant that grows below such lamps soon loses the lowest leaves and only a few thin shoots grow toward the light. And I am only speaking of the most durable plants.

A flowering plant actually needs five times as much light as a leaf plant, which needs 5,000 lux. That means a fluorescent light at 10 inches distance from the plant and an installed capacity of 100 watts per square meter. An African violet blooms and grows nearly year-round, so providing artificial light will consume a lot of energy! Besides, many lights are not even that attractive. When plants are grown with just artificial light, the result is almost always disappointing. If some daylight is available and artificial light is used

Left and below: Any plant light must be strong enough, or close enough to the plant, to keep photosynthesis going. Light strength decreases rapidly as distance is increased. A movable fluorescent light is often a workable light source.

as an additional supplement (perhaps during the winter seasons), then the situation can be positive for the plants. In that case it would be sensible to consider an artificial-light installation.

Influence of day length on growth

The number of daylight hours appears to influence the budding of many flowers. Short-day plants form buds when daylight is shorter than 12 hours. Long-day plants develop buds only when daylight is longer than 12 hours. Other plants are indifferent; for them, the day length has no effect.

When we know that a certain plant belongs to the long- or short-day type, we can confuse them into flowering by manipulating dark and light. That is the way the commercial grower forces his pot chrysanthemum to bloom in the spring and his poinsettias to get their colored blossoms ready by Christmas (in nature they would appear much later). You can make use of this knowledge by forcing an African violet or begonia to flower in the winter. To just extend the daylight, a normal light bulb is sufficient, for even a distant street lamp can sometimes fool a houseplant or even garden plants. Place your plant under a table lamp and it will bloom longer. Give a gloxinia some additional artificial light and it blooms prematurely.

For bud development it is often necessary that the day length correspond with the temperature. This necessity has been documented for most plants, but it would lead too far afield to go into details here.

TEMPERATURE

The plants we grow indoors come from various climate zones, where they grow under different temperature conditions. If we want our plants to thrive indoors, then it is necessary to create favorable conditions, particularly regarding temperature. But we can look at the problem from another angle; i.e., buy only plants that are suited to the temperature in our homes. This increases the chance for success, although the selection of plants will be limited.

Temperature in nature and in the home

In the tropics there is a fairly constant temperature. However, the night does bring some coolness to the lower elevations, and in tropical mountain areas, it often cools off considerably. The temperature in the subtropics fluctuates much more, not only every 24 hours, but also throughout the year. In these areas, there are very definite seasons.

In the past, the temperature in our homes fluctuated a lot as well. Even in heated rooms, areas near drafty windows were a lot colder than the centers of the rooms. Houses today are better insulated and almost all of them have central heating. The result is a constant temperature throughout the house year-round. If you think that this is a plus for the plants you want to grow, you are mistaken. In those drafty old houses you could grow azaleas, camellias, cyclamens, primulas and many other plants that like a cool spot, especially in the winter. In our modern houses, we are basically limited to growing tropical plants, such as *Ficus* and *Dieffenbachia*, that thrive in a constantly warm environment.

Differences in temperature

To know the exact temperature at the spot where your plants stand, use a minimum-maximum thermometer that is placed between the plants, but not in the sun. This is especially important in greenhouses, but even in the house you can achieve some unexpected results by how you control the temperature. If your windows are not insulated, and you pull the curtains at night, as the conservationists advise, then the temperature on the window sill could drop below freezing on a cold night. That drop will damage any plants, of course. In contrast the temperature in the summer by the window can rise far above 85°F and that also is not too helpful for most plants. All in all it is much easier to first find out the temperature extremes of a particular spot and then choose your plants accordingly.

Decreasing nighttime temperature

The temperature in nature is generally lower at night than in the daytime. Sometimes it is only a few degrees, but the difference in the desert can easily be 80°F, as described on page 50. In the daytime processes inside the plant differ from those at night. This is primarily determined by the presence of light, but also by the temperature. In general, plants grow better in our homes and green-

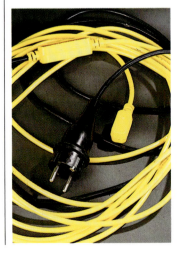

Houseplants differ strongly in their needs for warmth. The Dracaena *above can be kept at around 68°F (20°C) all year. The cyclamen to the left, however, requires a much lower average temperature and also a dormant period.*

Far left: *A 20 volt heating cable, suitable for both soil and space heating, can possibly be used in combination with a thermostat.*

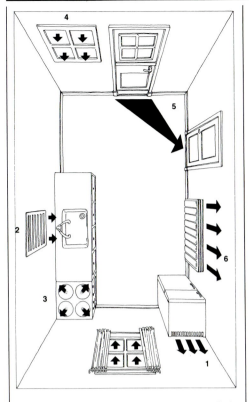

houses if we can provide them a nightly lowering of temperature similar to what they experience in nature. If you have the heat set at 68°F in the daytime, you can turn it down at night to 60°F, or even 55°F. But check a thermometer to be sure it does not get too cold close to the window, as some plants can be damaged even at 55°F. A nightly lowering of temperature is easy to achieve with a computerized thermostat. The purchase price is quickly recovered with the energy saved on heating.

Soil temperature
We have been talking about the air temperature, but the temperature of the soil in the pot is also important to the long-term health of plants. The soil is often considerably lower than the air temperature because of evaporation and/or the pot's placement on a cold surface, such as a stone floor or marble windowsill. Evaporation through the sides of a pot also takes heat from the soil. That is why inside a terracotta pot the soil is a few degrees cooler than inside a plastic pot, since no moisture evaporates through the sides of such a pot. Many tropical plants only function well when the temperature of the soil remains above 68°F. That soil temperature would be impossible to maintain in a pot where the room temperature is only 68°F. The solution is to provide some extra bottom heat. A good location in this case is on a wide window sill with a radiator underneath. A heat cable can also be used successfully, especially under the benches in a greenhouse.

Special attention is necessary for plants that spend the winter in a cold greenhouse. The floor of a greenhouse can be quite cold. In such conditions the potting soil can freeze. An oleander, for instance, will not do well with this treatment at all; the roots will rot and the plant will die. In earlier times, one placed these plants on a foot warmer in which hot coals burned. Nowadays, we simply place them on a piece of foamcore, and the problem is solved.

Seasonal differences
In nature, temperatures vary not only every day, but also throughout the season. The lowest temperature of the year determines the survival of the plant. A flamingo plant will die when it is exposed to 55°F for longer than 24 hours. Because nights are always colder than days, in the plant lists I have given minimum night temperature as the survival limit.

We can divide plants into three categories:

grow cool	minimum 37–50°F
grow rather warm	minimum 50–60°F
grow warm	minimum 60–68°F

In the first two groups are those plants that appreciate a change of season (see also discussion of dormancy on page 62–63), while the plants in the last group prefer a constant temperature year-round.

Damage, caused by too low a temperature, is often visible by the yellowing and dropping of leaves. Sometimes, these indications take considerable time to become apparent. The *Pandanus* does not immediately show the effects of a temperature drop below 50°F, but even if it takes a few months, its time is up.

Far left: *Differences in temperature in a kitchen: 1. heat from the top of a refrigerator; 2. cold air form an air conditioner; 3. heat from a stove; 4. heat from the sun's light through a window; 5. cool drafts from beneath doors; 6. heat from a radiator.*
Left: *Soil warmth from a tray on top of a radiator.*

Also, when plants become too hot, they droop. Often this happens because of lack of water. High temperatures are easier for a plant to tolerate when it is well watered, there is good light and the humidity is fairly high. With a temperature over 110°F inside a plant, it will die. Never leave plants in a closed car in the sun, as the inside temperature can run up to 140°F.

Influence of temperature on the development of the bud
The temperature can influence a plant's bud development. Sometimes, the length of the days plays an important factor as well, sometimes not. (See page 55.)

A period of lower temperatures is often important for the forming of flower buds, particularly with succulents and almost all subtropical plants. When the buds appear on such houseplants, the temperature can be allowed to rise, so that the flowers will develop. The plant descriptions clearly indicate when you have to lower the temperature and when it should go up again. Usually, flowers only develop when the temperature continuously stays above a certain level.

Temperature and humidity
There is a correlation between temperature and relative humidity. When you turn off the heat, the relative humidity in the air rises immediately. See page 64.

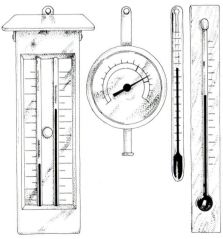

Above: *Different types of thermometers.*
Left: *Two different thermometers indicate that the soil in the plastic pot to the left is about two degrees warmer than the soil in the terracotta pot to the right. The discrepancy is due to a difference in evaporative ability between pots.*

WATER

Water is the staff of life for a plant. Without water, a plant will eventually die. It seems obvious to give your plants a little bit of water every day, but unfortunately, there is more to it than that. The following four pages offer an explanation.

Why is water necessary?

A plant utilizes water in various ways. As is explained on page 55, water is an important element in the growth of a plant, as inside the plant it is split into hydrogen and oxygen. Secondly, water is vital to a plant as a means for transportation of nutrients. All nutrients that are absorbed from the soil in one way or another, are transported in a dissolved state, via water to the area of the plant where they are needed, particularly the leaves. After being converted into starches and sugars via photosynthesis, they are transported to places where growth occurs or where surplus nutrients are stored. The third function of water is temperature regulation. In a process called transpiration, water vapor moves from the leaf into the atmosphere. As long as a plant evaporates water, it can keep cool, since evaporation withdraws heat. Transpiration is crucial when a plant stands in full sunlight. Otherwise, the temperature will rise too high and the plant will die. Finally, water provides the plant with the rigidity or strength, or the turgor, that keeps the plant standing up; woody plants have an additional source of strength, the heartwood.

What exactly happens?

Plants in general absorb water via the root hairs. In the roots is a layer of cells that is dependent on the water pressure in the plant; the concentration of food allows water to enter or not. We should not underestimate that pressure. Roots have a pressure capacity that you cannot match with your lungs; in fact, one that is four times the pressure in a car tire.

Water is transported through the plants via a system of veins. It arrives at the leaves, where it escapes into the atmosphere via the stomata (small openings or pores), with which the plant can regulate, up to a point, the amount of transpiration. With bright light and high humidity, stomata open as far as possible; when it is dark or when there is not much humidity in the air, they close.

Too much water or too little

Balance is the most important issue in nature, which applies to the water system of plants as well. The intake of water and the transpiration rate have to be in balance. If the plant does not lose enough water through transpiration, then the water flow in the plant stops, no nutrients are transferred and subsequently growth stagnates. If the plant loses too much water, then the cell pressure decreases, the plant wilts and, if this situation continues, the plant will dry up.

Each plant is different in how it regulates water intake and transpiration, depending on the climate where it originated. Some plants can stay alive for years without a drop of water. As soon as it rains, they quickly develop and store water. Other plants are adapted to life in a tropical forest with nearly 100 percent humidity; these plants do not have many roots, but plenty of possibilities for transpiration. To determine when and how to water your plants, it is useful to know where they originate.

It is absolutely impossible to be precise about watering; i.e., you can't count on "2 cups a day." How much is necessary depends on the extent of the transpiration and that varies from day to day. When the weather is sunny, you have to water more; some plants, especially those in small pots, may even need watering three times in a day. With overcast weather that same plant will transpire less and consequently needs less water. If the air or the soil is cold, then the absorption of water by the plant is practically nil. Watering in that case is hardly necessary. This applies to all plants, such as succulents, that go through rest periods in the winter. (See

A large terrarium with houseplants and epiphytic plants.

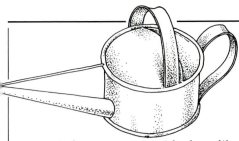

It can be difficult to find a good watering can. It needs to be large enough, yet comfortable to handle, and have a long spout for reaching between plants.

Below: Left: *Two misters.* Right: *An exceptional water system.*

Far below: Left: *A humidity meter, ideal for those people unsure of how much water to add.* Right: *A plant is dipped.*

On the following pages: Hemerocallis 'Catherine Woodbury.'

rest periods on page 62.) With plants like bulbs, there is very little need for water before they develop, since there is no surface where transpiration can occur. In short: If you always keep the water/transpiration balance in mind, you will make fewer mistakes watering your plants.

Dry or wet?

In the plant descriptions, I always indicate whether a particular plant needs to grow wet, moist, moderately moist or quite dry. What do these directions mean?

Wet cultivation means that water may stay in the bottom of the pot or in the plant tray. There are not many plants that can tolerate these conditions, but there are a few.

Moist means that the soil never dries out; when the soil is pressed it should feel damp, but no water should remain in the tray.

Moderately moist means that the soil never dries out completely, but it can become quite dry between waterings. If the plant starts to droop, the soil is too dry.

Dry cultivation means that the soil can get rather dry, but not bone dry. These plants often need a rest period during which less water is given. The drainage has to be perfect, so no water can collect in the bottom of the pot.

How you find out

A person with a green thumb can stick his or her finger in the soil and know instantly with which of the four conditions he or she is dealing. Try it yourself! If that fine-tuned touch is lacking, buy a moisture meter. Stick it in the soil and read the scale. What works too is the weight test. If the plant and pot feel light, then the soil is dry. Keep in mind that sandy soil holds less water than a soil rich in humus. The

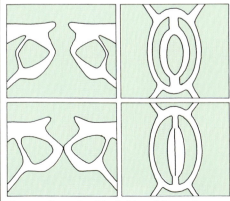

Stomas from the side (left) and from above (right), open and closed.

latter generally should be kept more moist.

The best way to water

You run into fewer problems with watering if you use pots with a good drainage hole. A waterproof saucer should be used under the pot to catch the water. Inexpensive plastic saucers are available everywhere. There are also decorative pots on the market with drainage holes and saucers. In my opinion, pots from the Middle East are the best; you can see them in many photographs in this book. Unfortunately, they are expensive and not always available.

You can water a plant either by pouring water directly on the soil or into the saucer. In the latter case, the plant draws the water up through the soil. If there is

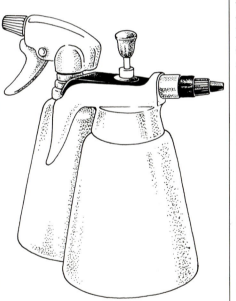

no soil at the bottom of the pot because of a thick layer of drainage material, this method of watering will not work. Clay pots themselves will also absorb water. One way of watering is not better than the other. However you do it, always remove the excess water that collects in the saucer.

Plants with fragile or hairy leaves, like African violets, do not appreciate getting water on them. With these plants, it is better to pour the water into the saucer. In cool weather, or for a plant in a cool corner, it is advisable to bring the water up to room temperature (68°–85°F). The fact is roots do not absorb cold water very well.

Dipping

Many woody houseplants appreciate being dipped—immersing the whole pot in water. This method allows air bubbles to escape from between the roots. After the ball of earth is completely saturated, let the excess water drip out, so fresh air can enter the soil. This dipping method also cleanses the soil.

PLANTS THAT NEED A DORMANT PERIOD

There are seasons in most climate zones in the world and the plants that grow in each naturally have adapted to their particular situation. If the season is favorable for growth and bloom, grow and bloom they will. If the situation is less favorable, they take a rest. We should try to imitate these circumstances as much as possible at home, to allow plants to grow their best. If we neglect this aspect of plant care, it can lead to weak, disease-sensitive plants. And for many plants if there is no dormant period, there will be no flowers.

Natural causes for dormancy

A plant goes into a dormant state when the temperature is too low or there is not enough water. Often a combination of both factors plays a role. In a temperate climate, the cold temperature is the most important factor. In winter, perennials completely die off above the ground, and deciduous plants shed their foliage to protect themselves against freezing. In a desert or savanna climate, the dormant period is determined by the lack of water. Succulent plants are equipped with various devices to limit the loss of water and resist the drought. During dormancy, growth stagnates almost completely, although inside the plant the living processes continue but at a very low level. Transpiration and assimilation still function. Furthermore during dormancy, preparations are made for future flowering: Bud construction takes place, but the flower buds do not grow until adequate conditions (warmer temperature, more water) arrive. At this point, the flowers will develop quite quickly.

Dormancy but not enough light

When there is no light, growth will also stop, but not for long. If there is sufficient water and the temperature is high enough, the plant still tries to grow and develop shoots and leaves. In nature this phenomenon hardly ever occurs; plants just do not grow in places where they do not belong. Plants imported into a temperate climate will sometimes exhibit this undesired growth because they are not in their natural habitat. Most houseplants fit into that "imported" category.

When a plant tries to grow in insufficient light, it exhibits thin, weak growth. The shoots become elongated (often seen in succulents) and the leaves turn yellow-green, because not enough assimilation of carbohydrates and sugars is taking place to maintain the plant. Eventually the whole plant wilts. To prevent these symptoms, give your plants an artificial rest period, by lowering the temperature and giving less water.

Dormancy occurs mostly in the winter

It is logical that in a temperate climate in the northern hemisphere the dormant period for plants occurs during the winter, because there is less light available. Dormancy in general starts around October and ends in April. As with all things in nature, there are exceptions. An arum, for instance, needs a rest period after blooming in May or June. Other plants originating in the southern hemisphere have not succeeded in changing their growing rhythm; to successfully cultivate them, we have to accommodate their wishes.

Plants can be fooled

To get them to bloom at a point other than their normal time, we can fool plants by changing the amount of light and water. Sometimes, they will even flower twice a year, but they do not sustain this pattern for very long; a plant forced from its natural rhythm often dies. In commercial cultivation, this out-of-season forcing is brought about on purpose to bring particular flowering plants to market at a certain time—for instance, chrysanthemums in early spring. It is a complicated process of darkening, artificial light and controlled temperatures.

On page 62: *A tray with plants in winter storage, in a cool, light shed.*
Right: *A balcony-built greenhouse can be kept frost free in the winter with the help of electric heating.*

Below: *The garage is often an ideal spot for storing dormant plants. It is suitable for rather large container plants, such as palms, which can then be moved outdoors in the summer.*

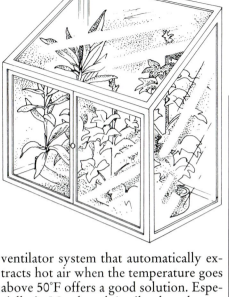

Rest areas in and around the house

The temperature in a modern home is kept constant year-round, not a suitable environment for plants that want a cooler period. It is possible, however, to keep one or more rooms cooler for the plants. A temperature between 40° and 50°F will keep most plants dormant. Watch carefully to be sure the temperature never goes below 40°F.

If you can heat your garage, it can be a good place for plants that should stay cool over the winter. A workable solution is the suggested addition to the garage, shown in the drawing. Subtropical plants that are woody and drop their leaves in the winter can be buried in a pit in the garden at least two feet deep toward the middle of November. Cover with sand and dig up again at the end of March. Sometimes, this technique can work with other plants as well, for instance the *Agapanthus*.

A cold or a moderate greenhouse is ideal for dormant periods. (See also pages 44–47, where greenhouses are discussed.) There is sufficient light in a greenhouse and the temperature can be regulated to your satisfaction. Even a small protected balcony (drawing above right), can serve as an excellent spot for dormant plants.

Watering and ventilation

Dormant plants in general have little need for water. I know of many cactus lovers who do not water succulents at all from November until the end of March. The drier they are, the more durable they are against cold. If they still have a lot of leaves, plants do need some water, but the soil can stay rather dry as long as the temperature is low.

It can sometimes be a real challenge to keep the temperature low, especially on a bright sunny day in the middle of winter when the inside temperature can easily rise as high as 68°F. Try to avoid these temperature changes, because the plants will start to grow too early. When the temperature does rise, you have to ventilate immediately, even if the temperature is still freezing outside! A greenhouse equipped with automatic ventilation windows is an easy solution. Also, an electric

ventilator system that automatically extracts hot air when the temperature goes above 50°F offers a good solution. Especially in March and April, when the sun is already quite strong, be careful to keep the greenhouse cool. Personally, I would rather put the container plants outside in the shade and protect them with plastic when a freeze is expected.

Timing

When the time comes to end the dormant period, the plants should gradually be exposed to warmer temperatures and receive more water. Do not make the mistake of immediately placing a dormant plant in a sweltering room. In much of the country, the possibility of frost can still occur through May and many container plants will not survive that exposure. Only after all danger of frost is over can they be safely put back on the terrace. But even then, extreme temperature vari-

ations should be avoided. I once bought a big myrtle that had been cultivated in a greenhouse. At the end of May, I brought it outside because of the nice weather. But the following night was cold and windy, which certainly did not do the plant any good. Most of the leaves fell off and only much later when the weather was warmer did new leaves appear.

When the plants go from their cool dormant spot into a warm room, mist them often to help them to acclimate to the drier air, and still try to keep them rather cool.

Right: *Tropical foliage plants can be cultivated warm all year; however, the amaryllis requires a strict dormant period if it is to flower a second time.*

HUMIDITY

When an enclosed space is heated, the air feels drier, an experience everybody has felt in the winter. This lack of humidity is one of the major reasons why houseplants have such a hard time in the winter. Why the air becomes so dry and what you can do about it is described below.

What is relative humidity?

The warmer the air, the more water vapor it can absorb. At 41°F one square yard of air holds a maximum ¼ oz of water; at 68°F, ⅔ oz. In both cases, the relative humidity is 100 percent. The absolute humidity does not particularly interest us. What happens is that a room with a temperature of 41°F contains, for example, 3½ oz of water vapor. With heating, you bring the temperature up to 68°F. If the room is well insulated, the amount of water vapor stays exactly at 3½ oz. But because the warmer air has the capacity to contain much more water vapor, the relative humidity will drop. Result: The air feels drier, not only to people but also to the plants. The same air in the same space becomes drier when it is heated and relatively more humid when the heat is turned off.

A fern and a cactus have very different evaporation rates.

Relative humidity influences evaporation

The drier the air, the more moisture people and plants will lose through evaporation. In the desert, one loses so much that you have to drink extra water to survive. On the other hand, in very humid air we have difficulty perspiring and sweat stays on our skin in drops and hardly evaporates. Plants that originate in the desert will not suffer very much from the dry air in our rooms. They do not have many stomata and those they have close tightly. But plants from tropical forests, that are used to living in high humidity, quickly are drained of moisture in dry air. They lose so much water through transpiration that it is impossible for the roots to make in up, and the plant dries up.

To measure humidity

The relative humidity of the air is easy to measure with an hygrometer. In many combinations of barometer/thermometer, a hygrometer is also included. These instruments are not 100-percent accurate. If you want to know the humidity exactly, then you need a so-called "wet-ball-thermometer." In my opinion, the need for this preciseness in the home is a bit exaggerated.

A reading of 100 percent means that the air is saturated to its maximum with water, usually only in the bathroom during the use of the shower. In the tropics, the relative humidity fluctuates between 60 percent and 90 percent. A manageable classification for home use is:

below 50%	low
50–60%	moderate
above 60%	high

In severe winters, the relative humidity can drop as low as 30 percent. You suffer from dry mucous membranes, which makes you susceptible to colds, wood furniture shrinks, paper becomes hard and brittle and plants have a hard time.

Ventilating does not help

Some people think that opening a window is a cure against dry air. The cold air outside is after all more humid. In reality, however, the air in the room only becomes drier with such ventilation. The inside air needs more humidity, so you bring in cold, relatively humid air from outside. But when that air has reached room temperature, it will have become relatively much drier than the original air!

Through heating, the relative humidity drops, as we know. If you have heating stoves with an exhaust system (wood-burning stoves, fireplaces, etc.), then the hot air disappears through the chimney. Fresh air from outside is drawn in from gaps around doors or windows. In fact, this is a simple way of ventilating. Gas heaters do not function in this manner. They suck air in and dispose of it without letting it enter the room.

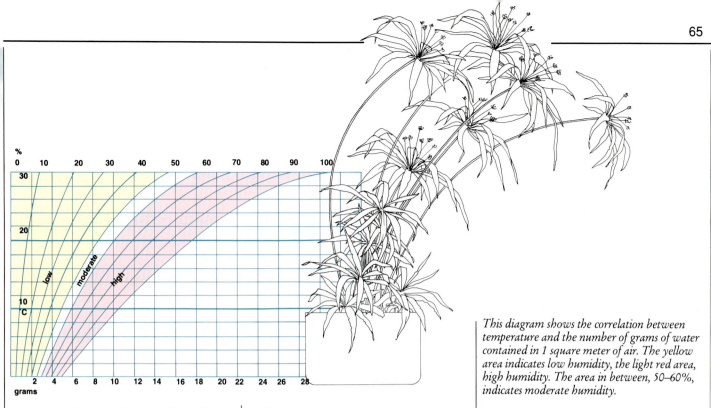

This diagram shows the correlation between temperature and the number of grams of water contained in 1 square meter of air. The yellow area indicates low humidity, the light red area, high humidity. The area in between, 50–60%, indicates moderate humidity.

Hot-air heating is a totally different matter. In most cases the air circulates around the rooms and the boiler, but sometimes it is possible to draw in fresh air from the outside. That is a kind of ventilation also, but one that has a drying effect. (If we know the relative humidity outside and inside and both temperatures, then we can find out exactly if the relative humidity inside will drop or rise—but that requires too much detail to explain.)

If you have a hot-air heating system with an air humidifier it is relatively easy to raise the humidity in the house. This is the ideal situation. But for people without this type of heating system there are solutions.

Increasing the humidity

It is much better for you, your plants and the piano, etc. to raise the humidity in the winter. Moreover, it does not cost anything, as we will see. In the past one put clay trays filled with water on the radiators; later these trays came in plastic often with a paper filter inserted. But the amount of water that can evaporate in a day is very small and scarcely effects the humidity.

It is also useful to mist the plants, only you must do it often, since the moisture dries up very quickly. If the heat is turned up high, it is not an exaggeration to mist the plants ten times a day. But who has the patience to do this? A pebble tray with water under the plants is another well-known way to raise the humidity locally. The water evaporates and the damp air strikes the leaves. Naturally this only helps rather small plants. If you have floor tiles, you can wet the floor with water every night. Especially if you have floor heat, keeping the floor wet is very effective in raising humidity. However, few people like to wet their beautiful floor, except perhaps in the bathroom. Pity, because it is a big help to the plants.

Serious measures

I do not take any of the above measures to raise humidity very seriously, because one has to evaporate over two gallons of water a day in a normal-sized living room to see a rise on the hygrometer. If the room is completely closed off from outside air, then less water is needed. But doors are always opened and closed, and besides, no room is hermetically sealed off.

You can evaporate two gallons of water, the amount you need, with a vaporizer. Vaporizers are equipped with small turbines, driven by an electric motor. The water lands on it and is subsequently blown into the room in very small drops.

The disadvantages are the noise these machines make and the deposits of water left on furniture and other objects.

Finally there are humidifiers. They consist of rather large water reservoirs (1½ to 2½ gallons) with an electric heating element. The water is kept at a constant temperature of over 200°F, so that it evaporates quickly; when all the water is used, the machine shuts off automatically. This modern version of the tea kettle on the stove operates practically noiselessly and lasts a long time. The only maintenance consists of replenishing the water and occasionally cleaning the reservoir, in which sediments from the water collect. That is when you will see how dirty your tapwater really is.

Save on gas by using electricity

An electric vaporizer uses only a small amount of electricity. Because air moistened by the vaporizer feels warmer than dry air, you can set your thermostat lower. I am not going to figure out the costs, but it is obvious that the electric power for the vaporizer does not cost you anything, since you earn back the money in savings on your heating costs.

Right: With a hygrometer, the exact relative humidity of the air can be measured. A humidifier and electric evaporator can produce the proper cultivation conditions for your plants.

THE RIGHT SOIL FOR EACH PLANT

Not so long ago, one just dug some earth from the garden and hoped that the houseplants would flourish in it. Today, one buys a bag of potting soil in the supermarket and assumes it is fine for the plants. Both approaches are wrong, although I have to admit that 75 percent of all houseplants do rather well in the packaged potting soil.

All-purpose potting soil

Something akin to a "standard" potting soil is available in every country. Local experts develop a recipe (or several) and manufacturers regularly use these standard recipes so that their potting soil mix gets the label "approved." A good, basic all-purpose potting mix consists of:

1 part sterilized garden soil
1 part peat moss
1 part clean builder's sand
1 tablespoon ground limestone per quart (to raise the pH to a moderately acid one)

The acid level of an all-purpose potting soil should fluctuate around pH 6 (see page 68–69), which makes it suitable for a whole range of houseplants. In the plant descriptions, I always indicate which type of potting soil is most appropriate for the growth of a particular plant. Unless it is obvious, I will indicate which soil or rather which growing mix should be used. These standard mixtures exist in many countries.

Rooting mediums

All-purpose potting soil is usually too heavy and contains too many nutrients for very young plants, such as seedlings and cuttings. Special rooting mediums are widely available for this purpose. This is a very fine mixture that is light and porous and contains few nutrients. After about four weeks the young plants should be repotted in normal potting soil, where they get more nourishment.

Extra acidic potting soil

For acid-loving plants such as azaleas, *Anthurium*, *Calceolaria*, *Camellia*, *Gesneria*, *Sinningia*, *Primula*, etc., an all-purpose soil is not very suitable. These plants cannot absorb sufficient iron at pH 6, so their leaves will yellow. The best pH for acid-loving plants lies around 4.8, which is achieved by adding less limestone to the mixture.

Potting soil with loam or clay

Very little commercial potting soil contains real earth such as loam or clay. Nevertheless, this substrate, which usually has a high pH level, is very good for some plants. Palms and many other plants from the tropics and the subtropics in particular grow better in a mixture that contains clay. One can make an appropriate potting soil by mixing the commercial soil with 20–40 percent loam or clay. You can dig clay or loam from the earth but it must be cleaned and made friable or it will be hard to mix. If this is difficult, you can purchase rock powder or lava powder in many nurseries.

Various additions

Separate mixtures for bromeliads, *Maranta*, ferns and many other plants can be bought commercially. Other supplements to potting soil are also available, such as dried cow manure, soil from coniferous woods, compost, etc.

Today more and more synthetic products like vermiculite and perlite are being added to potting soil mixtures or being

used alone for some purposes. Vermiculite is a lightweight mica product that is highly water absorbent. Perlite is a kind of puffed rock that is very airy and drains well while still holding some moisture.

How to mix your own all-natural potting soil

Because there are so many soil mixtures on the market, it is not really necessary to make your own. But if you enjoy it, you can do it. If you want to make a purely organic potting mixture, start with sterilized garden soil and well-decayed farmyard manure. If you can find molehills in the fields, the earth of molehills is a good addition to the mixture. Next add de-

Many ready-made potting soils are available, but you can mix it yourself, too, using clay, bark, coarse sand, peat moss, lime, etc., depending on what soil type is required by the plant.

An orchid in rock wood flakes.

cayed leaf mold, coniferous mold (often redwood), as well as some builder's or river sand (well rinsed and free of calcium) for drainage. If you want to keep it completely organic, then add bonemeal as a fertilizer. You can try various mixtures: Add more clay and some lime for plants that like a high pH, or peat moss and a lot of coniferous mold for acid-loving plants. Mix well and put it away for a few months. A well covered heap stays well preserved outside for a long time.

Mixture for cacti and other succulents

Cactus soil is often sold as a special product. But many cactus fans make their own mixture. The pH, for most species, should be between 5.5 and 6.5. In any case, the cacti do not like a heavy limestone substrate. But the mixture must be airy and porous and should drain well. A small percentage of humus (peat moss or leaf mold) should be sufficient. Other helpful ingredients include perlite, basalt powder, lava, rinsed river sand or builder's sand.

1 part builder's sand
1 part all-purpose potting soil
1 part perlite, lava powder or basalt powder
1 part loam or clay

Most small ball-formed cacti grow well in this mixture. It does not contain much nourishment, so fertilizing is necessary. Cactus food is used in this case (see page 74), dissolved in water. Epiphytic cacti, such as *Epiphyllum*, prefer a mixture that contains more humus and therefore retains more water. Peat moss has the same effect. What is important for cacti applies to most other succulents as well: a permeable soil with good drainage.

Soil mixtures for orchids

Mixtures for orchids, even more than for cacti, have always been shrouded in a certain mystery. Every orchid lover has his own recipe. Traditionally, chopped fernroots, milled sphagnum (moss) and leaf mold were mixed together. All are acidic elements, partially decayed and organic in origin, and equivalent to the humus that one finds in tree holes in the tropical forest. More recently pieces of bark, styrofoam, perlite, clay granules, cork, etc. are used. Orchids do not like lime; the pH of the substrate has to be around 5–5.5. Furthermore, it has to be extremely permeable, because stagnant water is disastrous to an orchid: It rots the roots. When you water it should practically run through the pot. Orchid roots have an ability to take up the water immediately; the soil does not have to do that for them. In warm weather, it is usually necessary to water more frequently or better yet to mist. Today, rock wool is generally used. Most of these materials contain no nourishment and therefore, you must add dissolved plant food to the water on a regular basis.

That advice pertains to the epiphytic orchid. But there are also terrestrial, or soil-growing, plants in the family. These need more humus in the soil mixture, sometimes even clay or loam. The correct mixtures are given in the plant descriptions.

Tree fern for orchids and bromeliads

One often sees pieces of tree fern used as a support for various sorts of orchids or bromeliads, especially the gray *Tillandsia*. Useful for small plants, the plants together with some humus are tied to the tree fern with copper wire. Give water and nutrients by taking the whole piece and dipping it in water.

FLOWER POTS AND POTTING SOIL

A plant is usually anchored in the soil by roots. But not always! Some plants grow on trees, where they are sustained by humus found in the axils of the tree branches. There are even plants that do not need any soil: Spanish moss simply hangs from a branch and absorbs food and dew water from the air. Even for houseplants, we rarely use earth anymore. Almost all potting soil comes from factories and synthetic elements increasingly are being added. It is therefore better to speak of a growing medium or substrate.

From decorative antique flower pots to plants that grow on pieces of bark, almost everything is possible with houseplants. At far right is a soil acidity test.

What is the purpose of a growing medium?

The substrate in which the roots grow has various functions. First of all, it holds the plant so that it cannot fall over. This does not apply to all plants, as climbing plants for instance hold on to walls, branches or wires. But one usually refers to a substrate as providing a firm grip for the roots. Secondly, the growing medium should supply the plant with nourishment. Even this is not an absolute, because some plants absorb their nutrients primarily via the leaves. But these plants do not have many roots and the substrate is less important. Absorption of food by the roots is explained in detail on page 50. Such absorption is only possible when the substrate contains nourishment. The growing medium may contain natural nourishment, but we usually add to it as well. On the other hand it should not contain too much, or you will burn the plant. Only when the concentration of food in the growing medium is lower than the concentration in the plant, does the plant absorb the nutrients. The substrate must also be capable of holding some water, because only nutrients that are dissolved in water can be absorbed by the plant. This balance between moisture and drainage varies widely, depending on the growing medium one uses. The exact nutrients that plants need are explained on pages 74–75.

The level of acid in the growing medium

The pH scale indicates whether something (in this case the growing medium) is acid, neutral or alkaline. The pH scale is a measurement of the concentration of hydrogen ions and goes from 1 (acidic) to 14 (alkaline); 7 is the median or neutral. Houseplants only grow between pH 4 and pH 8. So we only need to consider that area on the scale. The lower the pH is, the more acid is in the growing medium. By adding alkaline elements to the soil or plant water, we raise the pH level and the soil becomes less acid. That sounds very illogical, but is nevertheless true. By adding acid elements or acid plant water, the pH or acid level becomes lower and the soil becomes more acid. I explain this in such detail, because the exact acid level is of vital importance for all houseplants. If you provide the wrong acid level for a plant, it will die, even if the rest of the care is excellent.

Each plant has its own acid level

Many plants are quite sensitive to the acid level of their growing medium. In that small range between pH 4 and 8 lies a world of difference. An azalea only grows well in acid soil, between pH 4 and 5. If you try to cultivate an azalea in a less acid medium, then the plant will not get sufficient iron, fewer leaves will form and they will quickly turn yellow and photosynthesis will stop. An *Acacia*, on the other hand, does not like acid soil; these plants grow better in a medium with a pH between 6 and 7.

Fortunately, we do not have to mix a separate growing medium for each houseplant. By far most plants prefer a pH around 6, which means they can grow

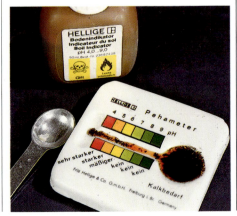

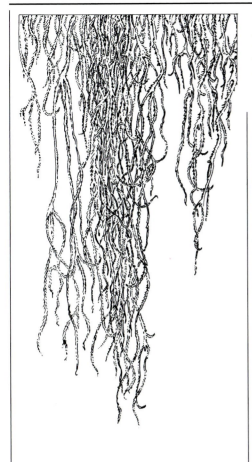

Epiphytic plants do not need much soil at all, and rely on the small amount of humus that collects in the axils of tree branches for their nutrients. These plants often absorb moisture and food through their foliage.

well in packaged potting soil. The exceptions are succulents, orchids, members of the heather family, as well as azaleas and a whole range of tropical plants, all of which should be cultivated in more acid soil.

How to measure the pH yourself

Test sets and meters are available with which you can determine the pH of your garden soil or potting soil. They are not expensive and give reasonably accurate measurements, although only a research laboratory can give absolute figures. I find it useful to be able to test the pH myself, because it contributes to a better understanding of the growing conditions. To measure is to know.

The acid level changes depending on the care

As I've already mentioned, the pH level of the soil can change depending on how you care for your plants. If alkaline water is used on a plant, then the pH level will rise and the soil will become less acid. If you do not take it seriously, and if your tapwater is also hard, your azaleas will probably die within a couple of months. Of course, you can reverse this process by providing extra acid water. You can even add acid in chemical form, but to do that you need a precise knowledge of chemical reactions. It is not simple.

How much water can the substrate hold?

If there are sufficient materials in the growing medium that do not hold water, such as rough sand or stone, then the growing medium dries up rather quickly. Plants with very fine root hairs can hold water because of their capillary action. That applies also to humus products, such as peat or peat moss. Peat moss can absorb eight times its own weight in water, but that liquid is held together with such a pressure that plant roots can only use half of it. That is still more than in any other product, which is why peat moss is often part of a growing medium. Some plants really flourish best in a substrate that dries out almost completely between waterings; others do better in a constantly moist soil. Therefore, it is logical that we cultivate plants from the first group in a sandy soil, and the plants from the second group in a more humus substrate.

The kind of pot and drainage

If you water too much and it cannot drain out, you will drown the plant. The water displaces the air in the potting soil and the roots die. Every flower pot should have a good drainage system, so that no surplus of water remains in the pot. Some plants are more sensitive to bad drainage than others. Orchids cannot stand stagnant water, which is why one fills the pots for these plants half full of drainage material. But this is a good practice for other plants as well. Put broken pieces of old-fashioned clay flower pots on the bottom of the pot before adding the potting soil. This technique will also prevent the roots from growing into the drainholes.

If you want to cultivate plants in a completely closed plant container, then add a drainage layer of at least two inches on the bottom. This will not completely avert the danger from excess water, because with overwatering you can float the drainage layer. For that reason, I devised a viewing tube: a plastic tube that slides down to the bottom of the container. You can easily observe with a flashlight if any water has collected in the bottom. In that case, do not water until the bottom is dry again.

Below: *Different models of plastic pots.*

At left: *An azalea, which requires acid soil, and a palm, which benefits from the addition of lime to its soil.*
Left: *A cutaway view of a large container shows how pottery shards can be used to improve drainage.*

REPOTTING

In nature most plants have enough space to grow. When the roots have exhausted a certain area, they just grow deeper or further out to find new food. Although most houseplants are satisfied with the limited space of a flower pot or container, if the soil is depleted of nutrients or the soil is spoiled, then the plant will die. Therefore, repotting is a necessity from time to time.

Poisonous concentrations in the potting soil

When you start with a properly prepared potting soil, either your own or a commercial one, conditions are close to ideal for the plant, with nutrients present in the right proportion, the pH factor in order, etc. But this situation changes quickly. When the plant grows, it consumes nutrients, which you replenish with fertilizer. But with the water you provide, you also bring in undesirable elements, particularly if the water is hard, and as a result the pH in the soil will gradually rise. Furthermore, tapwater often contains a high concentration of minerals that stay behind in the soil. They are often visible as white crusts on the outside of clay flower pots. With the environmental situation today, you may have to repot, not because the pot is too small but because the soil is polluted.

When is the pot too small?

When the commercial grower delivers the plant to the garden center, the pot is in fact already too small. Pots and soil cost money, so from his point of view, the smaller, the better, as long as the quality of the plant does not suffer. This basically means that you will have to repot your plant soon after bringing it home. Cacti in pots only a few inches wide, or large plants that do not stand up without support all suffer because the pots are too small.

It is difficult to explain exactly how big the pot for a particular plant should be. The size of the root mass and the plant above ground should be in balance. For aesthetic reasons as well, there should be harmony between the size of pot and plant. If the plant falls over, then for sure the pot is too small. A plant in a container that is proportionally too large looks strange, but the plant itself will not suffer from it. Some people assert that certain plants grow better in small pots, but this is not always the case.

When to repot

It is often said that you should only repot when the plant is dormant. The end of the rest period, usually spring, is of course a good moment to give the plant new soil, but if it is necessary, you can safely repot at other times, including when the plant is flowering. The secret is not to disturb the roots. Fast-growing plants, such as the *Abutilon*, often outgrow their pots in 4–6 weeks. If they are repotted immediately, then they continue to grow; otherwise the growth stops. To repot four to five times during a growing season is not exceptional for these plants. On the other hand, a very slow-growing plant can stay in the same soil for at least three years, if pollution does not make it necessary to repot before. In other words, how often to repot depends upon the speed of growth.

Take the plant out of the pot

Plants are usually easy to remove from plastic pots. Clay flower pots can give more problems, especially if the pot has a narrow top, and the ball of soil usually comes free. Tap the pot on the edge of a table. If not, you will have to cut the ball loose with a knife or even break the pot.

In the case of a valuable pot you don't want to lose, you can force the plant out with a strong stream of water, but this is a laborious process.

Do not disturb the roots

Cut away any diseased or decaying roots, but otherwise never cut them unless you are dividing the plant for propagation purposes. Every disturbance of the roots sets back growth, as the plant has to recover from the injury. Roots always grow toward the outside of the pot, so that you will find the largest concentration of roots against the sides. There are often fewer roots, and certainly no fine roots, inside the ball of soil. It is important to remove the old soil inside the root ball during the repotting process. This is easier to do when the soil is dry; by kneading the ball of soil, the soil will loosen and drop, without hurting the roots.

The new pot a big larger

When the plant has become pot-bound in its existing pot, the new one should be larger than the old one. A space of about an inch around the ball of soil is sufficient, but it can be more. Carefully check the depth of the plant as well, as it should not sit much deeper than it did before. Remember to put drainage material in the bottom of the pot so that excess water can

When the roots of a potted plant grow too big for its pot, it is better when replanting to break the pot open rather than pull the plant straight out, which may damage the roots.

Repotting, from left to right: *Remove the plant form its pot by tapping, insert a new drainage layer in the new pot, fill around the existing soil with new potting soil, allow a ¾ in space at the top of the pot for watering.* Far right: *Make sure that the plant stands as deep in the soil as it did in the old pot.*

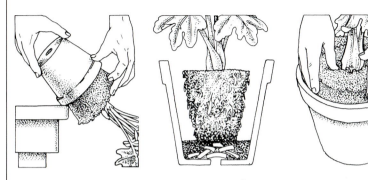

run off. Broken pot pieces and pebbles are effective as drainage material.

Add a layer of potting soil over the drainage material and then the root ball of the plant. Add new soil around the root ball and press down, so there are no air holes and the plant stands upright in the middle of the pot. There should be space at the rim for additional soil; also, for watering ease, allow about ¾ of an inch between the soil and the top of the pot. If you do not have sufficient space, select a larger pot.

After repotting, water the pot well and temporarily keep the plant away from sunlight. It is also a good idea to mist the plant more often than usual. After a week the plant will have probably recovered from possible root damage, and can be returned to its normal location.

Repotting cacti
Most cacti are repotted in the spring. Minimum size plastic pots are 3½ inches in diameter. Wear a sturdy glove to hold the plant or use special repotting tongs or simply a folded towel. Drain thoroughly, then continue as explained above.

Repotting orchids
The sympodial-growing orchids have to be set to one side of the pot or basket when they are repotted. The young new shoot should point toward the middle of the pot. The next time you repot, turn it, so that it will grow to the other side. Air plants, such as bromeliads that are grown on bark, are tied to these pieces with copper wire, which does not corrode. After some time these epiphytes will be self-supportive.

Right: *The roots of this* Clivia *begin to gradually work themselves out of the soil. When repotting, place this plant deeper in the soil, so the roots are again covered.*

Left: *Because roots tend to grow out toward a pot's sides, they often layer the pot's inside walls. Many people assume incorrectly that this layer can be removed when repotting; the loss of those roots will in fact considerably decrease a plant's ability to absorb food and water.*

Below: *When repotting a cactus, it is easier (and safer) to use special tongs or even a piece of folded cardboard or a towel.*

Far below: *If repotting seems too much work or just not necessary, simply replace the top, most polluted layer of pot soil.*

HYDROPONICS AND WATER SYSTEMS

With only a few exceptions, plants in nature grow in the earth or something similar, like a layer of humus. But in the 19th century, Justus von Liebig discovered that plants are able to grow in water, provided appropriate nutrients are supplied. At first, little use was made of this discovery, but today, this way of cultivation, called hydroponics, or water culture, is widely used both commercially and by hobbyists.

Different kinds of roots

Plants that grow in water have somewhat different roots than plants that grow in soil. When you rinse off a plant that has grown in soil and put it in water, it will experience a period of shock at first, until it has formed new (water) roots. It is the same process that happens when you plant a cutting in soil that has been growing in a glass of water. After you plant that cutting in potting soil, its growth will stop for a while until new (soil) roots have formed. This phenomenon has to do with the fact that roots need air (oxygen) to be able to function, as well as water. In porous potting soil, sufficient air is always available, but that is less so in water. Fortunately, plants adapt by creating another type of root, which is capable of absorbing oxygen from the water. These roots are less blanched and have fine long root hairs. When you purchase a houseplant, you always should indicate if you want a hydroplant; i.e., a plant that has been cultivated in water from the start. Plants cultivated in soil can readjust to water, but they often fail. Hydroplants are more expensive in general than plants cultivated in soil because they are grown in special nurseries and often there are fewer of them.

Advantages and disadvantages of hydroponics

The biggest advantage to hydroponics is the fact that the plants need less care. Watering is only necessary at great intervals and it is practically impossible to overwater. These advantages may be true, but I am not particularly in favor of methods that lessen the time we spend with our plants. Repeatedly in this book I have emphasized that the fun of caring for plants lies in the fact that it creates a bond between man/woman and plant. Nonetheless, I can imagine there are circumstances in which it is useful and maybe even necessary, because otherwise the plants would be totally neglected. Nowadays, many people work, and plants are left to themselves for long periods. Large containers in offices are usually designed for some type of hydroponics and under those circumstances the system is helpful.

Hydroponics is also a hobby, which means one is not doing it out of convenience but because one enjoys cultivating plants in water. In a nutshell: The advantage seems to be minimal care for companies and people who are away from home often. Disadvantages: high expenses for plants and containers, and less contact between the owner and the plant.

Do plants grow better in water?

Supporters of hydroponics always insist that plants grow better in water. That is true, if you compare them with plants in soil that do not get optimal care. But when proper care is equally applied to both growing methods, then I have never been able to see a difference. It is known, however, that some species do not grow well in water, probably because these plants have difficulty making water roots.

Support for hydro-plants

When a plant grows in a water solution, it will fall over, which is why pots and containers for hydroponics are always filled with material that provides a firm support. At the moment expanded clay particles or clay pebbles are the most frequently used, but other materials can be

On page 72: *Young hydro-cuttings.*
Below: *With hydroponics, plants generally sit in clay particles. A part of the root system is situated in water and withdraws food, another part grows between the clay and can absorb oxygen.*

Middle, left: *A food patty for hydroponics.* Middle, center: *A water level meter, used in hydroponics and watering systems.* Middle, right: *A porous tape is used to suck up water for a plant in a watering system.*

Below, left: *For watering during an extended vacation, cotton threads can be pulled through the soil and placed in a water tray beneath the plant.*
Below, right: *This "mushroom" is another way to keep potting soil moist automatically.*

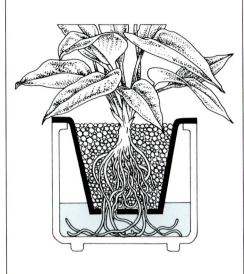

used as well, if they do not give the plant any nourishment. Cultivation of plants on rock wool is a kind of hydroculture too, although this material has a much finer texture than clay particles. This method of growing is increasingly popular in the professional world of hydroponic cultivation.

Water level
Pots and containers for hydroponics have to be supplied with a meter that shows the lowest and the highest level of the water. The containers are only partly filled with water. Clay pebbles are exposed at the top, so that some roots can grow above the water. The caretaker has only to fill up the container when the water level drops to the lowest point. Since the water slowly gets somewhat polluted, once a year it is pumped out and replaced with fresh water. Only when the plants completely outgrow the container is it necessary to repot. But that can take years.

The nourishment of hydro-plants
I refer the reader to page 74–75, where nourishment of all plants is discussed.

Watering systems
When I speak of watering systems, what I mean is a built-in system that semi-automatically regulates watering of plants growing in soil. This happens in hydroponics as well, but the plants grow in water. In fact, watering systems try to combine the advantages of hydroponics with the advantages of cultivation in soil, resulting in less maintenance, an optimal level of moisture in the soil and yet the use

of ordinary, cheaper plants with soil roots. This method can be quite successful, again especially in offices, where we see many containers with watering systems. We see these containers less in homes, because pots with built-in watering systems are a lot more expensive than simple plastic or clay flower pots. This is unfortunate, because after years of experience, I have come to the conclusion that many plants grow exceptionally well in pots with a watering system. The reason for the success is the consistency of moisture in the soil. The plant itself decides on the amount of water it wants to absorb. Even plants that are very sensitive to the moistness in the soil, such as ferns, grow better with a watering system.

How does it work?
In most cases, a reservoir for water is located in the bottom of the unit. Over that is a fine grid and on top of that is the potting soil and the plant. Via a wick or (more often) via a small part of the potting soil that always touches the water, the moisture is absorbed. The more liquid the plant loses the drier the soil becomes and the more liquid is drawn from the reservoir. This all happens by capillary action. For that reason, this system functions best with a potting soil containing humus,

which is true of most all-purpose potting soils. It would not work with clay particles. The reservoir can be refilled via a cap in the unit. A meter or float to measure the water level is used just as with hydroponics. In some units there is a layer of air between the water and the grid, so that air can enter the soil. This appears to provide an extra advantage.

Suitable for all plants?
All plants cultivated in soil can be put in a container with a watering system. Very small pots are available as well as very large containers. If you keep the reservoir filled with water, the soil will stay constantly moist. Some plants, for instance cacti, prefer that the soil get completely dry between waterings. You can do this with a watering system by letting the reservoir go dry and leaving it for a week before filling it up again. In this way, you can also provide periods of rest in the winter. But personally, I would rather cultivate plants in normal pots and only apply the watering system to plants that need constant moisture year-round.

NOURISHMENT FOR HOUSEPLANTS

There are only a very few plants that can live just on air, plants that seemingly have no need for food and still grow. Furthermore, all plants need quite a lot of nitrogen, phosphorus, potassium, magnesium and a whole range of micronutrients (boron, cobalt, copper, zinc, etc.). As explained on page 50, the plant factory "burns" these nutrients together with carbon dioxide, which is withdrawn from the air and the water.

Need for nutrients depends on growth

I am always amazed to see advertisements for houseplant food in the winter months. There is almost no plant that is growing during that period. It is counterproductive to give food at that time. If you continue to fertilize, the nutrients accumulate in the soil and pose the danger of poisoning the plant. This is because an overdose of nourishment can scorch a plant, as you read on page 50. You should only feed plants when they are growing. Enough nutrients will remain in the soil to maintain the plant. Small plants that grow slowly need less fertilizer than large ones. People frequently fail to consider this fact. Consequently, small plants receive too much food and large plants not enough.

What should the food contain?

Good soil contains all the necessary nutrients already, so when freshly potted up, a plant does not need fertilizing. But as the plant grows, the major elements, nitrogen, phosphorus and potassium, run out and must be replaced. Every fertilizer is subject to government inspection, so bad and harmful fertilizers do not exist. Although the formulas vary, reflecting the different needs of various plants, most houseplant fertilizers list three numbers indicating the percentages of nitrogen, phosphorus and potassium they contain. Most fertilizers for houseplants are synthetic, available in powdered form, in liq-

Right: *A 'lacecap' hydrangea grown as a houseplant requires much fertilizer and acidic soil.*

uid and sometimes pellet form. Powder is of course cheaper, because liquid fertilizer is nothing more than powder dissolved in water with a pretty color added. Many people, however, prefer liquid fertilizer, because it is easier to administer the proper dose.

Organic fertilizer is available as well, produced from manure or made of animal remains. If it contains enough nutrients, this type of fertilizer functions as well as the synthetic, although its absorption by the plant is significantly slower. A special type of fertilizer releases the nutrients gradually. It works over a long period so that you only have to fertilize once a season.

How much fertilizer each time?

Because it is so important, I repeat it again: You do not do your plants any favor by giving them a lot of fertilizer all at once. It is much better to fertilize more frequently but in smaller concentrations. Most plants are content with a concentration of ½ ounce or ½ fluid ounce to a quart of water. Sensitive plants like orchids and other epiphytic plants get only ⅕ of an ounce or fluid ounce to a quart of water. Plants that need a lot of fertilizer have to be fertilized during the growing season approximately twice a week. Plants with a normal growth rate should receive fertilizer once a fortnight and slow growers once a month. If there is little or no potting soil, so that food cannot be stored, then you need to provide fertilizer more regularly but in very low concentrations. This is necessary, for instance, with orchids that are cultivated on pure rock wool.

Absorption mostly via the roots

The nutrients are absorbed primarily by the roots, but the leaves of most plants are able to take in small quantities as well. There are special leaf fertilizers, which, strongly diluted, can be given to the plant with a watering can. For plants that produce few roots this is the only way to fertilize.

Fertilizing does not make repotting superfluous

Many people think that a good fertilizer makes repotting almost superfluous. The nutrients that the soil lacks are replenished after all. I would agree to that, were

Four methods of fertilizing houseplants.
1. dissolve liquid or powder fertilizer in plant water
2. use leaf fertilizer, dissolved in water and sprayed over the plant with a mister
3. renew the top soil
4. use fertilizer capsules, which when inserted into potting soil will slowly dissolve

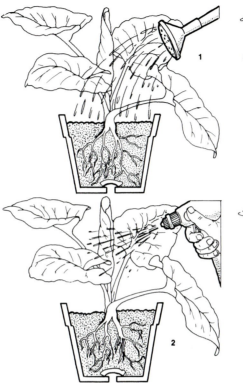

it not for the fact that watering can leave harmful deposits in the soil, especially if you have hard tap water. As a rule, repotting is advisable at least once a year and sometimes more often. Fertilizer is meant to replenish the shortages in between.

Nutrients with hydroponics or a watering system

With hydroponics, fertilizer is very important, because the clay particles (or other supporting material) and plain water do not contain nourishment. We add nutrients by dissolving special hydro-food in the water. When the growth slows, a smaller concentration is used than during the growth season. It is also important to be sure that the pH (acid level, see page 68) of the food solution is not too high. The pH should stay below 6.

A better way to nourish hydroplants is the method of ion-exchange. Small granules are often available in nurseries that provide nutrients to the water. That is not so exceptional; normal fertilizer does the same thing. But these granules also absorb elements that are harmful to the plant, such as calcium and magnesium. An exchange takes place, hence the name ion-exchange. This process continues for

about 4–6 months; then the solution (along with the tiny particles) is pumped out and replaced with a new solution. These particles can also be inserted as small capsules, which can be replaced. The beauty of this system is that one can never feed the plants too much because the ions are only exchanged when there is a surplus or shortage. This is one time it is good to use hard tapwater since it usually contains plenty of calcium and magnesium. With soft rainwater, there is no exchange possible and the particles do not work.

Since regular potting soil is used with a watering system, there will be sufficient nutrients for some time. But when these run out, it is time to fertilize. The best way is with a dissolved or dissolvable houseplant fertilizer, but an ion-exchanger works well also. As with hydroponics, magnesium and calcium are absorbed and nutrients delivered for months.

The water should always be poured into the tube so that it ends up directly in the reservoir. There, the ion-exchange takes place. If one waters the top of the soil, the magnesium and calcium remain there and will poison the potting soil, and there will be nothing to exchange in the bottom of the reservoir.

DAILY CARE FOR HOUSEPLANTS

Only when houseplants are given love and attention do they really flourish. If you feel it is an ordeal to make time for your plants, perhaps it would be better to buy artificial ones. Plants certainly do not ask to be abused.

A moment a day

That moment should be completely devoted to your plants. It is a plus for them, and it helps you to relax at the same time, as your mind is taken off your daily problems. Many people call this moment a talk with the plants. Of course you do not have to literally speak, although this happens more than you might imagine. It is always more important to listen and observe than to talk, and this maxim certainly applies to plants as well; you have to observe their small needs and fulfill them. One needs a bit more water, another, a good shower, the next shows its displeasure at the sun. It is really not hard to figure out a plant's needs, but most people in our society are so far removed from nature, that they find this difficult. The secret to a "green thumb" is simple: plant-oriented thinking.

Water

Watering the plants is the one thing you cannot really skip. For most plants it should be done daily, although there is nothing worse for a plant than to get the same amount of water every day. Each day is different depending on the weather; i.e., if the sun shines, there is more evaporation than on a foggy day. One should adapt the amount of water to conditions. Acquire a decent watering can, one that is manageable without dripping. Unfortunately good watering cans are rare—most models are clumsy and ugly. The plant mister is an important piece of equipment, too. To prevent spots on furniture and wallpaper, tie a piece of cloth to a pole, which you can hold behind the plant while you spray.

Keep an eye on the light

If the plants are located appropriately, they should not need to be screened on sunny days. Besides, this will only be possible if you are home a lot. It is much more sensible to place the plants in a spot that doesn't require screening or moving at all.

Cleaning the leaves

The leaves of houseplants can get so dusty that photosynthesis and breathing becomes difficult. If you use a leaf polish, then the dust will adhere even more. A gentle cleaning is a better solution. Use a cloth dipped in rainwater for the best result, since rainwater does not leave deposits. Lime can be dissolved by adding a bit of vinegar to the water. Work quickly and rinse off the leaves with clean water. Many people place their plants under the shower, which is fine, but watch that the pot does not flood. The same goes for plants that are put out in the rain. Also,

Many plants can be cut back drastically when they become too tall or too lanky. New shoots will eventually reappear from the leaf axils.

Left: *Careful, daily attention to your houseplants is the key to healthy growth.*

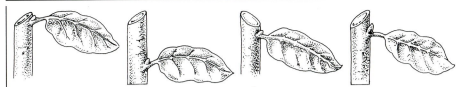

The right and wrong ways to cut plants. From left to right: *cut too low, cut too high, cut angled to the wrong side, cut correctly.*

do not take them out when there is a large difference in temperature between inside and outside.

Pruning

Pruning houseplants is not as difficult or complicated as pruning outdoor garden plants. Usually houseplants are pruned to sculpt the plant into a form or size we think is pretty. Some plants have too many branches so that they become disordered and tangled. Others will reach the ceiling too soon. In both cases, the pruning knife is the way out. Not all houseplants, such as ferns or African violets, for instance, need pruning.

One mostly prunes older woody plants that produce stems with leaves. Every leaf sprouts from a node on the stem. When a bud develops and grows into a leaf, another bud develops in the axil, the angle formed where the leaf joins the stem. Sometimes, this bud also sprouts and forms a lateral branch. But the bud node can also stay dormant. Only when the leaf is damaged or pulled off totally or when the top of the plant is lost, does this reserve bud develop and become a new leaf. One can take advantage of this growth habit by pruning right above a stem bud, giving the dormant bud the opportunity to sprout. Moreover, you will know the direction of the new shoot because it will grow straight from the axil. Thus by determining where to prune, you can direct the shape of the plant. Often a *Ficus* becomes more beautiful if you heavily prune it when young. Cut the top and the plant will branch out from the upper remaining axils. Do you want four instead of two branches? Then cut each branch back again after a few months. You will have a rubber plant with four stalks, instead of one. Do you want three or five stalks? It can be done. At first you allow four or six to grow and then you remove one or two undesired shoots.

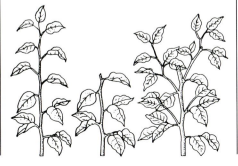

Pruning after repotting

During a drastic repotting operation where part of the roots either by accident or design have been cut away, you must prune a portion of the above-ground plant as well, in order to repair the balance between the roots and evaporation surface. Do not be afraid you are pruning too much; the plant will recover almost immediately.

Plants start to bleed

After pruning many plants discharge a white latex. You can put ash or charcoal on the wound, but this will not lessen the pressure from within. It is better for the plant to be put in a dark, cool spot so that photosynthesis and transpiration come to a stop. The bleeding will stop at the same time. Watch the latex so that it does not leave spots on furniture and clothing.

Pinching the top for better branching

Young plants that become thin and lanky instead of full and leafy can be forced to

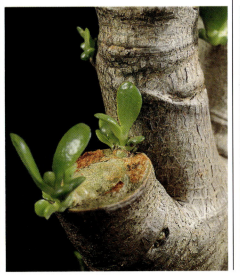

branch by pinching back the top. This is the way seedlings and cuttings are treated after new shoots sprout from dormant eyes. Sometimes it is necessary to prune the top two or three times (over a period of time) to reach the desired form. A better branched plant will develop more flowers.

To tie up plants

Most climbing plants are not capable of attaching themselves to a wall. Assist by tying them here and there to small hooks that you have attached to a wall or window frame.

You can also insert a support into the pot. Wire hoops that give support to plants with long tendrils, such as the *Stephanotis* or *Thunbergia*, are popular. The vines have to be led along the hoops. I cannot stand the ugly plastic supports; there must be something else one could use!

Many climbers are grown on moss poles. These should be sprayed to keep the moss moist. Spraying can be somewhat difficult in the living room, but still it is better for the plant when the pole stays moist. You can also make your own moss pole, which is perforated and sealed on the bottom, so that you can both give water and keep the moss wet at the same time.

Left: *Cutting the top of a plant.* Below, left: *The same shoot before, just after, and well after being cut. Notice the better branching.* Below, middle: *New buds appear after a drastic cutting.* Below, right: *Long vines can be attached to a wire for support.*

78

HOUSEPLANTS FROM SEEDS

More houseplants than you imagine are cultivated from seed. Many more plants than the familiar cacti, avocados, peanuts and bananas are raised from seed. The advantage of seeds is that they can easily be distributed all over the world. You can acquire exotic houseplants for very little money this way.

How seeds germinate
Many seeds can be stored for a long period and still retain their ability to germinate. But there are also seeds that must be sown immediately after ripening, or they will lose that ability. Generally a seed germinates when it becomes moist and warm. But some seeds will absolutely not germinate even though they are kept nice and warm. These cold germinators need temperatures between 32°F and 40°F. After they germinate they like higher temperatures, but still in most cases not above 60°–68°F. Other seeds need the stimulus of an actual freeze before they are able to germinate. We can artificially provide the stimulus by storing the sown seeds in trays in the freezer for a few weeks. After that keep them warm, and they will germinate. There are not many houseplants that need this treatment, but for the sake of completeness, I mention it.

The slow germinators are very irritating. These are seeds that just stay the same for months, sometimes a year, before they spring into action. The houseplants *Ardisia*, *Cissus* and *Stephanotis* belong to that group. Another group are the light germinators. While most seeds germinate best in the dark, lightly covered with soil, light germinators prefer to remain on top of the soil. Most succulents, but also bro-

meliads, *Plumbago*, *Saintpaulia* and *Streptocarpus*, will germinate better in the light. To stimulate the germinating of some hard-coated seeds, soak them in lukewarm water first, or file away the hard skin (be careful not to damage the germ).

Finally, another important point that is not discussed in most books: the exact pH (acid level) of the seed bed. The seeds of plants that like to grow in acid soil when they are developed should be sown in acid soil. Experiments have shown they do not germinate well in highly alkaline soils. So you see, sowing is a science of its own.

Time for sowing
Most seeds can germinate at any time of the year, but there should be enough light for the seedlings to grow after germination. Therefore, seeds are sown mostly in the spring, so that the young plant will enter a good growing season. Lack of light can be alleviated with artificial light,

because one fluorescent light bulb right above the seed bed can provide sufficient light. (See page 54–55.)

The sowing soil
It is better to speak of a sowing medium, because usually no soil is used at all. Most seeds germinate readily on moist filter paper or in sand, vermiculite or milled sphagnum moss. The sowing medium should be moist in almost all cases (and stay moist) and also allow air to circulate. Little nutrients are needed because young roots cannot digest "adult food." That is why regular potting soil is not well suited to seed. Potting soil can be mixed half and half with coarse sand or vermiculite to make it more suitable for seeds. But nowadays specially prepared sowing soil is commercially available, and suitable for most seeds. Characteristics of such soil are: few nutrients, a fine texture with some moisture retention, pH around 6 and good drainage. The base is often peat. There are also special growing blocks or pallets on the market; these are first watered thoroughly and then one or two seeds are planted in each block.

The sowing
I have found it best to sow in 2–3-inch high, square plastic seed boxes with drainage holes, but, naturally, one can use small pots as well. Fill up the box or pot to the rim with the sowing medium and press down firmly. Then add more until the tray is totally filled to the rim. The surface should be nice and smooth. Large seeds are placed in the sowing soil one by one. Fine seeds can be sprinkled right from the package. A common mistake is

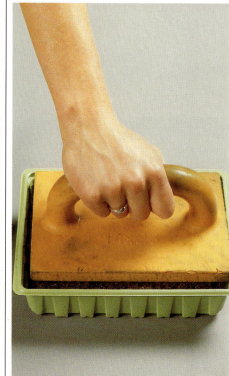

to sow too thickly. If the seed box is 6 x 6 inches square, do not sow more than 100 seeds, and even then, try to divide them evenly over the surface. If you have more seed and want many plants, fill a second tray. For seeds that can be covered (most of them), lightly spread silver sand over the seeds. Silver sand is available in plastic bags in hardware stores or garden centers. The layer of sand should be twice the thickness of the seeds. While sprinkling the sand, you will be able to see exactly when the often darker-colored seeds disappear under the white sand. Continue to sprinkle for a moment longer.

Watering from the top will wash the seed bar again. To avoid this I put the seed trays in a larger tray filled with water and let the sowing medium absorb the water. As soon as the water reaches the surface, you will notice the sand turn darker. Remove the trays from the water and let them drain. Finally, cover the pots with a glass top or a plastic bag.

The surface of the seed boxes, in spite of the sand cover, may rather quickly become covered with green algae growth. Since this growth will block off the soil from the air, you should prevent it by keeping the trays in the dark for the first few days. (This instruction does not apply to seeds that germinate in light.) Just cover them with newsprint. As soon as the plants break through the surface, remove the papers and keep an eye on the trays every day.

Give extra warmth

Some seeds need a relatively high temperature to germinate, often 68°–77°F, sometimes as much as 85°F. The temperature needed is that of the sowing medium, not the room temperature. To achieve extra warmth quickly, place the seed box on a warm base. Room terrariums, supplied with heat cables or other heating systems, are ideal. It is not necessary to regulate the supply of heat with a thermostat, but it is wise to watch the temperature, so insert a minimum/maximum thermometer. The sowing soil can sometimes get too hot and then the seeds will die. A warm window ledge above a radiator provides sufficient heat. Do not ever put seed trays in the full sun.

Transplanting seedlings

After the seeds sprout, you will see one small seed leaf on the *Monocotyledons* and two with the *Diocotyledons*. Next, the true leaves appear. As soon as this happens, the small seedlings, now about 1–2 inches high, should be transplanted to individual pots to give each more space. It is safest to use a tweezer when you prick out the often small and fragile seedlings. Cover the tweezer on the inside with some soft material, such as rubber.

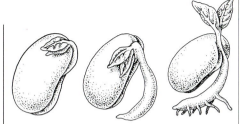

The germination of a seed, here a bean. At first, a root appears, followed by seed leaves that contain reserve nutrients.

Transplant only the strongest seedlings. Frequently, even after weeks, seeds may germinate, so do not dispose of the tray too soon.

You can use sowing soil again in these pots or a soil mixture that is suitable for the final cultivation of the plant. (See plant descriptions.) Keep the just-transplanted seedlings under glass or plastic for a while. As soon as they begin to grow, gradually accustom them to the drier air, by opening up the cover a little more each day. Because they grow too big for their assigned space, these seedlings often need to be transplanted a second time before being settled in a permanent spot.

From far left, on page 78: Materials to begin sowing, a heated terrarium with seed tray; pressing the soil; sowing seeds; sprinkling sifted sand; soaking in water; and finally, the planting out of germinated plants.

CUTTINGS AND OTHER METHODS OF PROPAGATION

The most popular way to multiply houseplants is by taking cuttings. If you are careful, you can take cuttings from almost every plant. The advantage is that your new plant will be exactly the same as your original, something that is not always the case with seeds. Cuttings go hand to hand from plant lover to plant lover. They form an important alternative circuit of plant distribution.

How cuttings grow

It is easy to make new plants from cuttings, because plants have an enormous regenerative capacity. In principle, new shoots and new roots can grow from every node of a plant. To assure quicker rooting, always cut the stem right below a node.

Preventing evaporation

When there are green leaves on the cutting—and this is almost always the case with cuttings from houseplants—the most important concern is to prevent evaporation, because the cutting has no roots and therefore no possibility of absorbing water. Yet transpiration continues in the leaves. Since the biggest danger is that cuttings will dry out, they are always placed under glass or plastic. Sometimes commercial growers keep them in a constant fine water mist. Cuttings also need light, but not direct sun, because photosynthesis and transpiration still continue in the leaf.

A second danger that threatens cuttings in a humid and warm environment is rotting. Cuttings from succulents are especially sensitive to rotting. One can prevent the forming of fungus by dipping the cuttings into an anti-fungal substance, such as Captan.

Below, from left to right: *Propagation from cuttings. Cut off a slip just above a node (remove the lower leaves), cut off the leaf ends, put the cutting in a pot, and to eliminate evaporation, place in a plastic bag.*

Warmth from the bottom is important

Roots form faster in most cases if the planting medium is warm. How to warm sowing soil is described on page 79. A temperature between 68–85°F is ideal for most woody plants. Sometimes a temperature as high as 95°F is needed. Rooting for many plants can be speeded up by treating the cutting with rooting hormone. This powder is available at garden centers; dip the cut end in the powder, and plant the cuttings as usual.

Soil for rooting cuttings

It is more accurate to speak of a cutting "medium," because often there is absolutely no soil in the mixture used for rooting. Cuttings can be rooted in sand, in special rooting soil, in a mixture of coarse sand and potting soil, in rock wool, in milled sphagnum moss, vermiculite, perlite, etc. One can also root many types of cuttings in water, but as explained on page 72, they will develop water roots, which sometimes cause problems after the cutting is planted in soil. The rooting medium should be porous, hold water well so it can remain constantly moist, yet be coarse enough to allow air to circulate easily, and the pH should be neither too high nor too low. A drier rooting medium is better for succulent plants, as it lessens the danger of rotting.

Harden off and pot

As soon as roots are formed, small new leaves will begin to develop. From that moment on, you can slowly start to harden off the cutting. One hardens off a new plant by gradually cutting down on humidity until the plant can tolerate normal conditions. Lift the glass or open the plastic bag a bit more each day. After a week, transplant the new plant to a pot with appropriate soil. Continue to supply some extra humidity, until a sufficient root structure develops. Only then will the new plant be in balance between transpiration in the leaves and water absorption in the roots.

Cuttings from the top or the middle

A tip cutting is one taken from the terminal end of a stem or branch and includes only a few leaves. A good length is 2–3 inches. Cut right below the node and remove the lowest leaves. If the cutting is of a woody branch leave a strip of the bast. A halfway cutting is one taken further

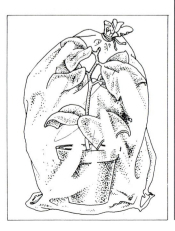

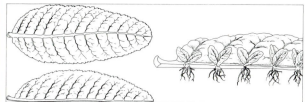

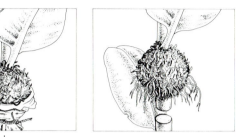

On page 80: *Electrically heated mini-greenhouse with thermostat for controlling air temperature and tray temperature. A small window in the top allows for ventilation. Even the most difficult cuttings will grow given this environmental control.*
Left: *Leaf cutting from a* Streptocarpus.
Below: *Air layering. From left to right: Make an incision and keep it open; wrap the area with moist moss and plastic; after roots form, cut off and plant the new growth.*

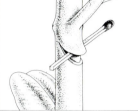

down the stem, about the same length, but without the terminal bud. These cuttings do not continue to grow, but rather produce new shoots in the axil.

Eye cutting

In general, this method is used for cuttings from plants with large leaves, like the *Ficus*. A stem section about ¾ inch long is cut above and below one leaf node. To reduce transpiration the leaf, especially if it is a large one, is often rolled up and secured with a rubber band. The stem, the node and part of the leaf stem are inserted in the rooting medium. Shortly, both a new shoot and roots will develop at the axil.

Leaf cuttings

A leaf with part of a leaf stalk is often sufficient for a successful cutting. Even fragments of begonia leaves as small as ½ square inch, laid flat on the cutting medium, are sufficient for rooting. The long leaves of *Streptocarpus* are cut in half along the middle vein and each half inserted upright in the rooting medium. Small new plants will develop along the cut vein. The thick, round leaves of some *Sedum* plants will develop roots when they drop off into the potting soil.

Stem cutting

Pieces of stem with one or more eyes can root as well, if they are placed in a warm rooting medium and given humidity. One can succeed not only with species like the *Dracaena*, but with *Anthurium* as well.

Below, left: *An eye cutting of a* Ficus *will bleed for a while.*
Below, middle: *Dividing plants.*
Below, right: *Special cutting container filled with a gel that allows the young plants to form roots without much effort.*

Root cuttings

The roots of some species have the capacity to develop new shoots from the eyes that are on the roots. The roots in this case are cut into pieces and placed in a humid and relatively warm rooting environment.

Propagating by division

Plants that have more than one stem or stalk coming out of the soil can be propagated by division. The plant is removed from the pot, divided into two or more pieces (sometimes, you will need a sharp knife, or you can pry the plant apart by hand) and each part is replanted in a separate pot. Each portion should possess at least one shoot and some roots. Tuber growths can easily be divided in this way also. The best time to do it is before the tubers bud. Each portion should have at least one eye. Bulbs can be divided by separating the young bulbs.

Air layering

This process is like making a cutting on the plant. The cutting is removed from the mother plant only after the roots have formed. Air layering is a method that is used mostly by people who do not really dare to take a cutting, but still want to do something about an overgrown plant. To air layer a plant, such as a *Ficus*, make an incision two-thirds of the way through the stem at the spot where you want roots to develop. That incision should be made right below a node, and it should slope upward. A wooden match is inserted in the wound to keep it open. Then wrap the whole section in moist sphagnum moss, cover with plastic and seal. It can take several months before roots develop; be sure to keep the moss moist. When a sturdy bunch of roots has grown, the trunk can be cut through just below the roots, and the new growth planted.

ADVANCED PROPAGATION

Anybody can successfully take cuttings from a geranium or a spiderplant. On these pages, we will look at more difficult methods of propagation, such as grafting, which demand particular skills. But if you can master them, these are very satisfactory ways to increase your indoor garden.

Cuttings from succulents
Cuttings from exceptionally juicy plants, such as succulents, can rot if put into soil immediately after cutting. Therefore, let them dry for several days and for very juicy plants even a few weeks. Do not put them in full sunlight during this period, because they will dry too fast. When the tissue has shrunk, plant the cutting in a very permeable medium such as perlite or sharp sand. Cover with glass or plastic but leave a gap. Water after the roots form.

Bromeliad "offspring"
Besides the old rosette, most bromeliads produce one or more offspring plants. Initially, they live off the nourishment of the dying rosette. For that reason, don't remove them too early. Only when the old plant is truly dying, can you safely remove the offset and plant them separately. Give the new plants the same care as indicated for the bromeliads. The pineapple has a crown of leaves, which can be cut off and successfully used as a cutting. Let it dry well, put it in sharp sand and roots will soon develop.

Left: *A cactus shoot.*
Below: *The top of a pineapple can be used as a cutting.*

Below: *A new growth on a bromeliad. The old rosette dies off slowly, but as it does it continues to feed the young plants it spawned. Do not remove the new plant too soon.*

Right: *A crowned tree (here a geranium) can be grown by guiding the plant straight up with a support stake and by cutting back all the side branches. When the trunk grows tall enough, remove the top so side branches will develop, and then cut again, if desired.*

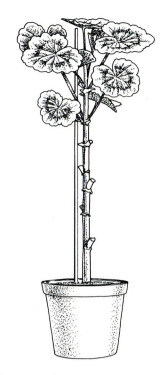

Combine two different species

Two different plants can sometimes be successfully combined. This technique is called grafting. In reality it only happens with plants that (in northern climates) do not have strong enough roots to survive on their own. These scions are grafted onto the lower part of the trunk of a plant that shows sturdy growth and has enough capacity to send up nourishment to the scion. The species have to be somewhat related. Various ways of grafting are known, following basically the same principle: the layer of cambium of the graft touches the cambium of the trunk and the two grow together. This can occur by binding the two together, for instance with a rubber band, or by inserting the scion in an incision made in the trunk or root stock, etc.

Grafting cacti

Grafting is done mostly with cacti, which do not grow well in northern climates. First one provides a strong base trunk or root stock, which should be about 3 inches, because it is the green part of the trunk that matters. These base trunks (for instance *Eriocereus jusbertii*) are cultivated from seed and cut off at the crown after 6–8 months. The small cacti that is to be grafted can be grown from seed or broken off a larger plant. Both sections should fit together reasonably well, although the lower trunk can be wider than the scion. Press both sections together with an elastic band or weight; after a few weeks the two will have united.

Making standard trees

It is possible to make standard trees from various houseplants; for instance, fuchsias or geraniums. Again, one starts with a cutting. The new shoot is guided up along a stake and all lateral shoots that the plant wants to produce are removed as they develop. When the plant has reached the desired height, the top is pinched back, so it can branch out. New shoots are pinched again after an interval and allowed to branch out once again. After this, one allows the plant to grow and a standard tree is created.

Grafting a cactus. The graft (yellow ball) is cut off and connected to the green growth below. At some time, the plants will grow as one.

DISEASES

When we speak of plant diseases, we mean afflictions caused by bacteria, insects, fungi or viruses. There are also maladies of shortage or excess, which are caused by the lack or overabundance of certain nutrients.

Something is not right
A disease in a plant is any variation from its healthy state. In other words, something is wrong. It is possible that the plant was already sick when you bought it, but diseases are almost always caused by mistreatment. In other words, if one takes care of plants as this book recommends, then they should stay healthy. Most parasites prefer soft, weak leaves or shoots, which they can bite easily. Sturdy leaves with thick skin are ignored. Weak growth occurs especially in the winter months, when there is less light for good photosynthesis and the indoor temperature is kept so high that growth continues. (See page 62, rest periods.) Other reasons for poor growth include: small pots, potting soil depleted of nourishment, accumulated deposits of old fertilizer, etc. Plants growing in such conditions are very susceptible to diseases.

Keep observing
During daily care, carefully observe the condition of your plants. Often, the color or the position of the leaves can alert you that something is not right. If you suspect bugs, study the plant closely. Often, a magnifying glass is necessary to observe the small offenders. Try, on the basis of the descriptions in this book, to determine what kind of small insects have infested your plant and take the recommended measures. You will see in a day or two if they worked.

The danger of chemicals
Much has been written about the danger of pesticides for people, and fortunately, before a toxic substance can be sold for household use today, it must be tested quite thoroughly. Therefore, we have some assurance that if it is used sensibly, it will not be harmful. This does not mean that we can safely spray indiscriminately. Keep all pesticides out of reach of children and avoid spraying inside. Take the plant to the garden or balcony and treat it there. Spray in the direction of the wind and do not breathe the mist. If the weather allows, leave the plant outside for a while and bring it in later.

Above: *Microscopic picture of eelworms.*
Below: *A greenhouse locust. Both these and the eelworms can cause a lot of damage.*

Be extremely careful with small children and pets, especially fish and birds. The smallest drop of disulfate in your aquarium kills all fish, for example. Birds are vulnerable as well.

Spraying is unnecessary if you use the granular form of these chemicals. The poison in the granule dissolves in the soil and is taken up via the roots, to the plant.

For hydroponic gardening there is a special substance available that can be added to the water. By using this substance, the whole plant becomes poisonous to small insects, which die when they eat from the plant.

Alternatives to chemicals
Because of the danger inherent in many chemical products, people are more actively looking for safe alternative remedies. Often, the old-fashioned folk remedies are rather effective. But they are poisonous, too, so be careful.

A few alternative nontoxic controls follow below:

1. **Soap/alcohol.** Dissolve ⁷⁄₁₀ ounces of hand soap in ⅓ fluid ounce alcohol. Spray with a plant mister. Do not spray in full sun.

2. **Pure alcohol.** Brush this substance on with a paintbrush to ward against scale bugs; may burn the leaves.

3. **Equisetumtha.** An extract from *Equisetrales.* Boil 10 ounces of dried herb in 1 quart of water for half an hour. Filter and add .15 fluid ounce of the tea to 1 quart of water, and spray with this mixture as a remedy against mildew caused by fungus.

4. **Nicotine from tobacco.** Pure nicotine, as was once used against insects, is a very effective poison. Do not buy, but soak

cigarette butts or tobacco in water. Use this nicotine tea to combat all kinds of insects. Sprinkle a little tobacco over the potting soil, as it will kill any insects in the soil.

5. **Pyrethrum.** This used to be extracted from the flowers of the chrysanthemum. Nowadays, it is made mostly from synthetic pyrethroids. Often used for insect control, it is very popular and available in retail stores.

6. **Sulphur.** Usually in liquid form or as sulphur compounds. Excellent against mildew.

Biological controls

In commercial greenhouses it is possible to control insects biologically, with the use of natural enemies. Thus robber ants kill the spidermite and the ichneumon wasp kills the whitefly. The problem for the home is that this system can only work in an isolated situation, where the various insect species keep each other in balance. The insects should not be able to escape from the greenhouse and the natural predators should be fed continually so they can survive if there are no pests to eat. To successfully do this in a private greenhouse would be very difficult.

An adult beetle.

The most important diseases and pests affecting plants in the house or greenhouse

Not all diseases are mentioned. If you cannot figure out a symptom, have an expert take a look. Many garden centers offer this service as well as local botanical gardens and arboretums. Also, check with the American Horticultural Society (1-800-777-7931), which may be able to assist. Their address is available from a phone directory.

Ants. Not very harmful for plants. They are attracted by the sweet discharge of aphids and white flies (honeydew). Control by placing ant traps.

Aphids. See greenfly and scalefly.

Beetles. There are two kinds, the grooved and the spotted. Both 4 inches long, they eat happily from leaves and buds. The white larvae eat the roots. Control the larvae living underground by inserting a disulfoton solution. Remove the creatures when you repot. The beetles can be caught in pots filled with woodshavings, where they will hide in the daytime. Another way to combat them is to poison the leaf with synthetic pyrethroids.

Blackflies. They are elongated insects, ½-inch long, dark brown with a red rump. After they attack and suck a leaf, silver-colored spots appear that later develop into large brown areas. Blackflies thrive in a hot, humid environment. Control by spraying with pyrethrum, with disulfoton or with dimethoate.

Botrytis. Afflicted plants are covered with a brown-gray fungus. Young plants that are kept too humid are especially prone to botrytis. Provide good ventilation, and do not pour water on the plant itself.

Brown spots on leaves. This condition could be caused by cold or lack of calcium. If you spill water on hairy leaves, light brown spots may also appear.

Burning. Caused by too much fertilizer or by feeding when the potting soil is very dry. The nutrients are not absorbed properly. In fact the plant cannot function due to the excess of nutrients. The result is dried leaf edges and curled leaves. Remove the plant from the pot, clean the roots as much as possible and repot in fresh soil.

Calcium damage. Water used on the plants can contain salts that can be harmful. Growth slows down. Repot and use water that contains less calcium, such as rainwater.

Calcium deficiency. Older leaves especially will turn yellow and dry at the edges. The color of the leaves becomes dark green or somewhat blue. Feed with a fertilizer that contains potassium.

Caterpillars. These are the larvae of various butterfly species, and they like green leaves. Control them by catching them, and if there are too many, spray with pyrethrum.

Centipedes. See root centipedes.

Chloride excess. Under this condition, the plant stops growing, but the leaf stays dark green. Often, the edges of the leaves are dried, and the symptoms may seem to indicate a lack of calcium. Use water that contains less chloride, such as rainwater, and avoid fertilizers that contain chloride.

Chlorosis or a shortage of iron. Yellowish leaves, especially between the veins; caused by the inability of the plant to absorb iron, magnesium or copper, and therefore the plant is not able to produce enough chlorophyl. Causes can be soil that is too cold or too wet, a pH (acid) level that is not right or poor light conditions. Use low-pH water and repot in acidic potting soil. Spray temporarily with iron-chelate.

Cicadas. Roundish sleek insects, green or brown, that jump when touched. When they suck on leaves, small white spots appear. Try to control with a substance that contains pyrethrum. If this does not work, try a dicofol-based insecticide.

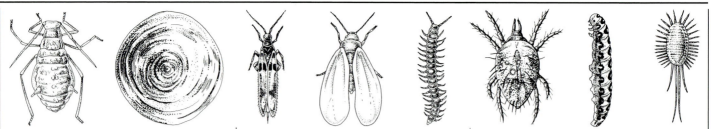

Cockroaches. Large insects with a flat body, sometimes as long as 1½ inches with long legs and feelers. They eat tender, young plant parts at night. You can spot them with a flashlight, or fill a large glass jar with beer, syrup or other sweets. The insects will jump in and drown.

Cottony maple scales. See scale bug.

Cyclamen mites. See mites.

Dampening-off disease. See seedling disease.

Earwigs. Dark brown, jointed insects with tongs at their abdomen. At night, they eat parts of the plants, but they also can be very useful because they eat greenflies. Catch them by placing jars containing woodshavings between the plants.

Eelworms. See worms.

False mildew. An off-white fungus floss that develops on the underside of the leaf. Control with sulphur/zineb (Thiram against fungus).

Flea beetle. Small, metallic or yellow-marked beetles that jump around and eat holes in the leaves. Control by spraying repeatedly with a substance containing pyrethrum.

Florida mouths. Gray-brown butterflies that only fly at night. The inch-long green caterpillar stage is harmful, as the caterpillars eat leaves, shoots and flowers. Often found in greenhouses. Close off the greenhouse and spray with pyrethrum.

Greenflies. Insects with rather large legs, colored green or yellow. They assemble in groups, mainly on young shoots, where they suck the juices. The excrements of the flies leave a sticky film on the leaves, and black fungus thrives on this.

A few well-known enemies of houseplants. Top, from left to right: scale bug; the hiding shield of a scale; blackfly; whitefly; millipede; red spider; caterpillar, aphid.
Right: Aphids in action. They belong to a suborder of bugs that includes aphids and scales.
Far right: Affliction brought on by scales.

Control by spraying a few times with a solution of soap/alcohol.

Greenhouse locusts. Insects of a little over an inch in length with very long feelers. They feed on the plants at night. Control by closing the greenhouse and spraying with pyrethrum. Smoke tablets are effective too.

Greenhouse whiteflies. Usually just called whiteflies. They are tiny white insects that fly when touched. They are often found in greenhouses, where they cause a lot of damage. Control by repeatedly spraying with pyrethrum. This does not, however, kill the eggs. A biological solution to combating this pest is to bring in ichneumon wasps. The greenhouse has to be sealed off, otherwise the wasps will escape.

Iron deficiency. See chlorosis.

Leaf loss. Excessive loss of leaves can result from a changed growing condition,

such as moving the plant, drought or excess water. Check the soil with the hydrometer. Also, the soil could be too acidic and repotting may be necessary.

Mice. Early in winter, mice will often enter the greenhouse. Control with mouse poison, put in places where pets and children cannot get at it.

Mildew. A fungus that causes white, cloudy spots on the leaf. Often impossible to avoid with plants that are sensitive to this affliction. Prevent by stimulating growth with fertilizing and repotting. Control with anti-mildew agents, of which sulphur is the best known. Thiram (mildew-spray) is available in retail outlets.

Millipedes. Elongated animals with more legs than centipedes. The body is round, instead of flat. At night, they gnaw at the young parts of the plants and the roots. The larvae are more greedy than the parents. To catch them, cut a potato in half

Below, left: *Red spider mites (above), and a blackfly (below).*
Below, right: *Greenflies often appear on houseplants, but are easy to get rid of.*

and hollow it out; position it in such a way that the creatures can crawl inside. To shoo away, sprinkle tobacco between the plants.

Mites. There are many different kinds of mites, each of which prefers its own particular plant (begonia mites, cactus mites, cyclamen mites). Red spiders are mites too, but so small you need a magnifying glass to be able to see them. Most of the time they are located on the underside of the leaf and suck the chlorophyll. The foliage will look dull and gray. Mites thrive in a dry environment, so misting helps. Control by spraying with anti-mite herbicide, for instance a dicofol-based insecticide, or bromophos.

Mosquitoes. When these are about ⅛ inch long larvae that look like small sticks of glass with dark heads, they eat young plants, seedlings and cuttings. When full grown, they are not harmful to plants.

Control mosquitoes by fumigating the greenhouse or spraying with pyrethrum.

Nitrogen deficiency. Young as well as older leaves turn light green to yellow-green in this situation and the plant does not grow well. The remedy is to feed with a fertilizer containing an appropriate amount of nitrogen for the particular plant.

Red spider. See mites.

Root centipede. Small white centipedes that move very fast. They eat roots. Control with lindane.

Root lice. White or off-white lice that eat roots. Control by pouring dicofol on the soil.

Root rot. See wilting.

Scale bugs. In this category belong cottony maple scales, woody aphids and

woolly root aphids. Hidden by their scales, these creatures suck at parts of the plants. They are difficult to control because of their scales. Rub off a small amount with a match, and then wipe the plant with a solution of alcohol. Spray large areas with disulfoton or insert plant arrows in the soil. If the whole plant is poisoned, all the scale bugs will be too.

Seedling disease. A fungus disease that causes the young seedlings and cuttings to rot at the soil. Also called "dampening-off." Preventative measures include light, sterilized potting soil and allowing more space between the plants. Air them from time to time, so that the humidity does not become too high. Chemical control is possible by spraying or misting with fungicide, for instance thiram.

Slugs. These are the larvae of moths (gray caterpillars), which eat parts of the plant both under and above the soil, especially at night. In the daytime, they hide curled

88

Above, left: *A Clusia with burnt leaves, caused by too much sunlight.*
Above, right: *The beginning signs of a nitrogen deficiency on a* Ficus lyrata *leaf.*
Below, left: *A young avocado plant with chlorosis.*
Below, right: *False mildew on a* Hebe.

up below the surface of the soil. Control by catching the creatures during repotting and watering with a solution of nicotine.

Snails. It is usually snails without shells that eat young plants at night, mainly in greenhouses. Control by putting down a snail control that contains metaldehyde. Be careful around children and pets.

Sooty mold. A black fungus that thrives on the discharge of lice or whiteflies. If you find sooty mold, you have to fight both symptoms—the pest as well as the fungus. The fungus disappears after spraying with thiram.

Spittlebugs (cicadas). The larvae live in small clouds of foam. They are not very harmful and easy to remove with water or a soap/alcohol solution.

Springtails. Small insects that jump when touched. They live often between the pot and an outside decorative pot where it is more humid. The white species do damage by eating the roots. Clean and dry the pots regularly. If this is not effective, sprinkle some tobacco on the areas where the insects are.

Sunburn. Light and brown spots on leaves caused by exposure to too much sun. Shade plants that are placed in an unscreened south window can also exhibit this symptom. Prevention: Screen against strong, direct sunlight.

True bugs. Green and brown insects with flat bodies, six legs and long feelers. They move very quickly. Some species have four wings. They suck young parts of plants, as well as the flowers, resulting in small holes. Control with dicofol-based insecticide.

Leaf rollers (tortrizids). Symptoms are webs spun between the leaves of the plant. In the webs are small brown or green writhing caterpillars, which eat the buds. Control by removing the webs or

by spraying with pyrethrum, so that the caterpillars drop from the webs.

Virus. There are many different viruses, and their symptoms differ as well. Often the leaf exhibits yellow spots or circles, dead spots, curling, etc. Control is impossible. Start with healthy material: Never take a cutting from a plant that has a virus. Green flies and other insects can also be carriers of viruses. Control these particular insects.

Whiteflies. See greenhouse whiteflies.

Wilting. Caused by vascular parasites, root rot and foot rot. To prevent, always use new sterilized potting soil. There is no herbicide available at retail to control this condition.

Wood lice. Flat, gray creatures with many legs. Found mainly in wet spots, especially under the benches in a greenhouse. At night, they eat plant parts. Easy to catch by using a hollowed-out potato.

Woolly aphids. See scale bugs.

Worms. These are very small worms, barely visible, of which there are different groups, such as eelworm, cystworms (which live in cysts or small tumors), stalkworms, rootworms, tuberworms and root lesionworms. The latter penetrate the roots and cause lesions or dead spots. Symptoms can vary, from dying leaves to disfiguring at the leaf, stalk and roots, to root rot. The control of worms is only possible with very poisonous remedies that are not available at retail. Your only remedy is to dispose of the afflicted plant. Leaf and stalkworm can spread via cuttings as well, so be sure to use only pure worm-free sterilized potting soil.

Yellow leaf. Deciduous plants often have beautiful colored leaves in the fall. This is quite normal. Even an occasional yellow leaf on a green plant is no cause for alarm. But if suddenly many leaves turn yellow, something is wrong. Possibly the plants were kept too dry, or too wet, for too long. Moreover a draft can cause the leaves to turn yellow. Too much sun on a plant that basically does not like sun can cause the leaves to turn yellow as well.

ALPHABETIC PLANT DESCRIPTIONS

In the following section, 1,000 plants are illustrated, and many more are described. The text has been kept brief, allowing the photographs to speak for themselves. After a general description of the plant, there follows a section on **care**, dealing with daily maintenance, dormant periods, etc., and on **propagation**. At the end of each entry is information on the plant's needs for **temperature (temp)**, **water**, **humidity (hum)** and **soil**. This information is provided in a shortened format; more detailed information can be found on pages 52–71.

The plants are arranged in alphabetical order, according to the latest nomenclature. If you can't locate a plant under its scientific name, refer to the index, where both Latin and common names are listed. If you do not recognize the plant's name, use the illustrations as an identification guide.

Abromeitiella brevifolia

Bromeliaceae

Sod-forming bromeliad from the mountains of Argentina and Bolivia. The small, thick leaves store moisture.
Care: Care is similar to that for cacti. Keep in a very sunny spot in the summer and do not water much. Apply cactus food once a month. Keep cool and dry in the winter. It is prettiest when planted in the full soil of a greenhouse. Its crawling way of growing does not really show in pots.
Propagation: By division.

Light:	Full sun.
Temp:	Moderately warm to warm, in the winter 40–50°F (5–10°C).
Water:	Keep rather dry, in the winter almost completely dry.
Hum:	Low to moderate.
Soil:	Cactus soil.

Abromeitiella brevifolia

Abutilon X hybridum

Malvaceae

These hybrids are the result of cross-fertilization between various original species. They come in different colors, such as yellow, orange and red, and the cultivars are often named. The leaves are almost always green.
Care: Because hybrids have more chlorophyll than the variegated cultivars, they can be put in darker locations, though a lot of light stimulates flowering. The plants may be grown outside in containers. Give plenty of water in the summer and add some nutrients once a week. Keep cool in the winter and prune in the spring.
Propagation: One can take cuttings from the hybrids, as with many other sorts, but one can grow them from seeds too. Seeds germinate easily when the temperature is between 60–68°F (15–20°C).

Light:	Slightly screened sunlight.
Temp:	In the summer cool to warm; in the winter, a minimum of 54°F (12°C).

Abutilon-hybr.

Abutilon-hybr. 'Golden Fleece'

Water:	Keep rather moist.
Hum:	Moderate (50–60%).
Soil:	Standard potting soil.

Abutilon megapotamicum

Malvaceae

Variegatum

In southern Brazil, its country of origin, this is an evergreen bush with branches that hang down. This species does not grow that tall as a houseplant, no more than about 3 feet (1 meter). The hanging flowers have the colors of the Belgian flag: red calyx, yellow top and, below, the almost-black stamen. The cultivar used most often is the variety 'Variegatum.' It has light yellow spotted leaves.
Care: This species needs a lot of light, and can endure almost full sunlight. The plant can be placed on a wind-protected spot on a terrace from June onward. Do not let the soil dry out and, during the growing period, give nutrients every week. The best temperature during hibernation is 50–60°F (10–15°C), but even in a warm room, it will survive the winter. Repot in the spring and prune to keep the shape compact. Tying up the branches is necessary most of the time.
Propagation: In the summer, top cuttings of nonflowering shoots root easily with a temperature around 68°F (20°C).

Light:	Plenty of light, almost full sun.
Temp:	In the summer, cool to warm.
Water:	Keep rather moist.
Hum:	Moderate (50–60%).
Soil:	Standard potting soil.

Abutilon megapotamicum

Abutilon pictum

Malvaceae

This is the strongest and also the best-known *Abutilon*, especially in the cultivar 'Thompsonii,' shown in the picture, with yellow spotted leaves. It can grow several feet high when it has enough space and is repotted when necessary (and that is often). The bell-shaped orange flowers appear in large numbers.
Care: Place in a light spot and fertilize every week after it begins growing. Can be grown outside in a plant container. The stems are rather thin, so tying them up is necessary. In winter, the temperature may be lowered to 54°F (12°C), but is not necessary. Prune back considerably and repot in the spring.
Propagation: One can take cuttings throughout the summer from nonflowering shoots, which will make roots, given a temperature between 68–77°F (20–25°C).

Light:	Plenty of light, almost no screening.
Temp:	Cool to moderately warm in summer.
Water:	Keep rather moist.
Hum:	Moderate (50–60%).
Soil:	Standard potting soil.

Abutilon pictum 'Thompsonii'

Acacia armata

Leguminosae

Mimosa tree

This is a relative of the tree from which mimosa branches are cut. A densely branched little bush from Australia, it does not grow taller than 10 feet and much less indoors. Fortunately, this species flowers at an early age, so that we can enjoy the yellow, fragrant little round flowers around Easter.

Care: We can only enjoy the plant for a second year if the plant spends the winter in a cool spot. In the summer, it can be put outside. Give adequate water and fertilize every two weeks.

Propagation: From seed, which must be soaked in warm water. Cuttings are possible, too. Take cuttings July–August and let them make roots under plastic, with slight heat.

Light:	Full sun in the summer.
Temp:	In the summer cool to warm, in the winter between 39–43°F (4–6°C).
Water:	Give plenty of water during growth; do not let it dry out during the winter.
Hum:	Moderate, 50–60%.
Soil:	If possible mix some clay into the standard potting soil.

Acacia armata

Acalypha hispida

Acalypha hispida

Euphorbiasceae

Chenille plant

This plant is marketed in bloom in the summer, looking very attractive with its long, red tails. There is also a species with white flowers, called 'Alba.'

Care: Grow warm and in a moist environment. It's possible to get it through the winter, but young plants are often more beautiful. In the summer, feed weekly.

Propagation: Take tip cuttings in February and keep roots at a temperature of 77°F (25°C). Pinch out the tips once or twice to achieve a better branching. After three months the plants are able to bloom.

Light:	As light as possible, but no direct sunlight.
Temp:	In the summer between 68–86°F (20–30°C); minimum winter temperature 61°F (16°C).
Water:	Keep moderately moist.
Hum:	High, best around 80%.
Soil:	Acidic potting soil.

Acalypha pendula

Euphorbiaceae

Purple loosestrife

A species with small leaves, hanging stalks and many short cat's tails.

Care: The cultivation is not very different from the one discussed above. Warm, but not in the sun. Provide a rather high humidity and only fertilize once a week during the growing season. Surviving the winter is possible, but keep the plants cool. Repot in the spring.

Propagation: Root the tip cuttings in the early spring at 77°F (25°C) under glass. Pinch off the tips of young plants a few times for better branching.

Light:	Much light, no full sunlight.
Temp:	Grow warm, in the winter at least 61°F (16°C).
Water:	Moderately moist.
Hum:	High, above 60%.
Soil:	Standard potting soil mixed with peat moss.

Acalypha pendula

Acalypha wilkesiana

Euphorbiaceae

Jacob's coat

A relative of the previous plant, with more interestingly colored leaves. The hybrid 'Musaica' has darker, spotted orange leaves, 'Marginata' has leaves with light-colored edges, 'Godseffiana' has light green leaves with white zig-zag edges. There are even more varieties of cultivar.

Care: Grow in a warm, humid environment. During the growing season fertilize once a week. Winter survival is possible, but the air is generally too dry, and the plants suffer too much.

Propagation: Take tip cuttings in February, with a soil temperature of 77°F (25°C). After rooting, pinch out the tips once or twice for better branching.

Light:	Much light, no direct sunlight.
Temp:	68–86°F (20–30°C); in the winter at least 61°F (16°C).
Water:	Keep rather moist.
Hum:	High, well above 60%.
Soil:	Acidic potting soil.

Acalypha Wilkesiana-hybr.

Acanthocalycium violaceum

Cactaceae

A bullet- or column-shaped cactus, which grows in Argentina at 33,000 ft. It flowers easily.
Care: Place the plants in a light spot, but screen against the bright afternoon sun. Do not grow too warm; in the summer these cacti can go outside, but not in the rain. Once a month provide cactus food. Keep cool and dry in winter.
Propagation: From seed. Soil temperature 68–77°F (20–25°C).

Light: Much light, screen against bright sun.
Temp: Grow moderately warm, keep 40–50°F (5–10°C) in the winter.
Water: Rather dry, almost completely dry in the winter.
Hum: Can be low.
Soil: Cactus soil.

Acanthorhipsalis monacantha

Cactaceae

Epiphytic cacti with flat and triangular sections that are thorned along the edges (the unthorned version is called *Rhipsalis*).

Acanthorhipsalis monocantha

Care: These plants do not belong in a cactus greenhouse, because they have to be kept rather warm the whole year. A winter dormancy period is not needed. Just before they flower, around October, keep them fairly dry for two months. They do no like full sun; use water without lime, because the plants need a low pH. At least once every two weeks fertilize during the growing period. One can hang the plants in a tree in the summer. Do not forget to water.
Propagation: Use the cut-off sections for cuttings, after they dry.

Acanthocalycium violaceum

Light: Much light, no full sun.
Temp: Grow warm, minimum 64°F (18°C).
Water: Keep rather moist, less so during dormancy.
Hum: Moderate to high.
Soil: Bromeliad soil or another mixture that is acidic (i.e. humus) and permeable, preferably planted in lattice baskets.

Acca sellowiana

Myrtaceae

A lesser-known greenhouse or potted plant, often called *Feijoa sellowiana*.
Care: With care this plant could grow outside in a wine-growing climate. In the north it is grown in a greenhouse, and put outside sometimes on warm days. As a potted plant, it is a borderline case. It can survive some frost. Give plenty of water in the summer and dissolve some food in it once every two weeks. In the fall, the plant has to be brought inside for the dormant period. Give enough warmth so the leaves do not fall.
Propagation: Root head cuttings under glass in July. Minimum temperature 77°F (25°C).

Light: Full sun.
Temp: Grow moderately warm to warm, in the winter 40–50°F (5–10°C).
Water: Keep moist, drier in the winter.
Hum: Moderate, 50–60%.
Soil: Standard potting soil mixed with extra loam and clay.

Acca sellowiana

Acer buergerianum

Aceraceae

A maple from Japan whose leaves have three lobes. In Japan it is a large tree, and when grown in our climate is quite hardy. In the picture you see a bonsai tree in the Shokkan style, about 40 years old. Other maple trees also are suitable for this cultivation.
Care: Trees such as these that lose their leaves in the winter cannot be kept in a warm room. A light, shaded spot outside is ideal, where the

Acer buergerianum

small trees can profit from the fresh rain and air. In the summer, they need nutrients on a regular basis. Furthermore, one should watch the ball of soil, so it doesn't dry out too much. They can endure a bit of frost, though the leaves drop. But to avoid freezing of the ball of soil completely, one should place it in a greenhouse. To bury the pot in ground, if the ground is not too wet, would be a solution. For more information about bonsais, see pages 28–29.
Propagation: From seed.

Light:	Shadow.
Temp:	Grow cool, minimum 32°F (0°C).
Water:	Moderately moist with rainwater.
Hum:	Moderate to high.
Soil:	Standard potting soil mixed with clay or loam, well drained.

Achimenes hybrids

Gesneriaceae

Copious flowering plants that grow from small rootstocks. In general only cross-fertilized hybrids are available, with flowers in red-purple, purple and purple-violet tints, though white varieties exist as well.
Care: A flowering plant can be indoors for some time, but usually the air is too dry. For long-term cultivation we need a greenhouse. Use soft water and add some food every two weeks. At the end of the summer, the plant may die off completely. Dig up the rootstocks and store dry. From the end of December, they can be potted again with a minimum temperature of 68°F (20°C). By resting dormant in dry soil, growth can start in March.

Achimenes-hybr. 'Johanna Michelsen'

Propagation: By dividing the rootstocks or from head cuttings. Soil temperature 72°F (22°C).

Light:	Much light, never full sun.
Temp:	68–86°F (20–30°C), in the winter at least 50°F.
Water:	Always rather moist in the growing period. Always use soft, luke-warm water.
Hum:	High, if possible 80%.
Soil:	Special, acidic and very light mixture, such as peat dust, leaf mold, sharp sand and cow manure.

Achimenes-hybr. 'Paul Arnold'

Acokanthera oblongifolia

Apocynaceae

An evergreen bush that can grow as high as a few yards in Natal (Brazil). But the fragrant flowers appear when the plants are very young. The whole plant is very poisonous. Often called *Carissa spectabilis*.
Care: Preferably, grow in a greenhouse, but the plant can also be placed indoors. Give much light, full sun is allowed. Feed every two

weeks. Allow dormancy in a moderate greenhouse. Blooming takes place in early spring.
Propagation: Head cuttings under glass, root with soil temperature of 77°F (25°C).

Light:	Much light, can have full sun.
Temp:	Moderately warm to warm, in winter a minimum of 54°F (12°C).
Water:	Rather moist, preferably rainwater.
Hum:	High, above 60%.
Soil:	Standard potting soil mixed with finely powdered clay and loam.

Acokanthera oblongifolia

Acorus gramineus

Araceae

A modest little plant with crawling rootstock, with striking lined leaves. The common sort has solid green leaves and is therefore less visually interesting. The cultivar 'Argenteostratus' has leaves with white lines. One should not expect flowers when it is grown indoors.
Care: Do not grow too warm and keep the potting soil wet. Fertilize every two weeks.
Propagation: By division in the spring.

Light:	Much light, no bright sun.
Temp:	Grow cool; in the winter even below 32°F (0°C).
Water:	Keep soil soaking wet.
Hum:	Moderate, 50–60%.
Soil:	Standard potting soil.

Acorus gramineus 'Argenteostriatus'

ADENIUM

Adenium obesum

Apocynaceae

A plant that has received a lot of attention lately. The flowering period is extremely long and the plant appears to survive well indoors, especially when it is grafted onto the trunk of the *Merium oleander*. All parts of the *Adenium* are very poisonous.
Care: These succulent plants store water in the trunk (which, when it is older, is very thick). If the plant is grafted, then the trunk stays thin. Watch the trunk so that it does not break off at the graft point. Put the plant in full sunlight (also outside) and never give too much water, especially when it grows on its own roots. Feed every two weeks. Give it a dormant period in the winter at a lower temperature; the leaves can drop.
Propagation: From seed and grafting by incision (see page 83) on a trunk of *Nerium oleander*, ½ inch (1 cm) thick.

Light: Full sun.
Temp: Grow warm, in the winter a minimum of 54°F (12°C).
Water: In the summer rather wet, if grafted; rather dry if not grafted. In the winter almost completely dry; grafted plants some water.
Hum: Low to moderate.
Soil: Standard potting soil mixed with finely powdered clay or loam. Drain plastic pots well.

Adenium obesum

Adiantum hispidulum

Adiantaceae

Maidenhair fern

A rather strong room fern that is short and hairy. The young plant is reddish and later it turns green.
Care: No sun allowed; keep the ball of soil moist. Provide high humidity, grow warm. Give fertilizer in the growing period every two weeks, using half the normal concentration. In the winter, this species can be kept cooler than others.
Propagation: By division, or by sowing the spores.

Adiantum hispidulum

Light: Shade, no bright sunlight.
Temp: Grow warm, at least 60°F (15°C).
Water: Keep moist constantly; if possible, use a pot with a watering system.
Hum: High, above 60%.
Soil: Standard potting soil with extra peat.

Adiantum peruvianum

Adiantaceae

Maidenhair fern

These lesser-known ferns are striking because of their large, somewhat leathery leaves. One would expect that they had more resistance against the dry air indoors than the thin, fine leaves of other plants.
Care: Definitely no sun and mist often. In case the leaves get dry, try to save the plant by pruning it back rigorously. During the growth period, give fertilizer every two weeks at half concentration.
Propagation: By sowing the spores (difficult) or by division.

Light: Shade, never bright light.
Temp: Daytime 68–77°F (20–25°C), at night at least 64°F (18°C).
Water: Keep rather moist, with great care (use, if possible, a watering system); use rainwater.
Hum: As high as possible, 80% or higher.
Soil: Standard soil with extra peat.

Adiantum peruvianum

Adiantum raddianum

Adiantaceae

Maidenhair fern

A species often cultivated with delicate small leaves, which are often reddish in color when they sprout. There are quite a lot of species that differ in the form of the leaves and tint, such as the 'Brillantelse,' 'Fragrantissimum,' 'Goldelse,' 'Glorytas,' 'Fritz Luthi,' etc.
Care: The delicate foliage does not agree with dry air, therefore it is not a fern that survives well indoors, especially in the winter. Misting helps somewhat. It is not a problem in greenhouses. Fertilize in the growing season, every two weeks, half concentration.
Propagation: By division.

Light: Shade, never bright sunlight.
Temp: Daytime 68–77°F (20–25°C), at night a minimum 64°F (18°C).
Water: Keep moist constantly.
Hum: High, at least 80%.
Soil: Standard potting soil with extra peat.

Adiantum raddianum 'Fragrantissima'

Adiantum raddianum 'Glorytas'

Adiantum tenerum

Adiantaceae
Maidenhair fern

A fern with even finer foliage than the last. This variety grows a bit sturdier. The 'Scutum roseum' variety pictured has reddish foliage. The leaf stalks are ink-black and wider at the top.
Care: This fern becomes rapidly less pretty with dry air. So spray a lot, and grow preferably in a greenhouse, otherwise the beauty does not last very long. During the growth period, fertilize every two weeks, half concentration.
Propagation: By division; with common species via spores as well.

Adiantum tenerum 'Scutum Roseum'

Light:	Shade, never sunlight.
Temp:	Daytime 68–77°F (20–25°C), at night at least 50°F (10°C).
Water:	Keep constantly moist.
Hum:	High, preferably 80% or more.
Soil:	Standard potting soil mixed with extra peat.

Adromischus cooperi

Crassulaceae

Variety of small succulents with thick, beautifully marked leaves in rosettes. The white or red little flowers appear as spikes.
Care: Give it a spot in the full sun and do not give much water. When the plant grows, once a month provide some cactus fertilizer (poor

Adromischus cooperi

in nitrogen). In the winter keep cool and do not give any water. At the end of April the plants can start to grow, possibly after repotting.
Propagation: Break off the leaves, let them dry for a few days and stick them in a sandy mixture.

Light:	Full sun.
Temp:	Grow moderately warm to warm, keep between 40–50°F (5–10°C) in the winter.
Water:	Give little water, nothing in the winter.
Hum:	Can be low.
Soil:	Cactus soil.

Aechmea chantinii

Bromeliaceae

A striking bromeliad, not too big, with horizontal stripes on the leaves, which stand in a rosette.
Care: The rosette dies after blooming. The tips for care below apply only when you want to cultivate the young plants. A little bit of water once in a while is enough for the plant to continue and finish its blooming period. Plants that are still growing get fertilizer every two weeks in the growing season, half concentration. You have to pour the water into the plant's funnel.
Propagation: Next to the old rosette, new plants begin growing. You can cultivate these separately, keeping a part of the original rosette attached. After about a year, they will flower. Read the section on bromeliads on pages 18–19.

Aechmea 'Friederike'

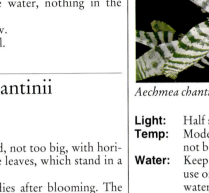

Aechmea chantinii

Light:	Half shade.
Temp:	Moderately warm to warm, at night not below 64°F (18°C).
Water:	Keep rather moist; for cultivation, use only soft water. In the summer, water is allowed to remain in the funnel.
Soil:	Bromeliad or anthurium mixture.

Modern hybrids of Aechmea

There are 150–180 species of the genus *Aechmea*, mainly in Brazil, where the plants grow predominately in trees and rarely on the ground. Many species pollinate themselves, others are dependent on pollination via hummingbirds. The grower nowadays plays the role of the hummingbird, creating wonderful hybrids, such as the pictured 'Friederike,' a creation of the bromeliad grower Bak, in Holland.

Aechmea fasciata

Bromeliaceae

This is the most well-known representative of the extended genus of bromeliads. The light red scaly leaves that protect the purple flowers have sharp thorns. The plants can grow rather large.
Care: The same rules as for the last sort of bromeliad apply to this plant. If you do not want to keep this plant, you only have to give it a little water during the flowering period. After that, you can dispose of it. For instructions on keeping it through the winter, see pages 18–19.
Propagation: By taking cuttings, or from seed.

Light:	Half shade.
Temp:	Moderately warm to warm, not below 64°F (38°C) at night.
Water:	Moderately moist; use soft water.
Hum:	Moderate, 50–60%.
Soil:	Bromeliad or anthurium mixture.

Aechmea fasciata

Aechmea fulgens

Bromeliaceae

From the rosette of this well-known bromeliad appear long stalks with small pure red flowers. In South America, this species almost always grows on trees. The shafts fill with rainwater, and in times of drought they use this as reserve.
Care: Do not bother too much about fertilization or light if you only want the plant as long as it flowers. After flowering, the old rosette dies off.

Aechmea fulgens

Propagation: By taking cuttings and growing them separately, or from seed. See pages 18–19 for more details.

Light:	Half shade.
Temp:	Moderately warm to warm, not below 64°F (18°C) at night.
Water:	Moderately moist, preferably rainwater.
Hum:	Moderate, 50–60%.
Soil:	Special mixture for anthurium or bromeliads.

Aechmea weilbachii

Bromeliaceae

A lesser-known, but nevertheless pretty, species of the extended genus of bromeliads. The shining leaves can grow to a length of 2 ft (60 cm) and are slightly ragged. The flower consists of pure red scaly leaves and light purple small flowers.

Aechmea weilbachii

Care: Only for further cultivation after flowering is good care necessary. In that case, one needs to fertilize every two weeks during the growth period, using half concentration.
Propagation: It takes a long time from seed, and from cuttings it can take one or two years before the rosettes bloom again.

Light:	Half shade.
Temp:	Moderately warm to warm, at night not below 64°F (18°C).
Water:	Keep constantly moist.
Hum:	Moderate, 50–60%.
Soil:	Special mixture for anthurium or bromeliads.

Aeonium arboreum

Crassulaceae

Succulent with thick, meaty, shiny leaves in rosettes. Although most species originate from the Canary Islands, this well-known species comes from Morocco. It is a strong plant, which forms an elegant habit as it grow older. The cultivar 'Atropurpureum' has dark-colored leaves.
Care: You can put it outside from the end of May on a sunny, protected terrace. Keep cool during dormancy; keep the soil almost dry. During growing periods, give it cactus fertilizer once every two weeks.
Propagation: Take off a leaf, let it dry a few days and stick in sandy soil to root. Seeds work, too, but often result in totally different plants.

Light:	Full sun.
Temp:	Grow cool, in the winter not much lower than 50°F (10°C).
Water:	Not much water, almost none in the winter.
Hum:	Can be low.
Soil:	Preferably a mixture that contains clay.

Aeonium arboreum

Aeonium holochrysum

Crassulaceae

A beautiful, bush-like species from the Canary Islands that has been around for a long time. Its flowers are yellow.

Care: Grow in a sunny environment; can be outside from the end of May, in a protected spot. Not too much water; once every two weeks some cactus fertilizer (one that does not contain much nitrogen). In the winter, keep cool and dry; the plant should not grow.

Aeonium holochrysum

Propagation: Cut off leaves, dry for some time, then plant. Young plants appear before the leaf touches the soil. Soil temperature 68–77°F (20–25°C).

Light:	Full sun.
Temp:	Grow cool to moderately cool, in the winter a minimum of 50°F (10°C).
Water:	Keep rather dry, in the winter almost completely dry.
Hum:	Can be low.
Soil:	Mix standard potting soil with finely powdered clay, loam, or rock wool.

Aeonium tabuliforme

Crassulaceae

A species with striking flat rosettes that have a light green tint. The leaves have a ciliate structure, which can be very pretty. The flow-

Aeonium tabuliforme

ers of these plants are light yellow, in long plumes.

Care: A light-to-sunny spot in the window, or outside in the summer. Keep cool during dormancy, around 50°F (10°C); do not water much. Only use cactus fertilizer when growing.

Propagation: Only by seed. Cutting is possible with cristate form.

Light:	Full sun.
Temp:	Grow cool, in the winter a minimum of 50°F (10°C).
Water:	Little, almost none in the winter.
Hum:	Low.
Soil:	Some clay in the mixture is preferable.

Aërangis rhodosticta

Orchidaceae

Epiphytic orchid from Ethiopia and Kenya. It has no pseudobulb, but does have many aerial roots. The flowers stay in bloom a long time.

Care: Grow moderately warm the whole year. At night, the temperature can go down to 54°F (12°C), for this stimulates the flowering. Keeping them dry from August until about mid-October stimulates the flowering as well. When the plant is growing, fertilize every 14 days.

Propagation: By division or seeds.

Light:	Much light, not full sun.
Temp:	Grow moderately warm, minimum 54°F (12°C).
Water:	Water, or dip in rainwater.
Hum:	High, above 60%.
Soil:	This plant is cultivated mainly on a piece of tree fern. Attach plants upside down on a piece of wood with copper wire or a piece of nylon.

Aërangis rhodosticta

Aëridis falcatrum

Orchidaceae

A monopodial orchid from Southeast Asia that does not produce pseudobulbs. Besides this species, there are dozens more like it. They all produce long flower stalks with bunches of fragrant little flowers.

Care: Always grow warm, without a dormant period. No direct sunlight allowed. Throughout the whole year, water a lot with water that does not contain much or any lime. Fertilize with low concentrations, as long as the plant grows. Provide a high humidity and a ventilator.

Propagation: Take rooted side shoots from old plants, or from seeds.

Light:	Much light or half shade, never bright sun.
Temp:	Grow warm, a minimum of 64°F (18°C).
Water:	Keep moderately moist.
Hum:	High, considerably above 60%.
Soil:	A mixture of clay particles and pieces of fern tree is advised, and even rock wool. Cultivation preferably in lattice baskets, so that excess water can drain easily.

Aërides falcatum

Aeschynanthus hildebrandii

Gesneriaceae

A species from Burma that is very suitable for the living room. The original species is also used for hybridization, so that there are various hybrids on the market.

Care: Although this plant originates from a warm, humid climate, with some extra care it is possible to keep it in the living room for a long time. The problems mainly arise in the winter, when the air is too dry. To prevent this, one can spray a lot or—even better—grow it in a greenhouse. The formation of flower buds

Aeschynanthus hildebrandii

is stimulated by the plants, after they are full grown, and when kept on the dry side for two months at a temperature of 54–60°F (12–15°C). Fertilize once every two weeks, low on lime content.

Propagation: Quite easy via top cutting, soil temperature 77–86°F (25–30°C). Cover with plastic.

Light:	Much light, no bright sun.
Temp:	68–77°F (20–25°C), except during dormancy.
Water:	Moderately moist with water low in lime, drier during dormancy.
Hum:	High, above 60%.
Soil:	Airy and acidic; for example bromeliad soil.

Aeschynanthus radicans

Gesneriaceae

The most well-known species, also called *A. pulcher*. Bell-shaped flower buds are located in the hairy, tubular calyxes, which later develop into flowers. Look for these small bells when you buy this plant.

Care: Keep out of the full sun and provide high humidity by spraying often. Give fertilizer low in lime and nitrogen during the

Aeschynanthus radicans

growth period. In the winter, provide a rather dry and cool rest period (54–60°F [12–15°C]) for 2 months.

Light:	Much, but no direct, sunlight.
Temp:	68–77°F (20–25°C), except during dormancy.
Water:	Moderately moist, less when dormant.
Hum:	High, above 60%.
Soil:	Airy and acidic, for instance, bromeliad soil.

Aeschynanthus tricolor

Gesneriaceae

A species we don't see much of these days. The pure red calyx and crown are hairy. When the crown opens a bit, one can spot black and yellow stripes on the inside.

Care: Grow with quite a bit of light, but not in full sun. Spray often to obtain a moist atmosphere. Fertilize once every two weeks during the growth period. Let it rest dormant for two months in the winter at a low temperature.

Aeschynanthus tricolor

Propagation: From top cutting, soil temperature 77–86°F (25–30°C).

Light:	Much light, no full sun.
Temp:	Grow warm, keep between 54–60°F (12–15°C) when dormant.
Water:	Moderately moist, during dormancy rather dry.
Hum:	High, above 60%.
Soil:	Airy, acidic soil, for instance, a mixture suitable for bromeliads.

Agapanthus praecox ssp. orientalis

Lilaceae

African lily

A well-known potted plant with meaty roots, belt-like leaves and beautiful blue (or white) flowers.

Care: In warmer areas, this plant can stay in the ground in the winter, but most of the time the *Agapanthus* is grown in large pots or containers. These can be placed on a sunny, protected terrace or balcony at the end of May. Water moderately and when the plants grow, add some fertilizer every week. They can en-

Agapanthus praecox ssp. *orientalis*

dure some frost, but in the winter these plants should be moved to a frost-free space. Add very little water, but do not let the leaves die off. Repot in the spring and bring it back to growth again.

Propagation: By division.

Light:	Full sun.
Temp:	Grow cool, a minimum of 32°F (0°C).
Water:	Moderately moist in the summer, almost dry in the winter.
Hum:	Moderate, 50–60%.
Soil:	Standard potting soil mixed with large parts of clay and loam.

Agathis macrophylla

Agave americana

Agave macroacantha

Agathis macrophylla

Araucariaceae

A conifer from Polynesia that can grow to 100 ft. (30 m). There are more species that we occasionally see as potted plants. This plant is akin to the more well-known conifers we see in houses.
Care: If required, cultivate outside from the end of May. It can stay in a cool room as well. Fertilize every 14 days. Bring it inside in the fall and place in a cool spot. In a warm room, the air is much too dry. Do not place it in a warm spot too early; repot in April, allow it to flower again, harden and bring it outside at the end of May.
Propagation: From new seeds or via tip cuttings. Soil temperature 68–77°F (20–25°C).

Light:	Much light, no bright sun.
Temp:	Grow cool, in the winter 40–50°F (5–10°C).
Water:	Keep moderately moist.
Hum:	Moderate, 50–60%.
Soil:	Mixture of ⅔ part standard potting soil and ⅓ part clay or loam.

Agave americana

Agavaceae

Not a real succulent, but certainly a tropical plant. It's grown often as a potted plant, which in summer can survive in a sheltered place. The plants grow bigger every year. They almost never flower, and if it happens, the first rosette dies. Other than the common green species, there are 'Argenteovariegata' and 'Aureovariegata,' which have yellow stripes in the middle of the leaves.
Care: It's better to cultivate indoors, but always grow it outside in the summer. The plant has to stay in a cool place in the winter, minimum temperature 40°F (5°C). A lot of light is not necessary then, and you do not have to water it much. In the summer, provide cactus fertilizer (low in nitrogen) once every two weeks. Repot small specimens each spring, and large ones every two or three years.

Propagation: From seed, or by taking the young rosettes that are formed at the foot of the old plant.

Light:	Full sun.
Temp:	Cool to warm, in the winter at least 40°F (5°C).
Water:	Rather dry; in the winter, almost no water at all.
Hum:	Low, can be below 50%.
Soil:	Standard potting soil, possibly mixed with some clay or rock wool.

Agave americana 'Aureovariegata'

Agave macroacantha

Agavaceae

A heavily armed species from Mexico. The leaves can grow to a maximum length of 24 in. (60 cm).
Care: Place in a sunny spot, inside or outside (from the end of May). In the summer, they do not need much water. When the plant is outside, provide the pot with good drainage, so that excess water can drain after a heavy rain shower. Fertilize every two weeks with cactus food. Bring the plant inside in the fall and place in a light spot for dormancy at a low temperature.

Propagation: From seed. Sometimes lateral rosettes are formed that can be used for propagation.

Light:	Full sun.
Temp:	Grow cool, in the winter 40–50°F (5–10°C).
Water:	Rather dry to moderately moist, in the winter very little water.
Hum:	Can be low.
Soil:	Mix standard potting soil with finely ground clay or loam.

Agave parviflora

Agavaceae

An agave that stays small, usually not higher than 4 in (10 cm). The leaves are not wider than .4 in (1 cm). White lines decorate the leaves, and white threads sprout along the edges.

Agave parviflora

Care: Due to the small size, this specimen is easy to place in a window sill. The plant does not take up much space for winter storage either. Put it in an airy location though. It can go outside in the summer. Feed the same way as the previous species.
Propagation: From seed (soil temperature 68°F [20°C]) or from removed shoots.

Light:	Full sun.
Temp:	Cool to warm, in the winter a minimum of 40°F (5°C).
Water:	Rather dry, in the winter almost nothing.
Hum:	Can be low.
Soil:	Standard potting soil, if possible mixed with some clay or loam.

AGAVE

Agave victoriae-reginae

Agavaceae

A very well-known species that does not grow very large, generally 20 in (50 cm). The green leaves are edged in white and they are striped. The top is hollow. This is one of the few species that does not form shoots.

Care: Like all the other species, grow in sun; it can be outside on a sheltered terrace from the end of May till end of September. Provide a cool dormant period, but one a little warmer than for the other species we discussed.

Propagation: Only from seed, because no shoots are formed.

Light:	Full sun.
Temp:	Cool to warm, in the winter a minimum 50°F (10°C).
Water:	Rather dry, in the winter even less.
Hum:	Can be low.
Soil:	Standard potting soil if possible mixed with clay soil.

Agave victoriae-reginae

Aglaonema commutatum

Aglaonema commutatum

Araceae

The most well-known species, it has many diverse varieties. The 'Silver Queen' shown is the most famous species, but 'Pseudobracteatum' and 'San Remo' are quite spectacular with their fascinating spotted leaves. The plants do bloom sometimes, with flowers resembling the arum. After that, red fruits are formed. One can observe this in the photograph.

Care: It is unfortunate that these plants require so much humidity. This need makes them less suitable for the living room. Only in the winter, when the heat is turned on, will one notice this. Spraying often improves the condition somewhat, but a greenhouse is the most preferable place. During periods of growth, feed once every two weeks. During the winter, do not lower the temperature much.

Propagation: From seed, by division and from tip cutting.

Light:	Much light for the strongly spotted species.

Temp:	Grow warm, not below 68°F (20°C). In the winter not lower than 60°F (15°C).
Water:	Continuous, rather moist with soft water.
Hum:	High, preferably above 60%.
Soil:	An airy, rather acidic mixture that contains, for example, coniferous soil.

Aglaonema costatum

Araceae

This species stays smaller than the previous one. The leaf is a shiny green with a very distinctive marking. In July, the plant can have a greenish flower.

Care: *A. costatum* is somewhat stronger than the previous plant, but it too does not do well in dry room air. This is especially cumbersome in the winter. One can help the plant by placing it in a cooler spot. During the growth periods, feed once a month.

Propagation: From seed, tip cutting and division.

Light:	Half shade.
Temp:	Grow warm, in the winter a minimum of 60°F (15°C).
Water:	Continuous moderate moisture with water low in lime.
Hum:	Preferably above 60%.
Soil:	Can be standard potting soil, rather than a mix with coniferous soil.

Aglaonema costatum 'Foxii'

Aglaonema crispum
Araceae

A very elegant species, also known as *Aglaonema roebelinii*. The leaves can grow up to a length of 12 in (30 cm) and the leaf stalk another 8 in (20 cm). The surface of the leaf is marked very prettily. The cultivated species 'Roebelinii' is shown in the picture and is the most famous. But there are more varieties that vary in their markings.
Care: The large leaves are sensitive to dry air, which is especially a threat in the winter. The plant also hates "cold feet." Feed every two weeks during growth periods.
Propagation: By division or via top cuttings.

Light:	Much light, no sun.
Temp:	Grow warm
Water:	Keep moderately wet continuously with soft water.
Hum:	High, above 60%.
Soil:	Humus, rather acidic, preferably with extra coniferous soil.

Aglaonema crispum 'Roebelinii'

Albizia julibrissin

Leguminosae

A tree from Asia with fern-like, double-feathered leaves, an obvious relative of the mimosa. Older specimens can have pink, bulleted flower heads at the end of the branches.
Care: This species does well as a potted plant in our climate. That is to say, in the summer, from the end of May, outside on a sheltered, sunny terrace. Give plenty of water when the weather is warm and fertilize every two weeks from the beginning of August.
Propagation: From seed.

Light:	Full sun.
Temp:	Grow cool, keep around 37–46°F (3–18°C) in the winter.
Water:	Moderate in the summer, drier in the winter.
Hum:	Moderate, 50–60%.
Soil:	Standard potting soil mixed with clay and loam.

Allamanda cathartica
Apocynaceae

A creeper from Brazil with yellow, trumpet-shaped, quite fragile flowers. Selections are cultivated like the 'Grandiflora' and the 'Hendersonii.'
Care: This is more of a greenhouse plant than a houseplant, especially because it requires so much moist air. Nevertheless, some people succeed in keeping these plants indoors and in good condition for a long time. Keep slightly cooler in the winter, repot in the spring and prune back well. Tie the shoots up when they regrow and spray them often. Feed weekly during growth periods.
Propagation: From tip cutting or middle cutting, soil temperature 77°F (25°C).

Light:	Much light, no full sunlight.
Temp:	Grow warm, not below 64°F (18°C) in the winter.
Water:	Keep moderately moist.
Hum:	Moderate to high, in any case above 50%.
Soil:	Standard potting soil.

Allamanda cathartica

Albizia julibrissin

Alloplectus capitatus

Alloplectus capitatus

Gesneriaceae

A plant from Colombia and Venezuela with red, velvety leaves. The stalks are meaty and reddish. The plant has yellow flowers with a red calyx. After flowering, numerous red seeds are formed.
Care: Considering it requires so much warmth and moist air, the plant is more suitable for a greenhouse. In the summer, though, it can stay indoors. Feed once every two weeks during growth periods.
Propagation: From tip cutting or middle cutting, or from seed. Soil temperature 77–86°F (25–30°C).

Light:	Much light, no full sun.
Temp:	Grow warm, in the winter not below 64°F (18°C).
Water:	Always moderately moist.
Hum:	High, above 60%.
Soil:	Standard potting soil.

Alloplectus schlimii

Gesneriaceae

A rather "new" plant that flowers easily. The leaves are a shiny green, and it has knobby flowers that bloom in a reddish purple.
Care: Like the last species, it requires moist air. If this becomes too difficult in the winter, let the plant die off and keep the tubular roots in the soil at a minimum of 54°F (12°C). Bring to flower again in the spring, preferably in a greenhouse. Feed once every two weeks during the growth period.
Propagation: From seed, tip cutting or middle cutting. Soil temperature 68–77°F (20–25°C).

Light:	Much light, no bright sun.
Temp:	Moderately warm, 61–68°F (16–20°C).
Water:	Keep moderately moist, dry in the winter.
Hum:	High, above 60%.
Soil:	Standard potting soil.

Alloplectus schlimii

Alocasia lowii

Araceae

The beautifully marked leafs of this plant resemble some *Anthurium* species. There are many different species of *Alocasia*, though only one is shown.
Care: These plants can only stay indoors for a short period, because of their need for warmth and moist air. It would be better to keep them in a greenhouse. In the winter,

Alocasia lowii

water less and lower the temperature somewhat. Feed once every two weeks during growth periods.

Propagation: From seed, by removing the shoots or by dividing the rootstocks.

Light:	Much light, no full sun.
Temp:	Grow warm, 70–77°F (22–25°C). In the winter lower to 64°F (18°C).
Water:	Always moderately moist with soft water.
Hum:	High, not below 60%
Soil:	Preferably a special mixture of peat moss.

Aloë aristata

Aloë humilis

Aloë arborescens

Liliaceae

Candelabra plant

This is a strong plant that grows bushy and flowers easily.

Care: Place in the garden or on the balcony, if possible in a sheltered and sunny spot from the end of May. Do not give too much water and feed once a month. Bring inside in the fall and keep cool during dormancy: This gives you more chance for flowers.

Propagation: Cut off a side shoot, let dry for a day and plant it in rather dry, sandy soil.

Light:	Full sun.
Temp:	Grow cool, in the winter 40–50°F (5–10°C).
Water:	Keep rather dry, in the winter almost completely dry.
Hum:	Can be low.
Soil:	Mixture of ⅓ part standard potting soil, ⅓ part clay and loam, ⅓ part sharp sand.

Aloë arborescens

Aloë aristata

Liliaceae

A beautiful, regular, dark green rosette of thick small leaves, covered with white warts and spiked at the edges. Orange-red flowers can grow on the long stalk.

Care: Grow very sunny in the summer (outside or in) and do not give too much water. Feed it cactus food once a month. Keep especially cool from the end of October so that the rosette shrivels somewhat.

Propagation: From seed or by removing the side shoots. Let dry for some days and plant.

Light:	Full sun.
Temp:	Grow cool, in the winter about 40°F (5°C).
Water:	Rather dry, in the winter almost completely dry.
Hum:	Can be low.
Soil:	Standard potting soil mixed with sharp sand and clay or loam.

Aloë humilis

Liliaceae

A rosette with thin, meaty leaves, again covered with clear papillas, as is often the case with this genus. The flowers are striking, and flowers of other species look very similar.

Care: Place in a sunny spot in the summer, possibly outside. Do not give too much water, and give it cactus food once a month (as long as it contains little nitrogen). Keep cool in the winter and provide only a little water.

Propagation: From seed or by removing and striking slips from side rosettes.

Light:	Full sun.
Temp:	Grow cool, in the winter about 40°F (5°C).
Water:	Give sparse water, almost nothing in the winter.
Hum:	Can be low, below 50%.
Soil:	Mixture of standard potting soil, clay or loam and sharp sand.

Aloë variegata

Liliaceae

Probably the most well-known species, the one most often sold as a small plant. This aloe does not grow taller than 12 in (30 cm). Orange-red flowers can appear on the long stalks.

Care: It can stay in the room the whole year, although a cooler dormancy is in fact better. Do not give it too much water or food, and place in a light spot.

Aloë variegata

Propagation: From seed or by striking slips from the side shoots. Let them dry well before planting.

Light:	Much light, full sun allowed.
Temp:	Grow cool to moderately warm, in the winter no lower than 40°F (5°C).
Water:	Very sparse, nothing at low temperatures to avoid rotting.
Hum:	Can be low, below 50%.
Soil:	Standard potting soil mixed with sharp sand and clay or loam.

Alpinia sanderae

Alpinia sanderae

Zingiberaceae

A member of the ginger family, originally from western Iran. The plant does not grow taller than 18 in (45 cm) and has a creeping rootstock. The elongated leaves sprout in rows of two. When grown in northern climates, it doesn't often flower.
Care: The plant requires high humidity and therefore is not very suitable for the living room. It will flourish in a greenhouse, however. The winter temperature should not be too low. Feed once every two weeks during growth periods.
Propagation: By dividing the rootstock.

Light:	Much light, no full sun.
Temp:	Grow warm, in the winter not below 64°F (18°C).
Water:	Always moderately moist.
Hum:	High, above 60%.
Soil:	Standard potting soil, possibly mixed with extra loam or clay.

Alsobia dianthiflora

Gesneriaceae

A plant that is better known under the name *Episcia dianthiflora*. Unfortunately, the striking flowers are often covered by the leaves.
Care: This plant flourishes in a greenhouse, but can survive in the living room during the summer, as long as it does not get any sun. Try to keep the humidity as high as possible. Feed once every two weeks during the growth period. In the winter, keep it in a greenhouse, where the temperature cannot get too low.

Propagation: By removing the rooted shoots or by tip cuttings, which can root under glass at 68–77°F (20–25°C) soil temperature.

Light:	Half shade.
Temp:	Grow warm, a minimum 61–64°F (16–18°C).
Water:	Moderately moist, preferably with soft water or rainwater.
Hum:	High, above 60%.
Soil:	Standard potting soil.

Alsobia dianthiflora

Alternanthera ficoidea

Amaranthaceae

A half-bush with beautiful colored leaves; they were often used in mosaic beds. As the picture shows, the small plants can grow in a large moss ball that you can hang somewhere. They are available in various colors.
Care: Requires much sunlight to maintain the beautiful colors of the leaves. Do not forget to water. In the summer, feed once a week. A few plants may be kept dormant in order to strike a slip in the spring.

Propagation: Remove tip cuttings of hibernated plants in January. Soil temperature 68–77°F (20–25°C). Cut the tips frequently to achieve bushy plants.

Light:	Full sun.
Temp:	Grow cool, in the winter a minimum of 54°F (12°C).
Water:	Keep moderately moist.
Hum:	Moderate, 50–60%.
Soil:	Standard potting soil.

Alternanthera ficoidea

Amaryllis belladonna

Amaryllidaceae
Belladonna lily

Amaryllis usually refers to *Hippeastrum*, the bulbous plant with very large flowers. (See p. 249.) This plant is the "real" *Amaryllis*, which does not have a hollow stalk, as does the other bulbous plant.
Care: They flower only in the summer months; it is not possible to force them to flower at any other time. It is advisable to treat this as a potted plant: In the winter keep it in a greenhouse, in the summer, a protected spot

Amaryllis belladonna

outside. It may possibly bloom indoors. Fertilize once every two weeks during the growing period. Provide dormancy at low temperatures in the winter; not all the leaves should drop. Repot only once every three years.

Propagation: From seed. These plants take three years before they flower.

Light:	Full sun.
Temp:	Grow cool, in the winter a minimum 40°F (5°C).
Water:	Moderately moist in the summer, in the winter quite dry.

Amorphophallus bulbifer

Amorphophallus bulbifer

Araceae

An unusual but interesting bulbous growth that can be considered a dry flowering plant. The flower is an arum with a thick, ill-smelling spathes.

Hum:	Moderate, 50–60%.
Soil:	Standard potting soil.

Care: The tuberous roots have to be kept completely dry and rather warm. In the spring, the flower develops without any water or soil. Only after this can you pot them and provide some water. Gradually water more as the large leaves appear. Little brown bulbs develop often on the leaf stalk. After May, the plant can be placed outside in a sheltered spot. Feed every week. Let the leaves die by withholding water in the fall and store the newly formed bulb dry again.

Propagation: By removing the new bulbs from the stalk.

Light:	Much light, but screen against bright sun.
Temp:	Grow cool to moderately warm, in the winter not below 60°F (15°C).
Water:	Keep moderately moist during growth, completely dry when dormant.
Hum:	Moderate to high.
Soil:	Standard potting soil with at least ⅓ loam or clay.

Ampelopsis brevipedunculata

Vitaceae

Virginia creeper

From the variety *maximowiczii*, the spotted form called 'Elegans' is always in cultivation. A long name for a long viny plant.

Ampelopsis brevipedunculata
var. *maximowiczii* 'Elegans'

Care: The plant can grow along a wall, but needs some support. Cool cultivation is the key to success. Terrace and balcony are suitable places, but a frost-free dormancy is necessary to survive. In the winter, the leaves may drop, but that is no problem. Give plenty of water with some food added in the summer.

Propagation: Tip cutting or middle cutting, soil temperature 60–68°F (15–20°C).

Light:	Much light, no full sun.
Temp:	Grow cool, frost-free in the winter.
Water:	A lot in the summer, keep moist in the winter.
Hum:	Moderate, 50–60%.
Soil:	Standard potting soil.

Ananas species

Bromeliaceae

Pineapple

A bromeliad species that everybody recognizes by the edible fruit. Most of the time, we see it as the houseplant *Ananas comosus* with yellow-edged leaves, commonly called 'Variegatus.' It forms a small fruit (not edible) and upon that appears a new rosette with leaves. There are smaller species, for example the *nanus*, shown in the photograph.

Care: As with all the bromeliads, the old rosette dies off after flowering. During and just after flowering, the care is not so important. If you decide to grow the small plants, then warmth and moist air are needed. Fertilize once every two weeks during the growth period.

Ananas nanus

Propagation: By removing the newly formed rosettes or by striking a slip from the leaf rosette, situated above the fruit. Dry the cutting for a few days. Soil temperature 77–86°F (25–30°C).

Light:	Much light, no full sun.
Temp:	Grow warm, in the winter not below 64°F (18°C).
Water:	Always moderately moist.

Ananus comosus 'Aureovariegatus'

Hum:	Moderate, between 50–60%.
Soil:	Standard potting soil.

Anastatica hierochuntica

Cruciferae

A desert plant that is not much more than a dried, curled-up rosette (below, left). When put in water, it will unwrap itself again, as in the glass bowl on the right. One could repeat this a few times with the same result. Another

Anastatica hierochuntica

plant with the same capacity is called *Selaginella lepidophylla*, which closely resembles *A. hierochuntica*. No plant food is necessary.

Care: It is almost impossible to root the rosette because it has actually died off already. As such, this isn't considered a serious houseplant.

Angraecum eburneum

Propagation: It is possible from seed, but these are hard to come by commercially.

Light:	Full sun.
Temp:	High.
Water:	Moderate.
Hum:	Low.
Soil:	Standard potting soil.

Angraecum eburneum

Orchidaceae

Rather large orchids for the greenhouse or a closed plant window. The fragrant, white flowers have spurs and are assembled in a bunch.

Care: The plants grow almost all year round and do not require a dormancy period, although less water is needed after a growth period. The sunlight has to be screened in the summer; in the winter weak sunlight is allowed. While the plant is growing, feed with orchid food once every two weeks.

Propagation: By division, or from seed.

Light:	Much light, no full sun.
Temp:	Grow warm, in the summer at least 64°F (18°C), in the winter 61°F (16°C).
Water:	Plenty of (rain)water during the growth period, provided that there is a good drainage system.
Hum:	High, above 60%.
Soil:	Preferably a mixture of pieces of fern'tree and osmunda, in a well-draining lattice basket.

Ansellia africana var. *nilotica*

Ansellia africana

Orchidaceae

An easily cultivated orchid from tropical Africa. Flowers appear in winter and last a long time.
Care: Preferably grown in a greenhouse; it needs light, but avoid the bright afternoon sun. When growth starts in the fall, provide sufficient water and every two weeks add orchid fertilizer. The dormant period follows the flowering, which occurs during the summer in our climate, and less water is required. No food is necessary when the plants' growth stops.
Propagation: By division.

Light:	Much light, no bright sun.
Temp:	Grow warm, in the winter 33–64°F (1–18°C).
Water:	Keep moderately moist during the growth period, with not much water during dormancy.
Hum:	High, above 60%.
Soil:	Mixture of chopped fern tree and fern roots, or pure rock wool flakes. Put a drainage layer in the pots.

Anisodontea capensis

Angraecum rhodostica

See *Aerangis rhodostica*.

Anigozanthos flavidus

Haemodoraceae

Once a rare plant, this is now frequently available at most florists. By spraying with growth retardants, it is made into an agreeable houseplant. The flowers are pretty before they even open, though this won't happen if there is not enough light.
Care: Grow with much light in the summer, but screen against the brightest sun. From the end of May the plant can go outside, but keep it sheltered. Give it plenty of water and food every two weeks. It needs a dormant period in the winter.
Propagation: By division or from seed.

Light:	Much light, no bright sun.
Temp:	Grow cool to moderately warm, in the winter, at 50–54°F (10–12°C).
Water:	In the summer, always moist. Drier in the winter.
Hum:	Moderate, 50–60%.
Soil:	Standard potting soil.

Anisodontea capensis

Malvaceae

A thrifty plant, usually called *Malva* or *Malvastrum* by growers. A hardy, full-flowering species, which does well indoors. The small bush can grow to a height of 5 feet (1.5 meters).
Care: In a sunny window or outside in the summer. Fertilize once every two weeks. It can endure a temporary drought, but it is advisable to water the plant on a regular basis. Store it cool in the winter. Prune in the spring, repot and allow it to grow again.

Light:	Much light, full sun included.
Temp:	Grow cool to moderately warm, in the winter 54°F (12°C).
Water:	Keep moderately moist, in the winter quite dry.
Hum:	Low to moderate.
Soil:	Standard potting soil.

Anigozanthos flavidus

Anthurium Andreanum-hybr.

Anthurium Andraeanum hybrids

Araceae

Flamingo lily

This is a relative of the flamingo flower, which is discussed under its own heading on this page. It is used less as a houseplant, and is cultivated by growers mainly as a cut flower.
Care: Requires a high temperature and very moist air. Nevertheless, some people succeed in growing this plant indoors; moreover, many find that this plant is easier to care for than the flamingo flower. Keep dry and cool for six weeks in the winter to stimulate bud formation. Feed every two weeks in the summer.
Propagation: By dividing the large plants or from trunk cuttings; possibly from seed. Soil temperature 77–86°F (5–30°C).

Light:	Half shade, never full sun.
Temp:	Grow warm, in the winter a minimum 60°F (15°C).
Water:	Always moderately moist and use only soft, lukewarm water.
Hum:	High, above 60%.
Soil:	Special mixture for anthurium, consisting of peat dust, peat pieces, coniferous soil and perlite for extra permeability.

Anthurium crystallinum

Araceae

The elegantly marked leaves are the main attraction of this plant. There are more species with this quality, often a velvety green shade or with a metallic gloss.
Care: This greenhouse plant is hard to keep in a warm living room, especially in the summer. Grow warm and moist. In the summer, fertilize once every two weeks.

Anthurium crystallinum

Propagation: From seed, by division and via trunk cutting.

Light:	Half shade, never full sun.
Temp:	Grow warm, in the winter a minimum 64°F (18°C).
Water:	Always keep moderately moist, use only soft water.
Hum:	High, above 60%.
Soil:	Anthurium mixture, see previous species.

Anthurium Scherzeranum hybrids

Araceae

Flamingo flower

One of the most popular species of houseplant, with its red, orange or all-white flowers. When this plant flowers, it is very pretty, but the blooms do not keep that easily.
Care: Unfortunately, this plant desires high humidity, making it less attractive as a houseplant. It thrives best in a greenhouse environment. By keeping the plant dry and cool for six weeks in the winter, flower buds will start to develop. Feed only during growth periods, once every two weeks.
Propagation: From seed, by division and via trunk cutting.

Anthurium Scherzeranum-hybr.

Light:	Half shade, never full sun.
Temp:	Grow warm, at least 68°F (20°C) in the winter a minimum 60°F (15°C).
Water:	Keep moderately moist with lime-free water. Avoid stagnant water.
Hum:	High, minimum 60%, preferably higher.
Soil:	Special mixture, see *A.* Andreanum-hybrids.

Aphelandra aurantiaca

Acanthaceae

A special species, also known as cv. *roezlii*. The orange flowers are elongated.

Care: Always keep in a moist atmosphere. During the flowering period, the plant can be kept in the living room, but the air becomes too dry in the winter. Let it sit dormant in a greenhouse. Avoid bright sunlight and give fertilizer once a week during growth periods. After the flowering period, cut the flower stalks and place the plant in a cool spot. In the spring—after repotting—let it grow in a very moist environment (greenhouse or plant window) and keep warm (77°F) (25°C), otherwise, there will be no flowers.

Propagation: Root tip cuttings under glass with a soil temperature of 77°F (25°C).

Aphelandra aurantiaca var. *roezlii*

Light:	Much light, no full sunlight.
Temp:	Grow warm; during dormancy (winter), continue at 50–58°F (10–14°C).
Water:	Keep moderately moist with soft water.
Hum:	High, above 60%.
Soil:	Standard potting soil or a mixture that contains coniferous soil.

Aphelandra maculata
Acanthaceae

Aphelandra maculata

Better known as *Stenandrium lindenii*. A small plant with very beautifully marked leaves and small yellow flowers in bracts.
Care: Suitable for areas with a warm and moist atmosphere, such as plant windows or vitrines. It has a creeping way of growing. Feed once

Aphelandra sinclairiana

every two weeks during growth periods. Lower temperatures in the winter are allowed.
Propagation: By division and via tip cuttings which root at 86°F (30°C) under glass.

Light:	Much light to half shade, no sun.
Temp:	Grow warm, minimum 56°F (13°C).
Water:	Keep moderately moist with soft water.
Hum:	High, above 60%.
Soil:	Acid-soil mixture, as coniferous soil and decayed cow manure, peat particles, etc.

Aphelandra sinclairiana

Acanthaceae

A rare *Aphelandra*, suitable for those with access to a greenhouse. There are many exotic specimens, all of which share similar cultivation requirements.
Care: Grow light, warm and moist. Protect against bright sunlight. Feed weekly during the growth period. Cut back after flowering and place in a cooler spot. Repot in the spring and try again.
Propagation: Root middle cuttings or eye cuttings under glass at a soil temperature of 68–77°F (20–25°C).

Light:	Much light, no full sun.
Temp:	Grow warm, in the winter a minimum 54°F (12°C).
Water:	Keep moderately moist, use water without lime.
Hum:	High, above 60%.
Soil:	Mixture of peat particles, standard potting soil, loam and clay.

Aphelandra squarrosa

Acanthaceae

The most cultivated *Aphelandra*, of which there are various genera. It is the hardiest, although still difficult to keep in a living room. The flowers are like dense spikes and are yellow or yellow-orange.

Care: In the summer, this plant does well indoors, but in the winter, it has a hard time because of the dry air. Feed weekly during the growth period. Prune after flowering and place in a cooler spot. Next, bring back to growth again: Bud development is stimulated by a period of low temperature, as well as by the length of the day and strength of the light.

Propagation: By middle cutting or eye cutting, soil temperature 68–77°F (20–25°C).

Light:	Half shade, never full sun.
Temp:	Grow warm; in the winter, for three months keep at 48–54°F (9–12°C).
Water:	Always moderately moist with soft water.
Hum:	High, above 60%.
Soil:	Standard potting soil.

Aporocactus flagelliformis

Aphelandra squarrosa

Aporocactus flagelliformis

Cactaceae

Rattail cactus

A cactus that grows on trees in the wild. The long stalks hang down, so grow in a hanging pot. It can be a strong and long-living plant indoors, and one that flowers plentifully each year. Grafted specimens grow quicker and flower even more.

Care: Hang outside from the end of May, but not in the bright sunlight. Give cactus food once every two weeks. Do not turn the plant away from the light after the bud forming has taken place, because the buds will fall off. Dormancy occurs in the winter; keep dry and cool.

Propagation: Quite easy from cuttings, which have to dry the first few days. From seed too, and by grafting, on, for instance, *Selenicereus*.

Light:	Much light, no full sun.
Temp:	Grow cool, in the winter a minimum 36°F (2°C).
Water:	In the summer moderately moist, in the winter hardly any water.
Hum:	Can stay below 50%.
Soil:	Cactus soil.

Arachis hypogaea

Leguminosae

Peanut

Peanuts are not related to other nut species. The flower stalks extend after pollination, penetrate the soil and make fruits there.

Arachis hypogaea

Care: The plant is an annual and can be cultivated from seeds. Provide good drainage, because stagnant water is very damaging. Give it a sunny spot in the greenhouse or window. When the plant is growing, fertilize once every two weeks.
Propagation: Germinate a few unroasted peanuts at a soil temperature of 68°F (20°C).

Light:	Much light, full sunlight allowed.
Temp:	Grow warm.
Water:	Rather dry to moderately moist with lukewarm water.
Hum:	Moderate, 50–60%.
Soil:	Standard potting soil.

Arachniodes aristata 'Variegatum'

Araucaria heterophylla

Araucariaceae
Norfolk Island pine

In the southern hemisphere, this tree can grow 122 ft (40 m) high, but in our climate it functions as a decorative houseplant. The lower branches come off over time, but this is not a drawback, especially when you have a specimen with more stalks, or more than one specimen in a pot.
Care: The biggest threat to this plant is the dry room air in the winter. Keep the plant as cool as possible during the winter months, as this will increase the humidity. In the summer, the plant can go outside, but not in the full sun. Feed once every two weeks during growth periods.
Propagation: Top cutting, though rooting is hard. Use a growth hormone and provide a 77°F (25°C) soil temperature.

Light:	Much light, no full sun.
Temp:	Grow cool, in the winter not below 40°F (5°C).
Water:	Keep moderately moist with lime-free water.
Hum:	High, possibly above 60%.
Soil:	Preferably coniferous soil.

Araucaria heterophylla

Arbutus andrachne

Arbutus andrachne

Ericaceae
These bushes come from countries around the Mediterranean; in the north they are suitable as potted plants. The species *andrachne* and *unedo* are more agreeable indoors. After the small, urn-shaped flowers are gone, orange or red fruits are formed.
Care: From the end of May, keep outside in a sheltered and sunny spot. Water regularly, and be careful; if the soil dries out, the plant will die. The same will happen if the water cannot drain and the soil gets too wet. Add food to the water once every two weeks. In the fall, the plants should go inside again and be placed in a cool, airy and light spot. Give less water then, but do not let it dry out. The foliage should stay on.
Propagation: From seed and via top cuttings, removed from well-flowering plants. They root under glass at 68–77°F (20–25°C).

Light:	Full sun.
Temp:	Grow cool, in the winter 40–50°F (5–10°C).
Water:	Always keep moist with lime-free water.
Hum:	Moderate, 50–60%.
Soil:	Acidic soil rich in humus, for instance, half standard potting soil and half peat dust, garden peat or leaf mold.

Arachniodes adiantiformis

Arachniodes species

Aspidiaceae
Holly fern

A fern better known under the name *Polystichum*. See there for other specimens.
Care: These ferns can survive dry room air quite well because of its leathery foliage. Still, it would help to spray the leaves a few times a day in the winter. An alternative is to provide a dormant period at a lower temperature, which increases the humidity. Keep the plants from the sun, provide a very regular watering system and give fertilizer weekly at half concentration during growth periods.
Propagation: By division and by sowing the spurs. Germination temperature 64–68°F (18–20°C).

Light:	Shade, never sun.
Temp:	Grow moderately warm, in the winter a minimum 50°F (10°C).
Water:	Keep constantly moist with soft water.
Hum:	Moderate, 50–60%.
Soil:	Mix standard potting soil with ⅓ part peat dust.

On the following pages: *Araucaria heterophylla*

Ardisia crenata

Myrsinaceae

This plant immediately begins the next season's fruit development while still bearing berries. The cv. 'Alba' has white berries. In the thickened edges of the leaves the bacteria *Bacillis foliicola* exists in harmony with the plant.

Care: Brush the pollen during flowering to stimulate pollination. Keep cooler in the winter, less water and spray the leaves.

Propagation: Multiply from ripe, new seeds or from top cuttings. Soil minimum warmth 77–86°F (25–30°C).

Light: Half shade.
Temp: Grow moderately warm, in the winter a minimum 54°F (12°C).
Water: Always keep moderately moist, but provide good drainage.
Hum: Moderate, 50–60%.
Soil: Standard potting soil.

Ardisia crenata

Arisaema candidissimum

Ariocarpus fissuratus

Cactaceae

Peculiarly formed cactus, with knobs that resemble leaves, especially when the plant is very young, as in the picture. No thorns. Not easy to grow.

Care: In the summer, keep warm and sunny and do not water much, even less than other cacti. Never pour water over the plant itself. Feed cactus food once a month.

Ariocarpus fissuratus

Propagation: From seed; the plants grow slowly and flowering takes years.

Light: Full sun.
Temp: Grow warm, in the winter 32–40°F (0–5°C).
Water: Keep rather dry, completely dry during dormancy.
Hum: Can be low.
Soil: Permeable and without humus. Mixture of clay or loam and perlite is suitable.

Arisaema candidissimum

Araceae

This plant grows from root tubers that sometimes can be ordered from a mail-order company.

Care: Order the tubers early, because growth starts in the middle of the winter. Plant tubers and do not keep them too warm, or too light. Give more water as soon as the plants start to grow. Place indoors during the flowering. After that, preferably in a greenhouse, keep half shaded and not too hot. Feed every two weeks. The plants die off at the end of the summer. The tubers can stay in the pot and new shoots will appear.

Propagation: By division of the roots.

Light: Half shade to much light, no full sunlight.
Temp: Grow cool, in the winter a minimum 50°F (10°C).
Water: Keep rather moist in the summer, completely dry in the winter.
Hum: Moderate to high.
Soil: Mix standard potting soil with extra peat moss or leaf mold.

Aristolochia grandiflora

Care: Although they are provided with reserve organs in the form of pseudotubers, these plants do not desire a strict dormant period. At most, you could limit the watering after the full growth of the pseudotubers. Provide an airy space out of the full sun, preferably in a greenhouse. Give orchid fertilizer once every two weeks during the growth period.
Propagation: By division and from seed.

Light:	Much light or half shade, no full sun.
Temp:	Grow moderately warm, minimum 61°F (16°C).
Water:	Keep moderately moist; drain the rainwater.
Hum:	High, above 60%.
Soil:	Grow in well-drained pots or lattice baskets, filled with a mixture of pieces of fern and sphagnum.

Asarina barclaiana

Scrophulariaceae

Genus of beautiful climbing plants, also known by the name *Maurandya*. They are usually grown from seeds each year.
Care: Grow in a light, airy greenhouse, sunroom, plant window or winter garden that can be ventilated on warm days. In southern areas, the plant can grow outside as well. In the summer, plenty of water and food once every two weeks. Support the vines. The flowering period starts in the summer and can last to the fall. The greenhouse does not have to be heated, because it is not worth keeping them dormant.
Propagation: Sowing from February, soil warmth 32–40°F (0–5°C). Grow warm, plant in pots, gradually harden off and plant at the end of May, preferably in the ground.

Light:	Much light, sun too.
Temp:	Grow cool.
Water:	Keep moderately moist.
Hum:	Moderate, 50–60%.
Soil:	Standard potting soil.

Asarina barclaiana

Aristolochia grandiflora

Aristolochiaceae

Plants for the greenhouse with enormous flowers. They are related to a hardy climbing shrub known as the "German pipe." The species shown is known by the name *gigantea*. Smaller in size is the species *elegans*, although it's easier to grow.
Care: Grow in shade in a rather large greenhouse. Tie up the long vines. If possible, plant in the ground of the greenhouse, otherwise in large containers. Provide food once a week during growth. Only when the plants are a few years old will they really start to flower. But there's always the chance they may suddenly die, so keep cuttings.
Propagation: Root middle cuttings under glass at 77–86°F (25–30°C), the whole year.

Light:	Much light or half shade, no sun.
Temp:	Grow warm, not below 64°F (18°C).
Water:	Keep moderately moist with soft water.
Hum:	High, above 60%.
Soil:	Mixture of standard potting soil, leaf mold and loam or clay.

Arpophyllum spicatum

Orchidaceae

Orchids with long, sleek pseudotubers and spectacular flower bunches.

Arpophyllum spicatum

ASCLEPIAS

Asclepias curassavica

Asclepias curassavica

Asclepiadaceae

Milkweed

A delicate half-bush from Florida and Central America.
Care: Grow in a very light room; give much sun and fresh air. In the summer, it can go outside in a very sheltered place. Give plenty of water and add food once every two weeks. In the winter, this plant has to be stored in a light, cool spot. The flowers bloom earlier the second year, but the plants possess less strength for growth then. For that reason, it's best to grow from seeds each year.
Propagation: Sow from January with soil temperature 68–77°F (20–25°C). Prick out the seedlings, cut the tips once for better branching and pot them. The flowers appear from the beginning of August.

Light: Much light, full sun as well.
Temp: Grow cool to moderately warm, in the winter 54–60°F (12–15°C).
Water: Keep moderately moist.
Hum: Moderate.
Soil: Mix standard potting soil with ⅓ part clay or loam.

Asparagus densiflorus 'Sprengeri'

Asparagus asparagoides

Liliaceae

Smilax

A decorative asparagus that differs from other species in its broad, heart-shaped leaves. The vines have been used in bridal wreaths and

Asparagus asparagoides

table decorations because they do not wilt quickly. The white flowers smell like oranges, and are followed in the growth period by purple berries.
Care: Grow in the shade, not too warm. If they have long vines, they have to be tied to sticks or ropes for support. Give plenty of water and fertilize weekly. In the winter, they can be kept cool.
Propagation: Sow from January at soil temperature 32–40°F (0–5°C).

Light: Much light, no bright sunlight.
Temp: Grow moderately warm, in the winter a minimum 46°F (8°C).
Water: Keep moderately moist.
Hum: Moderate to high.
Soil: Standard potting soil.

Asparagus densiflorus

Liliaceae

Asparagus plant

You can see the well-known 'Sprengeri' and the much prettier species 'Meyerii' in the pic-

Asparagus densiflorus 'Meyerii'

tures. Both are equally strong and very suitable for indoor growth.
Care: This asparagus species can stay in a warm room throughout the year, but can be grown at a lower temperature as well. When the plant grows, usually in the spring, fertilize weekly.
Propagation: These genera only propagate by division. The regular species can be cultivated from seed.

Light: Half shade, east-facing window.
Temp: Moderately warm to warm, 54–60°F (12–15°C).
Water: Keep moderately moist.
Hum: Moderate, 50–60%.
Soil: Standard potting soil.

Asparagus falcatus

Liliaceae

Another relative of the edible asparagus, in this case a species with linear leaves. It has enormous vitality and can produce shoots at least 3 ft (1 m) in length. The stalks hang down and have thorns.
Care: The plant is even stronger than the previous species; it can grow anywhere. A warm room is a suitable place, but a cooler one is fine as well. If you want to grow larger plants, then it is important to repot every year and to fertilize weekly during the growth period with a concentration of .06 oz. per quart (2g per liter).
Propagation: From seed, but the plants seldom form seeds. Division is somewhat difficult.

Light: Half shade, or even less.
Temp: Moderately warm to warm, 54–77°F (12–25°C).
Water: Always keep moderately moist.
Hum: Moderate, 50–60%.
Soil: Standard potting soil.

Asparagus falcatus

Asparagus setaceus

Liliaceae

A species that was often grown for ornamental greenery, now used less for that reason. There are different cultivars, such as 'Nanus,' 'Plumosus' and the pictured 'Pyramidalis.' The last is quite suitable as a potted plant.

Care: This species, unfortunately, needs a higher humidity than, for instance, *falcatus*. So grow in a greenhouse, or spray frequently. Give food weekly during the growth period.

Propagation: From seed.

Light: Half shade to much light, no bright sun.

Temp: Grow moderately warm, in the winter a minimum of 50°F (10°C).

Water: Keep moderately moist.

Hum: High, above 60%.

Soil: Mix standard potting soil with ⅓ peat dust or leaf mold.

Asparagus setaceus 'Pyramidalis'

Aspasia lunata

Aspasia lunata

Orchidaceae

Rare orchids from tropical Central and South America, which nonetheless are easy to grow.
Care: The plants have pseudotubers and so need a dry dormant period. With this plant, dormancy should follow the flowering. For the rest of the year, grow warm, providing plenty of water and fresh air. Put orchid fertilizer in the water during the growth period.
Propagation: By division, or from seed.

Light: Half shade, never full sun.
Temp: Grow warm, a minimum of 64°F (18°C).
Water: Except for the dormant period, always provide plenty of rainwater or dip in rainwater.
Hum: High, above 60%.
Soil: Can be grown on pieces of ferntree, but also in pots, filled with rock wool flakes and clay particles.

Aspidistra elatior

Liliaceae

Known for quite a while as a strong houseplant that doesn't need much light. Warmth is necessary. There is a also a spotted cultivar called 'Variegata' that needs more light. Sometimes, just above the soil, a few little flowers can appear.
Care: The common green species can be placed in a north-facing window. Feed once a month during the growth period. Winter temperatures can be lower, but you can keep the plant alive at room temperature.

Propagation: By division.
Light: Half shade or shade.
Temp: Warm to moderately warm, in the winter a minimum of 45°F (7°C).
Water: Keep moderately moist.
Hum: Moderate to low.
Soil: Standard potting soil.

Aspidistra elatior

Asplenium bulbiferum

Aspleniaceae
Mother Fern

A fern that is not very often available, but thrives indoors. There are buds all over the foliage, where the new plants appear. There are a few other species with the same habit, such as *Asplenium daucifolium*.

Care: Provide a shady spot and a humid atmosphere. Feed once every two weeks during the growth period. Keep cooler in the winter, which is favorable for humidity.
Propagation: Wait until the newly formed plants have a few roots, remove these and plant them.

Light: Half shade to shade, never sun.
Temp: Moderately warm to warm, in the winter a minimum of 54°F (12°C).
Water: Keep constantly moist.
Hum: High, above 60%.
Soil: Standard potting soil mixed with extra peat dust or peat moss.

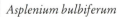

Asplenium bulbiferum

Asplenium marinum

Aspleniceae

A fern that originates along rocky coasts, where it grows in fissures. This culture doesn't do well in the garden, but it thrives in a moderately heated space or cold greenhouse.
Care: Keep out of the sun. Spray frequently once every two weeks during the growth period. Keep cool in the winter.
Propagation: From spurs and by division.

Light:	Shade, never sun.
Temp:	Grow cool, a minimum of 40°F (5°C).
Water:	Keep constantly moist.
Hum:	Moderate to high.
Soil:	Acidic potting soil, for instance coniferous soil mixed with standard potting soil and peat moss.

Asplenium marinum

Asplenium nidus

Aspleniaceae

Bird's-nest fern

A fern with single, large light green leaves that form a funnel-shaped rosette resembling a nest. There is a species of this kind that has carved leaves, called 'Fibriantum.'
Care: A large bird's-nest fern is very attractive, but difficult to maintain during winter in a warm room; the air is too dry. In the summer, however, it will thrive. Feed every two weeks, during the growth period. Keep cooler in the winter and somewhat drier. Spray the leaves very frequently with lukewarm, soft water. Avoid fluctuations in temperature and light, for this will cause disfiguring of the leaf.
Propagation: From spurs, germinate at 32–40°F (0–5°C). The cultivation progresses slowly.

Light:	Half shade.
Temp:	Grow warm, in the winter a minimum of 61°F (16°C).
Water:	Keep constantly moist with soft water.
Hum:	High, above 60%.
Soil:	A special mixture of peat moss with sphagnum and leaf mold.

Asplenium nidus

Astrophytum asterias

Cactaceae

Sea urchin

A flat ball-shaped cactus divided into eight equal segments, completely without thorns. Yellow flowers can develop. Often this species is grafted onto a lower trunk.
Care: Only screen against the brightest afternoon sun. Water sparsely and give cactus food once a month. Keep dormant at lower temperatures and with very little water in the winter.
Propagation: From seed.

Light:	Screen against bright sun.
Temp:	Grow warm to moderately warm, keep at 40–50°F (5–10°C) in the winter.
Water:	Keep rather dry, almost completely dry during dormancy.
Hum:	Can be low.
Soil:	Cactus soil.

Asplenium nidus 'Fibriantum'

Astrophytum asterias

Astrophytum myriostigma var. *strongylogonum*

Astrophytum myriostigma

Cactaceae
Bishop's cap

Very regularly featured cactus with four to five ribs, covered with delicate white dots. There are different varieties that all differ somewhat in shape. Shown here is the *strongylogonum*, which has less angular ribs than some other species. Yellow flowers may appear.
Care: Grow very light, but avoid too much sunlight. In the summer, water moderately and provide cactus food once a month. During dormancy the plant should be kept cool and without a drop of water. Only a misting in the spring is required.
Propagation: From seed, seedlings can be grafted.

Light:	Much light, not too bright.
Temp:	Grow warm, in the winter a minimum of 45°F (7°C).
Water:	Moderate in the summer, in the winter practically dry. Use rainwater.
Hum:	Low, can be below 50%.
Soil:	Cactus soil.

Astrophytum ornatum

Cactaceae

At first ball-shaped, later more column-shaped, this cactus has eight ribs, large thorns and delicate white spots. The flowers are yellow.
Care: Keep warm in the summer and rather light. Cactus food provided once a month is sufficient. A cool dormancy is important; without this, the flowers will not appear.

Propagation: From seed or, if possible, cuttings from the shoots, but these seldom develop.

Light:	Much light, though careful in the bright sun.
Temp:	Grow warm, in the winter cool, a minimum of 45°F (7°C).
Water:	Moderate, almost nothing in the winter.
Hum:	Can be low, below 50%.
Soil:	Cactus soil.

Aucuba japonica

Cornaceae
Japanese laurel

In fact a true garden plant, though it thrives indoors as well, and you can always plant it in a garden later. The spotted varieties 'Crotonifolia,' 'Picturata,' and 'Variegata' are widely cultivated.
Care: This plant is suited to a cool room, especially in the winter. Suitable for a second, occasionally unheated home as well, where it may have a winter dormant period with some frost. Fertilize once every two weeks during the growth period. Prune when it grows too tall. You will only see berries if both male and female specimens are present, and helped by pollinating bees.
Propagation: Cuttings from half-mature wood at 68°F (20°C).

Light:	Half shade.
Temp:	Grow cool, in the winter some frost is allowed.
Water:	Always moderately moist.
Hum:	Moderate, 50–60%.
Soil:	Standard potting soil.

Astrophytum ornatum

Aucuba japonica

Barkeria spectabilis

Orchidaceae

Orchid from Middle America, also called *Epidendrum lindleyanum*. The plants do not have real pseudotubers, but thick stalks, which function as reserve organs.

Care: Preferably grow in a warm greenhouse, with light shade. Give plenty of water in the summer and add orchid food once every two weeks. After the new stalks are full-grown, the plants need a strict dormancy, during which they will lose their foliage. Only after a few months can you start giving them some water again.

Propagation: Divide when you repot.

Light:	Much light, no direct sun.
Temp:	Grow warm, a minimum of 64°F (18°C).
Water:	Plenty of water during growth, provide sufficient drainage.
Hum:	High, above 60%.
Soil:	Grow on pieces of fern tree or in pots filled with rock wool flakes.

Barkeria spectabilis

Bauhinia punctata

Leguminosae

Bushes and trees from the tropics, although grown in greenhouses in our moderate climate. There are various species, such as *acu-*

Bauhinia punctata

minata, which has white flowers and is recommended because this plant flowers at an early age.

Care: Grow light, but screen against bright sunlight. Give plenty of water in the summer and fertilize weekly. In the winter, the temperature may be lower for one species more than another. The species in the picture and *yunnanensis* need to be kept above 40°F (5°C), *acuminata*, 54°F (12°C). Cut back quite a bit in the winter, repot in the spring.

Propagation: From seed or via top cuttings, which root under glass at 86°F (30°C), but only after a long time.

Light:	Much light, no sun.
Temp:	Grow moderately warm, for winter temperatures see above.
Water:	Moderately moist, drier in the winter.
Hum:	Moderate to high.
Soil:	Mixture of standard potting soil and finely ground clay or loam.

Beaucarnea recurvata

Agavaceae

Elephant's foot

A plant that we see more and more of lately. It is often still called *Nolina*. It grows to a height of 33 ft (10 m) in Mexico. The foot is swollen and functions as a water-reservoir.

Care: This plant does not dry out easily, but you can kill it with too much water. It prefers to be outside in the summer in a sheltered spot. Keep the plant cooler in the winter and withhold water. If you repot it once a year or more, fertilization is not needed.

Propagation: From seed or via shoots.

Light:	Full sun.
Temp:	Grow cool to warm, in the winter around 50°F (10°C).
Water:	Very moderate, in the winter almost nothing.
Hum:	Can be low, under 50%.
Soil:	Standard potting soil or cactus soil.

Beaucarnea recurvata

Begonia albopicta

Begoniaceae

A hanging begonia with strange, slanted leaves, called 'Guinea wing.' The surface is marked with silver-white spots. Green and white flowers can appear.

Care: Grow in a north- or east-facing window and keep moderately moist. Fertilize every two weeks during the growth period. To stimulate growth, repot the plant again during the growing season. Keep cooler and drier in the winter, prune in the spring if necessary to encourage new growth.

Propagation: From top cutting or middle cutting. Soil temperature 68°F (20°C).

Light:	Shade to half shade, no sun.
Temp:	Grow moderately warm, in the room a minimum 54°F (12°C).
Water:	Keep moderately moist, preferably with rainwater.
Hum:	Moderate to high.
Soil:	Mixture of standard potting soil and peat dust, peat moss or leaf mould.

Begonia albopicta

Begonia boweri

Begoniaceae

A foliage begonia that stays small, with dark red rootstocks. The leaf is handsomely marked, especially the 'Nigromarga' (see photo). Along the edges of the leaves are beautiful cilia. In the winter, the plant may produce little white flowers, but they are not very spectacular.

Care: A rather hearty houseplant provided you keep it cool in the winter, when the air is less dry. Feed once every two weeks during the growth period. If the plant struggles, prune, place in a cool, dry spot for a while, and bring back to grow.

Propagation: From top cutting or middle cutting.

Light:	Much light, screen against brightest sun.
Temp:	Grow cool to moderately warm; in the winter a minimum 54°F (12°C).
Water:	Keep moderately moist with soft water.
Hum:	Moderate to high.
Soil:	Standard potting soil mixed with at least ⅓ part peat dust or leaf mould.

Begonia 'Cleopatra'

Begoniaceae

A hybridization with brightly marked, maple-shaped leafs. Light red, fragrant little flowers can appear in bunches.

Care: Do not grow in the sun, but not too dark either, otherwise the pretty markings dis-

Begonia boweri 'Nigromarga'

Begonia 'Cleopatra'

appear. Provide a humid atmosphere. Feed once every two weeks during growth period.
Propagation: Plant a piece of the rootstock with a leaf. Soil temperature 68°F (20°C).

Light:	Much light to half shade.
Temp:	Grow moderately warm, in the winter a minimum 60°F (15°C).
Water:	Keep moderately moist.
Hum:	Moderate to high.
Soil:	Acidic and permeable, for instance, standard potting soil mixed with a large amount of leaf mold or peat dust.

Begonia coccinea

Begoniaceae

A terrific shrubby begonia that can reach 10 ft (3 m) in length and bloom lavishly. In a mild climate, the plant can be put outside, but protect it against the bright sun. Give plenty of water and feed weekly. Bring inside for the fall and let it rest dormant rather cool. Prune the

Begonia coccinea

plant if it becomes too large. Repot in the spring and bring back to growth.

Light:	Much light, screen against bright sun.
Temp:	Grow cool to moderately warm, in the winter a minimum of 54°F (12°C).
Water:	Keep moderately moist with soft water.
Hum:	Moderate to high.
Soil:	Standard potting soil mixed with ⅓ part peat dust and leaf mold.

Begonia Corallina hybrids

Begoniaceae

A shrubby begonia that resembles the species we discussed before, *Begonia 'Cleopatra.'* The genera most frequently cultivated— 'Luzerna,' 'Mad. Charrat' or 'President Carnot'—are hybrids with coccinea blood. The large leaf is covered with silver-colored spots. Often, it reaches 6.5 ft (2 m) in height. By that time, the plants are fully decorated with large flower bunches.
Care: You can only grow these plants very large if you repeatedly repot and fertilize. Do not allow too much sun or warmth. In warmer areas, the plant can go outside in the summer, but it is generally considered to be a houseplant. In the winter, the temperature can be lower. Prune plants that grow too big and repot in the spring.
Propagation: It's advisable to strike plenty of top and middle cuttings, because older plants can become less attractive and die from disease.

Light:	Much light, screen against bright sun.
Temp:	Grow moderately warm, in the winter minimum 54°F (12°C).

Begonia Corallina-hybr.

Water:	Keep moderately moist with soft water.
Hum:	Moderate to high.
Soil:	Standard potting soil mixed with a large dose of peat dust or leaf mold.

Begonia X credneri

Begoniaceae

A hybridization of the species *metallica* and *scharffiana*. It inherited its shiny leaves from the first, and its compact way of growing from the second. It is a beautiful small bush begonia for the living room, which produces light-red flowers.
Care: Grow indoors in a light north- or east-facing window. Stimulate growth in the summer by fertilization and repotting. The temperature can be lower in the winter because growth stagnates in that season. In the spring, when necessary repot or grow from new cuttings.
Propagation: From top or middle cuttings.

Light:	Shade or half shade, no sun.
Temp:	Grow moderately warm, in the winter 54–60°F (12–15°C).
Water:	Keep moderately moist with soft water.
Hum:	Moderate to high.
Soil:	Mix standard potting soil with a large part peat dust or with leaf mold.

Begonia X *credneri*

Begonia Elatior-hybr.

Begonia Elatior hybrids

Begoniaceae

Begonia

This is the most popular begonia, often called a Rieger begonia. In the picture, you can see a few species in various colors, but there are plenty more. They are not very durable as houseplants, but they do have striking flowers.

Care: You will get the most pleasure from these plants when they are grown rather cool and kept from sunlight. Fertilize every two weeks. You have to prune the plant and store it cooler and drier for a period, if you want it to live past dormancy. Try to stimulate growth after this, though most of the time, this does not work. The plant can be forced to continue its growth by artificial light. When the artificial light is discontinued, the plant starts to develop buds. In the summer, a similar effect is achieved by putting the plant in darkness.

Propagation: From leaf cutting or middle cutting. Soil temperature 68–77°F (20–25°C).

Light:	Half shade.
Temp:	Grow moderately warm.
Water:	Keep moderately moist with soft water; drier after flowering.
Hum:	Moderate, 50–60%.
Soil:	Standard potting soil.

Begonia X erythrophylla

Begoniaceae

This well-known houseplant was created by the hybridization of the species *hydrocotyli-folia* and *manicata*. The plant has a thick, often horizontal rootstock, that very soon will outgrow the pot. There are a few different cultivars, such as 'Bunchii,' which has curled leaf edges.

Care: The shiny, leathery leaves can endure dry room air quite well, so that this plant can stay in the living room the whole year. Of

Begonia X *erythrophylla*

course, a lower temperature is preferred in the winter. The plant grows more in width than height. Fertilize every two weeks during the growing season.

Propagation: Pieces of rootstock with a leaf root easily in potting soil.

Light:	Half shade, no direct sun.
Temp:	Moderately warm to warm, in the winter a minimum 54°F (12°C).
Water:	Keep moderately moist.
Hum:	Moderate, 50–60%.
Soil:	Standard potting soil with extra peat dust or leaf mold.

Begonia X *erythrophylla*, detail

Begonia grandis

Begoniaceae

A tuberous begonia, that is somewhat hardy, and able to survive light frost. Also known as the species *evansiana*, which in fact is the name of the variety.

Care: Always grow cool, preferably outside. When frost is expected, bring the plants into a greenhouse. In the summer, provide plenty of water and feed every two weeks.

Propagation: Small tubers develop in the leaf axils. They can be used for propagation. Propagation is possible by dividing the tubers as well.

Light:	Half shade.
Temp:	Grow cool, in the winter just keep frost-free.
Water:	Keep moderately moist.
Hum:	Moderate to high.
Soil:	Acidic soil, containing much peat dust or leaf mold.

Begonia grandis var. *evansiana*

Begonia heracleifolia

Begonia heracleifolia

Begoniaceae

An elegant foliage begonia with thick, brown rootstocks and hand-shaped leaves with pretty markings. White and light red flowers can appear.
Care: Preferably grow in a greenhouse, though the plant will survive the summer indoors as well. No direct sunlight. Only feed during the growth period and repot each year (this applies to all species).
Propagation: Divide the rootstocks.

Light:	Half shade.
Temp:	Moderately warm to warm.
Water:	Keep moderately moist with soft water.
Hum:	Moderate to high.
Soil:	Standard potting soil.

Begonia hispida var. cucullifera

Begoniaceae

A peculiar plant with green, hairy leaves, in which—along the prime veins—from so-called adventitious buds small plants seem to appear. In fact, they are only minor outgrowths. They almost never produce flowers.
Care: Continuous care, no full sun. Keep cooler in the winter. Give food every two weeks during the growth period. Prune when plants grow too big, or strike cuttings.

Propagation: From middle cutting.

Light:	Half shade.
Temp:	Moderately warm to warm.
Water:	Keep moderately moist.
Hum:	Moderate to high.
Soil:	Standard potting soil.

Begonia hispida var. *cucullifera*

Begonia imperialis

Begoniaceae

A low, creeping species with emerald green leaves from which only the variety 'smaragdina' is grown. The little white flowers hardly rise above the foliage.

Care: Preferably grown in a greenhouse with sufficient warmth and humidity. Give food every two weeks in the winter. Do not keep the plant too cold in the winter, because this species from Mexico is not hardy enough.
Propagation: By division.

Light:	Much light, no full sun.
Temp:	Grow warm, a minimum 64°F (18°C).
Water:	Keep moderately moist, preferably rainwater.
Hum:	High, above 60%.
Soil:	Acidic, humusy soil, e.g. standard potting soil with extra peat dust or leaf mold.

Begonia imperialis 'Smaragdina'

Begonia tuber-forming hybrids

Begoniaceae
Tuberous begonia

Tuberous begonias, scientifically indicated as *Begonia X tuberhybrida*, are often used in gardens, but the plants are also well-suited for the living room, provided it is not too warm. The hanging types with small flowers, for example, 'Bertinii,' are especially suitable for sheltered, shaded balconies. They are available in dozens of shapes and colors.

Care: The tubers can be sent dry, a help to the mail-order firms. Root the tubers after receiving in March–April, in moist peat dust, temperature around 68°F (20°C). Pot the sprouted tubers, keep moderately warm at first and harden off later, so that the plants, which are not that hardy, can go outside at the end of May. No sun in the summer; give plenty of water and fertilize every two weeks. Withhold water for half of September so that the leaves dry. Store the tubers in a cool environment and in dry soil till the next spring.

Propagation: As soon as the tubers sprout they can be divided. It is possible to grow young shoots with a piece of tuber attached. Do not wet the soil too much, because tubers and cuttings rot easily.

Light:	Half shade, never bright sun.
Temp:	Grow cool, in the winter minimum 43°F (6°C).
Water:	Keep moderately moist.
Hum:	Moderate, 50–60%.
Soil:	Standard potting soil mixed with a half part peat dust.

Begonia X tuberhybrida 'Renaissance'

Begonia limmingheiana

Begoniaceae

One of the many beautiful hanging begonias, these look their best when they hang above a window sill. The plant shown, in fact, is a hybridization, and one that flowers more plentifully than the original species.

Begonia limmingheiana X *solananthera*

Care: A clear window facing north is very suitable for this plant, because it cannot have much sunlight. Provide, if possible, a high humidity and keep the plants cooler in the winter. Feed every two weeks during the growth period. Repot each year.

Propagation: By middle cutting; root at 68–77°F (20–25°C).

Light:	Half shade, no direct sun.
Temp:	Moderately warm to warm.
Water:	Always keep moderately moist.
Hum:	Moderate to high.
Soil:	Standard potting soil.

Begonia Lorraine hybrids

Begoniaceae

A group of hybrids, created in the last century, by hybridization between *Begonia dregei* and *Begonia socotrana*. They are also called small-flowered, winter-blooming begonias. Lately they are grown less than the Rieger types (see Begonia hybrids).

Care: The plants stay in better condition when they are not too warm; 64°F (18°C) is sufficient. Decidedly no sun. Give food once every two weeks during the growth period. After the flowering period, prune back, place in a cooler, drier spot and after that try to bring back to growth. This is not an easy task, which

makes this species—like the Rieger types—a disposable plant.

Propagation: In the winter from leaf cutting, from the middle of March via middle cutting. Soil temperature for leaf cutting 64°F (18°C), for middle cutting 70°F (22°C).

Light:	Half shade, no sun.
Temp:	Moderately warm.
Water:	Keep moderately moist.
Hum:	Moderate, 50–60%.
Soil:	Standard potting soil.

Begonia Lorraine-hybr.

Begonia maculata

Begoniaceae

This is one of the many beautiful shrubby begonias, a plant for a real enthusiast, but one that is not very often available commercially. They can become, with good care, up to 6.5 ft (2 m) high and densely flowered with light red or white flower bunches. The genus shown, 'Picta,' has larger white spots than the usual kind of begonia.

Care: Thrives in a window facing east or a bay window facing north. Never allow exposure to the afternoon sun. Give food weekly during the growing period and repot once or twice. It has great vitality.

Propagation: Easy from top cutting or middle cutting.

Light: Half shade or shade, never full sun.

Begonia maculata 'Picta'

Temp:	Grow moderately warm, winter time a minimum of 54°F (12°C).
Water:	Keep moderately moist, preferably with rainwater.
Hum:	Moderate to high.
Soil:	Standard potting soil mixed with a large amount of peat dust or leaf mold.

Begonia manicata

Begoniaceae

A species easily recognized by its hairy leaf stalks. On the underside too are tufts of red

Shrubby begonias, for example the species *coccinea, maculata, manicata* and *metallica*, are not often available in stores. They are mostly distributed in the form of cuttings, on the "gray" market by plant enthusiasts. The key to success in growing these is a combination of the right location, plenty of fertilizer, frequent repotting and new cuttings each year, because older plants decline rapidly. People who do not heat their homes too much in the winter, for instance those that live in the country, often have terrific specimens.

Begonia manicata

hairs. The cultivar with light yellow leaves is called 'Aureomaculata.' 'Crispa' has frizzy leaf edges.

Care: The plant—often with a twisted, short stalk—grows more in width than in height. Keep away from strong sunlight. Give plenty of water and fertilize regularly during the growth period, at least once every two weeks. In the winter, the temperature can be much lower. Prune back, if necessary, in the spring, repot and bring back to growth.

Propagation: Root pieces of stalk with a leaf. Strike slips often, preferably each year, to ensure the growth of new plants.

Light:	Much light, no full sun.
Temp:	Grow moderately warm, in the winter 54°F (12°C).
Water:	Keep moderately moist, preferably with soft water.
Hum:	Moderate to high.
Soil:	Two-thirds part standard potting soil, ⅓ part peat dust or leaf mold.

Begonia manicata 'Aureomaculata'

Begonia X margaritae

Begoniaceae

A hybrid of the species *echinosepala* and *metallica*. A moderately sized shrubby begonia with shiny, somewhat hairy, leaves and light red flowers.

Care: Do not grow too warm, and provide humidity. Do not spray the hairy leaves, for it may leave deposits. Feed weekly during the growth period. In winter, lower temperatures for dormancy.

Propagation: By division and via middle and eye cuttings.

Light:	Shade or half shade, no sun.
Temp:	Grow moderately warm, in the winter a minimum of 54°F (12°C).
Water:	Keep moderately moist.
Hum:	Moderate to high.
Soil:	Standard potting soil, mixed with ⅓ part peat dust or leaf mold.

Begonia X margaritae

Begonia masoniana

Begoniaceae

A foliage begonia with a very specific leaf marking in the shape of an iron cross. Therefore, the plant is mainly called 'Iron Cross,' but this is not its genus. The plant grows from a rootstock, and the leaf surface is quite bumpy.

Care: Keep from the sun at all times, but do

Begonia masoniana

not place it in too dark a spot because the markings will disappear. Try to keep it continuously in a humid atmosphere. Feed every two weeks during the growth period. Keep cooler in the winter.

Propagation: A leaf with a stalk is sufficient for growing a new plant. Take a cutting at least once a year, because older plants can lose their vitality.

Light:	Much light, no direct sun.
Temp:	Grow moderately warm, in the winter a minimum of 54°F (12°C).
Water:	Always keep moderately moist.
Hum:	Moderate to high.
Soil:	Standard potting soil mixed with a half part peat dust.

Begonia metallica

Begoniaceae

One of the so-called shrubby begonias, plants that can grow easily to 3.3 ft (1 m) high. They

Begonia metallica

have hairy, metallic leaves and light red flowers. They are often used for hybridization.

Care: A suitable houseplant for a shaded window (north- or east-facing). It is a fast-growing plant and may need to be repotted a few times a year. By stimulating growth, you avoid diseases in the plants. Start frequently with new cuttings. Feed weekly during the growth period. Keep cooler in the winter.

Propagation: Via middle cutting, temperature of 68–77°F (20–25°C).

Light:	Half shade.
Temp:	Moderately warm to warm.
Water:	Keep moderately moist.
Hum:	Moderate to high.
Soil:	Standard potting soil mixed with 50% peat dust.

Begonia Rex hybrids

Begoniaceae

Leaf begonia

This species is available everywhere as the 'leaf begonia.' As you most likely know, there are many more varieties of leaf begonias. Almost all the leaf begonias produce flowers, but these are not the main attraction. The leaves of these hybrids—there are dozens—are marked in an exceptionally beautiful way. A number of genera are named, but most of the time they are sold as hybrids and not by their specific names.

Care: These begonias also need high humid-

Begonia Rex-hybr.

ity. They are more durable when placed in a cooler spot. They really flourish in a cool greenhouse. Feed every two weeks during the growth period. Keep somewhat drier and cooler in winter.

Propagation: Easy to propagate by leaf cuttings, or even small pieces of root. Place flat on the soil and lightly sprinkle with sharp sand, so that they stay down. Cover with glass or plastic and keep at a temperature of 68–77°F (20–25°C). Bed out young plants and keep under glass. Mixed species can be grown from seed.

Light:	Half shade, no direct sun.
Temp:	Grow moderately warm.

Water:	Always keep moderately moist.
Hum:	Moderate to high.
Soil:	Standard potting soil.

Begonia rotundifolia

Begoniaceae

Bush-like begonia with parachute-shaped round leaves and scaled leaf stalks.

Care: Grow in a warm, rather light location, for instance in a window facing east or maybe north. Feed every two weeks during the growth period. Provide a high humidity, if possible, especially in the drier winter, when the heat comes on. In the winter, the temperature can be lower, which will help keep the relative humidity up.

Propagation: From leaf cutting or middle cutting. Soil temperature 68–77°F (20–25°C).

Light:	Half shade.
Temp:	Grow moderately warm, in the winter a minimum of 54°F (12°C).
Water:	Keep moderately moist.
Hum:	Moderate to high.
Soil:	Mixture of 50% standard potting soil and 50% peat dust.

Begonia rotundifolia

Begonia rotundifolia

Begonia serratipetala

Begoniaceae

A species from New Guinea with olive-green carved leaves, marked with reddish purple spots. Light red flowers can appear.

Care: Preferably grown in a greenhouse, but in the summer the plant can survive indoors. Do not allow direct sunlight. During the growth period, fertilize every two weeks. Grow this species warmer than the larger bush begonias, even in the winter.

Propagation: Via top or middle cutting.

Light:	Much light, no direct sunlight.
Temp:	Grow moderately warm, in the winter a minimum of 61°F (16°C).
Water:	Keep moderately moist, if possible with soft water.
Hum:	High, above 60%.
Soil:	Standard potting soil with ⅓ part peat dust or leaf mold.

Begonia serratipetala

Summary of discussed begonias suitable for growth indoors or in a greenhouse:

Winter-flowering begonias
  Elatior hybrids
  Lorraine hybrids
  socotrana

Bush begonias
  coccinea
  Corallina hybrids
  maculata
  manicata
  X margaritae
  metallica
  rotundifolia
  venosa

Hanging begonias
  limmingheiana

Leaf begonias
  boweri
  'Cleopatra'
  X credneri
  heracleifolia
  hispida
  masoniana
  Rex hybrids
  serratipetala

Flower and leaf begonias
  X erythrophylla
  imperialis

Tuberous begonias
  grandis
  tuberous hybrids

Begonia venosa

Begonia venosa

Begoniaceae

A peculiar species, notable for its large leaves, which are completely covered with a wax layer. White, fragrant flowers can develop.

Care: Provide plenty of space and regular care. In the winter place in a somewhat cooler and drier spot. Prune when the plants become too large or too ugly. Repot each year. During the growth period, fertilize once every two weeks.

Propagation: From middle cutting.

Light:	Half shade, no direct sun.
Temp:	Moderate to warm, in the winter a minimum of 64°F (18°C).
Water:	Always moderately moist.
Hum:	Moderate to high.
Soil:	Standard potting soil.

Beloperone guttata

Acanthaceae

Shrimp plant

A small bush from Mexico that is easy to grow indoors. The decorative appeal lies in the orange bracts, from which a few little white flowers hang.

Care: The shrimp plant is one of the few that likes full sun. A south-facing window is an excellent place. A sheltered and sunny terrace is suitable for the *Beloperone* as well. If you want to keep the shrimp plant for a second year, then store it in a cooler location over the winter, pruning it back considerably first if the plant has become too large. In the spring, keep it warmer at first so that the plant will grow, then lower the temperature to 54–59°F (12–15°C) during budding. Feed weekly in summer.

Propagation: Root half-ripened top cuttings at 68–77°F (20–25°C) under glass, in the summer or fall. It is possible from seed as well.

Light:	Full sun, screening, at most, only in the middle of the day.
Temp:	Grow cool, a minimum of 54°F (12°C) in the winter.
Water:	Plenty in the summer, less in the winter.
Hum:	Moderate, 50–60%.
Soil:	Standard potting soil.

Beloperone guttata

BELOPERONE

Bergeranthus scapiger

Bergeranthus scapiger

Aizoaceae

One of the many kinds of so-called stalkless mesembryanthemums: succulents that are not hardy in a moderate climate and therefore have to rest dormant inside.
Care: In the summer, these small plants do well outside in the full sun. They do not take up much space and can survive in a pot on the balcony. It is not too serious an error to forget to water them sometimes. Too much water can be life-threatening. Therefore, always grow these plants in very well-drained pots and containers. Feed once every two weeks. In the fall, bring them inside to a cool, frost-free and completely dry space. Too much moisture stimulates rotting. In the spring, they only need some misting before the plants will begin growing again.
Propagation: Remove leaf cuttings, let them dry for a week and plant. Soil temperature 60–68°F (15–20°C).

Light:	Full sun.
Temp:	Grow cool, in the winter 40–50°F (5–10°C).
Water:	Keep rather dry, almost completely dry in the winter.
Hum:	Can be low.
Soil:	Standard potting soil mixed with ⅓ part perlite or sharp sand.

Bertolonia marmorata

Melastomataceae

Small plants from Brazil that need a very high relative humidity. There are various species

Bertolonia marmorata

and hybridizations, some with beautifully marked leafs.
Care: Always grow under glass in high humidity. The humidity cannot be achieved with spraying, because the leaves turn ugly when water falls on them. Fertilize once a month during the growth period. Keep warm in the winter too, for a dormant period is not needed.
Propagation: From seed and via top cuttings that root under glass at 86–95°F (30–35°C) soil temperature. Take cuttings frequently because only the young plants are pretty.

Light:	Much light or half shade, never sun.
Temp:	Grow warm 68–77°F (20–25°C), in the winter a minimum 64°F (18°C).
Water:	Keep moderately moist with soft water.
Hum:	Very high, well above 60%.
Soil:	Coniferous soil in wide, shallow bowls, well-drained.

Bifrenaria harrisoniae

Orchidaceae

A genus of orchid from Brazil with pseudotubers and strikingly beautiful flowers.
Care: The plants are easy to grow (in a greenhouse). They desire light, only need screening from bright sun. In the growth period, provide

Bifrenaria harrisoniae

plenty of (rain)water, and dissolved food once in a while. After the new pseudotubers are formed, there should be a dormant period of a few weeks, during which very little water is allowed and the temperature should be lowered.
Propagation: By division.

Light:	Much light, no bright sun.
Temp:	Moderately warm to warm, during dormancy a minimum of 54°F (12°C).
Water:	Plenty of water in the summer, but watch for stagnant water in the tray.
Hum:	High, above 60%.
Soil:	Grow in baskets with clay particles, rock wool flakes etc. Do not repot that often.

Billbergia nutans

Bromeliaceae

With every bromeliad the old rosette dies after blooming. But this species forms so many side shoots that there always will be some rosettes flowering. For that reason, this is the most easily cared for bromeliad that exists. All the more strange that it is almost never available! Fortunately, some plant enthusiasts give each other cuttings, which grow very easily. And there are also a few other related species for sale that require similar care.
Care: This species is very strong and can be kept outside in the summer. In the winter the plant can stay in the living room; with some spraying, it will survive the winter. A dormancy period is not needed, but you could provide a cooler space. Fertilize every two weeks during the growth period and repot each year.
Propagation: By division.

Light:	Half shade, not too much sun.
Temp:	Grow cool to moderately warm, in the winter a minimum of 58°F (14°C).
Water:	Moderately moist.
Hum:	Moderate.
Soil:	Standard potting soil.

Billbergia nutans

Blechnum species

Blechnaceae

Blechnum brasiliense, *gibbun* and *moorei* are the most well-known species available. The attractively carved leaves form a rosette, and the plants can grow up to 3.3 ft (1 m) high.
Care: With some care these pretty ferns will thrive indoors, at least during the summer. In the winter they may be put in a cooler spot, and one where the air is less dry. Decidedly no sun. Water very regularly (preferably with pots that have a watering system). Feed once a month, using half concentration, dissolved in water.
Propagation: From spurs. Soil temperature 68–77°F (20–25°C).

Light:	Half shade.
Temp:	Moderately warm to warm, in the winter a minimum of 54°F (12°C).
Water:	Moderate to heavy in the summer, in the winter a bit drier, when the plant cools.
Hum:	Moderate to high.
Soil:	Standard potting soil mixed with extra peat dust, coniferous soil or peat particles (acidic and porous).

Blechnum brasiliense

Blechnum spicant

Blechnum spicant

Blechnaceae

A wintergreen fern that can grow outside as well as indoors. The leathery leaves form a rosette, but some individual leaves grow taller. These are the fertile leaf feathers, and they carry reproductive spores.

Care: Grow as cool as possible. In the summer, keep the plant outside in a sheltered location. Always keep moist and feed every two weeks, with half of the normal concentration. Provide a cool dormancy, barely frost-free is warm enough.
Propagation: From spores and by division.

Light:	Half shade.
Temp:	Grow cool; in the winter, keep frost free.
Water:	Always keep moist.
Hum:	Moderate to high.
Soil:	Standard potting soil mixed with peat or coniferous soil.

Blechnum gibbum

Bloomeria crocea

Liliaceae

Tuberous plant that is available once in a while by mail order. It is not hardy.
Care: After receiving the tubers in the spring, pot them in rather large containers or in the full soil of the garden. When the bulbs have sprouted, give plenty of water during the summer, adding food every two weeks. In the fall gradually withhold water, so that the leaves die off. Keep the bulbs frost-free in the ground. Repot in the spring and bring to growth again.
Propagation: From seed or via small newly formed bulbs.

Light:	Full sun.
Temp:	Grow cool, in the winter 40–50°F (5–10°C).
Water:	Constantly keep moist, completely dry during dormancy.
Hum:	Moderate, 50–60%.
Soil:	Mixture of ⅔ part standard potting soil and ⅓ part loam.

Bloomeria crocea

Blossfeldia liliputana

Cactaceae

Genus of very small cacti, no bigger than 0.2–0.6 in (0.5–1.5 cm) in height. The small bulbs have ribs and no thorns. Because these cacti often grow in groups, there can be a beautiful floral display during the flowering period.

Blossfeldia liliputana

Care: In a moderate climate, it is advised to graft this species onto the lower trunk of another cactus. The natural form gets somewhat lost this way, but the growth and flowering become much better. Give cactus food once a month. Keep dry and cool in the winter.
Propagation: By removing the side sprouts and regrafting.

Light:	Full sun.
Temp:	Moderately warm to warm.
Water:	Keep rather dry, in the winter almost completely dry.
Hum:	Low to moderate.
Soil:	Cactus soil.

Bomarea caldasii

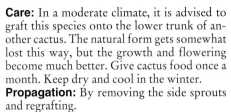

Bomarea caldasii

Liliaceae

Climbing plant from the Andes, where this plant grows at an altitude of 11,500 ft (3,500 m). It is related to the *Alstroemeria*, a famous garden plant and cut flower.
Care: This culture does not do well in pots. Therefore, plant in the full soil of a greenhouse, shading against the bright afternoon sun. Ventilate well during summer nights; the greenhouse temperature can drop considerably. Give plenty of water during the growth period and fertilize every two weeks. Keep drier and very cool in the winter, but frost-free. The plant will come out again in the spring, when large flower bunches will begin to appear. Give support when needed.
Propagation: By division of the rootstocks or from seed.

Light:	Much light, no full sun.
Temp:	Grow moderately warm, in the winter 32–40°F (0–5°C).
Water:	Keep moderately moist, drier in the winter.
Hum:	Moderate to high.
Soil:	Improve the soil in the greenhouse by adding leaf mold or potting soil and provide good drainage.

Borzicactus species

Cactaceae

A member of the column cactus family from South America. The name is confusing: Various species are classified under other genera, for instance *Matucana* and *Oreocereus*. The columns rarely stand straight: They mainly lie flat on the ground.
Care: A real collector's item because the columns often bloom at an early age. Grow sunny in the summer, possibly outside in a sheltered location, but ideally in a greenhouse. Plant out in the full soil of the greenhouse. Give moderate amounts of water and cactus food once a month. During the winter dormancy, keep

Borzicactus samaipatanus

cool, but not as cool as is necessary for most other cacti. Keep drier, too.
Propagation: From seed. Seedlings will grow when grafted onto *Trichocereus spachianus*.

Light:	Full sun.
Temp:	Grow moderately warm, in the winter 50–60°F (10–15°C).
Water:	Keep rather dry to moderately moist.
Hum:	Low to moderate.
Soil:	Cactus soil or standard potting soil.

Bougainvillea spectabilis

Nyctaginaceae

A climbing plant that we find in gardens in subtropical countries all over the world. This species is a very popular houseplant, and there are several hybrids available with differently colored bracts, for instance orange-red or white. The flowers are always white.
Care: These plants like sun and fresh air, but they are not hardy. For that reason, they have to lay dormant in a cool but frost-free spot. The leaves may drop. After the flowering period, you can prune considerably. During the growth period, feed once a week.

Borzicactus aureispina

Propagation: Root half-wooded middle cuttings in the spring at a soil temperature of 77°F (25°C).

Light:	Full sun.
Temp:	Grow moderately warm to warm, in the winter a minimum of 45°F (7°C).
Water:	Plenty of water in the summer, less during the cool dormancy.
Hum:	Low to moderate.
Soil:	Standard potting soil.

Bougainvillea spectabilis

Bouvardia hybrids

Rubiaceae

Famous, fragrant cut flowers, they last for a long time in water. They are known less as houseplants, but can be grown and kept in the house. Besides the hybrids, pure species are also considered for this purpose.

Care: Grow in an airy, light-protected greenhouse. It can also be grown outside from the end of May in a sheltered location. Always provide plenty of water and feed once a week. Bring inside at the end of the winter and store cool. Divide in the spring, repot and bring to growth again. Cut the tops at least two times for better branching. Tie up if necessary.

Propagation: Grow young cuttings in the early spring with a soil temperature of 68–77°F (20–25°C). Cut the tops a few times.

Light:	Much light, screen against bright sunlight.
Temp:	Grow cool to moderately cool, in the winter 40–50°F (5–10°C).
Water:	Keep moderately moist, somewhat drier in the winter.
Hum:	Moderate, 50–60%.
Soil:	Standard potting soil with extra-decayed cow manure or leaf mold.

Bouvardia-hybr. 'Mary'

BOWIEA

Bowiea volubilis

Liliaceae

A very ornamental and peculiar plant that consists of a large bulb, from which grow hanging or climbing stalks with smaller flower-stalks, which function as leaves.
Care: The bulb stores water. When the green part dies off entirely, the bulb can be stored for months without water at a low temperature. The fading of the foliage starts as early as the summer. From then on, withhold water, otherwise the plant will rot. New shoots appear in the winter, but be careful when first watering. Place in a warm spot, though. When the plant really starts to grow, water moderately and place in a light location. Feed once a month.
Propagation: By dividing the bulbs.

Light: Full sun.

Bowiea volubilis

Temp:	Grow warm to moderately warm, during dormancy 43–50°F (6–10°C).
Water:	Keep rather dry, completely dry during dormancy.
Hum:	Low to moderate.
Soil:	Mixture of standard potting soil with loam or clay and perlite.

Brachychiton rupestris

Sterculiaceae

Bottle tree

This is one of the 'bottle tree' species that can become 50 ft (15 m) high in Australia. Water is stored in the very thick, bottle-shaped trunk. The picture shows a young specimen with a strange twisted trunk.
Care: These plants like plenty of sun and can be outside in a sheltered spot in the summer. In the winter, place in a cooler location and water sparsely.
Propagation: From seed or top cuttings from ripe shoots.

Brachychiton rupestris

Light:	Much light, full sun allowed.
Temp:	Grow moderately warm, in the winter not below 54°F (12°C).
Water:	Keep rather dry.
Hum:	Can be low.
Soil:	Standard potting soil with 50% sharp sand.

Brasiliopuntia brasiliensis

Cactaceae

A prickly pear related to the *Opuntia*, originally from South America, where it can grow up to 13 ft (4 m) high.
Care: This strong, rough-looking cactus grows effortlessly and can be outside in the summer. Allow a cool and very dry dormant period in order to get flowers on the older specimens. During the growth period provide cactus food once a month.
Propagation: From seed, or by removing the discs, letting them dry for a couple of days and planting.

Brasiliopuntia brasiliensis

Light:	Full sun.
Temp:	Grow cool, in the winter not below 40°F (5°C).
Water:	Keep rather dry, withhold water in the winter.
Hum:	Low.
Soil:	Cactus soil or standard potting soil.

Brassaia actinophylla

Araliaceae

Often called *Schefflera*, the name of this species has recently changed. Young plants have compound leaves with 3–7 blades, older plants, 7–15 blades. As far as I know, they do not flower.
Care: Grow in a light and airy environment; in the summer, the plant can go outside. A cooler dormancy is very important, because the leaves will get damaged by warm, dry air. Prune plants that grow too large and repot. During the growing season, fertilize weekly.
Propagation: Most successfully from imported, new seeds. Cuttings are problematic.

Brassaia actinophylla

Light:	Much light, little sun.
Temp:	Grow cool, in the winter a minimum of 50°F (10°C).
Water:	Always keep moderately moist.
Hum:	Moderate to high.
Soil:	Standard potting soil.

Brassavola flagellaris

Orchidaceae

These orchids are quite easy to grow, and have rather small flowers on the ends of long, thin, cylindrical pseudotubers, topped by a long, narrow, meaty leaf. If they are provided with a high humidity, they can be cultivated indoors.

Care: The plants desire much light, but hate bright afternoon sun. Give plenty of (rain)water in the summer and spray frequently. Give orchid food once every two weeks. When the new pseudotubers are full grown, a dormancy of a few weeks is needed. Withhold water then and keep cooler.

Propagation: By division, when you repot. Do not repot too often.

Light:	Much light, no bright sunlight.
Temp:	Grow warm to moderately warm, a minimum of 54°F (12°C) while dormant.
Water:	Plenty of water provided there is a sufficient drainage. Keep dry during rest periods.
Hum:	High, above 60%.
Soil:	Pot in baskets with good drainage, filled with a mixture of clay particles, rock wool flakes, possibly some organic material such as sphagnum, fern roots, etc. One can attach the plant to a piece of fern tree as well.

Brassavola flagellaris

Brassia maculata

Brassia maculata

Orchidaceae

Orchids from subtropical and tropical America, provided with flat pseudotubers with one to three large, leathery leaves. The rather small flowers are attached to very long stalks.

Care: Rather easy to grow, even in the living room. Provide humid air by spraying frequently. Much light is needed, so only screen against the brightest afternoon sun. Give plenty of water with dissolved food once in a while.

Propagation: By division or from seed.

Light:	Much light, screen against bright sunlight.
Temp:	Grow warm, during dormancy a minimum of 56°F (13°C) night temperature.
Water:	Plenty of water during the growth period, with soft water; otherwise quite dry.
Hum:	High, above 60%.
Soil:	Tie to pieces of fern tree, or grow in pots or baskets filled with rock wool flakes.

X *Brassocattleya thorntonii*

X Brassocattleya

Orchidaceae

A hybridization of the orchids *Brassavola* and *Cattleya*.
Care: Similar to *Cattleya*. Grow with a lot of light, screening only against the bright afternoon sun. Always provide plenty of water, but make sure the plant is well drained. Use only soft water. Add orchid food once every two weeks, as long as the plant grows, or give a very light concentration daily when the plant grows in nonorganic material. When the pseudotubers are full grown, the plants should be withheld water for a few weeks. The temperature can be lower in the winter.
Propagation: By division during repotting.

Light: Much light, screen only against the brightest light.
Temp: Grow warm, in the summer a minimum of 60°F (15°C), in the winter 54°F (12°C).
Water: Plenty of (rain)water in the summer, rather dry during the rest of the year.
Hum: High, above 60%.
Soil: Mixture of pieces of tree fern, bark, clay particle etc., but pure rock wool flakes work as well.

X Brassolaeliocattleya

Orchidaceae

A very complicated name that indicates the hybridization of the genera *Brassavola*, *Laelia* and *Cattleya*.

X *Brassolaeliocattleya*-hybr.

Care: Similar to *Cattleya*. Grow very light, screening only against the brightest sun. Give plenty of water during the growing season. Add a solution of orchid fertilizer every two weeks. The new pseudotubers need a few weeks to rest dormant after they're fully grown.

Light: Much light, screen against the brightest light.
Temp: Grow warm, in the winter a minimum of 54°F (12°C).
Water: Plenty of water in the summer, almost no water during dormancy.
Hum: High, above 60%.
Soil: Often grown in pure rock wool flakes, in which case add a little fertilizer to the water. Otherwise grow in pieces of fern tree, clay particles, etc.

Breynia disticha

Euphorbiaceae

A lesser known but pretty leaf plant suitable for the greenhouse, but durable indoors during the summer. Small bell-shaped flowers may appear. The spotted cultivar 'Rosea Pictum' is almost always available (see photo).
Care: Provide continually high humidity and keep out of the sun. Feed once every two weeks in the summer.
Propagation: In the summer, top cuttings or middle cuttings. Soil temperature 68–77°F (20–25°C).

Light: Much light, no full sun.
Temp: Grow warm to moderately warm, in the winter a minimum of 62°F (16°C).
Water: Keep continually moist.
Hum: High, above 60%.
Soil: Standard potting soil.

Breynia disticha 'Rosea Pictum'

Brosimum alicastrum

Moraceae

Almost everybody assumes this to be a *Ficus*, but it is a different genus. Not much is written about it, which is strange, because it is an excellent houseplant.

Care: Like the *Ficus*, this plant can be kept in a warm living room throughout the year. Do not allow bright sunlight; the plant can tolerate quite a lot of shade. Feed every two weeks during the growth period.

Propagation: Top cuttings root easily under glass at moderate temperatures.

Light: Half shade or shade, no sun.
Temp: Grow warm, a minimum of 64°F (18°C).
Water: Keep moderately moist.
Hum: Low to moderate.
Soil: Standard potting soil.

Brosimum alicastrum

Browallia speciosa

Solanaceae

Half bushes from South America that are mostly annual in our climate. They can bloom plentifully for a large part of the summer. There are various genera, generally in purple and violet-blue tints.

Care: Mostly available in the spring. Feed weekly and keep the plants in the light and not too hot. Remove old flowers. Dormancy is possible, but it is only worth keeping dormant in order to use the cuttings to root new plants.

Propagation: From seed or top cuttings (from newly sowed plants as well). Start this in December. Soil temperature 68–77°F (20–25°C). Put 4–5 young plants in the final pot. Because *Browallia* gets rather tall, growers often spray the plants with a growth inhibitor (alar). You can limit the growth by cutting the tops a few times.

Light: Much light, but not full sunlight.
Temp: Grow cool, in the winter a minimum of 45°F (7°C).
Water: Moderately moist.
Hum: Moderate, 50–60%.
Soil: Standard potting soil.

Brunfelsia species

Solanaceae

Some people are quite successful with these pretty houseplants. They are not very easy to care for, but this makes it quite rewarding when they flower.

Brunfelsia latifolia

Brunfelsia pauciflora var. *calycina*

Browallia speciosa

Care: The flowering plant needs food every two weeks. Keep from bright sunlight. Do not place in too warm a spot, and grow, if possible, in the garden or in a sheltered spot outside. Avoid large fluctuations in temperature. Yellow leaves can be caused by water that is too hard or too soft. Keep cool for at least six weeks from the end of October. This stimulates bud formation. Fertilize a few times during dormancy. Bring gradually to growth again.

Propagation: From top cutting or middle cutting, soil temperature 77°F (25°C). Use a growth hormone.

Light: Much light, never full sun.
Temp: Grow cool to moderately warm, in the winter a minimum of 60°F (15°C).
Water: Keep moderately moist, preferably with rainwater.
Hum: Moderate to high.
Soil: Standard potting soil.

Bulbophyllum 'Louis Sander'

Bulbophyllum species

Orchidaceae

Orchids with a creeping rootstock, from which the often triangular pseudotubers grow. A meaty leaf appears on these pseudotubers. The species and their hybrids look very similar. The natural species *longissimum* and *ornatissimum* combined, create the beautiful 'Louis Sander.'
Care: The plants need a very light location, but no direct sunlight should touch them. It is better to grow the plants on pieces of fern tree or in lattice baskets, because the long rootstock begins creeping out of the pot at an early stage. Plenty of water is necessary throughout the year, and a high humidity. Keep somewhat dry when the pseudotubers are full grown. Repot only when really needed.
Propagation: By division or from seed.

Light:	Much light, no bright sun.
Temp:	Grow warm to moderately warm, in the winter a minimum of 58°F (14°C).
Water:	Plenty in the growing period, provided there is sufficient drainage.
Hum:	High.
Soil:	Pieces of fern tree or rock wool flakes.

Bulbophyllum rufinum

Caesalpinia gilliesii

Caesalpinia species

Leguminosae

Evergreen and deciduous bushes or small trees from Asia and South America, which can be cultivated in a moderate climate or greenhouse, and in Southern Europe, outside as well. One of the species is called *coriaria*, better known as the Divi-divi tree of Aruba.
Care: The hardiest species, *Caesalpinia decapetala*, can be outside during the summer in a sunny and sheltered place. Give plenty of water and dissolved food every two weeks. The leaves will drop in the fall. Bring inside (a darker location is allowed) and keep until the spring at the minimum temperature of 54°F (12°C). Repot in April, prune if necessary, place in a warm spot and bring outside at the end of May.
Propagation: By layer, from seed or via top cuttings of side shoots. Soil temperature 77–86°F (25–30°C).

Light:	Full sun.
Temp:	Grow warm to moderately warm, in the winter a minimum of 54°F (12°C).
Water:	Keep moderately moist.
Hum:	Moderate to high.
Soil:	Mix standard potting soil with extra loam or clay. Drain pot well.

Caesalpinia decapetala

Caladium Bicolor hybrids

Aracea

Leaf plants with tuberous rootstocks. They have striking leaf markings. There are many genera, sometimes named, but this plant is mainly sold as an indeterminate mixture.
Care: These plants are best suited for a greenhouse, and they can only stay indoors for a short time during the summer. The plant needs high humidity. One way to deal with this species is to let it die off in the fall, so that the tubers can rest dormant in dry soil at 64°F

(18°C). Then you can bring the plant back in the spring, keeping the relative humidity rather high during the time the plant makes new shoots.
Propagation: By dividing the tuberous roots. Treat wounds against fungus and plant at a soil temperature of 68–77°F (20–25°C).

Light: Much light, never full sun.
Temp: Grow warm.
Water: Keep moderately warm, except during dormancy.
Hum: High during growth.
Soil: Special mixture, very permeable, humus-rich and rather acidic.

Caladium Bicolor-hybr. 'Frieda Hemple'

Caladium Bicolor-hybr. 'Candidum'

Calanthe triplicata

Orchidaceae

An evergreen species without pseudotubers. The flowers are situated along the very long stalk.
Care: This is a terrestrial (soil-growing) orchid that should never be allowed to become completely dry. Grow warm in the summer and provide enough water and humid air. Screen against direct sunlight. Feed at half concentration weekly during the growing period. After the new shoots have formed, give the plant a short dormant period, providing less water.
Propagation: By division.

Calanthe triplicata

Light: Much light, no bright sun.
Temp: Grow warm, a minimum of 64°F (18°C).
Water: Keep moderately moist, less water during dormancy.
Hum: High, above 60%.
Soil: Mixture with leaf mold, decayed cow manure, ground loam or clay and perlite for sufficient drainage. Use pots with a drainage system.

Calanthe vestita

Orchidaceae

A deciduous *Calanthe*, a species with pseudotubers. This culture varies from the species discussed before. There are many Vestita hybrids as well. Other species with pseudotubers are *labrosa* and *rosea*.
Care: Grow moderately warm in the summer, allowing light but never bright sunlight. Give plenty of water, but provide excellent drainage in the pots, so that water can flow easily, otherwise rotting will occur. Provide orchid food once every two weeks during the growth period. Continually add food to the water, unless you grow the plant in rock wool, in which case use very light concentrations. In the fall, when the new pseudotubers are full grown, the leaves will turn yellow and dry out. Remove old leaves. Give less water or even stop the water supply entirely. The plants will start to flower now. After the blooming, repot

and divide. Put each pseudotuber in a new pot, but temporarily stop watering. Keep cool. Only after the new shoots have reached a length of 2 in. (5 cm) can one gradually supply the plants with water and raise the temperature.
Propagation: By division.

Light: Much light, no bright sun.
Temp: Grow moderately warm, in the winter 50–58°F (10–14°C).
Water: Plenty of (rain)water in the growing period, almost dry during the winter.
Hum: High, above 60%.
Soil: Mixture of peat moss, fern tree and clay particles, or pure rock wool flakes.

Calanthe Vestita-hybr.

Calathea crocata

Marantaceae

The only species of this genus that is sold in bloom, though we have to put up with less interesting leaves.

Care: Always grow warm and provide humidity. During the flowering period—mainly in the spring—the plant can live temporarily in the living room. Give food in light concentrations, every two weeks in the summer. One can divide the larger plants in September. They come back to flower the following spring.

Propagation: By division.

Calathea crocata

Light:	Half shade, no full sun.
Temp:	Grow warm, not below 61°F (16°C).
Water:	Keep moderately moist, preferably with rainwater.
Hum:	High, above 60%.
Soil:	Coniferous soil with pieces of peat.

Calathea lancifolia

Marantaceae

A distinctive foliage plant with interesting marked, lancet-shaped leaves, tinted red on the leaves' undersides.

Care: The *Calathea* is suited to keep in the living room all year. Unfortunately, the humidity is often too low in the winter, causing the plants to decline. The temperature can rise above 68°F (20°C). Dormant periods are not necessary. Direct sunlight may burn the foliage, so always screen. If the plant is doing well you can give a light concentration of food once every two weeks (.033 oz. per quart); (1 g per liter).

Propagation: By division. Take young parts with at least three leaves.

Light:	Half shade, never full sun.
Temp:	Grow warm, a minimum of 61°F (16°C).
Water:	Keep moderately moist.

Calathea lancifolia

Hum: High (the professional grower gives 80%).
Soil: Acidic potting soil, pH 5.0–5.5. Rough peat is ideal, possibly mixed with coniferous soil.

Calathea makoyana

Marantaceae

Famous foliage plant with a prettily marked leaf that is reddish on the leaf's underside.
Care: This is probably the strongest of the many *Calathea* species, but this plant, too, needs a high humidity. It thrives in plant cases, between other plants, rather than in a solitary spot. Dormant periods are not needed; the temperature can be high all year. Much light is good, but never allow direct sun. During the growth period, fertilize once every two weeks in half concentrations.
Propagation: By division.

Light: Half shade, never direct sun.
Temp: Grow warm, a minimum of 61°F (16°C).
Water: Always keep moderately moist.
Hum: High, above 60%.
Soil: Acidic potting soil, pH between 5.0–5.5. Often used is a mixture of rough peat and coniferous soil.

Calathea makoyana

Calathea ornata 'Roseo-lineata'

Calathea ornata

Marantaceae

One of the most famous (and strongest) species, with long stalks and shiny green leaves that show clear lines between the veins.
Care: Never grow in the sun and provide high humidity, possibly by spraying frequently with (rain)water. Do not keep it too cool in the winter. In the growing season, feed once every two weeks in light concentration.
Propagation: By division.

Light: Half shade, never full sun.
Temp: Grow warm, never below 61°F (16°C).
Water: Keep moderately moist with soft water.
Hum: High.
Soil: Acidic, permeable potting soil, for instance peat moss mixed with coniferous soil.

Calathea roseopicta

Calathea picturata 'Argentea'

Marantaceae

An exceptionally pretty plant with large, interestingly marked leaves. Another genus is called 'Vandenheckei.' The dark green foliage is light green along the middle vein and has a light green, irregular ring along the leaf edge as well.
Care: Difficult to keep in a warm room, especially in the winter, the humidity becomes too low then. Much light is needed, but direct sun will lead to burning. Temperatures up to 86°F (30°C) are OK. Once very 14 days give a light fertilizing (.033 oz per quart; 1 g per liter).
Propagation: By division (in moderately sized pieces).

Light: Much light is favorable, but never direct sunlight.
Temp: Grow warm, a minimum of 61°F (16°C).
Water: Keep moderately moist.
Hum: High, above 60%.
Soil: Acidic potting soil. A mixture of rough peat and coniferous soil works well.

Calathea picturata 'Argentea'

Calathea roseopicta

Marantaceae

Perhaps the most beautiful species, with its striking marked leaves. Unfortunately, these are the most troublesome to cultivate, as is often the case.
Care: Preferably in a greenhouse or in a plant window, quite light, but screened against bright sun. In the summer, fertilize every week. Provide a high relative humidity. Keep warm in the winter as well.
Propagation: By division.

Light: Much light, no full sun.
Temp: Grow warm, a minimum of 64°F (18°C).
Water: Keep moderately moist with soft water.
Hum: High, far above 60%.
Soil: Acidic, humus-rich, permeable soil, for instance coniferous soil.

CALCEOLARIA

Calceolaria hybrids

Scrophlariaceae
Slipper flower

Annual plants that are available in large numbers around Mother's Day. They come in various colors. Keeping them alive long is barely possible, which makes them true disposable plants.
Care: If you want to enjoy this plant as long as possible, then it should have a cool spot and be kept from sunlight. Give plenty of water and fertilize once every two weeks in half concentration.
Propagation: The professional grower sows from June to the end of September. Cuttings are possible too, keeping the temperature no higher than 64°F (18°C). After six weeks, they can be planted out and after another six weeks, they should be placed in the final flower pot. By keeping the plants cool—around 46–50°F (8–10°C)—the flowerbuds will begin to develop. After this, put the plants under artificial light to stimulate the bud growth.

Calceolaria-hybr.

Light:	Never in the full sun.
Temp:	Grow cool, in the winter a minimum 64°F (18°C).
Water:	Keep moderately moist.
Hum:	High, above 60%.
Soil:	Extra acidic soil, the so-called *Calceolaria* soil.

Calliandra harrisii

Leguminosae

A bush from Mexico known in the United States as the Powderpuff. The ornamental flowers are formed by the long, thin, brightly colored stamens. Other species sometimes have nicely feathered foliage, such as the *Calliandra tweedii*.
Care: Grow light in a greenhouse or indoors during the summer. Screen against the bright sun. Fertilize every two weeks. In the winter place in a cool spot. Allow enough light that the plant stays green.
Propagation: Root top cuttings under glass at a soil temperature of 68–77°F (20–25°C).

Calliandra harrisii

Light:	Much light, no bright sun.
Temp:	Grow moderately warm, in the winter a minimum of 54°F (12°C).
Water:	Keep moderately moist.
Hum:	Moderate, 50–60%.
Soil:	Standard potting soil.

Callisia species

Commelinaceae

Rather strong houseplants, although the relationship with, for instance, *Tradescantia* is not always clearly recognizable. Some species suggest a bromeliad. The small, white flowers are scarcely noticeable.
Care: Grow preferably in rather large hanging pots, in a light spot, but not in the sunlight. Give plenty water and feed weekly. In the winter, allow for lower temperatures to achieve a higher humidity.
Propagation: Root the top cuttings under glass, soil temperature 68°F (20°C).

Light:	Half shade or much light. No sun.
Temp:	Grow moderately warm, in the winter a minimum 54°F (12°C).
Water:	Keep moderately moist.
Hum:	Moderate, 50–60%.
Soil:	Standard potting soil.

Callistemon citrinus

Myrtaceae
Myrtle

A quite rare and beautiful plant that can grow rather tall and is very suitable for a terrace in the summer.

Callisia elegans

Callisia fragrans

Callistemon citrinus

Camellia japonica

Care: The problem is to find a cool spot during the winter, where the plant can stay at a low temperature. A warm room is not a suitable spot for its dormancy. In the spring, repot if necessary, and bring to growth again. At the end of May put outside in a sunny, sheltered spot. Fertilize every two weeks. Prune after blooming to keep the plant compact.
Propagation: From top cuttings in August, soil temperature 68–77°F (20–25°C). Cut the tops of young plants a few times.

Light:	Full sun.
Temp:	Grow cool, in the winter 43–50°F (6–10°C).
Water:	Keep moderately moist with soft water, less water in the winter.
Hum:	Moderate.
Soil:	Extra acidic, so add coniferous soil or peat mold to the mixture.

Calocephalus brownii

Compositae

A completely gray, whimsical little bush that can grow 12–20 in (30–50 cm) high. The leaves are extremely small.

Care: The small plant can grow outside in the summer without trouble, given a sunny place. Feed once every two weeks. In the fall bring the plant inside and keep cool.
Propagation: Top cuttings can root in the spring as well as in the fall. Soil temperature 68–77°F (20–25°C).

Calocephalus brownii

Light:	Full sun.
Temp:	Grow cool, in the winter a minimum of 40°F (5°C).
Water:	Keep moderately moist, drier in the winter.
Hum:	Moderate, 50–60%.
Soil:	Standard potting soil.

Camellia japonica

Theaceae

The camellia is not often available as a houseplant, and to be honest, it is not very well suited as such. It is grown more as a container plant. There are a number of beautiful species for sale.
Care: A camellia has to grow cool and lie dormant almost frost-free. It flowers early in the year. If the temperatures are too high and the humidity too low, the buds will drop. Turning the plant in relation to the light can also cause this. Halfway through May, the flowering period is over and the plant can go outside, sheltered and somewhat shaded. Every 14 days, provide some lime-deficient food. Immediately after the flowering period, one can prune the plant if necessary. Halfway through October, bring the plant inside for a cool dormancy.
Propagation: From top cuttings. Use growth hormones and soil temperature of 68–77°F (20–25°C).

Light:	Half shade.
Temp:	Grow cool, in the winter just frost free.
Water:	Always keep moderately moist with soft water.
Hum:	High.
Soil:	Extra acidic soil, for instance coniferous soil.

Camellia sinensis

Theaceae
Tea plant

Once in a while, the tea plant is sold as a house-
or container plant. It is a pretty foliage plant;
the white flowers are small and do not appear
that often in our climate. The leaves are not
immediately suitable for making tea; only after
drying, fermenting and other processing can
the leaves be used for brewing tea.
Care: Grows best in a moderate to cold
greenhouse. Possibly, in the summer, the plant
can go outside in a very protected, shaded
location. Give it plenty of water and fertilize
once every two weeks. Do not keep too warm
in the winter.
Propagation: From top cuttings and from
seed, soil temperature 68–77°F (20–25°C).

Camellia sinensis

Light:	Much light, screen against the brightest sun.
Temp:	Grow cool to moderately warm, in the winter 46–50°F (8–10°C).
Water:	Keep moderately moist, with soft water or rainwater if possible.
Hum:	High, above 60%.
Soil:	Standard potting soil mixed with 50% coniferous soil or peat mould.

Campanula fragilis

Campanulaceae

Campanula fragilis 'Carol Foster'

Campanula isophylla 'Alba'

A richly flowering bell-shaped flower from
Italy, lesser known than the next species, but
very much worth discovering.
Care: Like the *isophylla*, grow airy and light,
only screening against bright sun. Feed
weekly in the summer. Dormancy is possible
if the plants are kept cool, and pruned considerably.
Propagation: Sow from January with moderate warmth, bed out and top cut a few times
for better branching.

Light:	Much light, screen against the brightest sun.
Temp:	Grow cool, in the winter at 50–54°F (10–12°C).
Water:	Keep constantly moist, in the winter somewhat drier.
Hum:	Moderate to high.
Soil:	Standard potting soil mixed as much as possible with extra clay (lime).

Campanula isophylla

Campanulaceae

An easy blooming plant that is available in
white and violet colors. Perennial plants in big
hanging pots can produce thousands of flowers.
Care: In the summer, the plant can be outside
(no draft) as well as indoors. It can endure sun
and shade, as long as the ball of soil does not
dry out. Prune back in the fall, allow a cool

dormancy and bring back to growth in the
spring again. By extending the day (see page
55), early bloom may occur.
Propagation: From mid-November, remove top cuttings of about 2 in (5 cm) and dip
in lukewarm water so that the latex solidifies.
After that put it in a rooting hormone and then
in the cutting soil. Soil temperature 68°F
(20°C). Cover well with plastic or glass. Roots
appear only after about five weeks. Three to
four cuttings fit in a pot and when they start
to grow, they have to be cut at the top a few
times to allow for better branching.

Light:	Light, but not bright sun.

Campanula isophylla 'Mayi'

Temp:	Grow cool, in the winter between 45–54°F (7–12°C).
Water:	Always moderately moist.
Hum:	Moderate, 50–60%.
Soil:	Standard potting soil.

Canna Indica hybrids

Cannaceae

A rootstock plant that quite often is grown in gardens. It is not hardy, so the rots have to be dug up in the fall, as with the *Dahlia*. Smaller species are sometimes sold as houseplants, as for example the hybrid pictured.

Care: When flowering, the plants are rather pretty, but it's not easy to keep the flowers in bloom. They flower more successfully in a garden. Feed weekly. In the fall, after the first frost, dig up and provide a dry dormancy, as for *Dahlia* tubers. In the spring, replant and bring back to growth with warmth. The plants will grow taller now.

Propagation: By division of the rootstocks.

Light:	Full sun.
Temp:	Grow cool to moderately warm, in the winter about 59°F (15°C).
Water:	Moderately moist, in winter very dry.
Hum:	Moderate.
Soil:	Standard potting soil.

Cantua buxifolia

Polemoniaceae

Canna Indica-hybr. 'Lucifer'

A not-very-well-known, but quite impressive evergreen container or greenhouse plant, originating in the Andes. They can grow to 6.6 ft (2 m) high.

Care: From the end of May these plants can be put in pots or containers in a very protected, sunny outdoor location. Give plenty of water then and feed once every two weeks until the beginning of August. In the fall, move the plant to a greenhouse and keep at a moderate temperature. Bind up older plants.

Propagation: Root half-ripe top cuttings under glass at a soil temperature of 60–68°F (15–20°C).

Light:	Full sun.
Temp:	Grow cool, in the winter 46–50°F (8–10°C).
Water:	Keep moderately moist, drier in the winter.
Hum:	Moderate to high.
Soil:	Mix standard potting soil with ⅓ part fine clay or loam.

Cantua buxifolia

Capparis spinosa

Capparaceae

Caper bush

This original caper bush comes from the Mediterranean. The flower buds are put in jars with vinegar and sold as capers.

Care: Grow in a cold greenhouse or as a container plant outside in the summer. Give plenty of water and feed once every two weeks. In the fall, move the plant inside and provide a frost-free dormancy.

Propagation: From seed and via top cuttings, which root under glass at 68–77°F (20–25°C).

Light:	Full sun.
Temp:	Grow cool to moderately warm, in the winter 40–50°F (5–10°C).
Water:	Keep moderately moist.
Hum:	Moderate, 50–60%.
Soil:	Lime-deficient, permeable soil, such as loam or clay, mixed with perlite.

Capparis spinosa

Capsicum annuum

Solanacea

Sweet pepper

Sweet peppers are related to the Spanish pepper and paprika families. The fruits are always edible, but have a strong taste. For instance, salsa can be made from them. Hybrids have various forms and various colored fruits.
Care: The fruits color nicely towards the end of the summer, following a period of warmth and sun. Keep them cool indoors. Watch for red spider mites and aphids. When the plants turn ugly, it is better to throw them out then try to salvage them because the plant will not survive dormancy.
Propagation: From seed. Sow in March, soil temperature 60–68°F (15–20°C). When the plants are in bloom, stimulate fruit forming by spreading the pollen over the flowers with a small brush.

Light:	Full sun.
Temp:	Grow cool.
Water:	Keep moderately moist.
Hum:	Moderate.
Soil:	Standard potting soil.

Caralluma X suaveolens

Asclepiadaceae

A succulent plant with thick, prettily marked stalks and small reddish brown flowers. These plants attract bluebottle flies with their fragrance, as does the more well-known *Stapelia*.
Care: Place in the sun in the summer and keep rather dry. In all seasons, the drainage should be excellent. Use hardly any fertilizer. In the winter, keep cool and very dry. With a wet culture root rot will occur. The dormancy should not be too warm, otherwise there will be no flowers (which is not *so* bad since they are not that noticeable).
Propagation: Cut off top of stalks, dry for a week and plant in sandy, dry soil.

Caralluma X suaveolens

Capsicum annuum

Light:	Much light, or full sun.
Temp:	Grow moderately warm, in the winter a minimum of 40°F (5°C).
Water:	Water sparsely.
Hum:	Can be low.
Soil:	Mixture of leaf mould, some loam, decayed cow manure and peat moss. Preferably grown in lattice baskets.

Carex brunnea

Cyperaceae

Sedges

Other sedge species are good garden plants, but this species is not that hardy and will therefore only survive inside. In the trade, one mainly comes across the gold-spotted cultivation 'Variegata.'
Care: Easy to grow as long as the ball of soil stays moist, but not so wet that water collects in the tray. In the winter, keep cool. Fertilize once a month while the plant grows.

Propagation: By division.

Light:	Much light, full sun allowed.
Temp:	Grow cool to moderately warm.
Water:	Constantly moist.
Hum:	Moderate, 50–60%.
Soil:	Standard potting soil.

Carex brunnea 'Variegata'

Carnegiea gigantea

Cactaceae

Gigantic cactus from the southern United States and Mexico. The columns, after a few hundred years, can reach the respectable height of 50 ft (15 m). Large white flowers develop and open at night. These are followed by edible fruits.
Care: Because young plants grow slowly, they often are part of a collection. Provide a sunny location in the summer and cactus food once every two weeks. In the winter keep cool and dry.
Propagation: From seed.

Light:	Full sun.
Temp:	Grow moderately warm to warm, in the winter a minimum of 40°F (5°C).
Water:	Keep moderately dry, in the winter almost no water.
Hum:	Can be low.
Soil:	Cactus soil.

Carnegiea gigantea

Carpobrotus acinaciformis

Carpobrotus acinaciformis

Aizoaceae

Hottentot fig

One of the many creeping plants in this family, usually called *Mesembryanthemum*. They come in various colors. In southern countries, they are used as ground cover. This species originates in South Africa.
Care: Very warm and sunny, otherwise the flowers won't form. A window sill is a suitable place, and in the summer, outside as well. This succulent plant does not need much water, even less food. Keep cold in the winter.
Propagation: Let top cuttings dry for a week and stick in sandy soil.

Light:	Full sun.
Temp:	Grow cool to moderately warm, in the winter a minimum of 40°F (5°C).
Water:	Keep rather dry, at least in the winter, otherwise the plants rot.
Hum:	Can be low.
Soil:	Cactus soil or another permeable mixture that has no lime deficiency.

Caryota mitis

Palmae

A palm from Southeast Asia that has leaves with a triangular shape.
Care: These plants should be grown rather warm, and so cannot be laced outside in the summer. Always provide enough water and in the summer give the plant food in dissolved solution, once every two weeks. A warm greenhouse is a necessity for effective growth.
Propagation: From seeds or via shoots.

Light:	Much light, never full sun.
Temp:	Grow warm, never below 61°F (16°C).
Water:	Always keep rather moist.
Hum:	High, above 60%.
Soil:	Standard potting soil mixed with fine clay or loam. Use tall pots.

Caryota mitis

Cassia didymobotrya

Leguminosae

Rarely grown, but richly flowering and rather simple to maintain container plants. A popular species is the *Cassia corymbosa* var. *plurijuga*, which closely resembles the species pictured. It has longer flower bunches, though.

Care: Place outside form the end of May, protected and sunny. Make sure to use tubs that are large enough for the plant and give plenty of water in the summer with fertilizer once a week (until about mid-August). The blooms start in July and last until the fall. Bring inside before the frost and provide a cool, light dormant period. The leaves should not fall, so continue giving water, but not much. In the spring, keep cool as long as possible.

Cassia didymobotrya

Propagation: From seed or via top cuttings, which root under glass at 60–68°F (15–20°C) soil temperature. Keep the substrate moderately moist.

Light:	Full sun.
Temp:	Grow cool, in the winter 40–50°F (5–10°C).
Water:	Keep moderately moist, in the winter somewhat drier.
Hum:	Moderate, 50–60%.
Soil:	Standard potting soil, if possible mixed with extra loam, clay or rock wool powder.

Catasetum maculatum

Orchideceae

A genus with at least a hundred orchid species. The flowers are strikingly beautiful, but do not last long.

Care: Rather easy to grow, at least in an airy and light greenhouse. The plants desire much light and in the summer much (rain)water as well. Mix orchid food with the water every two weeks, in lighter concentrations if grown in rock wool powder. After the pseudotubers are fully grown, the plants should be kept almost dry for a few weeks.

Propagation: By division or from seed.

Light:	Much light, screen against bright sunlight.
Temp:	Grow warm, in the winter not below 64°F (18°C).
Water:	Plenty of soft water in the summer. Avoid stagnation.
Hum:	High, above 60%.
soil:	Grow in pieces of fern tree or in lattice baskets, filled with pieces of fern tree or with pure rock wool flakes.

Catharanthus roseus

Apocynaceae

A richly flowering plant, which is still called *Vinca*. They appear in various colors with a differently tinted eye in many cases.

Care: Place in a light spot; the plant can endure full sun, too. From the end of May, it can be placed in a garden or a protected place on a balcony. Fertilize once every 14 days. It is possible to keep the plants dormant by placing them in a cool spot. Repot in the spring, prune a bit and bring back to growth.

Propagation: From cuttings or seed. Sow in February; soil temperature 68°F (20°C). Top cuttings can be removed in the spring or in

Catasetum maculatum

Catharanthus roseus

August; temperature 68–77°F (20–25°C). Young plants have to be cut at the top once or twice to allow for better branching.

Light:	Much light, full sun as well.
Temp:	Grow cool, in the winter not below 54°F (12°C).
Water:	Keep moderately moist.
Hum:	Moderate, 50–60%.
Soil:	Standard potting soil.

Cattleya species

Orchidaceae

Orchids that grow as epiphytes (on trees) in nature. They are provided with pseudotubers, from which one or two leaves grow. The flowers are often large and beautifully marked.

Care: When grown in a greenhouse, these plants are hardly problematic. Much light is needed, but in the summer, the roof of the greenhouse should be screened somewhat, although some species do desire full sun as well. The glass can be cleared in November, so that the winter sun can shine unobstructed on the plants, until mid-April, when the light should be screened again. Provide continuous water, mixed with fertilizer, in the growing period. When grown in inorganic material (rock wool, clay particles, or even pure sand) the food should be dissolved in water. When cultivated in organic material (fern roots, pieces of fern tree, sphagnum), fertilizer is needed once every two weeks. It is essential that the water can drain well. Either well-draining pots or lattice baskets are a good way to grow these plants. After the pseudotubers have formed, keep the plants dry for several weeks so that the tubers ripen thoroughly. As soon as new roots appear, one can water again.

Propagation: By division.

Light: Much light, never bright sun.
Temp: Grow warm, in the winter a minimum of 60°F (15°C).
Water: Give plenty of water in the summer, keep dry during dormancy. Always use rainwater or soft water.
Hum: High, above 60%.
Soil: Inorganic or organic mixture (see above) in well-draining containers. Repot when plants grow too big.

Cattleya walkeriana

Cattleya bowringiana

Cattleya forbesii

Celosia argentea

Amaranthaceae

Cockscomb

Annual plants with strangely shaped flowers. The cockscomb is a cristate form (var. *cristata*) and the spike cockscomb is var. *plumosa*. Various bright tints are delivered in short and tall growing genera. The short species are used in the garden, but often sold as houseplants as well.

Celosia argentea var. *plumosa*

Care: Keep inside in a sunny-to-light, shaded location, and not too warm. Keep the soil temperature around 68°F (20°C). Give dissolved food every two weeks. Dispose of the plant after the flowering period, because the plant will not survive a dormant period.
Propagation: Sow from February; soil temperature 68–77°F (20–25°C). After it sprouts, plant out and continue to grow warmer. Plant in final pot and slowly harden off.

Light: Much light, full sun allowed.
Temp: Grow moderately warm.
Water: Keep moderately moist.
Hum: Moderate to high.
Soil: Standard potting soil.

Centradenia floribunda

Melastomataceae

Evergreen half bush from Central America with red stalks and light red-purple flowers, which stay in bloom from February until June.
Care: Preferably in a warm greenhouse because these plants need humidity. Much light is necessary, but screen against the bright afternoon sun. In the growing season, give plenty of water and add dissolved food every two weeks. In the winter, too, the plant should be kept warm.

Centradenia floribunda

Celosia argentea var. *cristata*

Propagation: Root top cuttings under glass at 77–86°F (25–30°C) soil temperature. Cut the tops during growth. It would be sensible to strike slips each year, because older plants grow less pretty.

Light: Much light, never full sun.
Temp: Grow warm, a minimum of 64°F (18°C).
Water: Keep moderately moist.
Hum: High, above 60%.
Soil: Standard potting soil mixed with at least ⅓ part clay or loam.

Cephalocereus senilis

Cactaceae

Old man cactus

Completely gray-bearded cactus from Mexico. The hair serves as a protection against the sun for the cactus body. The light red-purple flowers common to this plant almost never occur in cultivation.
Care: As with all cacti, this species should be kept warm and sunny. Never place it in a drafty location. Give cactus food once a month during the summer. Keep cooler and rather dry in the winter.
Propagation: From seed.

Light: Full sun.
Temp: Grow warm, in the winter never below 60°F (15°C).
Water: Very moderate, in the winter even less.
Hum: Can be low.
Soil: Cactus soil.

Cephalocereus senilis

Cereus neotetragonus

Cereus neotetragonus

Cactaceae

A column-shaped cactus that branches easily, forming a forest of ascending stalks. In Brazil, it can grow 6½ ft (2 m) tall and blooms with reddish, funnel-shaped flowers.
Care: An easily-growing cactus, it can be cultivated in the living room if it gets full light. These plants are not grown for their flowers, so a cool dormancy is less important. But keep the plants cool anyway, so that they do not grow in the winter. Give some cactus food monthly during the summer.
Propagation: Sowing, or cuttings via the tops, after they have dried thoroughly.

Light:	Full sun.
Temp:	Moderately warm to warm, in winter a minimum of 41°F (5°C).
Water:	Moderate, in winter very little.
Hum:	Can be low.
Soil:	Cactus soil, if necessary regular potting soil.

Cereus peruvianus

Cactaceae

A common *Cereus peruvianus* grows in a column-shaped fashion and branches out as well. 'Monstrosus' is a freak of nature, a cristate form that occurs frequently with cacti. The plant forms a number of growing points that all show a little growth and a kind of rock landscape is created. Flowers do not appear.
Care: Place in the sun during summer, give a moderate amount of water and some cactus food once a month. Keep cooler in the winter to stop the growth.

Cereus peruvianus 'Monstrosus'

Cereus peruvianus

Propagation: Mainly from cuttings. Dry the cuttings first for a while.

Light:	Full sun.
Temp:	Grow moderately warm to warm, in the winter not below 40°F (5°C).
Water:	Sparse, when kept cool in the winter almost no water.
Hum:	Can be low.
Soil:	Cactus soil, and if needed standard potting soil.

Ceropegia woodii ssp. woodii

Asclepiadaceae

Lantern plant, rosary vine

Ceropegia is a large genus of succulent plants, form which the easy to cultivate lantern plant is probably the most well-known. It forms pretty, variegated leaves or thin, hanging stalks; small tubers develop that can be used for propagation. The small flowers have the form of old-fashioned lanterns. The species 'Emmy' in the picture has especially beautiful leaf markings.

Ceropegia woodii ssp. *woodii* 'Emmy'

Care: Grow in a hanging pot in front of a light (can be sunny) window. Do not give too much water, and always provide good drainage. Feed once a month. Keep cooler in the winter.
Propagation: By cutting from the stalk pieces, removing the little tubers with a stalk or from seed.

Light:	Much light, full sun, too.
Temp:	Grow moderately warm, in the winter not below 50°F (10°C).
Water:	Sparse, in the winter extremely sparse.
Soil:	Cactus soil, and if needed standard potting soil.

CESTRUM

Cestrum X newellii

Solanaceae

An evergreen bush also described as the species *fasciculatum*. There are different species too, some with yellow flowers. Grow as a container plant.

Care: Grow outside in the summer in a protected and sunny location. Give plenty of water and fertilize weekly. The plants will produce rich, hardy flowers. Bring inside in the fall and allow a light dormancy. Most leaves should stay on the plant, so do not keep it too dry.

Propagation: Root young top cuttings under glass in the spring at 68–77°F (20–25°C) soil temperature.

Light: Full sun.
Temp: Grow cool, in the winter 40–50°F (5–10°C).
Water: Keep moderately moist.
Hum: Moderate, 50–60%.
Soil: Standard potting soil, mixed with ⅓ loam, clay or rock wool powder.

Cestrum X newelii

Chamaecereus sylvestri

Cactaceae

This cactus is made up of numerous small columns growing next to each other. On these columns appear large flowers. There also exist somewhat deviant hybrids, created by hybridizations with *Lobivia* or *Rebutia*.

Care: Keep the plant in a light and airy spot in the summer; screen from the brightest sun, otherwise the "fingers" turn brown. Fertilize monthly with special cactus food (with low nitrogen content). With overcast weather, one should be careful not to water too much. Keep especially cool in the winter; when the soil is completely dry, the plant can even endure some degree of frost, which will only enrich the next flowering period.

Propagation: By cuttings of the shoots, and from seed as well.

Chamaecereus sylvestri

Light: Much light, avoiding the brightest sun.
Temp: Grow moderately warm to warm, in the winter very cool, even below 32°F (0°C).
Water: Keep moderately dry.
Hum: Can be low.
Soil: Cactus soil.

Chamaedorea elegans

Palmae

Parlor palm

A palm that stays small and flowers very easily with small, yellow balls. Still even smaller than the regular species is the cultivar 'Bella.'

Care: Place in a light location but avoid bright sunlight and give plenty of water during warm weather. Fertilize once every two weeks. In the winter, provide a cooler place to avoid the harmful effects of dry room air.

Chamaedorea elegans

Chamaerops humilis

Chamaeranthemum gaudichaudii
Chamaeranthemum venosum

Propagation: By division, and even easier from seed. Soak seeds in water at 86°F (30°C) for two days, then sow and keep the soil temperature at 86°F (30°C). Germination can take up to three months. Start the cultivation at 68°F (20°C) in the daytime and 64°F (18°C) at night.

Light:	Much light, no full sun.
Temp:	Grow moderately warm, in the winter keep dormant at a minimum of 54°F (12°C).
Water:	Moderately moist.
Hum:	Moderate to high.
Soil:	Standard potting soil using preferably high pots.

Chamaeranthemum species

Acanthaceae

Creeping little plants with nicely marked leaves and white to light-blue flowers that grow in spikes. Suitable for greenhouses, plant cases and plant windows.
Care: Watch the temperature and humidity continuously. Spray the foliage with lime-deficient water. During growth, feed every 14 days. In the winter, the barometric levels can fall, but this is not necessary.
Propagation: By division and from top cuttings. Strike slips often because young plants are the prettiest.

Light:	Half shade, never full sun.
Temp:	Grow warm, a minimum of 61°F (16°C).
Water:	Keep moderately moist, with water containing not much lime.
Hum:	High, above 60%.

Soil:	Standard potting soil mixed with peat dust, peat moss, leaf mould or coniferous soil. Use shallow well-draining bowls.

Chamaerops humilis

Palmae

A beautiful fan palm with a rather short trunk and spiky leaf stalks. On the Riviera, it grows naturally. Other species previously classified under this genus are now categorized with the *Trachycarpus*.
Care: This is a typical container plant which during summer thrives in a sunny and protected location (e.g. a terrace). Add some fertilizer to the water every week. Keep cool and airy in the winter; if the soil is moist enough, the temperature can fall below zero. A fairly well-lit garage can be a good place.
Propagation: From seed, sowing in the early spring; soil temperature 86°F (30°C).

Light:	Much light, only screen against bright sun.
Temp:	Grow cool, in the winter a minimum of 32°F (0°C).
Water:	Lavishly in the summer, in the winter very little.
Hum:	Moderate, 50–60%.
Soil:	Preferably a mixture that contains clay, loam or rock wool powder.

Chamelaucium uncinatum

Myrtaceae

A small bush from West Australia that can bloom abundantly and long. In retail stores it is still quite rare, but this could change soon.
Care: A typical container tub plant that can stay outside in the summer, but in the winter must be kept cool. Feed once every 14 days.
Propagation: From seed and from top cuttings, taken in the summer. Soil temperature 77–86°F (25–30°C). Cut the tops a few times.

Light:	Full sun.
Temp:	Grow moderately warm, keeping it frost free in the winter.
Hum:	Low to moderate.
Soil:	Standard potting soil.

Chamelaucium uncinatum

Cheiridopsis candidissima

Aizoaceae

Succulent plant from South Africa that produces thick leaves in pairs. The light red flowers do not form in northern climates because of a lack of sufficient light.
Care: The problem with this plant is that it grows in the winter, when, in the northern hemisphere, there is not enough light. Artificial lighting can offer a possible solution. Always keep on the dry side; administer water only during the summer dormancy when the leaves wilt. Fertilizer is not needed, as long as it is repotted each year.
Propagation: From imported seeds.

Cheiridopsis candidissima

Light:	Full sun.
Temp:	Grow moderately warm to warm, a minimum of 64°F (18°C).
Water:	Keep rather dry.
Hum:	Can be low.
Soil:	Cactus soil.

Chlorophytum comosum 'Variegatum'

Liliaceae
Spider plant

A very well-known houseplant that thrives almost anywhere. Only the white-striped species is cultivated. Sometimes called

Chlorophytum comosum 'Variegatum'

Chlorophytum capense. An interesting detail about the spider plant is that it can extract the poisonous gas formaldehyde from the air (when released from chipboard).
Care: Grown preferably in a hanging pot. Soon, little white flowers develop and after that small "mini-plants" at the ends of long stalks. Feed every two weeks in the summer. The spider plant can be kept cooler in the winter, and can survive the season indoors.
Propagation: By removing and planting the small growths. Large plants can be divided.

Light:	Much light, no full sun.
Temp:	Grow moderately warm.
Water:	Keep moderately moist.
Hum:	Moderate, 50–60%.
Soil:	Standard potting soil.

Chorizema cordatum

Leguminosae

Small evergreen bushes from Australia appropriate for potted cultivation. They are not readily available, though there are some other species and selections on the market.
Care: Grow cool and airy, in the summer possibly as a container plant. Keep moist with rainwater and fertilize during the growing period once every two weeks. Do not keep too dry, because without enough water the foliage will fall off and the plant will die.
Propagation: From seed or via top cuttings. Young plants have to be cut at the top a few times. Gradually harden off and let them get used to the sun. During the second year the plants become really beautiful.

Chorizema cordatum

Light:	Full light, full sun, too.
Temp:	Grow cool, in the winter 40–50°F (5–10°C).
Water:	Keep moderately moist.
Hum:	Moderate, 50–60%.
Soil:	Acidic potting soil, for instance, standard potting soil mixed with extra peat dust, or coniferous soil.

Chrysalidocarpus lutescens

Chrysalidocarpus lutescens

Palmae
Butterfly palm

Often sold under the name *Areca.* A nice plant from Madagascar.
Care: This palm is easy to keep indoors during the summer, but must be kept in a light spot, without full sun. If possible place the plant outside and keep it well protected. Feed once a month. Keep it somewhat cooler in the winter, and do not allow it to continue growing.
Propagation: From seed.

Light:	Much light, no full sun.
Temp:	Grow moderately warm to warm, at night not below 64°F (18°C). In the winter not below 54°F (12°C).
Water:	Keep on the wet side, in the winter somewhat drier.
Soil:	Standard potting soil mixed with extra clay, loam or rock wool powder.

Chrysanthemum hybrids

Compositae
Garden chrysanthemum

Lately, perennial garden chrysanthemums, belonging to the *Indicum* or *Koreanum* hybrids, have been offered as lavishly flowering potted plants. They are often grown as a tree plant.
Care: When a blooming plant is purchased in the fall, the most important thing is to keep it cool, so that it will bloom longer. The beauty (and flowers) will soon be gone in a warm room. Give plenty of water and spray the plant daily. To achieve an even larger specimen during the second year, one should provide a very cool dormant period, for example in a cool greenhouse. In the spring, repot into a bigger container. The shoots should be topped and the plant pruned, so that a compact form is created in the shape of a bowl or pyramid. Food should be administered weekly, while the plant is growing until the flower buds color.
Propagation: These chrysanthemums make good cuttings in the early spring. To grow a tree plant, keep one shoot and remove the side branches. By the time it reaches the desired height, remove the top and cut the new side branches a few times, to produce a strongly branched crown.

Chrysanthemum

Light: Much light, no full sun.
Temp: Grow cool to moderately warm, possibly outside in the summer. In the winter a minimum of 40°F (5°C).
Water: Keep moderately moist.
Hum: Moderate to high.
Soil: Standard potting soil.

Chrysanthemum Indicum hybrids
Compositeae
Potted chrysanthemum

The potted chrysanthemum is a small plant that is grown often, but is difficult to keep alive: a true disposable plant. By controlling periods of light and dark, it can be tricked into flowering throughout the year. With the aid of stunting substances, it can be kept at a manageable height. The plants are not hardy, so one cannot keep them in an outdoor garden.

Care: One can keep a flowering, recently purchased plant in good condition longer by placing it in a cool spot and keeping it from the bright sun. Give the plant dissolved food every two weeks. Either throw it away after the flowering period or store it at a low temperature. If kept in a garden after the winter, the plant will become much taller.

Propagation: Take cuttings from dormant plants in the early spring. Young shoots can be used as cuttings.

Light: Much light, never full sun.
Temp: Grow cool, in the winter a minimum of 40°F (5°C).
Water: Keep moderately moist.
Hum: Moderate, 50–60%.
Soil: Standard potting soil.

Chrysanthemum Indicum-hybr.

Chrysanthemum parthenium

Compositae

Mums

Usually called *Matricaria* by growers. A perennial plant by nature, it is nonetheless cultivated as an annual plant. The fragrance strongly resembles camilla. There are special, smaller varieties for cultivation in pots—with plump white, yellow or orange flowers.

Chrysanthemum parthenium

Care: Do not keep too warm, but do place it in a light spot. Supply with plenty of water and move it to a larger container immediately once the original pot seems too small. Every two weeks while the plant flowers, provide a plant food solution. Follow the instructions given for garden chrysanthemums in regard to dormancy.
Propagation: Sow from the end of January at a minimum warmth of 64°F (18°C). Plant out in pots and continue to grow under glass. Cut off the tops a few times for better branching. Harden off and place indoors.

Light:	Much light, sun allowed.
Temp:	Grow cool, in the winter a minimum of 40°F (15°C).
Water:	Keep moderately moist.
Hum:	Moderate to high.
Soil:	Standard potting soil.

Chrysanthemum Indicum-hybr.

Chrysothemis pulchella

Gesneriaceae

A rare tropical plant of the *Achimenes* family. It forms a tuberous rootstock and has bumpy, opposing leaves.
Care: Grow warm and moist, preferably in a greenhouse. In the summer place the plant temporarily indoors. Provide soft water and

Chrysothemis pulchella

feed during the growth season once every two weeks. Keep cooler and drier in the winter, or let the plant die off in the fall and store the tubers in dry potting soil.
Propagation: By division of the rootstocks. It will sprout at 77–86°C (25–30°C) under glass or plastic.

Light:	Much light, never full sun.
Temp:	Grow warm, in the winter not below 61°F (16°C).
Water:	Keep moderately moist with soft water. During dormancy, keep tubers dry.
Hum:	High, above 60%.
Soil:	Special, humus mixture with peat moss, coniferous soil, decayed manure, sphagnum etc. Possibly an anthurium or bromeliad mixture.

Chysis aurea

Orchidaceae

Epiphytic orchids from Central and South America that have an overhanging way of growing.

Chysis aurea

Care: Preferably grown in lattice baskets, hung in a greenhouse. In the summer these plants should be grown indoors. Give them lots of light, screening only against the brightest sunlight. Give plenty of water in the summer, assuming there is good drainage. Add some fertilizer at least once every two weeks, more often when the plant grows in an inorganic substrate. After the new pseudotubers are full grown, a dormant period is necessary, during which the plants are kept drier and cooler.
Propagation: By division.

Light:	Much light, screen only against brightest sunlight.
Temp:	Not too warm in the summer, 77–86°F (20–25°C), in the winter a minimum of 54°F (12°C).
Water:	Much (rain)water in the summer, drier in the winter.
Hum:	Moderate to high.
Soil:	Grow in lattice baskets, filled with ground tree fern or rock wool flakes.

Cissus antarctica

Vitaceae

A strong climbing plant with attractively formed, sturdy green foliage. The cultivation form 'Grandidentata' is even more hardy, but creates less vines.
Care: This plant can stay indoors the whole year because it endures dry air quite well. But much light is necessary, although no direct sunlight. The potting soil cannot be too cold, or it will cause the plant to drop leaves. During the growth period, fertilize every week. In the spring, if necessary, cut back and repot. Give the vines sufficient support.
Propagation: From middle cut or top cut. Soil temperature 77°F (25°C).

Light:	Much light, no full sun.
Temp:	Grow moderate warm to warm, in the winter a minimum 46°F (8°C).
Water:	Keep moderately moist.
Hum:	Moderate, 50–60% is preferable.
Soil:	Standard potting soil, with possibly some extra clay or loam.

Cissus antarctica

Cissus discolor

Vitaceae

In contrast to the last kind, this climbing plant with its beautifully marked foliage is hard to keep indoors. It originates in humid, tropical forests where there's always high humidity, sometimes even 90%. Small, yellow flowers can appear on older plants.

Cissus discolor

Care: Grow in a warm greenhouse, with a temporary stay in the living room, spraying very often with rainwater. In the growth period, give food once every two weeks. Keep warm, in the winter as well.
Propagation: From top or middle cutting; soil temperature 77–86°F (25–30°C).

Light:	Half shade, never full sun.
Temp:	Grow warm, in the winter not below 64°F (18°C).
Water:	Keep moderately moist with soft water.
Hum:	High, above 60%.
Soil:	Standard potting soil.

Cissus rhombifolia

Vitaceae

A very strong climbing plant with triad leaves, also known as *Rhoicissus*. There are various cultivations, such as the pictured 'Mandaiana'

Cissus rhombifolia 'Mandaiana'

Cissus rhombifolia 'Ellen Danica'

and 'Ellen Danica,' with carved leaves. But the common sort with small leaves is the strongest. Even in improbably dark spots, it still survives; just take a look in restaurants, where it often finds a home.
Care: Can be in a warm room all year long. The vines twist themselves along any support or hang down very decoratively. Feed weekly during the growth period and repot in the spring. The winter temperature can drop to 46°F (8°C), but it is not absolutely necessary.
Propagation: From top or middle cuttings.

Light:	Half shadow or shadow.
Temp:	Moderately warm or warm.
Water:	Keep moderately moist.
Hum:	Moderate to low.
Soil:	Standard potting soil.

Cissus striata

Cissus striata

Vitaceae

A charming, small climbing and hanging plant with palmate leaves. Occurs rarely.
Care: Prefers a half-shaded spot. Cannot endure afternoon sun very well. Give plenty of support when the plant has to climb against a wall. Keep sufficiently moist in the summer, tie up when necessary and feed every two weeks. In the winter, mist the foliage or keep the plant cool.
Propagation: Root ripened top or middle cuttings in August under glass. Soil temperature 77–86°F (25–30°C).

Light:	Half shade.
Temp:	Grow moderately warm, in the winter a minimum of 40°F (5°C).
Water:	Keep moderately moist.
Hum:	Moderate, 50–60%.
Soil:	Standard potting soil.

Foliage loss with Cissus varieties

Cissus antarctica or *rhombifolia* sometimes lose their leaves suddenly. The following causes should be taken into consideration:
- not enough light
- potting soil too wet
- high salt concentration in the potting soil caused by bad water or too much fertilizer
- pH too low [pH6.0 is right]
- potting soil too cold. The soil should not be colder than 64°F (18°C)

Cistus species

Cistaceae

Magnificent container plants that unfortunately are not found much in shops or in homes. There are white and reddish purple flowering species, some of which are hybrids.
Care: Place outside in a sunny, sheltered spot from the end of May. During the growth period, fertilize every week, because only effectively fertilized plants flower well. Stop feeding in August and bring inside, preferably to a cold greenhouse, in the fall before the frost starts. Give little

Cistus ladanifer

water, but enough to keep the foliage from falling off. Keep especially cool in the spring, so that the plant does not come out too early.
Propagation: From seed or from top cutting. Soil temperature 68–77°F (20–25°C). Young plants should be cut at the tops a few times for better branching.

Light:	Full sun.
Temp:	Grow cool, in the winter 40–50°F (5–10°C).
Water:	Keep moderately moist.
Hum:	Moderate, 50–60%.
Soil:	Standard potting soil, mixed with ⅓ part fine clay or loam, or with rock powder.

Cistus albidus

X Citrofortunella mitis

Rutaceae

Orange tree

This mini orange tree is popularly known as *Citrus microcarpa* or *Citrus mitis*. In reality, it is a cross-hybridization between *Citrus reticulata*, the mandarin, and a *Fortunella* species. The plant is designed as an ornamental tree; but it is also known to provide some people with sour fruits for marmalade.
Care: Grow this species somewhat warmer than other *Citrus* species. Nevertheless, the

X *Citrofortunella mitis*

plant can be placed outside in the summer, if it is well protected. Screen against the brightest afternoon sun. Watch the ball of soil so that it does not ever dry out and fertilize every two weeks. If there are no insects around, then one can sweep over the open flowers with a very fine brush to spread pollen. Keep cooler in the winter.
Propagation: Only from cuttings. Root top cuttings in the summer under glass with a soil temperature of 60–68°F (15–20°C).

Citrus reticulata

Light:	Much light, screen against bright sunlight.
Temp:	Grow cool to moderately warm, in the winter not below 46°F (8°C).
Water:	Keep moderately moist with soft water.
Hum:	Moderate, 50–60%.
Soil:	Acidic potting soil, created by mixing clay soil with peat mold or garden peat.

Citrus species

Rutaceae

Miniature orange tree

A family with many species: *Citrus Aurantium* ssp. *aurantium* is often used as a base for other related subtropical fruits. *C. limon* is the sour lemon, *C. maxima* is the pomelo, *C.* x *paradisi* the grapefruit, *C. reticulata* the mandarin and *C. sinensis* the sweet orange tree. Usually grown for the deliciously fragrant blossoms, though oranges do appear as well. These various species are easy to purchase through importers and since each cultivation is the same, I do not have to discuss them separately.
Care: To keep the citrus tree happy, give it a sunny, sheltered spot outside. This applies from mid-May, after the danger of frost is over. Fertilize once every two weeks and do not ever forget to water (a container with a watering system is ideal). When the leaves turn yellow, this indicates iron deficiency. The pH is very high in that case. Spray with iron chelate and lower the soil's pH level. In the winter, the citrus trees should be kept cool but frost-free. A cold greenhouse is ideal, but a frost-free garage that is not too dark or an unheated bedroom will do.
Propagation: Root top cuttings in the spring at 68°F (20°C). Sowing is a possibility too, but one often ends up with different plants that way.

Citrus limon

Citrus aurantium ssp. *aurantium*

Light:	Full sun is allowed.
Temp:	Grow cool, in the winter a minimum of 40°F (5°C).
Water:	Keep moderately moist with soft water, drier in the winter.
Hum:	Moderate, 50–60%.
Soil:	Has to be acidic, but an addition of clay is necessary. Clay or loam mixed with peat moss is a good compromise.

Cleistocactus strausii

Cleistocactus strausii

Cactaceae

Column cactus from Bolivia that are totally covered with fine white thorns. They can reach a height of a few yards.

Care: Plant in a greenhouse if possible, because the plant grows out of its pot quickly. Keep sunny in the summer and give cactus food once a month. Flowers only appear on older specimens.

Propagation: From seed or from cuttings.

Light:	Full sun.
Temp:	Grow warm, in the winter a minimum of 50°F (10°C).
Water:	Moderate, in the winter withhold almost all water.
Hum:	Can be low.
Soil:	Cactus soil.

Clerodendrum thomsoniae

Verbenacea

Bleeding heart vine

This is a climbing plant with vines up to 13.2 ft (4 m) in length. By spraying the plant with a growth stunting hormone such as Reducymol and cutting the tops a few times, one obtains a compact houseplant that flowers richly. The flowers consist of a white calyx and a red crown, and they do not last long.

Care: Place the flowering plant in a light spot, but never in the full sun. Give fertilizer once every two weeks. Provide dormancy. Most of the leaves will drop. Repot in the spring, cut back a bit and top the vines a few times. The

minimum winter temperature is 64°F (18°C). From mid-March, the plant should be subjected to the short-day treatment, till the blooming begins (see page 55). Daylight should not exceed nine hours.

Propagation: From middle cutting, soil temperature 68–77°F (20–25°C). Four cuttings to a pot is ideal.

Light:	Much light, no full sun.
Temp:	Grow moderately warm, in the winter keep dormant period at 50–54°F (10–12°C).
Water:	Keep moderately moist, drier during dormancy.
Hum:	Moderate to high.
Soil:	Standard potting soil, possibly mixed with some clay and loam.

Clerodendrum thomsoniae

Cleyera japonica 'Tricolor'

Cleyera japonica

Theaceae

A member of the tea family, almost always grown in the variegated form 'Tricolor.' It is a houseplant for cool spaces.
Care: Grow the plant in a light spot, but keep it out of the full sun. It can be placed outside in the summer in a sheltered spot. It's not absolutely necessary to bring it indoors for the winter, but in all cases leave it in a cool spot.

Spray the leaves frequently. Fertilize only during the growing period once every two weeks.
Propagation: Root top cuttings in the spring under glass at a soil temperature of 68°F (20°C).

Light:	Half shade to much light, no bright sunlight.
Temp:	Grow cool, in the summer at 46–64°F (8–18°C), in the winter 50–54°F (10–12°C).
Water:	Keep moderately moist with soft water, for instance rainwater.
Hum:	Moderate to high.
Soil:	Coniferous soil or standard potting soil mixed with peat mold.

Clianthus puniceus

Leguminosae

Glory pea

An evergreen bush from Australia, suitable for growing in greenhouses. The flowers have a very strange, striking form. Other than the species shown, there is also *Clianthus formosus*, which is available in the stores every once in a while. Neither are known to be strong houseplants.
Care: Preferably plant out in the full soil in a greenhouse. Tie up the shoots adequately. Feed once every two weeks. In the winter the temperature can drop considerably, as the plants begin dormancy. Often grown as an annual species.
Propagation: Take top cuttings in the summer, soil temperature 68°F (20°C). It's possible to sow in March as well. *Clianthus formosus* can only be propagated from seed and often dies after the blooming. Seedlings are frequently grafted on the trunk of the species *Colutea*.

Light:	Full sun.
Temp:	Grow moderately warm.
Water:	Keep moderately moist, in the winter almost no water.
Hum:	Low to moderate, do not spray the leaves.
Soil:	Standard potting soil.

Clivia miniata

Amaryllidaceae

A strong, long-established houseplant that is easy to keep and can flower plentifully every year. The strongest is the common green species. Variegated specimens require much light.
Care: The *Clivia* endures the dry room air rather well and so does not have to be cultivated in a greenhouse. But for the budding of the flowers, a dormant period is needed, in which almost all water is withheld and the temperature lowered. The dormancy has to start in October. Give just the right amount of water, so that the leaves do not shrivel. Consequently, a new flower stalk appears in the beginning of the new year. If one starts to give the normal amount of water at this point, then the stalk stops growing and the buds will half open between the leaves. For that reason, it is best to wait till the stalk is of the right length. Only then place it in a warmer spot and give water as usual. Always leave the plant with the same side turned toward the light as long as it flowers. From the moment the plant is placed in a warmer location, it should be fed once every two weeks. Repotting is possible right after the flowering period. The plant can be placed outside in the garden during the summer.

Clivia miniata 'Burvenich'

Clianthus puniceus 'Roseus'

Clivia miniata

Propagation: From seeds that sometimes form on the plant, and take a long period to germinate. Also possible by taking the shoots that appear at the base of the old plant.

Light:	Half shade, a window facing east or west is ultimately best.
Temp:	Grow moderately warm, during dormancy around 50°F (10°C).
Water:	Keep moderately moist, during dormancy almost dry.
Hum:	Moderate, 50–60%.
Soil:	Standard potting soil mixed with clay, loam or rock powder (for sale in nurseries).

Clusia rosea

Guttiferae

A 16 ft (5 m) high tree in Central America, often growing out of trees or rocks. Large, light red flowers may appear.
Care: This plant likes a warm and moist atmosphere, but with some care it can stay in a warm living room during the winter. Feed once every two weeks during the growth period.
Propagation: From top or eye cuttings. Root under glass at soil temperature 77–86°F (25–30°C).

Light:	Half shade.
Temp:	Grow warm, in the winter not below 64°F (18°C).
Water:	Keep constantly moist.
Hum:	Moderate, 50–60%.
Soil:	Standard potting soil.

Clusia rosea

Coccoloba uvifera

Polygonaceae

Anyone who has visited the Caribbean Islands knows this bush, which grows along the beaches. It is remarkably resistant against salt water. Flowers and fruits hardly occur when cultivated indoors.
Care: This plant is quite easy to grow indoors, but in the winter the air becomes too dry, so spray frequently or place it in a cooler spot. Give plenty of water in the growing season and add some food every week. If the plants grow too tall, they may be pruned.
Propagation: Take a top cutting in the summer and root this under glass at soil temperature of 86–95°F (30–35°C).

Light:	Much light, never full sun.

Coccoloba uvifera

Temp:	Grow warm, minimal 54°F (12°C).
Water:	Keep moderately moist.
Hum:	Moderate, 50–60%.
Soil:	Standard potting soil mixed with clay or loam.

Cochliostema odoratissimum

Commelinaceae

Rare, but exceptionally beautiful epiphytic plant with fragrant flowers from Central America.
Care: Because this plant needs high humidity, a greenhouse is necessary for cultivation. Allow for much light, but no bright sunlight. Always grow warm, even somewhat warmer than the average temperature for a greenhouse. Feed every two weeks in the growing season.
Propagation: Germinate fresh (imported) seeds at 68–77°F (20–25°C) under glass. After sprouting, plant out and continue to grow warm. The plants can start to bloom after two to three years.

Light:	Much light, no full sun.
Temp:	Grow warm, minimum of 68°F (20°C).
Water:	Keep moderately moist with rainwater or soft water.
Hum:	High, far above 60%.
Soil:	Bromeliad soil.

Cochliostema odoratissimum

On the following pages: *Clivia miniata*

COCOS

Cocos nucifera

Palmae

Coconut palm

It is interesting to watch a coconut sprout, but the post-sprout care of the palm is not so easy. It needs a lot of light—especially in the winter—high humidity and warmth.

Care: Due to its many needs, the coconut palm will not last long indoors. And in a small greenhouse, it will grow too tall in a short time. So as a compromise we are resigned to

Cocos nucifera

these pretty, already-sprouted coconuts that can be found in a flower shop once in a while. Give plenty of water and do not place the young plant in full sunlight. Feed once every two weeks. Grow indoors because the winter temperatures are too cold.

Propagation: From imported seeds (coconuts).

Light:	Much light, no full sun.
Temp:	Grow warm, in the winter at least 64°F (18°C).
Water:	Keep moderately moist.
Hum:	High, above 60%.
Soil:	Standard potting soil.

Codiaeum variegatum

Euphorbiaceae

Croton

Well-known and nicely marked foliage plants that still are stubbornly referred to as *Croton*, a genus name that is no longer officially used. The cultivated species are part of the variety *pictum*. The latex in the plants can be poisonous.

Care: It's a pity that these beautiful plants need so much humid air, because as soon as the heat is turned on in the winter they begin to wilt. Spraying with water does help, but is not always sufficient. I advise placing the plants in a cooler space, for instance the bathroom. Fertilize during the growth period once

every two weeks with a substance that contains plenty of potassium.

Propagation: From top cutting of ripe shoots. Soil temperature 77–86°F (25–30°C).

Light:	Much light, no full sun.
Temp:	Grow warm to moderately warm, in the winter not below 64°F (18°C).
Water:	Always keep moderately moist with soft water.
Hum:	High, above 60%.
Soil:	Mix standard potting soil with extra peat mould. Provide good drainage.

Codiaeum variegatum pictum 'Goldfinger'

Codiaeum variegatum var. *pictum*

Codiaeum variegatum var. *pictum* 'Norma'

X Codonatanthus

Gesneriaceae

This variety is a cross-fertilization of *Codonanthe* and *Nematanthus*. The plants are given fantastic names such as 'Aurora' and 'Tropic Night' and 'Vista.' Pretty hanging plants that can bloom beautifully.

Care: Preferably grown in hanging pots or hanging baskets in a light spot. Do not allow bright sun. Dip the pots in water from time to time or give plenty of water in any other way.

X *Codonatanthus* 'Aurora'

Feed in the summer once every two weeks by adding fertilizer to the water. Always grow warm, and spray in the winter as often as possible.

Propagation: Root middle cuttings under glass.

Light:	Much light, never full sun.
Temp:	Grow warm, not below 64°F (18°C).
Water:	Keep moderately moist with soft water.
Hum:	Moderately 50–60%.
Soil:	Acidic potting soil, for instance coniferous soil or a mixture with peat mold.

Codonanthe crassifolia

Gesneriaceae

A rather strong hanging plant with small, white flowers, which are slightly orange-tinged in the middle. After pollination small red fruits appear. In the trade, there are several more cross-fertilizations, such as 'Paula,' with hairy leaves and white flowers that appear throughout the year.

Care: Grow in a light but not too sunny location. Fertilize in the growing period once

Codonanthe crassifolia

every two weeks. Keep rather warm in the winter as well and mist the foliage frequently.

Light: Half shade or much light, never full sun.
Temp: Grow warm, a minimum of 64°F (18°C).
Water: Keep moderately moist with soft water.
Hum: Moderate, 50–60%.
Soil: Coniferous soil or standard potting soil with peat moss.

Coelia bella

Codonanthe 'Paula'

Coelia bella

Orchidaceae

Orchids with large, almost round pseudotubers, also known under the name *Bothriochilus bellus*.

Care: Grow very light, but never allow direct sunlight. Give plenty of water in the summer; in the winter only enough to prevent the pseudotubers from shriveling. Supply a continuously humid atmosphere. Provide orchid food every two weeks during the growing season. Repot only when truly necessary because these plants have very sensitive roots. Use relatively small pots or baskets.

Propagation: From division and from seed.

Coelogyne cristata

Light: Much light, no full sun.
Temp: Grow moderately warm, in the winter a minimum of 54°F (12°C).
Water: Always keep moderately moist, in the winter somewhat drier.
Hum: High, above 60%.
Soil: Chopped tree fern or pure rock wool flakes.

Coelogyne cristata

Orchidaceae

A strong and beautiful orchid that can be cultivated successfully indoors.

Care: A window facing east is very suitable, one where the sun disappears after about 11 o'clock. Screen against bright afternoon sun. Always give plenty of (rain)water and add orchid food once every two weeks in the growing period. After the pseudotubers are full grown, in about December, one can place the plant in a somewhat cooler spot and keep it drier. Also, after the flowering period in the early spring, do not give too much water for one or two months. The pseudotubers can shrivel a bit during dormancy, but watch for (and prevent) total dryness.

Propagation: From division or from seed.

Light: Much light or half shade, no full sun.
Temp: Grow moderately warm, in the winter a minimum of 54°F (12°C).
Water: Moderately moist during the growth, drier during dormancy.
Hum: Moderate to high.
Soil: Grow in lattice baskets, filled with chopped fern tree or with rock wool flakes.

Coffea arabica

Coffea arabica

Rubiaceae
Coffee plant

The coffee plant will flower after its third or fourth year and consequently produce fruit. Nevertheless the beans are no reason to start growing your own coffee, because one needs a lot of plants to cover even daily consumption. In any case, the red fruits have to be carefully roasted before they can be used for coffee and this is not easily done at home.

Colchicum autumnale

Care: With some care, it is possible to keep the coffee plant indoors throughout the year, but the foliage has to be misted frequently. If possible, it is advisable to move the coffee plant to a moderately cool spot for the dormant period. Give food once every two weeks during the growth period.
Propagation: From top cuttings or, more easily, from fresh seeds. Soil temperature 77°F (25°C). Cut the tops of young plants once or twice.

Light:	Much light, but no full sun.
Temp:	Moderately warm to warm, though the temperature is allowed to drop in the winter to 60°F (15°C).
Water:	Keep moderately moist.
Hum:	Moderate, 50–60%.
Soil:	Standard potting soil.

Colchicum autumnale

Liliaceae
Autumn crocus

It is always nice to surprise someone in September with a few dry tubers of autumn crocus. Advise them to plant the tubers in a windowbox. The flowers will appear without any water.
Care: Roots and leaves develop only after the flowering period, in the spring. By that time,

the tubers are probably already gone, but you can plant them in the garden before the frost, 4 in (10 cm) deep. Look for a location that is not too dark. The following fall, the tubers will flower and the colors will be even better the second time around. But remember that all parts of the plant—tuber, leaf and flowers—are very poisonous.
Propagation: Via new tubers.

Light:	Inside, not so important, in the garden, half shade or full sun.
Temp:	Grow cool.
Water:	Withhold all water while the plant blooms, for the rest of the time keep moderately moist.
Hum:	Moderate, 50–60%.
Soil:	Preferably soil containing clay, but humus-rich, sandy soil is a possibility, too.

Coleus blumei hybrids

Labiatae
Flame nettle

Simple, elegant plants with beautifully marked foliage. There are many variations of this plant, some named, many not. They germinate spontaneously by pollination among them-

Coleus Blumei-hybr.

selves, and by sowing. They are propagated by taking cuttings.

Care: To preserve the plants' beautiful color, much light is needed. Screen only against very bright afternoon sun. Give food weekly and plenty of water when the weather is warm. Because the plants remain pretty for only a short time, it is advisable to take frequent cuttings. Old plants can rest dormant over the winter, allowing one to take cuttings the following spring.

Propagation: From seed and from top or middle cuttings. Soil temperature 68–77°F (20–25°C).

Light:	Much light, screen against bright afternoon sun.
Temp:	Grow moderately warm to warm, in the winter a minimum of 54°F (12°C).
Water:	Moderate to plenty in the summer, considerably less in the winter. Use soft water.
Hum:	Moderate to dry.
Soil:	Standard potting soil mixed with extra peat moss.

Colletia cruciata

Rhamnaceae

A very unfriendly bush from South America with gray branches and lateral twigs in the form of sharp thorns. The small leaves soon drop. In the summer, white, fragrant flowers

Colletia cruciata

appear. An easy-to-grow container plant for somebody that wants something peculiar.

Care: Grow outside from the end of May in a sunny, sheltered location. Fertilize during the growing period until about mid-August, once a month. Bring the plant inside in the fall and provide a cool dormant period.

Propagation: From half-ripe top cuttings. Soil temperature 68°F (20°C). Rooting takes a long time. Growth from seed is possible as well. Young plants should be topped a few times for better branching.

Light:	Full sun.
Temp:	Grow moderately warm, in the winter at 40–50°F (5–10°C).
Water:	Keep rather dry, withhold water almost completely in the winter.
Hum:	Can be low.
Soil:	Mix standard potting soil with half-fine clay or loam.

Columnea X banksii

Gesneriaceae

These plants grow as epiphytes (on trees) in the wild, usually hanging down from branches.

Care: All species have a great need for humid air and this makes it rather difficult to keep them alive indoors, especially during the winter. The solution is to provide lower temperatures or extra humidity. Prune back considerably after the plant blooms to stimulate the forming of new shoots. Repot and in the summer feed once every two weeks. Flowers will develop if one gives the plant a dormant period of at least six weeks in the winter. Give as little water as possible in that time. Start providing more water and higher temperatures when the buds appear.

Propagation: From top cuttings and middle cuttings. Soil temperature 68–77°F (20–25°C). Place six rooted cuttings per pot.

Light:	Half shade, place in as light a spot as possible during the dormant period.
Temp:	Grow warm, except during dormancy. Minimum around 54°F (12°C).

Columnea gloriosa

Columnea X *banksii*

Water:	Keep moderately moist continuously except during dormancy. Use soft water.
Hum:	High, above 60%
Soil:	Light and acidic, for instance, standard potting soil mixed with peat moss particles, peat mold, perlite, sphagnum, etc.

Columnea gloriosa

Gesneriaceae

A well-known species, endemic to Costa Rica. The plant is very hairy. A cultivated form with dark tinted foliage is called 'Purpurea.'

Care: See the above species. Provide high humidity and a dry dormant period in the winter.

Propagation: From top and middle cuttings.

Light:	Half shade.
Temp:	Grow warm, cooler in the winter, a minimum of 46°F (8°C).
Water:	Keep continuously moist, except during the dormant period.
Hum:	High, above 60%.
Soil:	Special mixture with extra sphagnum, peat moss, coniferous soil, etc., or possibly an anthurium mixture.

Columnea microphylla 'Hostag'

Columnea microphylla

Gesneriaceae

A species with long, hanging stalks covered with very small leaves; reddish orange flowers may appear. The variety 'Hostag' is grown more or less as a foliage plant.

Care: If flowers are not wanted, a dormant period is not necessary (see the preceding descriptions). Nevertheless, a constantly high humidity is always needed. Fertilize during the growth period once every two weeks.

Propagation: From top or middle cuttings. Soil temperature 68–77°F (20–25°C).

Light:	Much light, no full sun.
Temp:	Grow warm, if kept dormant the minimum is 54°F (12°C).
Water:	Keep continuously moist, except during dormancy.
Hum:	High, above 60%.
Soil:	Light and acidic, for instance anthurium or bromeliad soil.

Conophytum species

Aizoaceae

Cone plant

There are various varieties of "stones," for instance *Lithops*. The small plants actually consist of two thick, entangled leaves, which

Conophytum glabrum

Conophytum cornatum

are able to store moisture. At the end of the summer a little flower appears in the center. In fall, dormancy begins and the old leaves wrinkle up. And from this new leaves start to grow the following spring.

Care: Conophytum can easily be killed by too much water. Watering should be given only by drops and even then exclusively in the growing period, which lasts from July until about October. The rest of the year this plant hardly needs any water at all. In the winter the temperature should be considerably lower, to prevent the plant from growing.

Propagation: From seed and by division.

Light:	Full sun.
Temp:	Grow warm to moderately warm, in the winter a minimum of 40–50°F (5–10°C).
Water:	Very sparse in the growing period, when dormant no water except maybe sporadic misting.
Hum:	Can be low.
Soil:	Cactus soil.

Convallaria majalis

Liliaceae

Lily of the valley

The small lily is in fact a hardy garden plant that has adapted to indoor flowering rather well. This usually occurs in nurseries, largely for the purpose as bridal bouquets. Beware, though, the plant is quite poisonous.

Care: To cultivate flowering lilies, one has to start with crowns. These are hardy, thick buds that have produced only foliage in previous years. Crowns can be kept in the refrigerator, allowing them to bloom in any season. Plant them and cover the tops with moist sphagnum or put the pot in a plastic bag. Keep it initially in the dark at 77°F (25°C) and bring into the daylight when the shoots are 4 in (10 cm) long. Keep the plant cool as long as it flowers, and they will last longer. Plant in the garden immediately after the flowering period. Fertilizing is not necessary.

Convallaria majalis

Propagation: The rootstocks develop new shoots by themselves on the outside. These shoots will produce crowns after a few years, which again can be used in starting new flowers.

Light: Half shade or shade.
Temp: Grow cool.
Water: Keep moderately moist.
Hum: High.
Soil: Standard potting soil.

Convolvulus sabatius

Convolvulaceae
Convolvulus

A perennial plant from the coastal Mediterranean. It is related to the annual, tricolor convolvulus that is grown often in flowerbeds. Besides the species shown, there are several more that are able to survive outside in a rock garden; however, they all have a better chance of surviving if they can rest dormant in a greenhouse.
Care: Grow outside from the end of May, in full sun. The long shoots crawl over the ground or hang, therefore these are quite suitable as hanging plants, though be sure the pot is not too small. Give enough water and feed once every two weeks. The blooms last throughout the summer. Bring inside in the winter and provide a cool dormancy.

Convolvulus sabatius

Propagation: From seed or via top or middle cuttings taken from a dormant plant that already has new shoots. Soil temperature 68–77°F (20–25°C). It would be sensible to propagate new plants every year.

Light: Full sun.
Temp: Grow cool, in the winter 40–50°F (5–10°C).
Water: Keep moderately moist.
Hum: Moderate, 50–60%.
Soil: Standard potting soil.

Copiapoa cinerea

Cactaceae

The genus *Copiapoa* consists of species with a grayish exterior (as in the species shown) that are hard to get to flower, as well as a small, brown-

Copiapoa cinerea

black cacti, which flowers effortlessly at a very early stage. The latter has a long, thick taproot.
Care: The plants originate in Chile and often cannot adapt their growing rhythms to the northern hemisphere. Consider this when watering. In case the growth stagnates in the summer, the plants should be provided with light shade. When plants show signs of growth, one can fertilize once a month. Be careful watering the species with the taproot, because its roots rot very easily.
Propagation: From seed and from the shoots that are formed after years of growth. Grafting is a possibility as well.

Light: Full sun, except when the plants are dormant in our summer.
Temp: Grow warm to moderately warm, in the winter a minimum of 54–60°F (12–15°C), in the summer on the cool side.
Water: Sparsely during dormancy and keep slightly moist in the fall and winter.
Hum: Low to moderate.
Soil: Cactus soil, add extra perlite for the species with a taproot.

Coprosma X *kirkii* 'Variegata'

Coprosma species

Rubiaceae

A crawling plant from New Zealand that is widely available in the variegated varieties: green with white and green with yellow. There also exist cross-fertilizations, such as *Coprosma* x *kirkii*, which grow more vertically. Cultivation of all species is similar.
Care: Use as ground cover in a plant container. Give enough light, but avoid the bright sun. Fertilize every two weeks during the growth period. A cool dormancy in the winter is desirable.
Propagation: Root in the spring under glass at 68–77°F (20–25°C) soil temperature. Cut the tops of young plants once or twice. The tops can be used as cuttings again.

Light: Much light, no bright sun.
Temp: Grow moderately warm, in the winter at 40–50°F (5–10°C).
Water: Keep moderately moist.
Hum: Moderate to high.
Soil: Acidic potting soil, for instance 75% garden peat with 25% perlite.

Coprosma baueri 'Marginata'

On the following pages: *Cordyline indivisa*

CORDYLINE

Cordyline australis

Cordyline fruticosa 'Red Edge'

Cordyline australis, C. indivisa

Agavaceae

Two species that are very similar. There exist both a green and a brown version, usually called *Dracaena*. The species *australis* has a green middle nerve, *indivisa* an orange and somewhat higher situated one. There is also the cultivated species *stricta*, which has very narrow, roughly edged leaves. The plants can grow very tall when planted in containers.
Care: From the end of May these plants do very well in a garden, in a container on a sheltered terrace, or planted in a container buried in the garden. Provide plenty of water and in the summertime feed once every two weeks. Bring inside in the autumn and provide a period of dormancy in a light space.
Propagation: From seed and via top cuttings. These plants bloom once again and again develop tops. Soil temperature 68–77°F (20–25°C).

Light:	Full sun.
Temp:	Grow cool, in the winter about 40°F (5°C).
Water:	Keep moderately moist, drier in the winter.
Hum:	Moderate, 50–60%.
Soil:	Standard potting soil, possibly mixed with clay or loam.

Cordyline indivisa 'Purpurea'

Cordyline fruticosa

Agavaceae

Extremely beautiful foliage plants, often with much red in the leaves, though there is also a completely green species. This plant is often still referred to as *Cordyline terminalis*, but this is an out-of-date synonym.
Care: In the summer the plants do quite well inside, but when the heat is turned on, the dry air quickly turns the leaves brown. Fortunately, the temperature can be lower in the winter, which then allows for more humidity in the air. Feed once every two weeks during the growing period.

Cordyline fruticosa 'Mme. André'

Propagation: From root cuttings or trunk cuttings. Soil temperature 77–86°F (25–30°C).

Light:	Much light, no full sun.
Temp:	Moderately warm to warm, a minimum 54°F (12°C) in winter.
Water:	Keep moderately moist with hard water.
Hum:	High, above 60%.
Soil:	Coniferous soil.

Corokia species

Cornaceae

These bushes native to New Zealand are rather unknown, but sturdy, houseplants that can produce small, white flowers and later, yellow-orange berries.
Care: In the summer the plants can be placed in a sunny to half-shaded window. Give plenty of water and feed once every two weeks. Prune back a bit after the winter, repot and bring back to growth.
Propagation: From top cuttings taken in August. Root at 68–77°F (20–25°C) under plastic.

Light:	Full sun or half shade.
Temp:	Grow cool, in the winter a minimum of 40°F (5°C).
Water:	Keep moderately moist, somewhat drier during the dormant period.
Hum:	Moderate, 50–60%.
Soil:	Standard potting soil.

Corokia **X** *virgata* 'Coppershine'

Correa backhousiana

Rutaceae

Wintergreen bush from Tasmania, which in moderate climates can be grown as a container plant. There are also other species with green, yellow and red flowers. The cultivation is the same.
Care: These plants can be outside in a sheltered spot, given a relatively dry summer. With extremely rainy weather, one should bring them inside. Water carefully on a regular basis, because both a shortage of water and too much moisture can cause problems. The best solution is to provide a pot with some sort of watering system that assures constant moisture. Add food to the water once every two weeks. In the autumn, bring the plant inside and provide a cool dormant period. Give less water but be sure that the leaves do not fall.
Propagation: From fresh seeds or via top cuttings that root under glass at a soil temperature of 68–77°F (20–25°C).

Light:	Much light, full sun as well.
Temp:	Grow cool in the winter 40–50°F (5–10°C).
Water:	Keep moist on a regular basis with rainwater or other soft water.
Hum:	Moderate, 50–60%.

Correa backhousiana

Corokia cotoneaster

Soil:	Coniferous soil or another acidic light soil.

Corynocarpus laevigatum

Corynocarpaceae

A relatively new plant that somewhat resembles a *Ficus*. In New Zealand edible fruits appear, but the seeds are extremely poisonous.
Care: A strong plant that may be placed in the full sun and can be outside during the summer. In the winter, it can be kept very cool, but this is not absolutely necessary. Fertilize once

Corynocarpus laevigatum

every 14 days in the growing season and repot each spring.
Propagation: From top cuttings or middle cuttings, as well as from seed. Soil temperature 68–77°F (20–25°C).

Light:	Full sun or light shade.
Temp:	Grow cool to moderately warm, in the winter minimum 40°F (5°C).
Water:	Keep moderately moist.
Hum:	Moderate, 50–60%.
Soil:	Standard potting soil.

Coryphantha elephantidens

Cactaceae

Variety of cactus with a tuberculate surface on the columnar cactus body. The flowers can be yellow, light red or light purple.
Care: These plants desire a lot of light, so if possible grow in a greenhouse just behind the glass. Do not use small pots and provide cactus fertilizer once a month in the summer. In the winter the plants should be kept cool and completely dry. Do not water too early in the spring, at the most misting a little.
Propagation: From seed or by taking side shoots.

Light:	Full sun.
Temp:	Grow warm, in the winter about 40°F (5°C).
Water:	Keep rather dry, during blooming somewhat more moist, in the winter withhold all water.
Hum:	Can be low.
Soil:	Cactus soil.

Coryphanta elephantidens

Costus cuspidatus

Costus cuspidatus

Zingiberaceae

Plants for a moderate greenhouse that bloom in the fall and winter. The species pictured is the only one that stays rather small, growing about 12–20 in (30–50 cm) high.
Care: Plant preferably in a greenhouse; the plant flourishes this way more so than in a pot, although the flower production will be the same. Screen against bright sun. In the summer, fertilize every two weeks. They usually flower in the autumn and winter. The temperature can be lower then. Prune in the spring and bring back to growth.
Propagation: Root top and middle cuttings under glass at 77°F (25°C). From seed is possible as well.

Light:	Much light, no bright sun.
Temp:	Grow moderately warm to warm, in the winter 54–60°F (12–15°C).
Water:	Keep moderately moist.
Hum:	High, above 60%.
Soil:	Coniferous soil.

Cotyledon species

Crassulaceae

Interesting succulent plants with thick, wavy leaves and often hanging, bell-shaped flowers on a long stalk. Suitable for both indoor cultivation and a moderate greenhouse.
Care: The plants are sometimes beautifully pruinose, but if one touches them they become less pretty. Keep sunny in the summer, and do

Cotyledon ladysmithiensis

not give too much water or fertilizer. Feeding once a month is plenty. In the winter keep them cool and dry, otherwise the plants will not flower again.
Propagation: From seed or via top cutting. Let the cutting dry before rooting. Soil temperature 68–77°F (20–25°C).

Cotyledon undulata

Light:	Full sun.
Temp:	Grow moderately warm, in the winter 40–50°F (5–10°C).
Water:	Keep rather dry, withhold all water in the winter.
Hum:	Can be low.
Soil:	Cactus soil.

Crassula arborescens

Crassulaceae

Crassula arborescens

A plant with a bushy way of growing that can sometimes reach a height of 6½ ft (2 m). The silver-grey leaves have a narrow red edge.
Care: This plant is very suitable for rather large containers, which can then be placed outside in a sheltered location in the summer. Do not give too much water and fertilize at the most once a month, so that the plants do not overgrow. Bring inside to a cool, light space toward the winter.
Propagation: Break off parts, let dry for some days to a week and plant in a sandy mixture.

Light:	Full sun.
Temp:	Grow cool, in the winter 40–50°F (5–10°C).
Water:	Keep rather dry, almost no water in the winter.
Hum:	Can be low.
Soil:	One third part standard potting soil, ⅓ part clay or loam and ⅓ part perlite.

Crassula coccinea

Crassulaceae

A plant that is available in full bloom in the spring when it looks truly magnificent. It is not, however, an easy task to get them to bloom a second time. This plant is often called *Rochea coccinea*.
Care: Place in a light spot, but not in full sun during the flowering period. Prune a bit after blooming and place outside; it can now receive sunlight. Water moderately and feed every two weeks. Bring inside in October and keep it dormant in a greenhouse at low tempera-

Crassula coccinea

tures. Keep cool in the spring until flower buds have formed.

Propagation: Take top cuttings from non-flowering stalks and plant them in very sandy soil at a soil temperature of 60–68°F (15–20°C).

Light:	Much light, full sun allowed.
Temp:	Grow cool, in the winter 40–46°F (4–8°C).
Water:	Moderately moist in the summer, in the winter rather dry.

Crassula muscosa

Hum:	Moderate, 50–60%.
Soil:	Standard potting soil.

Crassula muscosa

Crassulaceae

The tall stalks of this plant are covered with very regularly overlapping leaves. The flowers are scarcely noticeable.

Care: Easy to keep healthy, even indoors on a warm, sunny window sill. Feed once a month with cactus fertilizer. The plant should be kept cooler in winter, otherwise it will become too leggy.

Propagation: By division or from cuttings.

Light:	Full sun.
Temp:	Moderately warm to warm, in the winter a minimum of 45°F (7°C).
Water:	Keep fairly dry, in the winter add almost no water.
Hum:	Can be low.
Soil:	Cactus soil.

Crassula ovata

Crassulaceae

A well-known, tree-like succulent, known previously as *Crassula argentea* or *C. portulacea*. This plant is relatively easy to grow indoors. Older plants can produce white flowers.

Care: Keep sunny in the summer, on the window sill or outside. Do not give too much food, some cactus fertilizer once a month at most. In the fall move inside and keep cool and frost free, withholding almost all water.

Propagation: From top cuttings, leaf cuttings or from seed. Let the cuttings dry first, then plant them in a very permeable soil mixture.

Light:	Full sun.
Temp:	Grow warm to moderately warm, in the winter a minimum of 40°F (5°C).
Water:	Rather dry, almost no water in the winter.
Hum:	Low.
Soil:	Standard potting soil or cactus soil.

Crassula ovata

Crassula pellucida 'Minuta'

Crassula pellucida

Crassulaceae

A small plant with limpy stalks and meaty, green leaves that turn somewhat red when grown in a sunny spot. The little flowers are white with red highlights. The form 'Minuta' is smaller in all parts than the species.
Care: An ideal hanging plant for a sunny location. It does not affect the plant very much if you forget to water it one time: in nature, it is used to receiving water on an irregular basis. Feed every two weeks during the growing period. In the winter, a dormant period is preferable, especially since the new shoots are not that pretty anyway.

Crassula perfoliata var. *falcata*

Propagation: Break off pieces, let dry and plant.

Light:	Full sun.
Temp:	Grow warm to moderately warm, in the winter 40–50°F (5–10°C).
Water:	Keep moderately dry, during growth withhold all water.
Hum:	Can be low.
Soil:	Cactus soil or standard potting soil mixed with clay or loam.

Crassula perfoliata var. falcata

Crassulaceae

This remarkable plant, with its pruinose leaves in two parallel surfaces, blooms with red flowers in broad bunches. It is still often called *Crassula falcata*.
Care: Grow rather warm and sunny in the summer and do not administer too much water. Provide cactus fertilizer once a month. It can be grown outside, but bring inside in the autumn and keep cool, adding little water.
Propagation: From top cutting or leaf cutting. Allow cuttings to dry for a few days, then plant in sandy mixture, soil temperature 68–77°F (20–25°C).

Light:	Full sun.
Temp:	Moderately warm to warm, in the winter not below 45°F (7°C).
Water:	Relatively dry, in the winter almost completely dry.
Hum:	Can be low, below 50%.
Soil:	Cactus soil.

Crassula perforata var. *falcata*

Crassula perforata

Crassulaceae

A *Crassula* that stays small, with a regular leaf system, through which the stalk grows.
Care: To preserve the beautiful shading, the plant is best grown in an especially sunny spot, without much water and very little fertilizer, at most some cactus food once a month. Keep cool in the winter so that the plant stops growing.
Propagation: Allow top cuttings to dry for a few days, then plant in relatively dry, sandy soil. Soil temperature 68°F (20°C).

Light:	Full sun.
Temp:	Grow cool to moderately warm, in the winter 40–50°F (5–10°C).
Water:	Keep rather dry, especially so in the winter.
Hum:	Can be low.
Soil:	Cactus soil.

Crassula perforata

Propagation: From seed or by growing new bulbs.

Light:	Full sun.
Temp:	Grow cool, in the winter a minimum of 40°F (5°C).
Water:	Moderately moist in the summer, almost dry in the winter.
Hum:	Moderate, 50–60%.
Soil:	Standard potting soil mixed with at least ⅓ part fine clay or loam.

Crassula rupestris

Crassula rupestris

Crassulaceae

A small horizontal bush with thin stalks that break off easily. The thick leaves grow like beads on a string. It can form little light red flowers.
Care: Keep well lit; this will cause the edges of the leaves to turn red. Water sparsely and provide cactus food once a month. For dormancy, keep it cool and rather dry.
Propagation: From leaf cuttings. Allow the leaves to dry first, then plant in a sandy mixture.

Light:	Full sun.
Temp:	Grow warm to moderately warm, in the winter not below 40°F (5°C).
Water:	Keep rather dry, in the winter very little water.
Hum:	Low.
Soil:	Cactus soil.

Crinum X *powellii*

Crinum X powellii

Amaryllidaceae

A bulbous plant with bottle-shaped bulbs that can grow very tall, similar to the *Hippeastrum*, but even bigger. The bulbs are not hardy and therefore cannot stay outdoors during the winter. Therefore, it is a typical container plant.
Care: Bulbs ordered by mail should be planted in the spring, with the neck of the bulb sticking out above the ground. Do not give too much water in the beginning, only when the plant is really growing. From the end of May, the plants can go outside in a sunny, sheltered location. Fertilize every two weeks. After the flowering period, withhold water gradually, with the bulb staying in the pot. The foliage shouldn't die off completely, but the plant should stop growing. If it continues to grow after the flowering period, then the temperature is too high.

Crocus vernus ssp. vernus

Iridaceae

Crocus

A crocus is not naturally a houseplant, but it is possible to force the small bulbs into flowering inside. It is usually a short-lived pleasure though.
Care: Pot the bulbs in October and bury them in the garden at a frost-free level. One can also store the pots in a cool, dark cellar. Once the tips are 3 in (7–8 cm) long and there are flower buds in the shoots, they can be allowed light. But keep them as cool as possible, because it will prolong their blooming. Fertilizer is not necessary. After the flowering period, one can plant the bulbs outside.
Propagation: From seed or via newly formed bulbs.

Light:	Keep from the sun.
Temp:	Grow cool.
Water:	Keep moderately moist.
Hum:	High, above 60%.
Soil:	Standard potting soil.

Crocus vernus ssp. *vernus* 'Pickwick'

Crossandra infundibuliformis

Acanthaceae

Firecracker flower

Although this plant is difficult to keep, it is quite popular, most likely because of its beautiful flowers.

Care: This is really a greenhouse plant that desires high humidity. Always use rainwater and administer food once every two weeks. One can keep it in the living room during the summer, but in the winter this usually does not work out. The temperature can be lower then, but not much.

Propagation: From seed or via top or middle

Crossandra infundibuliformis 'Mona Wallhed'

cuttings, which in May–June root at a soil temperature of 68–77°F (20–25°C). Use some growth hormones and cut the tops of the young plants a few times for better branching.

Light: Much light, no full sun.
Temp: Grow warm, in the winter a minimum of 60°F (15°C).
Water: Keep moderately moist with soft water.
Hum: High, above 60%.
Soil: Standard potting soil mixed with peat mould or coniferous soil.

Cryptanthus species

Bromeliaceae

These relatively small bromeliads are grown as foliage plants because the flowers are not very impressive. Often they play a subordinate part in mixed plant cases. In the picture are a small number of the many species and varieties that are available.

Care: As with all bromeliads, the rosettes die off after they flower. Sometimes side rosettes are formed, which can flower later. Generally they do not last longer than half a year, due to their need for high humidity. Water regularly and feed once every two weeks.

Propagation: By taking a growth of side rosettes. This can only happen when the old plant is dying.

Light: Half shade.

Cryptanthus

Temp: Grow warm, in the winter as well.
Water: Keep moderately moist.
Hum: Moderate to high.
Soil: Special mixture for bromeliads.

Cryptocereus anthonyanus

Cactaceae

A cactus with long, flat shoots and large flowers. Shows a resemblance to the *Nopalxochia*.
Care: Grow light, but not in full sun. In the summer, the plant can go outside. In the fall, the dormant period starts. Give very little water during this time and keep cool. The plant is allowed to shrivel somewhat. In the spring, once flower buds have formed, water more and do not turn the plant, otherwise the leaves will drop. From here on, give cactus

Cryptocereus anthonyanus

food every two weeks. After flowering, if one wishes, one can cut back the plant and let it rest dormant until the plant can go outside.
Propagation: Cut-off pieces from the shoots root easily. Allow to dry for a week, then plant in relatively dry, sandy soil. Soil temperature 68°F (20°C).

Light: Much light, no full sun.
Temp: Grow cool to moderately warm, in the winter 40–50°F (5–10°C).
Water: Keep moderately moist, in the dormant period almost completely dry.
Hum: Moderate, 50–60%.
Soil: Standard potting soil mixed with extra sharp sand or perlite. Provide good drainage.

Ctenanthe lubbersiana

Marantaceae

Foliage plants that resemble the more known *Calanthea* and *Maranta*. The cultivation is also the same.

Care: The common species is especially sturdy and grows very well in the summer. When the plant is kept in too dark a spot, the markings on the leaves will gradually disappear, though the plant will stay alive. The cultivar 'Variegata' needs more light than the common species. By keeping the temperature lower in the winter, one can provide a higher humidity, which is to the plant's advantage. Give food once every two weeks in the growing season.

Propagation: By taking and planting the shoots separately.

Ctenanthe lubbersiana

Light: Much light, but no full sun.
Temp: Grow moderately warm to warm, in the winter a minimum of 61°F (16°C).
Water: Keep constantly moist with soft water.
Hum: High, above 60%.
Soil: Standard potting soil with extra peat mold or peat moss. Use wide, well-draining pots or bowls.

Ctenanthe lubbersiana 'Variegata'

Ctenanthe oppenheimiana

Marantaceae

This species has beautiful leaf markings, but it is not easy to grow. Frequently, this cultivar is indicated as 'Tricolor.'
Care: The plant needs plenty of light to maintain the beautiful leaf markings, and a high humidity to grow well. This makes it a typical greenhouse plant, one that is only able to survive temporarily indoors (in the summer). Give some diluted fertilizer every two weeks.
Propagation: From shoots.

Light: Much light, but no full sun.
Temp: Grow warm to moderately warm, in the winter a minimum of 61°F (16°C).
Water: Keep moderately moist with soft water.
Hum: High, above 60%.
Soil: Humusy and permeable, e.g. a mixture with much peat moss, coniferous soil, etc. Grow in wide, well-draining pots or trays.

Cunonia capensis

Cunonia capensis

Cunoniaceae

Bush or small tree that grows in South Africa in relatively moist places. Grown as a container plant in moderate climate zones.
Care: Preferably, from May on keep in a sheltered, shaded location. The soil should be kept rather moist and food administered every two weeks. Bring to a cool, light, frost-free space in the fall. Give as much water as necessary to keep the leaves from falling off. Repot in the spring, place in a warmer spot and bring outside at the end of May.
Propagation: Via fresh, imported seeds.

Light: Much light, no bright sun.
Temp: Grow cool, in the winter 46–54°F (8–12°C).
Water: Keep constantly moist in the summer, drier in the winter.
Hum: Moderate, 50–60%.
Soil: Standard potting soil mixed with a large part of loam and clay.

Ctenanthe oppenheimiana 'Variegata'

Cuphea ignea

Cuphea species

Lythraceae

Before, gardeners usually only came across the species *ignea*, also called *platycentra*. On account of the tubular, flame-colored flowers, they are known as Firecracker plants as well. Lately, large numbers of the species *hyssopifolia* have come on the market, a plant that requires the same cultivation.
Care: Grow either outside or inside during the summer, but screen against the brightest sun. Feed every two weeks. Prune back toward winter and keep cool. Repot in the spring and bring back to growth. Sometimes this does not work for several years so it is better to take cuttings frequently.
Propagation: Sow in January, or take top cuttings in spring or fall. Soil temperature 68°F (20°C).

Light:	Much light, no bright sun.
Temp:	Grow cool, in the winter around 45°F (7°C).
Water:	Keep moderately moist.
Hum:	Moderate, 50–60%.
Soil:	Standard potting soil.

Cupressus macrocarpa

Cupressaceae

Indoor cypress

This is a typical example of a plant that until recently was rarely seen in people's houses but that has sprung up all over many living rooms lately. It is very durable. Shown above is the species 'Goldcrest.'
Care: The plant can be placed anywhere but if you want it to grow, then it should receive some light, but never full sun. In the summer, the plant can go outside in a sheltered location, with no bright sun here as well. Feed every two weeks. In the winter, the temperature can be much lower. That is better for the foliage, too.
Propagation: Root top cuttings under glass at 68–77°F (20–25°C).

Cuphea hyssopifolia 'Rubra'

Cupressus macrocarpa

Light:	Half shade.
Temp:	Grow cool to moderately warm, in the winter not below 40°F (5°C).
Water:	Keep moderately moist, drier in the winter.
Hum:	Moderate, 50–60%.
Soil:	Standard potting soil.

Cussonia spicata

Araliaceae

A lesser known evergreen from South Africa. Grown as a bush in our regions, fares well in a moderately warm living room, but can be outside as a container plant in the summer.

Cussonia spicata

Care: Do not place in the sun, not even when it is outside during the summer. The ball of soil should never dry out and should be fed every two weeks. Bring the plant inside in the fall and provide a dormant period at low temperature. Give less water in this period.
Propagation: From seed. Soil temperature 50–60°F (10–15°C).

Light:	Much light or half shade, no full sun.
Temp:	Grow cool, in the winter 40–50°F (5–10°C).
Water:	Keep moderately moist, drier in the winter, but the leaves should not fall off.
Hum:	Moderate, 50–60%.
Soil:	Standard potting soil.

Cyanotis kewensis

Commelinaceae

A crawling or hanging plant with succulent leaves and small, violet flowers.

Care: Grow light, but screen against the brightest sunlight. Place it in a hanging pot large enough to accommodate the plant. Do not give too much water; it is a succulent plant, and so can store much water. Feed only during the growth period.

Propagation: By division, via seed and from top cuttings, which easily root after drying for a day.

Cyanotis kewensis

Light:	Much light, no bright sun.
Temp:	Grow moderately warm, in the winter 50–54°F (10–12°C).
Water:	Moderately moist in the growing period, drier in the winter.
Hum:	Moderate, 50–60%.
Soil:	Standard potting soil.

Cycas revoluta

Cycadaceae

Sago palm

It is not a real palm nor a real fern. The plant belongs to a separate family over 200 million years old. In China and Japan, these plants grow in the wild. They are extremely decorative, but unfortunately, do not easily keep well.

Care: Keep in the light during summer, possibly in a sunny location outside. Give fertilizer every two weeks, but only while the plant grows. Keep the plant cooler in the winter and drier as well.

Propagation: From seeds, which germinate at 68–77°F (20–25°C).

Light:	Much light, but screen against the brightest light.
Temp:	Grow cool to moderately warm, in the winter not below 54°F (12°C), unless the plant is kept very dry.
Water:	Keep moderately moist, drier in the winter.

Cycas revoluta

Hum:	Moderate, 50–60%.
Soil:	Standard potting soil mixed with clay, loam or rock powder.

Cyclamen persicum

Primulaceae

Cyclamen

Richly flowering houseplants in numerous colors and shapes, such as the fringed variety in the picture. The so-called mini-cyclamen has become increasingly popular, and is also referred to by its creator's name, Wellensiek.

Care: The modern ability to maintain a constant temperature indoors, especially with well-insulated double-paned windows, has reduced the cyclamen's chances of surviving as a houseplant, since it prefers a spot by a cool, drafty window. Water by placing a tray of water beneath the plant's pot. If after half an hour the water is not sucked up, then dispose of it; this plant shouldn't be moist constantly or it will rot. After flowering, give less and less water until the leaves dry and fall off. The tuber stays in the pot and can be kept in that state for a month. Next, repot and bring back to growth. From the end of May, the plant can go outside and grow in a cool and shaded spot. Bring inside in the fall and keep especially cool. It is advisable to forget about a dormant

Cyclamen persicum

period for this species, and to continue to grow it, feeding once every two weeks. I suggest trying with and without a dormant period to see which one works best for your plant.

Propagation: Cyclamen are easy to sow. This can be done practically throughout the year, though a good time is in August. The pH of the sowing soil should be 5.6. The seeds have to be covered with .2 in (5 mm) of soil and the sowing tray kept under black plastic at 62°F (17°C) for 25 days. After that, the plastic is removed as the young plants gradually get used to the light. Keep at a temperature of 68°F (20°C). Four weeks later, one can start to plant the seedlings in pots. After about six weeks, lower the temperature to 60°F (15°C). From the end of December on, continue to grow the plants until they start to flower. The earlier you sow, the sooner the plants will sprout flowers. Chemical substances can be used to prevent premature rotting, if this becomes a problem.

Light:	Much light, but no full sun.
Temp:	Grow cool.
Water:	Keep moderately moist, completely dry during dormancy.
Hum:	Moderate to high.
Soil:	Standard potting soil, possibly mixed with clay or loam.

Cyclamen persicum

Cyclamen persicum 'Mini'

Cycnoches chlorochilum

Cycnoches chlorochilum

Orchidaceae

Extremely elegant and relatively easy-growing orchids, originally from tropical South America.
Care: Always provide plenty of light, but screen against bright afternoon sun. A greenhouse is a good location, but many people are successful in growing these plants inside their homes. Keep it moderately moist during the growing period, though never too much water, because it can cause the pseudotubers to rot. Add orchid food to the water every two weeks. Ventilate during warm weather. After the new pseudotubers are full grown, a dormant period of a few weeks is needed, in which little water should be administered. The temperature can be lower in the winter.
Propagation: By division and from seed.

Light:	Much light, no bright afternoon sun.
Temp:	Grow warm to moderately warm, in the winter a minimum of 58°F (14°C).
Water:	Keep moderately moist with soft water or rainwater, almost dry in the dormant period.
Hum:	High, above 60%.
Soil:	Preferably a mixture of fern roots and chopped tree ferns in lattice baskets. Pure rock wool flakes can be used as well, but in that case feed more frequently.

Cymbidium hybrids

Orchidaceae

Interest in the flowers of the *Cymbidium*, often sold in plastic boxes, is decreasing somewhat. Try this orchid for a change in houseplants. Some people succeed wonderfully. The mini-varieties shown in the pictures are especially suitable for this purpose.
Care: The plants can stay indoors throughout the year in a light location, but never in the full sun. A real dormant period is not needed, although the temperature can be lower in the winter and at night. Also important is frequent

Cymbidium-hybr. 'King Arthur Salvador'

misting with soft water in the winter. A humidifier in the plant's room works wonders. The pots should be well-drained and not too small. Repotting is necessary only once every two years, and should be done after the flowering period. During the growth period, add some food once every 14 days in a half concentration.
Propagation: Larger plants can be divided when you repot.

Light:	Much light, no full sun.
Temp:	In the summer, daytime 68–84°F (20–28°C) and at night a minimum of 62°F (17°C). In the winter daytime around 68°F (20°C) and at night 60°F (15°C).
Water:	Keep moderately moist; in the winter drier, but never completely dry. Always use rainwater or other soft water.
Hum:	Moderate to high, always above 50%.
Soil:	Often grown in a mixture of standard potting soil with synthetic particles, clay particles or rock wool flakes. In all cases the substrate should be permeable and the drainage perfect, with a pH level between 5 and 6.

Cyperus albostriatus

See *Cyperus diffusus*

Cyperus alternifolius

Cyperaceae

Umbrella plant

This is the most well-known of the various *Cyperus* species. It is easy to keep indoors, as long as it always stands with its roots in water.
Care: The plant can stay in a warm room the whole year, though can be kept cooler in the winter. Constantly keep the roots in water; water is allowed to reach the ball of soil. Administer food during the growth period.
Propagation: By dividing the large plants and by taking cuttings of the leaf rosettes. Take a small umbrella, cut off the leaves of 2 in (5 cm) and take the leaf stalk with about 3 in (7 cm) below the leaves. Place the umbrella in a

Cymbidium-hybr. 'Flirtation'

Cyperus alternifolius

glass of water and after a while one can observe roots forming. After that, plant in pots. Propagation from seed is a possibility as well.

Light: Much light, but never full sun.
Temp: Grow moderately warm, in the winter a minimum of 54°F (12°C).
Water: Keep constantly moist; the ball of soil should always stay under water.
Hum: Moderate.
Soil: Standard potting soil.

Cyperus diffusus

Cyperaceae

Cypress grass, small umbrella plant

This is a small umbrella plant with short stalks, as easy to grow as the last species, but less decorative. **Care:** While the *Cyperus alternifolius*, this plant does not always require wet roots, though the soil should constantly be moist. In the summer feed once every two weeks. Keep cooler in the winter.

Cyperus diffusus

Propagation: By division.

Light: Much light, never full sun.
Temp: Grow moderately warm, in the winter a minimum of 54°F (12°C).
Water: Keep constantly wet, but don't allow the water to stagnate in the tray.
Hum: Moderate.
Soil: Standard potting soil.

Cyperus papyrus

Cyperaceae

Papyrus

This is the original Egyptian papyrus, from which paper was made. The plant can grow up to 6½ ft (3 m) tall. There is a mini version as well that is about 24 in (60 cm) tall, the *Cyperus haspan*. Both species are rather hard to grow

Cyperus papyrus

indoors because they need much light and a high humidity. But they are extremely decorative, and can be worth the effort.
Care: A very light location is needed, allowing some sunlight in the winter. The plant should always stand in a tray with water. Keep *Cyperus haspan* very moist, but without the "foot-bath." Feed once every two weeks during the growth period. In the winter the temperature can be lowered to keep the air more humid.

Light: Much light, in the summer no full sun.
Temp: Grow moderately warm, in the winter a minimum of 61°F (16°C).
Water: Keep constantly moist.
Hum: High, above 60%.
Soil: Standard potting soil possibly mixed with some clay or loam.

Cyphostemma juttae

Vitaceae

It is hard to believe that this peculiar plant is related to the well-known houseplant *Cissus*. It was actually once called *Cissus juttae*. The plant has a thick, succulent trunk, in which it stores moisture. When growing in its native land, Southwest Africa, large, thick leaves appear during the rainy season, which later fall off as soon as the rain stops.
Care: Preferably in a bright, moderate greenhouse. In the summer, it needs plenty of sun, and sparse water. Feed at most once a month. Keep cool in the winter and withhold all water.
Propagation: From seed.

Light: Full sun.
Temp: Grow moderately warm to warm, in the winter 50–54°F (10–12°C).
Water: Rather dry in the summer, dry in the winter.
Hum: Low.
Soil: Cactus soil.

Cyphostemma juttae

Cyrtanthus parviflorus

Amaryllidaceae

Bulbous growth that flowers in the early summer and can be put outside. But it is not that hardy, so bring the plant inside for the autumn.
Care: The bulbs, which can be ordered by mail, generally arrive in the spring. Pot them immediately and withhold almost all water at first. As they start to grow, gradually administer more water and in the summer add some food once every two weeks. The plants can stay in the garden or on a sheltered balcony all summer, until the foliage dies off. Store the bulbs dry, in pots. In the spring, repot and bring back to growth.
Propagation: From seed and via newly formed bulbs.

Light:	Full sun.
Temp:	Grow cool, in the winter 46–50°F (8–10°C).
Water:	Moderately moist in the summer, dry in the winter.
Hum:	Moderate, 50–60%.
Soil:	Standard potting soil.

Cyrtomium falcatum

Aspidiaceae

Japanese holly fern

A relatively strong fern for growing inside, because its flat, leathery foliage does not evaporate as much as the fine, soft foliage of other plants. There are various cultivars in cultivation such as 'Rochfordianum' with carved-in, sinuated leaves.
Care: This fern does not like high temperatures, so keep it as cool as possible. It may go outside in the summer given the appropriate climate. In the winter, the temperature should be considerably lower. Feed once every month in half concentrations.
Propagation: By sowing the spurs, or by division.

Cyrtanthus parviflorus

Light:	Half shade to shade.
Temp:	Grow cool, in the winter possibly 45–50°F (7–10°C).
Water:	Keep constantly moist (in a pot with a watering system), somewhat drier in the winter.
Hum:	Moderate to warm.
Soil:	Standard potting soil with extra loam or clay.

Cyrtomium falcatum

Cytisus X spachianus

Leguminoseae

Broom

An old, well-known houseplant that we do not see so much of anymore, perhaps because of its rather difficult indoor cultivation needs.

Cytisus X spachianus

Care: Keep especially cool in the spring. The leaves and flowers fall off easily in a warm room. Keep from sunlight. Prune back after the flowering period, place outside in a light, somewhat shaded spot and feed every two weeks. Bring inside in the fall for a cool dormancy.

Propagation: Root half-hardened top cuttings in the summer at a soil temperature between 60–68°F (15–20°C).

Light:	Much light, but no sun.
Temp:	Grow cool, 54–64°F (12–18°C), in the winter 40–46°F (4–8°C).
Water:	Keep moderately moist.
Hum:	Moderate to high.
Soil:	Standard potting soil.

Danaë racemosa

Liliaceae

A strongly branched evergreen with nondescript small leaves and flowers, and following flowering, red berries. Is also called *Ruscus racemosus*. In nature, the bush is quite hardy. In more northerly latitudes it grows as a pretty container plant.

Care: Place outside at the end of May, and keep it protected and shaded. Give plenty of water and fertilize once every two weeks (until around mid-August). Bring inside before the frost starts and provide a cool dormant period, but not so dry that the leaves drop.

Propagation: By division.

Light:	Half shade to shade.

Danaë racemosa

Temp:	Grow cool, in the winter 40–50°F (5–10°C).
Water:	Keep moderately moist, in the winter somewhat drier.
Hum:	Moderate, 50–60%.
Soil:	Standard potting soil.

Darlingtonia californica

Sarraceniaceae

Pitcher plant

These remarkable, carnivorous plants from California and Oregon have hairs, pointed downwards, inside the hollow leaves that prevent curious insects from crawling out again. Inside the leaves, the insects die from the decaying liquid of the plant. The flowers are brownish red. During the flowering period,

pollinate with a small brush to increase flower development.

Care: These are swamp plants that prefer to stand with their roots in water, at least 2 in (5 cm) deep. The humidity has to be high, the temperature moderate. In the winter, the plants become dormant, but they should be kept frost-free. Enthusiasts grow these plants in a cold tray with moss-covered sides. The plant feeds on insects.

Propagation: From seed. In moist peat mold they germinate well; do not cover seeds.

Light:	Half shade to shade.
Temp:	Grow cool to moderately warm, in the winter frost free.
Water:	Keep constantly wet with rainwater or soft water.
Hum:	Very high, 80–90%.
Soil:	Peat mould with decayed manure, all covered with living peat moss.

Dasylirion acrotrichum

Agavaceae

Impressive container plant with a short trunk, which carries a half-sphere rosette of long, narrow, thorny leaves. A jewel for a terrace in the summer.

Care: Inside, these plants are much too dangerous, especially for children. At the end of May, they can go outside in the full sun. Feed every two weeks and make sure the ball of soil does not dry out. In October, bring inside and keep very cool but frost free. Prevent the plant from growing too early in the spring.

Propagation: From seed. Soil temperature 68–77°F (20–25°C).

Light:	Full sun.
Temp:	Grow cool to moderately warm, in the winter not below 32°F (0°C).
Water:	Keep moderately moist, drier in the winter.
Hum:	Low.
Soil:	Standard potting soil mixed with clay or loam.

Dasylirion acrotrichum

Darlingtonia californica

Datura species

Solanaceae

Impressive container plants with large, trumpet-shaped flowers. Some species can grow to at least 16.5 ft (5 m) high. There are species with white, yellow or orange flowers and there are cross-fertilizations available. The treatment for all is the same.

Care: At the end of May, this plant can go outside in a sheltered, sunny spot. One should use a rather large pot or container because they are vigorous plants. Feed weekly during the growth period. Often, flowers appear in the summer and the fall, and a few species bloom in the winter. Before the first night frosts destroy the plant, it has to be brought inside, preferably to a greenhouse. Prune back considerably in the spring, possibly repot and bring back to growth, but not too early.

Propagation: Take top cuttings in the spring from the young shoots and root them under glass or plastic at 68°F (20°C).

Light: Full sun.

Datura-hybr.

Datura aurea

Temp: Grow cool to moderately warm, dormancy at 40–50°F (5–10°C).
Water: Keep moderately moist, drier in the winter.
Hum: Moderate, 50–60%.
Soil: Standard potting soil mixed with clay or loam.

Davallia mariesii

Davalliaceae

A fern that grows with long, crawling, brown-scaled rootstocks. They look like hairy legs. Dry-stored rootstocks can come out after only months. The plant is sometimes hard to get, which is odd, because it is a pretty, strong houseplant.

Care: This plant can be kept indoors all year. The leaves are able to endure dry air fairly well. Regular watering is important, but can be made easier by installing a watering system. (This in fact applies to all ferns.) During the growth season, feed once every two weeks.

Davillia mariesii

Davallia mariesii

Propagation: By division, possibly via spurs.

Light: Half shade to shade.
Temp: Grow moderately warm to warm, a minimum of 64°F (18°C).
Water: Keep constantly moist.
Hum: Low to moderate.
Soil: Standard potting soil.

Delosperma species

Aizoaceae

Sturdy succulents that can be outside in the summer without a problem, provided that they do not catch too much rain. Often confused with *Lampranthus* and other varieties popularly known as *Mesembryanthemum*. The cultivation is the same.

Care: Grow in a sunny location, from the end of May possibly outside. Do not give too much water and add food to the water once a month. Cool and almost dry dormancy. Repot

Delosperma aberdeenense

Delosperma pruinosum

in the spring and keep warm. The small plants tend to grow quickly again.
Propagation: Allow the top cuttings to dry for a while, after that plant them in sandy soil. Soil temperature 68°F (20°C). Or from seed.

Light:	Full sun.
Temp:	Grow cool to warm, in the winter 40–50°F (5–10°C).
Water:	Keep relatively dry, water very sparsely in the winter.
Hum:	Low.
Soil:	Standard potting soil, mixed with perlite. Cactus soil as well.

Dendrobium aggregatum

Orchidaceae

These Dendrobium species belong to a group that is suitable for moderate greenhouses. So keep cooler in the winter, but not as cold as the plants in the following category. Some species are *aphyllum, anceps, bellatulum, brymeranum, chrysanthun, devonianum, fimbriatum, pendulum* and *speciosum*.
Care: Allow for much light in the early spring, though screen against bright sunlight in the summer. Keep warm in the growth period. Use plenty of water with food added regularly, especially when the plants grow in

Dendrobium aggregatum

a substrate that does not contain any nutrients, such as rock wool. After the new pseudotubers are full grown (usually in the fall), administer less water, but continue to allow much light. Keep cooler in the winter and withhold all water.
Propagation: By division.

Light:	Much light, screen against bright sunlight.
Temp:	Grow warm, dormant period a minimum of 54°F (12°C).
Water:	Plenty of rainwater or soft water in the summer, practically dry in the winter.
Hum:	High, above 60%.
Soil:	Many species are easy to grow on pieces of tree fern, or in pots and lattice baskets that have very good drainage systems and are filled with rock wool, peat moss pieces, etc.

Dendrobium nobile

Orchidaceae

A popular species, originating in high-altitude, rather cold regions. Other species for cool cultivation are, for instance, the species *hookeranum, pierardii* and *speciosum*. These species are labeled deciduous, though in cultivation, there is always some foliage on the plant during dormancy.

Dendrobium nobile

Care: Find a very light location, but screen against bright sunlight. During the flowering period the plant can come indoors. In the summer give plenty of water, grow warm and administer orchid food once every two weeks. By the time the new pseudotubers are full grown, lower the temperature and withhold almost all water in the winter, in order to stimulate the development of flower buds.

Propagation: By division, preferably after blooming.

Light:	Much light, no bright sun.
Temp:	Grow warm in the summer, in the winter between 46–54°F (8–12°C).
Water:	Give plenty of soft water or rainwater in the summer, provided that there is good drainage.
Hum:	High, above 60%.
Soil:	Grow in easy-draining pots or lattice baskets, filled with peat moss or rock wool flakes.

Dendrobium phalaenopsis

Orchidaceae

Those *Deodrobium* species from warm, tropical regions are evergreens, so-called because the leaves stay on. The dormant period is not as strict as with the species discussed before and low temperatures are not recommended. The most well-known species are: *atroviolaceum, bigibbum, brymeranum, chrysotoxum, dearei, densiflorum* (syn. *thyrsiflorum*), *findlayanum, formosum, infundibulum, loddigesii, moscha-tum, phalaenopsis, senile, stratiotes* x *superbiens, superbum* and *taurinum*.
Care: Grow warm the whole year and allow much light. Some species desire unscreened sunlight. Give plenty of water during the growth period and feed at least once every two

Dendrobium phalaenopsis

DICHONDRA

Dendrobium densiflorum

weeks. In the fall, after the complete growth of the pseudotubers, the dormant period starts. Keep the plants warm and do not withhold all water.
Propagation: By division.

Light: Much light; some species like full sun.
Temp: Grow warm, never below 64°F (18°C).
Water: Give plenty of water in the summer, provided the pot drains well. Less water in the winter. Always use soft water.
Hum: High, above 60%.
Soil: Airy and permeable, such as peat moss, clay particles, rock wool flakes or a mixture of the above.

Dichondra repens

Convolvulaceae

Low, crawling plant, also used as lawn cover in the subtropics. In northern climates, keep frost-free during the winter dormancy.
Care: Can grow outside in the summer, for instance on a balcony. Will endure heat as well as some drought. In the summer fertilize once

a week. Bring inside in the fall and keep cool. New shoots should develop by spring.
Propagation: By division or from seed.

Light: Full sun.
Temp: Grow cool to moderately cool, in the winter 40–50°F (5–10°C).
Water: Keep moderately moist.
Hum: Moderate, 50–60%.
Soil: Standard potting soil.

Dichondra repens

Dichorisandra reginae

Commelinaceae

A relative of the popular Tradescantia. The leaves have two silver-white lines that run lengthwise. Small bunches of purple flowers can appear.
Care: Grow warm and provide a relatively high humidity. Avoid sunlight. In the growing period, feed once every two weeks.

Dichorisandra reginae

Propagation: From top cuttings, seed or by dividing larger plants. Soil temperature 68–77°F (20–25°C).

Light:	Much light or half shade, no full sun.
Temp:	Grow warm, a minimum of 64°F (18°C).
Water:	Keep moderately moist.
Hum:	High, above 60%.
Soil:	Standard potting soil.

Dicksonia antarctica

Dicksoniaceae
Tasmanian tree fern

This plant, which can reach a length of 50 ft (15 m) in Australia, can really thrive in other regions as a houseplant, greenhouse plant or

Dicksonia antarctica

container plant, with good care.
Care: This tree fern can stand outside in a very sheltered location, but a greenhouse is preferable because of the higher temperature. Take special care in keeping the ball of soil from drying out, because the plant is very sensitive to this. Feed once every two weeks during the growth period.
Propagation: From spores.

Light:	Much light, but no full sun.
Temp:	Grow moderately warm to warm, in the winter the temperature can be lowered to 54°F (12°C).
Water:	Keep constantly moist.
Hum:	Moderate to high.
Soil:	A permeable, humus mixture of, for instance, peat moss, decayed manure, coniferous soil, etc.

Didierea madagascariensis

Didiereacea

A curious and rare relation of the cactus family with short, gray thorns, on which tubular green leaves grow. In our climate, flowers do not occur. It belongs to the oldest family of plants on earth and grows in desert areas on Madagascar.

Care: Grow warm and sunny, do not give much water. In the summer, give some cactus food every two weeks. In the winter, do not keep too cold and allow for extra light if possible.
Propagation: From seed (hard to obtain).

Didierea madagascariensis

Light:	Full sun.
Temp:	Grow warm, in the winter 58–61°F (14–16°C), no colder.
Water:	Keep rather dry, hardly any water in the winter.
Hum:	Low to moderate.
Soil:	Cactus soil.

Didymochlaena truncatula

Aspidiaceae

A beautiful but unfortunately not-so-strong fern with fresh green or somewhat brownish leaf feathers and brown-red stalks.
Care: The plant prefers high humidity and for that reason is not so suitable for a heated room. In the summer, however, it will be all right for a while indoors. Too much light is not desirable. In the winter, the temperature should be lowered to keep them alive. Feed during the growth period once every two weeks in half concentrations.
Propagation: From spores and by division.

Light:	Shady, north-facing window.
Temp:	Grow moderately warm, in the winter a minimum of 54°F (12°C).
Water:	Keep constantly moist.
Hum:	High, above 60%.
Soil:	Standard potting soil mixed with extra peat moss or leaf mold.

Didymochlaena truncatula

Dieffenbachia amoena

Araceae

Extremely popular houseplants that survive rather well, although they're not from the strongest plant family. Sometimes they produce arum-like flowers. The cv. in the picture, 'Tropic Snow,' is the most famous. The less white the plant is, the less light it needs. If the plant is situated in too dark a spot, all the leaves will turn green. All parts of the plant are poisonous, so do not keep them too close to children.
Care: Never full sun, always screen. The plants need to stay inside, because northern summers are even too cold (at least the nights). In the winter, the temperature can be lower. Fertilize during the growth period.
Propagation: Root top and trunk cuttings under glass at a soil temperature of 77°F (25°C).

Light:	Half shade to much light, never full sun.
Temp:	Grow moderately warm to warm, in the winter the temperature may be lowered to 60°F (15°C).
Water:	Always keep moderately moist with water that is not too cold or too soft.
Hum:	Moderate to high.
Soil:	A mixture of peat mold, peat moss or coniferous soil.

Dieffenbachia

Dieffenbachia bowmannii

Araceae

A species distinguished by an unmottled leaf stalk, which is not white at the base. The leaf is a strong cream-white color, especially on the shown 'Camilla' and the similar 'Marianne.' After a while the leaves become greener, which is noticeable in the picture.

Dieffenbachia bowmannii 'Camilla'

Care: Place where it can get a fair amount of light, but no full sun. Feed every two weeks during the growth period. In the winter the temperature may be lower.

Light:	Much light, never full sun.
Temp:	Moderately warm to warm, in the winter a minimum of 60°F (15°C).
Water:	Always keep rather moist with luke-warm soft water.
Hum:	High, above 60%.
Soil:	Standard potting soil mixed with much peat mould, peat moss or coniferous soil.

Dieffenbachia maculata

Araceae

Often called *Dieffenbachia picta*. The foliage is marked irregularly in cream-white and green. Variously marked selections are each named separate.
Care: Grow light, but avoid full sun. Feed once every two weeks in the growing season. Keep cooler in the winter to increase the humidity.
Propagation: From stem or top cuttings, soil temperature 77°F (25°C).

Light:	Much light, no full sun.

Dieffenbachia maculata

Dieffenbachia amoena 'Tropic Snow'

Temp: Grow moderately warm to warm, in the winter at least 60°F (15°C).
Water: Keep moderately wet constantly with soft, luke-warm water.
Hum: Moderate to high.
Soil: Mixture with much peat mould, peat moss or coniferous soil.

Dieffenbachia seguine

Araceae

A species with light green leaves that, along with the much-cultivated cv. 'Rudolph Roehrs,' is only dark green along the middle nerve and leaf edges. There are other species with a number of different shadings.
Care: Always grow warm, and not too dark, but always out of the sunlight. Mist or sponge the leaves frequently in the winter. It also helps if the temperature is lower, but not below 60°F (15°C).
Propagation: Root top cuttings or trunk cuttings under glass at a soil temperature of 77°F (25°C).

Light: Much light, no full sun.
Temp: Grow warm to moderately warm, a minimum of 60°F (15°C).
Water: Keep moderately moist, if possible use rainwater.
Hum: Moderate to high.
Soil: An acidic permeable mixture, with peat mold, peat moss or coniferous soil.

Dieffenbachia seguine

Dionaea muscipula

Dionaea muscipula

Droseraceae
Venus's flytrap

Carnivorous plants are enjoying an increased popularity among houseplant growers. It is quite engrossing to watch how an insect, taken by surprise, is imprisoned by the enclosing leaf parts. The plants digest the insect very slowly, and then sets up its trap again.
Care: Not suitable for a heated room. Cool temperatures and a high humidity are preferred, so it works well in a greenhouse. It also

works in a vitrine, provided it doesn't become too warm. I tried to grow the plant along the side of a small pond one summer, but it was not a great success. Plant food is hardly necessary when enough insects are caught.
Propagation: By division, leaf cuttings or from seed.

Light: Much light, screen only against the brightest sun.
Temp: Grow cool, temperature can be lower in the winter, 40°F (5°C).
Water: Keep moderately moist.
Hum: Very high, around 80%.
Soil: A mixture of sphagnum and peat moss.

Dipladenia sanderi

Apocynaceae

This twining plant from Brazil is not so easy to grow indoors, but due to its pretty flowers it is still very popular. There exist various cultivars, of which the picture 'Rosea' is the most well known.
Care: Needs light, but grow out of the sun, and provide a high humidity by misting often or vaporizing from below. Prune back a bit in the fall and keep cool. Give less water, but make sure that the plant does not dry out.

Propagation: From top or middle cuttings. Use growth hormones and soil temperature of 77°F (25°C).

Light: Much light, no full sun.
Temp: Grow moderately warm to warm, in the winter a minimum of 54°F (12°C).
Water: Keep moderately moist with soft water, and quite dry in the winter.
Hum: High, at least 60%.
Soil: Mix standard potting soil with extra peat moss or coniferous soil.

Dipladenia sanderi 'Rosea'

Dipteracanthus devosianus

Dipteracanthus makoyanus

Dipteracanthus devosianus

Acanthaceae

Tropical foliage plants, previously called *Ruellia*. These low, horizontal plants are suitable for ground cover in vitrines, greenhouses and bottle gardens. The species *devosianus* can produce white flowers with purple leaves. The species *makoyanus* is very similar but has light red flowers.
Care: Always keep warm and provide a humid atmosphere. No direct sunlight. Fertilize every two weeks in the growing season.
Propagation: Root top cuttings under glass at a soil temperature of 77°F (25°C). Take cuttings often to replace older plants that lose their beauty.

Light:	Half shade, never full sun.
Temp:	Grow warm, a minimum of 64°F (18°C).
Water:	Keep moderately moist, possibly with luke-warm rainwater.
Hum:	High, above 60%.
Soil:	Acidic, humus and permeable soil in shallow bowls with drainage. Coniferous soil is excellent, too.

Disa uniflora

Orchidaceae

Very beautiful orchids that differ from most other species in that the sepal, not the lip, is the most striking part of the flower. The species shown in the picture grows terrestrially (in the soil) with bulbous roots. Along with other species, there are hybrids as well.
Care: These plants are known to be difficult to cultivate. Keeping them constantly cool and fresh in a shaded greenhouse is important. Give plenty of water and mist during the growth period. Administer orchid food once every two weeks. When the part of the plant above the soil begins to die off, give less water. The temperature can go lower than the cold greenhouse level. Repot in the spring.
Propagation: By division during repotting.

Light:	Shade.
Temp:	Grow cool, in the winter 40–50°F (5–10°C).
Water:	Plenty of rainwater in the summer, provided that there is good drainage.
Hum:	High, above 60%.
Soil:	Mixture of coniferous soil, decayed leaf substrate and decayed manure bedded on a layer of clay particles or pottery shards. Cover with sphagnum moss after planting.

Disa uniflora

Dischidia pectenoides

Asclepiadaceae

A very strange climbing plant from the tropics. The upper leaves are normal, the lower ones are connected to a big bag in which water collects and the aerial roots of the plant will grow.
Care: Grow in a warm, shaded greenhouse. Provide a high humidity by misting fre-

Dischidia pectenoides

Disphyma crassifolium

Aizoaceae

Succulent from Australia, similar to *Delosperma* and *Lampranthus*. These small plants have been grown in Europe for a few centuries already, but are not often available in flower shops. Enthusiasts exchange cuttings and bring back small plants from their exotic journeys.
Care: Very easy to grow, outside (from the end of May, when the danger of night frost is over) as well as inside. Do not give much water and allow for full sunlight. Feed once every two weeks (cactus food is excellent). Bring inside in the fall for a cool, dry dormant period.
Propagation: Allow top cuttings to dry for a while, then plant them in permeable, relatively dry soil. Also possible from seed.

Light:	Full sun.
Temp:	Grow cool to moderately warm, in the winter 40–50°F (5–10°C).
Water:	Sparse, in the winter almost no water.
Hum:	Low.
Soil:	Standard potting soil mixed with sharp sand or perlite. Use pots with effective drainage.

Disphyma crassifolium

olive-green color. With the variety 'Gracillima,' the leaves are even narrower. The middle vein is white in this variety.
Care: The air in a heated room is too dry for this plant in the winter, so mist frequently, install a humidifier or allow the plant to have a cooler dormancy period. In the summer, fertilize every two weeks during the growth period.
Propagation: Fresh imported seeds, which germinate at 68°F (20°C).

Light:	Much light, no full sun.
Temp:	Grow moderately warm to warm, in the winter a minimum of 60°F (15°C).
Water:	Keep moderately moist with soft water.
Hum:	Moderate to high.
Soil:	Extra-acidic potting soil, for example coniferous soil.

quently. Add a little amount of fertilizer to the water.
Propagation: By division or from seed.

Light:	Much light or half shade, no full sun.
Temp:	Grow warm, minimum of 64°F (18°C).
Water:	Soft water or rainwater.
Hum:	Very high, well above 60%.
Soil:	Bromeliad soil when grown in a pot. But the plant can also be tied to a branch of another plant (for instance *Robinia*) and grown this way.

Dizygotheca elegantissima

Dizygotheca elegantissima

Araliaceae

False aralia

A very well-known houseplant with palmate (having four or more leaflets) leaves, constructed of very narrow, spiky leaves of an

Dizygotheca veitchii

Dizygotheca veitchii

Araliaceae

Another member of the aralia family with fine foliage, although the small leaves are wider than those of *D. elegantissima*. There are varieties with dark leaves available, too, such as the 'Castor,' pictured here.
Care: For optimal growth, the plant needs humidity, at least in the winter. Furthermore, there should be much light. In the summer months food is advised on a biweekly schedule. In the winter the plant can be kept cooler.
Propagation: Root top cuttings under glass at a soil temperature of 77°F (25°C).

Light:	Much light, but certainly no full sun.
Temp:	Grow moderately warm to warm, in the winter a minimum of 61°F (16°C).
Water:	Keep moderately moist with rainwater.
Hum:	Moderate to high.
Soil:	Extra-acidic mixture, for instance, coniferous soil.

DODONAEA

Dodonaea viscosa
Sapindacea

Bush from the southern United States and from Central America. Grown as a container plant in moderate climates. The greenish flowers are followed by reddish winged fruits.
Care: Grow outside from the end of May in a sunny and protected location. Water moder-

Dodonaea viscosa

ately and fertilize every two weeks. Bring inside in the fall and keep cool for the dormant period. Keep dry, but not so much that the leaves fall off. Allow adequate light while storing the plant over the winter, making sure that the bush stays cool so that it does not bloom too early.
Propagation: From seed, and via top cuttings, which root under glass at 68–77°F (20–25°C) soil temperature.

Light:	Full sun.
Temp:	Grow cool, in the winter 40–50°F (5–10°C).
Water:	Keep moderately moist, drier in the winter.
Hum:	Moderate, 50–60%.
Soil:	Standard potting soil mixed with 30% loam or clay.

Dolichothele baumii
Cactaceae

Effortlessly flowering, strong germinating cactus with yellow flowers that have a heavy scent.
Care: Grow with plenty of light, but screen against the brightest sunlight. Water sparsely and provide cactus food once a month. The temperature should be much lower in the winter to ensure the growth of flowers the following year. In the spring, mist it very lightly, until the flower buds appear.
Propagation: From seed and from cuttings.

Light:	Much light, even sun, but screen against bright sun.
Temp:	Grow moderately warm to warm, in the winter 40–50°F (5–10°C).
Water:	Rather dry, in the winter almost no water.
Hum:	Low.
Soil:	Cactus soil.

X Doritaenopsis
Orchidaceae

Orchids cross-fertilize very easily. This variety was created by the cross-hybridization of *Doritis* and *Phalaenopsis*. This variety gets the benefit of durability from the first variety, and the size of the flowers from the second. The cultivar is similar to *Phalaenopsis*.

X *Doritaenopsis* 'Jason Beard' X *manni*

Care: The plants do not have pseudotubers; water storage only takes place in the foliage. For that reason, never allow the leaves to dry out. Provide shade from March through October, when the plants are allowed full light again. Feed with orchid fertilizer (light concentration) once a month during the growth period. Before the blooming, keep somewhat cooler (54°F/12°C) and a bit drier. The timing of flowering differs from species to species. Repot only when necessary.
Propagation: By dividing larger plants.

Light:	Much light, but in the summer no direct sunlight.
Temp:	Grow warm, in the winter a minimum of 54°F (12°C).
Water:	Keep moist with rainwater or soft water.
Hum:	High, preferably 80%.
Soil:	Clay particles, rock wool flakes.

Doritis pulcherrima
Orchidaceae

An orchid with a strong resemblance to *Phalaenopsis*, which was often categorized with *D. pulcherrima*.
Care: The plants have no pseudotubers and therefore do not need a real dormant period; growth continues throughout the year. For

Doritis pulcherrima

that reason the temperature should always stay rather high. Screen against bright sun in the summer, but at the end of October the glass of the greenhouse can be wiped clean until around the beginning of April. Provide orchid food every two weeks while they are growing.
Propagation: By division.

Light:	Much light, no bright sun.
Temp:	Grow warm, a minimum of 66°F (18°C).
Water:	Keep moderately moist with rainwater.
Hum:	High, above 60%.
Soil:	Pure rock wool flakes or a mixture of clay particles, peat mold and fern roots.

Dolichothele baumii

Dorstenia elata

Moraceae

An extremely peculiar member of the *Ficus* family. The super-small blooms are situated on a round, communal flower bottom—quite an unusual sight. Is it a flower or a fruit, or something else entirely? (See overleaf.)
Care: Cultivation will only go well if the

Dorstenia elata

plant is grown in a greenhouse. Warmth and high humidity are essential. Direct sunlight should be avoided all the time. In the growing period, feed every two weeks.
Propagation: From seed and by top cuttings, which root under glass at a soil temperature of 77–86°F (25–30°C).

Light: Much light or half shade, no bright sun.
Temp: Grow warm, a minimum of 64°F (18°C).
Water: Keep moderately moist.
Hum: High, above 60%.
Soil: Standard potting soil.

Doryanthes palmeri

Agavaceae

A plant from Australia that forms a large rosette of 100 or more sword-shaped leaves. It resembles the *Yucca* somewhat. Flowers only appear after at least 10 years, but fortunately the plant is pretty without flowers. Grow as a container plant.
Care: Place outside at the end of May, keeping it sheltered and sunny. Give plenty of water and feed once every two weeks. In the fall, bring to a cool, light space for dormancy. If the plant starts to flower, then it does not die off, but forms side shoots at the base that can be grown separately.
Propagation: From the side shoots, also from seed.

Light: Full sun.
Temp: Grow cool to moderately warm, in the winter 40–50°F (5–10°C).
Water: Moderately moist in the summer, in the winter somewhat drier.
Hum: Moderate, 50–60%.
Soil: Mixture of standard potting soil and a large amount of clay or loam.

Doryopteris palmata

Adiantaceae

Ferns with very beautifully carved leaves. Unfortunately, they do not do very well in a heated room.
Care: Grow in a shaded spot in the summer and feed once every two weeks. If you keep the plant inside during the winter, then you have to mist it frequently. However, keeping the plant cooler would be a better solution.
Propagation: By sowing the spores.

Light: Shade.
Temp: Grow moderately warm to warm, in the winter 54°F (12°C).
Water: Keep moist on a very regular basis with soft water (preferably using a pot with a watering system).
Hum: High, above 60%.
Soil: Standard potting soil mixed with peat mold or peat moss.

Doryopteris palmata

Doryanthes palmeri

On the following pages: *Dorstenia elata*

DRACAENA

Dracaena deremensis

Agavaceae

Not everybody understands the difference between *Dracaena* and *Cordyline*. All the same, both genera are easy to distinguish from each other if you look at the roots. The roots of *Cordyline* are all white and the roots of *Dracaena* have a yellow-orange color. As houseplants go, the *Dracaena* is very important, because with some luck it can survive the winter while staying dry and warm indoors. One cannot say that about many plants. I photographed two cultivars from the often-grown *deremensis* species: 'Compacta,' with extremely compact rosettes, and 'Warneckii,' whose leaves have narrow white lines. The cv. 'Bausei' has white stripes as well. There are also varieties with yellow lines. The plants are often imported from Central America.

Care: The plants can stay in a warm room all year long, and a dormant period is not needed. Mist as often as possible in the winter, because dry air is not good for the plant and causes the leaves to dry out. Place in a light spot to preserve the leaf markings. If the plants do not get enough light the rosettes become very small and the leaf surface loses its markings. In the summer, feed once every two weeks. Repot in the spring.

Propagation: From trunk cuttings and shoot cuttings, soil temperature 68–77°F (20–25°C).

Dracaena deremensis 'Compacta'

Dracaena deremensis 'Warneckii'

Light:	Much light, no full sun. Half shade is adequate.
Temp:	Grow warm, in winter the temperature can be lowered to 56°F (13°C).
Water:	Keep moderately moist.
Hum:	Moderate, 50–60%.
Soil:	Standard potting soil.

Dracaena draco

Agavaceae

A very strong species with common green leaves in a rosette. It has supposedly grown on the Canary Island Tenerife for a few thousand years.

Dracaena draco

Care: To produce flowers, the plant should be grown as a container plant, and kept sheltered and sunny in the summer, cool and drier in the winter. Fertilize weekly while the plant is growing. Cultivation is possible in a warm room, but flowers are much less likely to bloom and the danger of disease is increased.
Propagation: From seed.

Light: Outside, full sun; inside, much light.
Temp: Grow cool to moderately warm, in the winter a minimum of 45°F (7°C).
Water: Keep moderately moist in the summer, drier in the winter.
Hum: Moderate, 50–60%.
Soil: Standard potting soil mixed possibly with extra clay or loam.

Dracaena fragrans

Agavaceae

Like the species *deremensis*, this plant is very popular. It also looks a bit like it, but forms larger leaves in a tighter rosette. The standard green species is very strong and can survive with little light. It is seldom available, however, because the variegated cultivars, such as 'Victoria,' have the much more attractive yellow strips along the edges of the leaves.
Care: Can be grown warm the whole year, but should be kept cooler in the winter. Mist the foliage frequently with soft water when the air is dry. Fertilize every two weeks during the growing season. Repot in the spring.
Propagation: From trunk cuttings, top cuttings or middle cuttings, soil temperature 68–77°F (20–25°C).

Light: Much light, no full sun. The green species will grow with little light.
Temp: Grow warm, in the winter a minimum of 56°F (13°C).
Water: Keep moderately moist.
Hum: Moderate, 50–60%.
Soil: Standard potting soil.

Dracaena fragrans 'Massangeana'

Dracaena marginata

Agavaceae

A species that, despite looking rather delicate, proves to be a very strong indoor plant that can even survive with very little light. (Whether the plant enjoys this or not is another question.) Shown is the variegated form 'tricolor,' which is somewhat weaker than other varieties. The older plants, which have several tops on a long, leafless trunk, are especially beautiful.

Dracaena marginata 'Tricolor'

Care: Can stay in a warm room the whole year, but in the winter the temperature can be lowered. During the growth period, fertilize once every two weeks. Repot in the spring.
Propagation: Works well with trunk cuttings, middle cuttings and from top cuttings. Soil temperature 68–77°F (20–25°C).

Light: The variegated form desires much light, but no bright sun. The basic green species can endure shade.
Temp: Grow warm, in the winter a minimum of 56°F (13°C).
Water: Keep moderately moist.
Hum: Low to moderate.
Soil: Standard potting soil.

Dracaena reflexa

Agavaceae

A houseplant previously known as *Pleomele*. The cultivar show, 'Song of India,' has pretty, yellow leaf edges. The plants branch easily.
Care: This species is also quite durable and can be kept inside the whole year. It is advisable to lower the temperature somewhat in the winter. Otherwise, mist frequently. In the growing season, fertilize once every two weeks. Repot in the spring.
Propagation: From top cuttings and trunk cuttings. Soil temperature 68–77°F (20–25°C).

Light: Keep rather light to preserve the variegated leaf markings, but never in the full sun.
Temp: Grow warm, in the winter a minimum of 55°F (13°C).
Water: Keep moderately moist.
Hum: Moderate, 50–60%.
Soil: Standard potting soil.

Dracaena reflexa 'Song of India'

Dracaena sanderiana

Agavaceae

A beautiful variegated species with leaves running 8" x 1⅓" (20 x 3 cm), which are narrowly stalk-shaped at the base. Along the leaf edges run wide, yellowish stripes.
Care: This species can be kept indoors permanently, but this requires a lower temperature and higher humidity. In the growing season, feed every two weeks and repot in the spring.
Propagation: From top cuttings, middle cuttings and trunk cuttings. Soil temperature 68–77°F (20–25°C).

Light: Much light, no full sun.
Temp: Grow warm, in the winter the temperature can be lowered to 50°F (10°C).
Water: Keep moderately moist.
Hum: Moderate, 50–60%.
Soil: Standard potting soil.

Dracaena sanderiana

Dracaena surculosa 'Florida Beauty'

Dracaena surculosa

Agavaceae

These *Dracaena* varies from other species. The spotted leaves are set on stalks at a distance from each other, so they do not form a rosette. This species is often called *Dracaena godseffiana*. Pictured is a cultivar with lively leaf markings, called 'Florida Beauty.'
Care: This species is not as strong as the others, despite the thick, leathery foliage. But with some luck, it can stay alive indoors throughout the year. But do keep it at a lower temperature in the winter. During the growth period, feed every two weeks. Repot in the spring.
Propagation: From top cuttings or eye cuttings.

Light:	Much light, no bright sun.
Temp:	Grow warm, in the winter a minimum of 50°F (10°C).
Water:	Moderately moist.
Hum:	Moderate to high.
Soil:	Standard potting soil.

Dracula troglodytis

Orchidaceae

A peculiar orchid with small flowers with long tails. Often called *Masdevallia*.
Care: Keep cool with plenty of water and fresh air. Much light is advised, but sunlight has to be screened. A lattice basket is necessary to allow the water to drain adequately. Provide orchid food once a month, at most. In the winter the temperature can be lower.
Propagation: From seed and by division.

Light:	Much light, no full sun.

Dracula troglodytis

Temp:	Grow cool, in the winter a minimum of 54°F (12°C).
Water:	Plenty of water in the summer and mist with pure rainwater.
Hum:	High, preferably 80%.
Soil:	Pure sphagnum or rock wool flakes.

Drosera capensis

Droseraceae

Sun dew

A carnivorous plant originating in South Africa. Insects are caught with the aid of the fine, sticky glandular hairs that run along the edges of the leaves.
Care: All species require a humid atmosphere. In the summer, one can grow the small plant along the side of a pond, with the pot pressed into the wet ground. Food is not needed if enough insects are caught. The plant should be brought inside in the winter because it will not survive the frost. A cool dormant period is necessary, preferably in a cold greenhouse.
Propagation: From rootstocks and via seed.

Light:	Full sun.
Temp:	Grow cool to moderately warm, in the winter keep around 40–50°F (5–10°C).
Water:	Keep constantly moist with soft water.
Hum:	High, above 60%.
Soil:	Pure sphagnum or peat moss.

Drosera capensis

Dryopteris affinis

Aspleniaceae

A fern grown in many European gardens, though it is not hardy everywhere. The ornamental plant with twisted leaves shown is called 'Crispa Congesta.' The rootstock is covered with brown scales.

Care: Grow especially cool, never in a warm room. The air must be humid. Spray the foliage a lot. During the growth period, feed once every two weeks at half concentrations.

Propagation: By dividing the rootstocks.

Light: Half shade to shade.
Temp: Grow cool, in the winter 40–50°F (5–10°C).
Water: Keep constantly moist.
Hum: High, above 60%.
Soil: Standard potting soil.

Dryopteris affinis 'Crispa Congesta'

Duchesnea indica

Rosaceae

Mock strawberry

A small houseplant that resembles the common strawberry plant, except for its yellow flowers. The small strawberries are not very tasty, but they're not poisonous.

Care: Grow as a hanging or climbing plant, and keep it somewhat cool, especially in the winter. The plant can survive the winter in a garden, but needs some covering as protection. Place in a well-lit spot, but screen bright sunlight.

Propagation: By cuttings of the young plants that form at the tips of shoots, and from seed.

Light: Much light, no full sun.
Temp: Grow cool, in the winter a minimum of 32°F (0°C).
Water: Moderately moist.
Hum: Moderate to high.
Soil: Standard potting soil.

Dudleya pachyphytum

Crassulaceae

This plant was previously a member of the genus *Echeveria* before reclassification as *Dudleya*. These plants are distinguishable by their non-angular flowers, while the crown leaves are thick and meaty.

Care: The elegant rosettes are pruinose (white-blooming), and disappear when the plant is sprayed. For that reason, only water at the bottom of the plant. Not much water is needed. Full sun makes the plant look better. Give cactus food once a month during growing season. Keep cool and dry in the winter, just below the glass of a cold greenhouse.

Propagation: Allow removed leaves to dry, then plant them in moist soil. Soil temperature of 68°F (20°C).

Light: Full sun.
Temp: Grow moderately warm to warm, in the winter 40–50°F (5–10°C).
Water: Keep rather dry, in the winter almost completely dry.
Hum: Low.
Soil: Cactus soil.

Duchesnea indica

Dudleya pachyphytum

Dyckia fosteriana

Bromeliaceae

A very strong bromeliad suitable for growth together with succulents, for instance, *Hechtia*. Works well indoors. The flowers are orange and sit on a long stem.
Care: Cultivation does not have to focus principally on the flowers, because the rosettes are pretty by themselves. If you want, bring these plants outside at the end of May, when sunlight is allowed. After the rosette has flowered the plant will die, but generally enough side rosettes are formed to allow for replanting. Water sparsely during the growing period and feed once every two weeks.
Propagation: By sowing the side rosettes. From seed too, but this takes a long time.

Light: Full sun.
Temp: Grow cool, 40°F (5°C) in the winter is sufficient.
Water: Keep moderately dry, in the winter almost completely dry.
Hum: Low.
Soil: Mixture of one part standard potting soil, one part loam or clay and one part sharp sand or perlite.

Dyckia fosteriana

Echeveria agavoides

Crassulaceae

Echeveria is an extended genus of succulents with thick, meaty leaves in rosettes.
Care: Succulents store moisture in their leaves for use in times of drought. To cultivate these plants successfully, never give too much water. A shortage of water does not harm them. The rosettes let you know when they really need some moisture by shriveling. Keep sunny in the summer. Water sparsely and keep at a low temperature during dormancy. Feed cactus food once a month.
Propagation: From leaf cuttings. Take a leaf, allow it to dry for a week, and plant it in rather dry sand.

Light: Full sun.

Echeveria agavoides 'Red Edge'

Temp: Grow cool to moderately cool, in the winter between 40–50°F (5–10°C).
Water: Keep rather dry, in the winter almost completely dry.
Hum: Low.
Soil: Cactus soil.

Echeveria derenbergii

Echeveria derenbergii

Crassulaceae

This species looks like many others of its kind. The orange flowers are carried on a long stem.
Care: Grow in full sun, possibly outside in the summer. The dormant period should be dry and cool, as with cacti, otherwise no flowers will appear and the rosette will rot. During the growth season, provide some cactus food once a month.
Propagation: After drying for a few days, loose leaves of the rosette can be planted. Propagation from seed is possible as well.

Light: Full sun.
Temp: Grow cool to moderately cool, in the winter between 40–50°F (5–10°C).
Water: Keep rather dry, in the winter almost completely dry.
Hum: Low.
Soil: Cactus soil.

Echeveria harmsii

Crassulaceae

A small bush with tiny, spatulate leaves in rosettes. With good care, this species can flower magnificently.
Care: Always grow in full sun and water sparsely. Give some low-nitrogen cactus food once a month. Allow a dormant period in the winter at a low temperature and water very sparsely. This is essential to get flowers the following season.
Propagation: From leaf cuttings. Let the leaves dry for some time, then plant them in sandy soil.

Light:	Full sun.
Temp:	Grow moderately warm to warm, in the winter 40–50°F (5–10°C).
Water:	Keep rather dry, in the dormant period, almost completely dry.
Hum:	Low.
Soil:	Cactus soil.

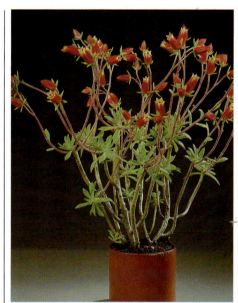

Echeveria harmsii

Echeveria pulvinata 'Ruby'

Echeveria pulvinata

Crassulaceae

A succulent with thick, white-haired leaves in a loose rosette. The edges of the leaves can turn a pretty light red color with enough light, as shown with the variety 'Ruby.'
Care: Keep well sunlit, possibly outside during the summer in a very sheltered location. Do not give too much water, and add cactus food once a month. Keep cool and dry in the winter; this plant must become absolutely dormant.
Propagation: Break leaves off a rosette, let them dry for a period, then plant. Make sure they are not too wet.

Light:	Full sun.
Temp:	Grow cool to moderately warm, in the winter between 40–50°F (5–10°C).
Water:	Keep rather dry, in the winter almost completely dry.
Hum:	Low.
Soil:	Cactus soil.

Echeveria setosa

Crassulaceae

A popular species that flowers effortlessly. It is usually available around Mother's day. The original *setosa* has hairy rosettes, though similar species are often not hairy.
Care: Place in full sunlight without too much water, and add cactus food once a month. Keep as cool as possible in the winter, otherwise there will be no flowers the following year.
Propagation: Allow leaves to dry and plant.

Light:	Full sun.
Temp:	Grow cool to moderately warm, in the winter 40–50°F (5–10°C).
Water:	Keep rather dry, in the winter almost completely dry.
Hum:	Low.
Soil:	Cactus soil.

Echeveria setosa

ECHEVERIA

Echinocactus grusonii

Cactaceae

A very well-known round cactus with regularly placed, very sharp thorns. The plants can grow to be over 4 ft (1.3 in) in diameter, but that takes decades. Flowers almost never appear.
Care: An easy cactus to grow, as long as it's kept warm and sunny, except in the spring, when it should be screened from sunlight a bit. Water moderately and add cactus food once a month. Keep cooler in the winter, but not cold.
Propagation: Seeds germinate at 77°F (25°C).

Light:	Full sun.
Temp:	Grow moderately warm to warm, in the winter between 54–60°F (12–15°C).

Echinocactus grusonii

Water:	Keep regularly moist in the summer and give less water in the winter.
Hum:	Low.
Soil:	Cactus soil.

Echinocereus species

Cactaceae

The large variety *Echinocereus* consists of growths that resemble a cross between a columnar cactus and a bullet-shaped cactus. It sometimes sprouts strongly, sometimes does not. The large flowers are thorned, as are the fruits.
Care: Give plenty of light and water during the growth period. However do not start watering too prematurely; in the spring, only

Echinocereus fitchii

Echinocereus viridiflorus

mist until the flowers have come out. Give cactus food once a month. Start gradually withholding water in the middle of the summer until the plant is completely dry in the fall. The plant should then rest dormant until spring.
Propagation: From seed and from cuttings of well-dried side shoots. Soil temperature 68°F (20°C).

Light:	Full sun.

Echinocereus pentalophus

Temp:	Grow moderately warm to warm, in the winter 40–50°F (5–10°C) for the green species, 40°F (5°C) for the densely throned or hairy species.
Water:	Keep rather dry, withhold water in the winter.
Hum:	Low.
Soil:	Cactus soil.

Echinocereus coccineus

Echinofossulocactus hastatus

Cactaceae

Previously known as *Stenocactus*, these cacti have characteristic wavy ribs and a dark stripe on the flower petals. The species pictured has extremely long middle thorns, which the flowers have worked themselves through in opening.

Echinofossulocactus hastatus

Care: The plants need a very light, but not sunny, location. Add some cactus food to the water once a month. Keep cool in the winter, but still in a light spot.

Propagation: From seed.

Light:	Much light, but no full sunlight.
Temp:	Grow moderately warm to warm, in the winter between 40–50°F (5–10°C).
Water:	Keep rather dry, withhold almost all water in the winter.
Hum:	Low.
Soil:	Cactus soil.

Echinopsis species

Cactaceae

A well-known and strong cactus, often grown by real plant enthusiasts. The flowers are impressive and appear in large numbers. Beyond the botanical species, there are large numbers of hybrids cultivated by home growers. These are mostly derived from the two species pictured.

Care: The night-blooming species (see box) should not get too much sun or have too high a humidity, which is why they generally flourish as a houseplant. They can be cultivated outside as well, for example under a roof eave, for protection against rain. Give cactus food once every two weeks during the growth period. In the winter the plants should be kept cool, but not as cold as most other cacti. At the same time, they should not be left completely dry. The day-blooming plants from the mountains need much sun, but less warmth than the plants that bloom at night. Keep these cool in the winter and withhold all water.

Propagation: From seed.

Light:	Night-blooming plants: much light, no full sunlight.
	Day-blooming plants: full sun.

Echinopsis eyriesii

Echinopsis tubiflora

Temp:	Night-blooming plants: moderately warm, in the winter 45–54°F (7–12°C).
	Day-blooming plants: cool in the winter 32–40°F (0–5°C).
Water:	Night-blooming plants: moderately moist, less in winter.
	Day-blooming plants: rather dry, in the winter withhold all water.
Hum:	Night-blooming plants: moderate, 50–60%.
	Day-blooming plants: low.
Soil:	Night-blooming plants: standard potting soil.
	Day-blooming plants: cactus soil.

Echium wildpretti

In the large genus *Echinopsis*, we can distinguish two groups: species from the mountain areas and species that grow in lower regions. The mountain species bloom in the daytime and the other species generally open their fragrant flowers at night, closing again the next afternoon.

Some night-blooming plants are, for example, *calochlora*, *eyriesii*, *leucantha*, *multiplex*, *oxygona*, *tubiflora* and the hybrids. Some day-blooming plants are, for example, *ancistrophora*, *ferox*, *mamillosa* and *obrepanda*.

Echium wildpretii

Boraginaceae

People who have visited around the Mediterranean probably have seen the magnificent *Echium* species (although the species pictured comes from the Canary Islands). In more northern latitudes, this makes a nice container plant, which becomes very impressive when it starts to bloom. Unfortunately, this can take a while.

Care: Place outside at the end of May, in sun and protected. Feed once every two weeks. Containers should be of adequate size. Bring inside in the autumn for a cool dormancy. Give a little water once in a while. Repot in the spring if necessary. Move it to a warmer spot in April and bring outside again in May.

Propagation: From seed.

Light:	Full sun.
Temp:	Grow cool to moderately cool, in the winter 40–50°F (5–10°C).
Water:	In the summer relatively dry to moderately moist, in the winter rather dry.
Hum:	Moderate, 50–60%.
Soil:	Fifty percent standard potting soil mixed well with 50% rough clay or loam.

Echium wildpretii

Elettaria cardamomum

Elettaria cardamomum

Zingiberaceae

Cardamom

An herb from the ginger family. Brown or green capsules contain dark seeds used as spices. It is not a very remarkable foliage plant.
Care: Grow with light, allowing it to gradually get used to it in the spring. Keep moderately moist in the summer and feed every two weeks. The temperature can be lowered in the winter, otherwise misting is necessary.
Propagation: From seed or top cuttings. Soil temperature 68–77°F (20–25°C).

Light:	Full sun.
Temp:	Grow warm, a minimum of 57°F (14°C).
Water:	Keep moderately moist.
Hum:	Moderate to high.
Soil:	Mix standard potting soil with ⅓ part clay or loam.

Encyclia species

Orchidaceae

Orchids that are often included in the genus *Epidendrum*.

Encyclia baculus

Encyclia cochleata

Care: These plants have pseudotubers, and are suitable for cultivation in a moderate greenhouse. During the growth period, give plenty of water and provide a high humidity. Feed once every two weeks with orchid food (unless it's planted in rock wool flakes, in which case feed more frequently and in lighter concentrations). When the new pseudotubers appear, the plants should be kept drier. Give them a dormant period with sparse water and a lower temperature the moment they reach maturity.
Propagation: By division or from seed.

Light:	Much light, no full sun.
Temp:	Grow moderately warm, in the winter a minimum of 54–60°F (12–15°C).
Water:	Plenty of pure (rain)water during the growth period.
Hum:	High, above 60%.
Soil:	Bark pieces, rock wool pieces or tree fern.

Ensete ventricosum

Musaceae

An extremely beautiful container plant that is easy to keep dormant if one has a cold greenhouse or cool sun room. It is also called *Musa ensete*.
Care: From the end of May the plant can go outside in a sunny and protected spot. Plant in a container or in the garden. In the summer, give plenty of water and feed weekly. Over warm summers, the plant's growth can be surprisingly vigorous. Bring inside in the fall, putting specimens that were planted in the garden in a container. One can cut back the roots somewhat. The dormancy should be light, cool and dry.
Propagation: These species do not produce root shoots, as does the common banana.

Ensete ventricosum

Epidendrum fragrans

Therefore, propagation is only possible from seed. Soil temperature 77–86°F (25–30°C).

Light: Full sun.
Temp: Grow cool to moderately warm, in the winter no warmer than 37–43°F (3–6°C).
Water: Keep moderately moist, drier in the winter.
Hum: Moderate, 50–60%.
Soil: Mixture of standard potting soil with fine clay or loam.

Epacris hybrids
Epacridaceae

Epacris is a plant that is closely related to our bell-heather, but isn't as hardy. It blooms in

Epacris-hybr. 'Diadem'

the middle of the winter. There are almost only hybrids among cultivated varieties.
Care: Preferably kept in a cold greenhouse. If it does not rain much in the summer, the pots and tubs can be outside. Feed once every two weeks in the growth period. After flowering, usually in May, the plants have to be pruned back considerably to keep them compact.
Propagation: Take middle and top cuttings in the spring or fall. They root under glass.

Light: Much light, screen against bright sun.
Temp: Grow cool, in the winter 40–50°F (5–10°C).
Water: Water regularly with soft water, preferably in pots with a watering system.
Hum: Moderate to high.
Soil: Acidic soil, such as coniferous soil.

Epidendrum fragrans
Orchidaceae

An orchid from Central and South America belonging to a group with rather large, club-shaped pseudotubers. This indicates that they need a definite dormant period, as do the species *radiatum*, *stamfordianum* and others with thick pseudotubers. Species with sleek, pencil-shaped pseudotubers do not have this requirement. The names can be confusing because the species *fragrans* and *radiatum* are often categorized with the genus *Encyclia*.
Care: Grow moderately warm in a light but not very sunny spot. Some people are even successful growing this species inside. Fertil-

ize once a month during the growth season, more frequently if the plant is standing in inorganic material. After the pseudotubers are full grown, around the beginning of the winter, a rather cool dormant period is needed, during which one should give considerably less water.
Propagation: By division during repotting.

Light: Much light, no full sun.
Temp: Grow moderately warm, in the winter a minimum of 54°F (12°C).
Water: Plenty of soft water in the growth period, during dormancy almost no water.
Hum: High, above 60%.
Soil: Mixture of pieces of tree fern with fern root (osmunda) or just rock wool flakes.

Epidendrum parkinsonianum
Orchidaceae

A wild orchid from Central America that hangs from trees in large bunches.
Care: This plant with sleek pseudotubers desires a shaded spot, with ample water in the summer. Excess water should be able to drain well, so grow it in lattice baskets. Add orchid food once a month. Keep drier and cooler in the winter.
Propagation: By division and from seed.

Light: Much light, no full sun.
Temp: Grow moderately warm, in the winter 54–60°F (12–15°C).
Water: Plenty of water in the growth season.
Hum: High, above 60%.
Soil: Pieces of tree fern, baskets with rock wool flakes.

Epidendrum parkinsonianum

Epipremnum pinnatum

Episcia cupreata

Episcia reptans

Epipremnum pinnatum

Araceae

I imagine that some people have been driven quite mad by the number of times this famous houseplant has changed names. Known originally as *Pothos*, then *Scindapsus* (which it is still called in many cases), after that *Rhaphidophora*—not an easy name—it is now called *Epipremnum*. For the reason names change so many times, read pages 12–13.

Care: This is a very strong houseplant, one which can stay in a warm room the whole year. The variegated form 'Marble Queen' needs lots of light, because it possesses little chlorophyll. If this plant is kept too dark, the foliage will turn mostly green. Feed once every two weeks during the growth period. The plant can be kept cooler in the winter, but this is not absolutely necessary.

Propagation: From top cuttings or middle cuttings. Soil temperature 68–77°F (20–25°C).

Light:	Much light, no full sun.
Temp:	Grow warm, in the winter a minimum of 60°F (15°C).
Water:	Keep moderately moist.
Hum:	Low to moderate.
Soil:	Standard potting soil.

Epipremnum pinnatum 'Marble Queen'

Episcia cupreata

Gesneriaceae

Though this is categorized as a foliage plant, some small flowers can appear sometimes. There are other varieties with tinted or marked leaves.

Care: These small plants are, in fact, only suitable for the greenhouse, where they should be planted on a bench. One can grow it as a hanging plant if the air is humid enough. Feed once every two weeks during the growth period. In the winter the temperature should be lowered slightly.

Propagation: From the shoots, top cuttings or even leaf cuttings. Soil temperature 68°F (20°C).

Light:	Much light, no full sun.
Temp:	Grow warm, in the winter not below 61°F (16°C).
Water:	Keep moderately moist.
Hum:	High, above 60%.
Soil:	Standard potting soil mixed with peat mold or coniferous soil.

Episcia cupreata 'Cleopatra'

Episcia reptans

Gesneriaceae

A species hard to distinguish from the last one. The leaves are brownish and the leaf stalks are shorter than *E. cupreata*.

Care: This species, too, should be grown warm and humid, preferably in a plant window. Fertilize during the growth period, once every two weeks. Keep somewhat cooler in the winter, but not too cold.

Propagation: Via shoots, top cuttings or leaf cuttings.

Light:	Much light to half shade.
Temp:	Grow warm, in the winter not below 61°F (16°C).
Water:	Keep moderately moist.
Hum:	High, above 60%.
Soil:	Standard potting soil mixed with peat mold or coniferous soil.

Erica gracilis

Ericaceae

Heath

This lavishly blooming heather species is often sold in the fall. Because it is difficult to make it last long, the plants are often disposed of after they bloom. Besides white, there are also red-purple species.

Care: To maximize the pleasure you can get from the purchase of blooming plants, place them in a large container outside in a garden or on a balcony. When kept in a warm room, the flowering period does not last long. They endure frost to some degree and, with luck, the plants will bloom until Christmas.

Propagation: In February, one can propagate from middle cuttings that were kept frost free. Cuttings of 1 in (2.2 cm) are sufficient. Soil temperature 64°F (18°C). The young plants should be topped repeatedly for better branching. Dormancy happens at 40°F (5°C). In the second year, clean the plants up a bit and grow outside. Fertilize frequently, but in low

Erica gracilis

concentrations. Spray against fungus diseases. The plants flower in the fall.

Light: Much light, second year full sun.
Temp: Grow cool, dormancy at 40°F (5°C).
Water: Keep constantly moist with soft water.
Hum: Moderate to high.
Soil: Acidic soil is a must, such as mixtures with much peat mold, garden peat or coniferous soil.

Erica X willmorei

Ericaceae

Heath

A cross-fertilization of unknown origin, replete with large, tubular flowers. It flowers around April or May.
Care: After the flowering period, prune back and continue to grow. Always use soft water and fertilize lightly every two weeks. Bring it inside in the fall and keep the plant cool. With some luck, it will flower a second time.
Propagation: From middle cuttings, soil temperature 68°F (20°C).

Light: Grow light, screen against bright sun.
Temp: Grow cool, in the winter a minimum of 40°F (5°C).

Erica X willmorei

Erica gracilis

Water: Keep constantly moist with soft water.
Hum: Moderate to high.
Soil: Acidic soil, such as mixtures with much peat mold, garden peat or coniferous soil.

Eriobotrya japonica

Rosaceae

Loquat, Japanese medlar

Evergreen bush from China and Japan. It has unextraordinary flowers, which are followed by yellow, edible fruits. The fruits can be eaten after ripening and made into jam or compote.
Care: From the end of May this plant can be put outside in a sunny and sheltered location. Give plenty of water and feed weekly until mid-August. The problem arises in the fall when you have to find suitable cool storage. After a few years it will grow into a small tree.
Propagation: From seed or via top cuttings, which root under glass at a soil temperature of 77°F (25°C).

Light: Full sun.
Temp: Grow cool, in the winter store at 40–50°F (5–10°C).
Water: Keep moderately moist, somewhat drier in the winter.
Hum: Moderate, 50–60%.
Soil: Standard potting soil mixed with ⅓ part fine loam or clay.

Eriobotrya japonica

On the following pages: *Episcia reptans*

ERIOBOTRYA

Erythrina crista-galli

Erythrina crista-galli

Leguminosae

Coral bush

An easily grown container plant that has striking butterfly-like flowers in the summer. Young plants can be ordered by mail.

Care: Grow in pots or other containers with good drainage. Place outside from the end of May, in full sun and protected from the elements. While they grow, fertilize weekly. In the winter, the plant lies dormant. Bring inside when it gets frosty and keep in a cool spot. The foliage is allowed to fall.

Propagation: From seed or via top cuttings, which root under glass at 77°F (25°C).

Light:	Full sun.
Temp:	Grow cool, in the winter 40–50°F (5–10°C).
Water:	Keep moderately cool, drier in the winter.
Hum:	Moderate, 50–60%.
Soil:	Mixture of standard potting soil, clay or loam and rough sand.

Erythrorhipsalis pilocarpa

Cactaceae

On first sight, one would not assume this to be a cactus. The thin, somewhat ribbed branches are weekly throned. Light yellow flowers may appear at the ends.

Erythrorhipsalis pilocarpa

Care: Grow in lattice baskets such as those used for orchids. The substrate should be moist at all times; direct sunlight is not good. Fertilize weekly in the summer. In an especially warm summer, the plants can be hung from a tree. Provide a dormant period of about six weeks in the fall. Keep rather dry until buds are formed. The fragrant flowers appear around Christmas.
Propagation: Via top and middle cuttings.

Light:	Much light, no full sun.
Temp:	Grow cool to moderately warm, in the winter a minimum of 54°F (12°C).
Water:	Keep moderately moist, except in the dormant period. Use only soft water.
Hum:	Moderate to high.
Soil:	Mixture of peat moss, coniferous soil, sphagnum on a layer of pottery shards.

Escobaria vivipara

Escobaria vivipara

Cactaceae

A beautiful and sturdy cactus, often called *Coryphantha vivipara*. The bullet-shaped cactus forms many shoots.
Care: Grow very light, just behind the glass of a greenhouse or cold vitrine. Never give too much water, slightly more while the plant is in bloom. Add cactus food monthly. In the winter this plant can be kept very cool. If it is also kept very dry, it will endure some amount of frost, lessening the need to use a greenhouse.
Propagation: From seed and by taking the shoots.

Light:	Full sun.
Temp:	Grow cool to moderately warm, in the winter normally 32–40°F (0–5°C), or even colder.
Water:	Keep rather dry, completely dry in winter.
Hum:	Low.
Soil:	Cactus soil.

Espostoa lanata

Espostoa lanata

Cactaceae

A column-shaped, completely gray, hairy cactus that can reach a height of 13 ft (4 m) in northern Peru. The young plants are very pretty as well, although they seldom produce flowers.
Care: The gray hairs grow to protect the cactus body from the sun. We have to grow the plant with lots of light and sun to make sure the hair stays. The plant can have more water than other cacti and a higher temperature in the winter. Give cactus food once a month in the summer.
Propagation: From seed.

Light:	Full sun.
Temp:	Grow warm, in the winter 50–60°F (10–15°C).
Water:	Keep moderately moist, drier in the winter.
Hum:	Low to moderate.
Soil:	Cactus soil.

Eucalyptus cinerea

Myrtaceae

A bush whose leaves are used in book binding. Known as the 'Silver Dollar Tree.'
Care: It is possible to grow the eucalyptus inside, though it does better on a sheltered terrace or patio. Over the long term, this plant

Eucalyptus cinerea

will grow very tall, but with pruning it can stay quite compact. During the growth period, fertilize every two weeks. Bring inside in the winter for dormancy at rather low temperatures. Repot in the spring and bring outside at the end of May.
Propagation: From seed.

Light:	Full sun.
Temp:	Grow cool to moderately warm, in the winter around 50°F (10°C).
Water:	Moderately moist.
Hum:	Moderate.
Soil:	Standard potting soil mixed with loam, clay or rock wool powder.

Eucomis bicolor

Eucomis bicolor

Liliaceae

A rather spectacular tuberous plant that will flower indoors without too much difficulty. Tubers can be ordered by mail. A bunch of leaves grows above the large blooming spike (which smells of boiled potatoes).
Care: Purchased tubers can be potted in February. Continue to keep cool until mid-May, then bring it outside or grow in a greenhouse—while it blooms keep it inside, of course. After the flowering period, grow outside in a sheltered spot and feed once in a while. Planting out in a garden works better than in small pots. Allow the foliage to dry completely at the end of the season; the tubers should be kept dry until February.
Propagation: By taking the newly formed tubers or from seed.

Light:	Full sun.
Temp:	Grow cool, minimum storage temperature 40°F (5°C).
Water:	Keep moderately moist in the summer, in the winter withhold all water.
Hum:	Low.
Soil:	Standard potting soil.

EUGENIA

Eugenia myriophylla

Euonymus japonica 'Albomarginata'

Eugenia myriophylla

Myrtaceae

Tree or bush that is also known by the name *Myrciaria*. This is an easily grown container plant that blooms in the spring with white flowers and long stamens. The plant is similar to myrtle. The name is rather misleading; most species of this genus are now called *Syzygium*.
Care: If possible, place outside in the summer. Fertilize every two weeks. Bring inside in the autumn for a cool dormancy.
Propagation: Root top cuttings under glass at 68–77°F (20–25°C). Young plants should be topped frequently for better branching. Cultivation of crown trees is a possibility as well.

Light:	Full sun.
Temp:	Grow cool, in the winter at 40–50°F (5–10°C).
Water:	Keep moderately moist, drier in the winter.
Hum:	Moderate, 50–60%.
Soil:	Standard potting soil, if possible mixed with some clay or loam.

Euonymus japonica

Celastraceae

The characteristic fruits of this genus that decorate so many garden bushes do not appear on the houseplant, which is a foliage plant. There are other varieties with white-variegated or yellow-variegated leaves.
Care: These somewhat hardy plants are only suitable inside if placed in cool rooms, for example halls or vestibules. The variegated species need much light to preserve their pretty markings, because with too little light the leaves turn all green. In the summer, all species can go outside. Feed every two weeks.
Propagation: From top cuttings, soil temperature 68–77°F (20–25°C).

Light:	Full sun to half shade.
Temp:	Grow cool, keep frost free in the winter.
Water:	Keep moderately moist, drier in the winter.
Hum:	Moderate, 50–60%.
Soil:	Standard potting soil.

Euonymus japonica 'Medio Picta'

Euphorbia balsamifera

Euphorbiaceae

Low, whimsically branched bushes from the Canary Islands. The leaves fall easily, except the ones at the top of the twigs.
Care: Instead of a jungle of small branches, one could, with precise pruning, shape this plant into a bonsai. The plants can grow very old when kept in pots and containers that are

Euphorbia balsamifera

Euphorbia caput-medusae

not too small. Place outside in the summer and keep cool and dry during dormancy. At the most add some cactus food once a month.
Propagation: From seed and via top cuttings.

Light:	Full sun.
Temp:	Grow cool to moderately warm, in the winter 40–50°F (5–10°C).
Water:	Keep moderately moist, withhold almost all water during dormant period.
Hum:	Low.
Soil:	Cactus soil.

Euphorbia canariensis

Euphorbiaceae

Anybody who has ever visited Tenerife or other Canary Islands knows this plant, which is so dense in some parts it is almost impossible to penetrate whole areas. The cactus-like columns branch out and can reach a height of at least 30 ft (10 m). Small yellow flowers appear. The plant is poisonous.

Euphorbia canariensis

Care: Place in a sunny and rather sheltered spot in the summer. Water sparsely and add cactus food no more than once a month; these plants should not grow too quickly. Bring inside in the winter and withhold almost all water.
Propagation: Break off parts, allow to dry and plant.

Light:	Full sun.
Temp:	Grow cool to moderately warm, in the winter a minimum of 40°F (5°C).
Water:	Keep rather dry, no water in the winter.
Hum:	Low.
Soil:	Cactus soil.

Euphorbia caput-medusae

Euphorbiaceae

A very peculiar *Euphorbia* that forms long thin stems covered with small leaves. Looked at as a whole, it somewhat resembles a frightening head wrapped in snakes, like the Gorgon Medusa, its namesake. There are quite a lot of species that look similar, which often causes confusion even though the care for all is the same. The plant has green flowers.
Care: Grow outside in the summer or keep in a succulent greenhouse. Keep rather dry and do not fertilize much. Keep cooler in the winter and withhold almost all water.
Propagation: If possible, from seed. Cuttings can work, too, but plants that grow from cuttings tend to be less regular in their features.

Light:	Full sun.
Temp:	Grow moderately warm to warm, in the winter a minimum of 54°F (12°C).
Water:	Very sparsely, in the winter only a little or nothing at all.
Hum:	Low.
Soil:	Cactus soil, with well-drained bowls or pots.

Euphorbia caracasana

Euphorbiaceae

A relatively unknown *Euphorbia*, originally from tropical areas. Branches are cut off there, exported and rooted elsewhere for use as houseplants. The plants grow shoots effortlessly.
Care: Keep light and warm, though not in the full sun. Keep relatively moist in the summer and feed them once every two weeks. It should not be kept too cold in the winter, so possibly bring indoors.
Propagation: The trunks can be sawed up in pieces and rooted at a soil temperature of 68–77°F (20–25°C).

Light:	Much light, no full sun.
Temp:	Grow warm, not below 64°F (18°C).
Water:	Keep moderately moist.
Hum:	Moderate to high.
Soil:	Standard potting soil.

Euphorbia caracasana 'Sanguinea'

EUPHORBIA

Euphorbia erythraeae

Euphorbia erythraeae

Euphorbiaceae

A vertically growing *Euphorbia*, which in Ethiopia grows as a large tree and in our area as a strong houseplant. It is also known as *Euphorbia candelabrum*. As with many species of *Euphorbia*, this too has a cactus-like stalk that can endure drought, with small leaves that fall quickly to reduce the need for moisture.

Care: It is possible to grow these and similar species in a warm room all year round, although a cooler dormant period in the winter helps the overall health of the plant. Growth that occurs without much light tends to be less healthy. If the leaves drop, provide a dormant period by keeping the plant cooler and drier. It will not die readily from drought, but will if it receives too much water. Fertilize moderately, at the most once a month during the growth period.

Propagation: From seed and via top cuttings. Cut off tops of 2¼ in (5 cm) and allow to dry for a long period before planting, to avoid rotting.

Light: Full sun.
Temp: Moderately warm to warm, in the winter a minimum of 54°F (12°C).
Water: Give moderate to little water, no water during the dormant period.
Hum: Low.
Soil: Standard potting soil or, better still, cactus soil.

Euphorbia fulgens

Euphorbiaceae

A popular flower for cuttings that is on the market especially in the autumn and winter months. There are varieties with white flowers. It is less known as a potted plant.

Care: Grow moderately warm at a relatively high humidity. It is, in fact, a greenhouse plant. Screen against bright sun and feed during the growth period. The flowering period can be advanced by a short-day treatment. Normally, these plants bloom in the early spring. After they bloom, prune the plants back and with-

Euphorbia fulgens

hold water to begin dormancy. Often new plants are grown from cuttings.

Propagation: Top cuttings have to dry for a while in the spring. Root under glass. Soil temperature 68–77°F (20–25°C). Cut the tops of young plants a few times.

Light: Much light, no bright sun.
Temp: Grow moderately warm, in the winter a minimum of 61°F (16°C).
Water: Keep moderately moist, almost dry after blooming.
Hum: High, above 60%.
Soil: Standard potting soil mixed with a part fine clay or loam.

Euphorbia grandicornis

Euphorbiaceae

Euphorbia grandicornis

A branched species from Kenya and South Africa that grows in several levels, often up to 6½ ft (2 m) high.

Care: Grow moderately warm to warm and sunny, giving moderate amounts of water in the growth period and feeding once every two weeks. In the winter the plant should be placed in light, and kept cool and almost dry. Plants that are too tall can be cut from the top, and will branch out again.

Propagation: Allow cuttings to dry, then provide a soil temperature of 68–77°F (20–25°C). It is easier from seed.

Light: Full sun.
Temp: Grow moderately warm to warm, in the winter a minimum of 54°F (12°C).
Water: Keep rather dry to moderately moist, almost dry in the winter.
Hum: Low.
Soil: Standard potting soil possibly mixed with some clay and loam.

Euphorbia leuconeura

Euphorbiaceae

A strange species, often confused with *Euphorbia lophogona*, which does look similar but produces white flowers on stems and stays smaller than *E. leuconeura*. The plant consists of a hairy trunk with four or five sides that is topped by a rosette of leaves. These drop quickly and leave distinct markings behind.

Care: A species easily grown indoors that only dies if the potting soil becomes too wet. When the leaves are gone, keep the plant drier

Euphorbia leuconeura

and cooler. After a while, new foliage will grow back, at which point keep the plant more moist. Fertilize monthly during the growth period.
Propagation: This plant becomes self-propagating after a while. Seeds are formed from inconspicuous little flowers, and these seeds pop off the plant audibly. They often land in the potting soil of other plants and germinate there easily. Plant outdoors and you will soon have a whole crop of plants.

Light:	Can stand full sunlight, but appreciates half shade as well.
Temp:	Warm the whole year, but the temperature could be lowered in the winter to 54°F (12°C).
Water:	Careful with water, almost dry in the dormant period.
Hum:	Low.
Soil:	Standard potting soil.

Euphorbia meloformis

Euphorbiaceae

A plant that resembles a cactus, except that it does not get thorns and typically *Euphorbia* flowers will appear.
Care: Strongly resembles a cactus, so keep sunny and do not water much, allowing a dormant period in the winter at low temperatures and with almost no water.
Propagation: From seed. Sometimes sprouts develop at the base, which can then be taken off for planting.

Light:	Full sun.
Temp:	Grow moderately warm to warm, in the winter a minimum of 45°F (7°C).
Water:	Keep rather dry, almost completely dry during dormancy.
Hum:	Low.
Soil:	Cactus soil.

Euphorbia milii

Euphorbiaceae

An old-fashioned, easy-to-grow houseplant with branched, thorned stalks and small, green leaves that come off easily. The plant originally had only red flowers (these are in fact deformed bracts) but with cross-fertilization other colors are now available. These are categorized under the name *Euphorbia* X *lohmii*.

Euphorbia meloformis

Euphorbia X *lohmii*

A species that remains small and blooms lavishly is known as the *imperatae* variety.
Care: As long as this plant receives water on a regular basis, the foliage will remain. If you allow the ball of soil to dry out, however, the leaves will fall off. And if, in drying to correct this, you start giving the plant plenty of water, you will drown it. It is better to give just small amounts of water after the leaves fall, and wait for the dormant period. After a while, new leaves appear and gradually one can increase the amount of water again. Fertilize once every two weeks in the summer. In the winter, the *Euphorbia milii* can be kept cooler, but it is not absolutely necessary, although one does have to prevent the plant from growing in the winter.
Propagation: Side shoots can be used as cuttings. Cut off, allow to dry and plant in sandy, rather dry soil. The bleeding from cutting can be stopped by holding the cut side in water of 95°F (35°C).

Light:	Full sun.
Temp:	Grow moderately warm to warm, in the winter a minimum of 54°F (12°C).
Water:	Keep moist on a regular basis, only a few drops during dormancy.
Hum:	Low.
Soil:	Standard potting soil.

Euphorbia milii

Euphorbia obesa

Euphorbia pulcherrima 'Marble'

Euphorbia obesa

Euphorbiaceae

A regularly shaped, cactus-like species with eight prettily marked colored ribs. At the top of this plant a few very small flowers appear. There are both masculine and feminine plants.
Care: Grow as a cactus, with much light, full sun and sparse water, even in the summer. Add some cactus food monthly. In the winter lower the temperature, water sparsely and provide a dormant period.
Propagation: From seed.

Light:	Full sun.
Temp:	Grow moderately warm to warm, in the winter a minimum of 54°F (12°C).
Water:	Keep rather dry, only a few drops in the winter.
Hum:	Low.
Soil:	Cactus soil.

Euphorbia pulcherrima

Euphorbiaceae

Poinsettia

A species with gigantic bracts around the flowers. They are red or off-white and are quite striking. It's no wonder this became the most popular *Euphorbia*, or as it's known by

Euphorbia pulcherrima 'Dorothé'

many growers, *Poinsettia*. With artificial lighting and darkening, one can force the plant to bloom at any desired moment. Nevertheless, still blooms mostly around Christmas.
Care: It is not easy to keep these plants alive for too long and they are almost always disposed of after their beauty fades. Still, if you want to try and preserve them, cut back the plant to half its size and keep it cooler, about 54°F (12°C). After some time, new shoots will appear. Then repot and grow warmer. Bring it

outside if possible in the summer. Feed once every two weeks with a fertilizer that contains micronutrients. Growth stunting hormones will keep the plants small. To get the plant to bloom a second time, it will need absolute darkness for 14 hours a day, for two months. If you do not provide them with darkness, the plants will bloom later than Christmas, sometime in the spring. This can be a big hassle and the chance of success is very small.
Propagation: Root top cuttings at 68°F (12°C) in a mixture of sand and peat mould. Dip cuttings in boiling water to stop bleeding.

Light:	Much light, no full sun.
Temp:	Moderately warm, a minimum of 60°F (15°C).
Water:	Keep moderately moist.
Hum:	Moderate, 50–60%.
Soil:	Standard potting soil.

Euphorbia pulcherrima 'Annette Hegg'

Euphorbia resinifera

Euphorbiaceae

A low bush of 20 in (50 cm) found in Morocco. The branched vertical stalks are square shaped.
Care: This is a strong plant that has to stand in a sunny window all summer. It can stay indoors during the winter, but the cooler a location, the better. During the growth period, give some cactus food monthly.

Euphorbia resinifera

Propagation: The tops of the side shoots can be used as cuttings. Allow to dry for a while before planting, because they rot easily otherwise.

Light:	Full sun.
Temp:	Grow moderately warm, in the winter a minimum of 54°F (12°C).
Water:	Keep rather dry, withhold all water during dormancy.
Hum:	Low.
Soil:	Standard potting soil.

Euphorbia submammillaris

Euphorbiaceae

A very low, horizontal, strongly branched bush from South Africa that should be grown in shallow bowls or pots. The stalks are covered with bumps.
Care: Can be placed in a sunny window all year, but it would be better if the plant stopped

Euphorbia submammillaris

growing for the winter. To achieve this, keep it cooler and drier. Feed moderately during the growth period, once a month at the most.
Propagation: Break off stalks, dry well and plant at a moderate soil temperature, making sure they do not rot.

Light:	Full sun.
Temp:	Grow moderately warm to warm, in the winter a minimum of 54°F (12°C).
Water:	Water sparsely, keeping it almost dry during dormancy.
Hum:	Low.
Soil:	Cactus soil.

Euphorbia tetragona

Euphorbiaceae

Wreaths of often square, succulent stems, provided with sturdy thorns that grow on a hexagonal or heptagonal trunk. In Southeast Africa this tree can reach a height of 50 ft (15 m), though it functions as a hardy houseplant in our region.
Care: Place inside in a sunny location and water moderately. Feed monthly. If possible, keep the plant cooler in the winter and give less water; the plant is strong and will survive a rather cool dormancy. When overwatered, it will die.
Propagation: Take 1½ in (7 cm) lengths from side shoots, allow to dry (about a week) and plant in dry, sandy soil.

Light:	Full sun.
Temp:	Grow moderately warm, in the winter not below 54°F (12°C).
Water:	Keep moderately moist, almost dry during dormancy.
Hum:	Low.
Soil:	Standard potting soil.

Euphorbia tetragona

Euphorbia tirucalli

Euphorbiaceae
Pencil plant

A plant with tubular stalks and occasionally some small leaves. Photosynthesis mainly takes place in the stalks.
Care: Grow inside in a moderately warm and sunny spot. Water moderately and only feed the plant while it grows, at the most once every two weeks. Keep cooler in the winter and water sparsely.
Propagation: Break off pieces of ripened stem at a node. Dry for a week and plant in sandy, dry soil.

Light:	Full sun.
Temp:	Moderately warm to warm, not below 54°F (12°C) in the winter.
Water:	Keep moderately dry, and during dormancy, add just enough to keep the leaves from shriveling.
Hum:	Low.
Soil:	Standard potting soil.

Euphorbia tirucalli

Eustoma grandiflorum

Eustoma grandiflorum

Gentianaceae

Prairie gentian

A plant known mostly by the name *Lisianthus*. It was grown as a cutting flower for a long time, but is now available as a potted plant as well. These low varieties are known as the 'Yodel' series, originally from Japan. Colors include white, red-purple and purple.

Care: If possible, the plant should be kept cool but frost free over the winter. It can be sowed at the end of the summer, though it is possible to purchase blooming plants in the spring. These will only keep for one season, after which they die. Keep the plant light and airy and fertilize once every two weeks as long as the bloom lasts.

Propagation: Sow in September for biennial cultivation, for annual cultivation, sow in March. Soil temperature 68–77°F (20–25°C). Plant seedlings out, continue to grow, harden off and keep dormant, or—with spring sowing—continue to grow. With annual varieties the bloom may arrive later.

Light:	Much light, full sun, too.
Temp:	Grow cool to moderately warm, in the winter 40–50°F (5–10°C).
Water:	Keep moderately moist.
Hum:	Moderate, 50–60%.
Soil:	Standard potting soil mixed with extra loam or clay.

Euterpe edulis

Palmae

Assai palm

A palm from Brazil with several trunks that each can grow to 100 ft (30 m) high. It is grown in our region as a small foliage plant, although it unfortunately will not last long indoors.

Care: Due to its large need for humid air, this plant will die in a dry, heated room in the winter. In any case, mist frequently and keep it from sunlight. Fertilize once every two weeks during the growth season.

Propagation: Fresh seeds germinate at a soil temperature of 68–77°F (20–25°C).

Euterpe edulis

Light:	Much light, no full sun.
Temp:	Grow warm, in the winter a minimum of 61°F (16°C).
Water:	Keep moderately moist.
Hum:	High, above 60%.
Soil:	Standard potting soil mixed with fine clay or loam or rock wool powder.

Exacum affine

Gentianaceae

German violet

A biennial plant that can be grown annually; these must be thrown out after blooming, however.

Care: Place a newly purchased blooming plant in a cool spot out of the sun. Drafts are harmful, but fresh air (from a sheltered terrace or balcony) is fine. Take off old flowers and feed once every two weeks. The ball of soil should stay moist at all times, otherwise the small flowers dry out quickly. Dispose of the plants once they are finished blooming.

Propagation: One can sow from December on, but February is easier. The germination temperature is 68°F (20°C). Germinated plants should be grown with a few together in a 3½ in (9 cm) diameter pot and grown at around 64°F (18°C). Remove the tops a few times for better branching. The plants can bloom three months from the original planting.

Exacum affine

Light: Much light, no full sun.
Temp: Grow moderately warm, 64–73°F (18–23°C).
Water: Keep moderately moist, do not allow the ball of soil to dry out completely.
Hum: Moderate, 50–60%.
Soil: Standard potting soil.

Fascicularia pitcairniifolia

Bromeliaceae

Bromeliads from Chile with very long, narrow leaves, ending in a sharp point.
Care: These are strong plants that can endure full sun and survive temperatures around 32°F (0°C). They are not very prevalent as potted

Fascicularia pitcairniifolia

plants, except among collectors. In Mediterranean regions they grow outside; to the north, as a container plant or greenhouse plant. Water sparsely and feed once every two weeks. Keep cool, light and almost completely dry.
Propagation: From seed or by taking side shoots.

Light: Full sun.
Temp: Grow cool to moderately warm, in the winter a minimum of 40–50°F (5–10°C).
Water: Keep moderately moist, withhold almost all water in the winter.
Hum: Low to moderate.
Soil: Cactus soil or other permeable soil with, for instance, a lot of perlite.

X Fatshedera lizei

Araliaceae

A very popular houseplant that has received less and less attention in recent years, and perhaps rightly so, since there are many more beautiful plants available now. The X in front of the name means that the plant is a cross-fertilization between two different genera: *Fatsia*, the finger-plant with large leaves, and *Hedera*,

X *Fatshedera lizei* 'Pia'

a climbing plant. There is also a variegated form called *Variegata*.
Care: Do not grow too warm, though it's possible to keep it outside in the summer. The green species can grow with little light, though the variegated species should have more. In the winter, the plants should be kept frost-free. Feed every two weeks during the growth period.
Propagation: From top cuttings or middle cuttings. Soil temperature 68–77°F (20–25°C). In general, it is best to plant three cuttings together.

Light: Will endure much shade, in a north-facing window. The variegated form demands more light, but no full sun.
Temp: Grow cool, in the winter a minimum of 45°F (7°C).
Water: Keep moderately moist.
Hum: Moderate, 50–60%.
Soil: Standard potting soil.

Fatsia japonica

Araliaceae

This is one of the parent species of the previous X *Fatshedera*. We often see the common green species, but the variegated 'Variegata' is, of course, more beautiful. The *Fatsia* is a strong plant, which can grow outside in a garden and will sometimes bloom there. During strong winters, though, it will freeze and die.
Care: A summer home is the ideal place to grow this plant, which will survive the winter in a cool spot without much light. Even some frost will not be harmful. One can leave it for two weeks without watering in a pot with a watering system. Feed once every two weeks in the summer.
Propagation: From top cuttings or middle cuttings. Soil temperature 68–77°F (20–25°C). The green species is easy to grow from seed; it will germinate at 50–60°F (10–15°C).

Light: This plant can have much shade, though the variegated species needs more light. No full sun.
Temp: Grow cool, some frost is allowed in the winter.
Water: Keep moderately moist.
Hum: Moderate, 50–60%.
Soil: Standard potting soil.

Fatsia japonica 'Variegata'

Faucaria tigrina

Aizoaceae
Tiger's jaw

An old-fashioned, well-known succulent with thick, closely-arranged leaves that have little teeth along the edges, resembling the open mouth of a ferocious animal. With proper cultivation the *Faucaria tigrina* blooms effortlessly with small yellow flowers. There is also a species *felina*, the cats' jaw, and *lupina*, the wolfs' jaw. They all require the same care.

Care: Grow sunny in the summer (possibly outside) and water moderately. Add cactus food monthly. To get flowers, a dormant period is needed in the winter at a lower temperature; water is hardly necessary then.

Propagation: From seed or via top cuttings taken in the summer. Allow them to dry for a few days, then plant in sandy dry soil. Soil temperature around 68°F (20°C).

Light:	Full sun.
Temp:	Grow moderately warm to warm; in the winter, dormancy at 40–50°F (5–10°C).
Water:	Keep moderately moist in the summer, in the winter almost dry.
Hum:	Low.
Soil:	Cactus soil.

Faucaria tigrina

Felicia amelloides

Compositae
Blue daisy

A half bush that is generally grown from seed and is often found in gardens. Once in a while, it may be bought as a potted plant. Very suitable for a balcony.

Felicia amelloides

Care: Grow sunny and airy, but do not place it in a drafty spot. Fertilize every two weeks. Dormancy is possible if you can provide a cool space with sufficient light. In this way, magnificent specimens can be grown with hundreds of flowers, just as with chrysanthemums.

Propagation: In the fall, one can use the top cuttings from the side shoots of existing plants. Soil temperature: 60–64°F (15–18°C). Air temperature: 50–60°F (10–15°C). If possible, give extra light during the winter. Cut off the tops of the growing plants a few times for better branching. One can also sow seeds in January, and cultivate as described above.

Light:	Much light, sun in the summer as well.
Temp:	Grow cool, winter temperature 45–54°F (7–12°C).
Water:	Keep moderately moist, somewhat drier in the winter.
Hum:	Moderate, 50–60%.
Soil:	Standard potting soil.

Fenestraria aurantiaca

Aizoaceae

Small plants with thick, elongated succulent leaves, topped by a transparent "window."

Fenestraria aurantiaca

These plants naturally grow underground, with only the small openings sticking out above the surface of the earth. Light falls through the clear water reservoir and reaches the chlorophyll that is inside the thick leaves.
Care: Grow very sunny and warm. Add small amounts of water to the soil. Add some cactus food once a month. After the flowering period, usually at the end of the summer, a dry and cool dormant period should be provided. Otherwise, the plants will not survive the shortage of light.
Propagation: It is easy to grow plants from seed.

Light:	Full sun.
Temp:	Grow warm, in the winter a minimum of 54°F (12°C).
Water:	Sparse, none during the dormant period.
Hum:	Low.
Soil:	Cactus soil, mixed with rough sand or pebbles.

Ferocactus species

Cactaceae

A genus of cacti with extremely powerful thorns. In Mexico and the southern United States, they can grow many feet tall and are

Ferocactus melocactiformis

often branched. There are mostly small, round or tubular plants in cultivation.
Care: Place in sun in the summer and give moderate amounts of water. Add cactus food once a month. The dormant period should be at a low temperature in a light spot.
Propagation: From seed. Germination temperature 68–77°F (20–25°C).

Ferocactus horridus

Light:	Full sun.
Temp:	Moderately warm to warm, in the winter 40–50°F (5–10°C).
Water:	Keep rather dry, withhold all water in the winter.
Hum:	Low.
Soil:	Cactus soil.

Ficus altissima

Moraceae

A tall tree from tropical parts of India and the Philippines. It is easy to recognize by the light leaf veins.
Care: Grow warm throughout the year and make sure that the air does not become too dry. Fertilize every two weeks in the growing period. Repot in larger containers, as size dictates.
Propagation: From top cuttings and eye cuttings. Soil temperature 68–77°F (20–25°C).

Light:	Half shade, no bright sun.
Temp:	Grow warm, not below 61°F (16°C).
Water:	Keep moderately moist.
Hum:	Moderate, 50–60%.
Soil:	Standard potting soil.

Ficus altissima

Ficus aspera 'Parcellii'

Moraceae

Clown fig

A lesser known *Ficus* with thin, marbled leaves and cherry-like, red- and white-veined fruits, which form at an early age.
Care: The thin foliage evaporates more moisture than the leaves of most other species, so that a high relative humidity is required. This will cause problems in the winter, especially when the temperature indoors cannot be lowered that much. Spraying the foliage with soft water is a good remedy. Fertilize the plant every two weeks during the growth period.
Propagation: From seed.

Light:	Much light, no full sun.
Temp:	Grow warm, minimum of 61°F (16°C).
Water:	Keep moderately moist.
Hum:	High, above 60%.
Soil:	Standard potting soil.

Ficus aspera 'Parcellii'

FICUS

Ficus benghalensis

Ficus benghalensis

Moraceae

Banyan

A tall tree from India. Aerial roots hang from the branches and form extra trunks where they touch the ground. Easy to recognize by the large leaves that are initially hairy, and light brown in color. A strong houseplant.
Care: Can remain indoors the whole year. During the growth period (and that is almost all year) feed every two weeks. Repot in the spring.
Propagation: From top cuttings or eye cuttings, soil temperature 86°F (30°C).

Light:	Half shade.
Temp:	Grow warm, in the winter a minimum of 60°F (15°C).
Water:	Keep moderately moist.
Hum:	Low to moderate.
Soil:	Standard potting soil.

Ficus benjamina

Moraceae

A very tall tree also grown in the tropics, it is reputedly the strongest *Ficus* for indoor cultivation. Older plants droop their branches in a very elegant way. There are various forms with small or somewhat differently shaped leaves; there is also a variegated (and weaker) form. In the picture from left to right are the leaves of 'Golden King,' 'Ryssenhout' and 'Exotica.'
Care: Warmth and relatively large amounts of light are sufficient to grow this *Ficus* without problems. Fertilize once every two weeks during the growth season. Repot if possible each spring to get rid of any harmful substances that have collected in the potting soil.
Propagation: From top cuttings, soil temperature 86°F (30°C).

Light:	Half shade.
Temp:	Grow warm, in the winter not below 61°F (16°C).
Water:	Keep moderately moist.
Hum:	Low to moderate.
Soil:	Standard potting soil.

Ficus benjamina

Ficus buxifolia

Moraceae

A fig with the foliage of the *Buxus*, or so it appears. A beautiful houseplant, but unfortunately not as strong as many other species with larger leaves.
Care: Always grow warm and spray the foliage frequently, or otherwise provide a high humidity. Fertilize every two weeks during the growth period.
Propagation: From top cuttings or middle cuttings. Soil temperature at least 77°F (25°C).

Light:	Half shade or much light, no bright sun.
Temp:	Grow warm, a minimum of 61°F (16°C).
Water:	Keep moderately moist.
Hum:	High, above 60%.
Soil:	Standard potting soil.

Ficus buxifolia

Ficus carica

Ficus deltoidea 'Variegata'

Ficus carica

Moraceae
Fig

This common fig is a deciduous *Ficus*, which in a moderate climate is somewhat hardy. In temperate wine-growing areas, the plant often grows against a sheltered wall. Farther north, it is grown as a container plant. Figs grow easily.

Care: When cultivated as a container plant, it should go outside at the end of May, somewhat shaded initially until the leaves have developed. Then move the plant into sun, and feed once every two weeks until the end of August. The fig can remain outside in the fall until it really starts to freeze, generally around

the end of December. Then bring it inside to a cool, dark storage space. Light is not needed after the plant's leaves fall. Plant in soil that is not too wet.

Propagation: Root middle cuttings in the early spring under glass at a soil temperature of 77°F (25°C).

Light:	Full sun.
Temp:	Grow cool, in the winter a minimum of 32°F (0°C).
Water:	Keep moderately moist, drier in the winter.
Hum:	Moderate, 50–60%.
Soil:	Standard potting soil mixed with at least ⅓ part fine clay or loam.

Ficus cyathistipula

Ficus cyathistipula

Moraceae

A species with sleek, shiny leaves. At an early age, red pseudofruits appear.
Care: The leathery leaves do not allow for much water evaporation, so this *Ficus* also flourishes in a heated room, where the humidity is not very high. During the summer fertilize once every two weeks and do not place the plant in full sunlight.
Propagation: Top cuttings or eye cuttings. Soil temperature 86°F (30°C).

Light:	Half shade.
Temp:	Grow warm in the winter at least 61°F (16°C).
Water:	Keep moderately moist.
Hum:	Low to moderate.
Soil:	Standard potting soil.

Ficus deltoidea

Moraceae

A plant that lives as an epiphytic species on other bushes. Previously known as *Ficus diversifolia*. The dark green foliage has small gold dots. The small green and yellow pseudofruits are formed effortlessly by the plant. 'Variegata' is the lesser known, variegated form.
Care: This species can be kept cooler than most other species. Nevertheless, much light is needed for adequate growth. Keeping the plant dry for a period will stimulate the forming of fruit. Fertilize during the growth period once every two weeks.
Propagation: From top cuttings or middle cuttings, soil temperature 86°F (30°C).

Light:	Much light, no full sun.
Temp:	Daytime around 66°F (19°C), at night 63°F (17°C). In the winter at least 60°F (15°C).
Water:	Keep moderately moist.
Hum:	Moderate, 50–60%.
Soil:	Standard potting soil.

Ficus deltoidea

FICUS

Ficus elastica

Moraceae
Rubber plant

A well-known species with large, often extremely shiny leaves. The stem does not branch very much in nature; it grows straight up until it reaches the ceiling. By cutting the top of the plant a few times, you can succeed in making the plant branch. A white latex, which when solidified is a kind of rubber, will flow from the cutting wounds. There exist various leaf shapes and some variegated varieties.

Care: This is a very strong houseplant that can remain indoors all year and endures dry air rather well. Fertilize during the growth period once every two weeks.
Propagation: Quite easy from eye cuttings. The large foliage is generally rolled up to prevent evaporation. (See page 81.) Plants that grow too tall are sometimes cut; it works but it takes more time. Soil temperature 86°F (30°C).

Light:	Half shade, never full sun.
Temp:	Grow warm, in the winter not below 61°F (16°C).
Water:	Keep moderately moist.
Hum:	Low to moderate.
Soil:	Standard potting soil.

Ficus leprieurii

Moraceae

A species better known as *Ficus triangularis*, for its triangular leaves. Fruits appear readily. There is also a variegated form, 'Variegata,' but this is rarer than the species *leprieurii*.
Care: Keep constantly warm, but out of the sun. Fertilize in the summer. Warm dormancy. This is not an easy species to grow, which is probably the reason why it is not often available.
Propagation: From top cuttings or middle cuttings. Soil temperature: 68–86°F (25–30°C).

Ficus elastica 'Doescheri'

Ficus elastica

Ficus elastica 'Schryveriana'

Ficus elastica 'Robusta'

Ficus elastica 'Decorata Variegata'

Ficus leprieurii

Light: Much light, no full sun.
Temp: Grow warm, not below 64°F (18°C).
Water: Grow moderately moist.
Hum: Moderate to high.
Soil: Standard potting soil.

Ficus lyrata

Moraceae

A very easily recognized *Ficus* with enormous, lyrate leaves with very expressive venation. It is not as easy to keep this *Ficus* as most other species. Nevertheless, it is quite popular, probably because of its impressive appearance.

Care: This species demands a humid atmosphere, especially in the winter, which can cause problems indoors. If you can lower the temperature somewhat, this would make a big difference. Allow as much light as possible in the winter, but keep the plant from the bright summer sun, to prevent the leaves from burning. Fertilize during the growth period once every two weeks. Repot each spring.
Propagation: From eye cuttings. Soil temperature 86°F (30°C).

Light: Much light, no full sun.
Temp: Grow warm, in the winter a minimum of 61°F (16°C).
Water: Keep moderately moist.
Hum: Moderate, 50–60%.
Soil: Standard potting soil.

Ficus microcarpa

Moraceae

Often called *Ficus* 'Panda,' it is now known as *Ficus microcarpa*. It is a strong houseplant that needs to be grown warm, just like most other *Ficus* species.
Care: Never place in full sun; allow some shade. Keep warm the whole year and provide sufficient water, but only add fertilizer once every two weeks. Make sure no excess water remains in the tray.
Propagation: From top cuttings or eye cuttings. Soil temperature 77°F (25°C).

Light: Much light or half shade, no sun.
Temp: Grow warm, not below 61°F (16°C).
Water: Keep moderately moist.
Hum: Moderate.
Soil: Standard potting soil.

Ficus microcarpa

Ficus pumila

Moraceae

Also known as *Ficus repens*. A very popular species with small leaves, grown as a hanging plant or climbing plant. The variety 'Minima' has even smaller leaves, about ½ in (1.5 cm) long, and 'Variegata' has spotted leaves.
Care: This species requires high humidity, but can be kept cooler than most other species of *Ficus*. Fertilize in the growing period every two weeks. If grown as a hanging plant, watch the ball of soil for drying and do not use pots that are too small (they have no water buffer).
Propagation: Roots are often formed where shoots touch the soil. Remove these pieces and plant them separately.

Light: Half shade.
Temp: Grow moderately warm to warm, in the winter the temperature can be lowered to 40°F (5°C).
Water: Moderate, drier at lower temperatures.
Hum: Moderate, 50–60%.
Soil: Standard potting soil.

Ficus pumila

Ficus lyrata

Ficus religiosa

Ficus religiosa

Moraceae

A sacred tree in India under which Buddha attained enlightenment. The large, thin leaves do not closely resemble the other *Ficus* species. The tops of the leaves often end in a long tail. The plants are mostly imported.

Care: The thin foliage is an indication that high humidity is needed. Often, these plants are not hardened sufficiently, and the foliage tends to droop soon after the plant is brought indoors. In any case, do not allow it sun and spray frequently, especially when the heat is turned on. The plants often recover and produce new leaves that are more resistant to dry air. Feed weekly in the summer.

Propagation: Via top cuttings or middle cuttings. Soil temperature: 77–86°F (25–30°C).

Light:	Much light or half shade, never sun.
Temp:	Grow warm, not below 64°F (18°C).
Water:	Keep moderately moist.
Hum:	High, above 60%.
Soil:	Standard potting soil.

Ficus retusa

Moraceae

A species with rather small leaves, strongly resembling *Ficus benjamina*. It is distinguishable by the small distance between its nodes, which makes the plant more compact. There are also some variegated varieties. The green species can be sold as an indoor bonsai, and is very suitable for this purpose.

Ficus retusa 'Hawaii'

Care: The variegated forms have to be kept light to preserve their leaf markings. Grow warm, and slightly cooler in the winter. In the growth season, fertilize every two weeks.

Propagation: From top cuttings, soil temperature 86°F (30°C).

Light: Much light, no full sun.

Ficus retusa

Temp: Grow warm, not below 61°F (16°C) in the winter.
Water: Keep moderately moist.
Hum: Moderate, 50–60%.
Soil: Standard potting soil.

Ficus rubiginosa

Moraceae

A strong, branched *Ficus* with medium-to-large leaves, available in green and variegated forms. The young leaves and leaf stalks are hairy and brownish. The stalks root where they touch soil.
Care: It is better for this species to be grown cooler than other figs, though the green species is especially strong and can stand warmer conditions. Feed every two weeks in the growth season.
Propagation: From top cuttings or eye cuttings. Soil temperature 86°F (30°C).

Light: Half shade, and for the variegated forms much light, but no full sun.
Temp: Grow moderately warm, keep around 60°F (15°C) in the winter, minimum 50°F (10°C).
Water: Keep moderately moist.
Hum: Moderate, 50–60%.
Soil: Standard potting soil.

Ficus rubiginosa

Ficus rubiginosa 'Variegata'

Ficus saggittata

Moraceae

A climbing species with small leaves, previously known as *Ficus radicus*. The long stalks root at the nodes. There is a variegated form as well, called 'Variegata.'
Care: A strong plant that does well as ground

Ficus sagittata

cover under a larger tree, especially the common green species, which can have much shade. Spray in the winter and keep the temperature rather high. Fertilize once every two weeks in the growing period.
Propagation: By taking the rooted stalks or via middle cuttings.

Light: Shade, or half shade.
Temp: Grow warm, minimum 64°F (18°C).
Water: Keep moderately moist.
Hum: Moderate, 50–60%.
Soil: Standard potting soil.

Ficus schlechteri

Moraceae

A species with relatively small leaves that resembles the species *rubiginosa*. In South and East Asia, this grows as a tall tree with hanging twigs like a willow.

Ficus schlecteri

Care: Very suitable for warm rooms. It will grow straight when tied up and pruned regularly. In the winter, spray often. In the summer, fertilize once every two weeks.
Propagation: From top cuttings and eye cuttings. Soil temperature 77°F (25°C).

Light: Half shade or much light, no full sun.
Temp: Grow warm, minimum 61°F (16°C).
Water: Keep moderately moist.
Hum: Low to moderate.
Soil: Standard potting soil.

Ficus stricta

Ficus stricta

Moraceae

A *Ficus* from Java with small leaves, recently available and not so easy to cultivate.
Care: Grow warm the whole year, but not in the sun. In the growing period, fertilize once every two weeks. If possible, tie the plant up so it grows straight, or keep it small by pruning regularly.
Propagation: Root top cuttings or eye cuttings under glass at a soil temperature of 77°F (25°C).

Light: Half shade, no full sun.
Temp: Grow warm, not below 64°F (18°C).
Water: Keep moderately moist.
Hum: High, above 60%.
Soil: Standard potting soil.

Fittonia verschaffeltii 'Argyroneura'

Fittonia verschaffeltii

Acanthaceae

Small plants with extraordinarily beautiful leaf markings. They are quite suitable ground cover in greenhouses, plant windows and vitrines. Besides the common species, there are two other cultivars, both pictured.

Care: The small plants do not stand dry air very well, so mist frequently with soft water, or, even better, provide a more humid atmosphere. In the winter, the temperature can be lowered, but not too much. Feed once every two weeks during the growth period.

Propagation: From top cuttings or by removing the shoots. Soil temperature 68°F (20°C).

Light:	Half shade.
Temp:	Grow moderately warm, around 68°F (20°C), now below 61°F (16°C) in the winter.
Water:	Always keep moderately moist with soft water.
Hum:	High, above 60%.
Soil:	Standard potting soil mixed with extra peat mould, peat moss, etc. Use shallow, wide bowls or pots with adequate drainage.

Futonia verschaffeltii 'Argyroneura'

Fitonnia verschaffeltii 'Pearcei'

Fortunella margarita

Rutaceae

Nagami, Oval Kumquat

A container plant that strongly resembles a citrus tree, but belongs to another genus. The sour fruits are sometimes used for marmalade, and are preceded in growth by small white, fragrant flowers.

Care: They are generally sold as bushes, grown on a trunk and are ideal as container plants. In the summer, they can go outside on a sunny, sheltered terrace. Give plenty of water, and feed every two weeks. Because these plants are not very hardy, they have to be brought inside in the fall for a cool dormancy. From this point on, they should be kept drier, but make sure that the foliage does not fall off. This is, after all, an evergreen.

Propagation: By grafting on *Poncirus trifoliata*, from seed or via top cuttings, which root under glass at soil temperature 68–77°F (20–25°C).

Light:	Full sun.
Temp:	Grow cool, in the winter 32–46°F (0–8°C).
Water:	Keep moderately moist, drier in the winter.
Hum:	Moderate, 50–60%.
Soil:	Standard potting soil mixed with loam or clay.

Fortunella margarita

Frithia pulchra

Aizoaceae

Baby toes

A small plant for a window with thick, gray stalks, translucent at the top to allow light to enter. The plants produce large flowers if they receive adequate care.

Care: Keep well sunlit and water sparsely during the growing period. Add cactus food once a month at most. In the winter keep cooler and almost completely dry. Only when the flowers appear (around April or May) should more water be given.

Propagation: From seed.

Light:	Full sun.
Temp:	Grow warm, in the winter between 45–54°F (7–12°C).
Water:	Keep fairly dry, almost completely dry in the winter.
Hum:	Low.
Soil:	Cactus soil.

Frithia pulchra

Fuchsia hybrids

Onagraceae

The nonhardy *Fuchsia* hybrids are extremely popular plants that bloom for a long period of time. The hanging flowers generally consist of a colored calyx with curled calyx leaves, and below that sits the flower crown. The stamen and pistil extend beyond the crown.

Care: Fuchsias are suitable for indoor growth, but most varieties prefer to be outside in the summer, in a not-too-windy but airy and shady spot. They do not like bright sunlight. Very beautiful plants can be obtained if grown in a white-chalked, cool greenhouse. A *Fuchsia* is best considered a container plant or greenhouse plant, to be kept outside in the summer and inside in the winter at a minimum temperature of 40°F (5°C). One can cut the plants back considerably before dormancy to save space. Since not everybody owns a greenhouse, it is good to know that one can ensile the *Fuchsia* underground. Once outdoor plants are subjected to their first frost, most of their foliage will drop. After this, cut back the bushes considerably. Then, dig a pit about 2 ft (60 cm) deep in a spot that is not too wet. Place the plants and their pots next to each other in the hole, and close it up just before the next frost is expected, sometime before December. The soil protects the plants from freezing. At the beginning of April, or even later, dig up the *Fuchsias*. They will look awful and barely able to recover. After repotting, the plants can be placed outside, but if they already have new shoots then they should be protected against night frosts, and perhaps kept inside briefly. If *Fuchsia* are grown temporarily in a greenhouse, they will come out sooner and will bloom earlier. This method of ensilage during dormancy can continue for years; the plants grow taller and taller and will produce more flowers each successive time. In the summer, fertilize weekly with a solution at normal concentration (2 g per liter).

Fuchsia-hybr. 'Saturnus'

Fuchsia-hybr. 'Isis'

Propagation: One of the reasons the *Fuchsia* is so popular is that it is easy to propagate from cuttings. This can happen as early as spring. If dormant plants are warmed early enough, the young shoots can be used as cuttings. But cuttings can also be taken from the partly wooded tops as late as August. Cutting temperature is 15–20°C. One can use some cutting powder, but this is not absolutely necessary. Place a few cuttings together in a pot and cut the tops for better branching when they begin to grow. Often it is even better to cut the tops a second time.

Light: Half shade to shade.
Temp: Grow cool, minimum 37°F (3°C).
Water: Always moderately moist.
Hum: Moderate to high, at least 50%.
Soil: Standard potting soil is good enough, but loam, decayed manure and leaf soil are good additions.

Fuchsia-hybr. 'Beacon'

Fuchsia-hybr. 'Wallington'

Furcraea foetida 'Striata'

Agavaceae

A plant from Brazil that needs a warm atmosphere. Also known as *Furcraea gigantea*. The cultivar 'Striata,' pictured, has wide white stripes on the leaves.
Care: In the summer, this plant can be outside if it is placed in a sheltered spot and does not receive full sun. Fertilize every two weeks. Bring inside in the winter for dormancy at a lower temperature and with moderate water.
Propagation: From seed and by taking shoots.

Light: Much light, especially for the varie-

Furcraea foetida 'Striata'

Temp: Grow moderately warm, in the winter a minimum of 54°F (12°C).
Water: Always keep moderately moist, drier during dormancy.
Hum: Moderate to high.
Soil: Mix standard potting soil with fine clay or loam.

Gardenia jasminoides

Rubiaceae

Cape jasmine

This plant is widely used for corsages, especially for men's boutonnieres, probably because of the flower's magnificent fragrance. If grown as a bush, it is possible to have fresh flowers at hand all summer.
Care: The plant can be placed outside in a large container as long as it is screened against the brightest sunlight. Feed every two weeks. At night, the temperature should not fall below 61°F (16°C), which could be problematic in cold summers. If this does happen, chlorosis will set in shortly after, indicated by yellow leaves. In the winter, the *Gardenia* has to be brought inside a moderate greenhouse with lower temperatures. In any case, it should not grow. When the buds have formed, the temperature at night should not rise above 63°F (17°C), otherwise they will fall off.
Propagation: Root top cuttings in the early spring under glass or plastic at a soil temperature of 77–86°F (25–30°C).

Light: Much light, no full sun.
Temp: Grow moderately warm, in the winter not below 54°F (12°C), and the soil temperature preferably even higher.
Water: Keep moderately moist.
Hum: Moderate, 50–60%.
Soil: Mix standard potting soil with clay or loam.

Gardenia jasminoides

Gasteria species

Liliaceae

Mouse-ear aloe

Succulent plants with a very short trunk and, quite often, leaves in double rows. There are various species available. When they bloom, small orange-red flowers appear on a long stem.
Care: Succulents such as these are easy to grow, and can only be destroyed by excess

Gasteria verrucosa

water. They like full sun in the summer, while in the winter a cool dormant period with sparse water is necessary for good health. Add very moderate amounts of cactus food, only once a month during the growth period.

Light: Full sun.
Temp: Grow moderately warm, in the winter a minimum of 40°F (5°C).
Water: Water sparsely, just enough in the winter so that the leaves do not shrivel.
Hum: Low.
Soil: Cactus soil.

Gasteria liliputana

Gazania-hybr.

Gazania hybrids

Compositae

Annuals grown mainly for flower beds, they are also now sold as potted plants. They can bloom for a long time in a sunny window.
Care: The plants like warmth, therefore in wet summers, indoors is a better place than the garden or a windy balcony. Water moderately with diluted food added once every two weeks. After blooming, dispose of the plants, because they will not survive a winter dormancy.
Propagation: Sow from February at a soil temperature of 68–77°F (20–25°C). Cover with glass. Plant out and continue to grow. In April, begin to harden them off.

Light:	Full sun.
Temp:	Grow moderately warm.
Water:	Keep moderately moist.
Hum:	Moderate, 50–60%.
Soil:	Standard potting soil.

Geranium palmatum

Geraniaceae

A family member of what is generally known as 'geranium,' but a very different species than what is listed in this book under the genus name *Pelargonium. Palmatum* is a brother to garden geraniums, which are perennials and always hardy. The species pictured does not have these qualities and has to be grown in a greenhouse. In many books, it is still described as *Geranium anemonifolium.*
Care: This plant can grow outside from the end of May, in a garden or on a balcony. Full sun to light shade. Water moderately and feed every two weeks if the plants are in pots. Better results can be achieved if the plants are put in a flower bed in mid-May. Bring inside in the autumn, putting grown plants in the earth for a cool and not too wet dormancy.
Propagation: By division or from seed.

Light:	Much light, full sun.
Temp:	Grow cool, in the winter 40–50°F (5–10°C).
Water:	Keep moderately moist, drier in the winter.
Hum:	Moderate, 50–60%.
Soil:	Humusy, loamy soil.

Gerbera hybrids

Compositae

Mostly known as cut flowers, it is possible to cultivate these varieties as potted plants. Species with short stems are sold for that specific purpose.
Care: Place newly purchased plants well into the sun, possibly in a sheltered location outside. The air temperature should not go below 61°F (16°C), while the ball of soil has to be even warmer. Keep the soil continuously moist and fertilize every two weeks. Take some leaves off in the fall and let rest dormant at a lower temperature. After a few years, the plants tend to bloom less, so for full blooming, replace them from time to time.
Propagation: In general, the potted plants are grown from seed. This happens in February at a soil temperature of 68°F (20°C). Division is possible too. Additionally, soil shoots can be used as cuttings, which should be kept under a water mist.

Light:	Much light, full sun.
Temp:	61–77°F (16–25°C) in the summer, in the winter 54–60°F (12–15°C).
Water:	Moderately moist.
Hum:	Moderate, 50–60%.
Soil:	Standard potting soil made extra permeable with peat moss or tree bark.

Gerbera-hybr.

Geranium palmatum

Glechoma hederacea

Labiatae

Ground ivy

A familiar wild plant that comes up spontaneously in many gardens. The variegated form 'Variegata' (see picture) is cultivated as a houseplant.

Care: Can be grown as a hanging plant in a cool room. In the winter the temperature can be much lower. Add plenty of water in the summer, with some food added once every two weeks. The green species can be kept in a dark spot, and the variegated species need more light.

Propagation: The long stalks root at the nodes, where they touch the soil. Take these shoots for cuttings.

Light:	Shade for the green species, half shade for the variegated form.
Temp:	Grow cool, in the winter a minimum 32°F (0°C).
Water:	Plenty of water in the summer, less in the winter.
Hum:	Moderate, 50–60%.
Soil:	Standard potting soil.

Glechoma hederacea 'Variegata'

Globba winitii

Globba winitii

Zingiberaceae

Tropical plant with extremely peculiar flowers, often grown in botanical gardens.

Care: Keep in a warm greenhouse the whole year, providing a humid atmosphere and light shade. In winter the foliage will die off, but the tuberous roots rest dormant in the soil. They should never dry out completely, so continue to give a little water even if nothing can be seen of the plant. In the spring, repot the tubers in new soil and bring back to growth.

Propagation: By division of the tubers.

Light:	Much light, no full sun.
Temp:	Grow warm, not below 64°F (18°C).
Water:	Keep moderately wet, water sparsely in the rest period.
Hum:	High, far above 60%.
Soil:	About half standard potting soil and half loam or clay.

Gloriosa rothschildiana

Liliaceae

A tuberous growth that is quite easy to get to bloom in a greenhouse as well as in a window. Tubers can be ordered by mail. It is a climber, so provide support.

Care: After receiving the tubers in the spring, keep them warm, under glass or plastic. Soil temperature 77–86°F (25–30°C). When the plants come out, harden them off, but provide a humid atmosphere and warmth, keeping the temperature above 64°F (18°C). Tie up the long shoots. After the flowering period, the plant will continue to grow for at least two months. Fertilize once every two weeks dur-

Gloriosa rothschildiana

ing this period. Administer less water at the end of the summer; the plants have to die off. The tubers can stay in the pots, but can also be taken out and stored dry, at around 63°F (17°C).

Propagation: Healthy growing plants develop new tubers. These in turn produce new plants the second year. Handle these plants with care, as each tuber has only one growth point.

Light:	Much light, screen against bright sunlight.
Temp:	Grow warm.
Water:	Always keep moderately moist in the summer.
Hum:	Moderate to high.
Soil:	Standard potting soil.

Glottiphyllum linguiforme

Aizoaceae

A succulent plant from South Africa that until recently was often grown as a houseplant. It is now somewhat rare. There are some other species available as well.

On the previous pages: *Gerbera* hybrid

Glottiphyllum linguiforme

Care: Grow sunny, for example, in a south-facing window. The plant can also go outside at the end of May. Do not give too much water and feed moderately, at most some cactus food once a month. A dormant period is advisable to stimulate the forming of new buds. The temperatures should be lowered considerably and almost all water withheld.

Propagation: By leaf cuttings.

Light:	Full sun.
Temp:	Grow cool to moderately warm, in the winter a minimum of 40°F (5°C).
Water:	Keep moderately dry, almost completely dry in the winter.
Hum:	Low.
Soil:	Cactus soil, in shallow, well-draining pots or bowls.

Gloxinia sylvatica

Gesneriaceae

Most plants called 'gloxinia' are described in this book under *Sinningia*. The species with the small flowers in the picture is an exception. It is often still identified as *Seemannia*. There is also a purple flowering species, *Gloxinia perennis*, and some cross-fertilizations as well. Their cultivation is similar.

Care: This is a greenhouse plant that requires high humidity. Nevertheless, it can be kept indoors during the flowering period, which starts in the fall. The temperature should never get below 63°F (17°C). When the blooming is over, add less and less water until the plant dies off. Store the dry rhizomes (underground stems) in the pot. In the spring, set out at 68–77°F (20–25°C). When they start to grow well, add more water and later on fertilize once a week.

Propagation: By dividing the rootstocks, but also from top cuttings or middle cuttings, which root at a soil temperature of 77–86°F (25–30°C) under glass.

Gloxinia sylvatica

Light:	Screened light.
Temp:	Grow warm, keeping rootstocks above 54°F (12°C) in the winter.
Water:	Give plenty of water during the growth season, withhold water during dormant period.
Hum:	High, above 60%.
Soil:	Very airy and acidic, for instance anthurium or bromeliad soil.

Goethea cauliflora

Malvaceae

A peculiar tropical plant that blooms directly from its trunk. Similar in cultivation to *Pavonia*.
Care: Preferably grown in a greenhouse or plant window, warm and lightly shaded in a humid atmosphere. Give plenty of water in the summer and feed once every two weeks. In the winter the temperature can be lowered. Cut back in the spring if necessary, repot and place in a warm spot again.
Propagation: Root top cuttings under glass or plastic at 86°F (30°C) in the spring.

Light:	Much light, no full sun.
Temp:	Grow warm, in the winter a minimum of 54°F (12°C).
Water:	Keep moderately moist with soft water.
Hum:	High, above 60%.
Soil:	Acidic and humusy, for instance coniferous soil.

Goethea cauliflora

Gomesa recurva

Gomesa recurva

Orchidaceae

A genus of rather small orchids, related to *Oncidium*, originating in Brazil. The flowers smell lovely.

Care: Give plenty of (rain)water during the growth season, but only if there is a functioning drainage system, for stagnant water makes the roots rot. Add food to the water once every two weeks. It is preferable to grow these in lattice baskets, hung high in a greenhouse in a light, sunscreened and well-ventilated location. When the new pseudotubers are developed, a rest period should follow, during which withhold water and keep temperatures low.

Propagation: By dividing older plants.

Light:	Much light, no full sun.
Temp:	Grow moderately warm, a minimum 54°F (12°C) during dormant period (usually in winter).
Water:	Plenty of rainwater during the growth season.
Hum:	High, above 60%.
Soil:	Tree bark sphagnum or rock wool flakes in lattice baskets.

Gomphrena globosa

Amaranthaceae
Bullet amaranth

A small annual garden plant that has lately become available as a potted plant, too. They come in a variety of very bright colors.

Gomphrena globosa

Care: A sunny spot by a window or on a balcony is excellent, but do not let it get too hot. Keep adequately moist and fertilize once every two weeks. Dispose of the plant after the flowering period.

Propagation: From seed in March or April, under glass. Soil temperature 60–68°F (15–20°C). Plant out shoots in pots and continue to grow at 68°F (20°C).

Light:	Full sun.
Temp:	Grow cool to moderately warm.
Water:	Keep moderately moist.
Hum:	Moderate, 50–60%.
Soil:	Standard potting soil.

Graptopetalum bellum

Graptopetalum species

Grassulaceae

Graptopetalum is a genus of succulents, comparable with the more famous *Echeveria*. The plants bloom easily and are quite pretty.

Care: Unlike most other succulents, full direct sunlight is not advisable. Allow much light, but screened as well. Water moderately and keep the soil practically dry in the winter while the plant is dormant at low temperatures. Feed lightly during the growth season.

Propagation: Take some leaves from a rosette, dry them and plant in relatively dry soil. Soil temperature 68°F (20°C).

Light:	Much light, no full sun.
Temp:	Grow moderately warm, and in the winter allow a rest period between 40 and 50°F (5 and 10°C).
Water:	Keep moderately dry, almost dry during dormant period.
Hum:	Low.
Soil:	Cactus soil.

Graptopetalum paraguayense

Graptophyllum pictum

Acanthaceae

A small bush found in many tropical gardens. The shiny green or purplish foliage is spotted irregularly in yellow. Dark red-purple flowers can appear.

Care: A humid atmosphere is necessary for successful cultivation, so it is really more a plant for a greenhouse. It can be placed indoors temporarily in the summer, if the location is not too sunny. Always provide adequate (rain)water and feed once every two weeks. The temperature should be rather high in the winter as well.

Propagation: Root top cuttings under glass at 68–77°F (20–25°C) soil temperature.

Light: Much light, or half shade, no full sun.
Temp: Grow warm, not below 64°F (18°C).
Water: Keep moderately moist with soft water.
Hum: High, above 60%.
Soil: Standard potting soil mixed with extra peat moss or coniferous soil.

Greenovia aurea

Greenovia aurea

Graptophyllum pictum

Greenovia aurea

Crassulaceae

A succulent from the Canary Islands that forms rosettes. In a moderate climate it is best suited for cultivation in a greenhouse, grown together with cacti and other succulents.

Care: Preferably keep in a cool, light greenhouse, though it can also survive in a sunny window. The plant can go outside in the summer as well, if the plants do not get drenched by too much rain. Give cactus food once a month. The temperature in the winter should be considerably lower, otherwise cultivation the following season will be a disaster.

Propagation: By taking side shoots and from seed.

Light: Full sun.
Temp: Grow cool to moderately warm, in the winter 40–54°F (5–12°C).
Water: Keep moderately dry, withhold almost all water in the dormant period.
Hum: Low.
Soil: Cactus soil.

Grevillea robusta

Proteaceae

Silky oak

The picture shows only the top of the *Grevillea robusta*, which in Australia can grow to a height of 165 ft (50 m). Indoors it can become too big. The plant can be pruned back for a more compact shape.

Care: Do not grow too warm, and certainly keep it cool in the winter. The plant does not do well in dry indoor air.

Propagation: Fresh (imported) seeds can germinate at 68°F (20°C). Attempts from cuttings are usually disappointing.

Light: Much light, no full sun.
Temp: Grow moderately warm, preferably not above 68°F (20°C), and in the winter 43–50°F (6–10°C).
Water: Keep moderately moist.
Hum: High, at least 60%
Soil: Standard potting soil.

Grevillea robusta

GREVILLEA

Guzmania species

Bromeliaceae

Bromeliads that have recently received more attention, especially the long-lasting, compact varieties, which are hybrids or variations on the species *lingulata*. The bracts are yellow, orange or red and form a compact rosette. The species *dissitiflora* (see detail) has a very different way of blooming. *Gusmania musaica* differs in shape too: The leaves are striped and the bloom is spherical, on a long stem. Care for all of these species is practically the same.

Care: The *Guzmania* blooms only once, like all bromeliads, and after that the rosette dies off. If mainly interested in the initial flowering (the beautiful bracts), then it does not matter very much how the plant is treated. Once in a while add some water, and do not keep it too cold. After a few months, when the plant begins to decline in beauty, dispose of it. But if you want to continue to grow the *Guzmania* from the new plants that spring up under the mother rosette, then particular care is required. First of all, place the plant in a light spot. Leave the small plants alone until the old rosette is clearly sucked dry. Then remove the young plants and continue to grow them in a greenhouse with high humidity. Use fertilizer in small doses, to avoid burning the plants.

After 12 to 15 months, the young plants are able to flower. If flowers do not appear, administer a chemical growth hormone.

Propagation: From the newly formed side plants.

Light: Much light, no full sun.

Temp: Grow warm, a minimum 61°F (18°C).
Water: Always keep moderately moist, in the summer water down the stem's funnel as well.
Hum: High, above 60%.
Soil: Bromeliad soil.

Guzmania lingulata

Guzmania dissitiflora

Guzmania musaica

Guzmania-hybr. 'Remembrance'

Guzmania-hybr. 'Wittmackii'

Gymnocalycium baldianum

Gymnocalycium species

Cactaceae

These cacti are well known, with their characteristic small red or yellow balls sitting atop green trunks, and they are sold by the millions. It is often thought that the colored ball is a flower, but this is certainly not the case. The red or yellow cactus top does not have any chlorophyll, and therefore is not capable of growing independently. It extracts food from the plant's trunk. (Read more about this on page 83.) Often there are species of *Gymnocalycium* grafted onto other cacti, of which you can see three in the picture. They bloom rather easily.
Care: The plants should be grown in a very light spot indoors or in a greenhouse, though in the spring, screen against the brightest sunlight. Keep quite dry. Give a rest period in the winter at lower temperatures and with hardly any water. Do not start watering too early in the spring. Begin by just misting once in a while.
Propagation: Shoots will form after grafting; also from seed.

Light:	Much light, no full sun.
Temp:	Moderately warm to warm.
Water:	Keep moderately dry, in the winter almost completely dry.
Hum:	Low.
Soil:	Cactus soil.

Gymnocalycium saglionis

Gymnocalycium, grafted forms

Gynura aurantiaca

Compositae

Primarily a foliage plant, this interesting species has purple hairs on its green leaves. Yellow flowers may appear, which unfortunately have a rather disagreeable smell.

Gynura aurantiaca

Care: Keep well lit, but not with too much sun. Keep moist in the summer and feed once a week. If possible, keep the plant cooler in the winter.
Propagation: Easy from top cuttings or middle cuttings; soil temperature 68–77°F (20–25°C). Take cuttings often because older plants are not very pretty.

Light:	Much light, no full sun.
Temp:	Moderately warm to warm, not below 54°F (12°C) in the winter.
Water:	Keep moderately moist.
Hum:	Low to moderate.
Soil:	Standard potting soil.

Haageocereus pseudomelanostele

Cactaceae

Relatively small column cactus that can grow to a height of over 3 ft (1 m). They are branched at the base. The columns have thorns that grow very close to one another. The species in the photo has brush hairs as well.
Care: Keep well lit and give plenty of water in the summer. The best results are achieved when this species is planted out in the bench of a greenhouse and not planted in pots. Give cactus food once every two weeks. In the middle of the summer, the growth stops for a while, so withhold water. But in the autumn, a second growth period begins. In December, when the winter dormancy begins, the plants should be kept warm, and drier as well.
Propagation: From seed and via top cuttings. Soil temperature 68–77°F (20–25°C).

Light:	Full sun.
Temp:	Moderately warm to warm.
Water:	Keep moderately moist in the summer, drier in the winter.
Hum:	Low.
Soil:	Standard potting soil or cactus soil.

Haageocereus pseudomelanostele

Habenaria xantholeuca

Habenaria xantholeuca

Orchidaceae

Deciduous, terrestrial (soil-growing) orchids with tuberous roots. There are hundreds of species, but most are rarely seen.
Care: Grow light in the summer, but not in bright sunlight. Place the pots outside in nice weather. Give adequate water and add some food once every two weeks. After the flowering period is over and the shoots begin to die off, one should give less water. In the dormant period, which lasts until about April, keep the soil only slightly moist. In the spring, the small tubers that are in the soil have to be planted in pots carefully. Then bring the plant back to growth again. Initially, water sparsely.
Propagation: By division during repotting.

Light:	Much light, no bright sun.
Temp:	Grow moderately warm, in the winter a minimum of 54°F (12°C).
Water:	Keep moderately moist in the summer, almost dry in the winter. Always use soft water.
Hum:	High, above 60%.
Soil:	Mixture for terrestrial orchids, such as fern roots, mixed with decayed manure, a little loam and perlite on a layer of clay particles.

Habranthus tubispathus

Amarayllidaceae

A bulbous plant related to *Zephyranthes*, with which it is often confused. The cultivation is the same.
Care: Bulbs can be ordered by mail. After delivery, pot in the spring, about 1.2 in (3 cm) under the soil. Initially, give only a little water, but keep warm to allow the bulbs to come out. As they do, add more water. The flowers ap-

Habranthus tubispathus

pear in summer. Fertilize once every two weeks. The pots can be outside or inside, always warm and sunny. Give less water in the fall but make sure that the foliage does not die off by keeping the plants cool through the winter. Bring back to growth in the spring. Repotting is necessary each year.
Propagation: By taking the bulbs and from seed.

Light:	Full sun.
Temp:	Grow cool to moderately warm, in the winter a minimum of 40°F (5°C).
Water:	Moderately moist in the growth period, drier during dormancy.
Hum:	Moderate, 50–60%.
Soil:	Standard potting soil.

Haemanthus albiflos

Haemanthus albiflos

Amaryllidaceae

A houseplant that, although rarely offered for sale, is often found in the homes of serious plant enthusiasts. The plants have long lives and tens of flowers can appear at the same time.
Care: Grow light in the summer, possibly in the sun, too. Give adequate water and add fertilizer every two weeks. Allow a rest period in the winter, but the foliage should not die off.
Propagation: By division. Occasionally, small plants develop along the edges of leaves that can be cut or broken off.

Light:	Much light, full sun as well.
Temp:	Grow moderately warm, keep at 54–60°F (12–15°C) in the winter.
Water:	Moderately moist in the summer, rather dry in the winter.
Hum:	Moderate, 50–60%.
Soil:	Standard potting soil mixed with ⅓ part fine loam, clay or rock wool powder. This plant does not do well when repotted, so try to leave the ball of soil as undisturbed as possible.

Haemanthus multiflorus

Amaryllidaceae

This plant does not resemble the last species very much. It grows from a bulb, which often can be ordered by mail.
Care: After receiving the bulb, one should pot in the spring and start off with a little water. Increase the moisture level when the plant begins to grow. Fertilize once every two weeks in the summer. Give less water at the end of the summer, until the foliage has completely died off. Keep the dormant bulb in its pot.
Propagation: From seed or by taking the bulbs and growing them separately.

Light:	Much light, no bright sun.
Temp:	Grow moderately warm, in the winter a minimum of 54°F (12°C).
Water:	Moderately moist in the summer, dry in the winter.
Hum:	Moderate, 50–60%.
Soil:	Standard potting soil.

Haemanthus multiflorus

Hamatocactus setispinus

Cactaceae

A species categorized by some experts as the genus *Ferocactus*, which requires a similar cultivation. With many species, the hook-shaped thorns are

striking; however, this is not true of the species pictured, which is perhaps the most popular. It blooms effortlessly, and at an early age.
Care: Keep well sunlit and make sure the ball of soil never dries out. Give cactus food monthly. In the winter, a dry and cool dormant period is needed.
Propagation: From seed.

Light:	Full sun.
Temp:	Grow moderately warm to warm, 40–50°F (5–10°C) in the winter.
Water:	Keep moderately moist in the summer, almost dry in the winter.
Hum:	Low.
Soil:	Cactus soil.

Harpephyllum caffrum

Anacardiaceae

A relatively unknown plant from South Africa that grows there as a tree with edible fruits. The foliage is feathered.

Harpephyllum caffrum

Care: Best to grow as a container plant, which could go outside in a sheltered spot during the summer. Provide a cool dormancy in the winter. Fertilize in the growing season once every two weeks. Indoors, avoid bright sunlight and keep at temperatures as low as possible in the winter. The foliage should remain.
Propagation: From fresh seeds. Grow in a greenhouse.

Light:	Much light, full sun as well.
Temp:	Grow cool, in the winter 40–50°F (5–10°C).
Water:	Keep moderately moist.
Hum:	Moderate, 50–60%.
Soil:	Standard potting soil mixed in large part with clay, loam or rock wool powder.

Hatiora bambusoides

Hatiora bambusoides

Cactaceae

A plant little reminiscent of a cactus, despite belonging to the cactus family. Small flowers can appear at the tops of the stems.
Care: Grow light, but do not allow much sun. In the summer, the plant can be grown outside fairly well, just like the Christmas cactus. Add cactus food once every two weeks. The dormant period falls during the winter, and requires low temperatures and little or no water.
Propagation: By growing parts that are taken off the plant and well dried.

Light:	Half shade.
Temp:	Grow cool to moderately warm.
Water:	Moderately moist in the summer, drier in the dormant period.
Hum:	Moderate, 50–60%.
Soil:	Cactus soil.

Hamatocactus setispinus

Haworthia species

Liliaceae

Most species are easily cared for succulents. The nicely marked foliage is the principal ornamental aspect of these plants. Small flowers on long stems may appear, but they are not very impressive. Some species grow naturally almost completely underground, and receive light from a small opening on the tips of the leaves.

Care: The most famous species, with small white pearls or horizontal stripes on the leaves (such as *Haworthia attenuata*, *H. fasciata*, *H. limifolia* and *H. reinwardtii*), prefer a sunny location behind glass in the summer. Water sparsely and do not water too much in between the leaves, rather water directly on the soil. Give cactus food once a month. The dormant period falls in the winter, at which time the plants can stay practically dry and at lower temperatures. The species with leaf openings are dormant in the summer and start to grow in October. These plants should have a warmer dormancy.

Propagation: From seed and by removing the side shoots. These should be dried for a while before planting.

Light: Full sun.
Temp: Grow warm, in the winter 40–50°F (5–10°C), for the window species a minimum of 61°F (16°C).

Haworthia limifolia

Water: Water sparsely in the summer, but keep the ball of soil moist. In the winter, the normal species do not need water at lower temperatures, and they can be allowed to shrivel somewhat.
Hum: Low.
Soil: Cactus soil in pots with good drainage.

Haworthia fasciata

Hebe species

Scrophulariaceae

These pretty bushes are related to species grown in outdoor gardens in England. In a more severe climate, though, they are not hardy, and are often available as houseplants. The plants come with both green and variegated foliage, while the flowers come in various colors.

Care: From the text above, one can infer that the *Hebe* does not like warmth. You will be most successful with a plant bought in bloom if you place it in a cool space, possibly even outside, if it does not freeze yet. After the bloom, keep it cool, but not dark (preferably in a greenhouse). In May, place outside on a sunny, sheltered spot in the garden. Fertilize every two weeks. The plant can bloom again in the fall.

Propagation: From top cuttings. Soil temperature 60–68°F (15–20°C).

Hebe speciosa

Light:	Full sun.
Temp:	Grow cool, in the winter a minimum of 54°F (12°C).
Water:	Keep moderately moist.
Hum:	Moderate, 50–60%.
Soil:	Standard potting soil.

Heliotropium aborescens

Helleborus niger

Ranunculaceae
Christmas rose

This is the real Christmas rose, not to be confused with the more popular pointsettia, which is listed under *Euphorbia*. The Christmas rose is in fact a garden plant that can be forced to bloom prematurely so that the flowers appear around Christmas. The plants are rather rare and expensive at present, but they do have much more charm than the mass-produced pointsettia.
Care: Large plants, grown in gardens, are dug up at the end of October and placed in large pots. The old foliage should stay on for a

Helleborus niger

while. Add enough water so that the ball of soil stays wet and the plant gets cleansed. Place in a greenhouse or cold container. Remove the old leaves in mid-November and bring the temperature to 40–45°F (4–7°C). The plants should then be covered completely with black plastic. After three weeks, the first flowers will appear. Bring blooming plants into a very cool space, and one can enjoy them for a long time. After the flowering period, place again in a frost-free greenhouse and then plant out in a garden at the end of April.
Propagation: By dividing from larger plants, and from seed, too.

Light:	Half shade.
Temp:	Grow cool, during the growth period a maximum of 60°F (15°C), before and after 40–45°F (4–7°C).
Water:	Keep moderately moist.
Hum:	High, above 60%.
Soil:	Standard potting soil mixed with extra peat moss.

Hemigraphis species

Acanthaceae

Small, creeping plants with shiny leaves that are reddish on the bottom. Besides the species *alternata* and *repanda*, there are also several hybrids. Suitable for plant windows, vitrines and small greenhouses.
Care: Provide a high relative humidity and keep the plants from the sunlight. Feed once every two weeks in the summer. No dormant period is necessary in the winter, only keep the plant warm and humid.
Propagation: Root top cuttings under glass at a soil temperature of 68–77°F (20–25°C).

Light:	Much light, no full sun.
Temp:	Grow warm, a minimum of 64°F (18°C).
Water:	Keep moderately moist with soft water.
Hum:	High, above 60%.
Soil:	Standard potting soil, fine loam and peat moss, ⅓ part of each. Use shallow, wide bowls with good drainage.

Hemigraphis alternata

Hemiographis 'Exotica'

Hemionitis palmata

Hemionitidaceae
Strawberry fern

A rather unknown small fern, whose leaves resemble the shape of a strawberry. Young plants can develop on the leaves.
Care: One can keep this plant in a warm room for a while, but in the winter, the air becomes too dry. It is more suitable for a plant window, vitrine or greenhouse. In the growth period, feed once every two weeks at half concentrations. Continue to grow warm in the winter, but if the plant stops growing, discontinue feeding. Never allow sunlight.
Propagation: By sowing the spores or by taking the young plants that are growing on the leaves.

Light:	Shade.
Temp:	Grow warm, not below 64°F (18°C).
Water:	Keep moist regularly, preferably with soft water and using pots with drainage systems.
Hum:	Moderate to high.
Soil:	Standard potting soil mixed with extra peat moss.

Hemionitis palmata

Heterocentron elegans

Hibiscus rosa-sinensis

Heterocentron elegans

Melastomataceae

Small, lavishly flowering plants that can be kept indoors or in a greenhouse during the summer.

Care: Never place in the full sun, but allow a lot of light. Water moderately in the summer and add food once every two weeks. Keep the plant alive in the winter and grow new plants from cuttings.

Propagation: Use new shoots for cuttings in the spring (soil temperature 77°F [25°C]). Cut off the tops of young plants a few times for better branching.

Hibbertia scandens

Light:	Much light, no sun.
Temp:	Grow moderately warm, in the winter a minimum of 54°F (12°C).
Water:	Keep moderately moist, if possible using soft water or rainwater.
Hum:	Moderate, 50–60%.
Soil:	Standard potting soil with extra loam or clay.

Hibbertia scandens

Dilleniaceae

A relatively unknown climbing plant for the greenhouse that is easy to grow.

Care: Can be grown in a greenhouse, with conditions similar to those for winter dormant cacti. It cannot tolerate any frost. Give much light and fresh air in the summer. By pruning the plant considerably in the spring, the shape remains compact. Administer some food once every two weeks during the growth period.

Propagation: From seed or top cuttings, which root under glass at 77°F (25°C) soil temperature.

Light:	Much light, full sun as well.
Temp:	Grow moderately warm, in the winter a minimum of 40°F (5°C).
Water:	Keep moderately moist.
Hum:	Moderate, 50–60%.
Soil:	Standard potting soil.

Hibiscus rosa-sinensis

Malvaceae

Chinese rose

The Chinese rose is a well-known houseplant, which nowadays can appear in different tints, as well as with full single flowers. Nevertheless, I miss the sturdy form with small flowers that one can find in gardens along the Medi-

terranean. This *Hibiscus* can become a yard high after a few years and bear hundreds of flowers. It is very difficult to grow such a magnificent specimen with large flowers from a hybrid. The variegated form is called 'Cooperi.'

Care: The Chinese rose is often grown in a warm room the whole year round, nevertheless, the plant naturally needs a cool dormant period. By continuing to grow the plant warm, flowers will appear, but the chance of infestation by lice is greater and after a certain point, the plant will become exhausted. Fertilize weekly during the growth period. When the buds have appeared, do not turn or move the plant, or the buds will fall off. Prune back in the spring to retain a compact shape. Hardier species can go outside as early as the end of May on a very sheltered, sunny terrace.

Propagation: Preferably from top cuttings, soil temperature 77–86°F (25–30°C). Often it is necessary to use cutting powder.

Light:	Much light, full sun for hardy genera.
Temp:	Grow moderately warm, in the winter around 54°F (12°C).
Water:	Keep moderately moist.
Hum:	Moderate, 50–60%.
Soil:	Standard potting soil.

Hibiscus rosa-sinensis 'Cooperi'

Hippeastrum-hybr.

Hippeastrum hybrids

Amaryllidaceae

Amaryllis

A bulbous growth that can be made to bloom indoors. The plant is still stubbornly called amaryllis, which creates some confusion because a plant quite like it is known by the Latin name *Amaryllis belladonna*. Cultivated varieties are solely hybrids, in various beautiful tints, with flowers either fully colored or with colored edges.

Care: When you buy the bulbs in the fall, make sure the roots are not damaged. Plant them carefully in a rather big plastic container. There are normal bulbs for sale, which will produce only one flower stem, and there are gigantic bulbs as well, from which more than one stem appears. The size of the pot for these bulbs should be bigger, too. Give a little water and place the pot in a spot where the soil will remain warm (above a radiator). Make sure that the ball of soil does not dry out, but at the same time do not keep it too wet. After some time, the flower stem appears, followed by the foliage. Now add more water. After the flow-

Hippeastrum-hybr. 'Laforest Morton'

ering period, cut off the flower stem and provide the plant with moderate amounts of water, with food added every two weeks. The leaves should grow considerably to store food reserves. The plant can go outside at the end of May. Withhold water from the beginning of September, so that the leaves dry up. Store the bulb in the pot at a temperature of 61°F (16°C). Repot in January and bring back to growth. Via temperature treatment, it is possible to produce an extra, early bloom, known in the trade as a prepared bulb.

Propagation: By taking the bulbs, which are then able to bloom after three years. It is also possible from seed.

Light: Much light, no full sun during the blooming; in the summer outside sun is allowed.
Temp: Cool to moderately warm.
Water: Keep moderately moist.
Hum: Moderate, 50–60%.
Soil: Standard potting soil.

Hippeastrum-hybr.

Hoffmannia ghiesbreghtii

Rubiaceae

Beautiful foliage plants, of which one variety exists with light-spotted leaves, called 'Vari-

Hoffmannia ghiesbreghtii

egata.' Suitable for spaces with high humidity, such as greenhouses, plant windows, etc.
Care: Grow continuously warm, humid and shaded. In the growing period, give moderate amounts of soft water and fertilize once every two weeks. Keep warm in the winter as well, but slightly drier.
Propagation: Root top cuttings under glass at 86°F (30°C) soil temperature.

Light: Much light, no sun.
Temp: Grow warm, not below 64°F (18°C).
Water: Keep moderately moist with soft water.
Hum: High, far above 60%.
Soil: Coniferous soil.

Homalocladium platycladum

Homalocladium platycladum

Polygonaceae

Interesting plant with wide, belt-shaped stalks, which take over the function of leaves to a large extent. One calls these stalks platyclades, because small leaves grow from them. Those plants known as phylloclades (see *Phyllanthus*) have stems that have completely taken over the function of leaves, and no leaves appear on them.
Care: Allow much light and even sun in the summer. The plant can be outside from the end of May. It is normal for the small leaves to fall off quite soon after appearing. Give moderate amounts of water and add food once every two weeks. Keep as cool as possible in the winter, to ensure that the growth stops.
Propagation: From seed or via top cuttings or middle cuttings, which root on the nodes at 68°F (20°C) soil temperature.

Light: Much light, full sun as well.
Temp: Grow cool to moderately warm, keep at 46–61°F (8–16°C) in the winter.
Water: Keep moderately moist.
Hum: Moderate, 50–60%.
Soil: Standard potting soil, possibly mixed with extra clay or loam.

Hoodia gordonii

Asclepiadaceae

These plants look a lot like cacti, but are not. They belong to the same family as *Stapelia*. Saucer-shaped, yellow-brown flowers should appear.
Care: Grow very warm and only give water when the sun shines. The plants rot quickly if they are kept too wet. Add some cactus food once a month. Give even less water in the winter, keep rather warm and place right behind the window glass.
Propagation: From fresh seed. Young plants can be grafted on *Ceropegia*, which makes them grow better.

Light:	Full sun.

Hoodia gordonii

Temp:	Grow warm, a minimum of 64°F (18°C).
Water:	Keep rather dry.
Hum:	Low.
Soil:	Cactus soil.

Howeia forsteriana
Palmae

Kentia palm

Famous hardy plant, originally from islands east of Australia. The other species of this genus is named *H. belmoreana*, and looks quite like the species in the picture, though it is not as strong.

Howeia forsteriana

Care: Relatively young plants are best suited for indoor cultivation, with a few specimens together in one pot. They cannot tolerate full sun as young plants. Give food once every two weeks during the growth period. Keep cooler in the winter, because the normal indoor air is too dry for this palm, in general.
Propagation: From fresh (imported) seed. Germination temperature 77–86°F (25–30°C).

Light:	Much light, no full sun.
Temp:	Grow moderately warm, in the winter 57–64°F (14–18°C).
Water:	Keep moderately moist, immerse in water once in a while.
Hum:	Moderate, 50–60%.
Soil:	Standard potting soil mixed with fine clay or loam. Use narrow, deep pots or containers.

Hoya bella

Asclepiadaceae

Small wax plant

A climbing plant from India with small, meaty leaves and fragrant flowers in hanging umbels (shaped like an umbrella). The picture is taken from below to expose the white flowers with the red-purple crowns.
Care: This species has to be grown warm at a high relative humidity, so a greenhouse is the best location. If the plant can be grafted on the trunk of *Hoya carnosa*, the bloom will be even richer than if propagated from cuttings. Tie up the vines well in the summer and feed monthly. Do not keep the plants too wet; it is a half succulent. Keep cooler and drier in the winter.
Propagation: Via grafting, top cuttings or middle cuttings. Soil temperature 68–77°F (20–25°C).

Hoya bella

Light:	Much light, no full sun.
Temp:	Grow warm, in the winter not below 64°F (18°C).
Water:	Keep moderately moist, somewhat drier in the winter.
Hum:	High, more than 60%.
Soil:	Coniferous soil or a mixture for bromeliads.

Hoya carnosa

Asclepiadaceae

Large wax plant

Better known and more easily grown than the small wax plant is the bigger species, *Hoya carnosa*. The thick leaves are much larger, and so are the fragrant flower umbels. This species, too, is a climber that grows long vines. There

Hoya carnosa

Hoya carnosa 'Compacta'

is a variegated form called 'Variegata,' and a strangely turned form 'Compacta.'
Care: The large wax plant can be grown cooler than the small species, especially in the winter, because the dormancy is more intense. If you allow the plant to continue growing, then this will almost certainly result in some sort of plant skin affliction. Feed once every two weeks in the growth period. When the buds are formed, do not turn the plant relative to the light, because there is a great chance that the buds will fall off prematurely. Planted out in a moderate greenhouse, the plant can grow high and reach a respectable old age.
Propagation: Top cuttings or middle cuttings root at 68–77°F (20–25°C).

Light:	Much light, no full sun.
Temp:	Grow moderately warm, keep between 50–57°F (10–14°C) in the winter.
Water:	Keep moderately moist, almost completely dry in the winter.
Hum:	Moderate to high.

Hoya linearis

Soil:	Standard potting soil mixed with clay or loam.

Hoya lacunosa
Asclepiadaceae

A relatively "new" species that is often sold under the name *Hoya micrantha*. It has small, fragrant flowers and a very small leaf.
Care: Grow as a hanging plant in a half shaded window. Keep warm in the winter, but somewhat drier; spray the foliage instead of the soil. Feed once every two weeks in the growth period. Always use rainwater or soft water.
Propagation: Root middle cuttings under glass at a soil temperature of 68–77°F (20–25°C).

Light:	Half shade, no full sun.
Temp:	Grow warm, a minimum of 64°F (18°C).
Water:	Keep moderately moist in the growing season, rather dry in the winter.
Hum:	Moderate, 50–60%.
Soil:	Coniferous soil in pots with good drainage.

Hoya linearis
Asclepiadaceae

A relatively unknown, hanging species, originally from the Himalayas.
Care: Preferably grown in a greenhouse, the plant can be placed indoors during the growing period. Do not allow bright sun. Do not water too much, because the plant evaporates little moisture. Always use soft water or rainwater. Feed once a month, and only while the plant grows. Keep it slightly cooler in the winter.
Propagation: Dry top cuttings or middle cuttings for a day, then plant at a soil temperature of 68–77°F (20–25°C).

Hoya lacunosa

Light:	Much light, no full sun.
Temp:	Grow warm, not below 64°F (18°C).
Water:	Keep moderately moist.
Hum:	Moderate to high.
Soil:	Coniferous soil.

Hoya multiflora
Asclepiadaceae

A lesser known wax flower from Malaysia with flowers that look like falling stars or comets. They have been called 'Shooting Stars.' The plant can produce flowers continuously throughout the summer and is therefore quite recommendable.
Care: As with the *Hoya bella*, this species has to be grown warm, with only a moderate dormant period in the winter. Give food once a month during the growth season.
Propagation: From top cuttings or middle cuttings, soil temperature 68–77°F (20–25°C).

Light:	Much light, no full sun.
Temp:	Grow warm, in the winter not below 64°F (18°C).
Water:	Keep moderately moist, drier in the winter.
Hum:	High, above 60%.
Soil:	Mix standard potting soil with coniferous soil or other permeable substrates.

Hoya multiflora

Huernia keniensis

Huernia keniensis

Asclepiadaceae

Succulents that grow with short, meaty, ribbed trunks form seeds after a while. The flowers smell awful, and attract bluebottle flies for pollination.
Care: Grow light and rather cool, but in the summer screen against bright sunlight. Water sparsely and give cactus food monthly. Keep cool in the winter and give enough water to prevent the foliage from shriveling.
Propagation: Break off small trunks, allow them to dry and plant in sandy soil. From seed as well. Soil temperature 68–77°F (20–25°C).

Light:	Much light, no bright sunlight.
Temp:	Grow moderately warm, in the winter 46–54°F (8–12°C).
Water:	Keep moderately dry, almost completely dry in the winter.
Hum:	Moderate, 50–60%.
Soil:	One-third part standard potting soil, ⅓ part clay and ⅓ part perlite. Use shallow, wide pots or bowls that drain well.

Huntleya meleagris

Orchidaceae

A family of rather difficultly grown orchids, of which only this species seems to appear in collections. The plants have no pseudotubers and the leaves are set in the shape of a fan. The fragrant flowers last for about a month.
Care: Grow quite cool and offer plenty of fresh air and humidity. The pots should drain well, because even the slightest excess of water can damage the roots. The base of the plant should be just above the planting medium, otherwise rotting will soon occur. A dormant period is not necessary. Give orchid food once in a while when the plant grows.
Propagation: From seed.

Light:	Half shade, never full sun.

Huntleya meleagris

Temp:	Grow rather cool, in the winter not below 54°F (12°C).
Water:	Keep moist regularly with soft water.
Hum:	High, above 60%.
Soil:	Rock wool powder or sphagnum.

Hyacinthus orientalis

Liliaceae

Hyacinth

Well-known bulbous plant, often forced to bloom indoors. There are various colors available. There are also prepared bulbs, which

Hyacinthus 'Blue Jacket'

bloom extra early, and 'Multiflora' hyacinths, which produce several flower stems per bulb.
Care: From the beginning of October, you can plant sturdy, healthy bulbs in soil or pebbles, or place in special hyacinth glasses that are filled with water. With pebble or water cultivation, the water level should be .04–.08 in (1–2 mm) under the bulb to prevent rotting. For rooting, a cool, dark period is necessary, with the temperature about 48°F (9°C). The pot can be ensilaged or covered with black plastic to keep out the light. With cultivating in pebbles or in hyacinth glasses, a period of absolute darkness is needed. Check once in a while to see if the bulbs are too dry or if they have formed a new shoot. Only when you can

Hyacinthus orientalis 'Blue Jacket'

clearly feel that the flower bud has left the bulb, can the bulb be placed in the light. Do not keep pots or bowls too warm—60°F (15°C) is right—or in the full sun, but provide light. Spray the leaves daily and watch the water level and the moisture level of the soil. Food is not needed. It is better to throw the bulbs away after they bloom, because forcing them into bloom a second time usually will result in a big disappointment.

Propagation: Hyacinths are multiplied via bulbs.

Light:	Much light or half shade.
Temp:	Grow cool.
Water:	Keep moderately moist.
Hum:	Moderate to high.
Soil:	Standard potting soil mixed with sharp sand, in a 1-to-1 ratio.

Hydrangea macrophylla

Saxifragaceae

Hydrangea

Although the hydrangea is mainly a garden plant (there exist various species, each different in shape), the subspecies *macrophylla* and from that the form *otaksa* are sold as houseplants. These forms are less hardy, although they can last a long time in a garden. For room cultivation, the plants' sensitivity to

Hydrangea macr. 'Blue Sky' (Teller-type)

Hydrangea macrophylla ssp. *macr.* f. *otaska*

Hydrangea macrophylla 'Sunset' (Teller-type)

frost is not of any consequence. Lately, the hydrangeas of the so-called 'lacecap'—or 'Teller'—type are sold more and more as houseplants. In the middle, they have fertile fruits which are surrounded by a wreath of flowers. Often, the flowers are pink. They can become blue by adding a chemical substance to the soil.

Care: A blooming hydrangea should be kept cool and certainly not in the full sun. Immerse in water once in a while to make the ball of soil thoroughly wet. Keep cool after the flowering period until the middle of May and then plant in a garden. It is advisable to prune the plant back at this moment. Give some food until the end of August. At the end of September, or mid-October, the plant should go inside again, but in a cool space, such as a garage or cold greenhouse. When the flower buds appear, the plant can be kept warmer, normally around February.

Propagation: Root top cuttings in the summer without any warmer soil temperatures.

Light:	Half shade, no sun.
Temp:	Grow cool, in the winter 43–50°F (6–10°C).
Water:	Keep moderately moist, use soft water.
Hum:	High, at least 60%.
Soil:	Extra acidic soil, for instance coniferous soil, garden peat, peat moss or mixtures of these ingredients.

Hymenocallis species

Amaryllidaceae

Ismene

These are less widely known, but beautifully exotic bulbous plants that are easy to force into bloom indoors. Bulbs of various species can be ordered by mail.

Care: Pot bulbs in February. Keep the pots warm and only moderately moist. Increase the amount of water when the plant grows. Give food once every two weeks in the summer. The foliage of some species dies in the winter, when the bulb should remain in the pot and not be watered much. Repot in the spring and bring back to growth.

Propagation: By taking the bulbs.

Light:	Much light, no full sun.
Temp:	Grow moderately warm, in the winter 60–68°F (15–20°C).
Water:	Keep moderately moist, on the dry side in the winter; completely dry when the foliage is dead.
Hum:	Moderate, 50–60%.
Soil:	Standard potting soil, if possible mixed with fine clay or loam.

Hyophorbe verschaffeltii

See *Mascarena verschaffeltii.*

Hymenocallis narcissiflora

Hymenocallis speciosa

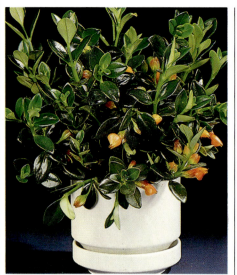

Hypocyrta glabra

Hypocyrta glabra

Gesneriaceae

A small, relatively strong houseplant with thick shiny leaves and bulky orange flowers. One can find a related species described under the genus *Nemantanthus*.

Care: The leathery leaves do not allow much moisture to evaporate, so it can endure dry indoor air pretty well. Much light is needed, screening only against bright light. Feed once every two weeks during the growth period. One can provide a dormant period in the winter and bring the plant outside at the end of May.

Propagation: From top cuttings and by division. Soil temperature 68°F (20°C).

Light:	Much light, no bright sun.
Temp:	Grow moderately warm, in the winter 50°F (10°C) is enough.
Water:	Keep moderately moist.
Hum:	Low to moderate.
Soil:	Standard potting soil.

Hypoestes phyllostachya

Acanthaceae

A small greenhouse plant with beautifully marked leaves. It is difficult to grow indoors in the winter.

Care: Provide high humidity and shade. Only feed during the growth period in the summer. Keep drier and cooler in the winter; prune back, repot and bring back to growth in spring.

Propagation: Root top cuttings at a soil temperature of 77–86°F (25–30°C). Propagation from seed is possible as well.

Light:	Much light, no full sun.
Temp:	Grow warm, in the winter not below 64°F (18°C).
Water:	Keep moderately moist.
Hum:	High, above 60%.
Soil:	Standard potting soil.

Illicium anisatum

Illiciaceae

Evergreen bush from Japan and Korea. It tends to be hardy in temperate areas, but not in northerly regions. The fruits are poisonous, unlike those of its relative *Illicium verum*, whose fruits are used as a medicinal herb and to flavor liqueurs.

Care: Can be grown as a container plant, and can be brought outside at the end of May, kept very protected and screened against the brightest sun. Water moderately and feed once every two weeks. Bring inside in the autumn for a cool dormant period.

Propagation: From seed and via top cuttings, which root at 68–77°F (20–25°C) under glass.

Light:	Much light, no bright sun.

Illicium anisatum

Hypoestes phyllostachya

Temp:	Grow cool, in winter no less than 40°F (5°C).
Water:	Moderately moist, in the winter enough to keep the leaves from shriveling.
Hum:	Moderate to high.
Soil:	Standard potting soil mixed with peat moss or coniferous soil.

Impatiens hawkeri

Balsaminaceae

A member of the balsam family with prettily marked leaves and many red-purple flowers. It has become increasingly popular.

Care: Keep well lit, screening only against the brightest sun. Provide large pots and plenty of water, and an additional amount of food once

Impatiens hawkeri 'Exotica'

a week, because these plants grow fast. Ensure dormancy at lower temperatures. Older plants lose their beauty quickly, but it's easy to grow new plants from cuttings.
Propagation: Root top cuttings without extra soil warmth.

Light:	Much light, no full sun.
Temp:	Grow cool, in the winter about 54°F (12°C).
Water:	Keep thoroughly moist, somewhat drier in the winter.
Hum:	Moderate, 50–60%.
Soil:	Standard potting soil.

Impatiens repens

Balsaminaceae

A creeping member of the impatiens family with thick red stalks and small leaves. Here and there a small yellow flower may appear.
Care: Use as ground cover in large plant cases, greenhouses and vitrines. This plant can grow outside in the summer as well, but only if protected against the brightest sun. Give fertilizer once every two weeks during the summer. In the winter keep the plant cooler and drier.
Propagation: Roots easily from top cuttings and middle cuttings. Take cuttings at least once a year, because older plants often become less pretty.

Light:	Half shade or much light, no bright sun.
Temp:	Grow cool, a minimum of 54°F (12°C).

Impatiens repens

Water:	Keep moderately moist.
Hum:	Moderate, 50–60%.
Soil:	Standard potting soil.

Impatiens walleriana

Balsaminaceae

Busy Lizzie

This small plant is so nicknamed because it grows and blooms inexhaustibly, as long as one provides water and food. Because it be-

Impatiens walleriana

comes less beautiful as it ages, I advise taking cuttings all the time.
Care: Keep well lit, but do not give too much sun. Do not grow them in small pots, or they dry out too fast. Keep dormant with lower temperatures, take cuttings and grow again in the spring.
Propagation: Top cuttings root very easily with almost no additional soil warmth.

Light:	Much light, no full sun.
Temp:	Grow cool, in the winter at 54°F (12°C).
Water:	Keep continuously moist, somewhat drier in the winter.
Hum:	Moderate, 50–60%.
Soil:	Standard potting soil.

Incarvillea mairei var. *grandiflora*

Incarvillea mairei var. grandiflora

Bignoniaceae

Garden gloxinia

As its popular name indicates, this is a garden plant, though it is sold more and more as a potted plant. This plant can flourish very well indoors, especially in the summer.
Care: The *Incarvillea* is not hardy in the garden. It likes a sunny location and cool dormancy. Water moderately in the summer and fertilize once every two weeks.
Propagation: From seed.

Light:	Much light, full sun, too.
Temp:	Grow cool, in the winter 32°F (0°C).
Water:	Keep moderately moist.
Hum:	Moderate, 50–60%.
Soil:	Standard potting soil.

Ipomoea batatas

Ipomoea batatas

Convolvulaceae

Yam root

Plant from tropical regions; the tuberous roots can be eaten. It is a nice hanging plant for a greenhouse or warm room.
Care: The tubers root in a jar with water. The long stalks create more roots in time. Grow warm and light and fertilize once every two weeks. It is advisable to allow the foliage to die in the winter in order to keep the tubers dry, just as with potatoes. In spring the plant will form roots again.
Propagation: By removing the rooted shoots or by dividing the tubers.

Light: Much light, full sun as well.
Temp: Grow warm, with dry dormancy a minimum of 54°F (12°C).
Water: Keep moderately moist, dry in the dormant period.
Hum: High, above 60%.
Soil: Standard potting soil.

Ipomoea tricolor

Convolvulaceae

Day flower

Annual climbing plant from tropical America. It is suited to a warm spot in a garden or on a balcony, but is also an excellent houseplant.

Ipomoea tricolor

Care: Keep warm and sunny and always provide enough water and food (once a week). Guide the long shoots along a fence or other form of support. The flower only blooms for one day but new flowers appear all the time if the plant is treated well.
Propagation: Sow immediately in pots, in mid-February. Plant 5–10 seeds in a pot 4¾ in (12 cm) wide. Soil temperature 68°F (20°C). Night temperature 64°F (18°C). Day temperature, up to 81°F (27°C).

Light: Much light, full sun, too.
Temp: Moderately warm to warm.
Water: Moderately moist.
Hum: Moderate, 50–60%.
Soil: Standard potting soil.

Iresine herbstii

Amaranthaceae

Often has red-colored foliage; form 'Aureoreticulata' has variegated leaves.
Care: Give a lot of light, full sun as well. A south-facing window is the best spot. The plants can go outside in the summer, too. Water moderately and add food once every two weeks. The temperature in the winter may be lowered somewhat; the plant will stay alive. Prune back considerably in the spring, repot and bring back to growth.
Propagation: Top cuttings root easily—even without soil warmth—in a bottle with water. Young plants should be topped a few times. Take cuttings often, because older plants lose their beauty.

Light: Full sun.

Iresine herbstii

Temp: Grow cool to moderately warm, a minimum of 54°F (12°C).
Water: Keep moderately moist.
Hum: Moderate, 50–60%.
Soil: Standard potting soil.

Iresine herbstii 'Aureoreticulata'

Isoplexis canariensis

and sheltered. Water moderately and feed once every two weeks. Bring inside in the fall, possibly after putting it in a pot, and provide a cool dormancy.

Propagation: Root top cuttings under glass at 68–77°F (20–25°C) soil temperature. Also possible from seed, but seeds often produce flowers with less color. Therefore, grow cuttings from the most beautiful plants and repeat this regularly, because old plants bloom less lavishly as time goes on.

Light: Full sun.
Temp: Grow cool to moderately warm, in the winter 46–50°F (8–10°C).
Water: Keep moderately moist, considerably drier in the dormant period.
Hum: Moderate, 50–60%.
Soil: Standard potting soil.

Ixora hybrids

Rubiaceae

When in bloom, these plants are magnificent, with large, round flower bunches. They are all hybrids and are becoming increasingly popluar as potted plants.

Care: Although originally a tropical climbing plant, this is hardly apparent from the plant in the picture. (The grower kept them low with growth-stunting substances.) Growth occurs under warm and humid conditions. Do not place it in the sun and spray the foliage frequently, preferably using rainwater. Fertilize once every two weeks. Prune in the fall and provide a dormant period in a warm greenhouse.

Propagation: Root top cuttings in the spring under glass at a soil temperature of 77–86°F (25–30°C).

Light: Half shade or much light, no full sun.
Temp: Grow warm, a minimum of 64°F (18°C).
Water: Keep moderately moist with soft water, somewhat drier in the winter.
Hum: High, above 60%.
Soil: Coniferous soil.

Ixora-hybr.

Iris reticulata 'Harmony'

Care: Plant the bulbs in October about 2¾ in (7 cm) deep in pots with good drainage or bowls. Ensilage these containers, preferably at a frost-free depth, or store them cool (48°F [9°C] is ideal) in the dark. By the time the bulbs have roots and the flower buds are clearly visible above the soil, the pots can be placed in a light spot. Keep as cool as possible to prolong the blooming. Fertilizer is not needed. Throw the plant away after the flowering period.

Propagation: Via bulbs.

Light: Much light, no full sun.
Temp: Grow cool, preferably 54–60°F (12–15°C).
Water: Keep moderately moist.
Hum: High, above 60%.
Soil: Standard potting soil mixed with extra lime.

Iris reticulata

Iridaceae

Some iris species can be successfully forced to bloom prematurely. This method is known as "home-forced" blooming. The most popular species used for this process is the *Iris reticulata*, pictured, but it also works very well with, for instance, *Iris aucheri* and *Iris bucharica*.

Isoplexis canariensis

Scrophulariaceae

A small bush from the Canary Islands, related to the foxglove. It's not hardy, so keep it frost-free during its dormant period.

Care: Grow as a container plant in the summer, or bedded out in the garden. Keep sunny

JACARANDA

Jacaranda mimosifolia

Bignoniaceae

Rosewood tree

A tree with elegant divided leaves that can grow to 130 ft (40 m). Young plants, which look very much like ferns, can be kept as houseplants.

Care: The plant needs warmth and humidity. The young plants especially should not be exposed to cold. By the time they are four years old, they can be treated as container plants, which means they can be placed outside in the summer in a sheltered location. It is possible that violet-blue flowers will appear. Feed once every two weeks in the summer.

Propagation: Seeds germinate at about 77°F (25°C).

Light:	Young plants need much light, but no full sun. Older specimens will endure sun.
Temp:	Young plants should not be grown under 64°F (18°C). Older specimens rest dormant at a minimum 54°F (12°C).
Water:	Always keep moderately moist, preferably with rainwater.
Hum:	High, at least with young plants.
Soil:	An acidic soil mixture, such as coniferous soil.

Jacaranda mimosifolia

Jacobinia carnea

Acanthaceae

A somewhat uncommon houseplant, it has short branches with large leaves, and above those a gigantic flower. It is not easy to grow.

Care: Preferably grown in a moderate greenhouse, because of the plant's high humid air requirement. Also, spray frequently. Allow much light, even sun is agreeable; with this, plants remain nicely compact and bloom more lavishly. Add food to the water weekly in the

Jacobinia carnea

summer. Provide a dormant period in the winter. Prune in the spring and repot.

Propagation: Root top cuttings of young shoots in February at 68–77°F (20–25°C) soil temperature.

Light:	Much light, full sun, too.
Temp:	Grow warm, winter dormancy at 54–60°F (12–15°C).
Water:	Keep moderately moist.
Hum:	High, above 60%.
Soil:	Standard potting soil.

Jacobinia pauciflora

Acanthaceae

Quite different in appearance from the last species, this plant is easier to cultivate.

Care: Keep outside from the end of May, sheltered and sunny. Behind a window is a good spot, too, provided it does not get too warm. Water moderately and feed weekly. Bring inside to a cool spot in the fall. The blooms come in winter. Prune back after that, repot and slowly bring back to growth.

Propagation: Take cuttings of nonblooming shoots in early spring. Soil temperature: 68–77°F (20–25°C). Cut off the tops of young plants a few times.

Light:	Full sun.
Temp:	Grow cool, in the winter 40–54°F (5–12°C).
Water:	Keep moderately moist.
Hum:	Moderate, 50–60%.
Soil:	Standard potting soil mixed with some clay or loam.

Jacobinia pauciflora

Jasminum officinale

Jasmine

There are several beautiful jasmine species that are occasionally sold as houseplants. They are of the family of bare-blooming jasmine, a climbing bush, that can often surprise one with small yellow flowers as early as December. It is not related to the Philadelphus, a white-blooming garden bush that is often called jasmine as well. The plant described here is not hardy. The other species, such as *Jasminum sambac* from Java, are also not hardy.

Care: Preferably grown planted out in a cold greenhouse, it can otherwise go in rather large containers, which can be placed outside from the end of May. Give the vines sufficient support. Feed weekly in the summer. Provide a very cool dormancy and keep the temperature low in the spring, too, by ventilation, because otherwise the plants will come out too early.

Propagation: In the summer, top cuttings or middle cuttings can be used. Soil temperature 68°F (20°C). Remove the tops of young plants a few times.

Light: Full sun.
Temp: Grow cool, in the winter 36–40°F (2–5°C).
Water: Keep moist, drier in the winter.
Hum: Moderate, 50–60%.
Soil: Standard potting soil mixed with fine clay or loam.

Jasminum officinale 'Grandiflorum'

Jatropha pandurifolia

Euphorbiaceae

A lesser known brother of the bottle plant, and less clearly a succulent. It is easy to grow.
Care: Keep warm and sunny in the summer. Do not give too much water. Adding some food once a month is adequate. Keep cooler in the winter, but do not provide a strict dormant period, for the foliage should remain on the plant.
Propagation: From seed and via top cuttings or middle cuttings. Soil temperature 68–77°F (20–25°C).

Jatropha pandurifolia

Light: Much light, full sun, too.
Temp: Grow moderately warm to warm, in the winter a minimum of 61°F (16°C).
Water: Keep moderately moist.
Hum: Moderate, 50–60%.
Soil: Standard potting soil.

Jatropha podagrica

Euphorbiacea

Bottle plant

A peculiar succulent that can store quite a lot of moisture in its thick trunk. It thrives when grown indoors, if one observes the following tips.
Care: Succulents store water for use in possible times of drought. Clearly, these periods do not occur when a succulent is grown as a houseplant; nevertheless, it is advisable to respect the natural rhythm of the plant. If and when the foliage falls, withhold water immediately and leave the plant alone until new leaves appear. The temperature does not have to be lower in this period, which will mainly occur in the winter. In the summer as well, be careful watering and fertilize once a month at the most.
Propagation: From fresh seed, which sometimes can form on the plant. Germination temperature 68–77°F (20–25°C).

Light: Full sun.
Temp: Grow warm, in the winter a minimum of 61°F (16°C).
Water: Keep rather dry, and just a drop when the foliage is gone.
Hum: Low.
Soil: Standard potting soil, preferably mixed with some clay or loam.

Jatropha podagrica

JATROPHA

KALANCHOË

Kalanchoë beharensis

Justicia carnea

See *Jacobinia carnea*.

Justicia panciflora

See *Jacobinia panciflora*.

Kalanchoë beharensis

Crassulaceae

A hairy, somewhat woody plant, which in its native Madagascar can grow to 10 ft (3 m) high. In the picture is the young, extremely hairy foliage. The stalks are covered with hairs as well.
Care: Grow very light and make sure the atmosphere does not become too dry. But avoid spraying the leaves, for this will cause ugly spots. This vigorously growing plant has to be repotted often and fed once a week during the growth period. The temperature can be lower in the winter. Prune back in the spring if necessary.
Propagation: From seed or via top cuttings. Soil temperature 79°F (25°C).

Light:	Full sun.
Temp:	Grow warm, in the winter a minimum of 54°F (12°C).
Water:	Keep moderately moist, drier in the winter.
Hum:	High, above 60%.
Soil:	Standard potting soil mixed with ⅓ part fine clay or loam.

Kalanchoë blossfeldiana

Crassulaceae

Under this name is classified the popular genus with large, zig-zag leaves and small flowers in rather short stemmed bunches. They can come in all kinds of bright tints.
Care: Give the plant much light, screening only against the brightest sunlight. Water moderately and feed monthly. In the winter, keep cooler and drier. Buds only appear the following year, when the days become shorter than 12 hours long (about November). If you want an early bloom you should give healthy plants a darkness treatment. The temperature in this case has to be 64–70°F (18–21°C).
Propagation: Top cuttings or middle cuttings, soil temperature 68–77°F (20–25°C).

Light:	Much light, screen against bright sunlight.

Kalanchoë blossfeldiana

Temp:	Grow moderately warm, in the winter 61–64°F (16–18°C).
Water:	Keep rather dry.
Hum:	Low to moderate.
Soil:	Standard potting soil.

Kalanchoë daigremontiana

Crassulaceae

This is one of the species previously known as *Bryophyllum*, now categorized with *Kalanchoë*. Along the leaf edges, small buds appear, which form roots and subsequently fall off.
Care: Can be kept in a warm room all year. The plant can become somewhat lanky over time, so it would be sensible to grow young plants from time to time, which is no problem, since it practically grows itself. Fertilizer is not needed.
Propagation: Put the new buds in pots.

Light:	Full sun.
Temp:	Grow moderately warm to warm, in the winter the temperature can be lowered to 40°F (5°C).
Water:	Keep rather dry, withhold water in the winter at low temperatures.
Hum:	Low.
Soil:	Standard potting soil.

Kalanchoë daigremontiana

Kalanchoë hybrids

Crassulaceae

From cross-hybridizations of various species, for instance *Kalanchoë manginii*, hybrids are created that distinguish themselves with large, tubular hanging flowers. 'Tessa' and 'Wendy'

Kalanchoë-hybr. 'Wendy'

Kalanchoë scapigera

are two relatively well-known cultivars. They are on the market mainly in the early spring.
Care: The care is not very different from that of *Kalanchoë blossfeldiana*. Grow these blooming plants moderately warm and quite sunny. Feed monthly during the growing season. Flower buds are formed only after a period of short days (less than 12 hours of light a day) of seven weeks' duration. During the short days, the temperature should stay under 63°F (17°C). If one does not observe these conditions, there will be no flowers!
Propagation: From top cuttings or middle cuttings. Soil temperature 64°F (18°C). Place three to five cuttings in a pot.

Light: Much light, screen against only bright light.
Temp: Grow moderately warm, in the winter a minimum of 54°F (12°C).
Water: Keep moderately moist.
Hum: Low to moderate.
Soil: Standard potting soil.

Kalanchoë orgyalis

Kalanchoë orgyalis

Crassulaceae

Small, magnificent, hairy rust-brown species. Yellow flowers may appear.
Care: Grow in a sunny window and do not drop water on the hairy leaves; it makes ugly spots. Feed once every two weeks. Keep cooler in the winter and give less water.
Propagation: Via top cuttings, which root at 77°F (25°C) soil temperature.

Light: Full sun.
Temp: Grow moderately warm to warm, in the winter a minimum of 54°F (12°C).
Water: Moderately moist in the summer, rather dry in the winter.
Hum: Moderate, 50–60%.
Soil: Standard potting soil mixed with some clay or loam.

Kalanchoë scapigera

Crassulaceae

Succulent leaves with a vertical way of growing and thick, gray-green leaves.
Care: Grow very light in the summer and do not give too much water or too much food. Add cactus food once in a while. Keep cool and dry in the winter to get flowers the next year.
Propagation: From leaf cuttings.

Light: Full sun.
Temp: Grow moderately warm to warm, in the winter a minimum of 40–50°F (5–10°C).
Water: Keep rather dry, almost dry in the winter.
Hum: Low.
Soil: Cactus soil.

Kalanchoë tomentosa

Crassulaceae

A beautiful succulent from Madagascar. The thick, spoon-shaped foliage is densely covered with soft, silver-gray hairs. With adequate light, the edges of the leaves become rust-brown.
Care: Grow sunny and rather warm. Do not add too much water because the plant does not evaporate much water due to its thick hairy skin. Allow a dormant period in the winter with lower temperature and almost no water. Feed once a month at the most during the growth period.
Propagation: From leaf cuttings. Allow removed leaves to dry for a few days, then plant. Soil temperature 68°F (20°C).

Light: Full sun.
Temp: Grow moderately warm to warm, in the winter a minimum of 45°F (7°C).
Water: Keep rather dry.
Hum: Low.
Soil: Cactus soil.

Kalanchoë tomentosa

On the following pages: *Kalanchoë tomentosa*

Kalanchoë tubiflora

Crassulaceae
Brood-leaf

Comparable to the species *daigremontiana*, but the buds are only at the top of the tubular leaves, rather than along the edges.
Care: This is a very strong plant, which can survive both a warm room and low temperatures in the winter. It can grow somewhat lanky with a warm cultivation, but by growing young plants frequently this is easy to avoid. Fertilizer is not necessary, and water sparsely.
Propagation: Plant the buds.

Light: Full sun.
Temp: Moderately warm to warm, a minimum of 40°F (5°C) in the winter.
Water: Keep rather dry, in winter lower the temperature and keep rather dry.
Hum: Low.
Soil: Standard potting soil.

Kalanchoë tubiflora

Koellikeria erinoides

Gesneriaceae

Small plants for a humid atmosphere. The cultivation is similar to that of the *Achimenes*.
Care: Provide a dormancy for those plants with rootstocks. If you have one, plant it in the spring in a pot and keep it warm. After sprouting, the plants should be grown warm and shaded in a greenhouse, vitrine, etc. Feed once every two weeks. In the autumn, the part above ground dies off again. The rhizomes can be stored dry in or outside of the pot until the spring.
Propagation: By dividing the rootstocks or via top cuttings, which root at a soil temperature of 68–77°F (20–25°C) under glass.

Light: Much light, no full sun.
Temp: Grow warm, in the winter a minimum of 50°F (10°C) for the dry roots.
Water: Keep moderately moist with soft luke-warm water. Keep dry in the winter.
Hum: High, above 60%.

Koellikeria erinoides

Soil: Acidic, airy soil, such as coniferous soil or a mixture of peat moss, leaf soil and sharp sand or perlite.

Kohleria hybrids

Gesneriaceae

Beautiful, tropical small plants that are sometimes known as *Isoloma* or *Tydaea*. Their cultivation is similar to that of the more well-known *Achimenes*.
Care: Begin with either a blooming plant or small rootstocks, which can be ordered by mail. These scaled roots have to be placed in a warm, moist substrate to be able to sprout; temperature 68–77°F (20–25°C), with a glass

Kohleria Eriantha-hybr.

cover. Even after the plant's growth is well on its way, maintain high humidity. Only while they bloom can the plants be kept in something other than a greenhouse. Give fertilizer once every two weeks during the growth period. Lower the temperature in the winter and give less water, but not so little that the foliage dies, as with *Achimenedes*. Repot in the spring and bring back to growth.
Propagation: By dividing the rootstocks in the spring, and also from top cuttings (soil temperature 68–77°F [20–25°C]).

Light: Half shade, never bright sun.
Temp: Grow warm, keep between 50–60°F (10–15°C) in the winter.
Water: Keep moderately moist with soft water.
Hum: High, above 60%.
Soil: Extra acidic, airy soil, for instance coniferous soil, or leaf soil with some standard potting soil. Add peat moss or perlite to make the mixture more permeable.

Lachenalia unifolia

Liliaceae

Bulbous plants, related to *Aloides* hybrids and *Lachenalia bulbiferum*. Flowers are whitish or orange. They're not hardy, and therefore are often forced into bloom inside. Bulbs can be ordered by mail.
Care: In September, the bulbs can be planted in containers and bowls, temperature 40–50°F

Lachenalia unifolia

(5–10°C), warmer for an early bloom. Artificial darkness is not needed. Keep potting soil moderately moist. The blooming may begin in December, or with cooler cultivation, in February through April. Fertilize during the growth period once every two weeks. In the summer, allow the foliage to die off gradually. Withhold water and then let the bulbs rest dormant in the pots. This can be done outside in a garden in a dry spot (e.g., under a roof). Start again in September as described above.
Propagation: By removing the newly formed bulbs.

Light:	Much light, full sun as well when outside.
Temp:	Grow cool, in the winter a minimum 40°F.
Water:	Relatively dry at the start, moderately moist during growth.
Hum:	Moderate, 50–60%.
Soil:	Standard potting soil.

Laelia cinnabarina

Orchidaceae

Beautiful, rather small orchids, which are related to *Cattleya* and often used for cross-fertilization. The pure botanical species, such as the one in the picture, are grown mainly by plant specialists.

Laelia cinnabarina

Care: These plants have pseudotubers, which means that a dormant period is needed. This falls in the winter. The temperature should be lower during dormancy and water sparse, until the new pseudotubers appear. Add some orchid food once a month in the summer.
Propagation: By division during repotting (after bloom).

Light:	Much light, but no bright sun.
Temp:	Grow moderately warm to warm, in the winter 54–60°F (12–15°C).
Water:	In the summer, plenty of soft water or rainwater; in the winter, water sparsely.
Hum:	High, above 60%.
Soil:	Grow in well-drained pots or lattice baskets. Fill these with peat moss, clay particles, tree bark or a mixture of all these.

Lagerstroemia indica

Lythraceae

Magnificent container plants with red-purple flowers. There are also cultivars with completely white flowers.
Care: Place outside from the end of May in a very sheltered, sunny location. Give moderate

Lagerstroemia indica

amounts of water and feed weekly. It is a deciduous bush, so the dormancy location does not have to be light. Ensiling the plant is a possibility as well. Prune back a bit in the spring, and if necessary repot and bring back to growth.
Propagation: From seed or via top cuttings, which root at 68–77°F (20–25°C) soil temperature.

Light:	Full sun.
Temp:	Grow cool, in the winter a minimum of 36°F (2°C).
Water:	Keep moderately moist, drier in the winter.
Hum:	Moderate, 50–60%.
Soil:	Standard potting soil mixed with ⅓ part clay or loam. Use rather big containers that drain well.

Lampranthus blandus

Aizoaceae

A simple succulent with curled-up round leaves, which are somewhat flat near the top.
Care: Place in a sunny window, or outside in a very sheltered, sunny terrace. Water carefully and fertilize monthly. Keep cool in the winter and withhold almost all water.
Propagation: From top cuttings (allow to dry) and from seed.

Lampranthus blandus

Light:	Full sun.
Temp:	Grow moderately warm, in the winter a minimum of 40°F (5°C).
Water:	Keep rather dry, in the winter almost dry.
Hum:	Low.
Soil:	Standard potting soil mixed with extra sharp sand.

Lantana camara-hybr.

Lantana camara hybrids

Verbenaceae

Mostly grown in gardens as an annual flower bed plant, but it is also currently sold as a houseplant, where it works excellently. There are hybrids in various colors.
Care: Grow moderately warm and sunny; fertilize once every two weeks. Dormancy is possible at lower temperatures. By the second year, one may already have a sturdy bush with hundreds of flowers, or even a tree, if you prune it back in the right way (see *Fuchsia*).
Propagation: Newly sprouted shoots can be taken in January. They root at 68–77°F (20–25°C). Also possible from seed.

Light:	Full sun.
Temp:	Grow moderately warm, in the winter a minimum of 45°F (7°C).
Water:	Keep moderately moist, drier in the winter.
Hum:	Moderate, 50–60%.
Soil:	Standard potting soil.

Laurus nobilis

Laureceae

Laurel

A very well-known container plant, often found at the entrances of shops or houses. The leaves can be used as an herb.

Laurus nobilis

Care: The laurel can be outside in the full sun from mid-May. Fertilize monthly and spray with insecticides from time to time to avoid the cottony maple scale. With proper pruning, any desired shape can be achieved. As long as it does not freeze, and is not too drafty, the laurel can remain outside. With the first frost, bring inside to a cool space (ventilate frequently), so that the plant does not form new shoots too early (not before April). Bring outside toward the end of May. If it is kept rather cold during dormancy, the plant may bloom as in the picture. Use rather large containers.
Propagation: Place top cuttings in sandy soil in the fall and keep cool, but allow frost-free dormancy. Roots appear in the spring.

Light:	Much light, full sun, too.
Temp:	Grow cool, in the winter 40–50°F (5–10°C).
Water:	Keep moderately moist.
Hum:	Moderate, 50–60%.
Soil:	Standard potting soil.

Ledebouria socialis

Liliaceae

A bulbous plant, previously known as *Scilla violacea*. This plant from South Africa is not hardy and is mainly grown for its attractive, spotted foliage. Small flowers can appear, too, as in the photograph.
Care: In contrast to many other bulbous plants, this small plant keeps its leaves all year. So, do not allow for too strict a dormant period, keeping the plant cooler in the winter and decreasing the water. Keep rather dry in the growing period and fertilize monthly. The plant can also go outside in the summer.
Propagation: By taking the bulbs.

Light:	Full sun.
Temp:	Grow moderately warm, in the winter a minimum of 40°F (5°C).
Water:	Keep rather dry.
Hum:	Moderate, 50–60%.
Soil:	Standard potting soil.

Ledebouria socialis

Leea guineensis 'Burgundy'

Leea guineensis

Leeaceae

A potted plant that has become increasingly popular the last few years. In most cases, the plant is still called *Leea coccinea*. Nobody expected that this plant from tropical Asia would flourish when grown as a houseplant. Besides the normal green species, there is also the cultivar 'Burgundy' with brown-red leaves. Red flowers may appear. The crystals that form on stalks and foliage do not indicate a disease but are part of the plant.
Care: Can be kept indoors all year. This plant does not like bright sun, stagnant water or the dry soil. 'Burgundy,' on the other hand, should be kept as light as possible. Feed once every two weeks while the plant grows (which is most of the year). Spray frequently in the winter and lower the temperature somewhat, if possible.
Propagation: The normal green species from seed. The species with the red leaves via top cuttings. Soil temperature 77–86°F (25–20°C).

Light:	Half shade, never full sun.
Temp:	Grow warm, in the winter a minimum of 61°F (16°C).
Water:	Keep moderately moist.
Hum:	Moderate to high.
Soil:	Standard potting soil.

Leea guineensis

Leptospermum scoparium

The plant is not hardy, and should be grown as a container plant. Various hybrids of the species in the picture are available with white or red-purple flowers.
Care: Place outside if possible in the summer, protected and in sun. Give plenty of water and feed once every two weeks. In the fall bring the plant inside and allow a cool and light dormancy. Prune back in the fall and spring for better branching.
Propagation: Top cuttings or middle cuttings that root at a soil temperature of 68–77°F (20–25°C) under glass.

Light:	Full sun.
Temp:	Grow cool, in the winter 37–46°F (3–8°C).
Water:	Keep moderately moist, drier in the winter.
Hum:	Moderate, 50–60%.
Soil:	Standard potting soil.

Leuchtenbergia principis

Cactaceae

A peculiar cactus from Mexico, though without the actual body of a cactus. It retains the knobs that decorate so many cacti, but which in this case are strongly elongated. At the end of each are papery thorns. The plant may bloom with large yellow flowers.
Care: Place well in the sun and do not give too much water. Add cactus food monthly. Withhold all water in the winter at low temperature.
Propagation: From seed, germination temperature 68–77°F (20–25°C).

Light:	Full sun.
Temp:	Moderately warm to warm, in the winter no water.
Water:	Keep rather dry, no water in winter.
Hum:	Low.
Soil:	Cactus soil.

Leuchtenbergia principis

Leptocladodia microhelia

Cactaceae

A genus of cacti that is newly separated from *Mammillaria*. The species from Mexico in the picture forms small columns that are covered with a very regular pattern of thorns, resembling small suns. The flowers are either yellow-white or light red.
Care: Keep well lit in the summer; full sun is fine, too, except in the early spring, when the plants are not yet used to it. Give food monthly and provide good drainage, because stagnant water makes the roots rot. Keep cool in the winter and withhold almost all water.
Propagation: From seed. Germination temperature 68–77°F (20–25°C).

Light:	Much light, full sun. too.
Temp:	Moderately warm to warm, in the winter 40–50°F (5–10°C).
Water:	Sparsely, almost nothing in the winter.
Hum:	Low.
Soil:	Cactus soil.

Leptospermum scoparium

Myrtaceae

Small bush or tree from New Zealand and Australia that blooms lavishly at an early age.

Leptocladodia microhelia

Leucothoë walteri

Ericaceae

A small bush from the heather family, mostly available in a beautiful variegated form, 'Girard's Rainbow.'
Care: Extremely suitable for cultivation in balcony containers and for cool spaces. If grown in pots, then make sure that not all of the soil freezes, because this evergreen plant will dry out. Provide shade and protection against the wind. In the summer, feed once every two weeks.
Propagation: Via top cuttings, soil temperature 68°F (20°C).

Leucothoë walteri 'Girard's Rainbow'

Light:	Half shade.
Temp:	Grow cool (the plant is hardy).
Water:	Keep moderately moist with soft water.
Hum:	Moderate to high.
Soil:	Acidic potting soil, for instance, coniferous soil.

Lilium hybrids

Liliaceae
Lily

Although lilies are primarily used for cut flowers, it is very possible to force the bulbs of

Lilium-hybr. 'Enchantment'

some hardy species (or genera) into blooming indoors. 'Enchantment' (pictured), 'Destiny,' the tiger lily 'Yellow Star' and 'White Europe' (a *longiflorum*-type) are all well suited for this.
Care: It is advisable to go with prepared lily bulbs, which can be ordered by mail. These bulbs are usually stored for a while at low temperatures and immersed in a bath of growth-stunting substances, so that the length of the plant will be limited to about 24–28 in (60–70 cm). Pot the bulbs under the soil surface of rather large containers with good water drainage. Keep cool at first (40–54°F [5–12°C]) and use little water. When the growth starts, place at 54–63°F (12–17°C) and keep moist. Add fertilizer every two weeks. After the blooming, ensilage the pot and bulbs in an outside garden. In the fall, bring inside and store the bulbs dry and in the pot at a minimum 40°F (5°C) until the next spring.
Propagation: By taking the bulbs.

Light:	Much light, full sun in the summer as well.
Temp:	First cool, later moderately warm.
Water:	Keep moderately moist.
Hum:	Moderate, 50–60%.
Soil:	Standard potting soil.

Liriope muscari

Liliaceae

Easily grown potted plants, of which a green and a variegated form exist. The green one is the strongest cultivar.
Care: These are by nature shadow plants, which are not hardy but can be kept cool; they grow well in a room that is not too warm. Give

Liriope muscari

a moderate amount of water, except in the dormant period. During the growth period, add food to the water once every two weeks.
Propagation: By division, and for the green species, from seed as well.

Light:	Half shade or shade.
Temp:	Grow cool, in the winter a minimum of 40°F (5°C).
Water:	Keep moderately moist.
Hum:	Moderate, 50–60%.
Soil:	Standard potting soil.

Lithops bromfieldii

Lithops bromfieldii
Aizoaceae
Living stone

Interesting succulents of which the species in the picture is only one example; there are numerous of species, all somewhat different, including some that are white-blooming. These are extremely succulent plants that can grow practically without any water. The whole plant consists of two very thick, disfigured leaves. A flower appears from the center of these leaves.
Care: After the end of the summer growth period, the leaves die off, while in the heart of the leaves a new leaf coupling develops. This absorbs the moisture of the old leaves. To water the plant during this process would be wrong. After the winter, start giving water again very gradually and sparsely, and if possible from beneath the soil. Fertilizing is not needed. The blooming period generally falls in August through September.
Propagation: From seed.

Light:	Full sun.
Temp:	Grow warm, in the winter 50–54°F (10–12°C).
Water:	Very sparsely, nothing in the winter.
Hum:	Low.
Soil:	Cactus soil.

Littonia modesta

Liliaceae

A climbing plant from South Africa that can be grown in a greenhouse, or possibly in a light window. Rootstocks can be ordered by mail. The cultivar 'Keitii' is primarily sold, because its flowers are bigger and more striking than most.

Care: Plant rootstocks in the spring and let them sprout by using warmth. Do not give much water at first, adding more later. In the summer, when they grow well, add food weekly. Grow light, even sun is allowed. In the fall the plant will die off, so withhold all water.

Littonia modesta

Keep the rootstocks dry during dormancy and bring back to growth again in the spring.
Propagation: From seed and by dividing the rootstocks.

Light:	Much light, sun, too.
Temp:	Grow moderately warm to warm, in the winter a minimum of 50°F (10°C).
Water:	Keep moderately moist, completely dry in the winter.
Hum:	Moderate to high.
Soil:	A mixture of standard potting soil, loam and clay.

Livistona chinensis

Palmae

A palm from China and Japan that has been grown in Europe for a long time. The broad foliage is cut through halfway down the leaf. On the similar *Livistona rotundifolia*, the extremely round leaves are cut only one-third of their length.

Care: Because generally only young plants are used, cultivation should consist of much light, but not bright sunlight. Give food in the summer once every two weeks. In the winter, this plant can be kept much cooler.
Propagation: From seed, germination temperature 68–77°F (20–25°C).

Livistona chinensis

Light:	Much light, no full sun.
Temp:	Grow moderately warm, in the winter 60–64°F (15–18°C).
Water:	Keep well watered in the summer, drier in the winter.
Hum:	Moderate, 50–60%.
Soil:	Standard potting soil mixed with fine loam or clay. Use rather large pots.

Lobivia species

Cactaceae

Lobivia, an anagram of the word Bolivia, are the most popular cacti for enthusiasts. And it's no wonder, since they are quite easy to grow and bloom at an early age with unbelievably large, beautifully-shaped flowers. It is typical of these flowers that one part of the stamen be situated under the flower, while the other part is much higher.

Care: Grow in full sun, but never keep too hot: Always ventilate in warm weather. Cold nights are especially good for the plants, so ventilate at night as well. If protected by a piece of glass, then they can be kept outside, too, during rainy summers. These plants will endure more water than most other cacti; nevertheless, water very carefully, especially in dark weather. Almost all species grow well by their own roots, so grafting is seldom necessary, as with other cacti. Give cactus food monthly in the growth period. In the winter, the temperature should be a lot lower and water given sparsely. In the spring, mist only until the buds are well developed, then gradually add more water.
Propagation: From seed and by removing and growing the side shoots.

Light:	Full sun.
Temp:	Grow cool to moderately warm, keep at 34–46°F (1–8°C) in the winter, no warmer.
Water:	Moderately moist in sunny weather, otherwise somewhat drier. Almost completely dry in the dormant period.
Hum:	Low.
Soil:	Cactus soil.

Lobivia aurea

Lobivia backebergii

Lobivia densispina

Lobivia jajoiana

Lockhartia lunifera

Orchidaceae

Also known as "woven" orchids because the stems' criss-cross leaves look like braids. Flowers appear at the ends of the stems; and the stems should not die off after they bloom.
Care: Grow out of the sun in a moderately warm spot (such as a protected greenhouse). Provide rainwater the whole year, but allow for good drainage. Add food once in a while in the summer, in light concentrations. Keep a bit cooler in the winter, but not cold. Repot only when the plants become too big.
Propagation: By division and from seed.

Light:	Much light, no full sun.
Temp:	Grow moderately warm, a minimum of 27°F (14°C).
Water:	Keep moderately moist with soft water.
Hum:	High, above 60%.
Soil:	Fill moderately sized lattice baskets with a mixture of pieces of tree fern and fern wood. Drain well.

Lockhartia lunifera

Lophomyrtus obcordata

Myrtaceae

A hardy houseplant from New Zealand, also known as *Myrtus*. Normally the foliage is entirely green, but there are some forms—for example the 'Gloriosa' in the picture and 'Travers'—with silver variegated leaves.
Care: This plant can remain in a warm room the whole year, but it is better to place it outside in the summer in a protected location and then move it to a cooler place inside in the winter. This will prevent the leaves from falling off. During the growth period, fertilize once every two weeks.
Propagation: Root top cuttings under plastic at a soil temperature of 77°F (25°C).

Light:	Much light, full sun, too.
Temp:	Grow cool to moderately warm, in the winter a minimum of 54°F (12°C).
Water:	Moderately moist.
Hum:	Moderate, 50–60%.
Soil:	Standard potting soil.

Lophomyrtus obcordata 'Gloriosa'

Lophophora williamsii

Cactaceae

Peyote

This cactus is frequently stolen from collections because it contains a substance that can be used as a drug. This drug is used in the religious ceremonies of some Native Americans. The picture shows a very young plant. Later, 7 to 10 ribs will form with small clouds of felt on the thornless areoles.

Care: Keep light in the summer and add some cactus food to the water at most once a month. Provide a cool and dry dormancy to generate flowers again the following year.

Light:	Full sun.
Temp:	Grow moderately warm to warm, in the winter cool but no less than 40°F (5°C).
Water:	Keep rather dry, drier in the winter.
Hum:	Low.
Soil:	Cactus soil.

Lophophora williamsii

flower stems with fragrant white flowers appear.
Care: Grow in a warm greenhouse at a high humidity level. Never allow direct sunlight and repot when necessary. Feed monthly when the plant grows. A real dormant period is not needed.
Propagation: From division and seed.

Light:	Half shade, no full sun.
Temp:	Grow warm, in the winter a minimum of 64°F (18°C).
Water:	Keep moderately moist with soft water.
Hum:	High, above 60%.
Soil:	A mixture of leaf mold, sphagnum, strongly decayed cow manure on a layer of clay particles.

Lotus berthelotii

Lotus berthelotii

Leguminoae

A hanging plant for a cold greenhouse that is very striking because of its bright red flowers.
Care: Grow sunny and airy in a cold greenhouse or possibly protected outside. Keep moderately moist continuously, because if the ball of soil dries out, the leaves fall off quickly. Therefore, it's advisable to use a pot with a watering system. Give food once every two weeks. Bring inside in the fall for a cool dormancy.
Propagation: From seed and via top cuttings or middle cuttings, which root under glass at 68–77°F (20–25°C).

Light:	Full sun.
Temp:	Grow cool to moderately warm, in the winter 40–50°F (5–10°C).
Water:	Keep moderately moist, drier in the winter (foliage may fall off in part).
Hum:	Moderate, 50–60%.
Soil:	Standard potting soil.

Ludisia discolor

Orchidaceae

Also known by the name *Haemaria*. It is a soil-growing orchid that looks like a normal small foliage plant until the winter, when long

Lycaste cruenta

Orchidaceae

A relatively easily grown orchid, which can be kept indoors with success.
Care: Give plenty of water in the summer, keep out of the sun and provide fresh air. Feed monthly. In the fall or winter, pseudotubers are formed and the old leaves drop. After this, withhold water for at least a few weeks. The temperature can be lowered during the dormant period.
Propagation: By division and from seed.

Light:	Half shade to shade, never full sun.
Temp:	Grow cool to moderately warm, in the winter a minimum of 45°F (7°C).
Water:	Plenty of rainwater in the summer, a dormant period in the winter with much less water.
Hum:	Moderate to high.
Soil:	Pieces of tree bark or clay particles.

Ludisia discolor

Lycaste cruenta

Macroplectrum sesquipedale

Macroplectrum sesquipedale

Orchidaceae

A large and strong orchid from Madagascar, where it is found growing on trees. Also known as *Angraecum sesquipedale*. There are no pseudotubers, but it does have big, leathery leaves. The flower has a long spore of at least 12 in (30 cm) in length (the green slip on the photograph).

Care: Grow in a warm greenhouse in a shaded area. In the summer, allow fresh air and frequently add soft water, provided that there is good drainage. Mist as often as possible when the weather is dry and sunny. Fertilize every two weeks with normal plant fertilizer. Keep drier in the winter, but do not give a strict dormant period. The temperature should stay relatively high.

Propagation: From seed.

Light: Half shade to shade, never sun.
Temp: Grow warm, during summer days up to 82°F (28°C), at night at least 61°F (16°C).
Water: Plenty of (rain)water in the summer, drier in the winter.
Hum: High, far above 60%.
Soil: Grow in pots or lattice baskets, filled with a mixture of pieces of tree fern and fern root.

Malpighia coccigera

Malpighiaceae

Mini-holly

A plant not seen very often, but with the increasing popularity of bonsai, more and more plants are imported that were previously unknown.

Care: One can cultivate this plant as a bonsai (see pages 28–29), although it is preferably grown in a greenhouse. The bloom comes out in the winter, with light red flowers. The plant only stays well indoors if provided a humid atmosphere. In the summer, it can go outside in an extremely protected place. It can receive sunlight. Feed once every two weeks in the growing period.

Propagation: From seed and top cuttings. Soil temperature 77–86°F (25–30°C).

Light: Much light, full sun as well.

Malpighia coccigera

Temp: Grow warm, in the winter not below 64°F (18°C).
Water: Keep moderately moist.
Hum: Moderate to high.
Soil: Standard potting soil mixed with some clay or loam.

Malvaviscus arboreus
Malvaceae

Bush from Central and South America that in moderate climates grows as a house or greenhouse plant.
Care: Grow sunny. From the end of May it can possibly go outside in a sheltered spot, otherwise keep in a greenhouse or a very well-lit window indoors. Give moderate amounts of water and feed once every two weeks. Bring inside to a greenhouse in the fall for a rather cool dormancy. It is generally too hot indoors during the winter for this plant. Prune back in the spring, repot, keep warm and bring outside again after hardening off, if desired.
Propagation: From seed and via top cuttings, which root under glass at 77–86°F (20–30°C) soil temperature.

Malvaviscus arboreus

Light: Full sun.
Temp: Grow cool to moderately warm, in the winter a minimum of 54°F (12°C).
Water: Keep moderately moist, drier in the dormant period.
Hum: Moderate, 50–60%.
Soil: Potting soil containing calcium, for instance, a mixture of standard potting soil and clay containing calcium or loam.

Mamillopsis senilis
Cactaceae

Elongated spherical cactus with white thorned edges, also called *Mammillaria senilis*.
Care: This is a very strong cactus that grows in Mexico at 10,000 ft (3,000 m) and can endure frost and snow. In the U.S. it is important to keep the plant in a sunny place all year long and especially important to keep it very cool and dry. Water sparsely in the summer and add cactus food monthly.
Propagation: From seed. Also, older plants make side shoots that can be removed and planted separately.

Mamillopsis senilis

Light: Full sun.
Temp: Grow moderately warm, cooler at night, in the winter 32–40°F (0–5°C).
Water: Keep quite dry, almost dry in the winter.
Hum: Low to moderate.
Soil: Cactus soil.

Mammillaria bocasana
Cactaceae

A spherical, sprouting cactus that normally has yellowish white flowers. Pictured is the variety *roseiflora*, which has considerably more beautiful flowers. Clear red fruits also appear.
Care: Grow sunny, so that the white hairs keep their color. Do not give too much water. Add cactus food monthly. In the winter, lower the temperature and keep almost dry.
Propagation: By removing the sprouts. Allow these to dry first before planting. Also possible from seed. Soil temperature 68°F (20°C).

Light: Full sun.
Temp: Grow moderately warm to warm, in the winter between 40–50°F (5–10°C).
Water: Keep rather dry, almost dry in the winter.
Hum: Low.
Soil: Cactus soil.

Mammillaria bocasana var. *roseiflora*

Mammillaria guelzowiana
Cactaceae

A spherical cactus with large, exceptionally beautiful flowers. Originally from Mexico.

Care: Provide a warm, sunny location and avoid stagnant water at all times by using well-draining pots. Give cactus food monthly. Keep cooler in the winter.
Propagation: Side shoots form on older specimens, which can be cut off and planted after drying. Also possible from seed, soil temperature 68–77°F (20–25°C).

Light: Full sun.
Temp: Grow warm, in the winter between 40–50°F (5–10°C).
Water: Keep rather dry, in the winter only a few drops.
Hum: Low.
Soil: Cactus soil.

Mammillaria guelzowiana

Mammillaria hahniana
Cactaceae

Spherical, seed-forming cactus with an elegant, white hairy cover and small red-purple flowers.
Care: The hairs only remain beautiful if the plant gets as much sunlight as possible. Add some special cactus food at the most once a month. Keep cooler in the winter and almost completely dry.
Propagation: By taking the shoots and planting them, and also from seed.

Light: Full sun.
Temp: Grow warm, in the winter 40–50°F (5–10°C).
Water: Keep rather dry, in the winter almost dry.
Hum: Low.
Soil: Cactus soil.

Mammillaria hahniana

MAMMILLARIA

Mammillaria prolifera

Cactaceae

Profusely sprouting, round cactus with rather small flowers, and interesting fruits, both of which are visible in the picture. This cactus will form seeds given enough time.
Care: Keep well lit in the summer. Preferably grown in shallow bowls that drain well. If possible, add water directly to the soil, adding cactus food once a month. Keep cool and dry in the winter, otherwise there will be no bloom.
Propagation: By division and from seed.

Light:	Full sun.
Temp:	Grow moderately warm to warm, in the winter between 40–50°F (5–10°C).
Water:	Keep moderately dry, in the winter almost completely dry.
Hum:	Low.
Soil:	Cactus soil.

Mammillaria prolifera

Mammillaria rhodantha

Cactaceae

Spherical to oval, easily blooming cactus. The flowers form a circle, as is often the case with *Mammillaria.*
Care: Keep light in the summer, screening only against the brightest sunlight. Add cactus food monthly. Keep cooler in the winter and practically dry.
Propagation: From seed, germination temperature 68°F (20°C).

Mammillaria rhodantha

Light:	Much light, screen against bright light.
Temp:	Grow moderately warm to warm, keep between 40–50°F (5–10°C) in the winter.
Water:	Keep rather dry, in the winter almost dry.
Hum:	Low.
Soil:	Cactus soil.

Mammillaria spinosissima

Cactaceae

A nonsprouting, quite large, oval cactus that grows and blooms easily. The flowers form a neat circle at the top.
Care: Keep well lit in the summer, even in full sun. Water sparsely, though this strong species could survive a complete dousing. Soft water is preferable. Add cactus food monthly. Keep cool and dry in the winter.
Propagation: From seed. Germination temperature 68–77°F (20–25°C).

Light:	Much light, full sun as well.
Temp:	Grow moderately warm to warm, in the winter between 40–50°F (5–10°C).
Water:	Keep rather dry to moderately moist, in the winter almost dry.
Hum:	Low.
Soil:	Cactus soil.

Mammillaria spinosissima

Mammillaria wildii

Cactaceae

Pictured is the form 'Cristata.' Cristate, or combination forms, occur quite frequently in cacti. They are caused by a fluke of nature that somehow disturbs the growth point, and produces the strange shapes shown in the photograph.
Care: This plant is easy to grow, and blooms at an early age. It has to be protected against the brightest sun. Water moderately and add cactus food monthly. Keep cool and almost dry in the winter.
Propagation: The normal species from seed; the cristate form by cutting off parts and treating them as cuttings. In general, cristate forms are grated onto other cacti.

Light:	Much light, screen against brightest sun.
Temp:	Grow moderately warm to warm, in the winter 40–50°F (5–10°C).
Water:	Keep rather dry, almost no water in the winter.
Hum:	Low.
Soil:	Cactus soil.

Mammillaria wildii 'Cristata'

Mammillaria zeilmanniana

Cactaceae

Spherical to oval cactus, which grows both singly and in a somewhat sprouting manner. It blooms easily around Mother's Day. The normal species has red-purple flowers, but there is also a white species.
Care: Easily grown in a light greenhouse or window. Much light, sun included, and do not give too much water. Add cactus food monthly. Allow to rest dormant in the winter at a low temperature.
Propagation: By removing the sprouts, which after drying can be planted. Also, from seed. Soil temperature 68–77°F (20–25°C).

Light:	Much light, full sun as well.
Temp:	Grow moderately warm to warm, in the winter between 40–50°F (5–10°C).
Water:	Keep rather dry, in the winter almost completely dry.
Hum:	Low.
Soil:	Cactus soil.

Mammillaria zeilmanniana

Mandevilla laxa

Mandevilla laxa

Apocynaceae

Twining plant from South America, which can grow in the ground or in large containers.
Care: This creeper can only bloom well outside in southern regions or in a very sheltered spot outside, tied up against a warm, sunny wall. When planted in a cold greenhouse, the bloom is all but guaranteed. Give support to the branches. Water moderately and fertilize weekly. In the winter, provide a dormant period, with considerably lower temperatures and less water. The foliage will fall off. Prune in the spring, repot and bring back to growth.
Propagation: From seed and via top and middle cuttings, which root under glass at 68–77°F (20–25°C) soil temperature.

Light:	Outside in the full sun, though screen against the brightest sun in a greenhouse.
Temp:	Grow moderately warm, in the winter 46–54°F (8–12°C).
Water:	Keep moderately moist in the summer, in the winter water sparsely.
Hum:	Moderate, 50–60%.
Soil:	Improve growing substrate with potting soil, leaf soil, etc.

Mandevilla sanderi
See *Diladenia sanderi*.

Manettia inflata

Rubiaceae

Climbing plant for a moderately warm greenhouse, sometimes sold as a potted plant.
Care: The long vines need adequate support, and with pot cultivation a hoop of wire will do nicely. Screen against the brightest afternoon sunlight. Grow moderately warm, which can work outside if conditions allow, but often a greenhouse or living room is the best place. Feed weekly in the growth period. Provide a dormancy at lower temperatures. Prune sharply in the spring, repot and bring back to growth.
Propagation: Root top cuttings at 68–77°F (20–25°C) soil temperature under glass.

Light:	Much light, no bright sunlight.
Temp:	Grow moderately warm, in the winter a minimum of 54°F (12°C).
Water:	Keep moderately moist.
Hum:	Moderate to high.
Soil:	Standard potting soil mixed with a large part loam or clay.

Manettia inflata

MANIHOT

Manihot esculenta

Euphorbiaceae

Cassava

These plants with edible rootstocks are grown in many tropical countries. The cassava root, used to make bread or tapioca, is an important food there. When grown as an ornamental plant, 'Variegata' is an excellent choice.
Care: Cultivate in a greenhouse or plant window for warmth and humidity. Allow a lot of light, but filter sunlight. Feed once every two weeks in the summer. The winter is a dormant period for this plant, so give less water then and do not fertilize. Most of the foliage will fall. Repot in the spring, keep warmer and bring back to growth.
Propagation: Root top cuttings under glass at 77°F (25°C) soil temperature.

Light: Much light, no full sun.
Temp: Grow moderately warm to warm, in the winter 54–60°F (12–15°C).

Manihot esculenta 'Variegata'

Water: Keep moderately moist, drier in the winter.
Hum: High, above 60%.
Soil: Mix standard potting soil with extra loam or clay.

Maranta leuconeura

Marantaceae

Prayer plant

Plants with tuberous roots and beautifully marked leaves. The species *bicolor* is sometimes known as the Ten Commandments plant because of the ten (or occasionally less) chocolate-brown spots that decorate the green leaves. Prettier, and grown more frequently, is the species *leuconeura*.
Care: These low-growing plants like wide and shallow bowls or pots and crave humid air. They last longest as ground cover grown in plant containers, as well as in greenhouses. Warm potting soil is a plus, so do not use terracotta pots (see page 57). Always keep them out of the sunlight and fertilize during the growth period, once every two weeks. In the winter, the temperature can be lower, but the soil should remain rather warm.

Maranta leuconeura 'Fascinator'

Propagation: By division and via top cuttings or middle cuttings. Soil temperature 68–77°F (20–25°C).

Light: Much light, never full sun.
Temp: Grow warm, in winter nights a minimum 57°F (14°C).
Water: Keep moderately moist with soft water.
Hum: High, above 60%.
Soil: Very airy and permeable, for example coniferous soil mixed with decayed cow manure.

Maranta leuconeura 'Kerchoviana'

Mascarena verschaffeltii

Palmae

A palm from around Mauritania, which has a ringed trunk. Young plants of this species, and also from the species *lagenicaulis* are sold in the U.S. as potted plants. They can stand dry air very well.
Care: These plants have to be kept warm throughout the year, with light, but no full sunlight. Give fertilizer once every two weeks in the growth period. When the heat is turned on, spray the foliage as often as possible and do not place above a radiator. Repot in the spring.
Propagation: From fresh (imported) seeds. It takes a few months before they germinate. Soil temperature 68°F (20°C).

Light: Much light, no full sun.

Mascarena verschaffeltii

Temp: Grow warm, no full sun.
Water: Keep moderately moist, immerse in water occasionally during the summer.
Hum: Moderate, 50–60%.
Soil: Standard potting soil with ⅓ part fine loam or clay.

Masdevallia species

Orchidaceae

There are many species of *Masdevallia*, orchids that grow in cool, humid mountain forests at 13,000 ft (4,000 m). These flowers have remarkable slips.
Care: The trick is not to keep these plants warm. It is often too hot in a greenhouse during the summer, therefore grow them outside from the end of May in a lightly shaded, airy spot. They can endure morning or evening sun very well. Growth usually occurs in the fall; the flowers appear in the spring or summer. Add orchid food once every two weeks in the growing period. When temperatures drop close to freezing, the plants have to be brought inside, where they should rest at rather low temperatures. A true dormant period is not necessary, however.
Propagation: By division, and from seed as well.

Masdevallia angulata

Masdevallia **X** *kimballiana*

Light:	Much light, screen against afternoon sun.
Temp:	Always grow cool, never above 77°F (25°C); in the winter between 40°F (5°C) at night, and 54°F (12°C) during the day.
Water:	Always keep moderately moist with soft water. Mist frequently. Do not pour water over the foliage in the winter.
Hum:	High, above 60%.

Soil:	Cultivate in pots that drain well; substrate can vary, rock wool flakes are sufficient.

Matucana currundayensis

Cactaceae

Spherical cactus from Peru. There are about 16 known species.

Care: These plants need much light to be able to bloom well. Therefore, grow directly behind a window, taking care that it doesn't get too hot by ventilating frequently. Cold nights can be withstood. In the summer add cactus food monthly. Keep cool and dry in the winter.

Propagation: From seed.

Light:	Full sun.
Temp:	Grow moderately warm, in the winter 40–50°F (5–10°C).
Water:	Rather dry, in the winter almost completely dry.
Hum:	Low.
Soil:	Cactus soil.

Maxillaria tenuifolia

Orchidaceae

Orchids with pseudotubers, often found in the collections of plant enthusiasts.

Care: The various species grow in nature under different circumstances, making it difficult to generalize about cultivation requirements. In all cases, a dormant period of about a month is necessary after the plant blooms, during which watering should be sparse. Otherwise, always provide sufficient (rain)water, and allow for easy drainage. During the growth period, fertilize monthly, but in light concentrations. Caution: direct sunlight causes the leaves to burn.

Propagation: By division, and from seed as well.

Light:	Half shade, never full sun.
Temp:	Grow warm, in the winter a minimum of 64°F (18°C). (Species originally grown in the mountains can be kept cooler.)
Water:	Always keep moderately moist, except during dormancy.
Hum:	High, above 60%.
Soil:	Pots or lattice baskets filled with fern roots, pieces of fern, clay particles, etc.

Matucana currundayensis

Maxillaria tenuifolia

Medinilla magnifica

Metrosideros villosus

Medinilla magnifica

Melastomataceae

A plant with impressive blooms. Unfortunately, it can only survive indoors temporarily, although some people are successful in cultivating the *Medinilla* for several years indoors with a lot of care.
Care: The problem here is the dry air that predominates in homes during the winter. In a greenhouse, however, the cultivation of large, lavishly blooming plants is absolutely no problem. In the winter, a dormant period at lower temperature is necessary. During the growth period, food is needed once every two weeks. Stop adding food at the end of August.
Propagation: Root top cuttings only under glass at a soil temperature of 86–95°F (30–35°C).

Light:	Much light, no full sun.
Temp:	Grow warm, in the winter, maintain a temperature around 60°F (15°C).
Water:	Keep moderately moist, drier in the winter.
Hum:	High, above 60%.
Soil:	Standard potting soil mixed with fine clay or loam, or rock wool flakes.

Melocactus maxonii

Cactaceae

Melon cactus

Interesting cactus, previously imported from the West Indies. Such specimens are generally

doomed to die, unfortunately, because they cannot make new roots in our climate. Off their native islands, only plants grown from seed flourish, and there are plenty available. The remarkable cephalon, the bloom top, is formed at an older age.
Care: Grow warm and sunny with moderate amounts of water. Add cactus food monthly. Keep cooler in the winter, but not as cold as most other cacti, and water sparsely.
Propagation: From seed. Germination temperature 68–77°F (20–25°C).

Light:	Full sun.
Temp:	Grow warm, in the winter between 50–60°F (10–15°C).
Water:	Keep moderately moist, much drier during dormancy.
Hum:	Low to moderate.
Soil:	Cactus soil.

Melocactus

Metrosideros villosus

Myrtaceae

Bushes from New Zealand reminiscent of the *Callistemon.* Cultivation for all species is the same.
Care: Keep outside from the end of May. Give moderate amounts of water and feed once every two weeks. Bring inside in the fall before it starts to freeze and provide a cool dormancy. Give less water, but not so little that the leaves fall off. Repot in the spring, keep warmer (not before April) and bring back to growth. If pruning is needed, do it just after the blooming period.
Propagation: Root top cuttings under glass at 68–77°F (20–25°C) soil temperature. The best time for this is midsummer.

Light:	Full sun.
Temp:	Grow cool, in the winter 40–50°F (5–10°C).
Water:	Keep moderately moist with soft water, drier in the summer.
Hum:	Moderate, 50–60%.
Soil:	Quite acidic, for instance coniferous soil or a mixture of standard potting soil and peat moss.

Melocactus maxonii

Microcoelum weddellianum

Mikania ternata

Microcoelum weddellianum

Palmae

Weddell palm

A very popular plant that can thrive in the warm indoor air for a while. But after at most two years, it succumbs; older specimens are rare.

Care: Contrary to the care requirements of most other plants, it is ok to leave excess water in the plant's tray. Spray frequently in the winter, because the palm hates dry air. During the growth period give food once every two weeks.

Propagation: Soak seeds in lukewarm water for a few days, then sow and allow to germinate at 77–86°F (25–30°C) soil temperature.

Light:	Much light, no full sun.
Temp:	Grow warm, not below 64°F (18°C).
Water:	Continuously moist.
Hum:	High, above 60%.
Soil:	Standard potting soil.

Microlepis speluncae

Dennstaedtiaceae

Nice indoor fern with large, soft, somewhat hairy leaves with triple or quadruple feathering.

Care: The large, soft foliage indicates immediately that it has a large evaporation capacity. This means that the plant cannot endure dry air very well. This creates no problems in the summer, as long as the plant is kept in the shade. In the winter, the atmosphere becomes too dry quite soon, so spray frequently and keep the temperature lower. Feed once every two weeks during the growth period.

Propagation: By division and by sowing the spores. Germination temperature 68°F (20°C).

Light:	Shade, never sun.

Temp:	Grow moderately warm, in the winter not below 60°F (15°C).
Water:	Keep very moist regularly (a pot with a watering system is ideal).
Hum:	High, above 60%.
Soil:	Standard potting soil.

Mikania ternata

Compositae

A creeping or somewhat climbing small plant, with palmate foliage that is completely cov-

Microlepis speluncae

ered by hair, which gives it a nice, matte green appearance. The underside of the foliage is purple-violet.

Care: Keep well lit in the summer; this plant could even get used to the sun. Do not pour water directly over the leaves, because it makes them ugly. Feed once every two weeks. In the winter, provide extra humidity or keep cooler.

Propagation: Root top cuttings under glass at a soil temperature of 68–77°F (20–25°C). Also possible by division.

Light:	Much light, full sun as well.
Temp:	Grow moderately warm, in the winter a minimum of 54°F (12°C).
Water:	Keep moderately moist.
Hum:	Moderate to high.
Soil:	Standard potting soil.

Miltonia roezlii 'Alba'

Mimosa pudica

Miltonia hybrids

Orchidaceae
Violet orchid

A popular orchid, from which there are many known hybrids. These plants have pseudotubers, but do not go through a strict dormant period.
Care: It is important to keep these plants cool, especially in the summer. So avoid the sun and look for an airy spot inside. During the growth period, give plenty of water and orchid food monthly. When the plant has bloomed, give less water. Do not screen light in the winter and keep the temperature low.
Propagation: By division and from seed.

Light:	Shade to half shade.
Temp:	Grow cool, never warmer than 77°F (25°C), in the winter 43–54°F (6–12°C).
Water:	Always use soft water. Much water in early summer, less when the growth stops, in the winter just enough to keep it moist.
Hum:	High, above 60%.
Soil:	All kinds of mixtures have been suggested. Nowadays soil with more clay particles, rock wool flakes or other mixtures without plant food are recommended. Fertilizing well is then necessary.

Miltoniopsis roezlii

Orchidaceae

An orchid that differs slightly from the last genus, and by some is considered to belong to *Miltonia*.
Care: Keep this species warm and lightly shaded. Give plenty of (rain)water in the summer, feeding once every two weeks. After the

pseudotubers are full grown, a dormant period of a few weeks should be provided. Give just enough water to keep the pseudotubers from shriveling.
Propagation: By division.

Light:	Much light, no full sun.
Temp:	Grow warm, a minimum 64°F (18°C).
Water:	Plenty of water in the summer, almost dry in the dormant period.
Hum:	High, above 60%.
Soil:	Grow in lattice baskets, and keep it well drained with pure rock wool flakes or a mixture of fern roots and peat moss.

Miltonia-hybr. 'Cella Wasserfal'

Mimosa pudica

Leguminosae
Touch-me-not

A small, peculiar plant that folds its leaves immediately at the slightest touch. This only works at temperatures above 64°F (18°C). After a while the leaves reopen to their original position. Light red-purple flowers can appear.
Care: Preferably grown in a greenhouse, because they need high humidity. Feed once every two weeks. Keep indoors only temporarily. Do not keep too cold in the winter. It is often better to grow new plants from seed each year.
Propagation: Sow in March under glass in a warm soil bed. Germination temperature: 68–77°F (20–25°C). Bed out and continue to grow in a moist atmosphere.

Mimosa pudica

Light:	Half shade.
Temp:	Grow warm, not below 64°F (18°C).
Water:	Keep moderately moist.
Hum:	High, above 60%.
Soil:	Standard potting soil.

Monstera adansonii

Araceae

Swiss cheese plant

A species of the genus *Monstera* that has leaves ridden with holes at a young age. As the plants age, the holes become slits, just as with the more popular *Monstera deliciosa*. Often, this plant is still referred to by its old species name, *pertusa*.
Care: This species is somewhat more sensitive than other *Monstera*. So provide a rather high humidity and always grow warm. Give food once every two weeks in the summer.
Propagation: Via top cuttings or eye cuttings, soil temperature 77–86°F (25–30°C).

Light:	Much light to half shade, never full sun.
Temp:	Grow warm, not below 64°F (18°C).
Water:	Keep moderately moist.
Hum:	High, above 60%.
Soil:	Standard potting soil.

Monstera adansonii

Monstera deliciosa

Araceae

Swiss cheese plant

A very popular and strong *Monstera*, which grows in nature as a climber that works its way around trees. Many aerial shoots are formed that root when they touch soil, though these can be cut if desired. Older plants can spread enormously along windows and other places that are not too dark. Full sun, however, is wrong. The white-variegated form needs more light than the green specimen. With too little light, no holes will form in the foliage. With good care, the leaves will become very large and the plant can even bloom with arum-like flowers. Fruits may develop, though this usually only happens in greenhouses.
Care: The plant can remain in a warm room the whole year. Spray the foliage frequently, though. During the growth period, feed once every two weeks. Repot in the spring to get rid of harmful substances that can build up in the soil. The vines need to be tied up in such a way that the leaves receive enough light, but not too much sun.
Propagation: From top cuttings or eye cuttings, soil temperature 68–77°F (25–20°C). Fresh seeds will also germinate.

Light:	Half shade.
Temp:	Grow warm, not below 64°F (18°C).
Water:	Always keep moderately moist.
Hum:	Low to moderate is sufficient, but with high humidity the leaves become much larger.
Soil:	Standard potting soil.

Monstera deliciosa

Monstera deliciosa 'Variegata'

Murraya paniculata

Rutaceae

Small plant for a moderate greenhouse that, nevertheless, with much care, can be grown indoors for a while. The white flowers are fragrant.
Care: These plants need moist air, so spray frequently.
Propagation: From fresh seed or via top cuttings. Soil temperature 86°F (30°C).

Light:	Much light, no bright sun.
Temp:	Grow moderately warm, in the winter a minimum of 54°F (12°C).
Water:	Keep moderately moist with soft water, somewhat drier in the winter.
Hum:	High, above 60%.
Soil:	Permeable and acidic, for instance, coniferous soil.

Murraya paniculata

Musa acuminata

Musa species

Musaceae
Banana

Growing ones own bananas seems a very attractive idea at first, but in reality, nothing much comes of it, indoors, at least. The plants need a lot of space and a humid atmosphere, and would do much better in a large greenhouse. There are various species available: *Musa acuminata*, the dwarf-banana, which cannot be cultivated from seed, but is nevertheless the best species for houseplant cultivation; *Ensete ventricosum* (see above), which can be grown from seed, but is not very suitable for room cultivation; and *Musa* X *paradisiaca*, the cultured banana, also seedless. The species *Musa rosacea* is now categorized as X *paradisiaca*.
Care: In the summer keep in a warm, light spot. Give food weekly when it grows. In the winter the air becomes too dry quickly and there won't be enough light either, at which point the growth stops and the problems begin.
Propagation: Seeds germinate at 68–77°F (20–25°C) under glass. Older plants make ground shoots after blooming that can be removed. This is the only way to propagate the seedless species.

Light:	Much light, older plants full sun, too.
Temp:	Grow warm, in the winter not below 54°F (12°C).
Water:	Keep moderately moist.
Hum:	High, above 60%.
Soil:	Standard potting soil, mixed with fine clay and loam.

Musa rosacea

Mussaenda philippica

Rubiaceae

Tropical plants originally from the Philippines that are completely covered by soft, sticky hairs. The small flowers are surrounded by white bracts.
Care: Has to be grown warm, and can be placed indoors in the summer for a while. Screen against the sun. Feed once every two weeks. Provide plenty of humid air in the winter, perhaps moving the plant to a greenhouse, if possible. Prune back somewhat in the spring, repot and bring back to growth.
Propagation: Root top cuttings under glass at a soil temperature of 77–86°F (25–30°C).

Light:	Much light, no full sun.
Temp:	Grow warm, not below 64°F (18°C).
Water:	Keep moderately moist with soft water.
Hum:	High, above 60%.
Soil:	Standard potting soil mixed with fine clay or loam.

Mussaenda philippica

Myoporum acuminatum

Myoporaceae

Evergreen bush from Australia grown as a container plant in a moderate climate.
Care: The plant can be placed outside from the end of May, very sheltered and in full sun. When it grows, give food once every two weeks. In the fall, before it starts to freeze, bring the plant inside to a light, slightly heated space (such as a cold greenhouse or bedroom) and let it rest dormant there with sparse water. Too much water in the winter is extremely bad. Most of the foliage should remain on the

Myoporum acuminatum

plant. Repot in the spring, keep warmer in April, harden off and bring back to growth.

Propagation: From seed or via top cuttings taken in August; these root at 68–77°F (20–25°C) soil temperature, under glass.

Light: Full sun.
Temp: Grow cool, in the winter 40–50°F (5–10°C).
Water: Keep regularly moist, considerably drier in the winter.
Hum: Moderate, 50–60%.
Soil: Acidic soil, for instance standard potting soil mixed with extra peat moss, leaf soil or coniferous soil.

Myrmecodia echinata

Rubiaceae

Peculiar, epiphytic plant from Southeast Asia, provided with large, thorned tubers. Within these tubers are corridors often inhabited by ants when found in nature. Grow in an orchid greenhouse.
Care: Provide a warm, shaded space with a high humidity. Water regularly with rainwater, so that the roots do not dry out. When the plant is growing, some orchid food can be administered once in a while. A real dormant period is not desired, so the temperature should remain quite high.
Propagation: Older plants can bloom with white flowers and will form seeds after that. This seed germinates easily at 68–77°F (20–25°C) soil temperature.

Light: Much light or half shade, no sun.

Myrmecodia echinata

Temp: Grow warm, during winter nights a minimum of 64°F (18°C).
Water: Keep moist very regularly with soft water.
Hum: High, well above 60%.
Soil: Grow in lattice baskets filled with a mixture of fern roots and sphagnum. It's probably ok to grow in rock wool flakes, but fertilize more in that case.

Myrtillocactus geometrizans

Cactaceae

Columnar cactus with a very regular shape and a beautiful, blue-green tint. Flowers do not appear in our climate.
Care: Keep well lit in the summer. Do not give too much water, and add cactus food once in a while. Do not overdo this, though, because the columns tend to overgrow. In the winter, keep warmer than most other cacti, and on the dry side. Since flowers are not expected, you can keep the plant in a warm room.
Propagation: Take a top cutting from older, branched plants. Allow to dry at first before planting. Fresh seeds will also work. Germination and cutting temperature: 68–77°F (20–25°C).

Light: Full sun.
Temp: Grow warm, in the winter not below 54°F (12°C).
Water: Keep rather dry.
Hum: Low.
Soil: Cactus soil.

Myrtillocactus geometrizans

Myrtus communis

Myrtaceae

Myrtle

The well-known myrtle provides deliciously fragrant flowers, which young brides often wore in their hair. It is a container plant, not a true houseplant.
Care: Myrtle can be outside from the end of May in a sunny, very sheltered location. Give food every two weeks. The flowers appear towards the beginning of fall. Bring it inside before the first frost and let rest dormant in a light space with low temperatures. Ventilate adequately in the spring so that the plant does not start to grow too early, because this foliage will just fall off when you bring the plant outside.
Propagation: Top cuttings taken from non-blooming shoots root in the summer at a soil temperature of 60–68°F (15–20°C). Seeds can be sown, too. Top the young plants frequently for better branching.

Light: Full sun.
Temp: Grow cool, in the winter 40–50°F (5–10°C).
Water: Always keep moderately moist with soft water.
Hum: Moderate, 50–60%.
Soil: Acid potting soil, e.g., standard potting soil mixed with much peat moss or garden peat. Coniferous soil is excellent, too.

Myrtus communis

NANDINA

Nandina domestica

Berberidaceae

An evergreen bush with the foliage of a *Berberis* and the growth pattern of bamboo. A spike with white flowers may appear, followed by red berries. In the fall, the leaves will color. This is a container plant.
Care: Grow outside in a lightly shaded place. Fertilize once every two weeks. In the winter, the plant should be kept dormant and frost free, and watered sparsely.
Propagation: Take top cuttings from side shoots in the fall. Soil temperature 60–68°F (15–20°C) under glass.

Nandina domestica

Light:	Half shade, no bright sun.
Temp:	Grow cool, in the winter frost free to 45°F (7°C).
Water:	Keep moderately moist.
Hum:	Moderate to high.
Soil:	Standard potting soil mixed with loam and clay.

Narcissus hybrids

Amaryllidaceae

Daffodil

Nearly all daffodils can be forced to flower indoors. Only the poet daffodils (of the *poeticus* group) are more difficult.
Care: Most daffodils need a cool rooting period, so plant the bulbs in the fall in bowls or pots and store at 46–50°F (8–10°C). No light should be allowed. (See p. 25 for information on how this works.) The genera 'Grand Soleil d'Or' (yellow) and 'Paperwhite' (white) do not have to be kept in darkness; these can be brought into a warm room immediately, in pots with soil as well as pebbles. Important for all these species and genera is a relatively cool cultivation. The bloom will not last very long in a warm room, which is a pity for all the effort involved. The flowers will last much longer if allowed to bloom in a space that is around 60°F (15°C), for instance a cool bedroom, hallway or corridor. Fertilizer is not needed.
Propagation: Buy new bulbs each year, because the old ones will not survive the winter.

Narcissus 'Paperwhite'

Light:	Half shade, no full sun.
Temp:	Grow cool, for a longer flowering period.
Water:	Keep moderately moist; when cultivating in gravel, the bulbs should not touch the water, thought the roots can.
Hum:	High, above 60%.
Soil:	Standard potting soil.

Narcissus 'Tête à Tête'

Nautilocalyx lynchii

Gesneriaceae

Rather rare, somber plants that can be used as contrast in larger collections because of their deep color. Yellow flowers may appear, but this is not guaranteed.
Care: Just as with most other species of the *Gesneria* family, this plant needs rather humid air, especially in the winter, when this can be a problem. Allow no sunlight and keep the temperature up. When the plant grows, fertilize every two weeks.
Propagation: Root top cuttings under glass at a soil temperature of 68–77°F (20–25°C).

Light:	Much light, no full sun
Temp:	Grow warm, never below 61°F (16°C).
Water:	Keep moderately moist with soft water.
Hum:	High, above 60%.
Soil:	Standard potting soil mixed with perlite for better drainage.

Nautilocalyx lynchii

Nematanthus hybrids

Gesneriaceae

For convenience sake, this plant was previously classified with the genus *Hypocyrta*. By cross-germination, hybrids were created, and by an intergenial hybridization of this

Nematanthus 'Gietvoz'

Nematanthus 'Tropicana'

Neomortonia nummularia

Neoporteria paucicostata

plant with *Codonanthe*, a new genus, X *Codonatanthus*, was introduced. The goal—to achieve larger, longer-lasting flowers in larger numbers—was achieved rather successfully.
Care: Keep light, but avoid bright sunlight. If you do not want flowers, then the plants can be kept darker. They endure dry room air quite well. Give food every 14 days while the plant grows. Keep cooler in the winter; this stimulates their growth. Repot in the spring.
Propagation: Root top and middle cuttings under plastic at a soil temperature of 68–77°F (20–25°C). Cut the tops off of the young plants a few times.

Light:	Half shade or much light, no bright sunlight.
Temp:	Grow moderately warm to warm, in the winter a minimum of 54°F (12°C).
Water:	Keep moderately moist, drier in the winter. Use soft water.
Hum:	Moderate, 50–60%.
Soil:	Coniferous soil or peat moss with perlite. Pots should drain well.

Neomortonia nummularia

Gesneriaceae

A long-lasting, flowering hanging plant from Central America, often sold under the name *Hypocyrta nummularia* or *Alloplectus nummularia*.
Care: Always grow in the shade and provide as high humidity as possible. Greenhouses and plant windows are ideal growing places. Provide plenty of (rain)water and feed every 14 days while the plant grows. In the winter, the temperature may be lowered, which stimulates the forming of new flowerbuds. Repot in the spring.

Propagation: Top cuttings or middle cuttings should be rooted at 68–77°F (20–25°C).

Light:	Much light or half shade, no full sun.
Temp:	Grow warm, in the winter 54–60°F (12–15°C).
Water:	Keep moderately moist with soft water, temporarily drier in the winter.
Hum:	Moderate to high.
Soil:	Acidic permeable soil, for instance bromeliad soil, coniferous soil or a mixture of peat moss and leaf mold.

Neoporteria species

Cactaceae

Spherical-to-elongated cacti with large, wide flowers that open in the spring and early summer. They even bloom if their location is not that sunny. Give cactus food monthly and keep cool and dry in the winter.
Propagation: From seed.

Light:	Much light or full sun.
Temp:	Moderately warm to warm, in the winter almost dry.
Hum:	Low.
Soil:	Cactus soil.

Neoporteria odieri

Neoporteria wagenknechtii

Cactaceae

This series of *Neoporteria* forms flowers whose inner petals do not open completely, and requires different care than the species last described. The bloom is generally in the fall or early spring. Other species within this group are *laniceps, nidus, subgibbosa* and *villosa*.
Care: These plants grow primarily in the fall; therefore, they should not be kept too dry or too cool, otherwise the flowers do not develop. On the other hand, they have to rest dormant in the summer, so give hardly any water then. Allow for much light, though. If the plant blooms in the fall or early winter, the temperature can be lowered, and water is hardly necessary.
Propagation: From seed.

Light:	Full sun.
Temp:	Grow moderately warm to warm, with a dormant period of 46–50°F (8–10°C) in the winter.
Water:	In both dormant and blooming periods, very sparse or nothing at all.
Hum:	Low.
Soil:	Cactus soil.

Neoporteria wagenknechtii

On the following pages: *Neoregelia carolinae* 'Flandria'

NEOREGELIA

Neoregelia concentrica

Neoregelia species

Bromeliaceae

These bromeliads are grown mainly for their beautifully marked leaves. The small, violet flowers are stuck within the cylinder, and often do not arise. The most famous species is the *carolinae*, and its cultivar, 'Tricolor.' The middle part of the leaf is cream-white. The species pictured on the overleaf (pages 286–287) is just the reverse; here the edge of the foliage is whitish.

Care: After the plant flowers, the rosette will eventually die off, as with all bromeliads. But to develop these species's beauty fully, allow plenty of light—though no full sun—and keep budding plants between 72–77°F (22–25°C). Keep cooler during winter.

Propagation: By cultivation of newly sprouted plants; see page 82.

Light:	Half shade or shade.
Temp:	Moderately warm to warm.
Water:	Keep moderately moist.
Hum:	Low; very high, though, for cultivation.
Soil:	Bromeliad soil.

Nepenthes hybrids

Nepenthaceae

Many plants can make vines at the end of their leaves, but with the *Nepenthes* these vine ends develop into a complete beaker, filled with a liquid that attracts insects for consumption. This interesting plant is easy to grow in a warm greenhouse and will act as flycatcher for a while.

Care: This plant needs a humid atmosphere, and should be grown in a greenhouse. Allow no direct sunlight. During growth, give a weak concentration of fertilizer once every two weeks. You can put some insects in the beaker if they do not end up there themselves. The temperature in the winter should not be lowered very much.

Propagation: Leaf cuttings can root in humid sphagnum at a soil temperature of 95°F (35°C).

Light:	Much light, no full sun.
Temp:	Grow warm, if possible all year round at 68–72°F (20–22°C), minimum of 64°F (18°C).
Water:	Keep regularly moist with pure (rain)water.
Hum:	High, above 60%.
Soil:	Preferably in lattice baskets filled with an acidic, very permeable mixture, such as fern roots, sphagnum, peat moss and decayed cow manure.

Nephrolepis exaltata

Nephrolepidaceae

These are probably the most splendid ferns for indoor cultivation. Large specimens are impressive and extremely elegant. They are often grown in shops, hotels, etc. Unfortunately, they do not last long when grown indoors, and depending on the care, can last from two to ten months. Naturally, there are always talented people who can keep them beautiful for several years. In general, the species *exalta* is cultivated, of which numerous cultivars exist, all distinguished by the grooved, curly foliage. Some examples are pictured.

Care: Grow specifically out of the sun and keep the soil very regularly moist. This plant works best in a pot with a watering system. During growth, add a half concentration of

Nephrolepis exaltata 'Bostoniensis'

fertilizer once every 14 days or a pH ion-exchanger in the water. Spray the foliage frequently. Keep somewhat cooler in the winter.

Propagation: By taking the shoots.

Light:	Shade.
Temp:	Grow warm, a minimum of 64°F (18°C).
Water:	Keep very regularly moist with soft water.
Hum:	Moderate to high.
Soil:	A mixture with a calcium deficiency, with, for example, coniferous soil or much peat moss.

Nepenthes-hybr.

Nephrolepis exaltata 'Corditas'

Nephrolepis exaltata 'Rooseveltii'

Nephrolepis exaltata 'Teddy Junior'

weeks. Do not allow the soil to become too cold in the winter, for the plant needs warm roots, while the air remains cool.
Propagation: Root top cuttings of non-blooming shoots in the summer, even in a bottle of water.

Light: Full sun.
Temp: Grow cool to moderately warm, allow dormancy in the winter at 40–50°F (5–10°C).
Water: Moderately moist to almost constantly moist in the summer, somewhat drier in the winter.
Hum: Moderate, 50–60%.
Soil: Standard potting soil.

Nerium oleander

Nertera granadensis
Rubiaceae
Coral moss

A small plant with attractive orange berries, but one that is not easy to keep.
Care: The secret is to grow in a very cool environment. In the summer, the small plant can be placed outside in a shaded location. Give enough (rain)water (do not spill water over the flowers) and feed once every two weeks. Keep cool in the winter. The bloom starts in early spring. The temperature has to stay under 55°F (13°C) all the time. Pollination will occur if you stroke the flowers with a small feather. When the berries start to grow,

Nertera granadensis

the temperature can rise above 61°F (16°C), otherwise the leaves overgrow them. In short, this is not a simple plant to grow, but it should be tried once.
Propagation: By division.

Light: Much light, no full sun.
Temp: Low in the winter, 54–60°F (12–15°C).
Water: Keep moderately moist, always adding directly to the soil.
Hum: Moderate to high.
Soil: Standard potting soil.

Nicotiana X sanderae
Solanaceae
Decorative tobacco

The *Nicotiana*, which is on the market in various colors, is mostly grown in gardens. Flowers appear throughout the summer, when the plant is placed in the shade. The plant is also available for room cultivation. For this purpose, use species that grow very compact.
Care: Grow indoors, not in the full sun, and keep ventilated. This plant will also grow on a balcony if it is not too drafty. Give moderate amounts of water and feed every two weeks. Dispose of it in the fall, because these plants are annuals.
Propagation: Sow under glass from February on. Soil temperature 68°F (20°C). Plant out, continue to grow at 61–64°F (16–18°C), place in its final pot and harden off.

Light: Much light.
Temp: Grow cool.
Water: Keep moderately cool.
Hum: Moderate, 50–60%.
Soil: Standard potting soil.

Nicotiana X sanderae

Nerium oleander
Apocynaceae
Oleander

A plant popular in the Mediterranean region that is also grown as a container plant. There are various tints available with a few single or multiple flowers. The plant is poisonous in all parts.
Care: This plant is easy to grow if you can provide a cool dormant period. The plant can be outside from the end of May. Watch that it does not come out too early in the spring; their shoots are attacked by insects quite often. During the growth period, feed every two

Nerium oleander

Nidularium fulgens

Bromeliaceae

Many of the species previously known under *Nidularium* can now be found under *Neoregelia*. The differences between genera are small, and cultivation is the same for both.

Care: The care mainly concerns the beautiful marked leaves, since the small flowers remain hidden in the plant's cylinder. Give some food once in a while, once a month is sufficient. The rosette dies off slowly, but it can last for months.

Propagation: It is possible to grow new plants from the shoots, which are formed at the base of the plant. For information on this, see page 82.

Light:	Half shade or shade.
Temp:	Moderately warm to warm.
Water:	Keep moderately moist.
Hum:	Moderate, 50–60%.
Soil:	Bromeliad soil.

Nidularium fulgens

Nopalxochia phyllanthoides

Cactaceae

Phyllocactus

For a long time, this plant was named *Phyllocactus*, then *Epiphyllum*, and now *Nopalxochia*. What this means is that each of the frequently grown hybrids are related to

Nopalxochia-hybr. 'Dante'

various genera and species. There are many cultivars on the market and even more created in the greenhouses of private growers. Some are named, while others remain nameless.

Care: Much light is desired, but direct sunlight is not. The plants can go outside in the summer, but should be well protected. Bring inside in the fall and allow the plant to rest dormant at low temperatures and with sparse water. When flower buds are being formed in the spring, do not turn toward the light, for the buds will fall off. Increase the watering amounts carefully. During and after the blooming, add cactus food once every two weeks. When the blooming period is over, shorten the longest shoots and allow the plant to rest dormant again for a few weeks. Then repot and bring to a garden.

Propagation: The removed parts are easy to grow. Allow to dry for a week before planting in a sandy mixture. Roots will even appear in water.

Light:	Much light, no bright sun.
Temp:	Grow cool to moderately warm, 40–50°F (5–10°C) in the winter.
Water:	Keep moderately moist, except during dormancy when the parts are allowed to shrivel a bit.
Hum:	Low to moderate.
Soil:	Add extra sand or perlite to standard potting soil. The pH has to be on the low side, about 5.5–6.0.

Nopalxochia phyllanthoides

Nopalxochia phyllanthoides

Notocactus species

Cactaceae

Spherical or somewhat elongated cactus from the pampas of South America. They are nice even without their flowers, as in the photograph of the species *magnificus*. Here the areoles are connected to one another by a white felt. Some species are lightly thorned, such as the species *graessneri*, while others have a more prominent green cactus body, like *uebelmannianus*. There are a number of beautiful species, all of which are popular with collectors.

Care: These cacti need regular care. They should not be too cold in the winter and the

Obregonia denegrii

lightly thorned species cannot stand bright sun. The soil should never dry out completely. Add some cactus food once a month.
Propagation: From seed, germination temperature 68–77°F (20–25°C).

Light:	Much light; the heavily thorned species full sun, the lightly thorned species screened sun.
Temp:	Grow moderately warm, in the winter 50–54°F (10–12°C).
Water:	Keep moderately moist in the summer, in the winter not completely dry, adding a drop of water once in a while.
Hum:	Low to moderate.
Soil:	Cactus soil.

Notocactus graessneri

Notocactus haselbergii

Obregonia denegrii
Cactaceae

A cactus that deviates from most other cacti by the fact that the nods have almost the makings of a rosette, formed by the small leaves. The flowers are white or very light red.
Care: This is not easy to grow. Half shade is necessary, for full sun is not healthy. The substrate has to be very permeable and should contain hardly any humus. Add food to the water once every two weeks. Allow a dormant period in the winter at low temperatures and withhold almost all water.
Propagation: From seed.

Light:	Half shade, no bright sunlight.
Temp:	Grow moderately warm to warm, in the winter 40–50°F (5–10°C).
Water:	Keep rather dry, almost completely dry in the winter.
Hum:	Low.
Soil:	Cactus soil with the addition of perlite.

Ochagavia carnea
Bromeliaceae

Relatively rare bromeliads that resemble the better known *Hechtia*. In the Mediterranean region, these plants can grow outdoors, where

Notocactus magnificus

Notocactus uebelmannianus

Ochagavia carnea

they bloom effortlessly. This, unfortunately, is not the case in northern regions.
Care: A bromeliad that does not need much water and warmth. They can be grown together with most cacti in the same greenhouse. Add food monthly in the summer, keep cool in the winter and water sparsely.
Propagation: By taking small newly formed plants, or from seed.

Light:	Full sun.
Temp:	Grow cool, in the winter 40–50°F (5–10°C).
Water:	Keep rather dry, almost dry in the winter.
Hum:	Low to moderate.
Soil:	One-third part potting soil, ⅓ part loam and ⅓ part perlite.

Ochna serrulata
Ochnaceae

Small bush from tropical Africa with leathery foliage, a quick-falling flower crown, a calyx that becomes red and lasts a long time, and green fruits, which turn black when ripe.
Care: A plant for a moderate greenhouse. You can place it outside in the summer in a protected location, but watch out for cold nights. Blooming occurs in the spring. Before that, allow for a dormant period, but do not keep it too cool. Give food every 14 days during the growth period.
Propagation: From seed and from top cuttings in August. Soil temperature 77°F (25°C).

Light:	Much light, full sun as well.
Temp:	Grow moderately warm, not below 45°F (7°C) in the summer.
Water:	Keep moderately moist.
Hum:	Moderate, 50–60%.
Soil:	Standard potting soil mixed with clay or loam.

Ochna serrulata

Odontoglossum bictoniense X
X *Odontioda* 'Hans Koch'

X Odontioda

Orchidaceae

The X in front of the name means that this is a cross-hybridization of two genera, in this case *Cochlioda* and *Odontoglossum*. Sometimes one can cross-fertilize a second time, which makes the lineage especially complicated. 'Hans Koch,' pictured, is an example of this process.
Care: The cultivation is similar to that of the *Odontoglossum* species from higher, cooler regions. Keep especially cool in the summer, well shaded and allow fresh air. Spray daily with soft water and add orchid fertilizer to the water every two weeks. With cultivation on pure rock wool, add food at low concentrations every time you water the plant. Allow for a dormant period after the flowering period by giving less water and keeping the plant cooler.
Propagation: By division.

Light:	Shade, never full sun.
Temp:	Grow cool, a minimum of 54°F (12°C).
Water:	Use soft water, keep continuously moist in the summer.
Hum:	High, above 60%.
Soil:	Various mixtures are offered, for instance clay particles with fern roots or pure rock wool.

X Odontocidium

Orchidaceae

Orchids that are created via cross-fertilizations between the genus *Odontoglossum* and *Oncidium*.
Care: Grow relatively warm, not in the bright sun, but allow for much light. Fresh air is favorable, too. The night temperature may drop lower than 63°F (17°C). Give plenty of (rain)water in the summer, though only if it can be drained easily. Keep rather warm in the winter as well, for this is when the plants generally bloom. A dormant period is not needed.
Propagation: By division.

Light:	Much light, no bright sun.
Temp:	Grow moderately warm to warm, daytime around 70°F (21°C), in the winter a minimum of 61°F (16°C).

X *Odontocidium* 'Tiger Hambuhren'

Water:	Keep moderately moist, in summer and winter.
Hum:	High, above 60%.
Soil:	Rock wool flakes.

Odontoglossum bictoniense

Orchidaceae

A species with a very long flower stem and small flowers. The photograph only shows a part of this stem.
Care: This is a relatively strong species that can possibly be grown indoors, provided that it is not too hot during the winter. A warm greenhouse, however, would be more favorable. After the bloom in the fall or winter, allow for a dormant period by giving less water and lowering the temperature somewhat. Repot in the spring and bring back to growth. Spray often, do not cultivate too warm in the summer and fertilize with special fertilizer every 14 days.
Propagation: By division when repotting.

Light:	Shade, never full sun.
Temp:	Grow cool, a minimum of 54°F (12°C).
Water:	Keep well watered and spray frequently during the growth period. Use soft water.
Hum:	High, above 60%.
Soil:	Mixture of clay particles, peat moss, rock wool flakes.

Odontoglossum bictoniense

Odontoglossum pulchellum

Odontoglossum pulchellum

Orchidaceae

A strong orchid that can be grown indoors with some success, at least in the summer. In the winter months, the plant should be kept considerably cooler than 68°F (20°C), the normal room temperature inside a house. Another strong species, *Odontoglossum grande*, is listed in this book under its new name, *Rosioglossum*.
Care: Grow moderately warm in half shade, for example, in an east-facing window. Fertilize once every two weeks during the growing period with special orchid food. After the new pseudotubers are full grown, a dormant period should be provided. The temperature may be lowered and water given less frequently, though not so little that the pseudotubers shrivel.
Propagation: By division.

Light:	Half shade, never full sun.
Temp:	Grow moderately warm, keep at 40–54°F (5–12°C) in the winter.
Water:	Plenty of (rain)water during growth, withhold almost all water during dormancy.
Hum:	Moderate to high.
Soil:	Mainly a mixture of chopped tree fern and fern roots, sometimes mixed with clay particles or peat moss. Grows well in pure rock wool, too.

Olea europaea

Oleacee

Olive

The well-known olive plant is grown for consumption in the countries around the Mediterranean Sea. They can also be grown as container plants in cooler regions. Plenty of flowers and fruits appear, but do not expect any edible olives, since northern summers are too cold for olive cultivation.
Care: If the weather allows, place outside in mid-May in a warm, protected, sunny location. Provide moderate amounts of water and add food once every 14 days. When the first frost arrives, bring inside for a cool dormancy.

Olea europaea

Ventilate especially well in the spring, so that the plant remains cool until at least mid-April.
Propagation: Root top cuttings in the summer at a high soil temperature, 95°F (35°C) under glass. Use cutting powder.

Light:	Full sun.
Temp:	Grow cool to moderately warm, in the winter a minimum of 40°F (5°C). If need be, frost can be endured.
Water:	Keep moderately moist.
Hum:	Low to moderate.
Soil:	Standard potting soil.

Oncidium microchilum

Orchidaceae

Oncidium species can be cultivated in warm, moderate and cold greenhouses, and even as a basic houseplant. This species feels the most at home in a moderate greenhouse. The bloom usually falls in the summer months or in the fall.
Care: This species requires much light, and can stand full sun. But give plenty of water, being careful to avoid stagnation, especially with newly formed shoots. Add food to the water in the growing season, with the quantity depending on the growth medium (see page 75). In the winter, keep cooler and, after the new pseudotubers are full-grown, water very sparsely for a few weeks to achieve good flower development.
Propagation: By division.

Oncidium microchilum

Light:	Much light, screen only against the brightest summer sun.
Temp:	Grow moderately warm, in the winter a minimum of 54°F (12°C).
Water:	Moderately moist in the summer, keep on the dry side during dormancy. Always use soft water.
Hum:	High, above 60%.
Soil:	Chopped tree fern in very well-drained pots. Rock wool flakes work, as well, though these necessitate more frequent fertilization.

Oncidium ornithorhynchum

Orchidaceae

A rather easily grown species, which will even flourish indoors. The flowers smell of vanilla. There are other species of this genus, such as *marshallianum*, but most of them require greenhouse cultivation.
Care: The care of the various species can differ considerably, but the species pictured grows well when it is kept moderately warm to warm. Give plenty of (rain)water in the summer, adding fertilizer once every two weeks. After the bloom falls in autumn, allow for a dormant period. Water sparsely, keeping the pseudotubers from shriveling. The temperature may be lowered. If necessary, repot in the spring and keep warmer.
Propagation: By division.

Light:	Much light, no bright sun.
Temp:	Grow moderately warm, the temperature may be lowered in the rest period to 54°F (12°C).
Water:	Plenty of water in the summer, if it drains well.
Hum:	High, above 60%.
Soil:	Pots that drain well or lattice baskets filled with a special mixture for orchids, such as chopped fern roots with sphagnum, clay particles, etc. Pure rock wool flakes work, as well.

Oncidium ornithorhynchum

Oncidium papilio

Orchidaceae

An orchid for a warm greenhouse resembling the species *kramerianum*. Both plants have small, oval pseudotubers.
Care: Grow lightly shaded in the summer, give plenty of water and spray frequently. Administer food once every two weeks. After the new pseudotubers are full grown, generally in the winter, a dormant period is given by keeping the plant on the dry side. The tubers, though, should not shrivel, and the temperature should not be much lower in this period.
Propagation: By division.

Light:	Shade, no bright sun.
Temp:	Grow warm, in the winter a minimum of 64°F (18°C).
Water:	Give plenty of soft water, keep rather dry in the dormant period.
Hum:	High, above 60%.
Soil:	Grow in pots or lattice baskets with a thick drainage layer of peat moss or clay particles, below a layer of rock wool flakes or organic material.

Oncidium papilio

OPHIOPOGON

Ophiopogon jaburan 'Vittatus'

Ophiopogon jaburan

Liliaceae

Snake beard

A rather unknown but strong and quite attractive houseplant. The variegated 'Vittatus' is prettier (although weaker) than the completely green plant. The plant looks like *Liriope* when in a nonblooming state (see page 268).
Care: If it is misted a bit in the winter, this plant can remain in a heated room all year round, though it can be placed in a considerably cooler spot, too. Furthermore, do not keep it too dark and fertilize every 14 days during the growth period.
Propagation: By taking shoots.

Light:	Much light, no full sun.
Temp:	Grow moderately warm to warm, in the winter a minimum of 40°F (5°C).
Water:	Moderately moist.
Hum:	Moderate, 50–60%.
Soil:	Standard potting soil.

Ophiopogon japonicus

Liliaceae

This species, which stays low, is even stronger than the species discussed previously. In warmer climates, the plant is hardy. The cultivar 'Minor' grows even lower than the common species. It is excellent ground cover in greenhouses.
Care: *O. japonicus* is very suitable for places where not much light enters. In the winter, this evergreen plant has to be kept frost-free. Water moderately in the summer and feed once every two weeks.
Propagation: By division.

Light:	Shade or half shade.
Temp:	Grow cool, in the winter just above 32°F (0°C).
Water:	Keep moderately moist.
Hum:	Moderate, 50–60%.
Soil:	Standard potting soil.

Oplismenus hirtellus 'Variegatus'

Ophiopogon japonicus 'Minor'

Oplismenus hirtellus

Gramineae

A small elegant grass with hanging stalks. The much cultivated cultivar 'Variegatus' has beautiful white-striped foliage, as well.
Care: This plant can stay in a heated room all year round, as long as it is sprayed in the winter. Prune back considerably in the spring, repot and allow to grow again. It is best shown off in a rather large hanging pot.
Propagation: Stalk pieces that are cut off root easily on the nodes at 68°F (20°C) soil temperature.

Light:	Much light, no full sun.
Temp:	Grow moderately warm, in the winter a minimum of 50°F (10°C).
Water:	Moderately moist.
Hum:	Moderate, 50–60%.
Soil:	Standard potting soil.

Opthalmophyllum jacobsenianum

Aizoazeae

These are living "stones" with little openings in the leaves, through which light can reach the tissue underneath. In the dormant period the contracting roots may pull the whole plant under the soil surface. Only a small hole will show where the plant was growing before.
Care: These small plants are highly succulent, so much so that an excess of water could be fatal. The species of this genus grow like *Conophytum*, when grown in the northern hemisphere in the winter. They have to be grown close to the window glass to receive as much light as possible. In the growing period, only sparse water is given. The temperature does not need to be that high. Nitrogen-deficient cactus food is needed at the most once a month. After the blooming, a dormant period occurs, when hardly any water should be given. This withholding should start when the small plants begin to shrivel up.

Opthalmophyllum jacobsenianum

Propagation: From seed.

Light: Full sun.
Temp: Grow moderately warm to war,m in the winter 41–50°F (5–10°C).
Water: Keep rather dry, all dry during dormancy.
Hum: Low.
Soil: Mixture of sifted standard potting soil with sharp sand and perlite.

Opuntia species

Cactaceae

Prickly pear

A very extensive genus of cast-iron cacti, most of which display thorned sections. In nature, they can grow to be very large, and hedges of *Opuntia* are virtually impenetrable. The most dangerous thorns are not even the largest ones. Almost all species also have very small thorns, called glochids. These thorns have hooks and will release from the plant easily. If you get one stuck in your skin, it may be very difficult to pull it out again and this often leads to infection. They say you can only grasp an *Opuntia* with your bare hands once in your life.

On occasion, some species of *Opuntia* will form small cylindrical leaves, which usually drop off quickly because they are not necessary for the plant's survival. The blooms of several of these species are quite large, while others are barely visible.

The cristate forms are very unusual; the growth point is somehow disturbed, resulting in a strange, twisting cactus, such as the very famous *clavarioides* 'Cristata.' These forms can only be propagated vegetatively.

Care: Most forms are easy to grow. They can stay in a living room throughout the whole year; just do not expect any flowers. Also, these indoor plants have a tendency to grow out looking quite ugly. A cool dormancy would help this. Naturally, during the dormant period very sparse water should be given. The cactus body may shrivel somewhat, but not too much. Some species can endure a very cool winter, for instance, *erinacea*, *fragilis*, *humifusa*, *phaecantha* and *polyacantha*, all of which can remain in a garden over the winter. If the soil does not get too wet, then they can survive some amount of frost. Planted out in the full ground of a greenhouse or in large containers, most species can reach considerable sizes. Adding food once every two weeks is sufficient.

Propagation: Cut-off or broken-off parts root relatively easily in a sandy substrate. Allow the parts to dry for a few days, though, otherwise rotting occurs.

Light: Full sun.
Temp: Grow cool to moderately warm, in the winter 40°F (5°C) is enough.
Water: In the summer, moderately moist, during dormancy give very little water.
Hum: Low.
Soil: Standard potting soil for the strong species, cactus soil for the rest.

Opuntia clavarioides 'Cristata'

Opuntia robusta

Opuntia cylindrica var. *cristata*

Opuntia subulata

Opuntia humifusa

Opuntia microdasys 'Albispina'

Opuntia tunicata

Opuntia vestita 'Cristata'

ORBEA

Orbea variegata

Asclepiadaceae

Most plant lovers will know this succulent plant by the name *Stapelia*; however, a number of species have been renamed *Orbea*. The flowers are beautiful, but give off a ghastly small meant to attract flies, which in turn take care of pollination.

Care: The species pictured is the most popular and the strongest of all. One can only kill it by giving too much water, which causes rooting. Therefore, always plant in well drained shallow bowls or pots, or lattice baskets. Keep rather dry in the summer, watering preferably from the bottom. Give cactus food monthly. Provide a dormant period in the winter, adding practically no water, at the most a few drops to prevent the plant from totally drying up. The temperature should be lowered in the winter.

Propagation: Cut off parts, dry for a few days and plant them in sandy soil. From seed is possible as well.

Light: Much light, screen against the brightest sun.
Temp: Grow moderately warm to warm, allow to rest dormant in the winter at 50–60°F (10–15°C).
Water: Keep moderately dry, in the winter almost dry. Use only soft water.
Hum: Moderate to high.
Soil: First, a thick drainage layer of peat moss or clay particles, then a layer of standard potting soil in which the roots grow. Cover with fine gravel to prevent rotting.

Oreocereus celsianus

Oreocereus celsianus

Cactaceae

Rather well-known column cactus with pretty white hairs. The species in the photograph was previously named *Orecereus trollii*. There are several different varieties, and the flowers for all are generally reddish.

Care: In nature, these cacti grow in high-altitude areas, where the temperature falls considerably at night. Therefore, these are less suited for room cultivation than growth in a very cold container or cold greenhouse. In the daytime allow full sun, and at night allow it to cool off to 32°F (0°C). With frost, cover the plant with glass. During growth, add some cactus food once every two weeks.

Propagation: From seed.

Light: Full sun.
Temp: Grow cool, a minimum of 32°F (0°C).
Water: Water sparsely, almost dry in the winter.
Hum: Moderate, 50–60%.
Soil: Cactus soil.

Oreopanax capitatus

Oreopanax capitatus

Araliaceae

Rather rare, but relatively strong houseplants, which can stay indoors the whole year but can be grown as container plants as well.

Care: It is possible to get these plants used to the full sun, but it should happen gradually. In the summer, one can cultivate them outside in a protected location. In the winter, they can stay in a space that is not too warm, but should be sprayed frequently, and fed every two weeks during growth.

Propagation: From top cuttings. Soil temperature 77–86°F (25–30°C), cutting powder is advised.

Light: Much light, full sun, too.
Temp: Grow cool, a minimum of 40°F (5°C).
Water: Keep moderately moist.
Hum: Moderate, 50–60%.
Soil: Standard potting soil.

Ornithogalum thyrsoides

Liliaceae

Chincherinchee

A bulbous growth from South Africa. This plant can grow outside in our climate, but the bulbs are not hardy and so have to be stored frost-free in the winter. Pot cultivation is possible as well.

Ornithogalum thyrsoides

Orbea variegata

Care: Bulbs can be ordered by mail. Pot in April and initially give sparse water. When the plants start to come out, gradually increase the water, and when they really grow, add food every 14 days. At first, the pots should stay inside at 60–68°F (15–20°C). At the end of May they can go outside, and they bloom in the summer. Allow the foliage to die off in the fall by withholding water gradually, and then store the bulbs dry in their pots. The following year, add new soil and bring back to growth.
Propagation: By taking newly formed bulbs.

Light:	Full sun.
Temp:	Grow moderately warm, store bulbs dry at a minimum of 54°F (12°C).
Water:	Moderately moist in the summer, dry in the winter.
Hum:	Moderate, 50–60%.
Soil:	Standard potting soil.

Oroya peruviana
Cactaceae

Oroya peruviana

Bullet-shaped, flat cacti that grow high in the mountains of Peru, at 11,500–13,000 ft (3,500–4,000 m).
Care: Grow very light, right behind a window, keeping it warm in the daytime. At night, the plant needs to cool, so open the window if possible. Keep somewhat more moist than other cacti. The soil should contain more humus, as well. Give cactus food monthly. Keep dry and cool in the winter.
Propagation: From seed.

Light:	Full sun.
Temp:	Grow warm, but cool at night, in the winter 40–50°F (5–10°C).
Water:	Moderately dry to moderately moist.
Soil:	One third part standard potting soil, ⅓ part peat moss and ⅓ part perlite.

Oscularia deltoides

Oscularia deltoides
Aizoaceae

Small, creeping succulent from South Africa that blooms lavishly and is very easy to grow.
Care: Grow warm and sunny, for example, in a window facing south; if very well protected, it can possibly go outside. Do not give too much water and add cactus food monthly. Store cool and quite dry in the winter. Because older plants bloom less, it would be sensible to take cuttings.
Propagation: Allow top cuttings to dry for a while, then plant in sandy soil. Soil temperature of 68°F (20°C).

Light:	Full sun.
Temp:	Grow cool to moderately warm, in the winter a minimum of 40°F (5°C).
Water:	Keep moderately dry, water very sparsely in the winter.
Hum:	Low.
Soil:	Standard potting soil mixed with sharp sand or perlite, in well-draining pots or bowls.

Osteospermum ecklonis
Compositae

Annually grown small plants resembling the more well-known *Dimorphotheca*. They can be grown in a garden, and as a potted plant as well.

Care: Grow sunny, inside or outside. Give food every two weeks. It is possible to keep the plants' dormancy cool and light, which makes them bloom extra-early the following year.
Propagation: Sow from January at a soil temperature of 68–77°F (20–25°C). After germination, plant out, cut off the tops one time for better branching, plant in pots and harden off.

Light:	Full sun.
Temp:	Grow cool, in the winter a minimum of 40°F (5°C).
Water:	Keep moderately moist.
Hum:	Moderate, 50–60%.
Soil:	Standard potting soil.

Osteospermum ecklonis

Oxalis species

Oxalidaceae

Clover sorrel

Oxalis deppei is sold as a good luck clover. It is, in fact, not a great plant for a warm room, for it requires coolness. This plant fares better in a garden, as is the case with the *Oxalis adenophylla* in the photograph. More suitable for indoor cultivation is *Oxalis megalorrhiza*, better known as *O. carnosa*, a species with succulent stems and leaves and yellow flowers.

Care: Purchased tubers should be planted in September, 2 in (5 cm) deep, with the temperature at 43–46°F (6–8°C). After the roots have formed, place in a warmer spot, at 54–57°F (12–14°C). Fertilizer is not necessary if fresh soil is used. After a temporary stay indoors, keep cool again. In May the plant can go outside in a sunny spot.

Propagation: By dividing the tubers.

Light:	Much light, in the summer full sun, too.
Temp:	Grow cool.
Water:	Keep moderately moist.
Hum:	High, above 60%.
Soil:	Soil containing loam.

Oxalis adenophylla

Oxalis deppei

Pachira macrocarpa

Pachira macrocarpa

Bombacaceae

Tropical trees with foliage like that of the chestnut tree. Young plants can be kept indoors.

Care: This plant needs a humid atmosphere, which can create problems in the winter in the form of dropping leaves. Therefore, keep it cooler in the winter, and spray frequently. It can possibly be placed outside, but keep it protected. When the plant becomes too tall, it may be pruned.

Propagation: From seed or via top cuttings. Soil temperature 77–86°F (25–30°C).

Light:	Much light, and it can bet used to sunlight.
Temp:	Grow moderately warm, in the winter a minimum of 54°F (12°C).
Water:	Keep moderately moist.
Hum:	Moderate to high.
Soil:	Standard potting soil mixed with clay or loam.

Pachycereus pringlei

Cactaceae

Columnar cactus that can grow to 40 ft (12 m) high in Mexico, with a yard-wide base. Of

Pachycereus pringlei

course, this is too big for the average living room, but young specimens are decorative enough with their splendid thorns. Flowers do not generally appear.

Care: In summer, keep in a sunny spot, water moderately, and do not feed (or they will grow too fast). In winter, provide a dormant period with lower temperatures and very little water.

Propagation: From seed.

Light:	Full sun.
Temp:	Moderately warm to warm, in the winter a minimum of 40°F (5°C).
Water:	Water sparsely, almost nothing in the winter.
Hum:	Low.
Soil:	Standard potting soil or cactus soil.

Pachyphytum oviferum

Crassulaceae

Succulent plants with very thick, meaty leaves where much moisture can be stored. These plants are related to *Echeveria* and can be cross-fertilized with them quite easily.

Care: The various species are easy to cultivate and can only be destroyed by keeping them too dark or too wet. If they are kept sunny and rather dry, the cultivation will go well. A winter dormant period will be better for the plants' health and will promote the blooming of small flowers on long stems, though they do not have much decorative value.

Propagation: Take some leaves, allow them to dry at least for a week and plant in sandy soil. Soil temperature 68°F (20°C).

Light:	Full sun.
Temp:	Moderately warm to warm, a winter dormant period at 40–50°F (5–10°C) is very healthy.
Water:	Keep moderately dry, during dormancy withhold almost all water (the plant may shrivel a bit).
Hum:	Low.
Soil:	Cactus soil.

Pachyphytum oviferum

Pachypodium species

Apocynaceae

Madagascar palm

Plants that remind one of cacti with leaves. They are not cacti, though, but succulents that collect reserve moisture in their trunks. In periods of drought, they can very easily go without leaves. In rare cases, flowers develop.
Care: A big mistake is to continue watering the plant after it's lost all its leaves. You must introduce a dry dormant period, at the end of which new leaves appear. Only then can you begin giving some water, though never too much. Add low-nitrogen cactus food once a month. You can decide for yourself when the Madagascar palm should rest dormant, for instance, in the winter. When you do, stop watering, lower the temperature and everything will happen as described above.
Propagation: From seed. Germination temperature 86°F (30°C).

Light:	Full sun.
Temp:	Grow moderately warm, in the winter a minimum of 55°F (13°C).
Water:	Keep moderately moist; do not let it dry out completely in the summer, because the leaves will fall off (which is not all bad, see above).
Hum:	Low to moderate.
Soil:	Standard potting soil mixed with fine clay or loam, and sharp sand.

Pachystachys lutea

Acanthaceae

'Pakistani'

A plant reminiscent of *Aphelandra*. Some time ago, it was sold mostly as a curiosity. Now, it is seldom seen, for it proves to be a difficult plant to keep alive.
Care: A humid atmosphere is needed, so spray frequently. Add food once every 14 days. Prune back considerably in the winter and keep cooler. When the plant comes out

Pachystachys lutea

Pachypodium lamerei

again, it will become much taller. This is not the result of meticulous care, but rather because it has not been sprayed with a growth retardant.
Propagation: Take top cuttings from non-blooming shoots. They root at 68–77°F (20–25°C) soil temperature.

Light:	Much light, full sun, too.
Temp:	Grow warm, in the winter, dormancy at 50–60°F (10–15°C).
Water:	Keep moderately moist.

X *Pachyveria haagei*

X *Pachyveria nigra*

Pachypodium saundersii

Hum:	Moderate to high.
Soil:	Standard potting soil.

X Pachyveria species

Crassulaceae

A genus created by cross-fertilization, primarily between *Echeveria* and *Pachyphytum*. The qualities of these species are somewhere in between the two. These are primarily foliage plants, although flowers do often appear.
Care: These succulent plants desire much sun, not too much water and a strict dormant period with no water and low temperatures. But since they are quite strong, some mistreatment can be endured. Do not give much food. Repotting once a year takes care of the need for food, in general.
Propagation: By planting side rosettes, and leaf cuttings as well. Allow cuttings to dry for a few days first.

Light:	Full sun.
Temp:	Grow moderately warm to warm, in the winter 40–50°F (5–10°C).
Water:	Keep moderately dry, almost completely dry in the winter.
Hum:	Low.
Soil:	Cactus soil.

Pandanus utilis

Pandanus species

Pandanaceae

Screw palm

Large, stately plants with sturdy, often striped, leaves that are attached to the trunk in a spiral. Along the edges of the leaves are fine prickles. The two most important species, *P. sanderi* and *P. veitchii*, resemble each other a lot. The strongest species is the *utilis*, shown blooming in the picture, which is actually a rare occurrence.
Care: A humid atmosphere is quite necessary for these plants, therefore spray the leaves frequently in the winter. A real dormant period is not necessary, although lower temperatures can be endured temporarily. Add fertilizer during the growth period every 14 days.
Propagation: When the top shoot is cut off, side shoots will form that can be used for

Pandanus sanderi

cuttings after a while. Soil temperature 68–77°F (20–25°C).

Light:	Much light, no full sun.
Temp:	Grow moderately warm to warm, a minimum of 54°F (12°C).
Water:	Keep moderately moist.
Hum:	Moderate to high.
Soil:	Standard potting soil, if possible mixed with some clay or loam.

Paphiopedilum concolor

Paphiopedilum X *harrisonianum*

Paphiopedilum species

Orchidaceae

Venus shoe

Extremely well-known and beautiful orchids, of which there are numerous species, genera and cross-fertilizations. Some can be cultivated indoors with extra care, although a greenhouse has its advantages, too.
Care: We can distinguish between two species, those with solid green leaves and those species with spotted leaves. The first category can be grown rather cool (moderate greenhouse), the second requires more warmth (warm greenhouse). The plants do not form pseudotubers, which indicates that a strict dormant period is not necessary. Always avoid bright sunlight, but do not keep the plants too dark, either. The pots have to drain well, and soft water is necessary for a healthy plant. The humidity should always be high, but the strongest species can survive indoors with frequent spraying. In the summer, administer some orchid food or other fertilizer in low concentrations once every 14 days.
Propagation: By division.

Light:	Half shade, no full sun.
Temp:	The all-green species, moderately warm, in the winter a minimum of 54°F (12°C). The spotted species, warm, in the winter a minimum of 64°F (18°C).
Water:	Keep moderately moist with soft water.
Hum:	High, above 60%.
Soil:	Traditionally, a mixture of equal parts fern root and sphagnum. But other substrates are possible, too, such as pure rock wool.

Paphiopedilum insigne

Paphiopedilum rothschildianum

Parodia aureispina

Parodia mutabilis

Passiflora caerulea

Parodia maassii var. *suprema*

Parodia species

Cactaceae

Rather small, spherical cacti that can produce huge flowers at an early age. There are many magnificent species, most of which are easy to grow. The thorns are closely spaced and they are woolly.

Care: Place in full light in the summer, but take care that it does not get too warm with frequent ventilation. Do not give too much water and administer cactus food every 14 days. Watch to make sure the soil does not dry out completely in the summer. In the winter, allow for dormancy, but keep the plant a little warmer than most other cacti.

Propagation: From seed. Seedlings grow very slowly the first time. By grafting them onto a base trunk that does not grow very fast, the seedlings' growth can be improved. Most species, though, grow well on their own roots.

Light:	Full sun.
Temp:	Grow moderately warm, in the winter 40–50°F (5–10°C).
Water:	Keep moderately moist, only a few drops in the winter.
Hum:	Low.
Soil:	Cactus soil.

Parthenocissus inserta

Vitaceae

Climbing plant from the grape family that can be grown outdoors, too. Another species, *P. henryana*, has a smaller leaf with white markings along the veins; this one cannot survive frost.

Care: An easy plant to care for, but one that has to be kept especially cool in the winter, not in a strongly heated room. During the growth period, add food once every 14 days. Pruning is always possible. Provide support if you want the plant to grow against a wall. Spray the foliage frequently.

Propagation: Root top cuttings in the summer at 68–77°F (20–25°C) soil temperature under glass. Cut off the tops of young plants a few times.

Light:	Full sun to half shade.
Temp:	Grow cool, in the winter the temperature can be as low as 32°F (0°C).
Water:	Keep moderately moist.
Hum:	Moderate, 50–60%.
Soil:	Standard potting soil.

Parthenocissus inserta

Passiflora alata

Passiflora species

Passifloraceae
Passion flower

A plant with extraordinarily striking flowers. The species *caerulea* is extremely strong and can be grown outdoors in milder conditions against a south-facing wall. Big orange fruits will appear then. The fruits of the species *alata*, which can only be grown in a greenhouse, are quite delicious.

Care: When cultivating indoors, place the plants in a well-lit spot and keep them cool in the winter. The dormant period is important for good blooming. In greenhouses, the plants may be planted out in the full ground. The vines can reach the top of a greenhouse over the long term. Cut back the side vines in the spring. Feed weekly during the growth period.

Propagation: Root top cuttings at 68–77°F (20–25°C) soil temperature under glass.

Light:	Much light, and the plant can be made to get used to full sun (when it is grown outside).
Temp:	Grow cool, in the winter a minimum of 40°F (5°C) (*P. caerulea* possibly lower, *P. alata* a minimum of 60°F [15°C]).
Water:	Keep moderately moist.
Hum:	Moderate to high.
Soil:	Standard potting soil.

Passiflora violacea

PAVONIA

Pavonia multiflora

Pavonia multiflora

Malvaceae

A small tropical bush with striking flowers. The red calyx leaves appear around the almost-black flower calyx.
Care: Not a strong houseplant, for it requires a high relative humidity. Spray frequently in the summer, do not place it in bright sunlight and feed every two weeks. Grow especially cooler in the winter, which automatically increases the humidity. Repot in the spring and prune.
Propagation: Root top cuttings at 86–95°F (30–35°C) soil temperature under glass. Use cutting powder.

Light:	Much light, no full sun.
Temp:	Grow moderately warm to warm, in the winter a minimum of 54°F (12°C).
Water:	Keep moderately moist.
Hum:	High, above 60%.
Soil:	Acidic potting soil, such as coniferous soil.

Pedilanthus tithymaloides

Euphorbiaceae

A peculiar plant with zig-zag-branching and curled foliage. Its poisonous latex marks it as a member of

Pedilanthus tithymaloides 'Variegata'

the *Euphorbia* family. The pictured form 'Variegata' is almost the only one cultivated.
Care: Grow warm the whole year and allow a lot of light, but screen against the bright afternoon sun. Give food every 14 days during the growth period. In the winter the temperature can fall a few degrees, but this is not necessary.
Propagation: Cut off top cuttings, immerse in warm water to solidify the latex, dry for a day and plant. Soil temperature 77°F (25°C).

Light:	Much light, no full sun.
Temp:	Grow warm, a minimum of 64°F (18°C).
Water:	Keep moderately moist.
Hum:	Low to moderate.
Soil:	Standard potting soil.

Pelargonium X blandfordianum

Geraniaceae
Foliage geranium

One of the many fragrant foliage geraniums, as these plants are called. Small flowers can appear, but this doesn't happen very often. The finely divided foliage of this cross-fertilization smells of musk.
Care: Can stay indoors all year, sunny or lightly shaded. Feed once every two weeks in the summer. The plant would appreciate a dormant period in the winter. Take a cutting once in a while, for older plants tend to become rather ugly and unwieldy.
Propagation: Very easy from top cuttings or middle cuttings. Allow cuttings to dry for a day.

Light:	Full sun to half shade.
Temp:	Grow cool to moderately warm, in the winter a minimum of 50°F (10°C).
Water:	Keep moderately moist, drier in the dormant period.
Hum:	Low to moderate.
Soil:	Standard potting soil.

Pelargonium X *blandfordianum*

Pelargonium X *citrosmum*

Pelargonium X citrosmum

Geraniaceae
Lemon geranium

A cross-fertilization with leaves that smell strongly of lemon. With careful cultivation, pretty flowers may appear.
Care: Grow sunny, giving moderate amounts of water during growth, and fertilize every two weeks. Keep as cool as possible in the winter, so that the plant stops growing. Administer less water then, too. Prune considerably in the spring if you want, and bring back to growth. Often, new plants can be grown from cuttings.
Propagation: Top cuttings and middle cuttings root easily after having dried for a while.

Light:	Full sun.
Temp:	Grow cool to warm, in the winter a minimum of 50°F (10°C).
Water:	In summer moderately moist, drier in winter.
Hum:	Low to moderate.
Soil:	Standard potting soil.

Pelargonium crispum

Geraniaceae
Foliage geranium

The variegated forms are especially beautiful foliage geraniums. These, too, smell of lemon.
Care: Grow in a well-lit spot to preserve the variegated leaf markings. The plant can be kept

Pelargonium crispum 'Queen of Lemons'

warm the whole year, but it would be better to provide a dormant period in the winter. Give moderate amounts of water in the summer and feed every two weeks. Cut back in the spring if desired and, of course, repot.
Propagation: Easy from top cuttings or middle cuttings. Dry first, then plant.

Light:	Full sun, or half shade.
Temp:	Grow cool to warm, in the winter a minimum of 50°F (10°C).
Water:	Keep moderately moist, drier in the winter.
Hum:	Low to moderate.
Soil:	Standard potting soil.

Pelargonium endlicherianum

Geraniaceae

An attractive species from Turkey, where it grows out of limestone.
Care: This plant can be kept outside in the summer if it does not rain too much. Do not give too much water and feed monthly. Keep under glass in the winter and water very sparsely, otherwise rotting will occur.
Propagation: Take top cuttings, dry well and plant.

Pelargonium endlicherianum

Light:	Full sun.
Temp:	Grow cool to moderately warm, in the winter 40–50°F (5–10°C).
Water:	Keep moderately moist, very sparsely in the winter.
Hum:	Low to moderate.
Soil:	Permeable and rich in calcium, for instance a mixture of perlite, sharp sand and rough clay soil.

Pelargonium X fragrans

Geraniaceae

A simple geranium that smells of nutmeg. The pictured genus, 'Variegatum,' has colored leaf edges.
Care: Grow light and sunny, outside or inside in the summer. Give moderate amounts of water and feed every two weeks. Keep rather dry and cool in the winter.

Pelargonium X fragrans 'Variegatum'

Propagation: Very easy from top cuttings or middle cuttings. Dry them first, then plant without any additional soil warmth.

Light:	Full sun.
Temp:	Grow cool to warm, in the winter a minimum of 40–50°F (5–10°C).
Water:	Moderately moist in the summer, rather dry in the winter.
Hum:	Low to moderate.
Soil:	Standard potting soil.

Pelargonium grandiflorum hybrids

Geraniaceae
French geranium

A group of cross-fertilizations with large, soft, all-green leaves and big flowers. They resemble azaleas a bit. These species are also known as *Pelargonium X domesticum*.
Care: These geraniums with large flowers are less suitable for cultivation outside. They bloom most splendidly when grown in a window or in a greenhouse. Flower buds are formed under the influence of a short day (day length less than 12 hours), or long days when the temperature remains steady at 46°F (8°C). The blooming can be forced by additional artificial lighting and a small rise in temperature to 60°F (15°C). To keep the plants small, spray them with growth-retardant substances. Without any artificial stimulation, the plants generally bloom in May. Give moderate amounts of water and feed weekly. Keep cooler

Pelargonium grandiflorum-hybr.

in the winter and keep rather dry. Repot in the spring and bring back to growth. In this way, one can grow large specimens.
Propagation: Top cuttings root easily in a sandy mixture. Allow the cuttings to dry for a day. August is the best cutting time. The rooted plants need to rest dormant and bloom the following year. If you strike cuttings later, use cutting powder.

Light:	Much light, full sun as well.
Temp:	Grow moderately warm, in the winter a minimum of 40°F (5°C).
Water:	Moderately dry to moderately moist, taking care that the water does not stagnate.
Hum:	Moderate, 50–60%.
Soil:	Standard potting soil, possibly with some extra lime and some sharp sand or perlite to make the mixture permeable.

Pelargonium graveolens 'Variegatum'

Pelargonium graveolens

Geraniaceae
Rose geranium

This is, in fact, a foliage geranium that is grown for its beautiful, fragrant foliage. In general, the most often-grown species is the white-edged form 'Variegatum.' Light purple flowers may appear.
Care: This is an extremely strong plant, which can stay in a warm room the whole year and will only die if one forgets to water it. However, if it is more convenient, the plant can be kept cooler in the winter. And by pruning it regularly, the plant will remain compact. Do not give too much food, otherwise it will grow even more than it already does without chemical help.
Propagation: Very easy from top cuttings.

Light:	Full sun to half shade.
Temp:	Grow moderately warm, in the winter a minimum of 40°F (5°C).
Water:	Moderately moist to relatively dry, rather dry during cool dormancy.
Hum:	Low to moderate.
Soil:	Standard potting soil.

Pelargonium radens

Pelargonium Zonale-hybr. 'Mrs. Pollock'

Pelargonium radens

Geraniaceae

Lemon geranium

The name is somewhat confusing, for many geraniums smell of lemon. This species has dissected leaves, which some think smell of earth or fungus.

Care: A powerfully fragrant plant that primarily produces leaves, but sometimes even flowers if its dormancy has been cool enough. It can stay in a warm room the whole year, but in this case the plant continues to grow and no flowers will appear. Give food every two weeks in the summer. Preferably keep cool in the winter. Cut back in the spring and repot.

Pelargonium Zonale-hybr. 'Frank Headly'

Propagation: Top cuttings and middle cuttings root easily when they are put in sandy soil after drying for a few days. Extra soil warmth is not needed.

Light: Much light or full sun.
Temp: Grow cool to moderately warm, in the winter 46–54°F (8–12°C).
Water: Moderately moist in the summer, keep rather dry in the dormant period.
Hum: Low to moderate.
Soil: Standard potting soil.

Pelargonium zonale hybrids

Geraniaceae

The most famous geraniums, recognized by the brownish ring on the leaves. There are numerous genera; nowadays, they are most often grown from seed (the so-called F1 hybrids). These hardy genera are primarily meant for garden and balcony cultivation. In some advanced collections exceptional forms, such as cultivars with splendidly colored leaves, with dissected foliage and with originally shaped flowers or tints are formed.

Care: Grow very light in the summer and water moderately. Add some food once every two weeks. Remove old flowers. Keep cool and rather dry in the winter. In general, strike cuttings in August, and then let young plants rest dormant; old ones can be thrown out. The dormant species can become very impressive the following year or even in their third year. Trunk forms can be grown as well, and this process is described on page 83.

Propagation: Via top cuttings from non-blooming shoots, preferably taken in August. Allow them to dry for a day and plant in a sandy mixture. 68°F (20°C) soil temperature is sufficient.

Pelargonium Zonale-hybr. 'Stadt Bern'

Light: Much light, full sun, too.
Temp: Grow moderately warm, in the winter a minimum of 40°F (5°C).
Water: Do not give too much water and provide drainage. The *Pelargonium* is somewhat succulent and therefore can endure drought. Withhold almost all water in the winter.
Hum: Low to moderate.
Soil: Standard potting soil is good enough, but the addition of some extra lime would help.

Pellaea falcata

Pellionia pulchra

Pentas lanceolata

Pellaea species

Sinopteridaceae

A relatively strong house fern. The most well-known species is *rotundifolia*, which has round, leathery leaves. There are species with triangular and elongated leaves, too, such as *Pellaea falcata*, shown above.

Care: This fern can stand dry air in a heated room rather well. Still, it would be beneficial to lower the temperature in the winter somewhat and spray the foliage frequently. Direct sunlight should always be avoided. Grow the plant in shallow but wide bowls or pots, or in lattice baskets. During the growth period, feed every two weeks in half concentrations.

Propagation: By division and by sowing the spores.

Light: Shade.
Temp: Grow moderately warm, in the winter preferably 54–60°F (12–15°C).
Water: Keep very moist regularly.
Hum: Moderate, 50–60%.
Soil: Humus and air mixture with some lime, for instance, leaf soil of beech trees.

Pellaea rotundifolia

Pellionia species

Urticaceae

Small ground covers, from Vietnam and surrounding regions, of which the two species

pictured occur most often. They grow very well in large plant containers.

Care: These plants really need humid air. This can become a problem, especially in the winter. Spray them frequently and possibly lower the temperature. Give fertilizer during the growth period once every 14 days.

Propagation: Root top cuttings at 77°F (25°C) soil temperature under glass.

Pellionia repens

Light: Much light to half shade, never bright sunlight.
Temp: Grow warm, a minimum of 54°F (12°C).
Water: Keep moderately moist with soft water.
Hum: High, above 60%.
Soil: Flat, well-drained pots or bowls filled with standard potting soil, mixed with extra peat moss or coniferous soil.

Pentas lanceolata

Rubiaceae

A rather rare but nice plant that can be grown best in a greenhouse. The colors of the flowers may vary from white to red-purple.

Care: Keep well lit, but avoid direct sunlight. Keep moist on a regular basis and add food to the water every 14 days. Make sure the pots drain very well. During the blooming, which usually falls in the autumn, the plant can be moved to a rather cool space. After that it should be moved to a moderate greenhouse for dormancy.

Propagation: Root young shoots in the spring at soil temperature 68–77°F (20–25°C). Cut off the tops of young plants a few times so that they branch better.

Light: Much light, no full sun.
Temp: Grow moderately warm, in the winter 54–60°F (12–15°C).
Water: Keep regularly moist with (rain)water. Keep somewhat drier after the plant blooms.
Hum: High, above 60%.
Soil: Standard potting soil mixed with fine clay or loam.

Peperomia argyreia

Piperaceae

One of the most striking species with peltate, hollow foliage, which is marked white between the veins. The small, thin, white spikes are the plant's flowers, from which almost every *Peperomia* can be recognized.

Care: Avoid bright sunlight. Give water carefully, the plants are half succulent and can easily receive too much too soon. Water should not remain in the tray beneath the plant. Warm the water a bit in the winter. One can grow the plants in lattice baskets as well. The temperature should not be much lower in the winter. When the plant grows, give food every 14 days.

Propagation: From leaf cuttings. Cut off a leaf with a small piece of the stalk, allow to dry for a day and plant in a sandy, permeable mixture. Soil temperature 68–77°F (20–25°C). Take care that the cutting does not start to rot (water first with a substances that prevents fungus).

Light: Much light, no full sun.
Temp: Grow moderately warm, a minimum of 54°F (12°C).
Water: Keep moist on a very regular basis with soft water.
Hum: Moderate to high.
Soil: An acidic mixture, for instance standard potting soil mixed with peat moss, coniferous soil, etc.

Peperomia argyreia

Peperomia caperata

Peperomia caperata

Piperaceae

A species with small, all-green, strongly wrinkled leaves. There are some variations. For instance, the cultivar 'Tricolor' has white leaf edges that are reddish at the base. This plant blooms effortlessly.
Care: They can endure quite a lot of shade, at least the green species. Give water carefully, and during the growth period give food every two weeks. Allow the plant some coolness in the winter, but it can remain in a heated room, too.
Propagation: Via leaf cuttings. Soil temperature 68–77°F (20–25°C).

Light:	Half shade to shade.
Temp:	Grow moderately warm, a minimum of 54°F (12°C).
Water:	Keep moist very regularly, with water that's not too cold.
Hum:	Moderate, 50–60%.
Soil:	Extra acidic, permeable potting soil.

Peperomia fraseri

Piperaceae

This is the *Peperomia* species with the nicest flowers, which are quite fragrant as well. These were previously called *resediflora*. The foliage is dark green.

Peperomia fraseri

Care: The plant endures much shade and therefore it can thrive in a window facing north. Keep continuously moist with lukewarm water. Add food to the water once a month in the summer. In the winter the plant can be kept a bit cooler, but it can stay in a heated living room as well.
Propagation: Root leaf cuttings at a soil temperature of 68–77°F (20–25°C).

Light:	Shade.
Temp:	Grow moderately warm, a minimum of 54°F (12°C).
Water:	Keep moderately moist with soft water.
Hum:	Moderate, 50–60%.
Soil:	Coniferous soil or standard potting soil with much peat moss.

Peperomia griseoargentea

Piperaceae

The strongly knobbed leaves are metallic gray. Small flowers are plentiful, appearing on very narrow, long spikes.
Care: Place in an area slightly lighter than for the species with dark green foliage. A window facing east or west is excellent. Add water carefully, never too much or too cold. Adding too little water is not as harmful as adding too much, for all *Peperomia* are somewhat succulent. Add fertilizer monthly in the growth period. In the winter the temperature can fall, but the plant can also stay in a heated room.
Propagation: Root leaf cuttings at 68–77°F (20–25°C) soil temperature.

Light:	Half shade, no full sun.
Temp:	Grow moderately warm, a minimum of 54°F (12°C).
Water:	Keep moderately moist with rainwater.
Hum:	Moderate, 50–60%.
Soil:	Acidic potting soil, bromeliad soil is sufficient, too.

Peperomia griseoargentea

Peperomia incana

Peperomia incana

Piperaceae

A species that is easy to recognize by its white velvety foliage.
Care: Do not place in sunlight, but grow quite light. Do not ever add cold water and avoid spilling on the leaves, because this will cause spots. Give fertilizer every two weeks while the plant grows. The temperature in the winter can be lowered, but this is not necessary.
Propagation: Via leaf cuttings or middle cuttings. Soil temperature 68–79°F (20–25°C).

Light:	Much light, no sun.
Temp:	Grow warm, in the winter a minimum of 54°F (12°C).
Water:	Keep moderately moist with soft, lukewarm water.
Hum:	Moderate, 50–60%.
Soil:	Acidic, permeable potting soil, for instance coniferous soil or bromeliad soil.

Peperomia obtusifolia

Piperaceae

A variegated species that is grown frequently, especially in the forms 'Greengold' and 'USA,' on which the markings are clearer.
Care: Because these plants have less chlorophyll, they have to be kept considerably light-

Peperomia obtusifolia

er than the dark green species, though full sun is too much. If they are kept in too dark a spot, then the foliage will turn a pale green. Add food to soft water once a month in the summer. In the winter the plant can be placed in a cooler spot, but this is not really necessary.
Propagation: Top cuttings or middle cuttings. Soil temperature 68–77°F (20–25°C).

Light:	Much light, no full sun.
Temp:	Grow moderately warm, a minimum of 54°F (12°C).
Water:	Keep moderately moist.
Hum:	Moderate, 50–60%.
Soil:	Acidic, permeable soil, for instance standard potting soil with extra peat moss, bromeliad soil, etc.

Peperomia puteolata

Peperomia pereskiifolia

Piperaceae

A species recognized at first by its vertical, and later more dropping, red-brown stems and green leaves, on which three lighter veins are visible. The species *blanda* looks very much like *pereskiifolia*, but its leaves have five veins, and the underside of the leaf is reddish. The species *puteolata* differs in its square stems and even more clearly marked veins.
Care: Grow out of the sunlight, and give food every two weeks during growth. In the winter, the temperature can fall, but do not allow the plant to cool off too much.
Propagation: From top cuttings. Strike just below a node, allow to dry for a day and plant in sandy soil. Soil temperature 68–77°F (20–25°C). No plastic cover is necessary.

Peperomia pereskiifolia

Light:	Half shade to shade.
Temp:	Grow moderately warm, a minimum of 54°F (12°C).
Water:	Give water on a very regular basis, but not to excess. Preferably use rainwater.
Hum:	Moderate, 50–60%.
Soil:	Extra acidic, airy and well drained.

Peperomia rotundifolia

Piperaceae

Previously, this plant was known as *Peperomia prostrata*, and is characterized by small round leaves on weak, thin stems. This is a perfect hanging plant, which soon covers the entire pot.
Care: *Peperomia* is suitable as a hanging plant, for they do not readily dry out when one forgets to water them. An excess of water is more deadly than a deficiency. Do not hang the pot in the sun and mist the foliage once in a while, especially in the winter. The temperature can be lower in the winter, but this is not absolutely necessary. Give food every two weeks in the growing season.
Propagation: Cut stems in pieces, allow to dry and plant. Even loose leaves with a piece of stem are able to root well. Soil temperature 68–77°F (20–25°C).

Light:	Half shade to shade.
Temp:	Grow moderately warm, a minimum of 54°F (12°C).
Water:	Not too much, keep rather dry during the cool dormancy.
Hum:	Moderate, 50–60%.
Soil:	Acidic and permeable, for instance coniferous soil with peat moss and some standard potting soil.

Peperomia rotundifolia

Peperomia serpens

Piperaceae

A peculiar hanging plant. In general, the yellow-spotted cultivation form 'Variegata' is most widely available.
Care: Grow in hanging pots or lattice baskets that drain well and are adequately sized. The location should not be sunny, but by growing it in the dark the variegation gets lost. A light-screened window facing south or east is suitable. Give food every two weeks in the growing season.
Propagation: Roto middle cuttings at 68–77°F (20–25°C) soil temperature.

Light:	Much light, no full sun.
Temp:	Grow moderately warm, a minimum of 54°F (12°C).
Water:	Keep moderately moist with soft, lukewarm water.
Hum:	Moderate, 50–60%.
Soil:	Coniferous soil or bromeliad soil.

Peperomia serpens 'Variegata'

Pereskia aculeata

Pereskia aculeata

Cactaceae

A rarity among the cactus family, a bush with leaves. Only here and there are scattered thorns visible, indicating that this is a unique plant. There are flowers as well, but these seldom appear in cooler climates. The cultivar 'Godseffiana' has yellowish foliage.
Care: Grow sunny and rather warm. Do not give too much water, but do not keep it too dry either, otherwise the leaves will fall off. Give fertilizer once a month. In the winter the plant may lose its leaves, indicating a dry dormant period is desired.
Propagation: Root top cuttings in the summer at soil temperature 68–77°F (20–25°C).

Light:	Full sun.
Temp:	Grow moderately warm to warm, in the winter 50–60°F (10–15°C).
Water:	Keep moderately moist, drier in the winter.
Hum:	Low to moderate.
Soil:	Standard potting soil in pots that drain well.

Perilepta dyeriana

Perilepta dyeriana

Acanthaceae

Tropical foliage plant with surprisingly beautiful markings. Unfortunately, they are difficult to keep indoors.

Care: A humid atmosphere is very important; only in the summer, when the heat can remain off, can the plant stay indoors with some success. Give moderate amounts of water and feed once every two weeks. In the winter, keep in a greenhouse. Pinch new slips regularly, because older plants lose their beauty.
Propagation: Top cuttings form roots under glass at a soil temperature of 77°F (25°C).

Light:	Much light, no bright sun.
Temp:	Grow warm, not below 64°F (18°C).
Water:	Keep moderately moist with soft water.
Hum:	High, even above 60%.
Soil:	Standard potting soil with extra peat moss or coniferous soil.

Peristrophe hyssopifolia

Acanthaceae

Small foliage plant from Java, especially beautiful in the variegated form 'Aureovariegata.' The small purple flowers are quite nice, too.
Care: Always grow warm and humid, ideally planted in a greenhouse or vitrine. Add fertilizer in the summer every two weeks. Strike slips often, because only young plants are pretty.
Propagation: Top cuttings form roots under glass at a soil temperature of 77–86°F (25–30°C).

Light:	Much light, no full sun.
Temp:	Grow warm, not below 64°F (18°C).
Water:	Keep moderately moist with soft water.
Hum:	High, above 60%.
Soil:	Standard potting soil.

Peristrophe hyssopifolia 'Aureovariegata'

Pernettya mucronata

Eriaceae

Small evergreen bushes with lovely colored berries. They are, in fact, garden plants, but not always completely hardy when planted outside. Therefore, they are often sold as small houseplants, too.
Care: Always place inside as cool as possible, and not in the bright sun. It can go outside in

Pernettya mucronata

the summer, in a garden or on a balcony. Give moderate amounts of (rain)water and feed once every two weeks. It is not worth the trouble to keep the bushes alive over the winter. Because the plants are deciduous, there needs to be a male present to fertilize the female bush; moreover, insects are needed to transport the pollen. With indoor cultivation, it is improbable that fruit will appear the second year.
Propagation: Top cuttings taken in August–September, root after some time in sandy, unheated soil.

Light:	Half shade, no full sun.
Temp:	Grow cool, in the winter 32–40°F (0–5°C).
Water:	Keep moderately moist with soft water.
Hum:	Moderate, 50–60%.
Soil:	Acidic humusy soil, for instance standard potting soil mixed with peat moss.

Persea americana

Lauraceae

Avocado

The pits of the avocado fruit are easy to grow and make nice plants for the home. One should not expect them to bear fruits, however.

Persea americana

Care: They will suffer somewhat in the winter because the air becomes too dry for them, so spray frequently or lower the temperature. Add food every two weeks in the growing period. Do not use water rich in calcium, otherwise the pH becomes too high and the plant will get chlorosis.

Propagation: Germinate a seed of an avocado in moist potting soil. Soil temperature 68–77°F (20–25°C). After germination, plant the seed in a pot, grow warm at first and then harden off.

Light: Much light, full sun as well.
Temp: Grow moderately warm to warm, in the winter a minimum of 50°F (10°C).
Water: Keep moderately moist.
Hum: Moderate to high.
Soil: Standard potting soil mixed with at least ⅓ part fine clay, loam or rock-powder.

Phaius tankervilleae

Phaius tankervilleae

Orchidaceae

A genus of terrestrial (soil-growing) orchids, of which the pictured species is the strongest and most popular. The flowers appear in the spring or early summer.
Care: Always grow warm and provide for much light, but screen against bright afternoon sun. Give orchid food in the growing period once every 14 days. After the new pseudotubers are full grown, a dry dormant period of three to four weeks has to be observed. Temperatures of 46°F (8°C) can be endured for a short period. Repot immediately after the plant blooms.

Propagation: By division.

Light: Much light, no full sun.
Temp: Grow war, normal winter temperatures not below 60°F (15°C).
Water: Plenty of (rain)water, especially in the summer, if the pot can drain well.
Hum: High, above 60%.
Soil: Mixture of ⅓ part rough clay or loam, ⅓ part decayed cow manure and ⅓ part chopped tree fern. Put this in plastic pots on a thick drainage layer of clay particles or pottery shards.

Phalaenopsis species

Orchidaceae

These species are the most popular orchids, at least as cut flowers. Many brides decorate their bouquets with white *Phalaenopsis* hybrids. These hybrids have all kinds of tints and colors, while pure species are only found in advanced collections.
Care: These plants have no pseudotubers, so water can only be collected in the thick leaves. For this reason, a strict dormant period is not

required. On the other hand, the temperature does have to be lower in the winter, which means that less water is needed then. Make sure that the water always drains well by putting a thick drainage layer in the bottom of the pot, or by growing on pure rock wool. In that case, during the growth period one should always add some fertilizer to the water. With use of a natural substrate, feeding once every 14 days is enough. The plants can also be grown on pieces of tree fern or in lattice baskets. Repotting is needed only once every year, preferably in May. From March on, the plants should be placed in shade at high relative humidity. In the summer, give plenty of

soft water, provided it drains well. In the winter allow for some sun.
Propagation: By division and from seed.

Light: Much light, but no sun in the summer. In the winter allow as much light as possible.
Temp: Grow moderately warm to warm, in the winter a minimum of 54°F (12°C).
Water: Use only rain or soft water.
Hum: High, quite above 60%.
Soil: Traditionally a mixture of tree ferns, osmundine, etc. Nowadays peat moss, clay particles and rock wool flakes are used more and more.

Phalaenopsis amboinensis 'Zauberrose'

Phalaenopsis-hybr. 'Lippstadt'

Phalaenopsis-hybr. 'Fifi X Marquise'

Phalaenopsis-hybr. 'Munsterland'

Philesia magellanica

Philesia magellanica

Liliaceae

A rather unknown evergreen container plant from southern Chile. It does not thrive in temperate regions, but is a real beauty when it blooms.

Care: It can be placed outside in the summer, protected and not too sunny. A humid atmosphere is important, therefore spray often. Water plentifully and fertilize once every two weeks. In the winter, move the plant into a cold-to-moderate greenhouse and keep drier, but not so dry that the leaves fall. Repot in the spring. If necessary, prune after the plant blooms.

Propagation: Top cuttings root slowly at 60–68°F (15–20°C) soil temperature.

Light:	Much light, no sun.
Temp:	Grow cool, ideally 50–60°F (10–15°C) over the whole year. Minimum 46°F (8°C).
Water:	Keep moderately moist, drier in the winter.
Hum:	High, above 60%.
Soil:	Decayed beech leaves with some old cow manure and loam.

Philodendron bipennifolium

Araceae

A strong, climbing species with heart-shaped, indented shiny leaves. With too little light, the

Philodendron bipennifolium

foliage becomes small and straight. This was previously called *panduriforme*.

Care: This is a strong plant that can remain indoors the whole year. Try to provide a humid atmosphere in the winter, when the temperature can be lowered, but not too much. In the summer, add fertilizer once every 14 days.

Propagation: Top cuttings or eye cuttings root at 68–77°F (20–25°C) soil temperature under glass or plastic.

Light:	Half shade to much light, but never bright sun.
Temp:	Moderately warm to warm, in the winter a minimum of 57°F (14°C).
Water:	Always keep moderately moist.
Hum:	Moderate, 50–60%.
Soil:	Standard potting soil.

Philodendron elegans

Araceae

A climbing species with aerial roots and noticeably dentate leaves. It makes a strong houseplant.

Philodendron elegans

Care: This plant can stay in a warm room the whole year, as long as it's protected against the bright sun. A window facing east is very favorable. In the growing period, give food every two weeks. Newly formed vines should be tied up carefully along the window. Repot in the spring and prune if necessary.

Propagation: Top cuttings and stalk cuttings root easily at 68°F (20°C) soil temperature, at least when you plant some aerial roots along with them in the soil.

Light:	Much light to half shade.
Temp:	Grow warm, in winter nights a minimum of 57°F (14°C).
Water:	Keep moderately moist.
Hum:	Low to moderate.
Soil:	Standard potting soil.

Philodendron erubescens

Araceae

An often-grown species with shiny leaves in an elongated heart shape. There are mainly cultivars in popular cultivation, such as the 'Emerald

Philodendron erubescens 'Emerald Queen'

Queen,' pictured, and the more reddish 'Red emerald.' Variegated forms exist, too.

Care: A strong plant, due in part to the shiny leaves, which do not evaporate so much water. It can remain indoors all year, although in the winter the air usually becomes too dry. So spray often with soft water or install a vaporizer. Give food once every two weeks in the growing season. Plants that grow well will have to be repotted each spring. In the winter, the temperature should be lowered, but not much, because they are, in fact, tropical plants.

Propagation: From top cuttings or eye cuttings. Soil temperature 68–77°F (20–25°C).

Light:	Half shade to much light, but never full sun.
Temp:	Grow moderately warm to warm, a minimum of 57°F (14°C).
Water:	Keep moderately moist.
Hum:	Moderate, 50–60%.
Soil:	Standard potting soil.

Philodendron melanochrysum

Araceae

Often called *Philodendron andreanum*, it's a climbing species with large, hanging leaves. When they first come out, they are reddish, later turning a velvety green. 'Melanochrysum' is the younger form, with short heart-shaped leaves; the adult form, 'Andreanum,' has elongated leaves. Both foliage forms can often be found on the same plant.

Philodendron melanchrysum

Care: Grow warm the whole year. Spray the foliage frequently and avoid direct sunlight. Give food every two weeks in the growing period. Support the vines as they grow.
Propagation: From top cuttings or eye cuttings, soil temperature 68–77°F (20–25°C).

Light: Much light to half shade, no sun.
Temp: Grow warm, not below 57°F (14°C).
Water: Keep moderately moist.
Hum: Moderate to high.
Soil: Standard potting soil.

Philodendron pedatum

Araceae

A strong and much cultivated species with lobed leaves. The leaf stalks are not hairy. It is called *laciniatum* as well.
Care: Can be kept in a warm room, but not in the bright sun. When left in a dark spot, the leaves will become very small and straight. In the growing period, give food every two

Philodendron pedatum

weeks. Spray the foliage, if the winter air is too dry. Tie up the vines very well for support.
Propagation: From top cuttings or middle cuttings. Soil temperature 68–77°F (20–25°C).

Light: Much light or half shade, no sun.
Temp: Grow warm, not below 57°F (14°C).
Water: Keep moderately moist.
Hum: Low to moderate.
Soil: Standard potting soil.

Philodendron rugosum

Araceae

A lesser known, but beautiful and strong *philodendron*, with magnificent texture to the leaves.
Care: Do not place in the direct sun, but grow warm all year, keeping the plant a bit cooler in the winter. Give some fertilizer once every two weeks in the growing period.
Propagation: From top cuttings or eye cuttings; soil temperature 68–77°F (20–25°C).

Light: Much light or half shade, never bright sun.

Philodendron rugosum

Temp: Grow moderately warm to warm, in the winter a minimum of 57°F (14°C).
Water: Keep moderately moist.
Hum: Moderate, 50–60%.
Soil: Standard potting soil.

Philodendron sagittifolium

Araceae

Pictured is the cultivar 'Ilsemannii,' often looked upon as merely a young form of *P. sagittifolium*, but also as an independent species *ilsemannii*. The plant has little chlorophyll, so to preserve the pretty markings, make sure to grow the plant in good light.
Care: It can be cultivated the whole year in a warm room, but is not so easy to keep as most other species. The need for light is great, but bright sun is absolutely inappropriate. Mist when the air is dry. Give food once every two weeks in the growing season.
Propagation: From top cuttings or eye cuttings. Soil temperature 68–77°F (20–25°C).

Light: Much light, no full sun.
Temp: Grow moderately warm to warm, in winter nights a minimum of 57°F (14°C).
Water: Keep moderately moist.
Hum: Moderate to high.
Soil: Standard potting soil.

Philodendron sagittifolium 'Ilsemannii'

Philodendron scandens

Philodendron scandens

Araceae

A busy climber with relatively small, heart-shaped leaves. This is a very strong species that is quite popular.
Care: It can stay in a warm room all year, although the temperature may be reduced some in the winter. Give sufficient support to the vines, or allow the plant to hang or crawl. During growth, add fertilizer once every two weeks.
Propagation: From top cuttings or eye cuttings. Soil temperature 68–77°F (20–25°C).

Light: Half shade, full shade, too.
Temp: Grow moderately warm to warm, a minimum of 57°F (14°C).
Water: Keep moderately moist.
Hum: Low to moderate.
Soil: Standard potting soil.

Philodendron selloum

Araceae

A species that differs a bit from other *Philodendron*, for it does not grow as a liana (woody long-stemmed plant). The leaves are heart shaped and strongly curved.
Care: These leaves are less leathery than those of the other species; therefore, there is a greater need for a humid atmosphere. So spray frequently, especially in the winter and/or lower the temperature. Feed once every two weeks in the summer.
Propagation: From seeds, which germinate at 68–77°F (20–25°C). Grow young plants at 72°F (22°C).

Light:	Much light to half shade, never full sun.
Temp:	Grow moderately moist, a minimum of 61°F (16°C).
Water:	Keep moderately moist.
Hum:	Moderate to low.
Soil:	Standard potting soil.

Philodendron selloum

Philodendron squamiferum

Araceae

A liana (woody long-stemmed plant) with long shoots that need to be well supported. The scaly red leaf stalks are very beautiful.
Care: The plant grows best when placed in half shade, for example in a window facing east. Avoid the afternoon sun. It can be kept warm the whole year, but the temperature may also be lowered in the winter. Spray the foliage frequently and fertilize every 14 days during the growth period.
Propagation: From top cuttings or eye cuttings. Soil temperature 68–77°F (20–25°C).

Philodendron squamiferum

Light:	Half shade.
Temp:	Grow moderately warm to warm, a minimum of 64°F (18°C).
Water:	Keep moderately moist.
Hum:	Moderate, 50–60%.
Soil:	Standard potting soil.

Philodendron tuxtlanum

Araceae

Also called *tuxtla*, after a place in the vicinity of Veracruz, Mexico, where the plant was discovered in 1959.
Care: This is one of the strongest species for warm room cultivation. While full sun cannot be endured, quite a lot of shade can. Give food once every two weeks in the growing season. Spray the foliage often in the winter or provide higher humidity in another way.
Propagation: From seed. Seeds germinate at 68–77°F (20–25°C) soil temperature. After about six weeks, plant out and after another six weeks plant them in the final pot before hardening off.

Light:	Half shade, no full sun.
Temp:	Grow warm, not below 64°F (16°C).
Water:	Keep moderately moist.

Philodendron tuxtlanum

Hum:	Moderate, 50–60%.
Soil:	Standard potting soil.

Phlebodium aureum

Polypodiaceae

An extremely strong house fern with blue-green foliage and a gold-colored scaled root-

Phlebodium aureum 'Areolatum'

Phlebodium aureum 'Mandaianum'

stock. There are some cultivars such as 'Mandaianum' with wavy, indented leaves, and others such as 'Areolatum' with foliage that is only wavy, not dentate, as shown.
Care: Its leathery leaves do not allow as much moisture to evaporate as most other ferns', and it is therefore very suitable for the dry air found indoors. Keeping the soil moist is very important. Give fertilizer once every 14 days in the growing season.
Propagation: By dividing the rootstocks.

Light:	Half shade to shade, never full sun.
Temp:	Grow moderately warm to warm, a minimum of 61°F (16°C).
Water:	Keep moist regularly.
Hum:	Low to moderate.
Soil:	Standard potting soil.

Phlebodium aureum

Phoenix canariensis

Palmae

Canary date palm

An extremely strong palm for indoor cultivation. The leaves stand straight up and are hard and stiff. Young plants are imported from regions around the Mediterranean, where they are grown outside.
Care: This plant can be placed outside in the summer, even in the full sun. It will thrive indoors, too, if not placed in too dark a spot. A cool dormant period at a considerably lower temperature is important for good plant

health. Give food once every two weeks during the growing season.
Propagation: From seeds, which have to be soaked before planting.

Light:	Much light, full sun as well.
Temp:	Grow cool, 40–50°F (5–10°C in the winter.
Water:	Keep moderately moist, completely immerse in water once in a while.
Hum:	Moderate, 50–60%.
Soil:	Standard potting soil mixed with fine clay or loam or rock powder, in shallow pots or buckets.

Phoenix roebelenii

Palmae

This looks like the last species, but grows less stiffly and the foliage feels softer.
Care: This palm needs more warmth than the *P. canariensis*. For that reason, it can stay in a warm room all year in a light, but not too sunny, spot. Spray the foliage frequently, at least in the winter, when the temperature can be lower as well. During the growth season, feed once every two weeks.
Propagation: From seed, or by division.

Phoenix roebelenii

Light:	Half shade or much light, no full sun.
Temp:	Grow moderately warm to warm, in the winter a minimum of 61°F (16°C).
Water:	Keep moderately moist.
Hum:	Moderate, 50–60%.
Soil:	Standard potting soil, possibly mixed with clay or loam.

Phormium tenax

Liliaceae
New Zealand flax

A grass-like plant from New Zealand that is also grown as a container plant. Older plants may bloom with a yard-high stalk. Often, white-variegated or yellow-variegated varieties are grown, and cultivars with brown-red foliage as well.

Phoenix canariensis

Care: Place outside from the end of May, protected and sunny or lightly shaded. Keep the soil constantly moist, for these are originally littoral plants (plants grown at water's edge). Feed each week. Keep light and cool in the winter. Light frost can be endured if it does not last that long.
Propagation: By division.

Light:	Much light, full sun as well.
Temp:	Grow cool, in the winter store at 40–50°F (5–10°C).
Water:	Keep constantly moist in the summer, drier in the winter.
Hum:	Moderate, 50–60%.
Soil:	Standard potting soil mixed with at least ⅓ part clay or loam.

Phormium tenax 'Aureomarginatum'

Phyllanthus angustifolius

Euphorbiaceae

Interesting plants that do not possess any leaves, but leaf-like wide stalks, called phylloclades. Small reddish flowers appear along the edges, and are not very remarkable.
Care: These are, in fact, plants for growth in a warm greenhouse because they require such a high relative humidity. A dormant period, or lowering of temperature, is not needed. If one keeps the plant indoors, then spray often in the winter. Do not give too much water, for this is a half succulent. Avoid the sun. Give food monthly during the growth period.

Phyllanthus angustifolius

Propagation: Stalk cuttings root at a soil temperature of 86°F (30°C) under glass. Sowing is possible, too.

Light:	Half shade, no bright sun.
Temp:	Grow warm, a minimum of 64°F (18°C).
Water:	Keep rather dry.
Hum:	High, above 60%.
Soil:	Standard potting soil.

Phyllitis scolopendrium

Aspleniaceae
Tongue fern

A quite hardy fern. The forms with curled foliage, such as the 'Cristatum' in the photograph, are grown especially for indoor cultivation.
Care: Grow cool and shady, for instance in a window facing north. Keep cooler in the winter, otherwise there will be problems resulting from the low humidity. During the growth period, administer food every 14 days. Grow the plant preferably in a pot with a watering system.
Propagation: The common tongue fern from spores, the cultivated forms by division.

Light:	Shade.
Temp:	Grow cool, a minimum of 37°F (0°C).
Water:	Keep very regularly moist.
Hum:	High, above 60%.
Soil:	Standard potting soil.

Phyllitis scolopendrium 'Cristatum'

Pilea species

Urticaceae
Artillery plant

The name artillery plant is derived from the fact that some species shoot pollen off forcefully, as soon as a blooming plant is moistened somewhat. Species and cultivars with strongly bubbled foliage, as the photographs show, are most often available.

Care: This small plant originated in tropical regions, which indicates that it has a need for humid air. When grown indoors, it usually does well until the heat is turned up, which causes the plant to wilt because of the increase in dry air. To quickly pinch off a slip is often the only way to regain beautiful plants the following year. Feed during the growth period every 14 days and make sure that the water does not stagnate in the pot. Do not spray too much water on the leaves, for this may cause spots.

Propagation: Top cuttings root quite easily at 68°F (20°C) soil temperature.

Light:	Much light, no full sun.
Temp:	Grow moderately warm to warm, in the winter a minimum of 54°F (12°C).
Water:	Keep moderately moist with soft water, and provide drainage.
Hum:	High, above 60%.
Soil:	Standard potting soil mixed with coniferous soil or leaf mold.

Pilea crassifolia 'Moon Valley'

Pilea cadierei 'Minima'

Pilea spruceana 'Norfolk'

Pinguicula moranensis

Lentibulariaceae
Crassula

A delicate succulent species. The sticky leaves catch insects, which are then digested.

Care: Just like most carnivorous plants, this succulent requires a shady, cool spot and a very humid atmosphere. Therefore, the plants are often grown in cold storage, covered with moist moss. Do not spill water on the leaves. Fertilizer is not needed, if enough insects are caught. Keep especially cool and somewhat drier in the winter.

Propagation: From leaf cuttings.

Pilea microphylla

Pilea spruceana 'Silver Tree'

Pinguicula moranensis

Light: Half shade, no sun.
Temp: Grow cool, in the winter 46–50°F (8–10°C).
Water: Keep constantly moist, somewhat drier in the winter.
Hum: High, above 60%.
Soil: Acidic, humusy soil, for instance peat moss with some sharp sand.

Pinus pinea 'Silver Crest'

Piper crocatum

Pisonia umbellifera 'Variegata'

Pinus pinea 'Silver Crest'

Pinaceae
Pine

This conifer was introduced a few years ago. I bought a specimen two years ago, kept it in a window, and it has since taken on a bonsai-like form. This plant is interesting in that it produces longer needles, seemingly wanting to expire, then reconsiders and begins forming shoots with short needles.
Care: Hard to believe, but this plant can stay in a warm room all year. It should be placed in a sunny window and watched so that the soil does not dry out completely, or the needles will fall off. When the plant grows give food every two weeks. With the right pruning, an interesting form can be achieved, as in the photograph.
Propagation: Root top cuttings under a mist of water at 77°F (25°C) soil temperature.

Light: Full sun.
Temp: Grow moderately warm to warm, a minimum of 40°F (5°C).
Water: Keep moderately moist.
Hum: Low to moderate.
Soil: Standard potting soil.

Piper crocatum

Piperaceae
Pepper

There are a lot of pepper plants, some of which are grown for their small fruit. The black pepper, *Piper nigrum*, is a climber with sturdy, leathery, dark green foliage. It can grow indoors as well as in a greenhouse. An especially beautiful species is the *Piper crocatum* in the photograph, often confused with *Piper ornatum* from Sulawesi

(Celebes). The latter has a rounder leaf, though, which is spotted more delicately.
Care: The beautifully marked foliage needs much light to stay magnificent, but not from direct sunlight. Give food every two weeks in the growth period. Keep cooler in the winter and let the plant rest dormant in a moderate greenhouse.
Propagation: From top cuttings or eye cuttings. Soil temperature 68–77°F (20–25°C). Cover with glass.

Light: Much light, no bright sun.
Temp: Grow moderately warm to warm, a minimum of 54°F (12°C).
Water: Keep moderately moist, possibly with rainwater.
Hum: High, above 60%.
Soil: Standard potting soil, mixed with leaf mold or coniferous soil.

Pisonia umbellifera

Nyctaginaceae

This plant is still sometimes called *Heimerliodendron*. Most widely cultivated is the cultivar 'Variegata' (pictured), with variegated foliage.
Care: Care is similar to that for a *Ficus*, so keep warm the whole year. Much light is necessary to keep the foliage nicely variegated, but avoid direct sunlight. Spray the leaves frequently in the winter or make the atmosphere extra moist in another way. When the plant grows add some fertilizer to the water.

Propagation: Root top cuttings and eye cuttings at a soil temperature of 77°F (25°C) under glass.

Light: Much light, no full sun.
Temp: Grow warm, a minimum of 64°F (18°C).
Water: Keep moderately moist.
Hum: Moderate, 50–60%.
Soil: Standard potting soil.

Pistia stratiotes

Araceae
Watercress

A floating plant that proliferates in the tropics' waterways. It can grow indoors in a shallow container.
Care: The water has to be kept at one continuous temperature and the plant needs light, but not full sun. Use shallow bowls or pots that allow the roots to reach the bottom. When you use glass containers, there is a danger of considerable algae growth. Fertilizing is not necessary.
Propagation: By division and from seeds, which are formed in the autumn. Keep the seeds in water and allow to germinate in the spring at 86°F (30°C) water temperature.

Light: Much light or half shade, no full sun.
Temp: Grow warm, water and air temperature 68–77°F (20–25°C).
Water: The plant floats on water.
Hum: Moderate to high.
Soil: None.

Pistia stratiotes

Pittosporum crassifolium

Pittosporum species

Pittosporaceae

Bushes with leathery, often shiny leaves and white, fragrant flowers that resemble the flowers of an orange tree. They are all container plants, and require a cool dormancy.

Care: If possible, grow outside in the summer on a sunny, protected terrace. Give food every 14 days and take care that the soil does not ever dry out. Before any night frost arrives, bring the plants inside for a cool dormancy, preferably in a greenhouse, with moderate lighting. Ventilate well when the temperature seems too high.

Propagation: Root top cuttings in August at a soil temperature of 77–86°F (25–30°C) under glass. The deciduous species can be grown from seed as well.

Light: Full sun.
Temp: Grow cool, in the winter 40–50°F (5–10°C).
Water: Keep moderately moist.
Hum: Moderate to high.
Soil: Standard potting soil.

Pittosporum tenuifolium 'Sunburst'

Pittosporum tobira

Pittosporum tobira 'Variegatum'

Pittosporum undulatum

Platycerium bifurcatum

Polypodiaceae
Buckhorn fern

A strong and quite popular fern that flourishes when hung on a wall in a warm room, largely because of a gray protective layer that covers the leaves and limits evaporation. If this layer is rubbed off, the plant will soon suffer.

Care: Never place in the sun. Place in rather big pots and water by taking the plant and fully immersing it. Add some fertilizer to the water during the growing season. Allow it to

Platycerium bifurcatum

drain and hang again. The pots should drain well. Lattice baskets are an excellent choice.

Propagation: By removing the shoots or by sowing the spores.

Light: Half shade to shade, never full sun.
Temp: Grow warm, in the winter the temperature can be lowered to 54°F (12°C), or even lower if the plant is dry.
Water: Keep moist on a very regular basis.
Hum: Low to moderate.
Soil: Coniferous soil.

Plectranthus coleoides

Labiatae

A nice plant with fresh, white-edged leaves, suitable for a cool room. This plant could easily be confused with *Plectranthus strigosus* 'Elegance,' and also with *Glechoma hederacea* 'Variegata' (variegated ground ivy).

Care: The plant can be outside in the summer without a problem, even in the full sun. But it is not hardy, so eventually bring it inside. Provide as a cool dormancy as possible, or

keep the plant warm and clip slips for growing new plants the following year. During the growth period, give food every two weeks.
Propagation: Top cuttings root easily, even without extra soil warmth.

Light: Much light, full sun, too.
Temp: Grow cool, a minimum of 40°F (5°C).
Water: Keep constantly moderately moist.
Hum: Moderate, 50–60%.
Soil: Standard potting soil.

Plectranthus coleoides 'Marginata'

Plectranthus fruticosus

Plectranthus fruticosus

Labiatae
Rheumatism plant

A vigorously growing plant with small violet flowers. Some people maintain that the presence of this plant in a room lessens rheumatic suffering. If it works, great.
Care: This plant is easy to grow and can remain indoors the whole year. Give moderate amounts of water in the growing period and feed once every two weeks. The temperature can be lowered somewhat in the winter. Because older plants tend to lose their beauty, it would be sensible to strike slips at least once a year.

Propagation: Top cuttings root very easily, even without soil warming or glass cover.

Light: Half shade or full sun.
Temp: Grow moderately warm to warm, in the winter a minimum of 54°F (12°C).
Water: Keep moderately moist.
Hum: Moderate, 50–60%.
Soil: Standard potting soil.

Plectranthus oertendahlii

Labiatae

A small creeping plant with oval leaves that are tinted white along the veins. Suitable as ground cover in plant containers or as a hanging plant.
Care: Screen against bright sunlight and spray frequently, more so in the winter, when the temperature can be lowered. Give food every two weeks in the growing period. When

Plectranthus oertendahlii

the plant starts to become ugly, clip some slips quickly and begin again.

Light: Half shade or much light, no bright sun.
Temp: Grow cool to moderately warm, a minimum of 54°F (12°C).
Water: Keep moderately moist.
Hum: Moderate to high.
Soil: Standard potting soil.

Pleione bulbocodioides

Orchidaceae

A beautiful orchid that is rather difficult to grow. It is sometimes sold for garden cultivation but also as a houseplant. These plants have pseudotubers, which means that they require a strict dormant period.
Care: Plants that are ordered by mail have to be kept inside after planting until foliage appears. Only give rainwater (but not excessively), and grow cool. Keep from the sun and mist frequently. In the growth season, fertilize lightly. Keep drier in the fall until all the leaves die off, then store the remains dry and frost free in the pot.
Propagation: By taking the small pseudotubers that form above the old ones during the summer.

Light: Half shade to shade.
Temp: Grow cool, in the winter a minimum of 40°F (5°C).
Water: Only in the summer keep moderately moist with soft water.
Hum: High during growth, above 60%.
Soil: Mixture of tree fern, chopped peat moss, clay particles, and a bit of cow manure in pots that drain very well.

Pleione bulbocodioides

Plumbago auriculata

Plumbago auriculata

Plumbaginaceae
Lead plant

This blue blooming lead plant is the most famous and most easily grown species of *Plumbago*, usually available as a container plant. Often it is still referred to by its old name, *Plumbago capensis*.

Care: Grow outside in the summer in a very protected spot. Screen only against the brightest afternoon sun. Support the long vines by winding them around a hoop. Give food every two weeks. Bring inside in the fall and continue to keep in a moderately warm space. When the winter comes, the plant can go in a cold greenhouse or other cool space. Repot in the spring and bring back to growth, but not too soon.

Propagation: Take half-ripe top cuttings in June. Soil temperature 68–77°F (20–25°C).

Light:	Much light, screen only against the brightest afternoon sun.
Temp:	Grow cool, in the winter a minimum of 40°F (5°C).
Water:	Keep moderately moist, somewhat drier in the winter.
Hum:	Moderate, 50–60%.
Soil:	Mix standard potting soil with fine clay or loam.

Plumbago indica

Plumbaginaceae

This species is more sensitive than the container plant described above, and is more a greenhouse plant than a houseplant.

Plumbago indica

Care: Grow preferably in a greenhouse, lightly shaded. It can possibly be grown indoors during the summertime. Water moderately during the growth period and give food every two weeks. Provide high humidity. Keep cooler in the winter and take special care in the spring that the plant does not come out too early.

Propagation: Strike slips from tops that have new shoots in the spring, and maintain a soil temperature of 68–77°F (20–25°C) under glass.

Light:	Much light, screen against the brightest sun.
Temp:	Grow moderately warm to warm, not below 55°F (13°C).
Water:	Keep moderately moist in the summer, drier in the winter.
Hum:	Moderate to high.
Soil:	Standard potting soil with at least ⅓ part clay or loam.

Podocarpus macrophyllus
Podocarpaceae

In a mild climate, this conifer can be grown in a garden, but when it gets really cold in the winter, it should be protected. It makes an excellent container plant as well, growing outside in the summer and inside during the winter, when the actual growth is limited.

Care: Grow outside in a protected, sunny, somewhat shaded location from the end of May. Add some food to the water every two weeks. By pruning, one can give it a distinct, personal shape. Bring inside in the autumn, but not too early; it can survive one night of frost.

Propagation: From seed or top cuttings, which root under glass at a soil temperature of 77°F (25°C).

Podocarpus macrophyllus

Light:	Much light, full sun, too.
Temp:	Grow cool, in the winter just frost free.
Water:	Keep moderately moist, drier in the winter.
Hum:	Moderate, 50–60%.
Soil:	Standard potting soil, possibly mixed with some loam or clay.

Polianthes tuberosa

Agavaceae
Tuberose

A tuberous plant, grown mainly for the strong smell of its flowers. Larger mail-order companies sometimes still carry them.

Care: After receiving the tubers in the spring, put them in pots; normally, three will fit in a pot

Polianthes tuberosa

6 in (15 cm) wide. Temperature: 54–60°F (12–15°C). After they sprout, start carefully giving water, gradually adding more. Do not allow the temperature to go up too much, otherwise the plants become too long. It takes about five months before they bloom. Give fertilizer every two weeks in the summer. Throw the tubers away in the fall; old tubers generally yield bad results.

Propagation: In principal, possibly by newly formed tubers, but in temperate climates, the cultivation is often not very successful. For that reason, the tubers have to be imported from warm countries.

Light:	Much light, full sun, too.
Temp:	Grow moderately warm.
Water:	Keep moderately moist during growth.
Hum:	Moderate, 50–60%.
Soil:	Standard potting soil.

Polyscias species

Araliaceae

Trees and bushes from the tropics. Nowadays the stocks can be imported, after which they sprout and root in a greenhouse. After that, the plants are made available to consumers. Unfortunately, they do not agree with dry indoor air very much. The species and cultivars with fine, dentate foliage are the weakest.

Care: Do not place in the full summer sun, and add food every 14 days till around mid-August. In the winter, place in a cooler spot and keep drier, although not so dry that the leaves start coming off. Repot in the spring and bring back to growth.

Propagation: Top cuttings root in the spring at 77–86°F (25–30°F) soil temperature under glass.

Light:	Half shade, never full sun.
Temp:	Grow moderately warm to warm, a minimum 60°F (15°C).
Water:	Keep moderately moist with soft water.
Hum:	High, above 60%.
Soil:	Standard potting soil mixed with fine loam or clay.

Polyscias balfouriana 'Pennockii'

Polystichum tsus-simense

Polystichum tsus-simense

Aspidiaceae

A rather hardy house fern that can survive without much warmth.

Care: The species pictured is most successful in a cool, shaded place in the house. Give water very regularly, preferably rainwater. Fertilize weekly with food in half concentrations. Keep rather cold in the winter; if this is not possible, then spray frequently.

Propagation: By division and by sowing the spores.

Light:	Shade to half shade, never full sun.
Temp:	Grow cool, in the winter a minimum of 40°F (5°C).
Water:	Water very regularly and grow preferably in a pot with a watering system.
Hum:	Moderate, 50–60%.
Soil:	Standard potting soil.

Polyscias filicifolia

Porphyrocoma pohliana

Acanthaceae

Relatively rare plants for a moderate greenhouse. The small violet flowers fall rather quickly, but the red bracts remain beautifully colored for weeks.

Care: Always provide humid air and light shade. Keep sufficiently moist in the growth season and feed weekly. In the winter the temperature can be lowered. Prune in the spring if necessary and bring back to growth again.

Propagation: Root top cuttings of young shoots under glass at 68–77°F (20–25°C). Cut off the tops of young plants a few times for better branching.

Light:	Much light, no full sun.
Temp:	Grow moderately warm, in the winter a minimum of 54°F (12°C).
Water:	Keep moderately moist, drier in the winter.
Hum:	High, above 60%.
Soil:	Standard potting soil, possibly mixed with some loam or clay.

Porphyrocoma pohliana

Polyscias quilfoylei 'Victoriae'

PORTULACA

Portulaca grandiflora

Portulaca grandiflora

Portulacaceae

Rose moss, ornamental purslane

A small garden plant and, in fact, a member of the edible purslane family. It proves to be very suitable for a sunny place indoors. A number of colors are available, single as well as full-blooming varieties.
Care: Grow preferably in a hanging basket in a very light, sunny spot. Temporary drought can be survived, and in any case avoid giving too much water. Add some food every two weeks. Dispose of the plant after the summer, for this plant is an annual.
Propagation: Sow from March in soil at 68–77°F (20–25°C) under glass. Plant and continue to grow warm.

Light:	Much light, as well as full sun.
Temp:	Grow warm.
Water:	Keep moderately moist.
Hum:	Low to moderate.
Soil:	Standard potting soil.

Portulacaria afra

Portulacaceae

Elephant bush

A bush from South Africa, which grows there up to 10 ft (3 m) high. There are few stalks, and the leaves are small and meaty. Its small, light red flowers are not very significant.

Portulacaria afra

Care: Grows without any effort in a light place indoors and can be easily pruned into a bonsai-like shape. Do not give too much water and certainly not too much fertilizer. Keep cool in the winter and on the dry side.
Propagation: From top cuttings, which have to dry first.

Light:	Full sun.
Temp:	Grow moderately warm, keep around 50°F (10°C) in the winter.
Water:	Keep rather dry, somewhat drier in the winter.
Hum:	Low.
Soil:	Mix standard potting soil with sharp sand and clay or loam.

Primula X kewensis

Primulaceae

A cross-fertilization between *Primula floribunda* and *Primula verticillata*, suitable for growth as a houseplant. The flowers appear early in the spring. These plants are not cultivated very often.
Care: Like all primroses, grow cool, so that the bloom lasts longer. Give plenty of water and feed every two weeks in half concentrations, for these plants are very sensitive to salt. Preferably use soft water or rainwater. One could try to keep these plants alive through the winter by placing them in a garden after they bloom and then bringing them inside the following winter to a cool space. However, it is much easier to grow new plants from seed.
Propagation: In July, one can begin sowing for a blooming in the following year. Soil temperature: 60°F (15°C). After germination, plant the young plants outside, in a cool spot without much sun. Cover them with glass in the fall and continue to grow at around 50°F (10°C).

Primula X kewensis

Light:	Much light, no sun.
Temp:	Grow cool, a minimum of 40°F (5°C).
Water:	Keep moderately moist.
Hum:	Moderate to high.
Soil:	Extra acidic potting soil, such as the mixture for *Calceolaria*.

Primula malacoides

Primulaceae

Primrose

A pretty, annual, fragrant primrose with leaves in rosettes and flowers in layers around the long flower stems. The flowers come in various colors.

Primula malacoides

Care: The cooler the location, the longer you can enjoy these plants. When the blooming is over, the plant usually dies off and can be disposed of. Never place it in the full sun and always give plenty of water; immersing is excellent, too. Fertilizer is not really necessary since the plant only grows for two months.
Propagation: One can sow in June–July for blooming in the following year. Do not cover the seeds with soil. Germination temperature: 61°F (16°C). Plant and continue to grow until the end of September, keeping it cool, preferably outside. Provide a dormancy at a maximum 50°F (10°C).

Light:	Much light, never full sun.
Temp:	Grow cool, if possible never above 50°F (10°C).
Water:	Keep continuously moist, without leaving excess water in the try.
Hum:	High, above 60%.
Soil:	Standard potting soil or (better) extra acidic potting soil, such as soil for *Calceolaria*.

Primula obconica

Primulaceae

Poison primrose

This primrose can induce rashes to form on people with sensitive skin. Not everyone is at risk, however. The flowers are clustered in semi-spherical umbrellas. This plant is principally a perennial.

Care: This species can be grown in a warmer place than most other primroses, but a cool place is fine, too. Add food at half concentrations during the growth season. Remove old flowers. After the plant blooms, keep it cool and bring it outside about mid-May to a shaded location. Bring inside in the fall and keep it rather cool and light until new flowers appear.

Propagation: Sowing can take place throughout the year. Sow for a spring bloom in July. Do not cover the seeds with soil. Germination temperature: 68°F (20°C). Plant and continue to grow cool.

Light:	Much light, never full sun.
Temp:	Grow cool, cultivation temperature 60–63°F (15–17°C). Allow to bloom at 50–75°F (10–24°C). The cooler the plant is kept, the longer the bloom lasts.
Water:	Give plenty of water, but do not leave excess water in the plant's tray.
Hum:	High, above 60%.
Soil:	Standard potting soil, preferably an extra acidic mixture (e.g., *Calceolaria* soil).

Primula obconica

Primula praenitens

Primulaceae

Chinese primrose

Better known as *Primula sinensis*. It is often sold in the spring as a houseplant.

Care: This species can survive warm indoor air better than most primroses. However, do keep it as cool as possible, for this lengthens the flowering period. Water moderately and add food in half concentrations weekly in the summer. Grow in light, but not full sun. Ventilate freely

Primula praenitens

in warm weather; cultivation outside is excellent as well. It is possible to keep the plants alive through the winter by keeping them very cool. But cultivation is not exactly easy.

Propagation: From seed. Sow from March until June for a blooming in the following spring. After germination, plant and continue to grow cool.

Light:	Much light, no full sun.
Temp:	Grow cool, in the winter 39–50°F (4–10°C).
Water:	Keep moderately moist, giving less water than the other *Primula* species.
Hum:	Moderate to high.
Soil:	Extra acidic potting soil (*Calceolaria* soil).

Primula vulgaris

Primulaceae

Often called *Primula acaulis*. This is, in fact, a garden primrose, but is grown rather often in small pots and sold in the spring for indoor cultivation. Various colors and cross-fertilizations are created with *Primula elatior* and *P. juliae*. These plants are perennials.

Care: An indoor room is much too warm for these brightly colored primroses. In any case, keep these plants as cool as possible (they will grow very well in a garden or on a balcony)

Primula vulgaris

and give plenty of water. Add food weekly in half concentrations.

Propagation: One can sow seeds between May and June for a blooming in the following spring. Germination temperature: 60°F (15°C). Grow cool and shaded, preferably outside. Bring inside in the fall and continue to grow cool.

Light:	Much light, no bright sun.
Temp:	Grow cool, in the winter 50°F (10°C).
Water:	Give plenty of water, and if need be, excess water can remain in the plant's tray.
Hum:	High, above 60%.
Soil:	Standard potting soil or extra acidic soil.

Prostanthera sieberi

Labiatae

Small bushes from Australia, which are not hardy outside of their native climate. They can be grown in a cold greenhouse, or if possible, outside.

Care: Grow in a sunny and rather warm place and watch for excess water. In warm summers, the plants can be outside from the end of May, kept in very well-drained containers. But if it rains a lot, they should be covered with glass temporarily. Add food every two weeks. Keep cool and rather dry in the winter. The flowers appear in the spring, after which, prune if needed and repot.

Propagation: From seed or by rooting top cuttings under glass at 60–68°F (15–20°C) soil temperature.

Light:	Full sun.
Temp:	Grow moderately warm, in the winter 46–50°F (8–10°C).
Water:	Rather dry to moderately moist; beware, excess water may kill the plants.
Hum:	Moderate, 50–60%.
Soil:	Mixture of standard potting soil, fine loam or clay and sand for better drainage.

Prostanthera sieberi

Pseuderanthemum species

Acanthaceae

Small, short foliage plants, often with brownish leaves, and mainly sold in the cultivated form 'Tricolor,' which is shown in the photograph. Sometimes other species are available, such as *sinuatum*. These species are suitable for greenhouses, vitrines and plant windows, and are sometimes called *Eranthemum*.
Care: Provide high humidity and do not grow in full sun. Fertilize during the growth period once every two weeks. In the winter, the temperature can be lowered.
Propagation: Top cuttings can be rooted under glass at 68–77°F (20–25°C) soil temperature. Because young plants are prettier than old, it is advisable to clip slips often.

Light:	Much light, no sun.
Temp:	Grow warm, a minimum of 61°F (16°C).
Water:	Keep moderately moist.
Hum:	High, above 60%.
Soil:	Standard potting soil in shallow, well-drained pots or bowls.

Pseuderanthemum atropurpureum 'Tricolor'

Pseudobombax ellipticum

Bombacaceae

A tree from Central America, sold elsewhere as a houseplant. The leaves are initially red-brown, and later turn green. Very beautiful flowers may appear, which open suddenly to display an abundance of light red stamens.

Pseudobombax ellipticum

Pseuderanthemum sinuatum

There is no guarantee these will appear given indoor cultivation.
Care: Grow in a very light place in the summer, providing high humidity. Give fertilizer once every two weeks in the summer. In the winter the foliage will fall, the temperature can be lowered and less water is needed. Repot in the spring and bring back to growth.
Propagation: From seed. These plants are often imported.

Light:	Much light or full sun.
Temp:	Grow moderately warm to warm, in the winter a minimum of 54°F (12°C).
Water:	Keep moderately moist in the summer, rather dry in the winter.
Hum:	High, above 60%.
Soil:	Standard potting soil mixed with at least ⅓ part loam, clay or rock wool powder.

Pseudomammillaria camptotricha

Cactaceae

Bird's nest cactus

A hardy sprouting cactus that is often still categorized with the genus *Mammillaria*. The plant has remarkably long cones, on which thin, light yellow thorns are implanted.

Pseudomammillaria camptotricha

Care: Grow in flat pots or bowls in full sun. Add cactus food monthly. Allow the plant to rest dormant in the winter at a low temperature, and withhold almost all water.
Propagation: By taking side shoots, and planting them.

Light:	Full sun.
Temp:	Grow moderately warm to warm, in the winter 40–50°F (5–10°C).
Water:	Keep moderately moist, almost no water in the winter.
Hum:	Low.
Soil:	Cactus soil.

Pseudopanax lessonii

Araliaceae

A rather unknown houseplant; the cultivation form 'Cyril Watson' is shown in the photograph. The plant is related to the more famous *Fatsia*.
Care: Grow in as cool a place as possible. In the summer, the plant can be placed outside, and in the winter it has to be kept frost free but cool. Much light is desired, however screen a little in the middle of the day. Give food every two weeks in the summer.
Propagation: The common species, from fresh seed; the cultivation forms only from

Pseudopanax lessonii 'Cyril Watson'

cuttings. Top cuttings root slowly. Do not give soil much warmth, but cover with glass or plastic.

Light:	Much light, but screen against bright sun.
Temp:	Grow cool, in the winter 40–54°F (5–12°C).
Water:	Keep moderately moist.
Hum:	Moderate, 50–60%.
Soil:	Standard potting soil.

Pteris cretica

Acrostichaceae

Wing fern

Ferns generally with single-feathered leaves. They appear in a large number of varieties, a number of which are shown in the photographs. These very ornamental plants can remain indoors for some time, though keeping them alive through the winter is difficult.

Pteris cretica 'Albolineata'

Care: Always provide the highest humidity possible, which in the winter, often creates problems. Lowering the temperature helps. Add water very regularly and administer food in half concentrations during the growing season.
Propagation: By division. Large numbers can be grown from seed as well. Soil temperature: 77°F (25°C).

Light:	Half shade to shade, no direct sunlight.
Temp:	Grow moderately warm, a minimum 54°F (12°C) for the green species and 61°F (16°C) for the variegated plants.
Water:	Keep very evenly moist with soft water. If possible use pots with a watering system.
Hum:	High, above 60%.
Soil:	Standard potting soil mixed with extra peat moss or coniferous soil.

Pteris ensiformis

Acrostichaceae

Wing fern

Another frequently grown wing fern, whose two most popular cultivars are 'Evergemiensis,' which has a very wide, white stripe in the middle, and 'Victoriae,' on which the light part is narrower and gray.
Care: Because the cultivars possess little chlorophyll, they have to be grown with much

Pteris ensiformis 'Evergemiensis'

Pteris cretica 'Roweri'

Pteris cretica 'Wimsettii'

light; however, avoid direct sunlight. Furthermore, provide a high relative humidity and a continuous water and food supply. The plants may be kept cooler in the winter.
Propagation: By division.

Light:	Much light, no bright sun.
Temp:	Grow moderately warm, in the winter a minimum 61°F (16°C).
Water:	Keep very regularly moist.
Hum:	High, above 60%.
Soil:	Standard potting soil mixed with extra peat moss or coniferous soil.

Pteris quadriaurita

Acrostichaceae

Wing fern

A fern with long, double- to triple-feathered leaves. They can be all green, but nicely variegated, too, as is the 'Argyreia' in the photograph or the 'Tricolor' variety.
Care: Keep well lit to preserve the clear foliage markings, but do not ever allow direct sunlight. Provide high humidity. In the winter, keep it cooler. Add food weekly in half concentrations during the growth season.
Propagation: By division.

Light:	Much light, no full sun.
Temp:	Grow moderately warm, a minimum 61°F (16°C).
Water:	Keep regularly moist.
Hum:	High, above 60%.
Soil:	Standard potting soil mixed with coniferous soil or peat moss.

Pteris quadriaurita 'Argyreia'

Punica granatum

Punicaceae

Pomegranate

The pomegranate is a true container plant. Outside of its native tropical regions, not much fruit will grow, but the flowers themselves are attractive. Often, the small cultivar 'Nana' is cultivated.
Care: In the summer, container plants are preferably kept outside. In the winter, they should be kept cool so as to discourage growth. Ventilate in the spring to keep the temperature from rising too much. Prune slightly, repot if necessary and bring outside in mid-May to a sunny, very well-protected spot.
Propagation: From seed and via top cuttings, which root at 77–86°F (25–30°C) soil temperature under glass.

Light:	Full sun.
Temp:	Grow cool, in the winter keep 40–50°F (5–10°C).
Water:	Keep moderately moist, in the winter almost dry.
Hum:	Low to moderate.
Soil:	Standard potting soil mixed with fine loam or clay, or rock wool powder.

Punica granatum 'Nana'

Puya chilensis

Puya chilensis

Bromeliaceae

A peculiar bromeliad with thorny leaves. Some species can reach 13 ft (4 m) in South America. They can even stand some frost.

Care: Outside of the tropics, the *Puya chilensis* does not grow that big. Greenish flowers may appear on a very long stem, but this does not happen very often. And when it does happen the rosette invariably drops off. It is usually grown in a cold greenhouse, but can be kept outside in a very protected and sunny spot in the summer. Add food in half concentrations once every two weeks. Keep frost free but cool during its dormant periods.

Propagation: From seed, and possibly by taking side rosettes, too.

Light:	Full sun.
Temp:	Grow cool, in the winter 40–50°F (5–10°C).
Water:	Keep moderately moist, quite dry in the winter.
Hum:	Moderate, 50–60%.
Soil:	Mix standard potting soil with much clay or loam.

Radermachera sinica

Bignoniaceae

A relatively new houseplant with light green, bushy leaves. In China, this is grown as a small

Radermachera sinica

evergreen tree on which yellow flowers can appear. These do not generally appear with indoor cultivation.

Care: Do not grow in too warm a place. In warm regions, this plant can be kept outside in the summer. Keep young plants in light shade. Give moderate amounts of water and feed every two weeks. The temperature should not be too high in the winter, otherwise the leaves will dry out.

Propagation: From fresh imported seeds and via top cuttings, which can produce roots under glass at 77°F (25°C) soil temperature.

Light:	Much light, no full sun.
Temp:	Grow moderately warm, in the winter 46–54°F (8–12°C).
Water:	Keep moderately moist, somewhat drier in the winter, but not so dry that the foliage falls off.
Hum:	Moderate, 50–60%.
Soil:	Standard potting soil.

Rebutia species

Cactaceae

Rebutia are rather small, often spherical cacti that can bloom lavishly at an early age. Numerous species are available.

Care: Grow in a light place; however, screen against the brightest afternoon sun. Also, the humidity should not be too low, so in warm, dry weather, spraying is more important than watering. The soil should never become totally dry in the summer. In the winter, allow the plant to rest dormant at low temperatures and with only a drop of water. The drier it's kept, the more cold can be endured, even a few degrees below zero. Start giving water again only when flower buds have appeared.

Propagation: From seed, with some species also by taking and planting side shoots.

Light:	Much light, screen only against brightest afternoon sun.
Temp:	Grow moderately warm, keep at 40°F (5°C) in the winter.
Water:	Relatively dry to moderately moist, almost completely dry in the winter.
Hum:	Moderate, 50–60%.
Soil:	Cactus soil.

Rebutia krainziana 'Albiflora'

Rebutia minuscula

Rebutia pygmaea

Rebutia senilis

Cactaceae

Small, flat spherical forms, covered with white thorns. There are varieties with yellow, red or orange flowers, all with somewhat different thorns.

Care: Tolerates more light than the last species because of its thorns, and screening is not necessary. Provide for a rather dry atmosphere, but do not let the soil dry out totally. Allow a dry and cool dormant period.

Propagation: From seed and by taking and planting the side shoots.

Rebutia senilis

Light: Full sun.
Temp: Grow moderately warm, in the winter a minimum of 40°F (5°C).
Water: Keep rather dry to moderately moist, almost no water in the winter.
Hum: Moderate, 50–60%.
Soil: Cactus soil.

Rehmannia elata

Gesneriaceae

A perennial plant reaching 5 ft (1.5 m) at most, grown as a container plant. The flowers resemble those of the foxglove.
Care: This plant is not hardy and has to spend its dormancy in a greenhouse. From the end of May, it can possibly be kept outside, if it has already started to bloom. Look for a protected, warm spot in the sun or in light shade. Add food every two weeks. Bring inside in the fall for a cool dormancy. This plant is usually sowed anew after a plant has bloomed; this way of cultivation seems more successful.
Propagation: Sow in March with soil temperature 68–77°F (20–25°C). Plant in rather large pots and continue to grow protected outside under glass, just as described above. The blooming will occur the following year.

Light: Much light, full sun, too.
Temp: Grow moderately warm, in the winter 40–50°F (5–10°C).
Water: Keep moderately moist, drier in the winter.
Hum: Moderate, 50–60%.
Soil: Standard potting soil mixed with loam or clay.

Rehmannia elata

Reinwardtia indica

Linaceae

Profusely flowering half bushes, suitable for a moderate greenhouse or for a cool room.
Care: This plant, originally from the mountains of northern India, hates warmth and full sun. If possible, grow outside in the summer, lightly shaded, otherwise grow in a cold greenhouse or in a room with considerable ventilation. Do not give too much water and fertilize

Reinwardtia indica

every two weeks. Keep cool and light in the winter.
Propagation: Take a cutting from ground shoots. Extra soil warmth is not needed.

Light: Much light, no full sun.
Water: Keep moderately moist.
Hum: Moderate, 50–60%.
Soil: Standard potting soil in very well-draining plastic pots.

Rhapis excelsa

Palmae

A palm that at first sight reminds one of bamboo. It is a strong plant, which can be grown inside as well as in a greenhouse.
Care: Do not place in the full sun; from the end of May, if desired, it can be moved to a protected location outside. Water moderately and add food every two weeks. Bring inside in the fall for dormancy, preferably in a cold greenhouse. The palm can stay indoors over the winter, too, though no warmer than 61°F (16°C) in a bedroom or hallway.
Propagation: By taking shoots.

Light: Much light, no full sun.
Temp: Grow cool, in the winter a minimum of 40°F (5°C).
Water: Keep moderately moist, somewhat drier and at low temperatures in the winter.
Hum: Moderate, 50–60%.
Soil: Standard potting soil mixed with ⅓ part clay, loam or rock wool powder.

Rhapis excelsa

Rhipsalidopsis gaertneri

Rhipsalidopsis species

Cactaceae

Eastern cactus

Besides the old reliable species *gaertneri*, there are more and more cross-fertilizations, sold under the name *Rhipsalidopsis* x *graeseri*. The flowers are bigger, often displaying colors other than the traditional red, and covering almost the whole plant.
Care: The plant, which is mostly sold in bloom in the spring, can stay indoors in a shaded spot. Give moderate amounts of water. Repot after the plant blooms and plant preferably in a shaded area in a garden. Watch out for snails and other pests. Give food every three weeks. Bring inside in the fall and keep dormant at a low temperature. Water very sparsely, but do not allow the plant's parts to shrivel. Increase the water only when the flower buds appear. Do not turn the pot to change the lighting, otherwise the buds fall off.
Propagation: Take top cuttings in May, allow them to dry for a day and plant in sandy soil; temperature 68–77°F (10–15°C).

Light: Half shade, no full sun.
Temp: Grow cool, in the winter keep between 50–60°F (10–15°C).
Water: Keep moderately moist in the summer, rather dry in the winter.
Hum: Moderate, 50–60%.
Soil: Bromeliad or anthurium soil.

Rhipsalidopsis X *graeseri* 'Evita'

Rhipsalis baccifera

Rhipsalis baccifera

Cactaceae

In the tropics, these cacti grow on trees with hanging, cylindrical parts and minuscule flowers, followed by white fruits that resemble berries.

Care: Much warmth is not necessary, and in the summer these plants can even be hung outside. Use absolutely soft water, adding food once every 14 days. Give a dormant period in October through November, keeping it drier and without fertilizer. The bloom generally follows in the winter or spring.

Propagation: From seed and by taking cuttings of the cylindrical parts.

Light:	Half shade, no full sun.
Temp:	Grow cool to moderately warm, in the winter a minimum of 54°F (12°C).
Water:	Keep moderately moist, except in the dormant period.
Hum:	Moderate, 50–60%.
Soil:	An acid-reacting mixture of, for instance, sphagnum, coniferous soil, fern roots, peat moss, etc.

Rhodochiton atrosanguineus

Scrophulariaceae

Strange climbing plant from Mexico generally grown in a cold greenhouse, but which in warm summers can be kept outside.

Care: The climbing stalks need sufficient support to guide them just behind a window or against a warm, sunny wall. Give moderate amounts of water and feed every two weeks. In general, these plants are grown each year from seed, but keeping them alive through the winter in a cold greenhouse is possible. Cut back considerably in the winter.

Propagation: Sow in February-March in soil at 60°F (15°C). Use fresh seeds, for they do not stay germinative very long. Plant in the final pot (6–8 in/15–20 cm in diameter), and harden off and possibly move outside around the end of May.

Light:	Full sun.
Temp:	Grow cool to moderately warm, in the winter 40–50°F (5–10°C).
Water:	Keep moderately moist, drier in the winter.
Hum:	Moderate, 50–60%.
Soil:	Standard potting soil.

Rhodochiton atrosanguineus

Rhododendron obtusum

Ericaceae

Japanese azalea

In comparison with the Indian azalea, described below, this group of hybrids has small flowers. The plants are more or less hardy, which means they can generally be grown outside, as well. They are easy to keep throughout the winter and can last decades.

Care: Cool cultivation is important, both inside and outside, when the plant blooms, usually in (early) spring. The plant can be placed in a living room temporarily, if it is not too

Rhododendron obtusum

warm. Spraying frequently is helpful. After the bloom, remove the old dead parts and keep the plant cool, preferably 43–50°F (6–10°C). Shoots at this point should be removed; only after mid-April should the plant be allowed to grow. Bring outside around mid-May to a protected, half-shaded location. Give plenty of water, in which some food is dissolved. In the fall, bring to a cool, humid, light space as late as possible and wait for the bloom there.

Propagation: Top cuttings root in the spring or in August at a soil temperature of 68–77°F (20–25°C) under glass.

Light:	Half shade, no direct sunlight.
Temp:	Grow cool, in the winter 32–45°F (0–7°C).
Water:	Keep moderately moist with soft water, immerse often.
Hum:	High, above 60%.
Soil:	Acidic soil, such as coniferous soil.

Rhododendron simsii

Ericaceae

Indian azalea

In contrast to the Japanese azaleas, this group of hybrids is certainly not hardy. They should be cultivated under somewhat warmer, but not in too hot, conditions.

Care: Growers often force this early-blooming genus into bloom with a daytime temperature of 61–68°F (16–20°C). Of course, this requires a high relative humidity. After the plant blooms, follow the same care as prescribed for the Japanese variety. This plant, too, can continue to grow in a garden. Bring inside eventually and do not place it in too warm a spot; the temperature should be kept at 54°F (12°C). Then, gradually increase the temperature and mist frequently until the flowers appear.

Propagation: Top cuttings root under glass at a soil temperature of 68–77°F (20–25°C).

Rhododendron simsii

Light:	Much light, no full sun.
Temp:	Grow cool to moderately warm, in the winter 54–68°F (12–20°C).
Water:	Keep well watered with soft water.
Hum:	High, above 60%.
Soil:	Acidic soil, such as coniferous soil.

Rhoeo spathacea

Commelinaceae

A rather well-known houseplant, usually sold in the white-striped form 'Vittata.' The small flowers are surrounded by shell-shaped bracts.
Care: Provide a continuously humid atmosphere and do not allow direct sunlight. In the winter, the plant can be kept cooler. During the growth period, fertilize every two weeks.
Propagation: From top cuttings or from side shoots, which form readily if the plant is topped. Soil temperature 68–77°F (20–25°C).

Rhoeo spathacea 'Vittata'

Light:	The variegated form 'Vittata' requires much light. The common green species can survive half shade or even full shade.
Temp:	Grow warm to moderately warm, in the winter a minimum of 60°F (15°C).
Water:	Keep moderately moist.
Hum:	Moderate to high.
Soil:	Standard potting soil.

Rhoicissus capensis

Vitaceae

A magnificent foliage plant from the grape family. This is the only species that is still grown as a houseplant, the rest have been moved to the genus *Cissus* (see pages 156–157).
Care: Absolutely do not grow too warm, preferably grow this plant in a cool corridor or hallway. The atmosphere should be quite

moist. Give food in the growing period once every two weeks. Keep below general room temperature, especially in the winter.
Propagation: Eye cuttings root at soil temperature 60–68°F (15–20°C) under glass or plastic.

Light:	Half shade, no bright sunlight.
Temp:	Grow cool, in the winter keep between 45 and 64°F (7 and 8°C).
Water:	Keep moderately moist.
Hum:	Moderate to high.
Soil:	Standard potting soil.

Rhynchostylis coelestis

Orchidaceae

These orchids do not have pseudotubers, so a real dormant period is not needed. They are used frequently for cross-fertilizations with other species, for they can bloom lavishly.
Care: Grow in very bright light. Screen slightly in the summer and in the winter keep it just behind a window. Provide high humidity and fresh air when it is very hot. Keep sufficiently moist and give orchid food every two weeks in half concentration. With rock wool cultivation, give food continuously in very light concentrations (.01 oz/.25 g per liter). Repot very carefully, for the plant will suffer damage if the roots are disturbed.
Propagation: From seed and by division.

Rhoicissus capensis

Light:	Much light, screen against the brightest sunlight.
Temp:	Grow cool to moderately warm, a minimum of 54°F (12°C).
Water:	Keep continuously moist with rainwater, avoiding the leaves.
Hum:	High, above 60%.
Soil:	Grows well in rock wool or clay particles, but also in a number of other mixtures.

Rhynchostylis coelestis

Rivina humilis

Rivina humilis

Phytolaccaceae

A little-known plant from the southern U.S. and Mexico. After its white flowers bloom, red berries appear.

Care: The plant can be kept indoors in the summer, provided with light shade. Give plenty of water and feed once every two weeks. Spraying the foliage is excellent, but do not spray the flowers, for it may harm the fruit development.

Propagation: Take top cuttings in the spring or sow ripe fruit. Soil temperature 68–77°F (20–25°C).

Light:	Much light or half shade, no full sunlight.
Temp:	Grow moderately warm to warm, in the winter a minimum of 54°F (12°C).
Water:	Keep moderately moist in the summer, in the winter somewhat drier.
Hum:	High, above 60%.
Soil:	Standard potting soil.

Rodriguezia secunda

Orchidaceae

Orchids with small blooms in large, multiflower bunches. They appear mostly in May-June; sometimes the plant blooms twice.

Care: Keep in a very light, warm and humid place (such as a greenhouse or plant window). Screen only against the brightest sun. The plant grows continuously throughout the year and much water is needed, provided that it can drain well. Give less water in the winter, but a real dormant period is not necessary, although the plant is provided with pseudotubers. Add orchid food every two weeks in the growing period. Only repot when it is really necessary; when grown undisturbed, these plants can become beautiful, large solitaires.

Propagation: By division.

Light:	Much light, no bright sun.
Temp:	Grow warm, not below 64°F (18°C).
Water:	Give plenty of water, always using soft water or pure rainwater.

Rodriguezia secunda

Hum:	High, above 60%.
Soil:	Grow in lattice baskets filled with chopped tree fern or rock wool flakes.

Rosa chinensis 'Minima'

Rosaceae

Mini-rose

These roses with small flowers are sold more and more as potted plants. They last quite a long time if they receive good care. The 'Rosamini' is a popular form and there are also several other cross-fertilizations grown.

Care: The plants can survive a long time indoors in the summer. They bloom several times when old flowers and a piece of the stem are removed. Feed them once every two weeks, and water moderately. For the health of the plants it is better to allow a dormant period in the winter, when the temperature

Rosa (mini-rose) 'Orange Rosamini'

should be lowered considerably. Prune in the spring, repot and bring back to growth.

Propagation: From seed and from cuttings. Top cuttings root easily with a soil temperature of 68°F (20°C). Cut off the tops a few times.

Light:	Much light, full sun, too.
Temp:	Grow cool, in the winter keep 32–50°F (0–10°C).
Water:	Keep moderately moist.
Hum:	Moderate, 50–60%.
Soil:	Standard potting soil.

Rosioglossum grande

Orchidaceae

A very hardy orchid that most people still refer to as *Odontoglossum*. The plant is cultivated indoors with success all year round, like many other species.

Care: Grow warm in the growing season, preferably in a window facing east. No full sun should be allowed. Give the plant some orchid food every two weeks when it grows. After the new pseudotubers are full-grown, a dormant period should be provided, during which just enough water is administered to prevent the tubers from shriveling. The temperature can be lower in dormancy, but this is not necessary.

Propagation: By division.

Light:	Much light or half shade, no full sun.
Temp:	Grow warm, somewhat cooler at night, cooler too in the dormant period. Minimum of 54°F (12°C).
Water:	Give plenty of soft water in the summer, and in the dormant period keep somewhat drier.
Hum:	Moderate, 50–60%.
Soil:	Clay particles with peat moss and/or rock wool flakes.

Rosioglossum grande

Ruellia devosiana

See *Dipteracanthus devosianus*.

Ruscus aculeatus

Liliaceae

Not a very hardy bush, but quite suitable as a container plant. The leaf-like branches (phylloclades), where the small flowers grow, are peculiar and are followed in growth by rather large red berries.
Care: In warmer climates, this bush is hardy, with some covering. More northerly, it is better to keep the bushes in a greenhouse. Keep outside, protected and sunny, in the summer. Water moderately and give food every two weeks. Bring inside when severe frosts begin and place in a cool, light spot. The foliage should not fall off.
Propagation: Sow seeds immediately after ripening. They germinate slowly (it may take a year).

Light:	Full sun.
Temp:	Grow cool, a minimum of 32°F (0°C).
Water:	Keep moderately moist, drier in the winter.
Hum:	Moderate, 50–60%.
Soil:	Mix standard potting soil with ⅓ part loam or clay.

Ruscus aculeatus

Sagina subulata

Caryophyllaceae

Star-moss

This is, in fact, a ground cover that is often sold as a small houseplant. With its linear leaves, the plant does make an excellent ground cover, especially when grown in plant containers.
Care: Grow as cool as possible and spray frequently. The temperature may drop considerably in the winter, and even a few nights of frost won't be a problem. Give moderate amounts of water in the summer and add food once every two weeks.
Propagation: By division.

Light:	Much light, avoid bright sun.
Temp:	Grow cool, a minimum of 32°F (0°C).
Water:	Keep moderately moist.
Hum:	Moderate to high.
Soil:	Standard potting soil.

Sagina subulata

Saintpaulia ionantha hybrids

Gesneriaceae

African violet

An extraordinarily popular plant; there are even societies of Saintpaulia lovers that have hundreds of different specimens in their collections. Relatively new are the 'Mini' cultivars, which are smaller overall than the normal African violet.

Saintpaulia Ionantha-hybr.

Care: These small plants may bloom all year long, when they receive some light in the winter. A common light bulb of 60 watts is sufficient for day lengthening (see page 55). It is also possible to grow the plants constantly under artificial light, with a light level around 5,000 lux. Indoors, the African violet needs a lightly shaded location, for instance in an east-facing window, which only receives some sun in the morning. In any case, screen against the bright afternoon sun. The ball of soil should never become too wet, and use soft water. Do not spill water on the leaves, for this causes spots. Remove old flowers. When new leaves appear, use fertilizer with a nitrogen deficiency or remove some foliage.
Propagation: Easy from leaf cuttings, leaving a small piece of the stem. Soil temperature 68–77°F (20–25°C).

Light:	Half shade to much light, no bright sun.
Temp:	Grow moderately warm to warm, in the winter a minimum of 61°F (16°C).
Water:	Keep moderately moist with lukewarm, soft water.
Hum:	Moderate to high.
Soil:	Standard potting soil mixed with much peat moss.

Saintpaulia Ionantha-hybr.

Saintpaulia Ionantha-hybr. 'Mini'

SANCHEZIA

Sanchezia nobilis

Acanthaceae

A not-very-often seen but beautifully marked foliage plant, a relative of the more popular *Aphelandra*. A second species *Sanchezia parvibracteata* 'Variegata' looks similar and is easily confused with *S. nobilis*. The cultivation is the same for both.

Care: A humid atmosphere is required, which does not make it an ideal houseplant. However, it is very suitable for greenhouses and vitrines, etc. Avoid bright sunlight, but grow light, otherwise the variegated markings fade away. Add food weekly in the growing period. In the winter, the temperature should not be lowered much.

Propagation: Top cuttings root easily under glass at a soil temperature of 68–77°F (20–25°C).

Light: Much light, no full sun.
Temp: Grow warm, a minimum of 60°F (15°C).
Water: Keep moderately moist with soft water.
Hum: High, above 60%.
Soil: Coniferous soil.

Sanchezia nobilis

Sandersonia aurantiaca

Liliaceae

Tuberous growth with weak stalks. Tubers can sometimes be ordered by mail.

Sandersonia aurantiaca

Care: Put the tubers in pots 1–2 in (3–5cm) under the soil. Keep warm and start giving water when they begin to grow. Grow these preferably in a greenhouse, but a windowsill is possible as well. Allow much light, but screen against the brightest sun. Give plenty of water in the summer and add food every two weeks. Decrease the water supply at the end of the summer, until all the foliage dies off. The tubers can then be stored dry in the pots. Repot in the spring and allow to sprout again.

Propagation: By dividing the tubers.

Light: Much light, screen the brightest sunlight.
Temp: Grow warm, in the winter not below 54°F (12°C).
Water: Keep moderately moist in the winter.
Hum: High, above 60%.
Soil: One-third part standard potting soil, ⅓ part fine clay or loam and ⅓ part decayed beech leaves.

Sansevieria trifasciata

Agavaceae

Sansevieria

Probably the most common and easiest to grow houseplant. One certainly doesn't need a green thumb to keep this plant happy. There is a green species with long leaves and another with small, short rosettes; both forms exist in yellow with green as well. Furthermore, there are some interesting species that one almost never sees. With the right care, flowers may appear.

Care: Thankfully, these can only be harmed by an excess of water. Forgetting to water them for a week will cause no harm, since these are originally desert plants. Only when the plant is bursting out of its pot should it be repotted. If you want the plant to grow faster, add food in the growing period once every two weeks.

Propagation: By division and by cutting a leaf into 3 in (7 cm) pieces and planting them. This only works with the green species; the yellow variegated species turns green after this process.

Sansevieria trifasciata

Sansevieria trifasciata

Light: Much light, preferably no bright sunlight; the plants can survive sunlight, but will fade.
Temp: Grow warm, never below 57°F (14°C).
Water: Keep rather dry.
Hum: Low to moderate.
Soil: Standard potting soil.

Sarcocaulon crassicaule

Geraniaceae

These plants are xerophytes, plants that are able to endure extreme drought. The knotty bushes can stay alive without water for a few years.

Care: The growing season starts in August. Only give water then and provide as much sunlight as possible, which can become a problem in the northern hemisphere in the fall. Give food monthly. Growth is concluded in the spring, when the small bush goes into a

Sarocaulon crassicaule

dormant period. Withhold all water until August. The temperature should stay high, which means that the plant can stay indoors in the winter, if it is kept in a south-facing window.
Propagation: From seed and by cuttings. Allow them to dry first.

Light: Full sun.
Temp: Grow warm, in the winter at least 54°F (12°C), though it can be warmer.
Water: Rather dry to moderately moist in the growing season, for the rest of the time, dry.
Hum: Low.
Soil: Very permeable, sandy soil mixed with some loam.

Sarmienta scandens

Gesneriaceae

Also known by the species name *repens*. A rather rare but pretty hanging plant for greenhouses or plant windows.
Care: Preferably grown in hanging pots or lattice baskets, with a humid environment in a shady location. Initially, water sparsely using rainwater. When the growth period begins, increase the amount, and add food weekly. In the winter, a strict dormant period should be observed, otherwise no flowers will appear the next year.
Propagation: Root top cuttings in the spring under glass at 68°F (20°C) soil temperature. Add fungus-preventing substances so that the cuttings do not rot.

Light: Half shade, no sun.
Temp: Grow moderately warm to warm in the summer, dormancy at 40–46°F (5–8°C) in the winter.
Water: Keep moderately moist with soft water, drier in the winter.
Hum: High, above 60%.
Soil: Bromeliad soil on a thick drainage layer of pottery pieces or clay particles.

Sarmienta scandens

Sarracenia flava

Sarracenia species

Sarraceniaceae

Carnivorous plants that lure insects into their long funnels. The insects cannot escape because the walls are too slippery. Slowly they decay, feeding the plant.
Care: Grow cool; in the summer the plant can grow by the edge of a pond, with its pot pressing into the wet ground. They are swamp plants. Keep cool through the winter, a cold greenhouse is an excellent place. Fertilizer is not needed since the insects serve this purpose.
Propagation: By division and from seed.

Light: Much light, screen against the brightest sun.
Temp: Grow cool, keep 32–50°F (0–10°C) in the winter.
Water: Keep constantly moist.
Hum: High, above 60%.
Soil: Pure peat moss is excellent.

Sauromatum guttatum

Araceae

A tuberous growth that when completely dry, without soil or water, can produce stinky, arum-like flowers.
Care: After the plant blooms, the tuber can be planted immediately in a garden, where it will

Sauromatum guttatum

Sarracenia purpurea

develop roots in early spring. Cover well against frost. A large, divided leaf on a long, spotted stem will then appear. In poor soil, fertilize once every two weeks in the summer. In the summer the foliage dies off, and the tuber can be brought inside after this to prepare it for blooming the following year. In this way one can continue to grow this plant for years, as long as the tubers do not freeze.
Propagation: By taking newly formed tubers.

Light: Half shade.
Temp: Grow cool, keep tubers frost free in the winter.
Water: Moderately moist during the growth period, for the rest of the time, dry.
Hum: Moderate, 50–60%.
Soil: Standard potting soil.

Sauromatum guttatum

Saxifraga cotyledon

Saxifraga stolonifera

Saxifraga cotyledon

Saxifragaceae

A hardy garden plant that produces a gigantic bunch of flowers out of a relatively small rosette. Growers can force older rosettes into blooming and sell them as houseplants.
Care: Keep indoors only when blooming, after which the rosette dies.
Propagation: Young plants can be removed from the old rosette. Grow outside in a sunny spot or in a rock garden. Excellent water drainage is very important. Give some food monthly. The rosettes may bloom by the second year. Cold and a long day are necessary for the development of flowers. If an early bloom is desired, then provide more light in the early spring (see page 55). During the beginning of the growth period, the temperature can stay quite low.

Light: Full sun.
Temp: Grow cool, in the winter keep just frost free when plants are inside, and during the process of forcing 50–60°F (10–15°C).
Water: Keep moderately moist.
Hum: Moderate, 50–60%.
Soil: Standard potting soil mixed with much sharp sand.

Saxifraga stolonifera

Saxifragaceae

Strawberry geranium

An easily grown houseplant with long shoots, on which small new plants appear. Shown in the photograph is the common, deciduous form. The cultivar 'Tricolor' is a bit weaker, and has light red and white marked leaves.
Care: Do not place in the bright sun and grow rather cool. Fertilize every two weeks during

the growth period. In the winter the temperature can drop considerably, with the variegated form somewhat less. These plants generally die after blooming.
Propagation: Grow new plants continuously by taking and planting young growths. They root easily.

Light: Half shade for the green species, much light for the variegated form. Never bright sun.
Temp: Grow cool, in the winter 32–50°F (0–10°C). The variegated form 57–64°F (14–18°C).
Water: Keep moderately moist.
Hum: Moderate, 50–60%.
Soil: Standard potting soil.

Schaueria calycotricha

Acanthea

Half bush from Brazil, also known as *Justicia calycotricha*.
Care: Preferably grown in a greenhouse, since there is a great need for humid air. Do not allow direct sunlight. Feed weekly in the summer. Repot in the spring and prune if necessary.

Schaueria calycotricha

Propagation: From seed, which are generally plentiful, and by top cuttings, which root under glass in the spring at 77°F (25°C).

Light: Much light, no sun.
Temp: Grow warm, a minimum of 60°F (15°C).
Water: Grow moderately moist with soft water.
Hum: High, above 60%.
Soil: Standard potting soil mixed with ⅓ part clay or loam.

Schefflera species

Araliaceae

Bushes with palmate leaves, originally from East Asia. Recently, more and more species, and especially cultivars, have appeared on the market. The names of the different cultivars are not that confusing, for almost everything seems to belong to the species *arboricola*. With a cool dormancy, the plant can bloom in the summer.
Care: Unfortunately, these plants require rather high humidity, and for this reason, they tend to suffer when kept in a heated living room. The solution is to lower the temperature considerably. Treat the plant as a container plant, for along the coast of the Mediterranean Sea they

Schefflera arboricola 'Renate'

Schefflera arboricola 'Trinette'

Water: Keep moderately moist with soft water.
Hum: High, above 60%.
Soil: Acidic and permeable, for instance coniferous soil or a mixture with leaf mold and peat moss.

Schismatoglottis picta

Schefflera digitata

are planted in gardens. Add food in the growing season once every two weeks.
Propagation: From fresh seed. Also from top and middle cuttings, which form roots at 68–77°F (20–25°C) soil temperature.

Light: Half shade, with indoor cultivation, no full sun. The variegated species need much light.
Temp: Grow cool, in the winter at 54–61°F (12–16°C), possibly even down to 40°F (5°C), but then the foliage falls off.
Water: Keep moderately moist.
Hum: Moderate to high.
Soil: Standard potting soil.

Schinus molle

Anacardiaceae

In the subtropics this grows as a street tree, but in moderate climates is only kept as a container plant. This plant is not seen very often.
Care: Place outside in the summer in a warm and protected location. Give moderate amounts of water and fertilize once every two weeks. These

Schinus molle

plants will pollinate (and form fruits) if you grow female plants next to male. In the fall, bring inside and keep cool, and provide a dry dormancy. The foliage should stay on.
Propagation: From seed and via top cuttings, which root under glass at 77°F (25°C).

Schefflera, flowering

Light: Full sun.
Temp: Grow cool to moderately warm, in the winter 40–50°F (5–10°C).
Water: Keep moderately moist.
Hum: Moderate, 50–60%.
Soil: Standard potting soil.

Schismatoglottis picta

Araceae

A plant that can very easily be confused with *Aglaonema* or *Syngonium*, which is not so serious because the cultivation is the same for all.
Care: Grow warm the whole year, as with most members of this family. The air should not be too dry, so spray frequently or, preferably, place in a warm greenhouse. Keep the plants from the sun, but do not place in too dark a spot, for then the foliage markings disappear. Give food once every two weeks in the growing period. Repot in the spring.
Propagation: By division.

Light: Much light, no full sun.
Temp: Grow warm, in the winter a minimum of 61–64°F (16–18°C).

Schizanthus pinnatus

Schizanthus pinnatus

Solanaceae

An annual growth that is often used in gardens. However, it is possible to grow these plants in pots. With proper sowing the preceding year, magnificent flowers can bloom in May, when they then can decorate either the greenhouse or a room indoors.
Care: During cultivation, fertilize a few times. Throw this plant away after it blooms.
Propagation: Sow for pot cultivation in August or September. Germination temperature 61°F (16°C). Plant a few seedlings together in large pots and continue to grow. Provide support for these plants as they grow.

Light: Much light, in the winter as well.
Temp: Grow cool, keep around 46°F (8°C) the whole winter.
Water: Keep moderately moist.
Hum: Moderate, 50–60%.
Soil: Standard potting soil.

Schlumbergera-hybr.

Schlumbergera hybrids

Cactaceae
Christmas cactus

Often indicated as *Zygocactus*. Where previously there was only one tint available, there are now hybrids that can bloom in various colors. The bloom occurs in the middle of the winter, but only if strict dormant periods are observed.

Care: For good bud development, the plant has to be kept completely dry and cool for about three months, usually starting at the beginning of August. After a month, the temperature can be raised to 68°F (20°C). When small buds become visible, gradually increase the amount of water given. After the plant blooms, allow it to rest dormant again for at least six weeks, possibly longer. During the dormant period the parts should not be allowed to shrivel due to lack of water. Repot in March or April and keep somewhat warmer. Grow outside from the end of May in a shaded, protected location and add cactus food every two weeks. Dormancy begins again in August, as described above.

Propagation: Top cuttings of older shoots can be planted in the spring. Allow them to dry for a few days, then plant in sandy soil with soil temperature 68°F (20°C). Grafting on another trunk is a possibility, too, which creates beautiful crown trees.

Schlumbergera-hybr.

Light: Half shade.
Temp: Keep moderately warm during growth, in the dormant periods around 54–60°F (12–15°C).
Water: Keep moderately moist with soft water, almost completely dry in the dormant periods.
Hum: Moderate, 50–60%.
Soil: An acidic, permeable soil mixture, for instance coniferous soil with beech leaves and cow manure. Use rather large, well-drained plastic hanging pots.

Scindapsus pictus

Araceae

Pictured is a true *Scindapsus*, the popular cultivar 'Argyraeus.' It is distinguished by its prominent leaf markings. Another species, *aureus*, is now classified under the genus *Epipremnum*.
Care: In a heated room in winter, this plant will suffer because of the dry air. Spraying frequently will help, as will growing it in a warm greenhouse. Do not allow direct sunlight. In the growing period, add food every two weeks.
Propagation: Top cuttings and eye cuttings form roots at 68–77°F (20–25°C) soil temperature.

Light: Much light, no full sun.
Temp: Grow warm, in the winter a minimum of 57°F (14°C).
Water: Keep moderately moist with soft water.
Hum: High, above 60%.
Soil: Mix standard potting soil with peat moss, perlite or coniferous soil, to make the medium extra permeable.

Scindapsus pictus 'Argyraeus'

Scirpus cernuus

Cyperaceae
Maidenhair

A green grass with very fine, thread-shaped, hanging stalks. It resembles a green wig.

Scirpus cernuus

Care: Grow cool in a humid atmosphere. It will noticeably suffer if grown in a heated room in the winter. Allow water to stand in the tray at the base of the pot (this is one of the few plants that requires such treatment). Feed every two weeks in the summer. Continuously acquire new plants, because older specimens tend to become unkempt rather quickly.
Propagation: By division.

Light: Half shade, no full sun.
Temp: Grow cool, in the winter at 60°F (15°C).
Water: Keep constantly moist.
Hum: High, above 60%.
Soil: Standard potting soil.

Scutellaria costaricana

Labiatae

Many species of this genus make hardy garden plants. The species pictured is a magnificent half bush grown in a moderate greenhouse.

Scutellaria costaricana

Care: Grow airy and screened against bright sunlight, preferably in a greenhouse, though cultivation is possible in the home in the summer, too. Water moderately and feed weekly. Keep cooler in the winter.

Propagation: Middle cuttings root quickly under glass at 68–77°F (20–25°C) soil temperature. Cuttings started in the fall will flower in the spring. Keep several cuttings together in one rather large pot and allow them to grow without cutting the tops off, for this will produce the largest flowers. It is sensible to grow new plants every year, disposing of the old ones.

Light: Much light, no bright sun.
Temp: Grow moderately warm, in the winter not below 54°F (12°C).
Water: Keep moderately moist.
Hum: Moderate to high.
Soil: Standard potting soil.

Sedum adolphii 'Golden Sedum'

Sedum species

Crassulaceae

Stonecrop

All *Sedum* species are succulents. They store water in their thick leaves and use this moisture in times of drought. They are not true houseplants, but many species are strong enough to be grown for this purpose.

Care: The plants look their best when grown in cold to moderate greenhouses, which recreate conditions most like their original habitats, which are most unlike cultivation in a heated room. Also, only plants that go through a strict dormant period will bloom. During the growth period in the summer, little water is necessary and at the most add cactus food once a month. These plants will easily grow out of their containers. Much sunlight is needed to stimulate the often interesting red-colored foliage.

Propagation: Dropped leaves root easily when they are put in soil for a while. Top cuttings root easily as well, but need to be dried for a while before planting in rather dry soil, to prevent rotting. Many species can be propagated from seed, also.

Sedum morganianum

Sedum sieboldii

Sedum pachyphyllum

Sedum sieboldii 'Variegatum'

Sedum lineare 'Variegatum'

Light: Full sun.
Temp: Grow moderately warm, keep 40–50°F (5–10°C) in the winter.
Water: Keep rather dry, in the winter just dry enough so the leaves do not shrivel.
Hum: Low.
Soil: Very permeable and not too acidic. Cactus soil is good, and can be made by mixing equal parts sharp sand or perlite, standard potting soil, and fine clay or loam.

Sedum stahlii

SELAGINELLA

Selaginella apoda

Selaginella martensii

Sempervivum arachnoideum tomemtosum

Selaginella species

Selaginellaceae

Moss

Short, small plants resembling moss that are suitable for cultivation in vitrines, greenhouses, etc. A species that can be stored in a dry form and opens up after soaking is called *Selaginella lepidophylla*. It looks like *Anastatica*, with which it is often confused.
Care: For successful cultivation, high humidity and shade is necessary. Furthermore, the plants are sensitive to water containing calcium, so always use soft water and administer water preferably to the soil. Once in a while mix in some food with the water.
Propagation: By division.

Light:	Much light, no full sun.
Temp:	Grow moderately warm to warm, a minimum of 60°F (15°C).
Water:	Keep moderately moist.
Hum:	High, above 60%.
Soil:	One-third part potting soil and ⅔ part peat moss mixed together.

Selenicereus grandiflorus

Cactaceae

Queen-of-the-night

A cactus that is famous for its large, fragrant flowers that bloom only at night (which is also a characteristic of many other cacti). The plants form shoots yards high, which makes it somewhat cumbersome to grow them indoors. But it works excellently in a greenhouse, if possible, planted out in the full soil.
Care: Grow light in the summer, but screen against the brightest sunlight. Give moderate amounts of water and cactus food every two weeks. Tie up the long shoots quite well or guide them along a sturdy support. Keep cooler in the winter and withhold almost all water. Only then will flowers develop.
Propagation: Cut off middle cuttings (parts of the stalks) of about 4 in (10 cm), allow them to dry for a few weeks and then plant. Soil temperature 68°F (20°C).

Light:	Much light to half shade, no full shade.
Temp:	Grow warm, in the winter 40–50°F (5–10°C).
Water:	Moderately moist in the summer, almost dry in the winter.
Hum:	Low to moderate.
Soil:	Standard potting soil.

Sempervivum arachnoideum

Crassulaceae

Cobweb houseleek

Small, rosette-shaped succulents, that are able to tolerate long-lasting drought. Some species

Selenicereus grandiflorus

can even endure frost. Various species are available as houseplants, for instance, the subspecies *tomentosum*, the delicate houseleek, which has small rosettes that look as though they're covered with cobwebs.
Care: Grow sunny and water very sparsely. In the winter, do not allow the plants to grow by keeping them cold and completely dry. The plants are suited for growth on a balcony, where they usually can remain throughout the year. Food is not necessary.
Propagation: By removing side rosettes and from seed.

Light:	Full sun.
Temp:	Grow cool to moderately warm, in the winter it can even go below freezing.
Water:	Very sparse, nothing during dormancy.
Hum:	Low.
Soil:	Poor soil, standard potting soil with at least half sharp sand is good, in well-drained pots or bowls.

Senecio cruentus hybrids

Compositae

Cineraria

This richly flowering plant is available in various colors around Mother's Day.
Care: If grown especially cool, the bloom will last longer. Spray frequently and keep sufficiently moist. Add some fertilizer to the water once in a while. Keeping it alive through the winter is virtually impossible, so throw the plant away after it blooms.
Propagation: Sow from mid-June to mid-October. Germination temperature 64°F (18°C); after planting in pots, this temperature should be maintained. When the plants have formed roots, continue to grow at 40–46°F (5–8°C), and do not give much water. The leaves may wilt in the daytime.

Light:	Much light, no bright sun.
Temp:	Grow cool (see above).
Water:	Keep moderately moist.
Hum:	Moderate, 50–60%.
Soil:	Standard potting soil.

Senecio Cruentus-hybr.

Senecio kleinia

Compositae

A well-known plant native to the Canary Islands. The thick, succulent stalks have numerous, linear leaves at the top. It is a very strong houseplant.
Care: This plant can endure drought by dropping a large chunk of its foliage; in the next growing season a new piece appears on the old stalk with new foliage. Grow sunny and do

Senecio kleinia

not give too much water. Do not feed too much.
Propagation: From seed and by stalk-end cuttings, which should dry for a while before planting.

Light:	Full sun.
Temp:	Grow moderately warm to warm, in the winter almost completely dry.
Water:	Keep rather dry, in the winter almost completely dry.
Hum:	Low to moderate.
Soil:	Standard potting soil with extra sharp sand or perlite.

Senecio macroglossus

Compositae

A climbing plant that at first sight reminds one of an ivy, especially the variegated form 'Variegatum,' which is a popular cultivar. However, the foliage is much thicker than that of a variegated ivy with small leaves; this plant is a leaf succulent.
Care: Avoid the bright sun and do not give too much water. In the winter, keep it cooler, because there will be not enough light for healthy growth. Support any weak shoots. In the summer give food once every two weeks.
Propagation: Top cuttings root with slight soil warmth.

Senecio macroglossus 'Variegatum'

Light:	Much light to half shade, no full sun.
Temp:	Grow moderately warm, in the winter a minimum of 50°F (10°C).
Water:	Rather dry to moderately moist, water very sparsely in the winter.
Hum:	Low to moderate.
soil:	Standard potting soil.

Senecio mikanioides

Compositae

A plant that often is confused with *Senecio macroglossus*. These leaves are bigger, though, and not meaty, and they are always green, never variegated. *Mikania* is the popular name.
Care: This species does not have the succulent characteristics of *S. macroglossus*, so always give plenty of water. Screen against the brightest sun. Grow preferably as a hanging plant, but the vines should be guided upwards. In the growing season, add food every two weeks. Repot in the spring.
Propagation: Root top cuttings with slight soil warmth.

Light:	Much light or half shade, no bright sun.
Temp:	Grow cool to moderately warm, in the winter a minimum of 54°F (12°C).
Water:	Keep moderately moist.
Hum:	Moderate, 50–60%.
Soil:	Standard potting soil.

Senecio mikanioides

Senecio rowleyanus

Compositae

Pea plant

There are a lot of *Senecio* species, all of which form small, thick leaves on hanging, thread-like stalks. With this species they look like peas, with *citriformis*, like green citrons, with *herreianus* they are elongated and with *radicans* they resemble mini-cucumbers.
Care: These are strong, succulent plants that can remain indoors all year long, but do well when given a cool winter dormancy. They do not need much water because they can store water in their foliage and evaporate little of it. Allow full sun, grow in hanging pots and fertilize only once a month.
Propagation: Cut the stalks in pieces and root in rather dry soil.

Light:	Full sun.
Temp:	Grow moderately warm to warm, in the winter 50–54°F (10–12°C).
Water:	Keep rather dry, almost completely dry in dormancy.
Hum:	Low.
Soil:	Cactus soil.

Senecio rowleyanus

Serissa foetida

Rubiceae

Rarely occurring, but attractive small potted plant, also sold as a bonsai. Almost always seen is the form 'Variegata,' with its variegated foliage. Small white flowers may appear.
Care: Do not place in full sun, but keep well lit, otherwise the pretty leaf markings will disappear. Water moderately in the summer and feed every two weeks. The small plant may be placed outside. In the winter keep frost free. Repot in the spring, if necessary, prune a bit and continue to grow.
Propagation: Take top cuttings from newly grown shoots. Soil temperature 68–77°F (20–25°C).

Light:	Much light, no bright sun.
Temp:	Grow moderately warm, in the winter 40–50°F (5–10°C).
Water:	Moderately moist, drier in the winter.
Hum:	Moderate, 50–60%.
Soil:	Mixture of ⅔ part standard potting soil and ⅓ part fine clay or loam.

Serissa foetida

Setcreasea pallida

Commelinaceae

Better known under the species name *purpurea*. A purple cultivation form is known as 'Purple Heart,' pictured.
Care: The beautiful purple leaf tint is only preserved if the plant is grown in a sunny place. It can be outside in the summer (there are even rumors that it has survived mild winters). The plant can stay alive without problems in a warm room without water for up to three months. Do not spray the foliage, or it will become ugly. Grow new plants often, for older specimens tend to lose their beauty. Feed very seldom: this plant should not grow that fast.
Propagation: Allow top cuttings to dry for a day and plant.

Light:	Full sun.
Temp:	Grow moderately warm, in the winter the temperature may fall to 32°F (0°C).
Water:	Water very sparsely; the plant could die of stagnant standing water.
Hum:	Low to moderate.
Soil:	Standard potting soil.

Setcreasea pallida 'Purple Heart'

Sibthorpia europaea

Scrophulariaceae

A hardy plant. There is also a variegated form that strongly resembles *Glechoma*. The small flowers are not very remarkable.
Care: Preferably plant in hanging pots, keeping it cool and shady. Keep constantly moist in the summer and feed once every two weeks. In the winter, the temperature can be lowered to just above freezing.
Propagation: By division.

Light:	Shade or half shade, keep the variegated form lighter than the deciduous species.
Temp:	Grow cool, in the winter 32°F (0°C) is sufficient.
Water:	Keep constantly moist, possibly drier in the winter.
Hum:	Moderate to high.
Soil:	Standard potting soil.

Sibthorpia europaea

Siderasis fuscata

Commelinaceae

A beautiful foliage plant with rust-brown hairs and small purple flowers, as well.
Care: This plant needs humid air, and is preferably grown in a greenhouse. Spraying is not advisable, for it causes ugly spots to form on the leaves. Do not allow full sun. In the grow-

Siderasis fuscata

ing period, add food once every two weeks. Keep it cooler in the winter, but not too cold.
Propagation: By division.

Light:	Much light, no bright sun.
Temp:	Warm to moderately warm, in the winter a minimum of 61°F (16°C).
Water:	Keep moderately moist.
Hum:	High, above 60%.
Soil:	Standard potting soil in especially well-drained plastic pots.

Sinningia cardinalis

Gesneriaceae

A plant almost always called *Rechsteineria*, and sometimes *Gesneria*, too. This is by far the most famous species.

Care: The tuberous rootstocks can be ordered by mail. After receiving the tubers, pot them and allow them to sprout at 68–77°F (20–25°C). Keep under glass for a while, for high humidity is a necessity. Don't ever allow full sun, but give plenty of light. After a while, harden off and bring indoors while the plant blooms. Add food every two weeks in the growing period. Decrease the water in September, until the plant dies off. Keep the rootstocks dry in the soil until the following year.

Propagation: By dividing the rootstocks that have shoots and from leaf or top cuttings. Also from seed. Soil temperature 68–77°F (20–25°C).

Light:	Much light, no full sun.
Temp:	Grow warm, during dry storage a minimum of 54°F (12°C).
Water:	Keep moderately moist with soft water.
Hum:	High, above 60%.
Soil:	Very permeable, humusy and acidic, for instance a mixture of coniferous soil, peat moss, beech leaf soil and decayed cow manure over an easy-draining layer.

Sinningia speciosa

Sinningia speciosa

Gesneriaceae

Gloxinia

An old-fashioned houseplant with striking flowers. They're not popular with everybody, but some people are quite successful with these plants, and can keep them for decades.

Care: A *Sinningia* is usually bought while blooming in the spring. Do not place it in the sun and try to keep the air as humid as possible (perhaps place a vaporizer underneath). Give plenty of water, for it evaporates easily off the leaves. Immersing in water is excellent as well. Always add some fertilizer (in half concentrations) to the water, for the plant really needs nutrients. After the blooming, continue to grow in a greenhouse if possible. Give less water starting in September, until the foliage dies off. Store the tuber dry in the pot. Repot in the spring and bring back to growth.

Propagation: Via leaf cuttings or by using the shoots. Sowing is possible, too, but it requires extra lighting to get young plants through the winter in good condition.

Light:	Much light, no full sun.
Temp:	Grow warm, not below 64°F (18°C). Minimum for dry stored tubers is 60°F (15°C).
Water:	Keep well watered with soft water.
Hum:	High, above 60%.
Soil:	A mixture of equal parts standard potting soil and peat moss.

Sinningia cardinalis

Sinningia speciosa

Skimmia japonica

Skimmia species

Rutaceae

Small bushes often grown in gardens, as well as in homes. The flower buds are light red, the flowers white. After the bloom, red berries may appear. The species *reevesiana* and *japonica* need similar care when grown as potted plants.
Care: Grow absolutely cool and keep outside in a lightly shaded location, where it can remain for some time; this plant can endure quite a lot of frost. If one does not have a garden, then the dormancy should be as cool as possible (cold room, hallway, etc.) Fertilize every two weeks in the growing season. Most species and cultivars are dioecious: To get fruit, a male and female specimen are required.
Propagation: Strike slips in August and allow a frost-free dormancy. In the spring, roots will appear.

Light: Half shade.
Temp: Keep cool in the winter, down to 32°F (0°C).
Water: Keep moderately moist.
Hum: High, above 60%.
Soil: Coniferous soil.

Skimmia reevesiana

Smithiantha hybrids

Gesneriaceae

Plants from rain forests in Central America. Mostly hybrids are grown, which are generally unnamed.
Care: Rootstocks can sometimes be ordered by mail. Lay them in moist peat moss or sphagnum and allow them to sprout under glass at a temperature of 68–77°F (20–25°C). Then plant them in pots and keep under glass for a while, for high humidity is necessary. Watch out for fungus growth. If possible, continue to grow in a greenhouse, keeping it indoors only for the few weeks that it blooms. Feed every two weeks. Continue to grow after the plant blooms until fall, adding gradually less water until the foliage dies off. Store the rootstocks dry in the pot, and start again the following year.
Propagation: By dividing the rootstocks, via leaf cuttings and from seed.

Smithiantha-hybr.

Light: Much light or half shade, never full sun.
Temp: Grow warm, with dry storage a minimum of 54°F (12°C).
Water: Keep moderately moist with soft water, no water in the winter.
Hum: High, above 60%.
Soil: An acidic and permeable soil mixture, for instance anthurium or bromeliad soil, or coniferous soil, leaf-soil and peat moss mixed together.

Solandra grandiflora

Solanaceae

Climbing bushes from Central America, suitable for a rather large greenhouse or for a wintergarden.
Care: In nature, these plants sometimes grow a few yards high, so give them space and much light, sun included. Give plenty of water in the summer and add food weekly. When the plants are well developed, a dormant period should be given by watering sparsely, until the leaves fall off. Following that, many flower buds form around August. In the winter maintain the temperature of a moderate greenhouse.

Propagation: From seed and via top cuttings or middle cuttings, which root under glass at 77–86°F (25–30°C) soil temperature.
Light: Full sun.
Temp: Grow warm, in the winter a minimum of 54°F (12°C).
Water: Give plenty of water in the summer, somewhat drier in the winter.
Hum: Moderate to high.
Soil: Standard potting soil mixed with a large part loam and clay.

Solandra grandiflora

Solanum pseudocapsicum

Solanaceae

Jerusalem cherry

This plant is not as lovely as the name suggests, for it contains a dangerous poison. Do not place it around children or pets.
Care: In general, the small fruits are colored in the fall. Much warmth is not needed, so do not immediately place the plant in a warm room. Spraying frequently limits evaporation. When the plant becomes less pretty, prune back considerably and keep dormant in a cool spot. Repot in the spring and after mid-May, plant it outside in its pot. Fertilize every two weeks. Flowers will then appear, and if insects take care of pollination, fruits will, too. Bring inside in the fall.
Propagation: Sow from mid-January, soil temperature 68°F (20°C); plant, and cut off the

Solanum pseudocapsicum

tops a few times. Continue to grow at 60°F (15°C), moving it outside later.

Light:	Full sun.
Temp:	Grow cool, in the winter 50–54°F (10–12°C).
Water:	Keep moderately moist.
Hum:	Moderate to high.
Soil:	Standard potting soil.

Soleirolia soleirolii

Urticaceae

A low, moss-like plant, also known as *Helxine*. The specimen in the picture has a layer of wire netting over the pot.
Care: The *Soleirolia* is very suitable grown as ground cover in large containers where the air is not too dry. It also grows well under tables in greenhouses; Always avoid the sunlight. Feed once every two weeks in the growing period. Keep cooler in the winter, divide in the spring, repot and bring back to growth.
Propagation: By division.

Light:	Half shade, no full sun.
Temp:	Grow cool, 50°F (10°C) in the winter is sufficient.
Water:	Keep moderately moist.
Hum:	Moderate to high.
Soil:	Standard potting soil.

Sonerila margaritacea

Melastomataceae

Soleirolia soleirolii

Small plants with very elegantly marked foliage and also pretty flowers. This species is not well suited for cultivation in the home.
Care: Because of the large need for humid air, grow this plant in a warm greenhouse, otherwise, spray frequently. Feed once every two weeks during growth. Always avoid sunlight and do not keep it too cool in the winter.
Propagation: Top cuttings can root under glass at 68–77°F (20–25°C) soil temperature.

Light:	Much light, no bright sun.
Temp:	Grow warm, a minimum of 64°F (18°C).
Water:	Keep moderately moist with soft water.

Sonerila margaritacea

Hum:	High, above 60%.
Soil:	Coniferous soil mixed with decayed cow manure. Use wide, shallow pots or bowls with good drainage.

Sophronitis cernua

Orchidaceae

Difficultly grown, very small orchids with pseudotubers.
Care: Grow in a cool, light greenhouse, where only the brightest sunlight is screened in the summer. When new pseudotubers are formed, a short dormant period should be given, for about a month, though the plant should not be kept completely dry. Add a

Sophronitis cernua

strongly diluted fertilizer solution weekly in the summer.
Propagation: By division.

Light:	Much light, screen only against the brightest sunlight.
Temp:	Grow cool to moderately warm, in the winter 50°F (10°C) is sufficient.
Water:	Keep rather moist in the summer with rainwater, drier in the dormant period.
Hum:	High, above 60%.
Soil:	Connect to a piece of tree fern or plant in rock wool flakes.

Sparmannia africana

Tiliaceae

A plant that was grown in homes quite a lot before the increased use of central heating, which seems to have limited this plant's usability.
Care: After blooming in the early spring, the plant should be kept cooler and given less water. At the end of May, place the plant on its side in a garden or on a balcony, so that any spare water can end up in its pot. Avoid the sun. Around the end of June, cut back to about 12 in (30 cm), repot and bring back to growth, possibly outside in a lightly shaded, protected location. Give food weekly in July and August. Bring inside before the night frosts and keep it cool, spraying frequently. The plant is best kept light and cool, for instance, in a corridor or hallway.
Propagation: Take top cuttings of side shoots on blooming plants. Soil temperature: 68–77°F (20–25°C). Cut tops of young plants a few times for a better branching.

Light:	Much light in the winter, in the summer half shade, no bright sun.
Temp:	Grow cool, in the winter a minimum of 40°F (5°C).
Water:	Keep moderately moist, except during dormancy. In the growing period, immerse the whole plant once in a while.
Hum:	Moderate to high.
Soil:	Standard potting soil, possibly mixed with clay or loam.

Sparmannia africana

SPATIPHYLLUM

Spatiphyllum wallisii

Spatiphyllum wallisii

Araceae

Plants with white, arum-like flowers. They are grown quite a lot, but not everybody seems to be able to keep them healthy inside their homes. **Care:** This plant needs a high relative humidity, which can cause problems in the winter. If the temperature can be lowered in the winter, it would help the humidity level. Otherwise, growing in a greenhouse would be a better idea. Fertilize once every two weeks in the growing period. **Propagation:** From seed and by division during repotting. Soil temperature 68–77°F (20–25°C).

Light: Much light, no full sun.
Temp: Grow warm, in the winter a minimum of 61°F (16°C).
Water: Keep moderately moist.
Hum: High, above 60%.
Soil: Acidic, airy soil, for instance a mixture of leaf mold, sphagnum and peat moss, provided with the necessary nutrients and some calcium.

Sprekelia formosissima

Amaryllidaceae
Gold-lily, Jacob's-lily

Sprekelia formosissima

Bulbs of this magnificent plant can be ordered by mail, and are usually delivered in the spring. **Care:** Plant the bulbs in pots with the neck just above ground. Keep the pot warm (68–77°F [20–25°C]) and do not give much water initially. The plant does not have to be kept dark. When the growth is well under way, increase the water and place in a cooler spot to prolong the blooming period. After the plants flower, allow them to continue growing, fertilize once every two weeks and add less water after the end of July, until the foliage dies off. Store the bulbs dry in their pots until the following year. **Propagation:** Via bulbs, which are removed and can be grown separately. Propagation from seed is possible as well.

Light: Much light, no full sun.
Temp: Grow cool, during dry storage a minimum of 60°F (15°C).
Water: Rather moist when the plant is growing.
Hum: Moderate, 50–60%.
Soil: Standard potting soil.

Stanhopea wardii

Orchidaceae

Orchids with extremely large flower buds that spring open with a snap. Unfortunately, the flowers only last for about three days. **Care:** Always grow in lattice baskets, over which the flowers hang, quite far. Do not grow too dark, but do not ever allow bright sun, either. Fertilize frequently with orchid food in low concentrations. After the forming of new pseudotubers, the plant should rest dormant

Stanhopea wardii

for a month, otherwise flower development does not occur.
Propagation: By division during repotting.

Light: Much light to half shade, no sun.
Temp: Grow moderately warm to warm, in the winter a minimum of 54°F (12°C).
Water: Give plenty of soft water in the summer, keep drier in the dormant period.
Hum: High, above 60%.
Soil: Peat moss, pieces of tree fern, rock wool, etc. provided there is always good drainage.

Stapelia X divaricata

Asclepiadaceae

Succulent plants with flowers that smell of carrion. The smell is meant to attract flies for pollination. Many species are now categorized

Stapelia X divaricata

with other genera, for instance *Caralluma*, *Huernia* and *Orbea*. The species pictured is a hybrid. The cultivation of all species is similar.
Care: Grow in a lightly shaded or sunny location, preferably in a greenhouse, in lattice baskets. Water carefully, for these plants rot quickly. Fertilizer is not needed. In the winter the temperature may be lowered considerably, and all water withheld.
Propagation: Dry broken-off stalks for a week and plant in almost dry soil. Soil temperature 68°F (20°C).

Light:	Much light or full sun.
Temp:	Moderately warm to warm, in the winter a minimum of 40°F (5°C).
Water:	Keep rather dry, completely dry in the winter. Use only soft water.
Hum:	Low to moderate.
Soil:	Mixture of loam, potting soil and perlite over a layer of clay particles or pottery shards.

Stenocarpus sinuatus

Proteaceae

Bush from Australia with strongly carved foliage, grown elsewhere as a container plant. Older bushes carry magnificent, yellow, orange and red flowers, but these do not appear so often in other climates, unfortunately.
Care: Can be outside from the end of May, very well protected against the brightest afternoon sun. Give moderate amounts of water and feed weekly. Bring inside in the fall and provide a cool dormancy. The foliage should stay on.
Propagation: From seed or via top cuttings, taken in August. Do not give additional soil

Stenocarpus sinuatus

warmth and rest dormant in a cold greenhouse. The roots appear in spring.

Light:	Much light, no bright sun.
Temp:	Grow cool, in the winter 40–50°F (5–10°C).
Water:	Keep moderately moist, drier in the winter.
Hum:	Moderate, 50–60%.
Soil:	Standard potting soil.

Stenotaphrum secundatum

Graminneae

A tropical grass species, almost exclusively grown in the form 'Variegatum,' with striped foliage. A nice hanging plant for a moderately warm room.
Care: The plant has to be kept well lit, or otherwise the foliage loses its beauty. Use rather large pots, for this lessens the chance that the plant will dry out. Add food to the water every two weeks. Repot in the spring, and if necessary cut back and bring back to growth.
Propagation: The long shoots often form roots, so one only has to cut these rooted parts and plant them.

Light:	Much light, full sun, too.
Temp:	Grow moderately warm, in the winter somewhat cooler, if possible, a minimum of 54°F (12°C).
Water:	Keep moderately moist.
Hum:	Moderate, 50–60%.
Soil:	Standard potting soil.

Stephanotis floribunda

Asclepiadaceae
Bridesflower

A climbing plant from the rain forests of Madagascar that is rather popular grown as a houseplant, and which with good care should be able to bloom for several years.
Care: It is very important that the plant stops growing in the winter, so give it a dormancy at lower temperatures than the normal living room temperature. Only then will the plant bloom well and stay healthy the following season. Fertilize once every two weeks in the summer and guide the long vines along a hoop or tie them up against a wall. If buds appear, then do not turn the plant any more. Add less

Stenotaphrum secundatum 'Variegatum'

water and food toward the fall, and keep cooler in November. At the end of the winter, after flower buds have appeared, gradually increase the temperature. The bloom can be forced by artificial lighting and higher temperatures. Repot after the plant blooms.
Propagation: Via middle cuttings with one leaf couplet. Soil temperature 68–77°F (20–25°C). Use cutting powder.

Light:	Much light, no bright sun.
Temp:	Grow moderately warm to warm, in the winter 54–57°F (12–14°C).
Water:	Keep moderately moist with soft water, drier in the winter.
Hum:	Moderate to high.
Soil:	Standard potting soil, possibly mixed with fine clay or loam.

Stephanotis floribunda

STRELITZIA

Strelitzia reginae

Strelitziaceae

Often sold as cut flowers and seldom in the form of houseplants. Cultivation is not that easy, for the plants need to be kept somewhat warm in the winter. Nevertheless, it is possible to produce flowers indoors every year.

Care: Use rather large containers and feed every two weeks in the summer. The plant should be kept quite warm and especially sunny. In warm summers, the *Strelitzia* can even be placed outside in an extremely protected spot (patio, terrace). Bring inside in the fall for dormancy at a moderate temperature and with less water.

Propagation: From fresh seed and by dividing older plants.

Light:	Full sun.
Temp:	Grow moderately warm, in the winter between 46–54°F (8–12°C).
Water:	Keep moderately moist in the summer, quite dry in the winter.
Hum:	Moderate, 50–60%.
Soil:	Standard potting soil mixed with 50% fine clay or loam. Use rather large containers and repot carefully, for the meaty roots rot easily.

Strelitzia reginae

Streptocarpus grandis

Gesneriaceae

One of the original parent species of the current hybrids (see below) available. This species has enormous leaves and very small flowers. With the hybrids, the aim is to achieve the opposite.

Care: Grow in half shade, with no afternoon sun. Keep moderately moist and fertilize every two weeks. In the winter, this plant can be kept cooler. Repot in the spring and continue to grow.

Propagation: From seed and from leaf cuttings.

Light:	Half shade.

Streptocarpus grandis

Temp:	Grow moderately warm, in the winter 54–60°F (12–15°C).
Water:	Keep moderately moist.
Hum:	Moderate, 50–60%.
Soil:	Standard potting soil.

Streptocarpus hybrids

Gesneraceae

A beautiful houseplant that can last for years if it is taken care of properly. Problems with the cultivation and transport of the plant have limited its popularity. Hopefully, this will soon change, for this plant is worth it.

Care: An ideal spot is one in a window facing east, where the sun disappears around 11:00 A.M. Full sun is bad, so screen against the afternoon sun. Remove old flowers in the summer and also some of the older branches. Give food every two weeks. In the fall, the bloom can be prolonged by hanging a normal light bulb above the plants. But in the winter, a dormant period with lower temperatures

Streptocarpus 'Laura Nimf'

Streptocarpus-hybr.

and less water is necessary. Repot in the spring and bring back to growth. When the days lengthen, the flowers will appear.
Propagation: From leaf cuttings. The long leaves have to be cut along the middle nerve and placed on their sides in soil. Soil temperature: 68°F (20°C). A whole row of young plants will form along the nerve.

Light:	Half shade.
Temp:	Grow moderately warm, in the winter 54–60°F (12–15°C).
Water:	Keep moderately moist, drier in the winter.
Hum:	Moderate, 50–60%.
Soil:	Standard potting soil.

Streptocarpus saxorum

Gesneriaceae

Besides the *Streptocarpus* hybrids, there is a whole range of botanical species with large leaves and small flowers. The species pictured has both small leaves and flowers, but it is still a very nice plant.
Care: The thick leaves contain much moisture, which indicates that the plant can endure periods of drought quite well. It is able to adapt to full sun, too. Do not give too much water and feed monthly. Allow a dormant period in the winter at low temperatures and with sparse water.

Streptocarpus saxorum

Propagation: From leaf cuttings. Allow the leaves to dry for a few days before planting.

Light:	Much light, full sun as well.
Temp:	Moderately warm to warm, in the winter 46–54°F (8–12°C).
Water:	Keep rather dry, even drier in the winter.
Hum:	Moderate, 50–60%.
Soil:	Standard potting soil, possibly mixed with clay.

Streptosolen jamesonii

Solanaceae

A bush from the mountains of Colombia and Ecuador. This plant can grow in a moderate greenhouse or inside the home.
Care: It is too cold to grow this plant as an outdoor container plant, so keep it in a greenhouse in the daytime (unless it is a really hot summer). However, allow it to cool off at night, for this happens in its natural habitat as well. Keep moderately moist and feed once every two weeks. Bring it inside in the winter for a cool and light dormant period. Flowers appear in the spring. After a plant blooms, prune back if necessary, repot and continue to grow.
Propagation: From seed or via top cuttings, which root easily under glass at 68–77°F (20–25°C) soil temperature.

Light:	Full sun.
Temp:	Daytime 68–86°F (20–30°C), at night 40–50°F (5–10°C), in the winter 54–60°F (12–15°C).
Water:	Keep moderately moist.
Hum:	Moderate, 50–60%.
Soil:	Standard potting soil with an extra ⅓ part of loam or clay.

Strobilanthes dyerianus
See *Perilepta dyeriana*.

Streptosolen jamesonii

Stromanthe amabilis

Stromanthe species

Marantaceae

This plant is often confused with *Calanthea* or *Ctenanthe*. It is not an easy houseplant to grow, though it is sold as such. *Stromanthe sanguinea* is the strongest species, and can be kept darker.
Care: The plant needs a humid atmosphere, which is usually lacking in the winter. Moreover, it has to be grown continuously warm. Avoid bright sunlight, but do not keep the plant too dark, otherwise the leaf markings disappear.
Propagation: By division.

Light:	Much light, no bright sun.
Temp:	Grow warm at a minimum of 64°F (18°C).
Water:	Keep moderately moist.
Hum:	High, above 60%.
Soil:	Standard potting soil mixed with perlite or peat moss for extra permeability. Use shallow pots or bowls with good drainage.

Stromanthe sanguinea

Sulcorebutia mizquensis

Sulcorebutia mizquensis

Cactaceae

A split-off from the better known genus *Rebutia*, consisting of spherically sprouting, very small cacti with large flowers. These are ideal for collectors, for they are beautiful and do not need much space.

Care: The plants have to be placed in a light and airy spot, even outside in the summer if it does not rain. Give cactus food monthly. After the plants bloom, from mid-June until mid-August, a dormant period should be given by keeping the plant rather dry. After that, let the plants continue to grow for another month, then add more water. At the end of October, the winter dormant period arrives, at which point the plants should be kept cool, and withhold almost all water. Mist only in the winter, until flower buds appear. Then add only a little bit of water to the soil.

Propagation: By taking side shoots, which can be used as cuttings. From seed as well.

Light:	Full sun.
Temp:	Grow cool to moderately warm, in the winter 37–45°F (3–7°C); with drought, they can endure some frost.
Water:	Keep rather dry, even drier in dormancy.
Hum:	Low.
Soil:	Cactus soil.

Synadenium grantii

Euphorbiaceae

A bush from Uganda and Tanzania with succulent stalks and thick leaves. The leaves contain latex. The green foliage is often marked with a wine-red color. The form with extra red leaves is called 'Rubra' (see photograph above).

Care: This plant belongs to the *Euphorbia* family and must always be grown warm and without much water. A dormant period is not necessary. Much light is needed; an appropriate spot would be a window facing south. Feed once every three weeks, but only when the plant grows.

Propagation: Allow top cuttings to dry for a few days, then plant in sandy soil. Soil temperature: 68–77°F (20–25°C).

Synadenium grantii 'Rubra'

Light:	Full sun.
Temp:	Grow warm, a minimum of 64°F (18°C).
Water:	Rather dry to moderately moist.
Hum:	Moderate, 50–60%.
Soil:	Mix standard potting soil with fine clay and sharp sand or perlite.

Syngonium podophyllum

Araceae

A member of the *Philodendron* family. It's a vigorous climber with small leaves. This houseplant can last a long while. In general, the variegated forms are most often available, since these are prettier, but they are less hardy than the green species.

Care: This plant can stay in a warm room all year, but should be provided with extra humidity in the winter, when the temperature can be lower, but not by much. Feed once every two weeks in the summer. Never keep it in the sun. Repot in the spring.

Propagation: From top cuttings or eye cuttings grown under glass. Soil temperature: 68–77°F (20–25°C).

Light:	Much light for the variegated forms, half shade for the green. Never allow full sun.

Syngonium podophyllum 'Greengold'

Temp:	Grow warm, a minimum of 60°F (15°C).
Water:	Keep moderately moist with soft water.
Hum:	Moderate, 50–60%.
Soil:	Standard potting soil, preferably mixed with coniferous soil.

Syngonium podophyllum 'Trileaf Wonder'

Tacca chantrieri

Taccaceae

Tropical plant with almost black flowers, suited for a warm greenhouse.

Care: Keep this plant in a greenhouse with high humidity and light shade all year. Feed once every two weeks in the growing period, possibly using rainwater.

Propagation: From seed or by division.

Light:	Much light, no full sun.
Temp:	Grow warm, never below 61°F (16°C).
Water:	Keep moderately moist with soft water.
Hum:	High, above 60%.
Soil:	A mixture of coniferous soil and sharp sand.

Tacca chantrieri

Tecoma castanifolia

Tecoma castanifolia

Bignoniaceae

Small tree from Ecuador, grown elsewhere as a container plant. It will not bloom as lavishly this way as in its native Central America.
Care: Place outside from the end of May in a sunny, protected spot. Water moderately and feed weekly. In the winter, a dormant period is necessary, but not so strict that the foliage falls off.
Propagation: Via top or middle cuttings, soil temperature 68–77°F (20–25°C).

Light: Full sun.

Tecomaria capensis

Temp:	Grow cool to moderately warm, in the winter 40–50°F (5–10°C).
Water:	Keep moderately moist.
Hum:	Moderate, 50–60%.
Soil:	Mixture of ⅔ part standard potting soil and ⅓ part loam or clay.

Tecomaria capensis

Bigoniaceae

A somewhat climbing evergreen bush from South Africa, where it blooms lavishly with trumpet-shaped flowers. When grown in a more moderate climate as a container plant, the bloom is less striking.
Care: Place outside in the summer, protected and sunny. Give plenty of water and feed weekly. Tie up the shoots if necessary. Bring inside in the fall, though do not keep it so cold that the foliage falls off. Prune considerably in the spring, so that the plant starts to grow more in the shape of a bush, which is easier to do when it's cultivated as a container plant.
Propagation: From seed, via top cuttings or middle cuttings and from shooting sprouts (lay long shoots in the soil). Soil temperature 68–77°F (20–25°C).

Light:	Full sun.
Temp:	Grow cool to moderately warm, in the winter 40–50°F (5–10°C).
Water:	Keep moderately moist.
Hum:	Moderate, 50–60%.
Soil:	Mixture of ⅓ part loam or clay, ⅔ part standard potting soil.

Testudinaria elephantipes

Testudinaria species

Dioscoreaceae

This plant originates in South Africa. Some species are taken from the genus *Dioscorea*. They are peculiar plants with large tubers that stick out halfway above the ground. In times of drought, the part above ground dies off and the tuber stays alive.
Care: The dormant period of these plants falls in the middle of the summer, and they should only be given enough water to keep the tuber from drying out completely. In the fall, the plants come out again (having previously sprouted in the spring). Keep them warm in the winter, moderately moist, and add food once in a while. Place the plant close to a window, for it needs a lot of light during the growth period. The ideal spot is in a warm greenhouse.
Propagation: From seed.

Light:	Much light; sun, too.
Temp:	Grow warm, a minimum of 64°F (18°C).
Water:	Keep moderately moist during the growing period, almost dry during dormancy.
Hum:	Moderate to high.
Soil:	Standard potting soil mixed with loam, clay or perlite.

Testudinaria sylvatica

Tetraclinis articulata

Tetraclinis articulata

Cupressaceae

Conifer from Morocco, Malta, etc. It is not hardy in northern regions, but can be grown as a houseplant there. Sometimes young, sown specimens are sold as houseplants, and on these the young blue cones have not yet appeared.
Care: It's best to treat this as a container plant, so keep it outside from the end of May, protected and lightly shaded. Water moderately and fertilize once every two weeks. Bring inside in the fall for a cool and light dormancy, during which the foliage should stay on. The plant can probably rest dormant in a warm room as well, just like some other conifers.
Propagation: From fresh seeds.

Light:	Much light, no full sun.
Temp:	Grow cool to moderately warm, in the winter a minimum of 40°F (5°C).
Water:	Keep moderately moist.
Hum:	Moderate, 50–60%.
Soil:	Standard potting soil with ⅓ part fine loam or clay.

Tetranema roseum

Scrophulariaceae

Rather unknown, but this potted plant blooms for a long period. It is also known under the species name *mexicanum*.
Care: It can be cultivated warm the whole year, preferably in a closed plant window, for the air is more humid there. Otherwise, spray

Tetranema roseum

frequently. Fertilize in the summer. In the winter the temperature may fall a few degrees, but this is not absolutely necessary. Repot in the spring and bring back to growth. Young plants bloom more richly, though.
Propagation: Sow from January at soil temperature 68–77°F (20–25°C). These plants may bloom the first year. Also possible from the parts of dormant plants.

Light:	Much light, no full sun.
Temp:	Grow warm, a minimum of 57°F (14°C).
Water:	Keep moderately moist.
Hum:	High, above 60%.
Soil:	Standard potting soil.

Tetrastigma voinierianum

Vitaceae

A climbing plant from the grape family with large, palmate leaves. It is very suitable for climbing stairs in hallways that are not heated much in the winter. The shoots can become many yards long.
Care: The young shoots appear in the most unexpected moments. Tie them up immediately, otherwise they break off soon. Give food every two weeks during the growth period. After that, the growth stops for a while and food is no longer necessary. If the plant becomes too tall, prune it back considerably; it will begin growing from the axils again.
Propagation: Root eye cuttings at a soil temperature of 77°F (25°C) under glass.

Light:	Much light to half shade, never full sun.
Temp:	Grow moderately warm, in the winter a minimum of 50°F (10°C). Best temperature is 57–64°F (14–18°C).
Water:	Keep moderately moist.
Hum:	Moderate to high.
Soil:	Standard potting soil.

Tetrastigma voinierianum

Thevetia peruviana

Thevetia peruviana

Apocynaceae

Yellow oleander

Evergreen bushes that are often found in tropical gardens. Just as with the common oleander (see *Nerium*), they are poisonous. The flowers have a fragrant bloom.
Care: Grow in a moderate greenhouse; in the south, possibly outside in the summer, but always protected. Allow full sun. Give moderate amounts of water and feed once every two weeks. In the winter the temperature may be lowered. Administer less water then as well, but not so sparse that the foliage dies off.
Propagation: From seed at soil temperature 68–77°F (20–25°C).

Light:	Full sun.
Temp:	Grow warm, in the winter a minimum of 54°F (12°C).
Water:	Keep moderately moist.
Hum:	Moderate, 50–60%.
Soil:	Standard potting soil, possibly mixed with extra loam or clay.

Thunbergia alata

Acanthaceae

Black-eyed Susan

An annual climbing plant that is grown from seed and can be found in shops in the spring.

Thunbergia alata

Thunbergia alata 'Alba'

There are also cultivated forms with white ('Alba') or more orange-colored flowers.
Care: When blooming, this plant should be kept well lit, with moderate amounts of water and fertilizer once every two weeks. After the bloom *Tialanta* is generally thrown away, but it is possible to keep it alive through the winter. Provide a dormancy in a cold greenhouse, cut back, repot and bring back to growth.
Propagation: In general, this is sown every year. This can happen under glass in December at a soil temperature of 64°F (18°C). Put three seeds in one pot. Going from seed to blooming plant takes 10–16 weeks.

Light:	Much light, full sun, too.
Temp:	Grow cool to moderately warm, a minimum of 40°F (5°C).
Water:	Keep moderately moist.
Hum:	Moderate, 50–60%.
Soil:	Standard potting soil.

Tibouchina urvilleana

Melastomataceae

A beautiful container plant, sometimes referred to as *Lasiandra semidecandra*. This bush displays its velvety leaves over the whole summer, and its beautiful purple flowers in the fall.
Care: Keep outside in a sunny, protected spot from the end of May. Give much water and feed once every two weeks until the end of August. When the plant starts to bloom, generally in October, it can stay indoors for a while. After that, it has to go to a dormancy space, where it can be kept until spring at low temperatures and with sparse water. It is probably possible to store the bush underground, after pruning it considerably. It is necessary, in any case, to cut it back in the early spring, for these plants have the unfortunate tendency to become rather weak.
Propagation: Young top cuttings make roots in spring under glass at a soil temperature of 68–77°F (20–25°C). Cut off the tops a few times for better branching.

Light:	Full sun.
Temp:	Grow cool, in the winter keep 40–50°F (5–10°C) for cool storage.
Water:	Keep moderately moist, drier in the winter.
Hum:	Moderate, 50–60%.
Soil:	Standard potting soil.

Tillandsia flabellata

Tillandsia seleriana

Tibouchina urvilleana

Tillandsia species

Bromeliaceae

Gray-scaled *Tillandsia* species differ considerably from other deciduous species. They do not have many roots and absorb moisture through the gray hairs on their foliage. The leaves form a rosette reminiscent of a bulb (see detail of *Tillandsia seleriana*).
Care: In nature, these plants grow as epiphytes (on trees or other plants) in regions where it is often foggy, but where dry periods also occur, with bright sun and cold. These conditions can be imitated. Add water by misting a few times a day and immerse in a bowl of water once a week. In the summer, the plants can hang outside, initially lightly screened, but later on in the full sun. Move to a greenhouse in the winter, where they can hang just below the glass at lower temperatures. Provide ventilation, for these plants are not supposed to get too wet.
Propagation: The rather small rosettes form many shoots, so that after a while a web of young and old (dying) rosettes may be formed. By dividing carefully, one can propagate the plants. From seed it is possible, too, but this requires much care.

Light:	Much light; full sun, too.
Temp:	Grow cool, in the winter 60°F (15°C).
Water:	Mist and immerse in rainwater.
Hum:	High, alternating with low.
Soil:	Tie up with copper wire or pieces of panty hose on pieces of bark, tree fern, etc. At the same time, tie some young shoots of conifers and the young plant together, using, for instance, small branches of *Juniperus* or *Thuja*.

TILLANDSIA

Tillandsia cyanea

Tillandsia usneoides

Tolmiea menziesii

Tillandsia cyanea

Bromeliaceae

One of the most well-known deciduous species, seen rather often in flower shops. Another species that looks much like *T. cyanea* is *T. lindenii*. The purple flowers have a white center. The plants are generally thrown away after they've lost their flowers.
Care: A blooming plant can stay in a warm room for a while. As the blooming rosette dies off, many new side rosettes are formed in the meantime. To cultivate them for flowering, a greenhouse is needed. High humidity, shade and high temperatures are also required. Water only with soft water and add some food once every two weeks.
Propagation: Remove side rosettes when they are half the size of the old plant and plant them in separate pots. Leave a piece of root with the old rosette.

Light:	Half shade, never full sun.
Temp:	Grow warm, never below 64°F (18°C).
Water:	Use rainwater or soft water and keep moderately moist.
Hum:	High, above 60%.
Soil:	Very permeable, acidic mixture for epiphytes, such as bromeliad soil.

Tillandsia ionantha

Bromeliaceae

One of the most well-known species with gray leaves, similar in cultivation to the species described on page 349.
Care: Hang outside in the summer. Immerse once a week in a fertilizer solution. Keep cooler in the winter, but still as light as possible.
Propagation: By division or from seed.

Light:	Much light, full sun, too.
Temp:	Grow cool, in the winter 60°F (15°C).
Water:	Mist daily and immerse once in a while.
Hum:	High, combined with low.
Soil:	Grow on pieces of tree fern, pieces of bark, etc.

Tillandsia usneoides

Bromeliaceae
Spanish moss

An extreme example of a plant that can live completely without roots. Spanish moss hangs on trees in regions with high humidity and subsists basically on air. It is a great example of a longitudinally growing bromeliad: The extremely small plants elongate themselves and in this way long vines are created.
Care: This is not difficult to grow in a greenhouse. Mist regularly, perhaps adding food to the water. In the winter, the temperature may be lowered, but this is not absolutely necessary.
Propagation: Simply by taking pieces of the plants.

Light:	Much light, no full sun.
Temp:	Grow moderately warm to warm, in the winter a minimum of 54°F (12°C).
Water:	Keep moist by spraying with soft water or rainwater.
Hum:	High, above 60%.
Soil:	None.

Tillandsia ionantha

Tolmiea menziesii

Saxifragaceae

A nice small plant that forms buds on the leaves, from which new plants grow.
Care: An easy, hardy plant that can remain in a warm room the whole year, although cooler conditions are excellent for it as well. It can be placed on a balcony in the summer, provided that there is no bright sunlight. Give some food every two weeks during the growth period.
Propagation: By division and by striking slips from an old plant with buds. Cut away the old leaves as much as possible and bury the remaining part with buds somewhat under the soil.

Light:	Shade or half shade, no sun.
Temp:	Grow cool to moderately warm, in the winter a minimum of 50°F (10°C).
Water:	Moderately moist.
Hum:	Moderate, 50–60%.
Soil:	Standard potting soil.

Torenia fournieri

Scrophulariaceae

A small annual plant that is commonly sold as a houseplant.

Tourenia fournieri

Care: Provide a light location, but avoid the sun. Much warmth is not necessary. The plant will continue to bloom if some food is given every two weeks. After that, it is better to throw the plant out, though a dormant period is possible.

Propagation: Sow in February under glass; soil temperature 64°F (18°C). After sprouting, plant out in the final pots, 5 to 10 plants per pot of 5 in (12 cm) diameter. Harden off and cut the tops off a few times for better branching.

Light:	Much light, no bright sun.
Temp:	Grow moderately warm.
Water:	Moderately moist.
Hum:	Moderate, 50–60%.
Soil:	Standard potting soil.

Trachycarpus fortunei

Palmae

A famous palm, also known by the name *Chamaerops excelsa* or *C. fortunei*. The difference is that with *Chamaerops* the leaf stalks are covered with bigger thorns than on *Trachycarpus*.

Care: This palm can grow rather tall and is suitable for large containers. In the summer, the plant can be placed outside; if it is young, keep lightly shaded, otherwise, older plants can endure the sun. Provide moderate amounts of water and feed every two weeks. Problems start only toward the winter, when a cool, frost-free storage spot has to be found for the palm. A cold greenhouse is ideal, but a part of the garage where enough light comes in is an alternative, too.

Propagation: Fresh seeds germinate at 77–86°F (25–30°C) soil temperature under glass.

Light:	Much light, later, full sun, too.
Temp:	Grow cool, store in the winter 32–45°F (0–7°C).
Water:	Keep moderately moist, drier in the winter.
Hum:	Moderate, 50–60%.
Soil:	Standard potting soil mixed with at least ⅓ part fine clay or loam, or with 15% rock wool powder.

Trachycarpus fortunei

Trachycarpus fortunei

Tradescantia species

Commelinaceae
Fatherplants

Nice, often variegated foliage plants that are most suitable as hanging plants. One can find some species regularly in plant shops.

Care: Do not keep the variegated species too dark; however, do not keep them in the full sun either. Always give plenty of water and add food every two weeks. Preferably place cooler in the winter: Room air often becomes too dry, which may harm the foliage.

Tradescantia albiflora 'Rochford Silver'

Tradescantia blossfeldiana

Propagation: Allow top cuttings to dry for a few days and then plant. They root very easily, without extra soil warmth.

Light:	Half shade to much light, no direct sun.
Temp:	Grow moderately warm, in the winter a minimum of 50°F (10°C).
Water:	Moderately moist in the summer, in the winter at low temperatures water sparsely.
Hum:	Moderate, 50–60%.
Soil:	Standard potting soil.

Tradescantia fluminensis 'Variegata'

Tradescantia sillamontana

TREVESIA

Trevesia palmata

Trichodiadema densum

Trevesia palmata

Araliaceae

Relatively rare house or rather greenhouse plants with strangely shaped leaves that somewhat resemble a duck's foot. Young foliage is covered with gray scales, which later disappear.
Care: Grow preferably planted in the full ground of a warm or moderate greenhouse, not in the sun. Otherwise keep indoors, though the air quickly becomes too dry. Water moderately and fertilize every two weeks. In the winter the temperature can be lower, but not too much. Give less water, but enough so that the foliage does not fall off.
Propagation: Top cuttings root under glass at 86–95°F (30–35°C).

Light:	Much light, no bright sun.
Temp:	Grow moderately warm to warm, in the winter 57–64°F (14–18°C).
Water:	Keep moderately moist, preferably with rainwater; drier in the winter.
Hum:	High, above 60%.
Soil:	Mixture of standard potting soil with about ⅓ part clay or loam.

Trichocereus spachianus

Cactaceae

Column cactus from Argentina, which grows there up to 7 ft (2 m) high. In other regions, the plant is often grown as a fast-growing trunk for other cacti that do not grow well on their own roots. (For information on how this works, read on page 83). A few other species can form big flowers, which generally open at night.

Care: This strong species (and a few other species as well) can grow outside in the summer. Water moderately and feed every two weeks. Keep cool and dry in the winter. Many species can endure light night frost then.
Propagation: Seeds germinate at 68°F (20°C) soil temperature. Striking slips is a possibility too, by cutting long trunks in 3 in (7 cm) pieces. Allow these to dry and plant in sandy soil.

Light:	Full sun.
Temp:	Grow cool, in the winter a minimum of 32°F (0°C).
Water:	Keep moderately moist in the summer, in the winter withhold all water at low temperatures.
Hum:	Low.
Soil:	Cactus soil.

Trichocereus spachianus

Trichodiadema densum

Aizoaceae

These small plants look exactly like cacti, but are not. They are afternoon bloomers and come from drought regions of South Africa. They bloom between January and March (which is summer there).
Care: Grow in full sun in a greenhouse or in a window. Possibly move outside in warm summers. Keep rather dry and feed monthly. In the fall bring inside and place it in a light spot. Do not keep it too cold and add enough water to grow on. Repot after blooming and continue to grow.
Propagation: From leaf cuttings and from seed.

Light:	Full sun.
Temp:	Grow moderately warm, in the winter a minimum of 64°F (18°C).
Water:	Keep moderately moist.
Hum:	Low.
Soil:	Mixture of standard potting soil with perlite and loam or clay (in equal parts).

Tritonia crocata

Iridaceae

Bulbous growth from South Africa, not hardy in moderate climates. It grows in our winters and rests dormant in the summer. The flowers appear in May through June.

Tritonia crocata

Care: Small bulbs can be ordered by mail. Plant in pots and keep warm. At first, do not give so much water; when the leaves develop increase the water supply. The temperature should not rise too much, so do not place in a warm room. But do place it in a very light, sunny window of a cool bedroom or hallway, or in a cold or moderate greenhouse. Feed monthly. After the plant blooms, gradually add less water, until all the foliage has died off. Store the bulbs dry and put them in pots again the following fall.

Propagation: Via bulbs.

Light:	Much light, sun as well in the winter.
Temp:	Grow cool to moderately warm, in the growing period (winter) at 46–60°F (8–15°C).
Water:	Moderately moist, withhold water in the dormant period.
Hum:	Moderate, 50–60%.
Soil:	Standard potting soil.

Tropaeolum species

Tropaeolaceae

There are various tuberous relations of the East Indian cress, a famous garden plant. Other than the species pictured, there are the species *tricolor* and *tuberosum*.

Care: These climbing plants should be grown in a cold greenhouse. Plant tubers in pots in the fall and initially give sparse water. Only when the growth starts, toward the end of January, should one gradually add more water. Provide wire netting or other support for the climbing shoots. In the summer, much light is needed and good ventilation, so that it does not get too hot in the greenhouse. In warm summers, they may be grown outside. Add food weekly. The flowers appear in late summer, though with the species *tricolor* it's usually in bloom by spring. Withhold all water after the plant blooms, so that the foliage dies off. Store the tubers dry for a while and bring back to growth.

Propagation: From seed, via middle cuttings or shoots (stalks lying under the soil often form small tubers).

Light:	Much light, sun, too.

Tropaeolum azureum

Tropaeolum pentaphyllum

Temp:	Grow cool to moderately warm, in the winter 40–50°F (5–10°C), warmer during the growing season.
Water:	Moderately moist, completely dry during dormancy.
Hum:	Moderate to high.
Soil:	Standard potting soil with extra peat moss or with leaf soil.

Tulipa hybrids

Liliaceae
Tulip

Tulips are not houseplants, but almost all species and cultivars can be forced into blooming inside. The old bulbs are worthless afterwards.

Care: After being placed in pots, tulip bulbs need a cool, dark period in which the roots are formed. Only when one can clearly feed the flower bud above the bulb in the shoot can the pots or bowls with tulips be placed in the light. The best temperature for forming roots is 48°F (9°C). Plant bulbs in pots or bowls in mid-October and ensilage them 20 in (50 cm) deep in

Tulipa 'Rosario'

a spot that will remain fairly dry. Cover the silage spot with reeds, otherwise it will be difficult to reach the pots when the ground freezes hard. Check in mid-January to see if a flower bud is touchable. If there is no garden available, then the rooting can occur in a dark cellar or in a frost-free, dark plant case on a balcony. Do not keep the containers with tulips too warm at first when they go inside: 60°F (15°C) initially is adequate. The bloom can last longer when the temperature is not so high.

Light:	Total darkness during rooting, much light from the moment that the flower buds are touchable, no full sun.
Temp:	Around 48°F (9°C) for the rooting, during growth 60–64°F (15–18°C).
Water:	Moderately moist.
Hum:	High, above 60%.
Soil:	Standard potting soil mixed with 50% sharp sand.

Tupidanthus calyptratus

Araliaceae

A not-very-well-known plant, related to the *Schefflera* and similar varieties in cultivation. In southern Europe the plant can be grown outside, though in more northerly regions it is a container plant.

Care: Possibly grow outside from the end of May, keeping it very protected and sunny (young specimens have to get used to the sun gradually). With indoor cultivation allow no full sun. Give food every two weeks. Bring inside in the fall for a cool but light dormancy. The foliage will stay on; it does fall off with very low temperatures, but the plant should stay alive.

Propagation: From fresh seed and also from eye cuttings. Soil temperature 68–77°F (20–25°C).

Light:	Much light, full sun, too.
Temp:	Grow cool, in the winter 50–60°F (10–15°C), possibly a minimum 40°F (5°C).
Water:	Moderately moist.
Hum:	Moderate to high.
Soil:	Standard potting soil, possibly mixed with extra clay or loam.

Tupidanthus calyptratus

Turnera ulmifolia

Turneraceae

Half-bush from Central and South America with foliage resembling the leaves of the nettle. It is generally grown elsewhere as a greenhouse plant.
Care: This plant requires humid air, and therefore it is difficult to grow in the home. Keep rather warm and give food during the growing period once every two weeks. Flowers appear in the morning, and the blooming period lasts from the early spring until the fall. Keep it a bit cooler in the winter, and cut back in the spring if necessary, repot and bring back to growth.
Propagation: From seed or from eye cuttings that root at soil temperature 68–77°F (20–25°C) under glass.

Light: Much light, no full sun.
Temp: Grow warm, in the winter 60–64°F (15–18°C).
Water: Keep moderately moist.
Hum: High, above 60%.
Soil: Standard potting soil mixed with extra loam or clay.

Turnera ulmifolia

Uebelmannia pectinifera

Cactaceae

A cactus family with only six species; the genus pictured was discovered in 1966. It's a rather threatening species with densely planted areoles. Green-yellow flowers and red fruits may appear.
Care: Somewhat differently from most cacti, these plants grow in nature in relatively humid humus. Water frequently in the summer and spray as well. In the winter the temperature should not be much lower. Growth proceeds slowly, so do not give an excess of food to try to force the growth.
Propagation: From seed.

Light: Much light, full sun, too.
Temp: Grow warm, in the winter not below 60°F (15°C).
Water: Keep moderately moist with rainwater.
Hum: Moderate to high.
Soil: A very acidic, humusy mixture, for instance leaf mold with coniferous soil, in pots with good drainage.

Urceolina grandiflora

Urceolina grandiflora

Amaryllidaceae
Brides-lily

A bulbous growth that is still generally called *Eucharis*. The flowers are often used in brides' bouquets. The bulbs can be forced into blooming indoors.
Care: Plant the bulbs 2 in (5 cm) under the soil in March or August; the pots do not have to be kept dark at first. Only start to give water when the plants begin to grow. Allow a month of dormancy after they bloom by sparsely adding water. A second blooming may follow. In the growing period, add food every 14 days.
Propagation: Via bulbs, which can be removed and grown separately (preferably in a greenhouse).

Light: Much light, no direct sun.
Temp: For sprouting bulbs 68–77°F (20–25°C). In the growing period 68°F (20°C), at night a few degrees lower. During dormancy 60°F (15°C).

Uebelmannia pectinifera

Water: Keep almost dry with the sprouting, during growth and blooming moderately moist, in the dormant period rather dry (the leaves do not have to dry out, though).
Hum: High, above 60%.
Soil: Standard potting soil mixed with clay or loam.

Vallota speciosa

Amaryllidaceae

A bulbous growth from South Africa that in appearance and in cultivation, too, resembles the *Hippeastrum* (amaryllis). Bulbs can be ordered by mail.
Care: After receiving the bulbs, plant them in pots with the tops just above ground, and keep rather warm. The bulbs do not need to be placed in darkness at first. Start to add water only when the growth period begins. Feed weekly in the summer. Add less water towards the fall, but not so sparsely that the leaves die (this would be all right, but is not necessary). The dormancy should be cool and rather dry.
Propagation: By removing and growing newly formed bulbs separately.

Vallota speciosa

Light: Much light, full sun, too.
Temp: Grow cool to moderately warm, in the winter 40–50°F (5–10°C).
Water: Initially very sparse, in the growing period moderately moist, rather dry during dormancy.
Hum: Moderate, 50–60%.
Soil: Standard potting soil.

Vanda coerulea

Orchidaceae

Monopodial orchids, plants that only grow at the top. Pseudotubers are not formed. The species in the photograph is one of the most well-known of the genus *Vanda*.
Care: These are orchids for a moderate or warm greenhouse, including the species pic-

Vanda coerulea 'Thailand Beauty'

tured. An extreme amount of light is needed, so screen only the brightest summer sun. The temperature can rise considerably, as long as the air does not become too dry. Spray frequently with rainwater. Add orchid food in the growing season, once every 14 days. In the winter the temperature may fall a bit, but a very strict dormant period is not necessary.
Propagation: By removing rooted side shoots, and from seed.

Light:	Much light, no bright sun.
Temp:	Grow moderately warm to warm, in the winter a minimum of 54°F (12°C).
Water:	Plenty of rainwater in the summer, somewhat drier in the winter.
Hum:	High, above 60%.
Soil:	Grow in pots, in lattice baskets and also on pieces of tree fern. Soil mixture should consist of clay particles, peat moss or pure rock wool, and should drain very well.

Veltheimia capensis

Liliaceae

Winter rocket

A delicate bulbous plant that can be ordered by mail. The flowers are reminiscent of those of the *Kniphofia*, a perennial garden plant.
Care: Bulbs should be planted in a pot immediately after delivery. They can be placed in the light right away. In the beginning, keep them rather dry, but as soon as growth has started, add more water. After sprouting, the temperature should be lowered. When flowers appear in the spring, the plant can be moved outside if temperatures remain above freezing. In this way, the bloom lasts longer. After the plant blooms, continue to grow and add food every two weeks. The dormant period falls in the middle of the summer; therefore, withhold water and food from the end of June, until all the leaves have dried up. The bulb can remain in the pot until the fall, then start again.
Propagation: By removing young bulbs or from seed.

Veltheimia capensis

Light:	Much light, full sun, too.
Temp:	Grow cool: when sprouting, 68°F (20°C), during bloom around 54°F (12°C), no warmer.
Water:	Mostly moderate during growth.
Hum:	Moderate, 50–60%.
Soil:	Standard potting soil mixed with some fine clay or loam.

Vriesea species

Bromeliaceae

One of the most famous bromeliads, the variety most frequently sold has long red dagger-shaped blooms. The colorful features of this plant are actually the bracts, for the flowers are not very remarkable and only remain for a short period. There are also *Vriesea* with branched blooms and also many cross-fertilizations have been created recently. The foliage is often beautifully cross-striped;

Vriesea carinata

sometimes it looks as though they contain signs (*Vriesea hieroglyphica*).
Care: The rosette of a bromeliad dies off after the plant blooms. This can take a while, but it happens. By giving the plant water and keeping it on the cool side (at least not in the sun) one can prolong its life span. The strength of the light does not make much difference. When the plant becomes less pretty, dispose of it. The cultivation of new bromeliads from the young plants that develop before the parent rosette dies is another case. These plants require a lot of light (no sun), a relatively high temperature and especially high humidity. A warm greenhouse is ideal for this purpose. During growth it should receive some food regularly. Water may be poured down the funnel in the summer, but in the winter keep this part dry. After about three years the new plants may bloom. If this does not happen, pour some chemicals in the funnel to stimulate blooming.
Propagation: The newly formed plants should be removed when they are as large as the parent rosette. If they do not appear to have enough roots, cut off a piece of the original rosette, too.

Light:	Much light, no full sun.
Temp:	Grow warm, a minimum of 64°F (18°C).
Water:	Keep moderately moist with soft water.
Hum:	High, above 60%.
Soil:	Bromeliad soil.

Vriesea-hybr. 'Vulkana'

Vriesea zamorensis

X *Vuylstekeara* 'Cambria Orange'

X Vuylstekeara hybrids

Orchidaceae

A peculiar though frequently grown orchid. It is a cross-fertilization from 1912, between the genera *Cochlioda*, *Miltonia* and *Odontoglossum*, which lately has gained more distinction. Mostly, the indicator 'Cambria' is used, after the name of one of the cross-fertilization results, but there are numerous others available.
Care: These plants are quite easy to grow, especially in a greenhouse. Always avoid direct sunlight. Give plenty of rainwater in the growing period, if it can be drained properly, adding some fertilizer to it in low concentrations. When new pseudotubers form, one should allow a dormant period with a lower temperature and less water. This generally happens in the winter.
Propagation: By dividing older plants and repotting.

X *Vuylstekeara* 'Edna Stamperland'

Light:	Much light to half shade, no full sun.
Temp:	Grow moderately warm to warm, in the winter 46–50°F (8–10°C).
Water:	Keep well watered with rainwater in the summer, quite dry in the winter.
Hum:	High, above 60%.
Soil:	Rock wool flakes.

Warscewiczella discolor

Orchidaceae

The right orchid for any collector familiar with the plant *Chondrorhyncha*. The flowers are very special.
Care: This orchid does not have pseudotubers, nor can it store moisture in meaty leaves, so a dormant period is not recommended. The cultivation should be continuously cool and airy, and shaded. Mist very frequently, making sure that no water remains between the leaves. When the plant grows, add some fertilizer in low concentrations to soft water. Keep cooler in the winter.
Propagation: By division and from seed.

Light:	Much light or half shade. Never full sun.
Temp:	Grow cool, a minimum of 54°F (12°C).
Water:	Keep quite moist in the summer (mist frequently), in the winter add less water, but not too dry.
Hum:	Very high, possibly 80–90%.
Soil:	Rock wool flakes.

Warscewiczella discolor

Washingtonia filifera

Palmea

Beautiful palms from the southern U.S., with leaves that split halfway down their length, and from which fine threads hang. An excellent, very decorative container plant.
Care: This plant can be placed outside in the summer in rather large containers or other well drained tubs. Young plants cannot endure sun, though older ones can get used to it gradually. Water moderately and add food

Washingtonia filifera

every two weeks during the growth period. In the winter this plant should be kept decidedly cooler, as with most other palms, and certainly not in a warm room.
Propagation: From fresh seeds, which germinate within a month of being planted.

Light:	Much light, including the afternoon sun for older specimens.
Temp:	Grow cool, in the winter 40–50°F (5–10°C).
Water:	Keep moderately moist, drier in the winter.
Hum:	Moderate to high.
Soil:	Standard potting soil mixed with ⅓ part fine clay or loam, or rock wool powder.

Weingartia species

Cactaceae

A generally yellow-blooming cactus from the Andes with dense thorns. These cacti can grow on their own roots, but can be grafted onto other species, too.

Weingartia densispina

Weingartia neocumingii

Care: Grow in light, airy spaces; in the summer set outside on sunny days. Keep quite moist regularly and add cactus food monthly. In the winter the plant should be kept almost dry and rather cool. A light night frost can be tolerated. Mist only in the spring, until buds appear. Then start to give more water very carefully.
Propagation: From seed.

Light:	Full sun.
Temp:	Grow cool, in the winter around 40°F (5°C).
Water:	Moderately moist in the summer, almost dry in the winter.
Hum:	Low to moderate.
Soil:	Cactus soil.

Whitfieldia elongata

Acanthaceae

These small tropical plants can be found occasionally in flower shops. Besides the species pictured, there is also *Whitfieldia lateritia*, with red flowers.
Care: This is difficult to keep in a warm room, for the air is much too dry in the winter; however, one can keep the plant inside in the summer. Avoid the sun and provide a humid atmosphere. Add some food to the water once every two weeks.
Propagation: Top cuttings root under glass at a soil temperature of 77–86°F (25–30°C).

Whitfieldia elongata

Light:	Much light, no full sun.
Temp:	Grow warm, a minimum of 64°F (18°C).
Water:	Moderately moist.
Hum:	High, above 60%.
Soil:	Mix standard potting soil with fine clay or loam.

Wilcoxia viperina

Cactaceae

Cactus from Mexico and Texas that grows in thin, long parts. Collectors generally grow these cacti grafted on, for instance, *Eriocereus jusbertii* or *Trichocereus spachianus*, which improves their growth and flowering.
Care: Grow very sunny in a greenhouse or a south-facing window. Give moderate amounts of water and cactus food monthly. Support the shoots, if necessary. For flowers in the second year, the plant should have a cool and dry dormancy. In the spring, mist only, waiting until buds appear before watering.
Propagation: Cut off shoots and graft.

Light:	Full sun.
Temp:	Grow moderately warm to warm, in the winter 45–54°F (7–12°C).
Water:	Keep moderately moist in the summer, in the winter almost completely dry.
Hum:	Low.
Soil:	Cactus soil.

Wilcoxia viperina

X Wilsonara hybrids

Orchidaceae

A cross-fertilization between the genera *Cochlioda*, *Odontoglossum* and *Oncidium*. They are pretty orchids that require care similar to that of the *Odontoglossum*.
Care: Always keep cool and well ventilated, except when it freezes. Spray a few times daily, avoid the sun and ventilate when growing in a greenhouse. Remove light screens from greenhouse windows in the winter, give less water, but still keep it sparsely moist. After the

X *Wilsonara* 'Hambuhren Stern'

pseudotubers are full grown, a short dormant period is advised (with very sparse water). Add orchid food during growth, every 14 days.
Propagation: By division.

Light:	Much light, screen against the brightest sunlight.
Temp:	Grow cool to moderately warm, in the winter a minimum of 54°F (12°C).
Water:	Keep moderately moist, withholding almost all water in the dormant period.
Hum:	High, above 60%.
Soil:	Rock wool flakes or clay granules with peat moss.

Xanthosoma lindenii

Araceae

Foliage plant with a tuberous rootstock and large, beautifully marked leaves. There are several species available.
Care: Preferably, grow in rather large pots or, even better, planted out in the ground of a greenhouse. Feed weekly in the summer. In the winter the temperature should still remain high; especially the soil temperature.
Propagation: By division.

Light:	Much light or half shade, never sun.
Temp:	Grow warm, a minimum of 64°F (18°C).
Water:	Keep moderately moist.
Hum:	High, above 60%.
Soil:	Mixture of standard potting soil with fine clay or loam and leaf mold.

Xanthosoma lindenii

Yucca species

Agavaceae
Palm lily

Since 1960, the *Yucca* has been very popular as a houseplant. Initially, the species *aloifolia* was mostly grown, but its sharp leaf ends caused many injuries, for instance poking the eyes of small children. Now it is chiefly the species *elephantipes*, also known as 'Elephant's-foot' or 'weak yucca,' that is primarily available. Dry trunks are usually transported from Central America for rooting elsewhere.

Care: The enormous popularity of this plant lies probably in the fact that it looks attractive and is relatively inexpensive, for almost all specimens die after a few years of cultivation as a houseplant. The *Yucca* is more of a container plant, which appreciates being kept outside in the summer and at low temperatures in the winter. When grown in this way, beautiful specimens will result. A sharp *Yucca* could even survive being outside in the winter. Only add food in the growing period, until the end of August. Bring inside in mid-October.

Propagation: By striking slips from side shoots. Trunks can be cut in pieces and planted after a period of drying. Soil temperature 68–77°F (20–25°C).

Light: Full sun.
Temp: Grow cool to moderately warm, keep at 40–50°F (5–10°C) in the winter, or if necessary even cooler.
Water: Rather moist in the summer, quite dry in the winter.
Hum: Low to moderate.
Soil: Standard potting soil mixed with ⅓ part fine clay or loam.

Yucca aloifolia

Yucca elephantipes

Yucca elephantipes 'Variegata'

Zamia pumila

Cycadaceae

A relatively rare plant from the family of palm ferns. This species does not grow as tall as most others and can be grown in a greenhouse.

Care: In the winter, the temperature can fall a few degrees, but then less water should be given, as well.

Propagation: From fresh seeds, which germinate at 86–95°F (30–35°C) soil temperature, but it takes a long time.

Light: Much light, no bright sunlight.
Temp: Grow moderately warm to warm, in the winter a minimum of 54°F (12°C).
Water: Keep moderately moist, drier in the winter.
Hum: Moderate, 50–60%.

Zamia pumila

Soil: Mix standard potting soil with clay or loam in pots that drain well.

Zantedeschia species

Araceae
Arum

Tuberous plants that can sometimes be kept as houseplants. With some extra care it is possible to keep these plants alive through the winter. They are often called *Calla*. The white species is the most famous; the yellow species is called *Zantedeschia elliottiana*, and the red species is *Z. rehmannii*, pictured. There are a large number of hybrids available as well.

Care: The white-blooming *aethiopica* produces flowers from January. The plant has to

Zantedeschia aethiopica

Zantedeschia rehmannii

be kept especially cool, no warmer than 60°F (15°C), and so certainly not in a living room. Add food every two weeks and always water moderately. The dormant period begins at the end of May; the plant can be laid in the garden, with the pot on its side. Water sparsely without fertilizer. Repot at the end of June and bring back to growth. Keep it sunny and well moistened. Again, provide another dormant period at the end of September, withholding all water so the foliage dies off. The rootstocks should remain in the pot, stored cool. The following January they will sprout again. Gradually add some water, slowly increasing the amount until flowers appear.
Propagation: By dividing the rootstocks.

Light:	Half shade or full sun.
Temp:	Grow cool, during the growth at 60°F (15°C), with dry rootstocks a minimum of 50°F (10°C).
Water:	Keep constantly moist in the growing period, during dormancy almost dry or completely dry.
Hum:	High, above 60%.
Soil:	Standard potting soil mixed with clay or loam.

Zebrina pendula

Commelinaceae

A plant often confused with the *Tradescantia*, which shares the same care requirements. The two species pictured are the most prevalent.
Care: Preferably grown as a hanging plant. Do not place in bright sunlight, but grow in light, otherwise the leaf markings disappear. Add food once every three weeks. In the winter, keep cooler. If the plants become ugly, cut them way back and allow them to grow new shoots.
Propagation: Top cuttings root very easily after having dried for a day. Additional soil warmth is not necessary.

Light:	Much light, no bright sun.
Temp:	Grow moderately warm, in the winter a minimum of 50°F (10°C).
Water:	Moderately moist, drier in the winter.
Hum:	Moderate, 50–60%.
Soil:	Standard potting soil.

Zebrina pendula 'Quadricolor'

Zebrina purpusii

Zephyranthes candida

Amaryllidaceae

A bulbous plant that is not very hardy and can be forced into blooming inside (and outside)
Care: Initially water very sparsely; when the plant begins to grow, add more water. Grow sunny, possibly outside in a protected spot. Feed every two weeks in the summer. Give less water after the plant blooms and keep frost free during dormancy; some leaves should stay on the plant. In warmer climates this plant can remain outside, covered, all year.
Propagation: By removing and growing young bulbs separately.

Light:	Full sun.
Temp:	Grow cool, in the winter 32–40°F (0–5°C).
Water:	Keep moderately moist, in the winter water very sparsely.
Hum:	Moderate, 50–60%.
Soil:	Standard potting soil.

Zephyranthes candida

Zygopetalon mackaii

Zygopetalon mackaii

Orchidaceae

Orchids that are not exceptionally difficult to grow, and which in nature grow both epiphytically as well as terrestrially.
Care: Provide much light, screening only against the brightest sunlight. Give plenty of water in the summer. Add some food once every two weeks. When the pseudotubers are fully grown, give a dormant period of a few weeks, which can be achieved by reducing the water added until the tubers almost shrivel. The growth medium should never dry out completely. The dormancy contributes to the development of the flowers, which appear in the fall or winter.
Propagation: By division.

Light:	Much light, no bright sun.
Temp:	Grow moderately warm to warm, in the winter a minimum of 54°F (12°C).
Water:	Keep regularly moist with soft water.
Hum:	High, above 60%.
Soil:	Mixture of pieces of tree fern and fern roots in pots with good drainage.

APPENDICES

To make houseplant choices easier, the plants reviewed in this book are categorized in the following appendices. The plants are grouped both by care requirements—light, location, temperature, humidity—and by plant type—foliage plants, flowering plants, ferns, cacti, etc.

The same plant may appear in several different lists if it fits more than one description; for example, a plant that is suitable for cultivation in a greenhouse and in the home. There are sure to be exceptions to the classifications made here, depending entirely on the skill of the grower.

These listings only provide cursory information. For more detailed plant descriptions, see individual species entries in the main text of the book.

LIGHT REQUIREMENTS

Plants that require or can endure full sun

Not that many indoor or greenhouse plants require or can endure unscreened sunlight, though they can get used to it. Cacti and other succulent plants are an exception. Also, most container plants like a place in the sun. It does make a difference if a plant is placed in full sun outside or inside behind a window pane. Behind glass, too much sunlight often produces too much heat, and not all plants like this even ones that can endure full sun. There is some overlap between this list and the following listing, plants that require much light.

Abromeitiella brevifolia
Acacia armata
Acca selloviana
Acokanthera oblongifolia
Adenium obesum
Adromischus cooperi
Aeonium arboreum
Aeonium holochrysum
Aeonium tabuliforme
Agapanthus praecox
Agave americana
Agave macroacantha
Agave parviflora
Agave victoriae-reginae
Albizia julibrissin
Aloë arborescens
Aloë aristata
Aloë humilis
Aloë variegata
Alternanthera ficoidea
Amaryllis belladonna
Anisodontea capensis
Arachis hypogaea
Arbutus andrachne
Ariocarpus fissuratus
Asarina barclaiana
Asclepias curassavica
Beaucarnia recurvata
Beloperone guttata
Bergeranthus scapiger
Bloomeria crocea
Blossfeldia liliputana
Borzicactus species
Bougainvillea spectabilis
Bowiea volubilis
Brachychiton rupestris
Brasiliopuntia brasiliensis
Caesalpinia decapetala
Caesalpinia gilliesii
Callistemon citrinus
Calocephalus brownii
Canna hybrids
Cantua buxifolia
Capparis spinosa
Capsicum annuum
Caralluma X *suaveolens*
Carex brunnea 'Variegata'

Carnegiea gigantea
Carpobrotus acinaciformis
Cassia didymobotrya
Catharanthus roseus
Celosia argentea
Cephalocereus senilis
Cereus neotetragonus
Cereus peruvianus
Ceropegia woodii ssp. *woodii*
Cestrum X *newellii*
Chamaedorea elegans
Chamaelaucium uncinatum
Cheiridopsis candidissima
Chorizema cordatum
Cistus species
Citrus species
Cleistocactus straussi
Clianthus puniceus
Colletia cruciata
Conophytum species
Convolvulus sabaticus
Copiapoa cinerea
Cordyline australis
Cordyline indivisa
Corokia species
Correa backhousiana
Corynocarpus laevigatum
Coryphantha elephantidens
Cotyledon species
Crassula arborescens
Crassula coccinea
Crassula muscosa
Crassula ovata
Crassula pellucida
Crassula perfoliata var. *falcata*
Crassula perforata
Crassula rupestris
Crinum X *powelii*
Cyphostemma juttae
Cyrtanthus parviflorus
Dasylirion acrotrichum
Datura hybrids
Delosperma species
Dichondra repens
Didiera madagascariensis
Disphyma crassifolium
Dodonaea viscosa

Doryanthes palmeri
Dracaena draco
Drosera capensis
Dudleya pachyphytum
Dyckia fosteriana
Echeveria agavoides
Echeveria derenbergii
Echeveria harmsii
Echeveria pulvinata
Echeveria setosa
Echinocactus grusonii
Echinocereus species
Echinopsis, day-blooming species
Echium wildpretii
Elettaria cardamomum
Ensete ventricosum
Eriobotrya japonica
Erythrina crista-galli
Escobaria vivipara
Espostoa lanata
Eucalyptus cinerea
Eucomis bicolor
Eugenia myriophylla
Euonymus japonica
Euphorbia balsamifera
Euphorbia canariensis
Euphorbia caput-medusae
Euphorbia erythraeae
Euphorbia grandicornis
Euphorbia leuconeura
Euphorbia meloformis
Euphorbia milii
Euphorbia resinifera
Euphorbia submammilaris
Euphorbia tetragona
Euphorbia tirucalli
Eustoma grandiflorum
Fascicularia pitcairniifolia
Faucaria tigrina
Felicia amelloides
Fenestraria aurantiaca
Ficus carica
Fortunella margarita
Frithia pulchra
Gasteria species
Gazania hybrids
Geranium palmatum
Glottiphyllum linguiforme
Gomphrena globosa
Greenovia aurea
Haageocereus pseudomelanostele
Habranthus tubispathus
Haemanthus albiflos
Hamatocactus setispinus
Harpephyllum caffrum
Haworthia species
Hebe species
Hechtia stenophylla
Hedychium gardnerianum
Heliotropium arborescens
Hibbertia scandens
Hibiscus rosa-sinensis

Homalocladium platycladum
Hoodia gordonii
Incarvillea mairei
Ipomoea batatas
Ipomoea tricolor
Iresine herbstii
Isoplexis canariensis
Jacaranda mimosifolia
Jacobinia carnea
Jacobinia pauciflora
Jasminum officinale
Jatropha pandurifolia
Jatropha podagrica
Kalanchoë beharensis
Kalanchoë daigremontiana
Kalanchoë orgyalis
Kalanchoë scapigera
Kalanchoë tomentosa
Kalanchoë tubiflora
Lachenalia unifolia
Lagerstroemia indica
Lampranthus blandus
Lantana Camara hybrids
Laurus nobilis
Ledebournia socialis
Leptospermum scoparium
Leuchtenbergia principes
Lilium hybrids
Lithops bromfieldii
Littonia modesta
Lobivia species
Lophohora williamsii
Lotus berthelotii
Malpighia coccigera
Malvaviscus arboreus
Mamillopsis senilis
Mammillaria bocasana
Mammillaria guelzoviana
Mammillaria hahniana
Mammillaria prolifera
Mammillaria spinosissima
Mammillaria zeilmanniana
Mandevilla laxa
Matucana currundayensis
Melocactus maxonii
Metrosideros villosus
Mikania ternata
Musa species
Myoporum acuminatum
Myrtillocactus geometrizans
Myrtus communis
Neoporteria species
Neoporteria wagenknechtii
Nepenthes hybrids
Nerium oleander
Notocactus species
Ochagavia carnea
Ochna serrulata
Olea europaea
Opthalmophyllum jacobsenianum
Opuntia species
Oreocerus celsianus

Oreopanax capitatus
Ornithogalum thyrsoides
Oroya peruviana
Oscularia deltoides
Osteospermum ecklonis
Pachira macrocarpa
Pachycerus pringlei
Pachyphytum oviferum
Pachypodium species
Pachystachys lutea
X Pachyveria species
Parodia species
Parthenocissus henryana
Parthenocissus inserta
Passiflora caerulea
Pelargonium X blandfordianum
Pelargonium X citrosmum
Pelargonium crispum
Pelargonium endlicherianum
Pelargonium X fragrans 'Variegatum'

Pelargonium graveolens 'Variegatum'
Pelargonium Grandiflorum hybrids
Pelargonium radens
Pelargonium Zonale hybrids
Pereskia aculeata 'Godseffiana'
Phoenix canariensis
Phormium tenax
Pinus pinea 'Silver Crest'
Pittosporum species
Plectranthus coleoides
Plectranthus fruticosus
Polianthes tuberosa
Portulacaria afra
Prostanthera sieberi
Pseudobombax ellipticum
Pseudomammillaria camptotricha
Punica granatum
Puya chilensis
Rebutia senilis
Rhodochiton atrosanguineum

Rosa chinensis 'Minima'
Ruscus aculeatus
Sarcocaulon crassicaule
Saxifraga cotyledon
Schinus molle
Sedum species
Sempervivum arachnoideum
Senecio citriformis
Senecio herreanus
Senecio kleinia
Senecio radicans
Senecio rowleyanus
Setcreasea pallida
Solandra grandiflora
Solanum pseudocapsicum
Stapelia X divaricata
Stenotaphrum secundatum 'Variegatum'
Strelitzi reginae
Streptocarpus saxorum
Streptosolen jamesonii

Sulcorebutia mizguinsis
Synadenium grantii
Tecoma castanifolia
Tecomaria capensis
Testudinaria species
Thevetia peruviana
Tibouchina urvilleana
Tillandsia, gray-scaled species
Trichocereus spachianus
Trichodiadema densum
Tupidanthus calyptratus
Uebelmannia pectinifera
Vallota speciosa
Weingargia species
Wilcoxia viperina
Yucca species
Zantedeschia species
Zephyranthes candida

Plants that require much light

Unprotected sunlight is just a bit too much for the indoor and greenhouse plants of this group. But even so, they require much light, and should only be screened against the brightest sunlight in the summer from 10:00 A.M. to 5:00 P.M., by means of a sunscreen. In the winter, these plants are able to endure unscreened sunlight, since it is weaker than in the summer.

There is some overlap with the previous listing, plants requiring full light, for some plants thrive under both conditions. There is also overlap with the listing of plants requiring half shade.

Abutilon X hybridum
Abutilon megapotamicum
Abutilon megapotamicum 'Variegatum'
Abutilon pictum 'Thompsonii'
Acalypha hispida
Acalypha pendula
Acalypha wilkesiana
Acanthocalycium violaceum
Acanthorhipsalis monocantha
Achimenes hybrids
Acokanthera oblongifolia
Acorus gramineus 'Argentroestriatus'
Aërangis rhodosticta
Aërides falcata
Aeschynanthus hildebrandii
Aeschynanthus radicans
Aeschynanthus tricolor
Agathis macrophylla
Aglaonema commutatum
Aglaonema crispum
Allamanda cathartica
Alloplectus capitatus
Alloplectus schlimii
Alocasia lowii
Aloë variegata
Alpinia sanderae
Amorphophallus bulbifer
Ampelopsis brevipendunculata
Ananas species
Angraecum eburneum
Anigozanthos flavidus
Anisodontea capensis
Ansellia africana
Aphelandra aurantiaca
Aphelandra maculata
Aphelandra sinclairiana
Aporocactus flagelliformis
Arachis hypogaea
Araucaria heterophylla
Arisaema candidissimum
Aristolochia grandiflora
Arpophyllum spicatum
Asarina barclaiana
Asclepias curassavica
Asparagus asparagoides
Asparagus setaceus
Astrophytum asterias

Astrophytum myriostigma
Astrophytum ornatum
Barkeria spectabilis
Bauhinia acuminata
Bauhinia punctata
Begonia 'Cleopatra'
Begonia coccinea
Begonia Corallina hybrids
Begonia imperialis
Begonia manicata
Begonia masoniana
Begonia serratipetala
Beloperone guttata
Bertolonia marmorata
Bifrenaria harrisoniae
Bomarea caldasii
Bouvardia hybrids
Brachychiton rupestris
Brassaia actinophylla
Brassavola species
Brassia species
X Brassocattleya species
X Brassolaeliocattleya species
Breynia disticha
Browallia speciosa
Brunfelsia species
Bulbophyllum species
Caladium Bicolor hybrids
Calanthe triplicata
Calathea picturata
Calathea roseopicta
Calceolaria hybrids
Calliandra harrisii
Callisia species
Camellia sinensis
Campanula fragilis
Campanula isophylla
Caralluma X suaveolens
Carex brunnea 'Variegata'
Caryota mitis
Catasetum maculatum
Catharanthus roseus
Cattleya species
Celosia argentea
Centradeis floribunda
Ceropegia woodii ssp. woodii
Chamaecereus sylvestri

Chamaerops humilis
Chlorophytum comosum 'Variegatum'
Chorizema cordatum
Chrysalidocarpus lutescens
Chrysanthemum Indicum hybrids
Chrysanthemum parthenium
Chrysanthemum, garden varieties
Chrysothemis pulchella
Chysis aurea
Cissus antarctica
X Citrofortunella mitis
Citrus species
Clerodendrum thomsoniae
Cleyera japonica
Coccoloba uvifera
Cochliostema odoratissimum
Cocos nucifera
Codiaeum variegatum
X Codonatanthus species
Coelia bella
Coelogyne cristata
Coffea arabica
Coleus Blumei hybrids
Columnea microphylla
Columnea microphylla 'Hostag'
Copiapoa cinerea
Coprosma species
Cordyline fruticosa
Corokia species
Correa backhousiana
Corynocarpus laevigatum
Costus cuspidatus
Crassula coccinea
Crocus vernus ssp. vernus
Crossandra infundibuliformis
Cryptocerreus anthonyanus
Ctenanthe lubbersiana
Ctenanthe oppenheimiana
Cunonia capensis
Cuphea species
Cussonia spicata
Cyanotis kewensis
Cycas revoluta
Cyclamen persicum
Cycnoches chlorochilum
Cymbidium hybrids
Cyperus alternifolius
Cyperus albostriatus
Cyperus papyrus
Cytisus X spachianus
Dendrobium species, moderate greenhouse
Dendrobium species, warm greenhouse
Dichorisandra reginae
Dicksonia antarctica
Dieffenbachia amoena
Dieffenbachia bowmannii
Dieffenbachia maculata
Dieffenbachia seguine
Dionaea muscipula
Dipladenia sanderi
Dischidia pectenoides

Dizygotheca elegantissima
Dizygotheca veitchii
Dolichothele baumii
X Doritaenopsis species
Doritis pulcherrima
Dorstenia elata
Dracaena deremensis
Dracaena draco
Dracaena fragrans
Dracaena marginata 'Tricolor'
Dracaena reflexa
Dracaena sanderiana
Dracaena surculosa
Dracula troglodytis
Duchesnea indica
Echinofossulocactus hastatus
Echinopsis, night-blooming species
Encyclia species
Epacris hybrids
Epidendrum fragrans
Epidendrum parkinsonianum
Epipremnum pinnatum 'Marble Queen'
Episcia cupreata
Episcia reptans
Erica gracilis
Erica X willmorei
Erythrorhipsalis pilocarpa
Euonymus japonica
Euphorbia caracasana
Euphorbia fulgens
Euphorbia leuconeura
Euphorbia pulcherrima
Eustoma grandiflorum
Euterpe edulis
Exacum affine
X Fatshedera lizei 'Variegata'
Fatsia japonica 'Variegata'
Felicia amelloides
Felicia amelloides
Ficus aspera 'Parcellii'
Ficus benjamina 'Variegata'
Ficus buxifolia
Ficus deltoidea
Ficus leprieurii
Ficus lyrata
Ficus microcarpa
Ficus religiosa
Ficus retusa
Ficus rubiginosa 'Variegata'
Ficus schlechteri
Furcraea foetida 'Striata'
Gardenia jasminioides
Geranium palmatum
Gerbera hybrids
Globba winitii
Gloriosa rothschildiana
Gloxinia sylvatica
Goethea cauliflora
Gomesa recurva
Graptopetalum species
Graptophyllum pictum

Grevillea robusta
Guzmania species
Gymnocalycium species
Gynura aurantiaca
Habenaria xantholeuca
Haemanthus albiflos
Haemanthus multiflorus
Harpephyllum caffrum
Hebe species
Hechtia stenophylla
Hedera helix, variegated varieties
Hedera helix ssp. canariensis 'Variegata'
Heticonia jacquinii
Hemigraphis species
Heterocentron elegans
Hibbertia scandens
Hibiscus rosa-sinensis
Hippeastrum hybrids
Hoffmania ghiesbreghtii
Homalocladium platycladum
Howeia forsteriana
Hoya bella
Hoya carnosa
Hoya linearis
Hoya multiflora
Huernia keniensis
Hyacinthus orientalis
Hymenocallis species
Hypocyrta glabra
Hypoestes phyllostachya
Illicium anisatum
Impatiens hawkeri
Impatiens repens
Impatiens walleriana
Incarvillea mairei
Ipomoea batatas
Ipomoea tricolor
Iris reticulata
Ixora hybrids
Jacaranda mimosifolia
Jacobinia carnea
Jatropha pandurifolia
Kalanchoë blossfeldiana
Kalanchoë hybrids
Koellikeria erinoides
Lachenalia unifolia
Laelia cinnabarina
Laurus nobilis
Leptocladodia microhelia
Lilium hybrids
Littonia modesta
Livistona chinensis
Lockhartia lunifera
Lophomyrtus obcordata
Malpighia coccigera
Mammillaria rhodantha
Mammillaria spinosissima
Mammillaria wildii
Mammillaria zeilmanniana
Mandevilla laxa

Manettia inflata
Manihot esculenta 'Variegata'
Maranta bicolor
Maranta leuconeura
Mascarena verschaffeltii
Masdevallia species
Medinilla magnifica
Microcoelum weddellianum
Mikania ternata
Miltoniopsis roezlii
Monstera adansonii
Monstera deliciosa 'Variegata'
Murraya paniculata
Musa species
Mussaenda phillipica
Myrmecodia echinata
Nautilocalyx lynchii
Nematanthus hybrids
Neomortonia nummularia
Neoporteria species
Nertera granadensis
Nicotiana X sanderae
Nopalxochia phyllantoides
Notocactus species
Ochna serrulata
X Odontocidium species
Oncidium microchilum
Oncidium ornithorhynchum
Ophiopogon jaburan
Oplismenus hirtellus 'Variegatus'
Orbea variegata
Oreopanax capitatus
Oxalis adenophylla
Pachira macrocarpa
Pachystachys lutea
Pandanus species
Parthenocisus henryana
Parthenocissus inserta
Passiflora alata
Passiflora caerulea
Passiflora violacea
Pavonia multiflora
Pedilanthus tithymaloides 'Variegata'
Pelargonium X blandfordianum
Pelargonium crispum
Pelargonium Grandiflorum hybrids
Pelargonium graveolens 'Variegatum'
Pelargonium radens
Pelargonium Zonale hybrids
Pellionia species
Pentas lanceolata
Peperomia argyreia
Peperomia incana
Peperomia obtusifolia 'Greengold'
Peperomia serpens 'Variegata'
Perilepta dyeriana
Peristrophe hyssopifolia 'Aureovariegata'
Persea americana
Phaius tankervilleae
Phalaenopsis species

Philesia magellanica
Philodendron bipennifolium
Philodendron elegans
Philodendron erubescens
Philodendron melanochrysum
Philodendron pedatum
Philodendron rugosum
Philodendron sagittifolium 'Ilsemannii'
Philodendron selloum
Phoenix canariensis
Phoenix roebelinii
Phormium tenax
Pilea species
Piper crocatum
Piper ornatum
Pisonia umbellifera 'Variegatum'
Pistia stratiotes
Plectranthus coleoides
Plectranthus fruticosus
Plectranthus oertendahlii
Plumbago auriculata
Plumbago indica
Podocarpus macrophyllus
Polianthes tuberosa
Porphyrocoma pohliana
Portulaca grandiflora
Primula X kewensis
Primula malacoides
Primula obconia
Primula praenitens
Primula vulgaris
Pseuderanthemum species
Pseudobombax ellipticum
Pseudopanax lessonii
Pteris endiformis
Pteris quadriaurita
Radermachera sinica
Rebutia species
Rehmannia elata
Reinwardtia indica
Rhapis excelsa
Rhododendron simsii
Rhoeo spathacea 'Vittata'
Rhynchostylis coelestis
Rivina humilis
Rodriguezia secunda
Rosa chinensis 'Minima'
Rosioglossum grande
Sagina subulata
Saintpaulia ionantha
Sanchezia nobilis
Sandersonia aurantiaca
Sansevieria trifasciata
Sarracenia species
Saxifraga stolonifera 'Tricolor'
Schaueria calycotricha
Schefflera species
Schismatoglottis picta
Schizanthus pinnatus
Scindapsus pictus

Scutellaria costaricana
Selaginella species
Selenicereus grandiflorus
Senecio Cruentus hybrids
Senecio macroglossus 'Variegatus'
Senecio mikanioides
Serissa foetida 'Variegata'
Siderasis fuscata
Sinningia cardinalis
Sinningia speciosa
Smithiantha hybrids
Sonerila margaritacea
Sophronitis cernus
Sparmannia africana
Spatiphyllum wallisii
Sprekelia formosissima
Stanhopea wardii
Stapelia X divaricata
Stenocarpus sinuatus
Stenotaphrum secundatum 'Variegatum'
Stephanotis floribunda
Streptocarpus saxorum
Stromanthe species
Syngonium podophyllum, variegated varieties
Tacca chantrieri
Testudinaria species
Tetraclinis articulata
Tetranema roseum
Tetrastigma voinerianum
Thunbergia alata
Tillandsia, gray-scaled species
Tillandsia usneoides
Torenia fournieri
Trachycarpus fortunei
Tradescantia species
Trevesia palmata
Tritonia crocata
Tropaeolum species
Tulipa hybrids
Tupidanthus calyptratus
Turnera ulmifolia
Uebelmannia pectinifera
Urceolina grandiflora
Vallota speciosa
Vanda coerulea
Veltheimia capensis
Vriesea species
X Vuylstekeara hybrids
Warscewiczella discolor
Washingtonia filifera
Whitfieldia elongata
Whitfieldia lateritia
X Wilsonara hybrids
Xanthosoma lindenii
Zamia pumila
Zantedeschia species
Zebrina pendula
Zygopetalon mackaii

Plants that require half shade

The term half shade means either filtered sunlight during the whole day, or a few hours of sun in the morning or evening and shade the rest of the day. East- or west-facing windows meet this description, but windows facing south work as well, as long as they are provided with a sunscreen. Many indoor and greenhouse plants in this group can be found in the group of plants that require much light, too. These plants will do well with either condition.

Acer buergerianum
Aërides falcata
Aglaonema costatum
Alsobia dianthiflora
Anthurium Andraeanum hybrids
Anthurium crystallinum
Anthurium Scherzeranum hybrids
Aphelandra aurantiaca
Aphelandra maculata
Aphelandra squarrosa

Ardisia crenata
Arisaema candidissimum
Aristolochia grandiflora
Arpophyllum spicatum
Asparagus densiflorus
Asparagus falcatus
Asparagus setaceus
Aspasia lunata
Aspidistra elatior 'Variegata'
Asplenium bulbiferum

Asplenium nidus
Aucuba japonica
Begonia albopicta
Begonia boweri
Begonia 'Cleopatra'
Begonia X credneri
Begonia Elatior hybrids
Begonia grandis
Begonia heracleifolia
Begonia hispida var. cucullifera
Begonia, tuberous hybrids
Begonia limmingheiana
Begonia Lorraine hybrids
Begonia maculata
Begonia X margaritae
Begonia metallica
Begonia Rex hybrids
Begonia rotundifolia
Begonia venosa
Bertolonia marmorata
Billbergia nutans

Blechnum species
Blecnum spicant
Brosimum alicastrum
Calathea crocata
Calathea lancifolia
Calathea makoyana
Calathea ornata
Calceolaria hybrids
Callisia species
Camellia japonica
Chamaeranthemum species
Cissus antarctica
Cissus discolor
Cissus rhombifolia
Cissus striata
Cleyera japonica
Clivia miniata
Clusia rosea
Codonanthe crassifolia
Coelogyne cristata
Columnea X banksii

Columnea gloriosa
Corokia species
Crocus vernus ssp. vernus
Cryptanthus species
Cupressus macrocarpa 'Goldcrest'
Cussonia spicata
Cyrtomium falcatum
Danae racemosa
Darlingtonia californica
Davallia mariesii
Dichorisandra reginae
Dieffenbachia amoena
Dipteracanthus devosianus
Dipteracanthus makoyanus
Dischidia pectenoides
Dracaena marginata
Dryopteris affinis
Epipremnum pinnatum
Episcia reptans
Euonymus japonica
Euphorbia leuconeura
X Fatshedera lizei
Fatsia japonica
Ficus altissima
Ficus benghalensis
Ficus benjamina
Ficus buxifolia
Ficus cyathistipula
Ficus elastica
Ficus microcarpa
Ficus pumila
Ficus religiosa
Ficus rubiginosa
Ficus saggittata
Ficus schlechteri
Ficus stricta

Fittonia verschaffeltii
Fuchsia hybrids
Glechoma hederacea 'Variegata'
Graptophyllum pictum
Hatiora bambusioides
Hedera helix, variegated varieties
Helleborus niger
Hoya lacunosa
Hytleya meleagris
Hyacinthus orientalis
Hydrangea macrophylla
Impatiens repens
Ixora hybrids
Kohleria Eriantha hybrids
Leea guineensis
Leucothoë walteri
Liriope muscari
Ludisia discolor
Lycaste cruenta
Macroplectum sesquipedale
Maxillaria tenuifolia
Miltonia hybrids
Mimosa pudica
Monstera adansonii
Monstera deliciosa
Myrmecodia echinata
Nandina domestica
Narcissus hybrids
Nematanthus hybrids
Neomortonia nummularia
Neoregelia species
Nidularium fulgens
Obregonia denegrii
Odontoglossum pulchellum
Ophiopogon japonicus
Pachiopedilum, spotted leaf species

Pachiopedilum, deciduous species
Parthenocissus henryana
Parthenocissus inserta
Pelargonium X blandfordianum
Pelargonium crispum
Pellionia species
Peperomia blanda
Peperomia caperata
Peperomia fraseri
Peperomia griseoargenta
Peperomia pereskiifolia
Peperomia puteolata
Peperomia rotundifolia
Peperomia serpens 'Variegata'
Pernettya mucronata
Philodendron bipennifolium
Philodendron elegans
Philodendron erubescens
Philoendron melanochrysum
Philodendron pedatum
Philodendron rugosum
Philodendron scandens
Philodendron selloum
Philodendron squamiferum
Philodendron tuxtlanum
Phlebodium aureum
Phoenix roebelinii
Phyllanthus angustifolius
Pinguicula moranensis
Pistia stratiotes
Platycerium bifurcatum
Plectranthus fruticosus
Plectranthus oertendahlii
Pleione bulbocodioides
Polyscias species
Polystichum tsus-simense

Pteris cretica
Rhipsalidopsis species
Rhipsalis baccifera
Rhododendron obtusum
Rhoicissus capensis
Rivina humilis
Rosioglossum grande
Saintpaulia ionantha
Sarmienta scandens
Sauromatum guttatum
Schefflera species
Schlumbergera hybrids
Scirpus cernuus
Selenicereus grandiflorus
Senecio mikanioides
Sibthorpia europaea
Skimmia species
Smithiantha hybrids
Soleirolia soleirolii
Sparmannia africana
Stanhopea wardii
Streptocarpus grandis
Streptocarpus hybrids
Syngonium podophyllum, deciduous trunk-type
Tetrastigma vionerianum
Tillandsia cyanea
Tillandsia lindenii
Tolmiea menziesii
Tradescantia species
X Vuylstekeara hybrids
Warscewiczella discolor
Xanthosoma lindenii

Plants that require shade

The indoor greenhouse plants in this group require no sun, and cannot endure direct sunlight. They can grow in a window facing north. They will grow in other locations of a house, too, for example, placed far enough from a window that direct sunlight cannot reach them. One should make sure, though, that the light is at least 1,000 lux, otherwise these plants will perish over the long term. A number of plants from this group can also be found in the listing for half shade plants.

Adiantum hispidulum
Adiantum peruvianum
Adiantum raddianum
Adiantum tenerum
Arachnoides species
Asparagus falcatus
Aspidistra elatior
Asplenium bulbiferum
Asplenium marinum

Begonia albopicta
Begonia X credneri
Begonia maculata
Begonia X margaritae
Brosimum alicastrum
Cissus rhombifolia
Cyrtomium falcatum
Danae racemosa
Darlingtonia californica

Davallia mariesii
Didymochlaena truncatula
Disa uniflora
Doryopteris plamata
Dracaena marginata
Dryopteris affinis
Epipremnum pinnatum
X Fatshedera lizei
Fatsia japonica
Ficus saggittata
Fuchsia hybrids
Hemionitis palmata
Liriope muscari
Lycaste cruenta
Macroplectum sesquipedale
Microlepis specluncae
Miltonia hybrids
Neoregelia species
Nephrolepis exaltata
Nidularium fulgens

X Odontioda species
Odontoglossum bictoniense
Oncidium papilio
Ophiopogon japonicus
Pellaea species
Peperomia blanda
Peperomia caperata
Peperomia fraseri
Peperomia pereskiifolia
Peperomia puteolata
Peperomia rotundifolia
Philodendron scandens
Phlebodium aureum
Phyllitis scolopendrium
Platycerium bifurcatum
Pleione bulbocodiodes
Polystichum tsus-simense
Pteris cretica
Sibthorpia europaea
Tolmiea menziesii

LOCATION REQUIREMENTS

Perennial houseplants

These plants can be grown in a warm room all year round. They do not need a dormant period to remain healthy, even if there is little growth in the winter due to lack of light. Fertilizer is barely necessary, and is not needed at all when growth stops. These plants generally endure dry room air quite well, but it is always advisable to spray the foliage frequently (except when it is hairy) or to install a vaporizer. Perennial houseplants are few, especially since they must stay healthy over the winter. Plants that can be grown successfully indoors but need a dormant period in the winter, or a period of time in a greenhouse, can be found in the listings that follow.

Abutilon X *hybridum*
Abutilon megapotamicum
Abutilon megapotamicum 'Variegatum'
Abutilon pictum 'Thompsonii'
Aloë variegata
Asparagus densiflorus
Asparagus falcatus
Aspidistra elatior
Aspidistra elatior 'Variegata'
Begonia X *erythrophylla*
Billbergia nutans
Brosimum alicastrum
Chlorophytum comusum 'Variegatum'
Cissus antarctica
Cissus rhombifolia
Clusia rosea

Corynocarpus laevigatum
Cupressus macrocarpa 'Goldcrest'
Cyperus alternifolius
Davallia mariesii
Dieffenbachia amoena
Dieffenbachia bowmannii
Dieffenbachia maculata
Dieffenbachia seguine
Dracaena deremensis
Dracaena draco
Dracaena fragrans
Dracaena marginata 'Tricolor'
Dracaena marginata
Dracaena reflexa
Dracaena sanderiana
Epipremnum pinnatum 'Marble Queen'

Epipremnum pinnatum
Euphorbia leuconeura
Euphorbia milii
Ficus altissima
Ficus benghalensis
Ficus benjamina
Ficus benjamina 'Variegata'
Ficus buxifolia
Ficus cyathistipula
Ficus elastica
Ficus lyrata
Ficus microcarpa
Ficus retusa
Ficus saggittata
Ficus schlechteri
Hedera helix ssp. *canariensis* 'Variegata'
Kalanchoë daigremontiana
Kalanchoë tubiflora
Leea guineensis
Monstera deliciosa
Monstera deliciosa 'Variegata'
Ophiopogon jaburan
Oplismenus hirtellus 'Variegatus'
Pelargonium X *blandfordianum*
Pelargonium graveolens 'Variegatum'
Pelargonium radens
Peperomia argyreia
Peperomia blanda
Peperomia caperata
Peperomia fraseri

Peperomia griseoargenta
Peperomia incana
Peperomia obtusifolia 'Greengold'
Peperomia pereskiifolia
Peperomia puteolata
Peperomia rotundifolia
Peperomia serpens 'Variegata'
Philodendron bipennifolium
Philodendron elegans
Philodendron erubescens
Philodendron melanochrysum
Philodendron pedatum
Philodendron rugosum
Philodendron scandens
Philodendron squamiferum
Philodendron rustlanum
Phlebodium aureum
Phoenix roebelinii
Pinus pinea 'Silver Crest'
Platycerium bifurcatum
Plectranthus fruticosus
Rhoeo spathacea 'Vittata'
Saintpaulia ionantha
Sansevieria trifasciata
Saxifraga stolonifera 'Tricolor'
Senecio mikanioides
Setcreasea pallida
Synadenium grantii
Syngonium podophyllum
Tolmiea menziesii

Semi-houseplants

The following are plants that with some luck and the proper care will stay healthy when grown indoors. The dry air in houses in winter can become a threat to the health of these plants, so try to increase the relative humidity. Many of these plants are also listed in the various greenhouse appendices.

Adiantum hispidulum
Adiantum peruvianum
Adiantum raddianum
Adiantum tenerum
Aglaonema commutatum
Aglaonema costatum
Aglaonema crispum
Alsobia dianthiflora
Ananas species
Anthurium Andraeanum hybrids
Anthurium Scherzeranum hybrids

Aphelandra aurantiaca
Arachis hypogaea
Asclepias curassavica
Asplenium nidus
Calathea crocata
Calathea lancifolia
Calathea makoyana
Calathea ornata
Calathea picturata
Codiaeum variegatum
X *Codonatanthus* species

Codonanthe crassifolia
Coffea arabica
Crossandra infundibuliformis
Cryptanthus species
Ctenanthe lubbersiana
Cymbidium hybrids
Dizygotheca elegantissima
Dizygotheca veitchii
Elattaria cardamomum
Euphorbia caracasana
Ficus leprieurii
Ficus religiosa
Ficus stricta
Guzmania species
Hoya lacunosa
Iresine herbstii
Ixora hybrids
Maranta bicolor
Maranta leuconeura
Mascarena verschaffeltii

Microcoelum weddellianum
Monstera adansonii
Mussaenda phillipica
Neoregelia species
Nephrolepsis exaltata
Nidularium fulgens
Odontoglossum pulchellum
Pedilanthus tithymaloides 'Variegata'
Philodendron sagittifolium 'Ilsemannii'
Philodendron selloum
Pisonia umbellifera 'Variegatum'
Pistia stratiotes
Pteris cretica
Pteris ensiformis
Pteris quadriaurita
Schismatoglottis picta
Scindapsus pictus
Tillandsia cyanea
Tillandsia lindenii
Vriesea species

Houseplants that require a dormant period

These are plants that generally flourish when grown indoors, but nevertheless require a cool and/or dry dormant period, which usually falls some time during the winter. It is important to provide a space where the temperature is lower than the average room temperature, and a greenhouse is always a good location. Specific information on temperature and dormancy can be found in individual species listings in the book.

Many of these species can also be found in the appendices for cold greenhouse plants and moderate greenhouse plants. There is also some overlap with container plants, for a number of species can be grown with similar conditions, though the dormant period often falls in a different season. See descriptions for details.

(Notice how many more plants require a dormant period than can survive a winter growing indoors.)

Abutilon X *hybridum*
Abutilon megapotamicum
Abutilon megapotamicum 'Variegatum'
Abutilon pictum 'Thompsonii'

Acacia armata
Adenium obesum
Adromischus cooperi
Aeonium arboreum

Aeonium holochrysum
Aeonium tabuliforme
Aeschynanthus hildebrandii
Aeschynanthus radicans
Aeschynanthus tricolor
Agathis macrophylla
Agave parviflora
Alloplectus schlimii
Aloë aristata
Aloë humilis
Aloë variegata
Alternanthera ficoidea
Ampelopsis brevipedunculata
Anigozanthos flavidus
Anisodontea capensis
Aphelandra aquarrosa
Aporocactus flagelliformis
Arachnoides species
Araucaria heterophylla
Ardisia crenata
Arisaema candidissimum
Asparagus asparagoides
Asplenium bulbiferum

Aucuba japonica
Begonia albopicta
Begonia boweri
Begonia 'Cleopatra'
Begonia coccinea
Begonia Corallina hybrids
Begonia X *credneri*
Begonia Elatior hybrids
Begonia heracleifolia
Begonia hispida var. *cucullifera*
Begonia, tuberous hybrids
Begonia limmingheiana
Begonia Lorraine hybrids
Begonia maculata
Begonia manicata
Begonia X *margaritae*
Begonia masoniana
Begonia metallica
Begonia Rex hybrids
Begonia rotundifolia
Beloperone guttata
Bergeranthus scapiger
Blechnum species

Bougainvillea spectabilis
Bowiea volubilis
Brachychiton rupestris
Brasiliopuntia brasiliensis
Brassaia actinophylla
Brassaia species
Brunfelsia species
Caesalpinia decapetala
Calliandra harrisii
Callisia species
Calocephalus brownii
Campanula isophylla
Carex brunnea 'Variegata'
Carpobrotus acinaciformis
Catharanthus roseus
Cephalocereus senilis
Cereus neotetragonus
Cereus peruvianus
Ceropegia woodii ssp. *woodii*
Chamaecereus sylvestri
Chamaedorea elegans
Cheiridopsis candidissima
Chorizema cordatum
Chrysalidocarpus lutescens
Chrysanthemum, tuinchrysanten
Chysis aurea
Cissus striata
X *Citrofortunella mitis*
Clerodendrum thomsoniae
Clivia miniata
Coccoloba uvifera
Coelogyne cristata
Coleus Blumei hybrids
Columnea— X *banksii*
Columnea gloriosa
Columnea microphylla
Columnea microphylla 'Hostag'
Convolvulus sabaticus
Coprosma species
Cordyline fruticosa
Corokia species
Correa backhousiana
Cotyledon species
Crassula arborescens
Crassula coccinea
Crassula muscosa
Crassula ovata
Crassula pellucida
Crassula perfoliata var. *falcata*
Crassula perforata
Crassula rupestris
Crassula X *powelii*
Cryptocereus anthonyanus
Cuphea species
Cussonia spicata
Cyanotis kewensis
Cycas revoluta
Cyclamen persicum
Cyperus albostriatus
Cyrtanthus parviflorus
Cyrtomium falcatum
Cytisus X *spachianus*
Delosperma species
Dichondra repens
Didymochlaena truncatula
Dipladenia sanderi
Disphyma crassifolium
Doryopteris palmata
Dracaena surculosa
Dryopteris affinis
Duchesne indica

Dudleya pachyphytum
Dyckia fosteriana
Echeveria agavoides
Echeveria derenbergii
Echeveria harmsii
Echeveria pulvinata
Echeveria setosa
Echinocactus grusonii
Echinopsis, day-blooming species
Echinopsis, night-blooming species
Epidendrum fragrans
Erica X *willmorei*
Espostoa lanata
Eucalyptus cinerea
Eucomis bicolor
Euonymus japonica
Euphorbia balsamifera
Euphorbia canariensis
Euphorbia erythraeae
Euphorbia grandicornis
Euphorbia meloformis
Euphorbia pulcherrima
Euphorbia resinifera
Euphorbia submammilaris
Euphorbia tetragona
Euphorbia tirucalli
Euterpe edulis
X *Fatshedera lizei*
X *Fatshedera lizei* 'Variegata'
Fatsia japonica
Fatsia japonica 'Variegata'
Faucaria tigrina
Felicia amelloides
Ficus deltoidea
Ficus pumila
Ficus rubiginosa
Ficus ribiginosa 'Variegata'
Fuchsia hybrids
Furcraea foetida 'Striata'
Gardenia jasminioides
Gasteria species
Geranium palmatum
Glechoma hederacea 'Variegata'
Gloriosa rothschildiana
Glottiphyllum linguiforme
Graptopetalum species
Grevillea robusta
Gymnocalycium species
Gynura aurantiaca
Habranthus tubispathus
Haemanthus albiflos
Haemanthus multiflorus
Harpephyllum caffrum
Hatiora bambusioides
Haworthia species
Hedera helix, variegated varieties
Helleborus niger
Heterocentron elegans
Hibiscus rosa-sinensis
Hippeastrum hybrids
Homalocladium platycladum
Howeia forsteriana
Hoya carnosa
Hoya multiflora
Hyacinthus orientalis
Hydrangea macrophylla
Hymenocallis species
Hypocyrta glabra
Impatiens hawkeri
Impatiens repens
Impatiens walleriana

Incarvillea mairei
Ipomoea batatas
Iris reticulata
Jacobinia pauciflora
Jatropha pandurifolia
Jatropha podagrica
Kalanchoë beharensis
Kalanchoë blossfeldiana
Kalanchoë hybrids
Kalanchoë orgyalis
Kalanchoë scapigera
Kalanchoë tomentosa
Lachenalia unifolia
Lampranthus blandus
Lantana Camara hybrids
Ledebouria socialis
Lilium hybrids
Liriope muscari
Littonia modesta
Livistona chinensis
Lophomyrtus obcordata
Lycaste cruenta
Malvaviscus arboreus
Manettia inflata
Microlepis specluncae
Mikania ternata
Musa species
Narcissus hybrids
Nemantanthus hybrids
Neomortonia nummularia
Nerium oleander
Nertera granadensis
Nopalxochia phyllantoides
Odontoglossum bictoniense
Odontoglossum pulchellum
Olea europaea
Oncidium ornithorhynchum
Ophiopogon japonicus
Opuntia species
Oreopanax capitatus
Ornithogalum thyrsoides
Oscularia deltoides
Osteospermum ecklonis
Oxalis adenophylla
Pachira macrocarpa
Pachycereus pringlei
Pachyphytum oviferum
Pachypodium species
Pachystachys lutea
X *Pachyveria* species
Pandanus species
Paphiopedilum, green leaf species
Parthenocissus henryana
Parthenocissus inserta
Passiflora caerulea
Pavonia multiflora
Pelargonium X *citrosmum*
Pelargonium crispum
Pelargonium endlicherianum
Pelargonium X *fragrans* 'Variegatum'
Pelargonium Grandiflorum hybrids
Pelargonium Zonale hybrids
Pellaea species
Pellionia species
Pereskia aculeata 'Godseffiana'
Pernettya mucronata
Persea americana
Phoenix canariensis
Phyllitis scolopendrium
Pilea species
Plectranthus coleoides

Plectranthus oertendahlii
Pleione bulbocodioides
Plumbago auriculata
Plumbago indica
Polianthes tuberosa
Polyscias species
Polystichum tsus-simense
Portulacaria afra
Primula X *kewensis*
Primula obconica
Primula praenitens
Primula vulgaris
Pseudobombax ellipticum
Pseudopanax lessonii
Radermachera sinica
Reinwardtia indica
Rhapis excelsa
Rhipsalidopsis species
Rhododendron obtusum
Rhododendron simsii
Rhoicissus capensis
Rivina humilis
Rosa chinensis 'Minima'
Rosioglossum grande
Sagina subulata
Sandersonia aurantiaca
Sarcocaulon crassicaule
Sauromatum guttatum
Saxifraga cotyledon
Schefflera species
Schlumbergera hybrids
Scirpus cernuus
Scutellaria costaricana
Sedum species
Sempervivum arachnoideum
Senecio citriformis
Senecio herreanus
Senecio kleinia
Senecio macroglossus 'Variegatus'
Senecio radicans
Senecio rowleyanus
Serissa foetida 'Variegata'
Sibthorpia europaea
Siderasis fuscata
Sinningia cardinalis
Sinningia speciosa
Smithiantha hybrids
Soleirolia soleirolii
Sparmannia africana
Spatiphyllum wallisii
Sprekelia formosissima
Stenotaphrum secundatum 'Variegatum'
Stephanotis floribunda
Strelitzia reginae
Streptocarpus grandis
Streptocarpus hybrids
Streptocarpus saxorum
Streptosolen jamesonii
Testudinaria species
Tetrastigma voinerianum
Thunbergia alata
Tradescantia species
Tritonia crocata
Tulipa hybrids
Tupidanthus calyptratus
Vallota speciosa
Veltheimia capensis
X *Vuylstekeara* hybrids
Yucca species
Zebrina pendula
Zephyranthes candida

Container plants

Container plants and conservatory plants are discussed at length on pages 26–27. Briefly, container plants are defined here as all plants that in moderate climates can be grown outside from the end of May to the end of September, including small plants. Many of these plants can also be found under the listing for cold greenhouse plants. There is also some overlap with the listing for houseplants that require a dormant period and even with some plants from the listing for perennial houseplants.

Container plants should spend their dormancies in a cold or moderate greenhouse, depending on the required minimum temperature. A few woody, deciduous plants can be ensiled. If no greenhouse is available, a cool room will suffice in many cases.

Abutilon X hybridum
Abutilon megapotamicum
Abutilon megapotamicum 'Variegatum'
Abutilon pictum 'Thompsonii'
Acacia armata
Acca sellowiana
Acer buergerianum
Adenium obesum
Aeonium arboreum
Aeonium holochrysum
Aeonium praecox
Aeonium tabuliforme
Agathis macrophylla
Agave americana
Agave macroacantha
Agave victoriae-reginae
Albizia julibrissin
Aloë arborescens
Aloë aristata
Aloë humilis
Aloë variegata
Amaryllis belladonna
Ampelopsis brevipedunculata
Anigozanthos flavidus
Araucaria heterophylla
Arbutus andrachne
Aucuba japonica
Beaucarnea recurvata
Begonia coccinea
Begonia grandis
Begonia, tuberous hybrids
Beloperone guttata
Bergeranthus scapiger
Blechnum spicant
Bloomeria crocea
Brachychiton rupestris
Brasiliopuntia brasiliensis
Brassaia actinophylla
Caesalpinia decapetala
Callistemon citrinus

Calocephalus brownii
Camellia japonica
Canna Indica hybrids
Cantua buxifolia
Capparis spinosa
Carpobrotus acinaciformis
Cassia didymobotrya
Cestrum X newellii
Chamaelaucium uncinatum
Chamaerops humilis
Chorizema cordatum
Cistus species
X Citrofortunella mitis
Citrus species
Cleyera japonica
Colletia cruciata
Convolvulus sabaticus
Cordyline australis
Cordyline indivisa
Corokia species
Correa backhousiana
Corynocarpus laevigatum
Crassula arborescens
Crassula ovata
Crassula perfoliata var. falcata
Crinum X powelii
Cryptocereus anthonyanus
Cunonia capensis
Cuphea species
Cupressus macrocarpa 'Goldcrest'
Cussonia spicata
Cycas revoluta
Cyrtomium falcatum
Cytisus X spachianus
Danae racemosa
Dasylirion acrotrichum
Datura hybrids
Delosperma species
Dichondra repens
Disphyma crassifolium

Dodonaea viscosa
Doryanthes palmeri
Dracaena draco
Duchesnea indica
Echeveria derenbergii
Echeveria pulvinata
Echium wildpretii
Ensete ventricosum
Erica gracilis
Erica X willmorei
Eriobotrya japonica
Erythrina crista-galli
Eucalyptus cinerea
Eucomis bicolor
Eugenia myriophylla
Euonymus japonica
Euphorbia balsamifera
Euphrobia canariensis
Fascicullaria pitcairniifolia
X Fatshedera lizei
Fatsia japonica
Ficus carica
Fortunella margarita
Fuchsia hybrids
Furcraea foetida 'Striata'
Geranium palmatum
Glottiphyllum linguiforme
Habranthus tubispathus
Harpephyllum caffrum
Hatiora bambusoides
Hebe species
Hechtia stenophylla
Hedera helix, variegated varities
Hedychium gardnerianum
Hibiscus rosa-sinensis
Illicium anisatum
Impatiens repens
Incarvillea mairei
Isoplexis canariensis
Jacobinia pauciflora
Jasminum officinale
Lachenalia unifolia
Lagerstroemia indica
Lampranthus blandus
Lantana Camara hybrids
Laurus nobilis
Leptospermum scoparium
Leucothoë walteri
Lilium hybrids
Liriope muscari
Lophomyrtus obcordata
Lotus berthelotii
Malvaviscus arboreus
Mandevilla laxa
Metrosideros villosus
Myoporum acuminatum
Myrtus communis
Nandina domestica

Nerium oleander
Nertera granadensis
Olea europaea
Oreopanax capitatus
Ornithogalum thyrsoides
Oscularia deltoides
Osteospermum ecklonis
Pachira macrocarpa
Parthenocissus henryana
Parthenocissus inserta
Passiflora caerulea
Pelargonium endlicherianum
Pelargonium X fragrans 'Variegatum'
Pelargonium Zonale hybrids
Pernettya mucronata
Philesia magellanica
Phoenix canariensis
Phormium tenax
Pittosporum species
Plectranthus coleoides
Plumbago auriculata
Podocarpus macrophyllus
Prostanthera sieberi
Pseudopanax lessonii
Punica granatum
Puya chilensis
Radermachera sinica
Rehmannia elata
Reinwardtia indica
Rhapis excelsa
Rhododendron simsii
Rosa chinensis 'Minima'
Ruscus aculeatus
Sauromatum guttatum
Schefflera species
Schinus molle
Serissa foetida 'Variegata'
Skimmia species
Solanum pseudocapsicum
Sparmannia africana
Stenocarpus sinuatus
Strelitzia reginae
Tecoma castanifolia
Tecomaria capensis
Tetraclinis articulata
Tibouchina urvilleana
Tillandsia, gray-scaled species
Trachycarpus fortunei
Trichocereus spachianus
Tupidanthus calyptratus
Vallota speciosa
Washingtonia filifera
Yucca species
Zantedeschia species
Zephyranthes candida

Plants for a warm greenhouse

As explained on page 44, the temperature in a warm greenhouse should never be lower than 64°F (18°C) in the winter, and the relative humidity should never drop below 60%. Once in a while, one can successfully grow plants of this category in the home, given the proper humidity level. If the plants are sprayed frequently, or if a vaporizer is used, these plants can often be grown indoors without trouble. When these plants bloom—generally in the summer—they can be brought indoors from the greenhouse without causing too much damage.

The conditions in a closed plant window or a plant vitirne, as described on pages 38–41, can be made similar to those in a warm greenhouse, and can house the following plants, as well.

Any plant with a minimum temperature requirement between that of a moderate greenhouse (54°F/12°C) and a warm greenhouse (64°F/18°C) is categorized in this group.

Acalypha hispida
Acalypha pendula
Acalypha wilkesiana
Acanthorhipsalis monacantha

Aërides dalcatum
Allamanda cathartica
Alloplectus capitatus
Alocasias lowii

Alpinia sanderae
Amorphophallus bulbifer
Angraecum eburneum
Anselia africana
Anthurium crystallinum
Aphelandra maculata
Aphelandra sinclairiana
Aristolochia grandiflora
Arpophyllum spicatum
Aspasia lunata
Barkeria spectabilis
Begonia imperialis
Begonia serratipetala
Begonia venosa
Bertolonia marmorata
Breynia disticha
Bulbophyllum species
Caladium Bicolor hybrids
Calanthe triplicata
Calathea roseopicta
Caryota mitis
Catasetum maculatum
Cattleya species

Centradenia floribunda
Chamaeranthemum species
Chrysothemis pulchella
Cissus discolor
Cochliostema odoratissimum
Cocos nucifera
Copiapoa cinerea
Ctenanthe oppenheimiana
Cycnoches chlorochilum
Cyperus papyrus
Dendrobium, warm greenhouse species
Dichorisandra reginae
Didierea madagascariensis
Dipteracanthus devosianus
Dipteracanthus makoyanus
Dischidia pectenoides
Doritis pulcherrima
Dorstenia elata
Episcia cupreata
Episcia reptans
Euphorbia fulgens
Ficus aspera 'Parcellii'
Fittonia verschaffeltii

Globba winitii
Graptophyllum pictum
Heliconia jacquinii
Hemigraphis species
Hemionitis palmata
Hofmannia ghiesbreghtii
Hoodia gordonii
Hoya bella
Hoya linearis
Hypoestes phyllostachya
Jacaranda mimosifolia
Lockhartia lunifera

Ludisia discolor
Macroplectum sesquipedale
Malpighia coccigera
Maxillaria tenuifolia
Medinilla magnifica
Miltoniopsis roezlii
Mimosa pudica
Myrmecodia echinata
Nautilocalyx lynchii
Nepenthes hybrids
X Odontocidium species
Oncidium papilio

Paphiopedilum, spotted-leaf species
Passiflora alata
Perilepta dyeriana
Peristrophe hyssopifolia 'Aureovariegata'
Phaius tankervillea
Phyllanthus angustifolius
Pseuderanthemum species
Rodriguezia secunda
Sanchezia nobilis
Schaueria calycotricha
Selaginella species
Sonerila margaritacea

Stromanthe species
Tacca chantrieri
Tetranema roseum
Trevesia palmata
Trichodiadema densum
Turnera ulmifolia
Uebelmannia pectinifera
Urceolina grandiflora
Whitfieldia elongata
Whitfieldia lateritia
Xanthosoma lindenii

Plants for a moderate greenhouse

These plants require a minimum temperature of 54°F (12°C) and grow well during the summer when kept warm, protected and in a humid atmosphere. They also require a dormant period. When these plants bloom they can be moved indoors temporarily. Conditions in a plant window or vitrine can be made similar to those of a moderate greenhouse.

Any plant with a minimum temperature requirement between that of a cold greenhouse (40°F/5°C) and a moderate greenhouse (54°F/12°C) is categorized in this group.

Achimenes hybrids
Acokanthera oblongifolia
Aërangis rhodosticta
Agave victoriae-reginae
Asparagus setaceus
Astrophytum asterias
Astrophytum myriostigma
Astrophytum ornatum
Bauhinia acuminata
Bifrenaria harrisoniae
Borzicactus species
Brassavola species
X Brassocattleya species

X Brassolaeliocattleya species
Caesalpinia gilliesii
Camellia sinensis
Cleistocactus strausii
Clianthus puniceus
Coelia bella
Costus cuspidatus
Cyphostemma juttae
Dendrobium, moderate greenhouse species
Dicksonia antarctica
X Doritaenopsis species
Cracula troglodytis
Echinocereus species

Encyclia species
Epidendrum parkinsonianum
Erythrorhipsalis pilocarpa
Euphorbia caput-medusae
Fenestraria aurantiaca
Frithia pulchra
Gloxinia sylvatica
Goethea cauliflora
Gomesa recurva
Haageocereus pseudomelanostele
Habenaria xantholeuca
Huernia keniensis
Hutleya meleagris
Jacobinia cornea
Koellikeria erinoides
Kohleria Eriantha hybrids
Laelia cinnabarina
Lithops bromfieldii
Mandevilla laxa
Manihot esculenta 'Variegata'
Melocactus maxonii
Murraya paniculata
Myrtillocactus geometrizans
Neoporteria species
Neoporteria wagenknechtii
Notocactus species
Ochna serrulata

X Odontioda species
Odontoglossum pulchellum
Oncidium microchilum
Orbea variegata
Passiflora violacea
Pentas lanceolata
Phalaenopsis species
Pinguicula moranensis
Piper crocatum
Piper ornatum
Porphyrocoma pohliana
Prostanthera sieberi
Rhipsalis baccifera
Rhynchostylis coelestis
Solandra grandiflora
Sophronitis cernua
Stanhopea wardii
Thevetia peruviana
Tillandsia usneoides
Vanda coerulea
Warscewiczella discolor
Wilcoxia viperina
X Wilsonara hybrids
Zamia pumila
Zantedeschia species
Zygopetalon mackaii

Plants for a cold greenhouse

The minimum temperature in this greenhouse is 40°F (5°C) during the winter, which is when most of these plants are dormant, requiring little or no water. Many cacti and other succulents are suitable for cold greenhouse cultivation. In the summer, these plants need much warmth, light and humidity. When these plants bloom they can be temporarily moved inside without much damage. There is some overlap here with container plants, which are often brought into a cold greenhouse or conservatory for the winter.

Abromeitiella brevifolia
Acanthocalycium violaceum
Acca sellowiana
Acorus gramineus 'Argenteostriatus'
Ariocarpus fissuratus
Asarina barclaiana
Asplenium marinum
Bauhinia punctata
Blossfeldia liliputana
Bomarea caldasii
Bouvardia hybrids

Caralluma X suaveolens
Carnegiea gigantea
Conophytum species
Coryphantha elephantidens
Darlingtonia californica
Dionaea muscipula
Disa uniflora
Dolichothele baumii
Drosera capensis
Echinocereus species
Echinofossulocactus hastatus

Epacris hybrids
Escobaria vivipara
Fascicularia pitcairniifolia
Greenovia aurea
Hamatocactus setispinus
Hibbertia scandens
Jasminum officinale
Leptocladodia microhelia
Leuchtenbergia principes
Lobivia species
Lophophora williamsii
Lotus berthelotii
Mamillopsis senilis
Mammillaria bocasana
Mammillaria guelzoviana
Mammillaria hahniana
Mammillaria prolifera
Mammillaria rhodantha
Mammillaria spinosissima
Mammillaria wildii
Mammillaria zeilmanniana
Masdevallia species
Matucana currundayensis

Miltonia hybrids
Obregonia denegrii
Ochagavia carnea
Opthalmophyllum jacobsenianum
Oreocereus celsianus
Oroya peruviana
Parodia species
Pseudomammillaria camptotricha
Puya chilensis
Rebutia senilis
Rebutia species
Rhodochiton atrosanguineum
Sarmienta scandens
Sarracenia species
Selenicereus grandiflorus
Stapelia X divaricata
Sulcorebutia mizguensis
Trichocereus spachianus
Tropaeolum species
Weingartia species

Plants for an office

The following rather large houseplants are suitable for an office, where a consistent temperature is maintained all year. This list includes some hanging and climbing plants as well.

Abutilon megapotamicum
Asparagus falcatus
Aspidistra elatior
Brosimum alicastrum
Cissus rhombifolia
Clusia rosea

Corynocarpus laevigatum
Cupressus macrocarpa 'Goldcrest'
Dieffenbachia amoena
Dieffenbachia bowmannii
Dieffenbachia maculata
Dieffenbachia seguine

Dracaena deremensis
Dracaena draco
Dracaena fragrans
Dracaena marignata
Dracaena reflexa
Dracaena sanderiana
Epipremnum pinnatum
Ficus altissima
Ficus benghalensis
Ficus benjamina
Ficus buxifolia

Ficus cyathistipula
Ficus elastica
Ficus lyrata
Ficus microcarpa
Ficus retusa
Ficus saggittata
Ficus schlechteri
Leea guineensis
Monstera deliciosa
Philodendron bipennifolium
Philodendron elegans

Philodendron erubescens	*Philodendron rugosum*	*Phlebodium aureum*	*Sansevieria trifasciata*
Philodendron melanochrysum	*Philodendron squamiferum*	*Phoenix roebelinii*	*Synadenium grantii*
Philodendron pedatum	*Philodendron tuxtlanum*	*Pinus pinea* 'Silver Crest'	*Syngonium podophyllum*

TEMPERATURE REQUIREMENTS

Warm cultivation

"Warm" refers to the temperature during the summer, which cannot go below 61–68°F (16–20°C) for the following plants. These plants cannot be placed outside, and should be monitored closely when grown in the home or in a greenhouse; the temperature shouldn't drop below 61°F. In the winter, some of these plants may require a dormant period. Check the individual species descriptions for information on the temperature during dormancy.

Abromeitiella brevifolia
Abutilon X *hybridum*
Abutilon megapotamicum
Abutilon megapotamicum 'Variegatum'
Acacia armata
Acalypha hispida
Acalypha pendula
Acalypha wilkesiana
Acanthorhipsalis monocantha
Acca sellowiana
Achimenes hybrids
Acokanthera oblongifolia
Adenium obesum
Adiantum hispidulum
Adiantum peruvianum
Adiantum raddianum
Adiantum tenerum
Adromischus cooperi
Aërides falcata
Aeschynanthus hildebrandii
Aeschynanthus radicans
Aeschynanthus tricolor
Agave parviflora
Agave victoriae-reginae
Aglaonema commutatum
Aglaonema costatum
Aglaonema crispum
Allamanda cathartica
Alloplectus capitatus
Alocasia lowii
Alpinia sanderae
Alsobia dianthiflora
Ananas species
Angraecum eburneum
Ansellia africana
Anthurium Andraeanum hybrids
Anthurium crystallinum
Anthurium Scherzeranum hybrids
Aphelandra aurantiaca
Aphelandra maculata
Aphelandra sinclairiana
Aphelandra squarrosa
Arachis hypogaea
Ariocarpus fissuratus
Aristolochia grandiflora
Asparagus densiflorus
Asparagus falcatus
Aspasia lunata
Aspidistra elatior
Aspidistra elatior 'Variegata'
Asplenium bulbiferum
Asplenium nidus
Astrophytum asterias
Astrophytum myriostigma
Astrophytum ornatum
Barkeria spectabilis
Beaucarnea recurvata
Begonia boweri
Begonia X *erythrophylla*
Begonia heracleifolia
Begonia hispida var. *cucullifera*
Begonia imperialis
Begonia limmingheiana

Begonia metallica
Begonia serratipetala
Begonia venosa
Bertolonia marmorata
Bifrenaria harrisoniae
Blechnum species
Blossfeldia liliputana
Bowiea volubilis
Brassavola species
Brassia species
X *Brassocattleya* species
X *Brassolaeliocattleya* species
Breynia disticha
Brosimum alicastrum
Bulbophyllum species
Caladium Bicolor hybrids
Calanthe triplicata
Calathea crocata
Calathea lancifolia
Calathea makoyana
Calathea ornata
Calathea picturata
Calathea roseopicta
Carnegiea gigantea
Caryota mitis
Catasetum maculatum
Cattleya species
Centradenia floribunda
Cephalocereus senilis
Cereus neotetragonus
Cereus peruvianus
Chamaeranthemum species
Cheiridopsis candidissima
Chrysalidocarpus lutescens
Chrysothemis pulchella
Chysis aurea
Cissus antarctica
Cissus discolor
Cissus rhombifolia
Cleistocactus straussii
Clusia rosea
Coccoloba uvifera
Cochliostemma odoratissimum
Cocos nucifera
Codiaeum variegatum
X *Codonanthus* species
Codonanthe crassifolia
Coffea arabica
Coleus Blumei hybrids
Columnea X *banksii*
Columnea gloriosa
Columnea microphylla
Columnea microphylla 'Hostag'
Conophytum species
Copiapoa cinerea
Cordyline fruticosa
Coryphantha elephantidens
Costus cuspidatus
Crassula muscosa
Crassula ovata
Crassula perfoliata var. *falcata*
Crassula rupestris
Crossandra infundibuliformis

Cryptanthus species
Ctenanthe lubbersiana
Ctenanthe oppenheimiana
Cycnoches chlorochilum
Cymbidium hybrids
Cyphostemma juttae
Davallia mariesii
Delosperma species
Dendrobium species, moderate greenhouse
Dendrobium species, warm greenhouse
Dichorisandra reginae
Dicksonia antarctica
Didierea madagascariensis
Dieffenbachia amoena
Dieffenbachia bowmannii
Dieffenbachia maculata
Dieffenbachia seguine
Dipladenia sanderi
Dipteracanthus devosianus
Dipteracanthus makoyanus
Dischidia pectenoides
Dizygotheca elegantissima
Dizygotheca veitchii
Colichothele baumii
X *Doritaenopsis* species
Doritis pulcherrima
Dorstenia elata
Dracaena deremensis
Dracaena fragrans
Dracaena marginata
Dracaena marginata 'Tricolor'
Dracaena reflexa
Dracaena sanderiana
Dracaena surculosa
Dudleya pachyphytum
Echeveria harmsii
Echinocactus grusonii
Echinocereus species
Echinofossulocactus hastatus
Elettaria cardamomum
Epipremnum pinnatum
Epipremnum pinnatum 'Marble Queen'
Episcia cupreata
Episcia reptans
Espostoa lanata
Euphorbia caput-medusae
Euphorbia caracasana
Euphorbia erythraeae
Euphorbia leuconeura
Euphorbia meloformis
Euphorbia milii
Euphorbia submammilaris
Euphorbia tirucalli
Euterpe edulis
Faucaria tigrina
Fenestraria aurantiaca
Ficus altissima
Ficus aspera 'Parcellii'
Ficus benghalensis
Ficus benjamina
Ficus benjamina 'Variegata'
Ficus buxifolia
Ficus cyathistipula
Ficus elastica
Ficus leprieurii
Ficus lyrata
Ficus microcarpa
Ficus pumila
Ficus religiosa
Ficus retusa
Ficus schlecteri
Ficus stricta
Frithia pulchra
Globba winitii

Gloriosa rothschildiana
Gloxinia sylvatica
Goethea cauliflora
Graptophyllum pictum
Guzmania species
Gymnocalycium species
Gynura aurantiaca
Haageocereus pseudomelanostele
Hamatocactus setispinus
Haworthia species
Hedera helix ssp. *canariensis* 'Variegata'
Heliconia jacquinii
Hemigraphis species
Hemionitis palmata
Hofmania ghiesbreghtii
Hoodia gordonii
Hoya bella
Hoya lacunosa
Hoya linearis
Hoya multiflora
Hypoestes phyllostachya
Ipomoea batatas
Ipomoea tricolor
Ixora hybrids
Jacaranda mimosifolia
Jacobinia carnea
Jatropha pandurifolia
Jatropha podagrica
Kalanchoë beharensis
Kalanchoë daigremontiana
Kalanchoë orgyalis
Kalanchoë scapigera
Kalanchoë tomentosa
Kalanchoë tubiflora
Koellikeria erinoides
Kohleria Eriantha hybrids
Laelia cinnabarina
Leea guineensis
Leptocladodia microhelia
Leuchtenbergia principes
Lithops bromfieldii
Littonia modesta
Lophophora williamsii
Ludisia discolor
Macroplectum sesquipedale
Malpighia coccigera
Mammillaria bocasana
Mammillaria guelzoviana
Mammillaria hahniana
Mammillaria prolifera
Mammillaria rhodantha
Mammillaria spinosissima
Mammillaria wildii
Mammillaria zeilmanniana
Manihot esculenta 'Variegata'
Maranta bicolor
Maranta leuconeura
Mascarena verschaffeltii
Maxillaria tenuifolia
Medinilla magnifica
Melocactus maxonii
Microcoelum weddellianum
Miltoniopsis roezlii
Mimosa pudica
Monstera adansonii
Monstera deliciosa
Monstera deliciosa 'Variegata'
Musa species
Mussaenda phillipica
Myrmecodia echinata
Myrtillocactus geometrizans
Nautilocalyx lynchii
Nemanthus hybrids
Neomortonia nummularia

Neoportenia species
Neoporteria wagenknechtii
Neoregelia species
Nepenthes hybrids
Nephrolepis exaltata
Nidularium fulgens
Obregonia denegrii
X Odontocidium species
Oncidium papilio
Opthalmophyllum jacobsenianum
Orbea variegata
Oroya peruviana
Pachycereus pringlei
Pachyphytum oviferum
Pachypodium species
Pachystachys lutea
X Pachyveria species
Pandanus species
Paphiopedilum, spotted-leaf species
Passiflora alata
Pavonia multiflora
Pedilanthus titymaloides 'Variegata'
Pelargonium X blandfordianum
Pelargonium X citrosmum
Pelargonium crispum
Pelargonium X fragrans 'Variegatum'
Pelargonium radens
Pellionia species
Peperomia incana
Pereskia aculeata 'Godseffiana'

Perilepta dyeriana
Peristrophe hyssopifolia 'Aureovariegata'
Persea americana
Phaius tankerivlleae
Phalaenopsis species
Philodendron bipennifolium
Philodendron elegans
Philodendron erubescens
Philodendron melanochrysum
Philodendron pedatum
Philodendron rugosum
Philodendron sagittifolium 'Ilsemannii'
Philodendron scandens
Philodendron squamiferum
Philodendron tuxtlanum
Phlebodium aureum
Phoenix roebelinii
Phyllanthus angustifolius
Pilea species
Pinus pinea 'Silver Crest'
Piper crocatum
Piper ornatum
Pisonia umbellifera 'Variegatum'
Pistia stratiotes
Platycerium bifurcatum
Plectranthus fruticosus
Plumbago indica
Polyscias species
Portulaca grandiflora
Pseuderanthemum species

Pseudobombax ellipticum
Pseudomammillaria camptotricha
Rhoeo spathacea 'Vittata'
Rivina humilis
Rodriguezia secunda
Rosioglossum grande
Saintpaulia ionantha
Sanchezia nobilis
Sandersonia aurantiaca
Sansevieria trifasciata
Sarocaulon crassicaule
Sarmienta scandens
Schaueria calycotricha
Schismatoglottis picta
Scindapsus pictus
Selaginella species
Selenicereus grandiflorus
Senecio citriformis
Senecio herreanus
Senecio kleinia
Senecio radicans
Senecio rowleyanus
Siderasis fuscata
Sinningia cardinalis
Sinningia speciosa
Smithiantha hybrids
Solandra grandiflora
Sonerila margaritacea
Spatiphyllum wallisii
Stanhopea wardii

Stapelia X divaricata
Stephanotis floribunda
Streptocarpus saxorum
Stromanthe species
Synadenium grantii
Syngonium podophyllum, variegated varieties
Syngonium podophyllum, green-leaf trunk type
Tacca chantrieri
Testudinaria species
Tetranema roseum
Thevetia peruviana
Tillandsia cyanea
Tillandsia lindenii
Tillandsia usneoides
Trevesia palmata
Turnera ulmifolia
Uebelmannia pectinifera
Urceolina grandiflora
Vanda coerulea
Vriesea species
X Vuylstekeara hybrids
Whitfieldia elongata
Whitfieldia lateritia
Wilcoxia viperina
Xanthosoma lindenii
Zamia pumila
Zygopetalon mackaii

Moderately warm cultivation

The plants in this category require a minimum temperature of 50–61°F (10–16°C), which generally means that they cannot be kept outside in early and late summer months when the temperature is cooler. There will be fewer problems when these plants are cultivated in the home or in a greenhouse. Some of these plants may require a dormant period in the winter. Check the individual species descriptions for information on the temperature during dormancy.

Abromeitiella brevifolia
Abutilon X hybridum
Abutilon megapotamicum
Abutilon megapotamicum 'Variegatum'
Abutilon pictum 'Thompsonii'
Acacia armata
Acanthocalycium violaceum
Acca sellowiana
Acokanthera oblongifolia
Adiantum tenerum
Adromischus cooperi
Aeonium holochrysum
Aërangis rhodosticta
Agave americana
Agave parviflora
Agave victoriae-reginae
Alloplectus schlimii
Aloë variegata
Amorphophallus bulbifer
Anigozanthos flavidus
Arachnoides species
Ardisia crenata
Arpophyllum spicatum
Asclepias curassavica
Asparagus asparagoides
Asparagus densiflorus
Asparagus falcatus
Asparagus setaceus
Aspidistra elatior
Aspidistra elatior 'Variegata'
Asplenium bulbiferum
Astrophytum asterias
Bauhinia acuminata
Bauhinia punctata
Beaucarnea recurvata
Begonia albopicta
Begonia boweri
Begonia 'Cleopatra'
Begonia coccinea
Begonia Corallina hybrids

Begonia X credneri
Begonia Elatior hybrids
Begonia X erythrophylla
Begonia heracleifolia
Begonia hispida var. cucullifera
Begonia limmingheana
Begonia Lorraine hybrids
Begonia maculata
Begonia manicata
Begonia X margaritae
Begonia massoniana
Begonia metallica
Begonia Rex hybrids
Begonia rotundifolia
Begonia serratipetala
Begonia venosa
Bifrenaria harrisoniae
Billbergia nutans
Blechnum species
Blossfeldia liliputana
Bomarea caldasii
Borzicactus species
Bougainvillea spectabilis
Bouvardia hybrids
Bowiea volubilis
Brachychiton rupestris
Brassavola species
Breynia disticha
Brunfelsia species
Bulbophyllum species
Caesalpinia decapetala
Caesalpinia gilliesii
Calliandra harrisii
Callisia species
Camellia sinensis
Canna Indica hybrids
Capparis spinosa
Caralluma X suaveolens
Carex brunnea 'Variegata'
Carnegiea gigantea

Carpobrotus acinaciformis
Celosia argentea
Cereus neotetragonus
Cerreus peruvianus
Ceropegia woodii ssp. woodii
Chamaecereus sylvestri
Chamaedorea elegans
Chamaelaucium uncinatum
Cheiridopsis candidissima
Chlorophytum comosum 'Variegatum'
Chrysalidocarpus lutescens
Chrysanthemum, garden varieties
Cissus antarctica
Cissus rhombifolia
Cissus striata
X Citrofortunella mitis
Clerodendrum thomsoniae
Clianthus puniceus
Clivia miniata
Codiaeum variegatum
Coelia bella
Coelogyne cristata
Coffea arabica
Coleus Blumei hybrids
Colletia cruciata
Conophytum species
Copiapoa cinerea
Coprosma species
Cordyline fruticosa
Corynocarpus laevigatum
Costus cuspidatus
Cotyledon species
Crassula muscosa
Crassula ovata
Crassula pellucida
Crassula perfoliata var. falcata
Crassula perforata
Crassula rupestris
Cryptocereus anthonyanus
Ctenanthe lubbersiana
Ctenanthe oppenheimiana
Cupressus macrocarpa 'Goldcrest'
Cyanotis kewensis
Cycas revoluta
Cycnoches chlorochilum
Cymbidium hybrids
Cyperus alternifolius
Cyperus albostriatus
Cyperus papyrus
Cyphostemma juttae
Darlingtonia californica

Dasylirion acrotrichum
Datura hybrids
Davallia mariesii
Delosperma species
Dichondra repens
Dicksonia antarctica
Didymochlaena truncatula
Dieffenbachia amoena
Dieffenbachia bowmannii
Dieffenbachia maculata
Dieffenbachia seguine
Dipladenia sanderi
Disphyma crassifolium
Dizygotheca elegantissima
Dizygotheca veitchii
Dolichothele baumii
Doryanthes palmeri
Doryopteris palmata
Drosera capensis
Dracaena draco
Dudleya pachyphytum
Echeveria agavoides
Echeveria derenbergii
Echeveria harmsii
Echeveria pulvinata
Echeveria setosa
Echinocactus grusonii
Echinocereus species
Echinofossulocactus hastatus
Echinopsis, night-blooming species
Echium wildpretii
Encyclia species
Ensete ventricosum
Epidendrum fragrans
Epidendrum parkinsonianum
Erythrorhipsalis pilocarpa
Escobaria vivipara
Eucalyptus cinerea
Euphorbia balsamifera
Euphorbia canariensis
Euphorbia caput-medusae
Euphorbia erythraeae
Euphorbia fulgens
Euphorbia grandicornis
Euphorbia leuconeura
Euphorbia meloformis
Euphorbia milii
Euphorbia pulcherrima
Euphorbia resinifera
Euphorbia submammilaris
Euphorbia tetragona

Euphorbia tirucalli
Eustoma grandiflorum
Exacum affine
Fascicularia pitcairniifolia
Faucaria tigrina
Ficus deltoidea
Ficus pumila
Ficus rubiginosa
Ficus rubiginosa 'Variegata'
Ficus saggittata
Fittonia verschaffeltii
Furcraea foetida 'Striata'
Gardenia jasminioides
Gasteria species
Gazania hybrids
Gerbera hybrids
Glottiphyllum linguiforme
Gomesa recurva
Gomphrena globosa
Graptopetalum species
Greenovia aurea
Grevillea robusta
Gymnocalycium species
Gynura aurantiaca
Haageocereus pseudomelanostele
Habenaria xantholeuca
Habranthus tubispathus
Haemanthus albiflos
Haemanthus multiflorus
Hamatocactus setispinus
Hatiora bambusioides
Hechtia stenophylla
Hedera helix ssp. canariensis 'Variegata'
Hedychium gardnerianum
Heterocentron elegans
Hibbertia scandens
Hibiscus rosa-sinensis
Hippeastrum hybrids
Homalocladium platycladum
Howeia forsteriana
Hoya carnosa
Huernia keniensis
Hutleya meleagris
Hymenocalis species
Hypocyrta glabra
Ipomoea tricolor
Iresine herbstii
Isoplexis canariensis
Jatropha pandurifolia
Kalanchoë blossfeldiana
Kalanchoë daigremontiana
Kalanchoë hybrids
Kalanchoë orgyalis
Kalanchoë scapigera
Kalanchoë tomentosa
Kalanchoë tubiflora
Laelia cinnabarina
Lampranthus blandus

Lantana Camara hybrids
Ledebouria socialis
Leptocladodia microhelia
Leuchtenbergia principes
Lilium hybrids
Littonia modesta
Livistona chinensis
Lobivia species
Lockhartia lunifera
Lophomyrtus obcordata
Lophophora williamsii
Lotus berthelotii
Lycaste cruenta
Malvaviscus arboreus
Mamillopsis senilis
Mammillaria bocasana
Mammillaria prolifera
Mammillaria rhodantha
Mammillaria sinosissima
Mammillaria wildii
Mammillaria zeilmanniana
Mandevilla laxa
Manettia inflata
Manihot esculenta 'Variegata'
Matucana currundayensis
Microlepis speluncae
Mikania ternata
Murraya paniculata
Nematanthus hybrids
Neoporteria species
Neoporteria wagenknechtii
Neoregelia species
Nerium oleander
Nidularium fulgens
Nopalxochia phyllantoides
Notocactus species
Obregonia denegrii
Ochna serrulata
X Odontocidium species
Odontoglossum pulchellum
Olea europaea
Oncidium microchilum
Oncidium ornithorhynchum
Ophiopogon jaburan
Oplismenus hirtellus 'Variegatus'
Opthalmophyllum jacobsenianum
Opuntia species
Orbea variegata
Ornithogalum thyrsoides
Oscularia deltoides
Pachira macrocarpa
Pachycereus pringlei
Pachyphytum oviferum
Pachypodium species
X Pachyveria species
Pandanus species
Paphiopedilum, green-leaf species
Parodia species

Passiflora violacea
Pavonia multiflora
Pelargonium X blandfordianum
Pelargonium X citrosmum
Pelargonium crispum
Pelargonium endlicherianum
Pelargonium X fragrans 'Variegatum'
Pelargonium Grandiflorum hybrids
Pelargonium graveolens 'Variegatum'
Pelargonium radens
Pelargonium Zonale hybrids
Pellaea species
Pentas lanceolata
Peperomia argyreia
Peperomia blanda
Peperomia caperata
Peperomia fraseri
Peperomia griseoargenta
Peperomia obtusifolia 'Greengold'
Peperomia pereskiifolia
Peperomia puteolata
Peperomia rotundifolia
Peperomia serpens 'Variegata'
Pereskia aculeata 'Godseffiana'
Persea americana
Phalaenopsis species
Philodendron bipennifolium
Philodendron erubescens
Philodendron rugosum
Philodendron sagittifolium 'Ilsemannii'
Philodendron scandens
Philodendron selloum
Philodendron squamiferum
Phlebodium aureum
Phoenix roebelinii
Pilea species
Pinus pinea 'Silver Crest'
Piper crocatum
Piper ornatum
Plectranthus fruticosus
Plectranthus oertendahlii
Plumbago indica
Polianthes tuberosa
Polyscias species
Porphyrocoma pohliana
Portulacaria afra
Prostanthera sieberi
Pseudobombax ellipticum
Pseudomammillaria camptotricha
Pteris cretica
Pteris ensiformis
Pteris quadriaurita
Radermachera sinica
Rebutia senilis
Rebutia species
Rehmannia elata
Rhipsalis baccifera
Rhodochiton atrosanguineum

Rhododendron simsii
Rhoeo spathacea 'Vittata'
Rhynchostylis coelestis
Rivina humilis
Saintpaulia ionantha
Sarmienta scandens
Schinus molle
Schlumbergera hybrids
Scutellaria costaricana
Sedum species
Selaginella species
Sempervivum arachnoideum
Senecio citriformis
Senecio herreanus
Senecio kleinia
Senecio macroglossus 'Variegatus'
Senecio mikanioides
Senecio radicans
Senecio rowleyanus
Serissa foetida 'Variegata'
Setcreasea pallida
Siderasis fuscata
Sophronitis cernua
Stanhopea wardii
Stapelia X divaricata
Stenotaphrum secundatum 'Variegatum'
Stephanotis floribunda
Strelitzia reginae
Streptocarpus grandis
Streptocarpus hybrids
Streptocarpus saxorum
Sulcorebutia mizguensis
Tecoma castanifolia
Tecomaria capensis
Tetraclinis articulata
Tetrastigma voinierianum
Thunbergia alata
Tillandsia usneoides
Tolmiea menziesii
Torenia fournieri
Tradescantia species
Trevesia palmata
Trichodiadema densum
Tritonia crocata
Tropaeolum species
Tulipa hybrids
Vallota species
Vanda coerulea
X Vuylstekeara hybrids
Wilcoxia viperina
X Wilsonara hybrids
Yucca species
Zamia pumila
Zebrina pendula
Zygopetalon mackaii

Cool cultivation

In the summer, the temperature or plants of this group can drop to 37°F (3°C), and they can generally be kept outside through the summer, beginning in late May and ending in September, always avoiding frosty conditions. Most plants from this list can be found under the listing for container plants as well. Also, many of these plants require a dormant period. Check the individual species descriptions for information on the temperature during dormancy.

Abutilon X hybridum
Abutilon megapotamicum
Abutilon megapotamicum 'Variegatum'
Abutilon pictum 'Thompsonii'
Acacia armata
Acer buergerianum
Acorus gramineus 'Argenteostriatus'
Aeonium arboreum
Aeonium holochrysum
Aeonium tabuliforme
Agapanthus praecox
Agathis macrophylla

Agave americana
Agave macroacantha
Agave parviflora
Agave victoriae-reginae
Albizia julibrissin
Aloë arborescens
Aloë aristata
Aloë humilis
Aloë variegata
Alternanthera ficoidea
Amaryllis belladonna
Amorphophallus bulbifer

Ampelopsis brevipedunculata
Anigozanthos flavidus
Anisodontea capensis
Aporocactus flagelliformis
Araucaria heterophylla
Arbutus andrachne
Arisaema candidissimum
Asarina barclaiana
Asclepias curassavica
Asplenium marinum
Aucuba japonica
Beaucarnea recurvata
Begonia coccinea
Begonia grandis
Begonia, tuberous hybrids
Beloperone guttata
Bergeranthus scapiger
Billbergia nutans
Blechnum spicant
Bloomeria crocea
Bougainvillea spectabilis
Bouvardia hybrids
Brasiliopuntia brasiliensis

Brassaia actinophylla
Browallia speciosa
Brunfelsia species
Caesalpinia decapetala
Calceolaria hybrids
Callistemon citrinus
Calocephalus brownii
Camelia japonica
Camellia sinensis
Campanula fragilis
Campanula isophylla
Canna Indica hybrids
Cantua buxifolia
Capparis spinosa
Capsicum annuum
Carex brunnea 'Variegata'
Carpobrotus acinaciformis
Cassia didymobotrya
Catharanthus roseus
Cestrum X newellii
Chamaecereus sylvestri
Chamaelaucium uncinatum
Chamaerops humilis

Chorizema cordatum
Chrysanthemum Indicum hybrids
Chrysanthemum parthenium
Chrysanthemum, garden varieties
Cistus species
X Citrofortunella mitis
Citrus species
Cleyera japonica
Convolvulus sabaticus
Cordyline australis
Cordyline indivisa
Corokia species
Correa backhousiana
Corynocarpus laevigatum
Crassula arborescens
Crassula coccinea
Crassula pellucida
Crassula perforata
Crinum X powelii
Crocus vernus ssp. vernus
Cryptocereus anthonyanus
Cunonia capensis
Cuphea species
Cupressus macrocarpa 'Goldcrest'
Cussonia spicata
Cycas revoluta
Cyclamen persicum
Cyrtanthus parviflorus
Cyrtomium falcatum
Cytisus X spachianus
Danaë racemosa
Darlingtonia californica
Dasylirion acrotrichum
Datura hybrids
Delosperma species
Dichondra repens
Dionaea muscipula
Disa uniflora
Disphyma crassifolium
Dodonaea viscosa
Doryanthes palmeria
Dracaena draco
Dracula troglodytis
Drosera capensis
Dryopteris affinis
Duchesnea indica
Dyckia fosteriana
Echeveria agavoides
Echeveria derenbergii
Echeveria pulvinata
Echeveria setosa
Echinopsis, day-blooming species
Echium wildpretii
Ensete ventricosum
Epacris hybrids
Erica gracilis
Erica X willmorei

Eriobotrya japonica
Erythrina crista-galli
Erythrorhipsalis pilocarpa
Escobaria vivipara
Eucalyptus cinerea
Eucomis bicolor
Eugenia myriophylla
Euonymus japonica
Euphorbia balsamifera
Euphorbia canariensis
Eustoma grandiflorum
Fascicularia pitcairniifolia
X Fatshedera lizei
X Fatshedera lizei 'Variegata'
Fatsia japonica
Fatsia japonica 'Variegata'
Felicia ammelloides
Ficus carica
Fortunella margarita
Fuchsia hybrids
Geranium palmatum
Glechoma hederacea 'Variegata'
Glottiphyllum linguiforme
Gomphrena globosa
Greenovia aurea
Habranthus tubispathus
Harpephyllum caffrum
Hatiora bambusioides
Hebe species
Hechtia stenophylla
Hedera helix, variegated varieties
Hedychium gardnerianum
Heliotropium arborescens
Helleborus niger
Hippeastrum hybrids
Homalocladium platycladum
Hutleya meleagris
Hyacinthus orientalis
Hydrangea macrophylla
Illicium anisatum
Impatiens hawkeri
Impatiens repens
Impatiens walleriana
Incarvillea mairei
Iresine herbstii
Iris reticulata
Isoplexis canariensis
Jacobinia pauciflora
Jasminum officinale
Lachenalia unifolia
Lagerstroemia indica
Laurus nobilis
Leptospermum scoparium
Leucothoë walteri
Lilium hybrids
Liriope muscari
Lobivia species

Lophomyrtus obcordata
Lotus berthelotii
Lycaste cruenta
Malvaviscus arboreus
Masdevallia species
Metrosideros villosus
Miltonia hybrids
Myoporum acuminatum
Myrtus communis
Nandina domestica
Narcissus hybrids
Nerium oleander
Nertera granadensis
Nicotiana X sanderae
Nopalxochia phyllantoides
Ochagavia carnea
X Odontioda species
Odontoglossum bictoniense
Olea europaea
Ophiopogon japonicus
Opuntia species
Oreocereus celsianus
Oreopanax capitatus
Oscularia deltoides
Osteospermum ecklonis
Oxalis adenophylla
Parthenocissus henryana
Parthenocissus inserta
Passiflora caerulea
Pelargonium X blandfordianum
Pelargonium X citrosmum
Pelargonium crispum
Pelargonium endlicherianum
Pelargonium X fragrans 'Variegatum'
Pelargonium radens
Pernettya mucronata
Philesia magellanica
Phoenix canariensis
Phormium tenax
Phyllitis scolopendrium
Pinguicula moranensis
Pittosporum species
Plectranthus coleoides
Plectranthus oertendahlii
Pleione bulbocodioides
Plumbago auriculata
Podocarpus macrophyllus
Polystichum tsus-simense
Primula X kewensis
Primula malacoides
Primula obconica
Primula praenitens
Primula vulgaris
Pseudopanax lessonii
Punica granatum
Puya chilensis
Reinwardtia indica

Rhapsis excelsa
Rhipsalidopsis species
Rhipsalis baccifera
Rhodochiton atrosanguineaum
Rhododendron obtusum
Rhododendron simsii
Rhoicissus capensis
Rhynchostylis coelestis
Rosa chinensis 'Minima'
Ruscus aculeatus
Sagina subulata
Sarracenia species
Sauromatum guttatum
Saxifraga cotyledon
Saxifraga stolonifera 'Tricolor'
Schefflera species
Schinus molle
Schizanthus pinnatus
Scirpus cernuus
Sempervivum arachnoideum
Senecio Cruentus hybrids
Senecio mikanioides
Sibthorpia europaea
Skimmia species
Solanum pseudocapsicum
Soleirolia soleirolii
Sophronitis cernua
Sparmannia africana
Sprekelia formosissima
Stenocarpus sinuatus
Streptosolen jamesonii
Sulcorebutia mizguensis
Tecoma castanifolia
Tecomaria capensis
Tetraclinis articulata
Thunbergia alata
Tibouchina urvilleana
Tillandsia, gray-scaled species
Tolmiea menziesii
Trachycarpus fortunei
Trichocereus spachianus
Tritonia crocata
Tropaeolum species
Tulipa hybrids
Tupidanthus calyptratus
Vallota speciosa
Veltheimia capensis
Warscewiczella discolor
Washingtonia filifera
Weingartia species
X Wilsonara hybrids
Yucca species
Zantedeschia species
Zephyranthes candida

HUMIDITY REQUIREMENTS

Plants requiring a high relative humidity

These are almost exclusively greenhouse, vitrine and plant window plants. They can be kept in the home as long as the heat is not turned on; once the heat is on, the relative humidity often drops below 60%, the minimum for these species. Spraying the plants may help their chances indoors, however.

Acalypha hispida
Acalypha pendula
Acalypha wilkesiana
Acanthorhipsalis monacantha

Acer buergerianum
Achimenes hybrids
Acokanthera oblongifolia
Adiantum hispidulum

Adiantum peruvianum
Adiantum raddianum
Adiantum tenerum
Aërangis rhodosticta
Aërides falcata
Aeschynanthus hildebrandii
Aeschynanthus radicans
Aeschynanthus tricolor
Aglaonema commutatum
Aglaonema costatum
Aglaonema crispum
Allamanda cathartica
Alloplectus capitatus

Alloplectus schlimii
Alocasia lowii
Alpinia sanderae
Alsobia dianthiflora
Amorphophallus bulbifer
Angraecum eburneum
Ansellia africana
Anthurium Andraeanum hybrids
Anthurium crystallinum
Anthurium Scherzeranum hybrids
Aphelandra aurantiaca
Aphelandra maculata
Aphelandra sinclairiana

HUMIDITY REQUIREMENTS

Aphelandra squarrosa
Araucaria heterophylla
Arisaema candidissimum
Aristolochia grandiflora
Arpophyllum spicatum
Asparagus asparagoides
Asparagus setaceus
Aspasia lunata
Asplenium bulbiferum
Asplenium marinum
Asplenium nidus
Barkeria spectabilis
Bauhinia punctata
Begonia albopicta
Begonia boweri
Begonia 'Cleopatra'
Begonia coccinea
Begonia Corallina hybrids
Begonia X credneri
Begonia grandis
Begonia heracleifolia
Begonia hispida var. cucullifera
Begonia imperialis
Begonia limmingheiana
Begonia maculata
Begonia manicata
Begonia X margaritae
Begonia masoniana
Begonia metallica
Begonia Rex hybrids
Begonia rotundifolia
Begonia serratipetala
Begonia venosa
Bertolonia marmorata
Bifrenaria harrisoniae
Blechnum species
Blechnum spicant
Bomarea cladasii
Brassaia actinophylla
Brassavola species
Brassia species
X Brassocattleya species
X Brassolaeliocattleya species
Breynia disticha
Brunfelsia species
Bulbophyllum species
Caesalpinia decapetala
Caesalpinia gilliesii
Caladium Bicolor hybrids
Calanthe triplicata
Calathea crocata
Calathea lancifolia
Calathea makoyana
Calathea ornata
Calathea picturata
Calathea roseopicta
Calceolaria hybrids
Camelia japonica
Camellia sinensis
Campanula fragilis
Cantua buxifolia
Caryota mitis
Catasetum maculatum
Cattleya species
Celosia argentea
Centradenia floribunda
Chamaedorea elegans
Chamaeranthemum species
Chrysanthemum parthenium
Chrysanthemum, garden varieties
Chrysothemis pulchella
Chysis aurea
Cissus discolor
Clerodendrum thomsoniae
Cleyera japonica
Cochliostemma odoratissimum
Cocos nucifera
Codiaeum variegatum
Coelia bella
Coelogyne cristata
Coleus Blumei hybrids
Columnea X banksii

Columnea gloriosa
Columnea microphylla 'Hostag'
Cordyline fruticosa
Costus cuspidatus
Crocus vernus ssp. vernus
Crossandra infundibuliformis
Cryptanthus species
Ctenanthe lubbersiana
Ctenanthe oppenheimiana
Cyclamen persicum
Cycnoches chlorochilum
Cymbidium hybrids
Cyperus papyrus
Cyrtomium falcatum
Cytisus X spachianus
Darlingtonia californica
Dendrobium species, moderate
    greenhouse
Dendrobium species, warm
    greenhouse
Dichorisandra reginae
Dicksonia antarctica
Didymochlaena truncatula
Dieffenbachia amoena
Dieffenbachia bowmannii
Dieffenbachia maculata
Dieffenbachia seguine
Dionaea muscipula
Dipladenia sanderi
Dipteracanthus devosianus
Dipteracanthus makoyanus
Disa uniflora
Dischidia pectenoides
Dizygotheca elegantissima
Dizygotheca veitchii
X Doritaenopsis species
Doritis pulcherrima
Dorstenia eleta
Doryopteris palmata
Dracaena surculosa
Dracula troglodytis
Drosera capensis
Dryopteris affinis
Duchesnea indica
Elettaria cardamomum
Encyclia species
Epacris hybrids
Epidendrum fragrans
Epidendrum parkinsonianum
Episcia cupreata
Episcia reptans
Erica gracilis
Erica X willmorei
Erythrorhipsalis pilocarpa
Euphorbia caracasana
Euphorbia fulgens
Euterpe edulis
Ficus aspera 'Parcellii'
Ficus buxifolia
Ficus leprieurii
Ficus religiosa
Ficus stricta
Fittonia verschaffeltii
Fuchsia hybrids
Furcraea foetida 'Striata'
Globba winitii
Gloriosa rothschildiana
Gloxinia sulvatica
Goethea cauliflora
Gomesa recurva
Graptophyllum pictum
Grevillea robusta
Guzmannia species
Habernaria xantholeuca
Hebe species
Hedra helix, variegated varieties
Heliconia jacquinii
Helleborus niger
Hemigraphis species
Hemionitis palmata
Hofmannia ghiesbreghtii
Hoya bella

Hoya carnosa
Hoya linearis
Hoya miltiflora
Hutleya meleagris
Hyacinthus orientalis
Hydrangea macrophylla
Hypoestes phyllostachya
Illicium anisatum
Ipomoea batatas
Iris reticulata
Ixora hybrids
Jacaranda mimosifolia
Jacobinia carnea
Kalanchoë beharensis
Koellikeria erinoides
Kohleria Eriantha hybrids
Laelia cinnabarina
Leea guineensis
Leucothoë walteri
Littonia modesta
Lockhartia lunifera
Ludisia discolor
Lycaste cruenta
Macroplectum sesquipedale
Malpighia coccigera
Manettia inflata
Manihot esculenta 'Variegata'
Maranta bicolor
Maranta leuconeura
Masdevallia species
Maxillaria tenuifolia
Medinilla magnifica
Microcoelum weddellianum
Microlepis speluncae
Mikania ternata
Miltonia hybrids
Miltoniopsis roezlii
Mimosa pudica
Monstera adansonii
Murraya paniculata
Musa species
Mussaenda phillipica
Myrmecodia echinata
Nandina domestica
Narcissus hybrids
Nautilocalyx lynchii
Neomortonia nummularia
Neoregelia species
Nepenthes hybrids
Nephrolepis exaltata
Nertera granadensis
X Odontioda species
X Odontocidium species
Odontoglossum bictoniense
Odontoglossum pulchellum
Oncidium microchilum
Oncidium ornithorhynchum
Oncidium papilio
Orbea variegata
Oxalis adenophylla
Pachira macrocarpa
Pachystachys lutea
Pandanus species
Paphiopedilum, spotted-leaf species
Paphiopedilum, green-leaf species
Passiflora alata
Passiflora caerulea
Passiflora violacea
Pavonia multiflora
Pellionia species
Pentas lanceolata
Peperomia argyreia
Perilepta dyeriana
Peristrophe hyssopifolia 'Aureovariegata'
Persea americana
Phaius tankervilleae
Phalaenopsis species
Philesia magellanica
Philodendron melanochrysum
Philodendron sagittifolium 'Ilsemannii'
Philodendron selloum
Phyllanthus angustifolius

Phyllitis scolopendrium
Pilea species
Pinguicula moranensis
Piper crocatum
Piper ornatum
Pistia stratiotes
Pittosporum species
Plectranthus oertendahlii
Pleione bulbocodioides
Plumbago indica
Polyscias species
Porphyrocoma pohliana
Primula X kewensis
Primula malacoides
Primula obconica
Primula praenitens
Primula vulgaris
Pseuderanthemum species
Pseudobombax ellipticum
Pteris cretica
Pteris ensiformis
Pteris quadriaurita
Rhododendron obtusum
Rhododendron simsii
Rhoeo spathacea 'Vittata'
Rhoicissus capensis
Rhynchostylis coelestis
Rivina humilis
Rodriguezia secunda
Sagina subulata
Saintpaulia ionantha
Sanchezia nobilis
Sandersonia aurantiaca
Sarmienta scandens
Sarracenia species
Schaueria calycotricha
Schismatoglottis picta
Scindapsus pictus
Scirpus cernuus
Scutellaria costaricana
Selaginella species
Sibthorpia europaea
Siderasis fuscata
Sinningia cardinalis
Sinningia speciosa
Skimmia species
Smithiantha hybrids
Solandra grandiflora
Solanum pseudocapsicum
Soleirolia soleirolii
Sonerila margaritacea
Sophronitis cernua
Sparmannia africana
Spatiphyllum wallisii
Stanhopea wardii
Stephanotis floribunda
Stromanthe species
Tacca chantrieri
Testudinaria species
Tetranema roseum
Tillandsia cyanea
Tillandsia, gray-scaled species
Tillandsia lindenii
Tillandsia usneoides
Trevesia palmata
Tropaeolum species
Tulipa hybrids
Tupidanthus calyptratus
Turnera ulmifolia
Uebelmannia pectinifera
Urceolina grandiflora
Vanda coerulea
Vriesea species
X Vuylstekeara hybrids
Warscewiczella discolor
Washingtonia filifera
Whitfieldia elongata
Whitfieldia lateritia
X Wilsonara hybrids
Xanthosoma lindenii
Zantedeschia species
Zygopetalon mackaii

Plants requiring a moderate relative humidity

"Moderate" refers to a relative humidity of 50–60%. With help from a vaporizer or by spraying regularly, this humidity level can be reached in a heated room. Plants of this group can often rest dormant in the home, provided the thermostat can be lowered somewhat, increasing the relative humidity.

Abromeitiella brevifolia
Abutilon hybrids
Abutilon megapotamicum
Abutilon megapotamicum 'Variegatum'
Abutilon pictum 'Thompsonii'
Acacia armata
Acanthorhipsalis monocantha
Acca sellowiana
Acer buergerianum
Acorus gramineus 'Argenteostriatus'
Adenium obesum
Agapanthus praecox
Agathis macrophylla
Albizia julibrissin
Allamanda cathartica
Alternanthera ficoidea
Amaryllis belladonna
Amorphophallus bulbifer
Ampelopsis brevipedunculata
Ananas species
Anigozanthos flavidus
Anisodontea capensis
Arachis hypogaea
Arachnoides species
Arbutus andrachne
Ardisia crenata
Arisaema candidissimum
Asarina barclaiana
Asclepias curassavica
Asparagus asparagoides
Asparagus densiflorus
Asparagus falcatus
Aspidistra elatior
Aspidistra elatior 'Variegata'
Asplenium marinum
Aucuba japonica
Bauhinia punctata
Begonia albopicta
Begonia boweri
Begonia 'Cleopatra'
Begonia coccinea
Begonia Corallina hybrids
Begonia X credneri
Begonia Elatior hybrids
Beognia X erythrophylla
Begonia grandis
Begonia heracleifolia
Begonia hispida var. cucullifera
Begonia, tuberous hybrids
Begonia limmingheiana
Begonia Lorraine hybrids
Begonia maculata
Begonia X margaritae
Begonia masoniana
Begonia metallica
Begonia Rex hybrids
Begonia rotundifolia
Begonia venosa
Beloperone guttata
Billbergia nutans
Blechum species
Blechnum spicant
Bloomeria crocea
Blossfeldia liliputana
Bomarea caldasii
Borzicactus species
Bougainvillea spectabilis
Bouvardia hybrids
Bowiea volubilis
Brassaia acitnophylla
Brisimum alicastrum
Browallia speciosa
Brunfelsia species
Caesalpinia decapetala

Caesalpinia gilliesii
Calliandra harrisii
Callisia species
Callistemom citrinus
Calocephalus brownii
Campanula fragilis
Campanula isophylla
Canna Indica hybrids
Cantua buxifolia
Capparis spinosa
Capsicum annuum
Carex brunnea 'Variegata'
Cassia didymobotrya
Catharanthus roseus
Celosia argentea
Cestrum X newellii
Chamaedorea elegans
Chamaelaucium uncinatum
Chamaerops humilis
Chlorophytum comosum 'Variegatum'
Chirozema cordatum
Chrysalidocarpus lutescens
Chrysanthemum Indicum hybrids
Chrysanthemum parthenium
Chrysanthemum, garden varieties
Chysis aurea
Cissus antarctica
Cissus rhombifolia
Cissus striata
Cistus species
X Citrofurtunella mitis
Citrus species
Clerodendrum thomsoniae
Cleyera japonica
Clianthus puniceus
Clivia miniata
Clusia rosea
Coccoloba uvifera
X Codonatanthus species
Codonanthe crassifolia
Coelogyne cristata
Coffea arabica
Coleus Blumei hybrids
Convolvulus sabaticus
Copiapoa cinerea
Coprosma species
Cordyline australis
Cordyline indivisa
Corokia species
Correa backhousiana
Corynocarpus laevigatum
Crassula coccinea
Crinum X powelii
Cryptanthus species
Cryptocereus anthonyanus
Cunonia capensis
Cuphea species
Cupressus macrocarpa 'Goldcrest'
Cussonia spicata
Cyanotis kewensis
Cycas revoluta
Cyclamen persicum
Cymbidium hybrids
Cyperus alternifolius
Cyperus albostriatus
Cyrtanthus parviflorus
Cyrtomium falcatum
Cytisus X spachianus
Danae racemosa
Datura hybrids
Davallia mariesii
Dichondra repenes
Dicksonia antarctica
Didierea madagascariensis

Dieffenbachia amoena
Dieffenbachia maculata
Dieffenbachia seguine
Dizygotheca elegantissima
Dizygotheca veitchii
Dodonaea viscosa
Doryanthes palmeri
Dracaena deremensis
Dracaena draco
Dracaena fragrans
Dracaena marginata 'Tricolor'
Dracaena marginata
Dracaena reflexa
Dracaena sanderiana
Dracaena surculosa
Duchesnea indica
Echinopsis, night-blooming species
Echium wildpretii
Elettaria cardamomum
Ensete ventricosum
Epacris hybrids
Epipremnum pinnatum 'Marble Queen'
Epipremnum pinnatum
Erica gracilis
Erica X willmorei
Eriobotrya japonica
Erythrina crista-galli
Erythrorhipsalis pilocarpa
Espostoa lanata
Eucalyptus cinerea
Eucomis bicolor
Eugenia myriophylla
Euonymus japonica
Euphorbia caracasana
Euphorbia pulcherrima
Eustoma grandiflorum
Exacum affine
Fascicularia pitcairniifolia
X Fatshedera lizei
X Fatshedera lizei 'Variegata'
Fatsia japonica
Fatsia japonica 'Variegata'
Felicia amelloides
Ficus altissima
Ficus benghalensis
Ficus benjamina
Ficus benjamina 'Variegata'
Ficus carica
Ficus cyathistipula
Ficus deltoidea
Ficus elastica
Ficus leprieurii
Ficus lyrata
Ficus microcarpa
Ficus pumila
Ficus retusa
Ficus rubiginosa
Ficus ribuginosa 'Variegata'
Ficus saggittata
Ficus schlechteri
Fortunella margarita
Fuchsia hybrids
Furcraea foetida 'Striata'
Gardenia jasminioides
Gazania hybrids
Geranium palmatum
Gerbera hederacea 'Variegata'
Gloriosa rothschildiana
Gomphrena globosa
Gynura aurantiaca
Habranthus tubispathus
Haemanthus albiflos
Haemanthus multiflorus
Harpephyllum caffrum
Hatiora bambusioides
Hebe species
Hechtia stenophylla
Hedera helix, variegated varieties
Hedera helix ssp. canariensis 'Variegata'
Hedychium gardnerianum
Heliotropium arborescens
Hemionitis palmata

Heterocentron elegans
Hibbertia scandens
Hibiscus rosa-sinensis
Hippeastrum hybrids
Homalocladium platycladum
Howeia forsteriana
Hoya carnosa
Hoya lacunosa
Hoya linearis
Huernia keniensis
Hyacinthus orientalis
Hymenocallis species
Hypocyrta glabra
Illicium anisatum
Impatiens hawkeri
Impatiens repens
Impatiens walleriana
Incarvillea hybrids
Ipomoeae tricolor
Iresine herbstii
Isoplexis canariensis
Jacobinia pauciflora
Jasminum officinale
Jatropha pandurifolia
Kalanchoë blossfeldiana
Kalanchoë hybrids
Kalanchoë orgyalis
Lachenalia unifolia
Lagerstroemia indica
Lantana Camara hybrids
Laurus nobilis
Ledebouria socialis
Leea guineensis
Leptospermum scoparium
Leucothoë walteri
Lilium hybrids
Liriope muscari
Littonia modesta
Livistona chinensis
Lophomyrtus obcordata
Lotus berthelotii
Lycaste cruenta
Malpighia coccigera
Malvaviscus arboreus
Mamillopsis senilis
Mandevilla laxa
Manettia inflata
Mascarena verschaffeltii
Melocactus maxonii
Metrosideros villosus
Mikania ternata
Monstera deliciosa
Monstera deliciosa 'Variegata'
Myoporum acuminatum
Myrtus communis
Nandina domestica
Nematanthus hybrids
Neomortonia nummularia
Nephrolepis exaltata
Nerium oleander
Nertera granadensis
Nicotiana X sanderae
Nidularium fulgens
Notocactus species
Ochna serrulata
Odontoglossum pulchellum
Olea europaea
Ophiopogon jaburan
Ophiopogon japonicus
Oplismenus hirtellus 'Variegatus'
Orbea variegata
Oreocereus celsianus
Oreopanax capitatus
Ornithogalum thyrsoides
Oroya peruviana
Osteospermum ecklonis
Pachira macrocarpa
Pachypodium species
Pachystachys lutea
Pandanus species
Parthenocissus inserta
Passiflora caerulea

Pedilanthus tithymaloides 'Variegata'
Pelargonium X *blandfordianum*
Pelargonium X *citrosmum*
Pelargonium crispum
Pelarognium endlicherianum
Pelargonium X *fragrans* 'Variegatum'
Pelargonium Grandiflorum hybrids
Pelargonium graveolens 'Variegatum'
Pelargonium radens
Pelargonium Zonale hybrids
Pellaea species
Peperomia argyreia
Peperomia blanda
Peperomia caperata
Pepromia fraseri
Peperomia griseoargenta
Peperomia incana
Peperomia obtusifolia 'Greengold'
Peperomia pereskiifolia
Peperomia puteolata
Peperomia rotundifolia
Peperomia serpens 'Variegata'
Pereskia aculeata 'Godseffiana'
Pernettya mucronata
Persea americana
Philodendron bipennifolium
Philodendron elegans
Philodendron erubescens
Philodendron melanochrysum
Philodendron pedatum
Philodendron rugosum
Philodendron sagittifolium 'Ilsemannii'
Philodendron scandens
Philodendron selloum

Philodendron squamiferum
Philodendron tuxtlanum
Phlebodium aureum
Phoenix canariensis
Phoenix roebelinii
Phormium tenax
Pinus pinea 'Silver Crest'
Pisonia umbellifera 'Variegatum'
Pistia stratiotes
Pittosporum species
Platycerium bifurcatum
Plectranthus coleoides
Plectranthus fruticosus
Plectranthus oertendahlii
Plumbago auriculata
Plumbago indica
Podocarpus macrophyllus
Polianthes tuberosa
Polystichem tsus-simense
Portulaca grandiflora
Primula X *kewensis*
Primula praenitens
Prostanthera sieberi
Pseudopanax lessonii
Punica granatum
Puya chilensis
Radermachera sinica
Rebutia senilis
Rebutia species
Rehmannia elata
Reinwardtia indica
Rhapsis excelsa
Rhipsalidopsis species
Rhipsalis baccifera

Rhodochiton atrosanguineum
Rhoeo spathacea 'Vittata'
Rhoicissus capensis
Rosa chinensis 'Minima'
Rosioglossum grande
Ruscus aculeatus
Sagina subulata
Saintpaulia ionantha
Sanseveria trifasciata
Sauromatum guttatum
Saxifraga cotyledon
Saxifraga stolonifera 'Tricolor'
Schinus molle
Schizanthus pinnatus
Schlumbergera hybrids
Scutellaria costaricana
Selenicereus grandiflorus
Senecio Cruentus hybrids
Senecio kleinia
Senecio macroglossus 'Variegatus'
Senecio mikanioides
Serissa foetida 'Variegata'
Setcreasea pallida
Sibthorpia europaea
Solandra grandiflora
Solanum pseudocapsicum
Soleirolia soleirolii
Sparmannia africana
Sprekelia formosissima
Stapelia X *divaricata*
Stenocarpus sinuatus
Stenotaphrum secundatum 'Variegatum'
Stephanotis floribunda

Strelitzia reginae
Streptocarpus grandis
Streptocarpus hybrids
Streptocarpus saxorum
Streptosolen jamesonii
Synadenium grantii
Syngonium podophyllum, variegated varieties
Syngonium podophyllum, green-leaf trunk type
Tecoma castanifolia
Tecomaria capensis
Testudinaria species
Tetraclinus articulata
Tetrastigma voinerianum
Thevetia peruviana
Thunbergia alata
Tibouchina urvilleana
Tolmeia menzeisii
Torenia fournieri
Trachycarpus fortunei
Tradescantia species
Tritonia crocata
Tropaeolum species
Tupidanthus calyptratus
Uebelmannia pectinifera
Vallota speciosa
Veltheimia capensis
Washingtonia filifera
Weingartia species
Yucca species
Zamia pumila
Zebrina pendula
Zephyranthes candida

Plants that can survive dry air

These plants are very suitable for indoor cultivation and can rest dormant in a heated room, unless of course their dormancies require a lower temperature (as with most cacti and other succulents). These plants will grow well in humid air as well as dry air.

Abromeitiella brevifolia
Acanthocalycium violaceum
Adenium obesum
Adromischus cooperi
Aeonium arboreum
Aeonium holochrysum
Aeonium tabuliforme
Agave americana
Agave macroacantha
Agave parviflora
Agave victoriae-reginae
Aloë arborescens
Aloë aristata
Aloë humilis
Aloë variegata
Anisodontea capensis
Aporocactus flagelliformis
Ariocarpus fissuratus
Aspidistra elatior
Aspidistra elatior 'Variegata'
Astrophytum asterias
Astrophytum myriostigma
Astrophytum ornatum
Beaucarnea recurvata
Bergeranthus scapiger
Blossfeldia liliputana
Borzicactus species
Bougainvillea spectabilis
Bowiea volubilis
Brachychiton rupestris
Brasiliopuntia brasiliensis
Brosium alicastrum
Caralluma X *suaveolens*
Carnegiea gigantea
Carpobrotus acinaciformis
Cephalocereus senilis
Cereus neotetragonus
Cereus peruvianus
Ceropegia woodii ssp. *woodii*

Chamaecereus sylvestri
Chamaelaucium uncinatum
Cheiridopsis candidissima
Cissus rhombifolia
Cleistocactus strausii
Clianthus puniceus
Colletia cruciata
Conophytum species
Copiapoa cinerea
Coryphantha elephantidens
Cotyledon species
Crassula arborescens
Crassula muscosa
Crassula ovata
Crassula pellucida
Crassula perfoliata var. *falcata*
Crassula perforata
Crassula rupestris
Cyphostemma juttae
Dasylirion acrotrichum
Davallia mariesii
Delosperma species
Didierea madagascariensis
Disphyma crassifolium
Dolichothele baumii
Dracaena marginata 'Tricolor'
Dracaena marginata
Dudleya pachyphytum
Dyckia fosteriana
Echeveria agavoides
Echeveria derenbergii
Echeveria harmsii
Echeveria pulvinata
Echeveria setosa
Echinocactus grusonii
Echinocereus species
Echinofossulocactus hastatus
Echinopsis, day-blooming species
Epipremnum pinnatum 'Marble Queen'

Epipremnum pinnatum
Escobaria vivipara
Espostoa lanata
Euphorbia balsamifera
Euphorbia canariensis
Euphorbia caput-medusae
Euphorbia erythraeae
Euphorbia grandicornis
Euphorbia leuconeura
Euphorbia meloformis
Euphorbia resinifera
Euphorbia submammilaris
Euphorbia tetragona
Euphorbia tirucalli
Fascicularia pitcairniifolia
Faucaria tigrina
Fenestraria aurantiaca
Ficus benghalensis
Ficus benjamina
Ficus benjamina 'Variegata'
Ficus cyathistipula
Ficus elastica
Ficus schlechteri
Frithia pulchra
Gasteria species
Glottiphyllum linguiforme
Graptopetalum species
Greenovia aurea
Gymnocalycium species
Gynura aurantiaca
Haageocereus pseudomelanostele
Hamatocactus setispinus
Haworthia species
Hoodia gordonii
Hypocyrta glabra
Jatropha podagrica
Kalanchoë blossfeldiana
Kalanchoë daigremontiana
Kalanchoë hybrids
Kalanchoë scapigera
Kalanchoë tomentosa
Kalanchoë tubiflora
Lampranthus blandus
Leptocladodia microhelia
Leuchtenbergia principes
Lithops bromfieldii
Lobivia species

Lophophora williamsii
Mamillopsis senilis
Mammillaria bocasana
Mammillaria guelzoviana
Mammillaria hahniana
Mammillaria prolifera
Mammillaria rhodantha
Mammillaria spinosissima
Mammillaria wildii
Mammillaria zeilmanniana
Matucanan currundayensis
Melocactus maxonii
Monstera deliciosa
Myrtillocactus geometrizans
Neoporteria species
Neoporteria wagenknechtii
Neoregelia species
Notocactus species
Obregonia denegrii
Olea europaea
Opthalmophyllum jacobsenianum
Opuntia species
Oroya peruviana
Oscularia deltoides
Pachycereus pringlei
Pachyphytum oviferum
Pachypodium species
X *Pachyveria* species
Parodia species
Pedilanthus tithymaloides 'Variega'
Pelargonium X *blandfordianum*
Pelargonium X *citrosmum*
Pelargonium crispum
Pelargonium endlicherianum
Pelargonium X *fragrans* 'Variegatum'
Pelargonium graveolens
Pelargonium graveolens 'Variegatum'
Pelargonium radens
Pelargonium Zonale hybrids
Pereskia aculeata 'Godseffiana'
Philodendron elegans
Philodendron pedatum
Philodendron scandens
Phlebodium aureum
Pinus pinea 'Silver Crest'
Platycerium bifurcatum
Portulaca grandiflora

Portulacaria afra
Pseudomammillaria camptotricha
Punica granatum
Sansevieria trifasciata
Sarcocaulon crassicaule
Sedum species

Selenicereus grandiflorus
Sempervivum arachnoideum
Senecio citriformis
Senecio herreanus
Senecio kleinia
Senecio macroglossus 'Variegatus'

Senecio radicans
Senecio rowleyanus
Setcreasea pallida
Stapelia X *divaricata*
Sulcorebutia mizguensis
Trichocereuse spachianus

Trichodiadema densum
Weingartia species
Wilcoxia viperina
Yucca species

PLANT CHARACTERISTICS

Foliage plants

The decorative value of these plants lies in their foliage, though this does not necessarily mean that they are unable to bloom. Many of these plants have beautiful flowers as well as leaves, and are also listed under flowering plants.

Acalypha wilkesiana
Acer buergerianum
Acorus gramineus 'Argenteostriatus'
Adromischus cooperi
Aeonium arboreum
Aeonium holochrysum
Aeonium tabuliforme
Agathis macrophylla
Agave americana
Agave macroacantha
Agave parviflora
Agave victoriae-reginae
Aglaonema commutatum
Aglaonema costatum
Aglaonema crispum
Alocasia lowii
Alpinia sanderae
Alternanthera ficoidea
Ampelopsis brevipedunculata
Ananas species
Anthurium crystallinum
Araucaria heterophylla
Asparagus densiflorus
Asparagus falcatus
Asparagus setaceus
Aspidistra elatior
Aspidistra elatior 'Variegata'
Aucuba japonica
Beaucarnea recurvata
Begonia boweri
Begonia heracleifolia
Begonia hispida var. *cucullifera*
Begonia imperialis
Begonia masonia
Begonia Rex hybrids
Bowiea volubilis
Brachychiton rupestris
Brassaia actinophylla
Breynia disticha
Brosimum alicastrum
Caladium Bicolor hybrids
Calathea lancifolia
Calathea makoyana
Calathea ornata
Calathea picturata
Calathea roseopicta
Callisia species
Calocephalus brownii
Camellia sinensis
Carex brunnea 'Variegata'
Caryota mitis
Chamaedorea elegans
Chamaerops humilis
Chlorophytum comosum 'Variegatum'
Chrysalidocarpus lutescens
Cissus antarctica
Cissus discolor
Cissus rhombifolia
Cissus striata
Cleyera japonica
Clusia rosea
Coccoloba unifera
Cocos nucifera

Codiaeum variegatum
Coffea arabica
Coleus Blumei hybrids
Columnea microphylla 'Hostag'
Coprosma species
Cordyline australis
Cordyline fruticosa
Cordyline indivisa
Corynocarpus laevigatum
Crassula arborescens
Crassula muscosa
Crassula perforata
Cryptanthus species
Ctenanthe lubbersiana
Ctenanthe oppenheimiana
Cupressus macrocarpa 'Goldcrest'
Cussonia spicata
Cycas revoluta
Cyperus alternifolius
Cyperus albostriatus
Cyperus papyrus
Cyphostemma juttae
Danaë racemosa
Dasylirion acrotrichum
Dichondra repens
Dicksonia antarctica
Didierea madagascariensis
Dieffenbachia amoena
Dieffenbachia bowmannii
Dieffenbachia maculata
Dieffenbachia seguine
Dionaea muscipula
Dizygotheca elegantissima
Dizygotheca veitchii
Dracaena deremensis
Dracaena draco
Dracaena fragrans
Dracaena marginata 'Tricolor'
Dracaena marginata
Dracaena reflexa
Dracaena sanderiana
Dracaena surculosa
Drosera capensis
Dudleya pachyphytum
Echeveria agavoides
Echeveria pulvinata
Elettaria cardamomum
Ensete ventricosum
Epipremnum pinnatum 'Marble Queen'
Epipremnum pinnatum
Episcia cupreata
Episcia reptans
Eriobotrya japonica
Eucalyptus cinerea
Euonymus japonica
Euphorbia balsamifera
Euphorbia canariensis
Euphorbia caracasana
Euphorbia erythraeae
Euphorbia grandicornis
Euphorbia leuconeura
Euphorbia resinifera
Euphorbia submammilaris

Euphorbia tetragona
Euphorbia tirucalli
Euterpe edulis
X *Fatshedera lizei*
Fatsia japonica 'Variegata'
Ficus altissima
Ficus aspera 'Parcellii'
Ficus benghalensis
Ficus benjamina
Ficus benjamina 'Variegata'
Ficus buxifolia
Ficus carica
Ficus cyathistipula
Ficus deltoidea
Ficus elastica
Ficus leprieurii
Ficus lyrata
Ficus microcarpa
Ficus pumila
Ficus religiosa
Ficus retusa
Ficus rubiginosa
Ficus rubiginosa 'Variegata'
Ficus saggittata
Ficus schlechteri
Ficus stricta
Fittonia verschaffeltii
Furcraea foetida 'Striata'
Glechoma hederacea 'Variegata'
Grevillea robusta
Gynura aurantiaca
Harpephyllum caffrum
Haworthia species
Hechtia stenophylla
Hedera helix, variegated varieties
Hedera helix ssp. *canariensis* 'Variegata'
Hemigraphis species
Hofmannia ghiesbreghtii
Homalocladium platycladum
Howeia forsteriana
Hypoestes phyllostachya
Impatiens repens
Iresine herbstii
Kalanchoë beharensis
Kalanchoë daigremontiana
Kalanchoë tomentosa
Kalanchoë tubiflora
Ledebouria socialis
Leea guineensis
Livistona chinensis
Lophomyrtus obcordata
Manihot esculenta 'Variegata'
Maranta bicolor
Maranta leuconeura
Mascarena verschaffeltii
Microcoelum weddellianum
Mikania ternata
Monstera adansonii
Monstera deliciosa
Monstera deliciosa 'Variegata'
Musa species
Neoregelia species
Nepenthes hybrids
Nidularium fulgens
Ochagavia carnea
Olea europaea
Ophiopogon japonicus
Oplismenus hirtellus 'Variegatus'
Oreopanax capitatus
Pachira macrocarpa
Pachyphytum oviferum

Pachypodium species
Pandanus species
Parthenocissus henryana
Parthenocissus inserta
Pedilanthus tithymaloides 'Variegata'
Pelargonium X *blandfordianum*
Pelargonium crispum
Pelargonium X *fragrans* 'Variegatum'
Pelargonium radens
Pellionia species
Peperomia argyreia
Peperomia blanda
Peperomia incana
Peperomia obtusifolia 'Greengold'
Peperomia pereskiifolia
Peperomia puteolata
Peperomia rotundifolia
Peperomia serpens 'Variegata'
Perilepta dyeriana
Peristrophe hyssopifolia 'Aureovariegata'
Persea americana
Philodendron bipennifolium
Philodendron elegans
Philodendron erubescens
Philodendron melanochrysum
Philodendron pedatum
Philodendron rugosum
Philodendron sagittifolium 'Ilsemannii'
Philodendron scandens
Philodendron selloum
Philodendron squamiferum
Philodendron tuxtlanum
Phoenix canariensis
Phoenix roebelinii
Phyllanthus angusitfolius
Pilea species
Pinguicula moranensis
Pinus pinea 'Silver Crest'
Piper crocatum
Piper ornatum
Pisonia umbellifera 'Variegatum'
Plectranthus coleoides
Plectranthus oertendahlii
Podocarpus macrophyllus
Polyscias species
Portulacaria afra
Pseuderanthemum species
Pseudobombax ellipticum
Pseudopanax lessonii
Rhapis excelsa
Rhoeo spathacea 'Vittata'
Rhoicissus capensis
Sanchezia nobilis
Sansevieria trifasciata
Saxifraga stolonifera 'Tricolor'
Schefflera species
Scindapsus pictus
Scirpus cernuus
Selaginella species
Senecio citriformis
Senecio herreanus
Senecio kleinia
Senecio macroglossus 'Variegatus'
Senecio mikanioides
Senecio radicans
Senecio rowleyanus
Sibthorpia europaea
Soleirolia soleirolii
Stenocarpus sinuatus
Stenotaphrum secundatum 'Variegatum'
Stromanthe species

Synadenium grantii
Syngonium podophyllum, variegated varieties
Syngonium podophyllum, green-leaf trunk type
Testudinaria species
Tetraclinis articulata
Tetrastigma voinierianum
Tillandsia usneoides
Tolmiea menziesii
Trachycarpus fortunei
Tradescantia species
Trevesia palmata
Tupicanthus calyptratus
Washingtonia filifera
Xanthosoma lindenii
Yucca species
Zamia pumila
Zebrina pendula

Flowering plants

The primary decorative value of these plants lies in their flowers, which again does not mean their foliage is unattractive. Several of the following species do have beautiful leaves and are also listed under foliage plants.

Abutilon X hybridum
Abutilon megapotamicum
Acacia armata
Acalypha hispida
Acalypha pendula
Acca sellowiana
Achimenes hybrids
Acokanthera oblongifolia
Adenium obesum
Aeschynanthus hildebrandii
Aeschynanthus radicans
Aeschynanthus tricolor
Agapanthus praecox
Albizia julibrissin
Allamanda cathartica
Alsobia dianthiflora
Amaryllis belladonna
Amorphophallus bulbifer
Anigozanthos flavidus
Anisodontea capensis
Anthurium Andraeanum hybrids
Anthurium Scherzeranum hybrids
Aphelandra aurantiaca
Aphelandra sinclairiana
Aphelandra squarrosa
Arachis hypogaea
Arbutus andrachne
Ardisia crenata
Arisaema candidissimum
Aristolochia grandiflora
Asarina barclaiana
Asclepias curassavica
Bauhinia acuminata
Bauhinia punctata
Begonia coccinea
Begonia Corallina hybrids
Begonia Elatior hybrids
Begonia grandis
Begonia, tuberous hybrids
Begonia limmingheiana
Begonia Lorraine hybrids
Begonia maculata
Beloperone guttata
Bergeranthus scapiger
Bloomeria crocea
Bomarea caldasii
Bougainvillea spectabilis
Bouvardia hybrids
Browallia speciosa
Brunfelsia species
Caesalpinia decapetala
Caesalpinia gilliesii
Calathea crocata
Calceolaria hybrids
Calliandra harrisii
Callistemon citrinus
Camellia japonica
Campanula fragilis
Campanula isophylla
Canna Indica hybrids
Cantua buxifolia
Capparis spinosa
Caralluma X suaveolens
Carpobrotus acinaciformis
Cassia didymobotrya
Catharanthus roseus
Celosia argentea

Centradenia floribunda
Ceropegia woodii ssp. woodii
Cestrum X newellii
Chamaelaucium uncinatum
Chorizema cordatum
Chrysanthemum Indicum hybrids
Chrysanthemum parthenium
Chrysanthemum, garden varieties
Chrysothemis pulchella
Cistus species
Clerodendrum thomsoniae
Clianthus puniceus
Cochliostemma odoratissimum
Codonanthe crassifolia
Colletia cruciata
Columnea X banksii
Columnea gloriosa
Columnea microphylla
Conophytum species
Convolvulus sabitacus
Corokia species
Correa backhousiana
Costus cuspidatus
Crassula coccinea
Crassula pellucida
Crinum X powelii
Crocus vernus ssp. vernus
Crossandra infundibuliformis
Cunonia capensis
Cuphea species
Cyclamen persicum
Cyrtanthus parviflorus
Cytisus X spachianus
Datura hybrids
Delosperma species
Dipladenia sanderi
Dipteracanthus devosianus
Dipteracanthus makoyanus
Disphyma crassifolium
Dodonaea viscosa
Dorstenia elata
Duchesnea indica
Epacris hybrids
Erica gracilis
Erica X willmorei
Erythrina crista-galli
Eucomis bicolor
Eugina myriophylla
Euphorbia fulgens
Euphorbia milii
Euphorbia pulcherrima
Eustoma grandiflorum
Exacum affine
Faucaria tigrina
Felicia amelloides
Fenestraria aurantiaca
Fortunella margarita
Frithia pulchra
Fuchsia hybrids
Gardenia jasminioides
Gazania hybrids
Geranium palmatum
Gerbera hybrids
Globba winitii
Gloriosa rothschildiana
Glottiphyllum linguiforme
Gloxinia sylvatica

Goethea cauliflora
Gomphrena globosa
Guzmania species
Habranthus tubispathus
Haemanthus multiflorus
Hebe species
Hedychium gardnerianum
Heliconia jacquinii
Heliotropium arborescens
Helleborus niger
Heterocentron elegans
Hibbertia scandens
Hibiscus rosa-sinensis
Hippeastrum hybrids
Hoodia gordonii
Hoya bella
Hoya carnosa
Hoya lacunosa
Hoya linearis
Hoya multiflora
Huernia keniensis
Hyacinthus orientalis
Hydrangea macrophylla
Hymenocallis species
Hypocyrta glabra
Illicium anisatum
Impatiens walleriana
Incarvillea mairei
Ipomoea batatas
Ipomoea tricolor
Iris reticulata
Isoplexis canariensis
Ixora hybrids
Jacobinia carnea
Jacobinia pauciflora
Jasminum officinale
Jatropha pandurifolia
Jatropha podagrica
Kalanchoë blossfeldiana
Kalanchoë hybrids
Koellikeria erinoides
Kohleria Eriantha hybrids
Lachenalia species
Lagerstroemia indica
Lampranthus blandus
Lantana Camara hybrids
Leptospermum scoparium
Leucothoe walteri
Lilium hybrids
Lithops bromfieldii
Littonia modesta
Lotus berthelotii
Malpighia coccigera
Malvaviscus arboreus
Mandevilla laxa
Manettia inflata
Medinilla magnifica
Metrosideros villosus
Murraya paniculata
Mussaenda phillipica
Myoporum acuminatum
Myrmecodia echinata
Myrtus communis
Nandina domestica
Narcissus hybrids
Nematanthus hybrids
Neomortonia nummularia
Nerium oleander
Nicotiana X sanderae
Ochna serrulata
Opthalmophyllum jacobsenianum
Orbea variegata
Ornithogalum thyrsoides
Oscularia deltoides
Osteospermum ecklonis
Pachystachys lutea

Passiflora alata
Passiflora caerulea
Passiflora violacea
Pavonia multiflora
Pelargonium endlicherianum
Pelargonium Grandiflorum hybrids
Pentas lanceolata
Philesia magellanica
Pistia stratiotes
Plumbago auriculata
Plumbago indica
Polianthes tuberosa
Porphyrocoma pohliana
Portulaca grandiflora
Primula X kewensis
Primula malacoides
Primula obconica
Primula praenitens
Primula vulgaris
Prostanthera sieberi
Punica granatum
Rehmannia elata
Reinwardtia indica
Rhodochiton atrosanguineum
Rhododendron obtusum
Rhododendron simsii
Rivina humilis
Rosa chinensis 'Minima'
Ruscus aculeatus
Saintpaulia ionantha
Sandersonia aurantiaca
Sarcocaulon crassicaule
Sarmienta scandens
Sarracenia species
Saxifraga cotyledon
Schaueria calycotricha
Schinus molle
Schismatoglottis picta
Schizanthus pinnatus
Scutellaria costaricana
Senecio Cruentus hybrids
Sinningia cardinalis
Sinningia speciosa
Skimmia species
Solandra grandiflora
Spatiphyllum wallisii
Sprekelia formosissima
Stapelia X divaricata
Stephanotis floribunda
Strelitzia reginae
Streptocarpus hybrids
Streptocarpus saxorum
Streptosolen jamesonii
Tacca chantrieri
Tacoma castanifolia
Tecomaria capensis
Tetranema roseum
Thevetia peruviana
Thunbergia alata
Tibouchina urvilleana
Tillandsia cyanea
Tillandsia lindenii
Torenia fournieri
Trichoiadema densum
Tritonia crocata
Tropaeolum species
Tulipa hybrids
Turnera ulmifolia
Urceolina grandiflora
Vallota speciosa
Veltheimia capensis
Whitfieldia elongata
Whitfieldia lateritia
Zantedeschia species
Zaphyranthes candida

Plants bearing fruit

The plants in this group bear fruit given the proper cultivation. (Please consult the individual species listings to see if the fruits are edible.)

Aglaonema commutatum
Alloplectus capitatus
Ananas species
Ardisia crenata
Asparagus asparagoides
Aucuba japonica

Capsicum annuum
X *Citrofortunella mitis*
Citrus species
Coconanthe crassifolia
Coffea arabica
Corokia species

Danaë racemosa
Dodonaea viscosa
Duchesnea indica
Eriobotrya japonica
Euphorbia leuconeura
Ficus aspera 'Parcellii'
Ficus carica
Ficus cyathistipula
Ficus deltoidea
Ficus leprieurii
Fortunella margarita
Illicium anisatum

Nertera granadensis
Olea europaea
Passiflora alata
Passiflora caerulea
Pernettya mucronata
Rivina humilis
Ruscus aculeatus
Schinus molle
Skimmia species
Solanum pseudocapsicum

Ferns

Many ferns make suitable houseplants, while others require the high humidity of a greenhouse, vitrine or plant window. Since all ferns are exclusively foliage plants that never bloom, they are not also listed under foliage plants.

Adiantum hispidulum
Adiantum peruvianum
Adiantum raddianum

Adiantum tenerum
Arachnoides species
Asplenium bulbiferum

Asplenium marinum
Asplenium nidus
Blechnum species
Blechnum spicant
Cyrtomium falcatum Davallia mariesii
Didymochlaena truncatula
Doryopteris palmata
Dryopteris affinis
Hemionitis palmata
Microlepia specluncae

Nephrolepis exaltata
Pellaea species
Phlebodium aureum
Phyllitis scolopendrium
Platycerium bifurcatum
Polystichum tsus-simense
Pteris cretica
Pteris ensiformis
Pteris quadriaurita

Cacti

All cacti belong to the same family. They are also part of a larger grouping called succulents; all non-cactus succulent plants are listed in the next appendix. Only the strongest species of cactus make suitable houseplants, most preferring cultivation in a cold or moderate greenhouse.

Acanthocalycium violaceum
Acanthorhipsalis monocantha
Aporocactus flagelliformis
Ariocarpus fissuratus
Astrophytum asterias
Astrophytum myriostigma
Astrophytum ornatum
Blossfeldia liliputana
Borzicactus species
Brasiliopuntia brasiliensis
Carnegiea gigantea
Cephalocereus senilis
Cereus neotetragonus
Cereus peruvianus

Chamaecereus sylvestri
Cleistocactus straussii
Copiapoa cinerea
Coryphantha elephantidens
Cryptocereus anthonyanus
Dolichothele baumii
Echinocactus grusonii
Echinocereus species
Echinofossulocactus hastatus
Echinopsis, day-blooming species
Echinopsis, night-blooming species
Erythrorhipsalis pilocarpa
Escobaria vivipara
Espostoa lanata

Gymnocalycium species
Haagercereus pseudomelanostele
Hamatocactus setispinus
Hatiora bambusoides
Leptocladodia microhelia
Leuchtenbergia principes
Lobivia species
Lophophora williamsii
Mamillopsis senilis
Mammillaria bocasana
Mammillaria guelzoviana
Mammillaria hahniana
Mammillaria prolifera
Mammillaria rhodoantha
Mammillaria spinosissima
Mammillaria wildii
Mammillaria zeilmanniana
Matucana currundayensis
Melocactus maxonii
Myrtillocactus geometrizans
Neoporteria species
Neoporteria wagenknechtii
Nopalxochia phyllantoides

Notocactus species
Obregonia denegrii
Opuntia species
Oreocereus celsianus
Oroya peruviana
Pachycereus pringlei
Parodia species
Pereskia aculeata 'Golseffiana'
Pseudomammillaria camptotricha
Rebutia senilis
Rebutia species
Rhipsalidopsis species
Rhipsalis baccifera
Schlumbergera hybrids
Selenicereus grandiflorus
Sulcorebutia mizguensis
Trichocereus spachianus
Uebelmannia pectinifera
Weingartia species
Wilcoxia viperina

Succulents

The following are all succulent plants included in this book with the exception of cacti, which are listed above. Succulents are able to store moisture in their leaves and stalks. Many species require a cool and dry dormant period that simulates the dry season of their native countries.

Adenium obesum
Adromischus cooperi
Aeonium arboreum
Aeonium holochrysum
Aeonium tabuliforme
Agave americana
Agave macroacantha
Agave parviflora
Agave victoriae-reginae
Aloë arborescens
Aloë aristata
Aloë humilis
Aloë variegata
Beaucarnea recurvata
Bergeranthus scapiger
Caralluma X *suaveolens*
Carpobrotus acinaciformis
Ceropegia woodii ssp. *woodii*
Cheiridopsis candidissima
Conophytum species
Cotyledon species

Crassula arborescens
Crassula coccinea
Crassula muscosa
Crassula ovata
Crassula pellucida
Crassula perfoliata var. *falcata*
Crassula perforata
Crassula rupestris
Cyanotis kewensis
Cyphostemma juttae
Delosperma species
Didierea madagascariensis
Disphyma crassifolium
Dudleya pachyphytum
Echeveria agavoides
Echeveria derengerii
Echeveria harmsii
Echeveria pulvinata
Echeveria setosa
Euphorbia balsamifera
Euphorbia canariensis

Euphorbia caput-medusae
Euphorbia erythraeae
Euphorbia grandicornis
Euphorbia leuconeura
Euphorbia meloformis
Euphorbia milii
Euphorbia resinifera
Euphorbia submammilaris
Euphorbia tetragona
Euphorbia tirucalli
Faucaria tigrina
Fenestraria aurantiaca
Frithia pulchra
Gasteria species
Glottiphyllum linguiforme
Graptopetalum species
Greenovia aurea
Haworthia species
Hoodia gordonii
Hoya bella
Huernia keniensis
Jatropha podagrica
Kalanchoë beharensis
Kalanchoë blossfeldiana
Kalanchoë daigremontiana
Kalanchoë hybrids
Kalanchoë orgyalis
Kalanchoë scapigera
Kalanchoë tomentosa

Kalanchoë tubiflora
Lampranthus blandus
Lithops bromfieldii
Opthalmophyllum jacobsenianum
Orbea variegata
Oscularia deltoides
Pachyphytum oviferum
Pachypodium species
X *Pachyveria* species
Pelargonium X *blandfordianum*
Pelargonium X *citrosmum*
Pelargonium crispum
Pelargonium endlicherianum
Pelargonium X *fragrans* 'Variegatum'
Pelargonium Grandiflorum hybrids
Pelargonium graveolens 'Variegatum'
Pelargonium radens
Pelargonium Zonale hybrids
Peperomia argyreia
Peperomia blanda
Peperomia caperata
Peperomia fraseri
Peperomia griseoargenta
Peperomia incana
Peperomia obtusifolia 'Greengold'
Peperomia pereskiifolia
Peperomia puteolata
Peperomia rotundifolia
Peperomia serpens 'Variegata'

Sedum species
Sempervivum arachnoideum
Senecio citriformis

Senecio herreanus
Senecio kleinia
Senecio radicans

Senecio rowleyanus
Setcreasea pallida
Stapelia X *divaricata*

Streptocarpus saxorum
Synadenium grantii
Trichodiadema densum

Orchids

Just as with cacti, all orchids belong to the same family, and since all orchids are flowering plants, all are listed here and not duplicated in the flowering plants appendix. Orchids are primarily greenhouse plants, though with care they can sometimes be cultivated in the home. Most orchids require soft water and are very sensitive to stagnant water. Water can be added plentifully during the growing period as long as it can drain properly. Orchids with water-reserve organs such as pseudotubers generally need a dormant period. The various species listed are grouped here by most appropriate greenhouse temperature.

Warm greenhouse
Aërides falcata
Angraecum eburneum
Ansellia africana
Arpophyllum spicatum
Aspasia lunata
Barkera spectabilis
Bulbophyllum species
Calanthe triplicata
Catasetum maculatum
Cattleya species

Cycnoches chlorochilum
Cymbidium hybrids
Dendrobium species, warm greenhouse
Doritis pulcherrima
Lockhartia lunifera
Ludisia discolor
Macroplectum seesquipedale
Maxillaria tenuifolia
Miltoniopsis roezlii
X *Odontocidium* species
Oncidium papilio

Paphiopedilum spotted-leaf species
Phaius tankervillea
Rodriguezia secunda

Moderate greenhouse
Aërangis rhodosticta
Bifrenaria harrisoniae
Brassavola species
Brassia species
X *Brassocattleya* species
X *Brassolaeliocattleya* species
Chyssis aurea
Coelia bella
Coelogyne cristata
Dendrobium species, moderate greenhouse
X *Doritaenopsis* species
Dracula troglodytis
Encyclia species
Epidendrum fragrans
Epidendrum parksinsonianum
Gomesa recurva
Habernaria xantholeuca
Huntleya meleagris
Laelia cinnabarina

Lycaste cruenta
X *Odontioda* species
Odontoglossum bictoniense
Odontoglossum pulchellum
Oncidium microchilum
Oncidium ornithorhynchum
Paphiopedilum, deciduous green-leaf species
Phalaenopsis species
Rhynchostylis coelestis
Rosioglossum grande
Sophronitis cernua
Stanhopea wardii
Vanda coerulea
X *Vuylstekeara* hybrids
Warscewiczella discolor
X *Wilsonara* hybrids
Zygopetalon mackaii

Cold greenhouse
Disa uniflora
Masdevallia species
Miltonia hybrids
Pleione bulbocodioides

Bromeliads

The different genera of bromeliads all belong to the same family. The characteristic rosette always dies off after these plants bloom, no matter what care is provided. A greenhouse is necessary to cultivate the newly formed plants that sprout up next to the parent rosette. Only a few species are strong enough for indoor cultivation, and these are listed under perennial houseplants.

Abromeitiella brevifolia
Ananas species
Billbergia nutans
Cryptanthus species
Dyckia fosteriana
Fascicularia pitcairniifolia
Guzmania species
Hechtia stenophylla
Neoregelia species

Nidularium fulgens
Ochagavia carnea
Puya chilensis
Tillandsia cyanea
Tillandsia, gray-scaled species
Tillandsia lindenii
Tillandsia usneoides
Vriesea species

Annual and biennial houseplants

These are plants that only live one or two years, or plants that are usually only cultivated for one year. In a few cases, common annual garden plants are sold in pots as houseplants, but this does not necessarily mean they are suitable for indoor cultivation. Once they lose their attractiveness, these plants can be thrown out; it's not worth the effort to keep them alive over a winter.

Arachis hypogaea
Asarina barclaiana
Asclepias curassavica
Browallia speciosa
Calceolaria hybrids
Campanula fragilis
Capsicum annuum
Celosia argentea
Chrysanthemum Indicum hybrids
Chrysanthemum parthenium
Eustoma grandiflorum

Exacum affine
Gazania hybrids
Gomphrena globosa
Heliotropium arborescens
Ipomoea tricolor
Nicotania X *sanderae*
Portulaca grandiflora
Primula malacoides
Schizanthus pinnatus
Senecio Cruentus hybrids
Torenia fournieri

Tuberous plants and plants with rootstocks

In most cases, the plants from this group require a dormant peirod, in which considerably less or no water is given. Often the foliage will die off, and the tubers or rootstocks need to be kept dry in the soil at a certain minimum temperature (see individual species descriptions). After the dormant period, the tubers or rootstocks can be brought back to growth with a gradual increase of temperature and water.

Amorphophallus bulbifer
Arisaema candidissimum
Begonia grandis
Begonia, tuberous hybrids
Canna Indica hybrids
Ceropegia woodii ssp. *woodii*
Cyclamen persicum
Eucomis bicolor
Gloriosa rothschildiana
Hedychium gardnerianum
Ipomoea batatas

Littonia modesta
Maranta leuconeura
Oxalis adenophylla
Polianthes tuberosa
Sauromatum guttatum
Sinningia cardinalis
Sinningia speciosa
Testudinaria species
Tropaeolum species
Xanthosoma lindenii
Zantedeschia species

Bulb plants

There is a clear distinction between tubers and bulbs. Bulbs are skirted by open, underground leaves that form a water reserve organ. A dormant period is necessary for most species, when bulbs receive less water and the plant parts above the soil die off. Bulbs should be kept dry in or outside the pot, at a certain temperature specified in each individual plant description.

Amaryllis belladonna
Bloomeria crocea
Bowiea volubilis
Crinum X *powelii*
Crocus vernus sp. *vernus*
Cyrtanthus parviflorus
Habranthus tubispathus
Haemanthus multiflorus

Hippeastrum hybrids
Hyacinthus orientalis
Hymenocallis species
Iris reticulata
Lachenalia unifolia
Ledebouri socialis
Lilium hybrids
Narcissus hybrids

Ornithogalum thyrsoides	*Tritonia crocata*	*Urceolina grandiflora*	*Veltheimia capensis*
Sprekelia formosissima	*Tulipa* hybrids	*Vallota speciosa*	*Zephyranthes candida*

Climbing plants and hanging plants

The plants in this group have long, thin, lanky stems, some of which grow vertically (with enough support) and some of which hang down when grown in hanging pots or lattice baskets.

Allamanda cathartica
Alsobia dianthiflora
Ampelopsis brevipedunculata
Aporocactus flagelliformis
Aristolochia grandiflora
Asarina barclaiana
Asparagus falcatus
Begonia limmingheiana
Bomarea caldasii
Bougainvillea spectabilis
Callisia species
Ceropegia woodii ssp. *woodii*
Chlorophytum comosum 'Variegatum'
Cissus antarctica
Cissus discolor
Cissus rhombifolia
Cissus striata
Clerodendrum thomsoniae
Clianthus puniceus
X *Codonatanthus* species
Columnea X *banksii*
Columnea gloriosa
Columnea microphylla
Columnea microphylla 'Hostag'
Convolvulus sabaticus
Coprosma species
Crassula pellucida

Crassula rupestris
Cyanotis kewensis
Dichondra repens
Dichorisandra reginae
Dipladenia sanderi
Dischidia pectenoides
Dracaena reflexa
Duchesnea indica
Epipremnum pinnatum
Epipremnum pinnatum 'Marble Queen'
Episcia cupreata
Episcia reptans
Ficus pumila
Ficus sagittata
Fuchsia hybrids
Glechoma hederacea 'Variegata'
Gloriosa rothschildiana
Hedera helix, variegated varieties
Hedera helix ssp. *canariensis* 'Variegata'
Hibbertia scandens
Hoya bella
Hoya carnosa
Hoya lacunosa
Hoya linearis
Ipomoea batatas
Ipomoea tricolor
Ixora hybrids

Littonia modesta
Lotus berthelotii
Mandevilla laxa
Manettia inflata
Mikania ternata
Monstera deliciosa
Monstera deliciosa 'Variegata'
Neomortonia nummularia
Nepenthes hybrids
Oplismenus hirtellus 'Variegatus'
Parthenocissus henryana
Parthenocissus inserta
Passiflora alata
Passiflora caerulea
Passiflora violacea
Peperomia rotundifolia
Peperomia serpens 'Variegata'
Philodendron bipennifolium
Philodendron elegans
Philodendron erubescens
Philodendron melanochrysum
Philodendron pedatum
Philodendron rugosum
Philodendron sagittifolium 'Ilsemannii'
Philodendron scandens
Philodendron squamiferum
Piper crocatum
Piper ornatum
Plectranthus coleoides
Plectranthus oertendahlii
Plumbago auriculata
Plumbago indica
Portulaca grandiflora
Rhodochiton atrosanguineum

Rhoicissus capensis
Sandersonia aurantiaca
Sarmienta scandens
Saxifraga stolonifera 'Tricolor'
Schlumbergera hybrids
Scindapsus pictus
Scirpus cernuus
Sedum species
Selenicereus grandiflorus
Senecio citriformis
Senecio herreanus
Senecio macroglossus 'Variegatus'
Senecio mikanioides
Senecio radicans
Senecio rowleyanus
Setcreasea pallida
Sibthorpia europaea
Solandra grandiflora
Soleirolia soleirolii
Stenotaphrum secundatum 'Variegatum'
Stephanotis floribunda
Streptocarpus saxorum
Syngonium podophyllum, variegated varieties
Syngonium podophyllum, green-leaf trunk type
Tecomaria capensis
Tetrastigma voinerianum
Thunbergia alata
Tolmiea menziesii
Tradescantia species
Tropaeolum species
Zebrina pendula

SELECTED READINGS

Anglade, Pierre, editor. *Larousse Gardening and Gardens.* Facts On File, New York, 1990.

Faust, Joan Lee. *The New York Times Book of Houseplants.* Times Books, New York, 1973.

Graf, Alfred B. *Exotica Four, 12th ed.* Macmillan Publishing Co., New York, 1986.

Graf, Alfred B. *Tropica III, 3d rev. ed.* Macmillan Publishing Co., New York, 1986.

Hawkes, Alex D. *Encyclopedia of Cultivated Orchids.* Faber & Faber, Winchester, MA, 1987.

Herwig, Rob. *Macmillan Book of Houseplants.* Collier Books, New York, 1986.

Herwid, Rob and Margot Schubert. *The Treasury of Houseplants.* Collier Books, New York, 1979.

Tootill, Elizabeth, general editor, and Stephen Blackmore, consultant editor. *The Facts On File Dictionary of Botany.* Facts On File, New York, 1984.

INDEX

Numbers in italic indicate illustrations and captions

INDEX

INDEX